Iran's Experiment with Parliamentary Governance

Modern Intellectual and Political History of the Middle East
Fred H. Lawson, *Series Editor*

SELECT TITLES IN MODERN INTELLECTUAL AND POLITICAL HISTORY OF THE MIDDLE EAST

Ethnicity, Identity, and the Development of Nationalism in Iran
David N. Yaghoubian

Hakibbutz Ha'artzi, Mapam, and the Demise of the Israeli Labor Movement
Tal Elmaliach; Haim Watzman, trans.

The International Politics of the Persian Gulf
Mehran Kamrava, ed.

The Iranian Constitutional Revolution and the Clerical Leadership of Khurasani
Mateo Mohammad Farzaneh

Mohammad Mosaddeq and the 1953 Coup in Iran
Mark J. Gasiorowski and Malcolm Byrne, eds.

National Symbols in Modern Iran: Identity, Ethnicity, and Collective Memory
Menahem Merhavy

Shaykh Yūsuf al-Qaraḍāwī: Spiritual Mentor of Wasaṭī *Salafism*
Sagi Polka

Why Alliances Fail: Islamist and Leftist Coalitions in North Africa
Matt Buehler

For a full list of titles in this series, visit https://press.syr.edu/supressbook-series/modern-intellectual-and-political-history-of-the-middle-east/.

Iran's Experiment *with* Parliamentary Governance

THE SECOND MAJLES, 1909–1911

MANGOL BAYAT

Syracuse University Press

Syracuse, New York 13244-5290

First Edition 2020
20 21 22 23 24 25 6 5 4 3 2 1

∞ The paper used in this publication meets the minimum requirements of the American National Standard for Information Sciences—Permanence of Paper for Printed Library Materials, ANSI Z39.48-1992.

For a listing of books published and distributed by Syracuse University Press, visit https://press.syr.edu.

ISBN: 978-0-8156-3676-2 (hardcover)
978-0-8156-3686-1 (paperback)
978-0-8156-5499-5 (e-book)

Library of Congress Control Number: 2020936512

Manufactured in the United States of America

To the memory of Thomas Philipp, my husband,
companion, and colleague.
His place is empty, as we would say in Persian.
And yet how powerful is his presence in his absence.

Contents

Preface

DURING THE PAST three decades, champions of cultural and religious authentic identity throughout the non-Western world and even in Europe, not to mention the United States, have tended to de-legitimize the secular legacy of the Enlightenment. Such an onslaught is noticeable in some studies of the Constitutional Revolution of 1905–11 in Iran written with the Revolution of 1979 as a subtext in mind, obscuring or downplaying the strong underlying secularist trends that characterized the very nature of the constitutional movement. To a great extent shaped by French revolutionary ideology, the Constitutional Revolution followed a pattern common to most nineteenth-century and early-twentieth-century revolutions elsewhere in the world. Its history is part of the history of the age, inextricably linked to its time.

Undoubtedly some of its champions in the period from 1905 to 1909 referred to Islamic texts and laws in defense of their ideas and programs. However, as I demonstrated in my previous study, *Iran's First Revolution*, the Islamic rhetoric by no means displayed a genuinely innovative trend originating from within the olama's ranks and distinct from the lay modernists' argument. It merely adopted modernist views, accommodating them to religious principles. In fact, the *mojtahed* (high-ranking cleric) Fazlollah Nuri and other olama who actively opposed the Constitution, regardless of their respective motives, represented the contemporaneous authentic voice of mainstream Islamic jurisprudence at that time.

Iranian constitutionalist leaders held diverse beliefs, but they all shared a similar conviction, rooted in the Enlightenment, that the olama's functions in the New Iran had to be curtailed. Freedom, they also believed, entailed equality of all Iranian citizens irrespective of their sectarian affiliation. In the early stages of the revolution, a formidable coalition of religious and secular forces compelled the reigning shah to promulgate the Constitution of 1906 and his successor to sign the Supplement of 1907.

In the second Majles (National Assembly or Parliament) and the Lesser Despotism interlude, conservative and constitutional olama played a role in determining the fate of Iran's experiment with parliamentary governance. However, I argue that once the Constitution was restored in 1909, its ardent olama champions eventually reversed course, even though nominally still in favor of the idea of constitutional government and combating its adversaries at home and abroad. Some of the legislated reforms had provoked their ire, which was then manipulated by conservative politicians to undermine, if not to defame, prominent Majles deputies, mostly Democrats. Religion was then used as a weapon to crush the constitutional movement, targeting so-called extremist, secular-nationalist constitutional leaders and thus facilitating a second assault on the Majles.

The period of the second Majles represents the second but most important Iranian experiment with parliamentary governance. My study consists of a much needed chronological examination of the second Majles's reforms from within its sociopolitical and financial context. It offers a detailed analysis of the important episodes, their main national and international actors, and the intricate political climate that engendered one crisis after another and ultimately led to the fateful end of the second Majles. I chose to focus on how a truly social revolution aimed at building new modern institutions alienated the country's traditional religious and political elite as well as the European powers with geopolitical and economic interests in the country. The conjunction of an innovative and highly centralized government in the capital and strong enforcement of the tax system, normally rife with corruption, was too new in the ruling elite's experience, hence intolerable.

My analysis of how the two major political parties, the Democrat and the Moderate, developed during the revolution and what their platforms were highlights their common goals, which I trace to the conceptual principles and values of the European Enlightenment. Moreover, I show how Freemasonry, specifically the Order of the Grand Orient de France, played a significant part in the revolution precisely because it propagated popularized ideas of the Enlightenment that many key figures of the constitutional leadership found most appealing. My analysis of Freemasonry's role in both the first and the second Majles presents a sharp contrast to existing, mostly Persian conspiracy theories depicting the organization's nefarious impact on the nation's cultural and political history.

Central to the legislators' narrative was the idea of governing the country as one indivisible, sovereign nation composed of a multiethnic, multireligious citizenry enjoying equality before the law. Following this idea often required compromise on the part of some Majles deputies. Contrary to the conventional understanding of the Democrat and Moderate Parties' role in the second Majles, I contend that no sharp ideological differences prevented the deputies from closing ranks when passing reform bills unanimously conceived as vital for the construction of the new Iran. The deputies' deep preoccupation was *not*, in fact, their ideological differences but rather their lasting legacy to the future they aspired to construct.

As elected representatives in the Majles, Democrats felt the need to prioritize reform projects and to work with Moderates and nonpartisans alike, lay and religious, who shared their goal. Indeed, lay or clerical, affiliated to a faction or not, most deputies willingly joined their voices to the Democrats. Again and again I show how the radical wing of the Democrat Party was sidelined as its parliamentary representatives favored a pragmatic approach to enact modernizing laws. I demonstrate that, contrary to some existing studies of the revolution, the majority of the legislators—regardless of their ideological or class differences, whether traditionalist Moslems, lay conservatives, or leftists—with few exceptions worked together in passing secularizing laws.

But I show how social and religious traditions weighed heavily on the legislators' effort to carry on their self-defined "sacred" tasks to radically transform the country's political culture. Thus, I argue that the centrifugal reforms, approved by majority vote, were paradoxically often inconsistent with some newly enacted laws, such as the electoral distribution of Majles seats based on the divisive but centuries-long sectarian and tribal definition of individual identity. I also describe how the most passionate advocates of modernization were fully aware of their country's dire financial situation and shortages of knowledgeable human resources. They fiercely defended their reforms, arguing that they were building the foundation for a better, freer, and more just Iranian society. I show how all political and financial factors affecting the reforms and their outcome were interwoven, and I contextualize them to shed light on how the dynamics of European countries' involvement helped shape the debt-ridden country's geopolitical environment.

The reformists' dominance established a consensus, which then evaporated when individual deputies and cabinet officials had personal reasons for backtracking or were powerless in resisting Anglo-Russian pressure to eliminate any policy deemed detrimental to British and Russian imperial interests. Politics came to trump policies when national and international actors fueled fierce debates, pitting the legislature against some members of the government most exposed to British and Russian pressure. I analyze the political and religious circumstances that turned the Majles into a theater of constitutional politics; all factions fought one another in the name of the Constitution. The successful implementation of financial reform measures by W. Morgan Shuster, the hired American financial adviser initially given absolute authority by both members of the Majles and cabinet ministers, regardless of their political affiliation, provided the pretext for the destruction of the second Majles. There exists no recent study of Shuster's brief tenure in this all-important post. He was treated as a unique threat to the norms of Anglo-Russian politics enshrined in the convention of 1907, a dangerous man likely to lead the newly awakened nation into rebellion against the two imperial powers. Hence, his forced resignation marked the end of Iran's steady experiment with parliamentary governance as it was halted by foreign forces beyond the control of its architects.

My historical perspective reflects a strong conviction that the past cannot be studied in the light of subsequent ideologically diverse events. I believe it is necessary to offer the interested public as well as scholars a judicious analysis of the attempts to lay the legal foundation for the modern Iranian nation-state as well as of the achievements and failures in those attempts.

Acknowledgments

I THANK Christopher Dadian for his invaluable help in preparing the final format of this manuscript.

I am grateful to Bryan Dolan for his patience and good humor in helping to rectify my numerous computer mistakes.

Volker Mulfinger in Germany never failed to come to my rescue to save pages of a day's work from falling down a computer memory hole.

The precious love and encouragement given by my daughter, Shirin; my son-in-law, John Higgins; and my grandchildren, Fiona, Dylan, and Quentin, have been a tremendous source of pure joy and strength. They give meaning to my life.

Iran's Experiment with Parliamentary Governance

Introduction

The Past as Prologue

EUROPE AND THE UNITED STATES in the eighteenth and nineteenth centuries experienced tensions arising from the secularizing changes in societies where religion still prevailed as a predominant factor in its citizens' life. In the United States, the separation of church and state guaranteed the right of those with diverse beliefs to worship freely, ensuring the protection of religion from state power. The French Revolution, which provided the basic model for most other European and Middle Eastern political reforms, established a state that would also protect individuals from ecclesiastical power by reducing ecclesiastical control over matters pertaining to public life. In both cases, the road to a secular state went through serious religious obstacles that threatened smooth passage to this destination. An account of the historical-ideological context of Iran in the early 1900s compared with the European experience may help in understanding how peculiarly Islamic, or universal, was the situation in premodern Iran.

In his classic study of the European intellectuals in the Middle Ages, the French sociologist Jacques Le Goff traces their origins to the monastic "*clerc*" through an analysis of the *rapport de force* (correlation of forces) among the church, the university, and the reigning dynastic power.[1] From the twelfth through the fifteenth century, he writes, the Christian scholastic and humanist thinkers emerged from within the monastery ranks, and they in turn gave rise to the Renaissance intellectuals. The fourteenth-century war waged between church and state, when dynastic powers mercilessly struggled against papal claims to temporal authority, ended with the emergence of the absolutist monarchy, its state founded upon the separation of public law from ecclesiastical jurisdiction, though with the church conferring upon the monarch a religiously legitimate aura. The war facilitated the evolutionary though stormy development of autonomous institutions of higher learning, disengaging speculative thought from theology. The eighteenth-century Enlightenment enshrined in the French Revolution's ideology then helped consolidate the status of the modern secular intellectual. Clashes between religious and secular institutions, however, persisted. The French Republic did not officially declare a separation of church and state until 1905.

This peculiarly western European tradition of warfare between church and state did not occur in premodern Iran or elsewhere in the premodern Moslem world.[2] Individual religious leaders periodically denounced some government officials as corrupt, but such denouncements were exceptional. Throughout the nineteenth century, high-ranking religious leaders (olama) living in Iran gained wealth and social status as members of the ruling elite. They formed a privileged class, rich and powerful. Some engaged in the power politics of their time, joining a political faction of their choice in alliance with lay politicians. Personal motives rather than doctrinal considerations oftentimes determined their choice. In fact, political clout consolidated the activist olama's status and influence within the religious institutions in Iran proper. Despite the divisive character of the political cabals, the Islamic traditional social order remained intact, preserving the close working relationship between the two mutually dependent centers of authority, state and religion. The religious leaders taught Islamic jurisprudence and presided over the religious courts of justice, but the enforcement of God's law was under state jurisdiction. The shah was not granted doctrinal legitimacy but was considered an integral and necessary part of the Islamic society and was referred to as "the Shadow of God on earth." Originally a pre-Islamic Persian attribute for the monarch, the title was revived by the Sunni Abbasid Caliphate of Baghdad (750–1258). As Fazlur Rahman, the late scholar of Islamic theology and philosophy, explained, for the olama this title "meant a point of cohesion against chaos and lawlessness, but in the popular belief, influenced by the ancient Iranian idea of kingship, this phrase assumed literal truth."[3] A medieval Moslem historian offered an even more concrete definition of the state/religion relationship: "Religion and kingship are two brothers, neither can dispense with the other. Religion is the foundation of kingship, and kingship protects religion. For whatever lacks a foundation must perish, and whatever lacks a protector disappears."[4] This tradition of mutual dependency between dynastic power and religious authority was firmly maintained with the advent of the Safavids to the restored Persian imperial rule in the early sixteenth century and survived through the Qajar period (1789–1925). The shah was also referred to as the *qotb*, the pivot, round which the universe rotates. The "universal ruler," to quote Gene Garthwaite's interesting analysis, "was identified with Iran."[5]

The traditional Qajar power structure positioned the sovereign's rule, *saltanat*, as transcending and hence distinct from the royal appointed government, the *dowlat*. Popular revolts rarely held the monarch responsible for wrongdoing. Thus, unlike the European experience in the High Middle Ages, up to the early twentieth century the speculative thinkers in Iran lacked any strong institutional backing in their struggle to free themselves from theology. Iranian reformers even lacked the military institutional backing that the Young Turks enjoyed in Ottoman Turkey, where modernization of the armed forces in the late nineteenth century had produced a new nationalist leadership. God's law was the law of the realm, as taught and enforced by its guardians, the *mojtaheds*, with no distinction made between the sacred and the profane, the religious and the secular. Knowledge was defined as knowledge of the divine. Shi'a mysticism in all its variety experienced an even deeper tension between the discipline of the law and a powerful messianic impulse, which the *mojtaheds* persecuted. The intellectual in premodern Iran thus remained a "*clerc*" in Le Goff's terminology.

It was only in the last two decades of the nineteenth century that, partly as a result of greater awareness of Europe—its knowledge, its institutions, and its political systems—that Iranian dissident thinkers found the historic opportunity and the political means to detach themselves from religious institutional authority. Throughout the constitutional period, 1906–11, the terms *monavvar al-fekr*, "enlightened thinker" in Arabic, and *oqala*, those using their "intellect" or "reason" (from 'aql in Arabic), dominated the revolutionary discourse to distinguish the emerging nationalist-modernist leadership from the established religious guardians of traditional values and sociocultural institutions. While *monavvar al-fekr* was also applied to some of the reform-minded olama who actively supported the Constitution, the term *oqala* was specifically used to contrast the lay modernists from the olama in general. The Persian term *rowshanfekr*, "enlightened thinker," was gradually coined, acquiring a secular, liberal meaning, in contrast to its Arabic equivalent, which had retained a semblance of Islamic legitimacy, if not authenticity. All three terms were European-inspired neologisms to designate the Iranian counterpart of the central European and Russian intelligentsia, reflecting the sociopolitical ideals of eighteenth-century Enlightenment philosophy. As the equivalent of an intelligentsia, the *rowshanfekr* included modernist reformers, bureaucrats, and politicians as well as publicists, journalists, and writers in general.

It is important to note here that the Iranian intelligentsia missed both the centuries-long evolutionary process and the necessary socioeconomic and scientific conditions that facilitated the social maturing of their western European counterparts. However, they benefitted from the well-marked trail established by European innovations: modern technology and communication, modern science, and modern educational institutions offered a tested model, a break-through path that enabled an accelerated process of change outside Europe. Moreover, the Iranian intellectual, who initially threw away his "*clerc*" mantle at the turn of the twentieth century, emerged as a political activist clamoring for modern reforms. The failure of nineteenth-century Shi'a schools of thought and religious movements, deemed heretical, to have any lasting impact on institutionalized religion dissuaded the activist intellectual from further pursuing the quest for change in this direction.[6] Politics then dominated this intellectual's debates and program of action, committed as he was to the belief that social and political problems were the central issues of life. Seeking pragmatic solutions to particular problems, he distanced himself from Islamic theology and mysticism, which he deemed "ancient," and looked to Europe for inspiration and emulation. The source of the profound schism that was later to occur between modern Iranian thought and its centuries-old Shi'a intellectual heritage goes back to this period.

No historical figure better symbolized the "*clerc*" than Seyyed Jamal ed-Din Asadabadi, known as "al-Afghani" (1838–97). Though much has been written about his Islamism and Pan-Islamist activities, al-Afghani was essentially a man in revolt against institutionalized religion and its hierarchical order, fighting for the intellectual "renewal" of Moslem societies. Reared in traditional religious schools, *madreseh*, he was more attracted to Islamic philosophy and dissident schools until, charged with heresy, he was forced into exile. Traveling to India, Egypt, and then Europe, he became acquainted with modern ideas and institutions. He rallied around him a small but potentially influential group of like-minded Egyptian and Syrian Islamist reformers. He vehemently criticized traditional Islamic teachings, holding the olama establishment responsible for the Moslems' intellectual and political decline. He hailed European thought and science as the source of Europe's power and assailed the olama for discouraging the faithful from learning from the non-Moslems. "They have not understood that science is that noble thing that has no connection with any nation, and is not distinguished by anything but itself." He thus persistently maintained the view that science "is not connected to any nation" and that "men must be related to science, not science to men."[7] He universalized the concept of knowledge, thus divorcing it from its traditional Islamic conception as knowledge of the divine and related religious disciplines, without distinction between the sacred and the profane. This intellectual standing best defines the legacy of al-Afghani's activism. It would be no exaggeration to state that al-Afghani had in fact initiated the process of de-sacralization of the concept of knowledge, despite his often confused and obscurantist rhetorical argument and action.

Al-Afghani also fought the absolute dynastic power then ruling over Iran. He seized the occasion of the Tobacco Concession Affair of 1890–92 to call for a revolt against the Qajar shah and to mobilize the *mojtaheds*' backing. He appealed to the doctrine of the Imamate, the sole legitimate source of authority, of which, he reminded them, they were the guarantors. Sheer political expediency lay behind this paradoxical move, an unprecedented strategy to mobilize a broad-based coalition in opposition to government policies. This strategy was to be emulated in 1906 by the Constitutional Revolution's major players in successfully forcing the shah to grant a constitution to the nation. It was also a strategy that inherently bore fatal weaknesses with lasting consequences, leaving unresolved tensions between the secular and the religious.

The secularist leaders who wished to undertake radical social and cultural reforms through a political revolution had to reconcile their ideas with the prevailing religious norms. The "normative vocabulary" of their time limited their freedom of maneuvering to what could be justified and rendered seemingly compatible to religious principles—hence, the complexity of the debates on constitutionalism. All groups involved adopted the innovative term *mashrutiyat*, defined to mean "constitutionalism," which provided a common leitmotif for their respective diverse and in some cases irreconcilable objectives. All had therefore to confront the same dilemma: how to justify resistance to the "Shadow of God" and the olama while at the same time proclaiming belief in the Islamic social order. Hence, some rationalized their right to resist tyranny through reference to the time-honored Shi'a tradition of dissent, which deemed illegitimate the Sunni state established following the death of the Prophet and the subsequent martyrdom of many of their imams. The olama's active participation in the events, however, precipitated the destruction of the old power structure.

The olama, whether supportive of or opposed to the Constitution, upheld the tradition of *saltanat* transcending *dowlat*. In their communication with the shah, they never failed to address him as the "Shadow of God," the king of Islam and the Moslems, putting the blame for the crisis on corrupt elements within his government. At the early stage of the constitutional movement, many lay leaders followed their example, sparing the "affectionate father of the nation"[8] from any responsibility of official wrongdoing. In his response, Mozaffar al-Din Shah (r. 1896–1907) would call upon the olama's duty to pray for his royal well-being, reminding them of their obligations to the throne and the government and insisting on his royal prerogatives and the authority bestowed upon him by divine grace. When he first decreed the Constitution in August 1906, he referred to his "royal self" as the "protector of all rights of the people of Iran, our true subjects" and expressed his "royal desire" for government reforms to be enacted by a "national consultative assembly."[9]

Most olama, including the conservative *mojtahed*s who had conveniently joined the constitutional movement when it gathered nationwide momentum, perceived the Majles as a means to check abuse of government power and to protect religion. The shah believed it would act as the guarantor of royal justice and would ensure the application of the holy law. At the opening ceremony of the first Majles, speakers made repeated references to "Mozaffar's justice" and expressed the people's gratitude to the compassionate Shadow of God, the shah of Islam. Because of the highly visible part that the constitutionalist olama—led in Tehran by Seyyed Abdollah Behbahani and Seyyed Mohammad Tabataba'i, in Tabriz by Theqat al-Islam, and in Najaf by Ayatollah Mohammad Kazem Khorasani—played as nominal leaders of the movement and the seemingly predominant aura of religious legitimacy it acquired, the shah mistakenly believed he was witnessing the erosion of kingly power and, conversely, the ascendancy of the olama's power in political affairs. Neither the moderate secularists nor the radical revolutionaries initially involved in shaping and directing the movement wished to dispel this illusion, at least not at this early stage. The increasing hostility of the newly crowned shah, Mohammad Ali Shah (r. 1907–9), to the Constitution, his court intrigues against the Majles, and his support of the anticonstitutionalist olama released the virulent energy of the radical wing of the movement from the tactical self-imposed constraints.

The intelligentsia, be they moderate or radicals, aristocrats or middle class, by then viewed the prevailing political culture as a formidable obstacle to their reforms. They still conceded hereditary rights to the Qajar dynasty, including the right to appoint the heir apparent. However, they now insisted that the Majles was the center of political authority, the guardian of the people's rights and obligations. They understood that institutional changes had to be carried out in order to build a modern state. Such a state would claim sovereignty and demand loyalty from all citizens, who were no longer regarded as mere subjects and to whom civic rights and equality before the law would be granted, regardless of their social status, tribal affiliation, or religious affiliation. The term *ra'iyat*, traditionally meaning "subjects of the sovereign," was now reinterpreted to mean "citizenry." However, the constitutionalist pamphlets of the time preferred a more populist terminology: *mardom* (people) and *mellat* (nation) as distinct from *saltanat* and *dowlat*. An unprecedented conception of the "will of the people" began to take root, decisively aimed at eroding the theological premises of Iran's political power structure. The old concept *saltanat* was redefined as radicals began to challenge the shah's "most holy" authority. Pamphlets circulating nightly in Tehran and Tabriz reminded him of the fact that his rule depended on the nation's right to confer it upon him. The people of Iran, he was told, "are no longer the same as they were five or six years ago. It is now evident to all that your power . . . rests on the nation's. . . . By God, if there is no nation there is no government; if there is no government, there is no shah."[10]

Mohammad Ali Shah, enjoying the full support of the conservative olama, turned reactionary, resisted any new legislation that curbed his royal prerogatives, and urged the official replacement of the term *mashrutiyat* with *mashru'iyat* (derivative of sharia holy law), which he deemed more compatible to the traditional Islamic political order. However, moderate elements of the intelligentsia did not hesitate to refer to the Crown–olama traditional balance of power to dissuade him from such a drastic reactionary step. He was warned that his suggestion would allow the olama to call for a religious government, hinting at the olama's potential claim to rule on the basis of their being the sole guarantors of the Islamic law. The shah withdrew his demand.

The chronicles of the Constitutional Revolution amply show how the olama, even those who espoused the movement from the start, formulated neither its concepts nor its objectives. They were willing to concede in theory, though not always in practice, to the Fundamental Law (Constitution) promulgated in 1906 (*qanun-e-asassi*, as distinct from *fiqh*, Islamic jurisprudence) jurisdiction over matters pertaining to political-public affairs provided state law was compatible with Islamic principles and values. In fact, clause 2 of the Supplement to the Fundamental Law that was promulgated in 1907, stipulated the formation of a council of five *mojtaheds* to determine the religious compatibility of all laws to be enacted by the Majles. But the clause did not grant the council the right to enforce sharia rule. Furthermore, this significant clause was overshadowed by the ruling giving the Majles the right to select by majority vote the council's candidates, a procedure that delayed the council's formation in both the first and the second Majles. At that time, opponents to the clause circulated pamphlets, stressing the importance to be given to such a distinction between the rules of the Qur'an and the imams for religious affairs, on the one hand, and the Fundamental Law for worldly matters, on the other; some even urged the olama to limit their function to theology and worship. A tiny faction from among the radicals that included middle-ranking dissident members of the religious institutions attempted to target the olama directly. But they were compelled to remain underground and mute their radicalism. Sparks of the verbal fire they periodically ignited would be swiftly extinguished.[11] Nonetheless, the constitutionalist olama's role in drafting the Fundamental Law was increasingly reduced to giving a mere seal of approval.[12]

Ayatollah Fazlollah Nuri had from the start fiercely combated the concepts of freedom of opinion and equality of all individuals before the law as contrary to Islam. Freedom is heresy, he repeatedly proclaimed, and so, together with fellow conservative olama, he stopped attending the Majles. Some deputies countercharged him with heresy and threatened to bring him and his "minions" to justice. The two opposing olama camps, for and against the Constitution, grew politically farther apart as extremist elements penetrated their respective ranks, fueling the dispute. Alarmed by the divisive consequences of the escalating hostility, the constitutionalist *mojtahed* Mohammad Tabataba'i angrily warned the Majles: "Only the olama can judge the olama. The nation in these matters has no right to intervene." Then he pleaded with Nuri to "join hands and work together to reform matters concerning the nation."[13] It would be dangerous and self-destructive, he told Nuri's associates, to take side against the Majles or the nation, for the Majles no longer allows the olama "to do what they wish to do," as they had in the past.[14] Nuri, however, had already identified his cause with the shah's, who by then claimed royal prerogative as the sole legitimate protector of the nation. He famously denied the right to share this responsibility with "just any grocer" who, "rifle in hand, causes riots and disturbs public safety."[15] A small group of lay and clerical deputies reportedly responded: "The grocer who elected us has the duty, rifle in hand, to protect us" from the unlawful deeds of a handful of court officials aiming to destroy the Majles's authority.[16] The shah reluctantly signed the Supplement to the Fundamental Law in October 1907. Article 35 declared the monarchy to be a "trust that the nation delegates" to the person of the shah. Clause 26 stressed the fact that the nation constitutes the basis on which all powers rest.[17]

The olama's initial acceptance of the Constitution and the later defection of those who came to realize the true secular nature of the entire movement underscore their personal motives for their participation in one camp or another. Beneath the highly visible role they collectively played in these fateful events lay considerable differences in temperament, ambition, and personal ability to comprehend the enormous implications of the term *constitution.* In a manner reminiscent of old Qajar political cabals but with graver repercussions for the nation at large, activist olama took sides with or against government officials then in power. However, the constitutional government, even though composed of members of the former political elite, was now accountable to the Majles and no longer to the shah, and its officials were men who genuinely or expediently supported the Constitution. The constitutionalist olama suffered no loss in social status, clout, and financial support for as long as the Majles–shah power struggle tilted in favor of the Majles. Conversely, their star would be tarnished and their religious opponents' would shine when in the summer of 1908 Mohammad Ali Shah, enjoying full Russian support and British acquiescence, struck a severe blow to the first Majles. Thus, the individual fate of the activist olama depended on the worldly political cause each espoused and on the fate of the cause's lay sponsors, just as it was for the old cabals. In other words, the balance of power between the two olama camps was determined by the corresponding balance of power between political factions outside the religious institutions.

With the shah's coup in 1908, Nuri and fellow conservative members of the olama, labeled "promoters of despotism" by their detractors, reimposed their religious authority in the capital. The fiercest battle of words engaged by the two rival clerical camps was fought out during this period, known in the historical annals as "the Lesser Despotism." Once more but even more virulently, they sent cables back and forth, charging one another with heresy, asserting the doctrinal credibility of their opposing views with references to scriptural evidence. It was impossible to know, lamented an eyewitness, who was the true Moslem.[18] Shortly after the closing of the first Majles, Nuri and his entourage met with Mohammad Ali Shah in private to submit a written statement pronouncing the Constitution contrary to the law of Islam and declaring the Majles the "abode of heresy."[19] Armed with this religious support, the shah revoked the Constitution, thus expressing his willingness, as *shahenshah* (king of kings) of the Moslems, to abide by the olama's wishes. The royal decree referred to the "divine command" that through the centuries had entrusted both the reigning monarch, the "king of the age," and the olama with the sacred task of safeguarding Islam. It stated that the shah and the olama were acting in conformity with their respective religious obligations.[20]

Meanwhile, the constitutionalist *mojtahed*s from Najaf, Mohammad Kazem Khorasani, Abdollah Mazandarani, and Mohammad Hosain Tehrani signed a series of cables stating, "To side with the opponents of the Constitution . . . is tantamount to fighting against the Imam of the Age," and "to consolidate the foundation of the Constitution is to protect Twelver Shiʿa religion and safeguard Islam from its enemies." They appealed to the shah to restore the Constitution and to call for new elections. Otherwise, they warned, civil unrest could result in a loss of countless lives. Their tone, however, remained respectful, true to the olama's long tradition of addressing the monarch as the lawful protector of Islam and Moslems. They counseled moderation and national reconciliation. "The king's children," they wrote, would gratefully pray for him and resume their normal life once peace and public safety were restored. But they were adamant in their condemnation of the "corrupt state of affairs" in the country and threatened to come to Tehran should it persist.[21]

Junior disciples of the constitutionalist olama in Najaf sent out several treatises in defense of the Constitution. These polemical writings aimed at refuting Nuri's statements, picking out each of his arguments and finding scriptural evidence to rebut his allegations. Despite the traditional Islamic rhetoric generally adopted by their authors, these essays reflected the lay intelligentsia's ideas and programs. In fact, constitutionalist olama in Najaf were kept continuously informed on the latest developments in Tehran, Tabriz, Istanbul, and the European capitals, where the exiled constitutionalists staged their return to power. Some essays, such as Mohammad Hosain Na'ini's, deduced innovative, modernist concepts of government, which they borrowed from the lay thinkers, out of a seemingly conventional reading of holy texts and classical theological commentaries.[22] Others preferred to demonstrate the right of the lay intelligentsia to govern. Thus, a *mojtahed* of Najaf, Shaikh Ismail Mahallati, wrote a treatise officially endorsed by Khorasani in defense of the Majles and the constitutional monarchy. He proclaimed the intelligentsia of the nation fully responsible for the establishment of the rule of law. Islamic scholars, he stated, who are well informed on the merits of the Constitution, know very well that a constitutional monarchy is not contrary to the holy law. In all languages of the universe, he explained, "constitutional monarchy" means preventing the shah from ruling arbitrarily and ensuring that his rule is in conformity with the Fundamental Law. Mahallati stressed the fact that in times of "tyrannical rule," which necessarily occurs until the advent of the rightful Shi'a ruler, the Constitution and the Majles help soften the oppression and fulfill the religious obligation to "enjoin the good and forbid the bad." The Majles, he added, also safeguards the country from chaos and lawlessness and from its foreign enemies. All Moslems must strive, each according to his individual ability, to preserve the constitutional monarchy in Iran in order to protect Islam. Mahallati refuted the "despots'" allegation that freedom is incompatible with Islamic values. Freedom, he argued, means national freedom from the king's despotic rule. Freedom of the pen is needed to protect individuals' freedom to pursue activities necessary for national development. It also means freedom for each individual, even the weakest, from being subjected to the power of anyone else, even the king's. Religious morality would be preserved and un-Islamic behavior forbidden. Fundamental laws in free countries, he noted, relatively differ, and the differences reflect each nation's morality, religion, and local characteristics.[23]

Events in Azerbaijan and Gilan, where a bloody struggle for the restoration of the Constitution was waged beginning in the summer of 1908, news of unrest in other regions, and, by the spring of 1909, the British renewed effort to work again with the Russian government to check Mohammad Ali Shah's growing despotism encouraged the Najaf olama to raise the tone of their denunciation. They called on all Iranians to unite to save the nation and Islam and to reestablish the Constitution. In the present age of the absence of the Righteous Imam, they argued, the governance of the Moslems belongs to the Moslem people.[24] Radical revolutionary organizations (*anjoman*) increased their underground activities and distributed pamphlets that in the virulence of their tone recalled those passed out during the earlier days of the revolution. Their prime targets were Fazlollah Nuri and other prominent royalist olama and fueled the prevailing paranoia that gripped the ruling circles as demands for the restoration of the Constitution increased in volume. On January 8, 1909, Nuri barely escaped an attempt on his life as he was coming out of a fellow *mojtahed*'s home, where government ministers were holding a meeting. He remained close to the shah, whom he advised till the very end of the monarch's battle to hold onto the Peacock Throne.

Nuri and fellow conservative olama represented mainstream Shi'a jurisprudence, whereas the constitutionalist olama followed an updated Islamic mystical/theological tradition of dissent. Both trends, often at war with each other, had through the centuries enriched Islamic cultures in all their diversity. However, the politically active olama in the early constitutional period became victims of their partisanship, drawn as they were to power politics, which at the time of the revolution had become too complex for them to survive unscathed. They proved to be useful instruments for their respective factional leaders. By granting their support for the movement, the constitutionalist olama were in fact conceding their acceptance of the conception of a Fundamental Law, *qanun-e asassi*, pertaining to matters of worldly affairs as distinct from the sharia. In practice, this concession allowed a greater delineation of the worldly from the religious realms than had the traditional *orfi* (customary law under court administration)and *shar'i* jurisdictions. The Constitution irrevocably de-sacralized the nature of political power and altered its structure. This inevitable consequence of the Constitutional Revolution and the legislative reforms of the first Majles would in turn hasten in the subsequent period the secularization of the vital social institutions that until then had remained in the olama's jurisdiction. The "*clerc*" would give way to the modern intellectual. Seyyed Hasan Taqizadeh and Seyyed Sadeq Tabataba'i (Mohammad Tabataba'i's son), two prominent deputies of the first Majles, were among many, mostly middle-ranking clerics who had symbolically expressed their distancing from the religious institutions by taking off their religious garb. The stage was indeed set for a new breed of Iranian secular nationalists to take over the task of shaping public opinion, constructing the "new Iran," and ushering in modernity. However, the Constitution and the political philosophy behind it were concepts still too alien for its detractors to concede defeat without a struggle.

1

Freemasonry and the Constitutional Revolution

BABIS, NIHILISTS, REVOLUTIONARIES, FREEMASONS! These were the defamatory epithets hurled at the most militant constitutionalists, often interchangeably, by reactionary royalists, lay or clerical, or just by those who feared a social explosion with fatal consequences to the traditional order. To be sure, in the early phase of the constitutional movement and during the period of the first Majles there were both Azali Babis and revolutionaries, but, as I have already demonstrated elsewhere, they all fought for secular reforms and restrained or were compelled to restrain their radicalism.[1] And there were Freemasons. Indeed, many prominent constitutionalists figured on some lists of Freemasonic lodges. Undeniably, European, especially French, Freemasons took an active part in the major events of the period in full support of the constitutionalists, leading some Iranian historians to conclude that these European Freemasons, acting as their imperialist governments' agents, plotted the whole affair to destroy the country's independence. Did they? To assess the validity of this conspiracy theory, it is necessary (1) to understand the nature of modern Freemasonry, its program and agenda, and (2) to evaluate, inasmuch as it is possible given the paucity of reliable evidence, its contribution to the Constitutional Revolution.

The history of Freemasonry—its origins, hierarchy, beliefs, and rituals—does not concern the present study, nor does its centuries-long tradition of controversies, myths, and occult power or its impact on local social mores. The multiplicity of orders with their respective chapters in different places as well as their differences and similarities are also set aside. It is the modern Freemasonry, emerging fully defined and structured with the second edition of the so-called Anderson Constitution (named after its main author), and its political activities, overt or covert, that have immediate relevance to an analysis of its involvement in the Middle East in general and in Iran in particular.

The Freemason constitution of 1736 emphasizes the concept of universalism based on a shared faith in one God, referred to as the "Grand Architect of the Universe." "In Freemasonry," writes Pierre Chevallier, a non-Mason historian of the French orders, "Mecca and Geneva, Rome and Jerusalem are identical. There are no Jews, no Mohammedans, no Papists and no Protestants; there are only brothers who have sworn to God, the Father common to all, to remain brothers forever."[2] Morality was linked to religious conscience, and belief in the immortality of the soul was enforced. In theory, though not always in practice, all religions were deemed equal. In the initiation rites, each new adherent's personal creed was taken into consideration, and he took the oath holding his own holy book in hand. Humanist values, however, transcended religious particularism, imposing an ecumenical framework built on the basic principles of tolerance, pluralism, and freedom of worship. Honor, loyalty, the practicing of good and the shunning of evil, brotherhood, strong belief in humanity as one and indivisible, the sharing of common goals and aspirations were lofty ideals uniting all in a common bond. Highly intellectual, eighteenth-century Freemasonry fully absorbed the philosophy of the Enlightenment, its faith in human reason, human perfectibility and progress, and, above all, liberty. By the end of the eighteenth century, Freemasonry increasingly identified liberty with patriotism and freedom with national independence and national sovereignty. It forged networks in Europe and the Americas, carrying the banner of humanism and universal brotherhood across the national frontiers.

French Freemasons saw their ideal realized with the French Revolution of 1789, which mobilized the masses with the concepts of liberty and patriotism. In the nineteenth century, viewing themselves as missionaries serving the cause of liberalism, they appropriated the revolutionary slogan "Liberty, equality, and fraternity" as their own.[3] They were Voltarian and, as such, fiercely anticlerical. They considered Catholicism in particular as amounting to superstition and fanaticism, and they wished to replace it with a "natural" and more "rational" religion. This is not to say that Freemasonry in general encouraged radical political activism or favored the eradication of institutionalized religion. In fact, although many individual Freemasons participated in the American and French Revolutions and some, such as General Lafayette, participated in both, many others remained loyal to the old political regime, fighting their "brothers" in the opposite camp. Both revolutionary states, the French and the American, adopted the principle of church–state separation.

Freemasonry in France

French Freemasonry during Napoleon Bonaparte's reign prospered, becoming a "state Freemasonry." The French emperor viewed it favorably as a "militia devoted to the interests of his regime and his personal glory."[4] However, Freemasonry, as Chevallier notes, always had representatives in governments in and out of power. This dualism allowed the Freemason dignitaries to serve two masters at the same time.[5] Throughout the nineteenth century, they encountered fierce hostility in many lay and religious circles, chief among them the Catholic Church, compelling the order's top hierarchy to impose a general ban on political activism. Many "brothers" outwardly complied but secretly continued their political activism, reinforcing the medieval conspiratorial aura Freemasonry held and thus increasing public mistrust in the order.

By the mid–nineteenth century, dissension severely divided the ranks of the Grand Orient de France, the order that played an important role in the Iranian Constitutional Revolution. A marginal group espoused socialism and positivism, transforming the order into an antimonarchical, anticlerical institution. This group's manifesto promoted the ideas of democratic republic, sovereignty of the people, direct universal suffrage, universal education under state jurisdiction, state financial support for needy children, and the rights of workers and farmers to improve their working conditions and raise their standard of living. As we shall see, the programs of the two political parties active in the second Majles were identical to the Freemasons', which reflected Enlightenment philosophy. Furthermore, the French revolutionary slogans were adapted to the radical Freemasonic manifesto, calling on all religions to respect liberty, to preach equality, and to practice fraternity.[6] But the official hierarchy of all Freemasonic orders in France condemned the manifesto and the political activism of its authors.

Freemasonry was at the time profoundly bourgeois, in favor of law and order. In August 1849, Grand Orient officials drafted and promulgated a constitution that reaffirmed belief in the existence of God and in the immortality of the soul and prohibited social and political debates deemed too controversial. The hierarchy turned autocratic, and the order lost its independence. Gradually, an elected body, the Supreme Council of the Order

(Suprême conseil de l'ordre) acquired greater authority, reducing the office of the grand master to an honorary function. Positivists' underground activities persisted, by 1865 succeeding in altering the constitution article concerning faith in God and the immortal soul with the inclusion of a sentence allowing membership to individual nonbelievers. Moreover, as the Catholic authorities intensified their assault on Freemasonry, the radical "brothers" dramatically increased their combative tone. Considering themselves the soldiers of freethinking, they proclaimed their readiness for battle "when Rome declares war on modern reason."[7] By 1871, the office of the grand master was also eliminated and replaced with an elected president; the Supreme Council retained its authority. This democratization of the Grand Orient leadership took place at a time when positivism was rapidly gaining ground within its ranks.

Freemasons rode the tide and drew advantage from the humiliating military defeat French troops suffered at the hands of the Prussian army in 1871. Until 1940, when Hitler's army invaded France, Freemasonry played an important role in the country's political life. A great number of politicians, high middle-ranking functionaries in the capital and the provinces, were active members of the Grand Orient lodges, translating into practice the principles of the Declaration of Human Rights, which many masons had helped formulate.[8] Freemasonry is commonly referred to as the "church of the Third Republic." In 1877, the Supreme Council revoked the articles of the constitution regarding the existence of God and immortality of the soul, instead asserting morality as independent from religion. Like the Third Republic itself, the order identified with the middle class and the petit bourgeois. It gave full support to the legislative reforms of the 1880s that secularized the entire public-education system.[9] Many lodges of the Grand Orient were the most belligerently secularist and positivist of the French orders.

French Freemasonic lodges, like their British counterparts, effectively spread out through international networks, promoting the republic's policies and national interests throughout the world. Short- or long-term alliances were forged, some even with clerical groups engaged in *missions evangelisatrices* (evangelical missions).[10] French Freemasons, however, were above all committed to *missions civilisatrices* (civilizing missions) in the non-European world, establishing cultural and social ties with the ruling elite of targeted countries. Here, too, they shared common goals with the French government, which, partly as a result of its colonial policies in competition with other European powers, promoted the French language and culture in different continents. Modern, secular, even republican values were to be exported to distant foreign lands, though presented as universal values that were by no means incompatible with the local national or religious values. To a large extent, one can say that French Freemasonic lodges popularized and attempted to universalize the ideals and slogans of the French Revolution abroad as they expanded their ateliers (auxiliary branches) in the Middle East and North Africa.

Ottoman Lodges and Their Persian Adherents

Several lodges were established in the Ottoman Empire, particular in its Balkan and Arab provinces and in Istanbul. However, the ateliers' bulletins and archival documents rarely provide concrete information on their work and divulge no clues as to their members' extracurricular activities. A brief look at them, however, can serve as a preliminary illustration and guideline for the role of Masonry in Iran in the same period.

Paul Dumont cites a document explaining the goals of the French Istanbul lodge Étoile du Bosphore. The goals formulated explicitly were general, expressing the desire to create a common alignment for men of goodwill living in a multinational, multisectarian, and diverse country and offering them services. But it also provided institutional protection and cover to Frenchmen devoted to the glory of their fatherland and the independence of Europe.[11] This dual function of the ateliers characterized all the Masonic activities in the region. As we shall see, this function by no means determined and even less guaranteed protection and ultimate success for the local national cause. When conflicts of interest arose, and there were many, French and generally European priorities eclipsed any solidarity with their Middle Eastern "brothers," to the point of betraying the cherished ideals of Freemasonry. By the same token, Middle Eastern "brothers" were not always as obedient in carrying out their Masonic instructions. Contrary to the prevailing grandiose conspiracy theory, Iranian constitutionalists were not docile agents of European imperialism acting in the guise of Freemasonic brotherhood.

We know that throughout the period 1876–1908 the Ottoman Freemasons formed the most effective organizations in opposition to the traditional sociopolitical order.[12] Founded in 1862 in Istanbul, the Union d'Orient, a lodge affiliated with the Grand Orient de France, began by recruiting Christian and Jewish members but by the late 1860s also began to admit Moslem high-ranking officials and military officers and even some olama, eventually becoming a "Moslem Masonic lobby."[13] The initiation was secret, and the lodge was defined as an organization essentially philanthropic and philosophically progressive, aiming at "moral and intellectual improvement of Humanity [*sic*]."[14] Its members' task was to instruct those who, although not Freemasons, were to play a great role as educators of the new generation. In the 1870s, Proodos (Progress), the most overtly political of all the lodges in Istanbul, attracted the membership of the Moslem ruling elite. The part played by Masonic lodges in the rise and triumph of the Young Turk Revolution of 1908 is now uncontested. A great number of the Committee of Union and Progress (Young Turk) leaders were either members or supported close companions who were. In early 1909, Mehmet Talaat, a Freemason and member of the new Turkish government, anxious to establish a distance from the Young Turks' French mentors/collaborators, assumed the position of grand master in a newly founded Grand Orient Ottoman lodge, autonomous from the French order. Freemasonry thus came out into the open in the Ottoman Empire, fashionable and respected, with increased membership.

In Istanbul, some prominent Iranian politicians and social reformers joined some lodges, Union d'Orient and Progress seemingly their favorite choices. The Persian ambassador to Turkey, Mirza Mohsen Khan Moshir al-Dowleh, and his fellow reform-minded politician Mirza Malkom Khan belonged to the Union d'Orient. Both also had membership in the Sincere amitie lodge of Paris, affiliated with the Grand Orient de France. Mohsen Khan was promoted to the rank of master of the Sincere amitie in 1860 and was awarded the Rose-Croix, a highly prestigious honor, at the Union d'Orient in Istanbul in 1874.[15] Both men reportedly became directly engaged with the Ottoman reform movement during their stay in the Turkish capital. Contact between Ottoman and Iranian reformers intensified in the summer and fall 1908, when many constitutionalists went into exile in Paris and Istanbul and the Young Turks' success offered a hopeful model to emulate.

Malkom Khan's Proto-Masonic Organizations

As far as we know, European Freemasonry did not officially begin its activities in Iran until the early twentieth century. In 1907, the Grand Orient established an atelier in Tehran called Le Réveil de l'Iran (Iran's Awakening) and referred to in Persian as Bidari-ye Iran.[16] The Grand Lodge of England did not inaugurate its presence in Iran until after the outbreak of World War I. Earlier discussions to set up lodges in Tehran and some provincial capitals apparently remained fruitless because there is no evidence of their official existence prior to 1907.[17] Mirza Malkom Khan's short-lived organization

House of Oblivion (Faramushkhaneh) resembles a Masonic lodge, but it had no affiliation with any European order, and none recognized it as such. However, Malkom Khan and many other prominent nineteenth-century politicians belonged to different French and English lodges in Europe. European Masonic institutions welcomed them and greatly facilitated their initiation, bypassing strict rules of procedure. The first to be officially acknowledged in a Masonic bulletin was Fath Ali Shah's ambassador at Napoleon's court. Admitted in a Paris chapter of the Grand Lodge of Scotland on November 24, 1808, he was promoted within three weeks to a higher grade, master.[18] Mirza Saleh Shirazi, one of the first Persian students sent to London in 1815 on a government scholarship, joined a chapter of the Grand Lodge of England in 1817. Mirza Saleh, back in Iran, played an important role ushering in the "new age," setting up a second printing press and editing the official government gazette.[19] In 1857, the shah's envoy to the Anglo-Iranian peace treaty in Paris and his entire diplomatic delegation, which included Malkom Khan, joined the Sincere amitie lodge. According to the *Bulletin du Grand Orient de France*, the Supreme Council viewed this initiation of the Iranian mission as a good diplomatic means to promote French cultural and political influence in Iran.[20] Upon his return from that trip to Europe in 1858, Malkom Khan founded his society.

Was the House of Oblivion a Masonic lodge? Opinions vary. Officially, there exists no evidence of any link it may have had with a European order. Some sources, however, regard it as a lodge.[21] Regardless of its official status, Malkom's society was indeed modeled on the Masonic system of secret cells, strict rules, and hierarchical structure. Its teachings and goals were almost identical to the Grand Orient's, with its positivist faith in science, progress, and humanity's ability to transcend divisive obstacles in its march forward. Freedom, rule of law, national representative government, human rights—all were concepts eagerly presented to House of Oblivion members as the path to follow for national redemption. They were told to shun evil, to strive to do good, to fight against oppression, and to seek and diffuse learning. Words such as *civilization* (in transliterated French), *humanity*, *order*, *law*, *universalism*, and *fraternity* kept on recurring in his writings. In fact, he is credited with introducing the term *qanun* (law) in the Persian vocabulary as distinct from *shari'at* (Islamic law).[22]

Malkom Khan was successful in attracting many reform-minded officials and students of the Dar al-Fonun, the newly established school offering a modern curriculum, where he also taught. He was initially successful in gaining the support of royal princes and government ministers and even, reportedly, the shah. Established olama of the capital also figured in the House of Oblivion's membership list: the *imam jom'eh* of Tehran Zain al-Abidin as well as the *mojtahed* Seyyed Sadeq Tabataba'i, father of his more famous son, Seyyed Mohammad Tabataba'i, who was to play a leading role in the Constitutional Revolution. The list also included many known members of European lodges abroad, such as Mirza Mohsen Khan Moshir al-Dowleh and Mirza Hosain Khan Sepahsalar, two officials who served as ambassadors in Istanbul,[23] and many others who were to join the Réveil de l'Iran lodge when it was set up in 1907. The royal prince Jalal al-Din Mirza, a great fan of modern European knowledge, a friend of many liberal intellectuals of his time, and a writer, offered Malkom Khan support and help in setting up the society, including the use of his house for the meetings. Both Jalal al-Din and Malkom were basically antireligious, the former openly hostile and the other discreetly opposed.[24] It is alleged that the prince hoped to use the House of Oblivion's network to ascend to the Qajar throne. But he was to die in 1872.[25] Mas'ud Mirza Zell al-Soltan, the governor of Isfahan, more cynically manipulated the society and others that were to emerge in the political scene decades later, assuming a liberal attitude simply to win their support for his acquisition of the shah's crown. Other dignitaries associated themselves with Malkom Khan and his society for the contacts they believed he had with European lodges, seeking either admission in prestigious orders or promotion in rank.[26]

Within five years, however, Malkom Khan and his circle suffered a severe reversal of fortune as his numerous enemies and rivals, enjoying some olama's support, caused his loss of favor with the shah. He was charged with sedition, republicanism, Babism, and conspiracy to eradicate Islam. He was also accused of attempting to create unity between Moslems and non-Moslems.[27] Although insisting that his society did not propagate ideas incompatible with Shi'a Islam, he in fact underlined his universal conception of knowledge: "Great truths are neither planted in French soil nor manufactured in English factories. The sun of knowledge has no particular sphere; it rises everywhere. If we are clear-sighted enough, we would see that the truth of these secrets belong neither to Europe nor India; it has no specific time or place."[28] This conception ran counter to religious leaders' teaching of Islam. Malkom Khan was forced into exile, other officials were dismissed from their posts, and many were kept under house arrest.

In 1862, Malkom Khan arrived in Istanbul, ready to make use of his Masonic contacts, chief among them the Persian ambassador, Mirza Hosain Khan, later known as "the Sepahsalar," commander in chief, from 1859 to 1871. The latter wasted no time in obtaining a royal pardon for him. Thus cleared, Malkom Khan settled comfortably in the Ottoman capital as a newly appointed special adviser to the ambassador, continuing to enjoy his protection against recurring troubles with the then minister of foreign affairs in Tehran and maintaining close ties with fellow Masons, including Ottoman statesmen. Significantly, all were active members of Masonic lodges most overtly involved in Ottoman politics, including the Union d'Orient and Progress.[29]

Other contemporary Iranian diplomats and Masonic "brothers" collaborated with Malkom Khan in writing essays and disseminating ideas about reforms. Mirza Yusef Khan Mostashar al-Dowleh, author of *Yek kalameh* (One Word), was a member of the Clemente amitie, another Paris lodge of the Grand Orient, which recruited adepts from among the Moslem ruling elite. In 1869, Mostashar al-Dowleh received the prestigious Rose-Croix at an elaborate ceremony held at the headquarters of the organization.[30] His famous essay introducing social liberalism and constitutionalism to Iran, written in Paris, is considered one of the most important Persian modernist works of the time. Like Malkom Khan, Mostashar al-Dowleh cloaked his ideas in Islamic terms, identifying *mashrutiyat* (constitutionalism) with *mashru'iyat* (based on Islamic law), and, again like Malkom, was a protégé of Mirza Hosain Khan. All three shared in common an admiration for the Ottoman Tanzimat reforms and a strong wish to accomplish parallel projects in Iran.

In 1871, Mirza Hosain Khan returned to Tehran to assume the title of *sepahsalar* and the post of minister of finance, then a few months later the post of prime minister. He invited Malkom Khan and Mostashar al-Dowleh to work with him as special advisers. For the first time, all three were in a position to put into practice in Iran their cherished administrative reforms and lay the legal basis for economic development. Centralized government, the rule of law, justice, military and educational reforms, banking and trade regulations—all were part of their ambitious program to modernize the country, emulating the Tanzimat experiments in the Ottoman Empire. As elsewhere in Europe and the Middle East, Freemasonic connections allowed both the sordid and the lofty ideals, fraudulent and authentic intentions, to work hand in hand. Extensive international networks facilitated financial transactions that mostly benefited their initiators and middlemen, often to the detriment of their government interests. The history of the second half of the nineteenth century in Iran is marred with the shady deals between foreign concessionaires and their Iranian representatives. Prominent Masons, including the Sepahsalar and Malkom Khan were heavily involved in negotiating such concessions, receiving huge monetary compensations for their services, which in the end caused the minister's downfall.

Masonic activity among Iranians abroad continued to have an aura of international prestige and glamour, a view duly encouraged by the European governments, especially France and Britain. For the aristocrats and high-ranking officials of these European countries, membership in a lodge was regarded as a token of diplomatic esteem on the part of the host honoring his guest, a symbol of cordial relations. More illustrious tokens were reserved for the shahs, Naser al-Din (r. 1848–96) and his successor, Mozaffar al-Din: portraits of the hosting sovereigns, adorned with precious stones and, even more glorious, the British Order of the Garter, an honorific title usually restricted to Christian noblemen judged to be of the highest merit.[31] Sir Arthur Hardinge, the British ambassador in Tehran from 1900 to 1905 and a Freemason, complained about some aristocratic Persian "brothers" using their Freemason connection to conspire with "Mahommedan fanatics and revolutionists whose views and objects are entirely different for purposes utterly alien to the principles of freemasonry."[32]

Malkom Khan had been appointed ambassador in London in early 1873, a post that he kept for sixteen years and that gave him plenty of opportunities to enrich himself while relentlessly campaigning for reforms in Iran and maintaining his Masonic contacts. Hosain Khan died in disgrace in 1881. Mirza Mohsen Khan Moshir al-Dowleh, however, prospered in his post as ambassador in Istanbul from 1873 to 1891, remaining an honored and active member of several lodges while closely collaborating with Malkom Khan and other reform-minded officials who belonged to Malkom's group of disciples. When Malkom Khan's political demise occurred in 1889, he turned into an unequivocal opposition leader, living in exile in London and publishing the newspaper *Qanun*, which played a vital role in popularizing liberal concepts among Iranians. Moreover, Malkom's voluminous correspondence with Iranian officials at home kept him in touch with events. Mozaffar al-Din Mirza, the crown prince at the time, corresponded with him regularly, seeking advice on reforms. "I am extremely fond of you," the prince wrote; "know that I am completely in accord and agreement with you." But he also expressed his reservations: "You yourself must be aware that matters cannot be accomplished all at once; they must ripen gradually."[33]

It was with *Qanun*, essentially a one-man enterprise, that Malkom fully expressed his Freemasonic-inspired views, which he introduced in his columns as the ideology and program of the League of Humanity (Majma'-e 'Adamiyat). There is no evidence that this organization actually existed with a fully-fledged membership, nor is there any link that would tie it to a European Masonic order. In the 1890s, its primary function was the distribution of the paper in Iran and abroad. It is important to note, however, that the league's structure, as described in *Qanun*, followed a European lodge model, with a similar hierarchy and strict rules and regulations, and that the ideology it propagated was Masonic both in content and in form. The first issue, appearing on February 12, 1890, bore the slogan "Union, justice, progress," which it kept until the last issue in 1898. The "principles of humanity" exposed a positivist outlook, with faith in reason and science and defining the essence of humanity as progress. Malkom's "Religion of Humanity" attempted to combine Judeo, Christian, and Moslem teachings into one creed and proclaimed people's right to worship freely but rationally as long as they abided by the "law of the world order." Malkom perceived humans as perfectible and progressive, able to avoid evil and accomplish good, and able to abolish tyranny. "Humanity means serving the world," he wrote,[34] insisting that only with accord and unity could such a goal be attained.

More than a decade before the revolution, *Qanun* was the first Persian paper to publicly call for a parliamentarian regime with the establishment of a national consultative assembly (*majles-e showra-ye melli*), to be popularly elected.[35] Paradoxically, however, in a clear attempt to win over the olama to his cause, Malkom proposed the formation of a higher assembly (*majles-e a'zam*) composed of olama to limit royal absolute power on the basis of Islamic principles.[36] In 1907, both the royalists and the olama turned constitutionalists took these proposals into consideration. Malkom upheld paradoxical religious and political views. Anticlerical and antireligious he may have been, but that did not prevent his adoption of a moderate program of reforms that would in no way antagonize the political and religious elite he hoped would execute them. He candidly confessed to Christians, Jews, and Moslems living in Iran that the Ottoman Empire and the Caucasus must be respected, that attacking their faith would attract their wrath and mistrust, so the reform objectives would not be reached.[37] Like many fellow Masons in

Europe, Malkom favored working with the political establishment to bring about the necessary reforms from within, but he also identified with the opposition political stand. He attacked the state of lawlessness in the country and the tyranny of the government and demanded laws to ensure security for life and property, echoing the French revolutionary slogans, but he opposed violence as a means to overthrow the regime.[38]

In 1896, Naser al-Din Shah had been assassinated by one such violent radical. Malkom adopted a more moderate tone, especially as Mozaffar al-Din Mirza ascended the Qajar throne. The new shah had had cordial relations with him, as already stated, and was reputed to have a more liberal mind than his predecessor. Malkom wasted no time in instructing all his "brothers" in the League of Humanity to obey the new ruler. "Woe to those ignorant and misguided ones who shall commit the slightest treachery to this sinless monarch upon whom depend all the hopes of Iran."[39] In 1898, he ceased publication of his paper. He was soon rehabilitated enough to obtain a post as ambassador in Rome, which he accepted rather than return to Iran and which he kept until his death in 1908. Although he no longer participated directly or indirectly in the politics of the time because he was getting on in age, he maintained the status of a patriarchal adviser to the major political players in Iran.

In 1905, on the occasion of Mozaffar al-Din Shah's trip to Paris, Malkom wrote another essay, "Neda-ye 'adalat" (The Call for Justice), in the form of a memorandum for reforms to be enacted to ensure national survival and the rule of law. Once more Malkom insisted on the formation of a committee of *mojtaheds* to review the compatibility of the new laws with Islamic principles, an idea that subsequently led to the insertion of clause 2 into the Supplement to the Fundamental Law of 1907. Freedom of speech should be permitted if based on the Qur'anic rule to "enjoin the good and prohibit the bad." This moderate, loyalist, yet liberal treatise and many of Malkom's other works were reprinted and circulated in Tehran as the Constitutional Revolution was gathering momentum, involving the highly visible participation of the leading *mojtaheds* in town. Stripped of its more blatantly Freemasonic ideas, Malkom's message read like a blueprint for a vast reform project best undertaken by the ruling elite, albeit only select, open-minded members, lay and clerical. Constitutionalism was expediently not identified as a revolutionary movement. That set the pattern for political behavior in the early stages of what British officials persistently referred to as the "Reform Movement."

Many members of the ruling elite in Iran used Freemasonry as a means for their own ends, a network for social and political self-promotion, and not necessarily as an ideological bond tying them to the order. The conversion of Ali Asghar Khan Amin al-Soltan, the prominent prime minister of successive Qajar monarchs, best illustrates the point. At an international gathering of Freemasons held at the Carlsbad luxury spa, presently in the Czech Republic, that was frequented by the European ruling elite, he met with several high-ranking European statesmen and professionals. He described them as "outstanding men from all over the world," occupied with serving humanity and planning the destinies of mankind, who revealed to him "unimaginable mysteries" and who "made a human being of me."[40] The "wise men of Carlsbad" encouraged his return to Iran and instructed him to establish the rule of law and justice there. As Hamid Algar points out, because Amin al-Soltan was determined to return to political life in Iran, he appreciated "the unseen but powerful support foreign Masonic connections could secure," and, perhaps, masonry proved an attractive "ideology preaching secular progress."[41] His "conversion" to Freemasonic ideals did not, however, convince his enemies. In 1907, at the height of the royalists' assault on the first Majles, he was assassinated in broad daylight. His violent death also frightened the anticonstitutionalists, however, and assured the passage of the Supplement to the Fundamental Law, which was until then seriously contested by Ayatollah Nuri and his supporters.[42]

The Alliance Française in Tehran

Liberal Iranian politicians of the second half of the nineteenth century had failed in implementing their ideas through any lasting reforms, and their tentative steps toward building new modern government institutions were obstructed both by Naser al-Din Shah's reluctance to pursue social changes he had initially espoused and by his successor Mozaffar al-Din Shah's ill health. The only institution that survived royal whims was the Dar al-Fonun school. Founded in 1851 by Amir Kabir, one of the first reform-minded ministers to have lasted in office long enough to achieve one accomplishment, the school emerged within half a century as the best institute of higher learning that offered a modern, European-style curriculum and educated children of the political elite and the wealthy. In the early 1900s, Nasrollah Khan Moshir al-Dowleh, then foreign minister, and his son Hasan Khan founded the Political Science Faculty, which was affiliated with the Dar al-Fonun. Its aim reportedly was to provide a solid modern education for the country's new generation of diplomats and political leaders.[43] Its graduates were guaranteed important government posts. At the turn of the century, they came to play a prominent role as the intellectual avant-garde, the intelligentsia riding the tide when not leading the various phases of the revolution.

From the start, the Dar al-Fonun hired European instructors and added European languages to its regular curriculum. By the late 1880s, however, French instructors and the French language began to dominate as close ties were formed with a newly established French cultural institute, the Alliance française, a branch of the Paris-based Association nationale pour la propagation de la langue française.[44] As the full name indicates, the Alliance, founded by the government in 1883, aimed at spreading French influence in the world through its intensive cultural mission, teaching French language and civilization. Its agenda was to acquaint people of diverse cultures and nationalities with French mores and customs, believing this would facilitate France's foreign relations and promote French products in the world markets. Branches were established in Germany, Russia, Belgium, Italy, Australia, and the United States as well as in Egypt and the Ottoman Empire. In each town, the Alliance set up a school with its own administrative board, a library, and an advisory committee recruited from among its employees, the local European community, and concerned local nationals. In 1889, Dr. Joseph-Desire Tholozan, the French physician of Naser al-Din Shah, after lengthy negotiations with the Alliance's Central Committee in Paris and high-ranking Iranian court officials, opened Alliance schools in Tehran and Shiraz. However, given the almost exclusive trade monopoly Britain and Russia enjoyed in Iran, tolerating no competition, Paris reluctantly reduced Tehran Alliance activities to teaching. Joseph Richard, a Frenchman who had spent decades in Iran and was a member of the Dar al-Fonun faculty, was appointed the first director of the school. The Central Committee, headed by Dr. Feuvrier, another French doctor at the royal court, included highly influential Iranian political figures: Ali Asghar Khan Amin al-Soltan, Naser al-Din Shah's powerful prime minister, and his nemesis, the reform-minded politician Mirza Ali Khan Amin al-Dowleh; Kamran Mirza Nayeb al-Saltaneh, the Qajar prince most active in court politics; and Ja'far Qoli Khan Nayer al-Molk, director of the Dar al-Fonun.

Paul Henri Morel, the Alliance Central Committee's first secretary, was an instructor of French at the Political Science Faculty and publisher of the French gazette *Echo de Perse* before its forced closure due to its liberal views. By the time he departed Iran in 1910, he had lived in the country for twenty-five years. Alphonse Nicolas, the French Orientalist turned diplomat, future French consul in Tabriz, an expert on Persian language and culture; Julien Bottin, a French engineer; and Dr. Tholozan's son-in-law, Jean-Baptiste Lemaire, the musical director at the shah's court and future director of the Alliance in Tehran—all figured in the committee's list, together with many other European and Iranian diplomats, businessmen, educators, and other professionals.[45]

The Alliance school similarly attracted the shah's suspicion. Rumors were spreading in Tehran that the Alliance's agenda was identical to the Freemasons', its "revolutionary" propaganda similar to the Babis', thus threatening the monarchy and Islam. The Comte de Montfort, the Austrian officer hired in 1879 to run the Tehran police, reportedly was adamantly opposed to the Alliance and its activities.[46] The English envoy was no less hostile to the French institution, regarding its cultural activities merely as a cover for French political and economic penetration of Iran. Generally speaking, Naser al-Din Shah and his conservative entourage feared the undue impact of "dangerous ideas" taught at foreign schools. The French envoy, who was the honorary chairman of the Alliance Central Committee, intervened with the shah, however, assuring him that the school was not adverse to either his religion or his government[47] and that its only concern was to teach the French language. In an effective manner aimed at putting an end to the malicious rumor mongering, he offered the shah the title of honorary chairman of the Alliance. The shah, delighted and somewhat reassured, agreed. A royal decree dated April 18, 1891, proclaimed the Alliance to be under his personal royal patronage and offered financial support. Classrooms at the Dar al-Fonun and the Political Science Faculty were put under the Alliance's disposal to teach its courses there.

The new friendly environment helped to increase student enrollment. However, Dar al-Fonun's full development occurred only when Dr. Justin Schneider took over its directorship. A physician attached to the French military, Schneider was appointed in 1894 by Kamran Mirza to join the circle of royal physicians in the capital. In 1899, he was appointed director of the school. He quickly expanded his activities and came to control the Anjoman-e Ma'aref, an educational association privately run by Iranian reform-minded politicians involved in establishing new schools and public libraries. In 1901, he joined an advisory board for the Ministry of Education, which declared the French language a compulsory subject for all students aiming at government service. He also established an exchange program with the University of Lyons in France to admit Iranian students on government scholarships. He succeeded in having the French Ministry of Education recognize the Alliance diploma as equivalent to the French baccalaureate, despite the obvious evidence to the contrary, thus allowing his school's graduates admission to universities in France. In his correspondence with Lyons and Paris, Schneider claimed his efforts could potentially benefit France because Iranian graduates from French establishments would work to promote French interests.[48] He also ensured that more and better instructors were hired from abroad. In 1900, Joseph Vizioz was brought from Istanbul to direct the school. Under the latter's leadership, which was to last till the outbreak of World War I, the school dramatically raised its academic standards and its enrollment. From the initial five students admitted in 1889, by 1907 it had 125 full-time students, a relatively high number for the time.[49] By then, the new shah, Mozaffar al-Din, was pronouncedly more lenient toward the reformers. The Alliance wished to cooperate with "men of good intentions," regardless of their faith or political affiliation—patriotic men who also considered France their second homeland.[50]

In 1899, a French-educated medical doctor, Zain al-Abedin Loqman al-Mamalek, founded a bilingual school in Tabriz. Known as "the Loqmaniyeh," from the start this school received full material and financial support from the Alliance française Central Committee in Paris. So did another school established by the constitutionalist Mirza Hasan Roshdiyeh, which came to be known by its founder's name and served as a model for other schools set up in Tehran in the early 1900s. Reportedly, the Loqmaniyeh was virtually run by the Alliance.[51] In October 1906, the French Orientalist Alphonse L. M. Nicolas was named consul in Tabriz and honorary chairman of the Alliance Central Committee. A close collaboration was then forged between the Alliance, the French consul, and the Azerbaijan *anjoman*, the Tabriz political organization that would later play a decisive role in the revolution. Nicolas attended this *anjoman*'s meetings regularly, where he was often requested to lecture on the French Revolution.[52]

On the eve of the Constitutional Revolution, court officials once more voiced their distrust of the "dangerous ideas" taught at foreign schools, which in turn compelled the Alliance to deny having any political objectives and to reiterate its sole interest in teaching French. School director Vizioz's added comments were more ambiguous: "France is the land of ideas," he explained, and the Alliance's aim was to "plant the seeds of its talents in the midst of people who were in the past overrun by floods."[53] The Alliance school also had its detractors from among the constitutionalists. Yahya Dowlatabadi accused it of wanting to teach French to the exclusion of all other European languages.[54] Dowlatabadi was a frequent visitor to the British legation. The Alliance school attracted the resentment of other educators, who regarded it as unfair competition for government financial and material support. So did the Dar al-Fonun, despite its close cooperation with the Alliance and its sharing of instructors and classrooms. Moreover, Russian and British diplomats in Tehran and elsewhere in the country were as disenchanted with these French educational activities. Their hostility was well founded.

By the early 1900s, the Alliance, an instrument of the French Republic's *mission civilisatrice*, emerged in Tehran and Tabriz as an important center where members of Iran's ruling elite, the intelligentsia, and the small but socially prominent international circle of diplomats and foreign residents mixed easily. Many were elected officers of the Alliance's various committees in charge of administrative or fund-raising tasks; others contributed generously to its libraries. Its school graduates helped in translating French books on liberalism and revolutionary history into Persian; and with the outbreak of the revolution, they addressed massive crowds gathered in mosques and later on the grounds of the British legation.

The Réveil de l'Iran Lodge

It was some of the most active members of the Alliance française who established the first officially recognized Masonic lodge in Iran. Bottin, Lemaire, Morel, Vizioz, and Schneider were acknowledged Freemasons affiliated with the Grand Orient and were to play a vital role in organizing, recruiting, and planning the Iranian lodge. Schneider, back in France prior to the Iranian lodge's establishment, maintained his contact with them and the Iranian "brothers." According to the archival sources, on November 29, 1906, Lemaire invited several French and Iranian Masons to his house to discuss the need for a lodge in Tehran where they all could meet regularly and discuss Masonic activities. A total of ten individuals met that evening, including the hosts, Bottin and Morel. Also present were Ibrahim Khan Hakim al-Molk, a physician who had spent ten years studying medicine in France from 1892 to 1902 and had joined the Mount Sinai lodge in the late 1890s, where he was promoted to master in 1900 and received the Rose-Croix in 1901; Mirza Fazlollah Lava' al-Molk, a high-ranking military officer; and Mohammad Hasan Shaikh al-Molk Sirjani, a publicist and recent member of the Clemente amitie. Hajj Sayyah Mahallati, a low-ranking cleric publicist and political orator, was admitted in 1872 to the Italia Risorta lodge and the Orient de Constantinople, both located in Istanbul. Hajj Hosain Amin al-Zarb, the wealthy merchant who played an important role in the early phase of the Constitutional Revolution, and his father, the equally influential Hajj Hasan Amin al-Zarb, were members of Malkom's society, the House of Oblivion. Entezam al-Saltaneh, a government official, had joined a Spanish rite lodge that Bottin also belonged to and that reportedly used to meet in Tehran in 1898, though its official existence at that time was denied.[55] The initial meeting for the new lodge in Lemaire's house was also attended by the court official and member of the Clemente amitie lodge Ahmad Khan known for the successive titles to his name "Vazir Hozur," "Qavam al-Dowleh," and "Qavam al-Saltaneh"; and by his brother, the equally active politician Hasan Khan Vothuq al-Dowleh, who apparently did not join the French lodge till 1910. Both brothers were appointed ministers to successive cabinets in the second Majles period. According to the list of the earliest members of Le Réveil de l'Iran filed at the Grand Orient de France Archives, most were affiliated with the Clemente amitie or the Sincere amitie, two Grand Orient lodges favored by non-European Masons. As already stated, the Grand Orient, founded in 1773, adopted a liberal and rationalist policy, identifying with the values of the Enlightenment and by the late nineteenth century with positivism and anticlericalism. Its lodges were also the most active in recruiting members from among non-Christian populations, especially in the Middle East.

At that first meeting, all agreed on the need for an official lodge to organize the Masons' activities in Tehran. Three days later, seventeen members, including the original ten, met at Hakim al-Molk's house and unanimously decided to have their lodge affiliated with the Grand Orient de France. On December 23, 1906, they all met in a new locality rented by Morel for that purpose and chose the name "Réveil de l'Iran" or "Bidari-ye Iran," for the lodge, opting for the Scottish rite, which continued to enforce the belief in the Supreme Being, Creator of the Universe, and in the immortality of the soul.[56] This choice was of the utmost importance, given the role religion played in Moslem societies and in the Middle East in general. On December 28, 1906, the newly elected committee, headed by Lemaire as the venerable (the title given to the lodge's president), wrote to the Supreme Council in Paris requesting admission to the Grand Orient federation. They promised loyalty and strict adherence to its constitution and general regulation, vowing to work for the development of Freemasonry and the welfare of humanity. It took almost a year for Paris to grant its consent.

Although the Réveil de l'Iran lodge was not officially incorporated into the Grand Orient until November 1907, the atelier acted as a fully-fledged chapter of the French order from the start. When Lemaire died in February 1907, Morel replaced him as venerable of the atelier. Indeed, by all accounts it was Morel, the energetic torchbearer of Freemasonic values and goals in Tehran, who shaped the organization and determined its policies, committing it to the constitutionalists' cause. In March 1907, in an eloquent letter to the Supreme Council, he appealed for speedier recognition as well as for help and guidance. "The current situation in Iran," he wrote, "puts us under the obligation to act. . . . The lodge can and must take benevolent action." And he explained that the majority of the Iranian "brothers" were already admitted to some Grand Orient lodges, that they loved and appreciated France and its culture, and that they had had a good command of its language.[57] Morel's friendly contacts with the Iranian intelligentsia and the ruling elite, which he had cultivated through the long years of his residence in Tehran, enabled him to provide the atelier with moral support and influence on public opinion at a time when Freemasonry was highly suspect and its adepts persecuted. His home was a safe house and a discreet meeting place for the "brothers."[58] The second Majles unanimously voted to grant him a retirement pension when, seriously ill, he resigned his post. He died on his way back to France in the summer of 1910.

In addition to the names already mentioned, the various Réveil de l'Iran membership lists[59] read like a who's who of prominent constitutionalists of the time: from the radicals (Seyyed Hasan Taqizadeh, Ali Akbar Dehkhoda, Malek al-Motakallemin, Jamal al-Din Va'ez, Mirza Jahangir Khan, Mirza Aqa Tabrizi, and the Tarbiyat brothers) to the moderates (Abol Hasan Mo'azed al-Saltaneh, Nasrollah Taqavi, Mohammad Ali Zoka' al-Molk [Foroughi], Yusef Khan Mostashar al-Dowleh, Nasrollah Khan Moshir al-Dowleh [Pirnia] and his two sons Hasan Khan and Hosain Khan, Adib al-Mamalek Farahani the poet, Morteza Qoli Khan Sani' al-Dowleh, and Isma'il Khan Momtaz al-Dowleh, whose brother Samad Khan Momtaz al-Saltaneh was then ambassador to Paris and a prominent member of the Clemente amitie lodge there) to the conservatives and reactionaries who infiltrated the lodge (such as the notorious Movaqqar al-Saltaneh—the shah's brother-in-law, who following the coup of 1908 would defect and reveal to the court all the lodge's secrets—Mas'ud Mirza Zell al-Soltan, Abol Fath Mirza Salar al-Dowleh, and Malek Mansur Mirza Sho'a' al-Saltaneh, three Qajar princes interested in promoting their respective claim to the throne. Seyyed

Mohammad Tabataba'i, the *mojtahed* of Tehran and staunch supporter of the constitutionalists, and one of his sons, Mohammad Sadeq, figure in all available lists as frequent participants in lodge meetings.[60] With the restoration of the Constitution in 1909, practically most members of the new government, including the Bakhtiyari brothers and Yeprem Khan, as well as a large number of the deputies in the second Majles would join the ranks of Le Réveil initiates. Contact between the Iranian Masons and their French "brothers" remained constant, with some of the latter often acting as mentors.

News of the formation of the Réveil de l'Iran lodge was received with jubilation in Paris. Thus, on March 24, 1908, the grand master of the Clemente amitie wrote to Adib al-Mamalek, the poet and one of the first members of the Réveil: "I have no doubt that, should our Masonic brothers in Tehran work together, they would be able to enlighten the most ignorant and most backward of its population. . . . A Masonic center in the East could, with the diffusion of its principles, revitalize the intelligent and knowledgeable members of the Iranian Parliament." He strongly urged his "brothers" to strive to have their compatriots believe in the worthiness of their work. "It is time," he wrote, "to show to the modern world that Iran is worthy of renewed life, that it can develop its resources, liberate the thought of its people. . . . Cry out loudly: we want to attain spiritual and material liberty, equality of all before the law, and fraternity of all in accordance to each individual's class, status, and mental ability; and promote these three concepts among all those who desire progress for their fatherland."[61]

The Réveil membership was highly selective from the start. Most of the members were, with very few exceptions, Moslem-educated, upper-class men, many of whom held government or court positions or were rising in prominence with their active participation in the constitutional movement as Majles deputies, journalists, or public orators. Each individual initiation began with a standard procedure of personal investigation by the atelier committee, followed by a vote in a special meeting (which had to be unanimous) and final approval from the Paris headquarters. An unnamed person's request for admission was denied when the investigation produced unfavorable reports. Paris was then notified to bar any attempt by the rejected candidate to seek membership in Paris.[62] According to a typical initiation certificate found in the lodge's file in Paris, the new adept signed an "obligation" and swore an oath by the Freemasonry constitution to fully accept its laws as inviolable and to keep secret everything he saw or heard concerning the order, unless explicitly authorized to reveal it in a manner specifically indicated. He promised to work with zeal, constantly and regularly, for the Masonic objectives. The atelier's venerable, always a Frenchman until 1912—when Mohammad Ali Khan Zoka' al-Molk (Forughi) was elected the first Iranian to hold that post—was directly accountable to the Grand Orient general secretary in Paris, to whom he sent regular reports on the budget and news of its members. The Supreme Council persistently refused permission for the translation of the Grand Orient constitution into Persian, and it ordered Tehran "brothers" to perform the rituals in French. Only in 1913 did it give the green light for Persianization. However, more often than not, the meetings were conducted in both Persian and French, and some preliminary translation of the constitution and the rules-and-regulation booklet was done prior to that date.[63] Both the unofficial and official translations were the result of the collaborative work of Nasrollah Taqavi, Vothuq al-Dowleh, and Mirza Hosain Khan Dabir al-Molk Badar, with additional assistance by Zoka' al-Molk and Joseph Vizioz for the version done in 1912.

The rules and regulations very specifically laid out the members' duties: solidarity, obedience, promotion of Masonic principles and concepts, regular attendance of meetings (i.e., no absenteeism without a valid excuse), regular payment of membership fees (nonpayment not acceptable, with the nonpaying member subject to expulsion upon the third warning, temporarily or permanently depending on each individual case). Disobedience, failure to execute responsibilities, and betrayal of secrets were to be very harshly punished. All members were accountable to the lodge committee and the Supreme Council of the Grand Orient in Paris. Members were to spread the mission as far as possible through personal instructions, lectures, publications, assembly meetings, establishment of new schools and newspapers in order to inform the public on the benefits of Freemasonic principles and philosophy: tolerance, liberty, freedom to pursue knowledge, humanism, and universalism. They were urged to replace divisive personal conflicts with union and accord and to combat laziness, self-complacency, and passive surrender to the status quo. "Awake from the slumber of ignorance" constituted the universal Masonic slogan.[64]

The Persian Secret Societies

Here, a pertinent question needs to be addressed. Was Nazem al-Islam Kermani's secret *anjoman*, founded under the auspices of the *mojtahed* Seyyed Mohammad Tabataba'i and his son Mohammad Sadeq Tabataba'i, both members of the French lodge, an auxiliary of the Réveil? Was the new school that the *mojtahed* had sponsored also fulfilling the Réveil's instructions? To be sure, the *anjoman*'s first meeting on February 7, 1905, predates that of the Réveil by some ten months. But future lodge members already knew each other and were well acquainted with Masonic goals and strategies to attain them. More important, the *anjoman*'s structure was modeled on a typical Grand Orient lodge, and its repeated slogan, "Awake from the slumber of ignorance," recalls the Masons'. In fact, Nazem al-Islam's famous chronicle of the revolution is titled *Tarikh-e bidari-ye Iraniyan*, (History of the Awakening of the Iranians).

Réveil, *bidari*, *awakening*: one identical key word of Grand Orient masonry active in North Africa and the Ottoman Empire. The *anjoman*'s program also reflected Freemasonic principles and concepts. Of the greatest significance, given its novelty in the Islamic world, is the concept of union of all members, regardless of their religious differences—all to be admitted on equal terms provided they share Iran as a common fatherland. Like the Masons, the *anjoman*'s members pledged to abide by its strict rules and regulations, which included the oath of secrecy, union, solidarity, and accord, in order to devote themselves selflessly to the cause. They were to uphold moral behavior: no lying, no cheating, working to promote the good, and shunning the bad in deed and thought. Their prime objective was to awaken people from their slumber of ignorance, to combat tyranny and injustice, and to spread the concepts of tolerance, humanism, and patriotism. In the initiation ceremony, each member pledged allegiance and took the oath while holding his holy book in hand, be it the Zoroastrian, Jewish, Christian, or Moslem holy book,[65] in a manner recalling the European Freemasons' traditional rite. Political moderation and respect for religion and religious leaders were nominally enforced.

In many of this *anjoman*'s meetings, more radical, revolutionary statements were uttered. Thus, in a March 1905 meeting Ahmad Majd al-Islam Kermani mentioned Seyyed Mohammad Tabataba'i's alleged republican goals as a fact, which Majd al-Islam viewed as not incompatible with the *anjoman*'s general objectives for government reforms and eradication of tyranny. Whether accomplished in the name of republicanism or constitutionalism, the end result should be the same, he reassured the members. "Republicanism is part of constitutionalism."[66] In yet another meeting, class consciousness was displayed as some members complained of the power of the rich and the helplessness of those who lacked political support. Money is all, they bitterly observed, and ignorance breeds tyranny. Nazem al-Islam ventured a more revolutionary proclamation. The House of Iran, he said, plundered for so long by the Qajar kings, is decaying. Total destruction is needed before building it anew. "As long as there is no revolution in the country, there can be no reforms. . . . Only a revolution can awaken."[67] Nonetheless, such occasional political extremism remained under check. The *anjoman*'s activities concentrated on forging alliances between groups and prominent individuals, spreading networks to gather information and divulge news, distributing pamphlets and newsletters throughout the country and across the borders into the holy cities, the Caucasus, and the Ottoman Empire. Its activities also involved subordinate players, low-ranking clerics and civil servants, in contrast to the Réveil lodge, the bulk of whose membership was European and Iranian upper-class men, palace courtiers, and politicians, some of whom were rising to prominence with recent events.

At about the same time, another secret society was formed by Malek al-Motakallemin and Jamal al-Din Va'ez, the two star orators of the first Majles and members of the Réveil lodge. This society held views and objectives identical to those held by Nazem al-Islam Kermani's society and had similar strategies, but it was more diverse in its membership. By 1907, it came to include many Réveil "brothers" such as Shaikh al-Ra'is, Zoka' al-Molk, Nasrollah Taqavi, Taqizadeh, Dehkhoda, Mo'azed al-Saltaneh, and many others. This "secret committee" often met at the home of Hakim al-Molk, another "brother."[68] It was through this committee that the constitutionalists were able to coordinate their program for legislative reforms in the Majles, to mobilize the masses in the mosques and public squares, and to publicize their views in newspapers and pamphlets. It was also this committee that organized the counterattack to the conservative *mojtahed* Fazlollah Nuri's relentless religious assault on the Constitution and the Majles deputies. This society, along with Nazem al-Islam's, also bore the brunt of the shah's wrath. Its members were subjected to the Russian-commanded Cossack troops' assault when the first Majles was besieged in the summer of 1908. In the massive arrests that ensued, Jamal al-Din Va'ez, Malek al-Motakallemin, and Jahangir Khan lost their lives, Seyyed Mohammad Tabataba'i the *mojtahed* and other constitutionalist olama were banished into exile, and hundreds were sent to prison—although a few were able to escape to Europe with the British and French legations' help.

Here again Morel's role sheds light on the nature of the Réveil lodge activities. In addition to the correspondence attesting to his participation in the revolution on the constitutionalists' side, there exists in the Réveil de l'Iran file a couple of letters he wrote to the Grand Orient's general secretary, yielding more of these rare glimpses into these activities. He intervened on behalf of Taqizadeh, Dehkhoda, and Mo'azed al-Saltaneh, organizing their safe departure to Europe with the French legation's help. Informing the Paris headquarters of their imminent arrival, he introduced the three refugees as certified members of the Réveil de l'Iran lodge since May 17, March 3, and June 11, 1907, respectively. They would need advice and instructions as well as letters of recommendation to "our brothers in London," he explained, requesting that the order give them "all possible help and assistance while in exile."[69] As always cautious, a few weeks later Morel asked the general secretary to inform the "brothers" Samad Khan Momtaz al-Saltaneh, the Persian ambassador, and Dr. Jalil Khan, an Iranian physician resident of Paris and member of the Clemente amitie lodge, of the exiles' arrival and to be prepared to identify all three personally. Only then, he added, should the enclosed certificates of adherence to the lodge be handed over to the exiles.[70] Proper identification was needed, lest the badge of the lodge fall into the hands of impostors. The lodge in Tehran mourned in private the death of three of its "brothers," Malek al-Motakallemin, Jamal al-Din Va'ez, and Jahangir Khan, and deplored the arrest and forced exile of others. Soon after the bombardment of the Majles, Morel declared the atelier to be temporarily suspended.

There is no doubt that the organization, concepts, and activities of Iranian secret *anjomans* owed a great deal to, if not outright borrowed from, European Masonic lodges. They spoke of the need to adopt the "new learning" and to teach European languages, science, and technology, which was to displace the study of mysticism and theological philosophy. Emphasizing the concepts of fatherland and patriotism, members of these secret societies reached out to non-Moslem compatriots and insisted on the equality of all Iranians before the law. Some were fiercely anti-olama, overtly or discretely, though not necessarily antireligious. They depicted tyranny as a two-headed monstrous institution, dynastic and cleric, and called for the secularization, or rather the laicization, of the country's judicial and educational institutions. The necessity to arouse national consciousness was considered a fundamental task for all to assume: whether cleric, civil servant, courtier, statesman, whether of aristocratic, middle-class, or lower-class background, whether Moslem, Zoroastrian, Jewish, or Christian. Members of these societies believed that the responsibility for guarding the fatherland was not exclusive to the olama; it fell to all learned individuals, be they Moslem or non-Moslem, provided they conceived of Iran as their *vatan* (fatherland).[71] Terms such as *liberty, equality, fraternity, accord, union, civilization, progress, human rights, rule of law*, and *constitutionalism* frequently appeared in constitutionalist pamphlets. Nasrollah Taqavi, prominent activist and member of the Réveil de l'Iran lodge and deputy of the first and second Majles, wrote, as mentioned earlier, an essay for mass circulation demonstrating the benefits of the Constitution and helped translate into Persian the constitution of the Grand Orient order. Furthermore, in the various episodes leading to the promulgation of the Persian Constitution in 1906, would-be members of the French lodge worked to mobilize Dar al-Fonun students and the Political Science Faculty to assemble crowds in public places, mosques, and *madresehs* (religious schools) and to participate in organizing requests for asylum at the British legation. All sources attest to the vital role of Dar al-Fonun students as instructors on the legitimacy of the constitutionalist cause and its objectives.

Even more significant, though, Iranian Freemasons were by no means acting in unison or aiming at identical political goals. Ideological differences, class distinctions, and personal ambitions divided their ranks, making them vulnerable to manipulation by compatriots or foreigners. The story of the League of Humanity is a case in point. With Malkom Khan's approval, it was established in 1904 by Abbas Qoli Khan Qazvini, a minor civil servant who emerged to prominence only through this organization. It had four branches in Tehran and many others in the provinces, all coordinated by a council of twelve trustees and directed by Abbas Qoli Khan. Its structure and rituals copied those of Malkom's secret society, the House of Oblivion; its membership was recruited from among the ruling elite and Qajar princes, some of whom were genuine constitutionalists, others reactionaries, and many mere opportunists. All contributed generously to the league. Persian members of the Réveil lodge distrusted Abbas Qoli Khan and his society, especially when Amin al-Soltan, the hated former ancien régime minister joined the League of Humanity. A week after his initiation into the league, Amin al-Soltan was assassinated by a member of the Transcaucasian Social-Democratic group secretly active in the revolution.[72]

The League of Humanity survived for a while longer, attracting members from among the conservative ruling elite close to Mohammad Ali Shah, who assumed the mantle of champion of human rights. Appalled by this new royal posturing, many defected from the society to form a separate *anjoman* called Hoquq (Rights). Among the defectors were two Qajar brothers, Solaiman

Mirza and Yahya Mirza, who would then join the ranks of the nationalists in defense of the Constitution against the shah's renewed onslaught within weeks of his initiation and would later join the Democrat Party. In 1909, following the restoration of the Constitution, the Réveil's first official act was to pronounce the League of Humanity pseudolodge illegitimate.

The French atelier Le Réveil would remain indirectly active in the politics of the second Majles, its prestige attracting the most prominent members of the successive cabinets, Majles deputies, and politicians in and out of office. But some of its earliest adepts stopped attending its meetings, Taqizadeh and Dehkhoda among them. The Réveil de l'Iran lodge pursued its cooperation with the Iranian "brothers," providing them with necessary concepts, strategies, protection, and even ways and means to propagate their ideas. It continued to appeal to the Supreme Council of the Grand Orient in Paris to use its influence with the French government and have selected Masons come to Tehran in different diplomatic or teaching posts.

Ideologically, the Réveil's impact proved invaluable, specifically in promoting concepts of constitutionalism and secularism. In this, its members were no different from those British diplomats in the country who had genuinely sympathized with the constitutionalists and offered help that proved to be vital to the unfolding events or from the Transcaucasian Social-Democrats who lent the constitutionalists a no less resourceful hand in their ideological and political combats. As this study shows, leading *anjoman* players shared identical values and goals with the Freemasons. But these values and principles were essentially those of the European Enlightenment, about which many had read independently from the lodges and their masters. Freemasonry alone could not claim paternity for the French or American Revolution or for the Young Turk Revolution, despite the more or less important part it played in each; the same can be said regarding the Constitutional Revolution in Iran. More significantly, the various *anjoman*s had overlapping membership, with an ideological composition ranging from West European liberalism to Russian social-democracy to Shi'a sectarian radicalism and Azali Babism, with the basic values of the Enlightenment forming an irresistibly attractive common ground. The constituency for Freemasonry was there, but only as fellow travelers to a destination that ultimately did not correspond to the European Masons'.

Positive in a self-serving manner or damning in a conspiratorial fashion, accounts of the role of Freemasonry in the Constitutional Revolution understate the authenticity of the movement for reform we now call modernization, with its principles best popularized in the lodges. They also overlook the fact that both British and the French Masons, no matter how genuine their sympathy, were ultimately powerless in preventing their respective governments from harming the cause they had espoused, resulting in a betrayal of the universal values of human rights and liberty they upheld. National interests and international power politics had priority over commitments to solidarity with their "brothers" in Iran. Thus, what we learn about the Freemasons' involvement in the revolution is less important than how this fact is woven into the revolution's history, constituting but one thread among many others.

2

The Politics of the Restoration of the Constitution

THE ROYALIST COUP against the Majles on June 23, 1908, leading to executions, mass arrests, and exile of prominent constitutionalist leaders, did not bring about an end to their movement. It temporarily restored the shah's power, backed by conservative, anticonstitutionalist olama and protected by the Russian-commanded Cossack Brigade. During this short-lived period of the Lesser Despotism, the monarch surrounded himself with reactionary court officials, while Vladimir Lyakhof, the brigade's commander, ruled over Tehran with an iron grip, enforcing martial law. However, secret *anjoman*s resumed their underground activities in the capital, while armed fighters carried on a bloody resistance struggle in Azerbaijan and Gilan. More important for the eventual fate of the movement, by the winter of 1908–9 Britain and Russia began a joint effort to compel the shah to reinstate the Constitution, albeit in a modified form. Much was at stake for the two powers' vested interests in the country, formally enunciated in the Anglo-Russian Convention of 1907. According to the convention's terms, northern Iran, including Tehran, was part of the Russian sphere of influence, where the fiercest opposition to the shah's absolute rule took place. As events were rapidly unfolding, the vital though numerically insignificant participation of Transcaucasians in the battlefield compounded Russia's sense of danger. Britain, bound by its commitment to the convention's agreements, was also concerned with the political instability it deemed detrimental to its own geostrategic and commercial interests. While Sir Edward Grey, the British foreign minister, was adamant about preserving the convention's terms and maintaining good relations with the tsarist government, he encountered strong opposition to his Iran policy from within his own Liberal Party as well as in Parliament and the liberal press. The "dissenters," to use Mansour Bonakdarian's word,[1] relentlessly attacked Grey's decision to support the coup regardless of its consequences in Britain and abroad. Furthermore, the Foreign Office had sent to Iran some liberally oriented diplomats who were more inclined to negotiate with the "moderate," "nationalist" elements. They undertook the delicate task of helping to bring about a more flexible Russian political stand in dealing with the crisis.

In St. Petersburg, the Russian liberal press and the liberal Duma deputies compelled Alexander Izvolski, then minister of foreign affairs, to defend publicly Lyakhof's action against the coup's detractors. Privately, however, he began to communicate to British diplomats his willingness to reinstate constitutional rule in Iran. Concerns with the European balance of power and the Russian minister's need for British support for his strategic policies in the Balkans lay behind the reversal of attitude. Nikolai Hartwig, the Russian envoy who had masterminded the coup, was recalled from his post and replaced by Evgeni Vasilevich Sablin, a more steadfast advocate of the Anglo-Russian Convention. Sablin closely cooperated with his British colleague George Barclay, who also had recently arrived in Tehran. Thus, according to Sir Arthur Nicolson, Izvolski belatedly recognized the necessity for the shah to dismiss his current advisers, "evil reactionary counsellors," and to replace them with a few men competent enough to "form a satisfactory cabinet" of ministers. He expressed "his earnest desire that the Anglo-Russian understanding would eventually result in re-establishing in Persia a Liberal and Constitutional Regime."[2] When the shah's anticonstitutionalist envoy to Moscow tried to warn both powers against the chaos that inevitably would ensue if the Constitution were restored, his British counterpart, Nicolson, retorted: "Both Powers are adamant in pursuing that course."[3] In Tehran, Barclay tried to convince a "short-sighted, stubborn" shah that his only hope of preserving Persia from disintegration, "or at least from the forcible dictation of terms by the Nationalists," rested on restoring the constitutional regime.[4]

The Exiles in Europe

Reportedly, some two hundred constitutionalists sought refuge in Europe, setting up centers for the Iranian opposition in Paris, London, and Yverdon, Switzerland.[5] The largest number went to the French capital, where former cabinet ministers and well-born Majles deputies emerged as the prominent leaders for "national reconciliation" and the restoration of the Constitution. Isma'il Khan Momtaz al-Dowleh, the former Majles Speaker; his brother, Samad Khan Momtaz al-Saltaneh, the Persian ambassador to Paris; Mehdi

Qoli Khan Mokhber al-Saltaneh; Mahmud Khan Ehtesham al-Saltaneh; and other constitutional monarchists in touch with the opposition networks active in Iran proper and elsewhere in Europe carried out the mostly covert and highly sensitive negotiations with British and French government officials. From the start, this aristocratic circle of moderate politicians encountered the mistrust of more radically oriented, middle-class intellectuals, chief among them Ali Akbar Dehkhoda, the poet-journalist editor of *Sur-e Israfil* (Trumpet of Israfil), and the paper's publisher, Mirza Abol Qasem Tabrizi. The latter group included some of the most prominent publicists and activist members of the first Majles deputies, who had most vigorously defended legislative reforms against royalists and conservative olama: Hasan Taqizadeh, the Tarbiyat brothers, Mohammad Reza Musavat, Nasrollah Taqavi (Akhavi), and Abol Hasan Mo'azed al-Saltaneh, to name only a few, formed their own vast networks linking exiles in Europe, the Caucasus, and the Ottoman Empire with networks in Iran.

Soon after arriving in Paris, Dehkhoda began to explore the possibilities for a European edition of *Sur-e Israfil*, his satirical paper founded during the first Majles, if only to combat his own idleness and mental depression. He fully realized the enormous obstacles to his political endeavor. "With three and a half francs in my pocket," he wrote sarcastically to Mo'azed al-Saltaneh, who was then in London, "I wish to overthrow Mohammad Ali Shah and restore the Constitution in Iran."[6] Mo'azed al-Saltaneh, who had by then (November 1908) emerged as the chief liaison for this group of exiled intellectuals in Europe, encouraged him to undertake the project, promising full financial support. The news of the resumption of publication of the most successful and fiercest organ championing the constitutional government rapidly spread among the exiles in Europe and beyond. The irony of his situation did not escape Dehkhoda, the greatest Persian satirical poet of his time. "People believe that I am the same person I was in Tehran," he wrote, recalling the period of his political journalism highly committed to the "good cause" and ideals shared with trusted friends. "They do not know how great is my despair nowadays, how extreme my hopelessness."[7]

Dehkhoda was not as isolated or alone as he claimed. As already stated, the Tehran leaders of the Masonic lodge Réveil de l'Iran had recommended him and other "brothers" to the Grand Orient Supreme Council, requesting full support for their stay in Paris. He had the company of other fellow expatriates, with whom he planned ways and means to undermine the shah's legitimacy in French public opinion. French Masons and French intellectuals sympathetic to the Persians' cause helped him translate and publish articles in prominent journals such as the *Debat* and the *Revue du monde Musulman.* Contact with Moslem expatriates from Ottoman Turkey and the Caucasus kept him and other Iranian exiles abreast of news of political and social change in that part of the world. It was during his short say in Paris that Dehkhoda frequented the meetings of a small group of Young Turk leaders and decided to adopt their political program for his group.

Prior to the coup in July 1908 that brought them to power in Istanbul, the Young Turks formed several loosely tied opposition groups, all styling themselves modernists in favor of radical political, cultural, and institutional transformation of society. They did not constitute a monolithic political movement, even when in 1902 the Committee of Union and Progress (CUP) emerged as an umbrella organization for all Young Turk factions. Until 1908, the CUP remained underground, its ideology, leadership, and ethnic composition constantly evolving. Şükrü Hanioğlu's study of the pre-1908 Young Turks opposition describes its original leadership as generally freethinking, promoting a single goal—"to replace religion with science"—and denigrating any effort to reconcile Western civilization and science with Islam and traditional values.[8] All had great faith in education as the most efficient means to eradicate the old order. Ottoman authorities viewed Ahmad Reza (1859–1930), a leader of the CUP and a convinced positivist follower of Auguste Comte's school of thought, as "a person who denies the existence of God and is an atheist," even though he attempted for a while to reconcile constitutionalism with the Islamic law.[9] As early as 1897, he had publicly commented in an interview in a French magazine: "Religion is not a matter of concern to the state but is merely a matter of private concern."[10] Other Young Turk leaders were less openly antireligious. Reportedly, they generally concealed their true ideology. "In virtually every domain, one can find evidence to show that whatever was claimed in the official organs of the movement was contradicted by decisions made by its executive branches,"[11] and what was published in European languages abroad contradicted views expressed in Turkish. The need for self-protection from charges of heresy and competing leadership could to a large degree explain the inconsistencies. Ahmad Reza believed that mass conversion to positivism had to be gradual, with the revolution being the most immediate objective. The enlightened Moslem elite would then take over the task of eradicating fanaticism.[12]

In Paris in the fall of 1908, Dehkhoda met Ahmad Reza. Duly impressed, recognizing in the Young Turk a kindred freethinker and radical social reformer, he labeled him the "Ottoman Voltaire" of their time. Both met at a Turkish-Iranian society La Fraternite Musulmane, which Reza directed. Founded in December 1907, this organization was frequented by Young Turk and Iranian constitutionalists in exile, though it included other Moslem nationals who shared similar aspirations for social reforms back home.[13] It is difficult to know whether the fraternity had any official Freemasonic affiliation. Neither Ahmad Reza nor Dr. Nazem Beg, his closest collaborator in the Young Turk movement, were Masons, but many colleagues in their entourage maintained close ties with or were Masons. The newly installed Turkish minister of justice, Rafik Beg, had openly proclaimed that the CUP recruited its members among Freemasons because it trusted their moral principles.[14] Various Masonic organizations welcomed with enthusiasm the success of the Young Turks Revolution. In November 1908, a delegation led by Nazem Beg and Ahmad Reza arrived in Paris to discuss the situation in the Balkans with French government officials. The Grand Orient Supreme Council gave a reception in their honor at its headquarters on Rue Cadet. At the banquet, Nazem Beg expressed his government's gratitude for the order's help and inspiration. "Our peaceful revolution," he said, "is more your achievement than ours; you gave us the ideas, and we resorted to your methods and means. . . . We followed your way to emancipate ourselves from the yoke obstructing our path to progress, and have accepted the separation of church from state."[15] By that time, the Grand Orient had advocated openly an intransigent socialist-positivist and antireligious trend.

The Young Turks delegation had taken to Paris with them a copy of the CUP political program of reforms, which reportedly was just a reformulation of the Tanzimat reforms, including freedom of worship. The program carried also a proposal for a Balkan confederation as a possible solution to the permanent crisis in the eastern European part of the Ottoman Empire.[16] Was this the program Dehkhoda wished to emulate? Freedom of worship, equality of all citizens before the law, and even tax reforms were already incorporated, in some form or another, into Iran's Supplement to the Fundamental Law of 1907. Perhaps it was the innovative federalist concept of government that appealed to his political radicalism. Whatever the reason, he succeeded in obtaining a copy of the written CUP political program of reforms from Ahmad Reza on the condition that he keep it fully confidential. In tune with the Young Turks' secretive tactics, Dehkhoda and his *Sur-e Israfil* collaborators meant to keep the program secret until the political conditions were ripe for its implementation. Only when Mohammad Ali Shah dies and the situation in Iran deteriorates, he wrote to Moʿazed al-Saltaneh, would the real struggle take place, demanding all their concerted effort and devotion to the cause, and only then would the program bear fruit.[17]

At about that time, early 1909, an anonymous Persian pamphlet circulating in Tabriz was published in the *Revue du monde Musulman* in French translation under the title *Les États Unis de Perse* (The United States of Persia),[18] a summary of the program for a Republic of the United States of Persia. It discussed Iran's prevailing tyranny, corruption, and social backwardness, calling for liberty, justice, and individual responsibility. The key terms, *order* and *progress*, certainly reflect the Young Turks' ideology, which was inspired by positivism. But Iranian intellectuals had been acquainted with Auguste Comte and his faith in science since the 1890s, and they were equally familiar with Vittorio Alfieri's conception of the dual tyranny, dynastic and clerical, obstructing the spread of scientific knowledge, which these tyrants deemed detrimental to their power because ignorance sustained their authority over the masses. It was the proposal for a federal form of government that Ahmad Reza and his colleagues had brought to Paris in November 1908. Some politically radical Iranians were already acquainted with this concept prevalent among Social-Democratic circles in the Caucasus. Quoting a "sage dictum" extolling human beings as "masters of their persons and property," the pamphlet warned that human liberty cannot be absolute, for each individual has obligations toward others and his fatherland. The worthiest elected individuals are to assume authority to ensure the general welfare of the nation. There can be "no more hereditary power," and a federal republic would replace the monarchy. The pamphlet described the function of the Parliament of the United States of Iran in charge of all foreign, defense, and financial affairs but granting each province a measure of autonomy for local political and economic affairs. This federalist, republican conception of government was rarely mentioned in other Persian publications in exile.

While the battle for the restoration of the constitutional regime was raging, the exiles in Europe were concerned with preserving a unity of purpose. Moʿazed al-Saltaneh, a moderate constitutionalist who would subsequently distance himself from his radically oriented fellow exiles, sounded truly revolutionary when he wrote to his brother: "Should I and four other persons depart, thousands would take our place. . . . No matter how much injustice the despotic government commits, the number of partisans for justice increases, and the foundation of constitutionalism gets stronger. . . . The tree of justice is always watered with blood."[19] He assumed the all-important function of fund-raiser, financial manager, and public-relations man, linking all groups and their foreign advisers to *Sur-e Israfil*'s editorial board.[20] Hailed as "the greatest memorial for the martyrs of Iran's liberty,"[21] the journal was relocated to Switzerland, first in Geneva and then in Yverdon, a small town where rent was much lower. Most exiles, regardless of their ideological differences, initially valued the paper as an important organ of the resistance to despotism and the dissemination of constitutional ideals. Nonetheless, the climate of mistrust setting apart moderates and radicals prevailed, as Dehkhoda bitterly resented his aristocratic compatriots' lavish lifestyle in Paris, which he contrasted to his own and his friends' modest standard of living. After having governed and embezzled their nation's wealth, the exiles in Paris now enjoy a sumptuous life in a free country, he complained in a letter.[22]

European Patronage

Mo'azed al-Saltaneh coordinated the journalists' work with Edward Granville Browne's crusading efforts on behalf of the constitutionalists.[23] It was Persia, as the Europeans persistently called Iran, that most fascinated the professor at the University of Cambridge, who was well versed in Arabic, Persian, and Ottoman Turkish languages and literature, and to which he gave priority in his professional and extracurricular activities. A liberal in the British political meaning of the term, he firmly believed in the possibility for Iran to realize its intellectual and socioeconomic potential if given the right kind of moral encouragement and logistical support for development. He vested all his hope in the constitutional movement and worked from his office at Pembroke College to help promote positive press coverage in Britain. His Cambridge address became the poste restante for all correspondence between the constitutionalists abroad and the constitutionalists in Iran as well as the olama in Najaf.

Browne also cultivated continued contact with an impressive network of former students and close acquaintances working at the Foreign Office, some of them attaining important diplomatic or ministerial posts: Walter Smart, Major Claude Stokes, R. B. Graham, and Sydney Churchill were assigned to Iran during the fateful years of constitutional struggles. More important, Browne had access to Sir Edward Grey, the British minister of foreign affairs, chiefly through Sir Cecil Spring-Rice, who headed the British legation in Tehran until the fall of 1908. But it was Henry F. B. Lynch who came to play a pivotal role in initially influencing Grey's policy toward Iran. A Liberal member of Parliament and a self-styled "liberal imperialist,"[24] Lynch set up the Persia Committee in association with Browne, which was composed of members of Parliament as well as other prominent figures in political and press circles critical of Grey's policy. The committee lobbied for the restoration of the Constitution in Iran and endeavored to bring together all the disparate political exiles active in Europe and beyond. Constitutionalist olama in Najaf fully supported the committee, hoping its expected activities would promote freedom and national independence.[25] The committee selected those figures most likely to succeed as leaders of a Qajar loyalist, constitutional monarchist opposition. Isma'il Khan Momtaz al-Dowleh, the former Majles Speaker, gained the committee members' favor as the spokesman best qualified to project to the British government the ideal image of moderate Iranian nationalism. William Barber, editor of the liberal paper the *Morning Post* and a member of the committee, suggested to Browne that he arrange in strict confidentiality a direct meeting between Lord Grey and Momtaz al-Dowleh. He believed the latter "voiced the organized opinion of the practical and conciliatory section among the nationalists."[26] However, Foreign Minister Grey declined, to Browne's disappointment.[27] The committee nevertheless pursued its plan to help rally the political exiles round Ali Qoli Khan Sardar As'ad, the Bakhtiyari tribal leader. In fact, Barber had in mind the formation of a Persian "Young Turks" group, with Isfahan as its Salonika,[28] an idea that Browne also promoted.

Ayatollah Mohammad Kazem Khorasani endorsed the plan of national reconciliation and wrote to the *anjoman* in Tabriz (Anjoman-e Tabriz) suggesting that a common national front be formed that would include Isma'il Momtaz al-Dowleh, Mehdi Qoli Khan Mokhber al-Saltaneh, Abol Qasem Naser al-Molk, and other grandees. Warning against the destructive consequences of divisive politics, he wrote: "Only unity protects the independence of Moslem countries."[29] It is important to note here that Momtaz al-Dowleh was also a favorite at the French Ministry of Foreign Affairs. Its minister, Stephen Pichon, was a Mason affiliated with the Grand Orient,[30] to which Momtaz al-Dowleh and his brother, Samad Khan, the Iranian ambassador to France, also belonged. When the shah, displeased with his envoy's support for the exiles, tried to recall Momtaz al-Dowleh from his post, Pichon promptly refused to allow his departure under the pretext of his unpaid debts to French creditors. "There the matter rests," Lynch wrote to Grey, "it shows how the wind blows."[31] However, Lynch had commercial interests in common with Sardar As'ad, one of the most ambitious and powerful

Bakhtiyari tribal khans. Lynch's family-owned firm had negotiated with the khans some lucrative contracts for the construction of highways and waterways in the southwestern region of Iran, which the Bakhtiyari tribe controlled. The Bakhtiyaris' accession to power in Tehran through the constitutionalists' ranks would ensure the Lynch Brothers Company's interests. Thus, Henry Lynch accorded Sardar As'ad a loan, negotiated through British consular services, to finance the Bakhtiyaris' military fight against the shah's forces.[32]

The Lynch–Bakhtiyari connection was no secret to the foreign diplomats in Tehran[33] or to British officials or to Browne. Lynch assured Grey that he desired to work in harmony with the Foreign Office: "Neither myself, nor any of my colleagues in the Persia Committee have any desire to advertise ourselves or to fry any fish of our own."[34] Lord Grey, forever mistrustful, not to say contemptuous, of the Iranian constitutionalists, had nonetheless lent his support to Lynch's role in coordinating the "national reconciliation," rallying all actions under one umbrella, and allowing Sardar As'ad a prominent part in the restoration of the Constitution.[35] Sardar As'ad and his brothers had also negotiated lucrative contracts with other British firms, including the d'Arcy Oil Company, which had successfully explored the potential wealth lying underground in Bakhtiyari territory.

Lynch had convinced fellow members of the Persia Committee that his broader interests corresponded with British interests in Iran's future. He was as interested as they were, he wrote to Browne, in "grooming" young Iranians to assume a leadership position in their government and to carry on pro-British policies.[36] From the fall of 1908 through the winter of 1909, he traveled repeatedly to Paris with Sardar As'ad, arranging meetings with the exiles and persuading them to accept the Bakhtiyari khan as a disinterested nationalist leader. Sardar As'ad, he promised them, would deliver his armed tribal forces to fight for the constitutional cause. Lynch also succeeded in organizing the exiles' action in Istanbul.[37] His chief goal was to convince all of the constitutionalists to reassure the shah that they were aiming solely at reestablishing security and order and that they wished him and his throne no harm. Lynch in fact firmly believed that the exiles, whom he described as competent men "who would certainly not discredit any European administration," were not aiming to destroy the monarchy.[38]

Fragmented as the nationalist front was abroad, the task of stage-managing the reconciliation was not easy. The major players resumed the art, developed throughout the period of the first Majles, of finessing internal tensions by in appearance yielding to stronger external arbiters while concealing their real objectives. More importantly, they came to fully realize that political skills were required for them to win cooperation without being the pawns of outside powers that had their own agendas.

Dissent among the Exiles

Browne was all in favor of the resumption of *Sur-e Israfil*, but he would have preferred England rather than Switzerland as its location. England is more important, he informed Mo'azed al-Saltaneh.[39] But the *Sur-e Israfil* group enjoyed their relative distance from both Paris and London, away from the ongoing negotiations between various political factions under British unofficial tutelage. Mo'azed al-Saltaneh kept them informed on the Lynch-sponsored meetings between Sardar As'ad and the former officials in Paris, who in December 1908 had called for a joint effort to stage a national reconciliation. Mo'azed al-Saltaneh also sent a cable to the shah requesting the restoration of the Constitution but also pledging loyalty to the Qajar monarchy.[40] Dehkhoda angrily rejected the very idea of such cooperation. "How could one trust four thieves," he wrote to Mo'azed al-Saltaneh, and other "charlatans in Paris" who, "now that the wind is blowing in our direction, offer to work with us?"[41] The whole *Sur-e Israfil* group vehemently opposed the Bakhtiyaris' inclusion in the constitutionalist ranks. Mohammad Ali Shah would die, and a Bakhtiyari would take his place on the throne, Dehkhoda warned. In fact, he ascertained, a powerful Bakhtiyari would be much more dangerous than a weak Mohammad Ali. Dehkhoda also dismissed the possibility of working with the titled officials, these "al-Saltanehs" and "al-Dowlehs," the "would-be ministers," as a total waste of time.[42] He believed that the leadership of the national resistance to despotism should be entrusted to the intelligentsia, the "brain trust of the nation," and not to Sardar As'ad. And he was incensed that Mo'azed al-Saltaneh showed the secret Young Turks' political program to the newly formed coalition leaders.[43] Sardar As'ad and people like him, he wrote, should deliberately be kept in the dark about the intelligentsia's objectives. They would be useful to the cause merely as an instrument, a means to attain the goal, until compelled to collaborate through coercion and intimidation. He reminded Mo'azed al-Saltaneh of the chief reason for the move to Yverdon, to set up a secret center, with the journal providing a convenient cover.[44] Other exiles shared Dehkhoda's misgivings. Mirza Aqa Farshi, the Azerbaijan deputy in the first Majles, a close friend of Hasan Taqizadeh, with whom he had fled to Europe, insisted that the issue at stake was not just persuading the shah to allow the reopening of the Majles, but what kind of Majles would be initiated.[45] This group of exiles opposed the decision made by Mokhber al-Saltaneh and his group to cable the shah their promise to guarantee his throne in exchange for the restoration of the Constitution.[46] Another prominent constitutionalist, Mo'ayyed al-Islam Kashani, editor of *Habl al-matin* (The Firm Cord), then in exile in Calcutta, India, proclaimed a better future for the nation could be ensured only through armed intervention and the overthrow of the shah.[47]

Sur-e Israfil resumed its publication on January 23, 1909, with Dehkhoda's column "Charand parand" (a nonsense title) addressing the issue of monarchy on its front page.[48] In countries where ignorance displaces science, might displaces right, and fear displaces truth, Dehkhoda argued, monarchy is conceived as a divine gift, which means that God the Almighty has given away to a single individual the power to dispose of the entire land, keeping its population under religious obligation to obey. It is of the utmost importance, he stated, for his readers and for any "rationally" religious person to study in depth the veracity of this conception. If it is true that monarchy is a divine gift and that obedience to the sovereign is an immutable condition, we should without hesitation or doubt submit to our fate. Human weakness does not permit resistance to divine commands, nor can it break the iron claws of fate. However, should monarchy, like any other human activity, be of our own making, he argued, then let us gather all the strength God has bestowed on us to fight it.

Dehkhoda then asserted that no divine command has so far been revealed to legitimize the monarch's authority, for it would be irrational to believe God the Just subjects the entire fate of his creatures to the power of a single man, especially one who does not recognize right from wrong or distinguish the innocent from the sinner; this belief would be tantamount to disbelief in God's justice. He then categorically dismissed the institution of monarchy as contrary to the Islamic belief in the Oneness of God, for belief in the "Shadow of God on earth" amounts to polytheism. Furthermore, he explained, reason never allows such superstitious belief in one man possessing absolute power over an entire nation to dispose of their life and property at will. Thus, both reason and the holy law refute the conception of the monarch's authority as divine. Dehkhoda argued that ignorance and human helplessness provoke individuals' "awe" when facing a display of wealth and power. In contrast, a reasonably knowledgeable man recognizes that his relation to the monarch is no different from his relation to a salesman, hired servant, or grocer. It is based on a contract, setting the monarch's limits and rights just as a buyer's or employer's are set. By the same logic, should the sovereign fail to fulfil his contractual obligations, he should be overthrown. This is the lesson of world history, Dehkhoda asserted, which clearly shows that human societies, when weak, ignorant, and defenseless, seek to bond themselves to the powerful, who are then believed to be the chosen of God, with hereditary right to rule. If we can imagine the person of the monarch stripped of his magnificent attire and material possessions, alone without his servile entourage, we will see an ordinary, feeble, miserable, and needy man, devoid of any holy aura. The article concluded with a strong message: it is possible to overthrow the monarch and replace him with a good, brave, and rational fellow compatriot, a defender of the fatherland. Monarchy is nothing but the exercise of one man's power over all people.

With this article, Dehkhoda was resuming his implacable war of the pen for the cause of political justice, which he firmly believed could be attained only through radical social transformation of the Iranian power structure and institutions. The article drew fire from several quarters, underscoring the ideological divides in the constitutionalists' ranks. The moderate elements in the resistance movement were dismayed by the virulence of its antimonarchy message. Mokhber al-Saltaneh, who had been mostly in favor of resuming publication of the journal, expressed his "sorrow" in concrete terms. The article, he wrote, is "contrary to our present interests."[49] Browne also communicated his worry of the possible harmful consequences of such a harsh essay. Without denying the veracity of its content, he warned against telling the truth. "I fear this issue may fall onto the hands of some court officials, who would show it to the shah, telling him the constitutionalists would only be satisfied with your overthrow. . . . May God prevent this issue of *Sur-e Israfil* from bearing bitter results, despite its author's good intentions."[50]

Dehkhoda's response to his critics was as virulent as his article, sarcastically dismissing "those individuals" who abide by the constitutional principles only if their personal interests are not harmed. With such interventions, he exclaimed, "the pen remains in the enemy's hands," and he threatened to resign should he have to temper his columns, difficult as it was for him to exert self-restraint.[51] Other members of the editorial board equally rejected such "censorship" and argued that even Mohammad Ali Shah, prior to the coup, had never succeeded in "sealing the lips" of those who wished to tell the truth. "Obstructions to the pen," they stated, render their hard work "fruitless."[52] But the journal raised too many controversies, allowing its adversaries to undermine its publishers' credibility in the eyes of prominent expatriates, including Sardar As'ad, who was rapidly gaining acceptance as a powerful leader of the opposition to the shah. Publication ceased after the third issue, on March 8, 1909. Soon after, both Dehkhoda and Mo'azed al-Saltaneh moved to Istanbul and, enjoying the Young Turks government patronage, established a new Persian journal, *Sorush* (Glad Tidings). Its first issue came out on July 1, 1909, a couple of weeks before the fall of Tehran.

The Anjoman-e Sa'adat

Established in Istanbul during the period of the Lesser Despotism, the Anjoman-e Sa'adat (Council of Happiness) received vital support from the newly empowered Young Turks regime, whose officials kept contact with the Persian exiles they had met in Europe.[53] It had begun its existence as essentially a loosely defined organization, where lay anticlerical and antimonarchical revolutionaries, including the Iranian Social-Democrats, worked together with their counterparts in Tabriz, Baku, and Mashhad. According to Malek al-Sho'ara Bahar, local and Caucasian Social-Democrats in Mashhad were mostly active in recruiting government employees, students of religious schools, and bazaar merchants as well as publishing underground antitsarist Russian newspapers.[54] The *anjoman* in Istanbul also included among its members representatives of Najaf constitutionalist olama, led by Shaikh Assadollah Mamaqani, a close aid of Khorasani. Khorasani in fact financially contributed to the organization.

Prior to the Young Turks Revolution of July 23, 1908, the Ottoman authorities in Baghdad had severely restricted Najaf constitutional activism, closely watching the olama's movement and intercepting their correspondence, forcing them to adopt cautious measures. Nonetheless, the most prominent *mojtaheds* succeeded in issuing a widely spread religious decree, or fatwa, that condemned the reactionary coup in Tehran, thus declaring holy war against the shah. After the Young Turks Revolution, the new regime in Istanbul reached out to the constitutionalist *mojtaheds* in Najaf, where the Young Turks' advent to power was greeted with "great enthusiasm." All restrictions previously enforced were immediately lifted, and communications between Najaf and constitutionalists active in the Ottoman Empire were allowed total freedom. The governor of Baghdad was a Young Turk partisan, and a local CUP branch reportedly worked closely with the *mojtaheds* in the Shi'a holy city.[55] Another local organization, the Iranian

Brotherhood (Okhuvat-e Iraniyan), acted together with local Young Turks activists as a liaison among Najaf, Baghdad, and Istanbul, keeping the olama and Iranian expatriates in Mesopotamia up to date on events in Tabriz and guiding them "onto the right path."[56] Ahmad Bey Aqaev, the Baku-born Social-Democrat who was then residing in Istanbul and about to receive Ottoman nationality, had forged a close alliance between the Young Turks' CUP and the Anjoman-e Sa'adat. The CUP reportedly offered "every kind of material and moral support" for the latter's activities, encouraging it to draft a program reflecting a common ideological stand.[57] Shaikh Assadollah Mamaqani participated in the meetings between the two organizations, further strengthening their close communication with Najaf.

Throughout the fall of 1908 and the winter of 1909, the more radical element predominated in the Anjoman-e Sa'adat, imposing its militant and uncompromising view and, despite its rather ideological incoherence, providing a much-needed center for international networking. Weapons were clandestinely bought in the Caucasus, paid for by concerned Iranian expatriates as well as mostly by Georgians and Armenians, and smuggled to Tabriz.[58] In his self-serving memoirs, Yahya Dowlatabadi, who had arrived in the Ottoman capital shortly after the coup in 1908, deplores the state of ideological disunity and dissentions prevailing among the *anjoman*'s members, the majority of whom were Azerbaijani. Angered by their "deeds," he tried to establish another, more moderate center for the constitutionalists in exile, bringing together former officials, but with no success.[59] The expatriates in Europe preferred to work with the Anjoman-e Sa'adat, which, Dowlatabadi admits begrudgingly, was the "officially recognized headquarters" of the constitutionalists' activities, rapidly becoming the sole reliable source for information on those activities.[60]

By the late spring of 1909, when Mo'azed al-Saltaneh arrived in Istanbul to take over the leadership of the Anjoman-e Sa'adat and was followed there by Dehkhoda, the more radical elements had lost ground as the *ordre du jour* was then to rally all constitutionalists under one common political umbrella. The *anjoman* seemed also to have begun to keep its distance from the Baku-based Social-Democrats who had helped the resistance in recruiting fighters and providing weapons.[61] A noticeably more focused and better-organized plan of action succeeded in coordinating the exiles' effort to attain their immediate common goal: the restoration of the Constitution. In his own memoirs, Taqizadeh asserts that the *anjoman* in Istanbul provided the only means of communication for the Tabriz resistance and the rest of the country because the royalists had cut off the telegraph line. "In fact, [the Anjoman-e Sa'adat] became the constitutionalist headquarters for all in Iran and abroad. All the leaders converged to Istanbul and joined its membership."[62] The *anjoman* also left its mark on events leading to the reconvening of the Majles as it toned down its radicalism and adopted a moderate reformist, constitutional-monarchist program. It appealed to the nation to seize upon the momentum gathered at both the international level and the national level to destroy tyranny. As already stated, the British entrepreneur Henry Lynch had succeeded in organizing the national reconciliation movement in the Turkish capital.

The exiles saw in the Young Turks' success a major source of inspiration and guiding principles. Taqizadeh writes that Browne, who was very pro–Young Turks, encouraged an Iranian-Ottoman rapprochement. In a speech given to honor Ahmad Reza Beg and Dr. Nazem Beg at the London headquarters of the Balkan Committee, which he helped establish as part of his active interest in solving political issues related to the Ottoman Empire, Browne warmly congratulated them and implored them to back the Iranians' own struggle and set aside the "Sunni–Shia feud."[63] Browne was in fact echoing most exiles' sentiment. In Istanbul, Anjoman-e Sa'adat leaders continued to cultivate close ties with and enjoy the protection of the new Turkish regime. They even "commissioned" Ahmad Reza to represent them when negotiating with European government officials.[64] Young Turk leaders referred to the *anjoman* members as their brothers-in-arms, the "Jeunes Persans," a self-identifying name often found in some Persian constitutionalists' private papers and memoirs as well as in their press.[65] An article published in an Istanbul gazette recognized publicly the influence of the Young Turks' victory in helping Iranians to "awaken from the slumber of ignorance" and overthrow their own despot.[66] In a meeting held in an upscale European quarter of Istanbul, assembling Iranian expatriates, Turks, Armenians, Kurds, and Europeans, Prince Sabbah al-Din pledged the Turkish government's full support. While all hailed the memory of "freedom's martyrs killed by the royalists in the 1908 coup" (Malek al-Motakallemin, Jamal al-Din Va'ez, and Mirza Jahangir Khan), the exiles loudly asserted the unity of all Iranians of Persian, Turkic, or Arab descent in one national identity. A Frenchman present in the assembly, speaking in the name of "freedom-seeking Europeans," urged Iranians to follow the French example and "do what the French nation did to despotism."[67] Much of the exiles' writings on the eve of and shortly after the restoration of the Constitution reflected their hosts' victorious slogans and vision for sociopolitical renewal.

By the spring of 1909, the moderate reconciliation trend was consolidated. A realistic assessment of the Europeans' geostrategic and political-commercial interests in the region led many exiles to reconsider their rhetorical tactics. In that sense, too, they emulated the Young Turks' movement, which had originally consisted of several small ideologically disparate groups rallying round one immediate goal, the overthrow of the reigning monarch. In a letter sent in March 1909 from Yverdon to the Anjoman-e Sa'adat leadership in Istanbul shortly before his departure for Istanbul, Dehkhoda expressed best the exiles' newly acquired willingness to work in unison for the desired common purpose. It is incumbent upon all patriots, he wrote, to rise in defense of Iran before it is too late, for the situation is getting worse; the country is about to be annihilated. The fate of its future generations lies in the hands of its present leaders, whether they will rise to the occasion and uphold the nation's ancient glory and honor or hand over its children to the "neighbors," meaning Russia and Britain, forever enslaving them. The root of all evil within a nation or a religion, he argued, lies in disunity, alienation, and conflict; only national unity and accord can achieve its rescue. At its zenith, Islam had shaken and taken over the world but began to decline with the emergence of sects and conflicting schools of thought. The divisive conflicts that "our freedom-seeking group" is experiencing nowadays are even worse, he wrote. Thus, it is imperative for all to march together toward one goal and overcome the "ideological distance separating our ranks."[68]

In this letter, Dehkhoda insisted on consolidating that union with only one program of action, one platform enunciating collective goals. Renouncing his earlier ideological intransigence, he argued that the Anjoman-e Sa'adat should emerge as the sole organization rallying all other groups under one umbrella, offering a unified program and propagating its merit within Iran and abroad. Hundreds of thousands of progressive-minded Iranian expatriates, he proclaimed, are ready to reach out and work together with their fellow countrymen to "liberate" Iran. Islam, he explained, had spread because of divine intervention and because it showed compassion, forgave the newcomers' heathen past, and was content with their attesting to Islam's first article of faith: "There is no god but God." The old strategy of threat and intimidation pursued so far must give way to acceptance by all who join the common cause, regardless of their ideological or tribal background. Citing Ahmad Reza, the Young Turk leader he had met a few months earlier in Paris, he extolled the virtues of faith in the validity of one's ideology and affection for all adherents to the cause, virtues that had propelled the CUP to its "miraculous achievement." The Anjoman-e Sa'adat must adopt the same principles.

Here, Dehkhoda explicitly praised Mohammad Vali Khan Naser al-Saltaneh Sepahdar (hereafter referred to as "the Sepahdar," "the Commander," in accordance with the references to Naser al-Saltaneh given in all documents), an official he had contemptuously dismissed a few months earlier as another member of the ruling elite turned constitutionalist. The Sepahdar, as we shall see, had defected from the royal forces to join the insurrection in Gilan, where he was appointed governor by the revolutionary groups. Dehkhoda conceded in the letter that this drastic political reversal had strengthened the movement in Rasht. Similarly, Dehkhoda set aside his previous mistrust of well-born constitutionalists and recognized the effective role they could play as spokesmen to the British government. The English, he wrote, attach importance to the words of Momtaz al-Dowleh, Mokhber al-Saltaneh, and Ehtesham al-Saltaneh, for these individuals are knowledgeable and well informed. They would communicate in clarity and moderation the views that Taqizadeh and Mo'azed al-Saltaneh had conveyed in London and, like them, would work hard to arouse English public opinion in the constitutionalists' favor. He admired "the unique English freedom" based on the power of the British press in affecting public opinion, which in turn affected government policies. "Opinion is the nation's opinion . . . there is no government opinion but this collective opinion of all individual members of one nation." Hence, it was important to have "prominent Iranians" working in London to combat the Russian disinformation campaign against the activities of the Anjoman-e Sa'adat and its leadership and to alert the British public against Lord Grey's pro-Russian policy of military intervention in Iran. Dehkhoda was fully aware of the objections his views would arouse among "some individuals" within the *anjoman*. "The fact is," he wrote, "the time of war is over. To resist Russian intervention we have no choice but to resort to *politics*,"[69] and politics, he surmised, is what can best "attract English attention." Dehkhoda had no objection to Momtaz al-Dowleh's move to London as the constitutionalists' new liaison with British officials.[70]

The "would-be ministers" exiled in Europe were taking over the national reconciliation movement, agreeing with Lynch that a united front of all exiles in Europe in alliance with the Bakhtiyari khans constituted a more reliable means to attain their goals. Sardar As'ad was invited to meet with Sir Charles Harding, the former ambassador to Iran and prominent member of the Foreign Office. Strategic benefits outweighed ideological differences. Thus, reality compelled the *Sur-e Israfil* group to accept the facts that London was the "source of world politics"[71] and that the imminent threat of further Russian military intervention necessitated a national united front in defense of the fatherland. They began to add their signatures to the moderates' dispatches to the shah calling for a reconciliation between him and the nation. Privately, though, they continued to fear the divisive impact of British politics on the expatriates, nursing bitterness toward their political mentors. "May God destroy the House of the English for the fire it had set in Iran, and still does," Mo'azed al-Saltaneh exclaimed in a letter to Dehkhoda, concluding that Russian politics and English politics were identical after all.[72]

Dehkhoda had indeed learned to censor his own views and rein in his firebrand rhetoric in order to better cope with the reality of national and international politics affecting the unfolding events in his country. He had decided to leave the safety of his life in exile in Europe to join Mo'azed al-Saltaneh in Istanbul, but not before taking the precaution of requesting Ottoman citizenship, thus emulating many of his countrymen, who similarly acquired foreign protection. In a highly interesting letter marked "confidential" to Mo'azed al-Saltaneh, Dehkhoda tried to justify this seemingly unpatriotic move by explaining his need for foreign protection against Iranian authorities. In Iran today, he explained, there is no respect left for customs, traditions, law, ethics, or religion. As in all despotic regimes, there is only fear of the rulers. He wished to return to Iran to look after his mother and siblings, whom he had left behind when forced into exile. "In my opinion," he wrote, "family responsibility comes before any other responsibility, even for the fatherland. A fatherland is, after all, the sum total of all families."[73] This candid expression of political detachment previewed Dehkhoda's later stand in the second Majles, where he won a seat and in a final reversal of his earlier avowed radicalism opted to join the Moderate Party, forsaking his revolutionary bedfellows. But even then he was recorded more often absent than present in most of the parliamentary sessions.

In that same confidential letter addressed to Mo'azed al-Saltaneh, Dehkhoda felt the need to explain his feelings that he could not change his nature with a mere change of passport. One cannot forget one's ancestors' graves, one's birthplace, or one's childhood playground, he remarked. "Just as today it is expedient to change one's citizenship for the safekeeping of one part of this fatherland, that is, the family, tomorrow, when the fatherland needs one's presence, the same change" of papers would take place. Dehkhoda then emphatically proclaimed: "Love of the fatherland is an innate thing"; it does not pass away. He praised Abdol Hosain Khan Vahid al-Molk Shaybani, the Persian constitutionalist journalist and Browne's protégé, who had apparently acquired British citizenship. "With the power of the passport he has in his pocket, hundreds of newspapers similar to the *Times* of London will inform the nation of their government's wrongdoing." If it were not for people like him, he asserted, many more constitutionalists would have perished at the time of the coup in 1908.

Taqizadeh's British Connection

Hasan Taqizadeh's safe departure from Iran following the coup was ensured by both the French Masons and the British diplomatic intervention on his behalf. Paul Henri Morel, the venerable of the Réveil de l'Iran lodge in Tehran, and Walter Smart, the English official at the embassy, offered him protection and support in their respective capitals. All the while, he kept contact with the national resistance taking place in the northern provinces of Iran, where members of the radical *anjoman* in his native town, Tabriz, played a central role.

Taqizadeh and his fellow constitutionalists had witnessed British and Russian power openly exercised in their country's domestic affairs. They despaired, feeling betrayed and alone in their struggle. "We have been fooled," Taqizadeh wrote to Browne in the early days of his exile; "they [British officials] told us neither we [the British] nor the Russians would intervene in national domestic affairs," whereas in fact they were secretly intervening. The constitutionalists, he went on, came bitterly to realize their own ineffectiveness in safeguarding the liberties they had so painstakingly won in the course of the first Majles.[74] Warned by the British against staging an armed struggle to protect their rights, threatened by an allegedly imminent Russian military occupation, they had opted for surrender and exile. Throughout the summer and fall of 1908, Taqizadeh would never miss a chance to remind all concerned groups and individuals, Iranian or foreign, of the painful choice he and other constitutionalists had made: they sacrificed liberty for the sake of national independence.

While still in Tehran, Taqizadeh, no doubt encouraged by Smart, who was by then in despair regarding British policy in Iran,[75] had composed a letter to British government officials in defense of the Majles and its deputies.

Inspired by the French and English model of civilization, he wrote, the Iranian people had demanded a constitution for their nation. Circumstances not of their own making had led them to lay the foundation of freedom on the ground of the British legation in Tehran, and they came to view the Constitution and the established Majles as Britain's "spiritual child." But Russia, he lamented, plotted its destruction, therefore violating the Anglo-Russian Convention of 1907, which had guaranteed foreign nonintervention in Persian national affairs. He pleaded with the British officials, the "protectors of freedom in the world," to come to the Iranian people's rescue.[76]

This emotional appeal, no doubt equally revealing Smart's own state of mind, may display a certain naïveté and even border on obsequiousness. But, above all, it demonstrates the utter sense of vulnerability of a rising political star, who had for a short while tasted the sweet fruit of freedom and power before having to swallow the bitter pill of a foreign state's decision to back the despised reactionary monarch. This acute sense of vulnerability was to affect Taqizadeh and many other prominent Iranian figures, blurring their vision of their role in shaping their country's political destiny and enfeebling their willpower. The young Tabrizi politician adopted a dual radical-moderate role, striving to ride the revolutionary tide whenever possible but also to avoid being wiped out by the low ebb that periodically threatened to erase all vestiges of the constitutional movement.

On his way to Europe following the coup in 1908, without warning his French and English sponsors, Taqizadeh had taken a long detour to the Caucasus in order to coordinate the resistance efforts, raising funds from wealthy Moslem Russian subjects and monitoring the purchase of arms and their shipment to Iran. From Tiflis, he wrote to Sattar Khan, Azerbaijan's leading antishah warrior, to explain his "delay" in joining him and his fellow combatants, mentioning that urgent political matters were forcing him to go to Europe. He informed Sattar Khan of the imminent arrival of massive help from the Caucasus, enjoining him to keep up the armed struggle, until Mohammad Ali Shah, "this Russia-worshipping, nay, Russian king," is overthrown. In that letter, Taqizadeh openly expressed his view of the need for a radical political solution to the prevailing situation in the country. Sattar Khan must seize power in Azerbaijan, depose the shah, and declare himself or someone else who is trustworthy as head of a provisional government in Tabriz, to be recognized throughout the country and abroad. A republic must be established until the lawful heir to the throne is installed and the monarchy restored. Taqizadeh also instructed Sattar Khan to send a cable to the French Parliament in the name of the "Azerbaijan nation," proclaiming unlawful any foreign loan granted to the disgraced monarch. A loan must be prevented at all cost, he wrote. "Without it, the shah is lost; with it, we are lost."[77] While still in the Caucasus, Taqizadeh also dispatched several letters, equally radical in tone, to expatriates in Istanbul, urging them to support Sattar Khan and denouncing the "irreligious traitor, the king."[78] He also advised them to keep close contact with the newly installed Young Turk government.

Once in Europe, Taqizadeh chose England as a more potentially productive place for refuge, staying in Paris just a few weeks. Browne, who had followed Taqizadeh's meteoric rise to power in the first Majles, largely through Smart's long reports, was ready to promote Taqizadeh's "moderate" cause by introducing him to influential statesmen and journalists sympathetic and equally ready to contribute their share to the task. He arranged a meeting with the editor of the *Morning Post*, William Barber, "a man of great influence" and a journalist hostile to the Anglo-Russian Convention and therefore sympathetic to the Persian nationalist cause.[79] Taqizadeh praised Browne highly: "You are to us Iranians what Lord Byron was to the Greeks . . . [t]he saviour of weak nations."[80] He followed Browne's and other British advisers' guidance and even toned down, though reluctantly, his own virulent attack on the British government for its quiescence regarding the shah's coup. Warned by all, he went so far as to deny any revolutionary characteristics or goals of his and other constitutionalists' program of action, insisting they were neither revolutionary nor antimonarchical but rather nationalist reformers.

The formulation of three different drafts of a famous article published in the *Times* on October 15, 1908, best illustrates the conflicting ideological pressure exerted on Taqizadeh and his collaborators to win British government officials' and the public's support. Raw anger permeates the first draft of what Iraj Afshar calls the "*Times* Manifesto." Obviously written after Taqizadeh left Tehran, either while he was still in the Caucasus or shortly after his arrival in Europe, it discusses forty-nine items related to the coup on the basis of the new information he had gathered from friends and fellow political activists in the Caucasus and Europe. It holds both Russia and Britain entirely responsible for the defeat of the nationalists, their respective embassies acting through their agents as de facto censors of the information the Majles tried to send to the provinces about the gravity of the situation. It argues that the shah merely executed the Russian embassy's instructions;

that Russia threatened the Iranian people with a military intervention should they undertake a "political revolution"; and that the British embassy acquiesced out of consideration for the terms of Anglo-Russian Convention of 1907. It reserves its most vehement attack for the shah, whom it depicts as a traitor to his nation and religion. It ends with a desperate plea for the people of Iran to be left alone to find their way to establish order, peace, and security.[81] In the second draft, written in London, where he was coached by Browne, Taqizadeh adopted a milder tone, was appreciative of British support and sympathy, and categorically denied that he or any member of his faction were revolutionary. But he proclaimed that the bond tying the people to the "person who now calls himself shah" was totally broken: "There is no hope whatsoever for reconciliation. . . . The Iranian nation must be free to attain its liberty," without any foreign interference on behalf of the "traitors to the fatherland."[82] The final draft that appeared in English in the *Times* of London, translated by Browne, is a tame version of the Persian text, leaving out its author's denunciation of British complicity and eliminating all the paragraphs referring to the shah in negative terms as well as the sentence denying the possibility of reconciliation.[83]

Browne and indirectly the Foreign Office looked favorably upon Taqizadeh, believing him to be "on the side of moderation."[84] The Cambridge professor reportedly provided "anonymous financial assistance" to Taqizadeh and his two relatives, the brothers Mohammad Ali and Ali Mohammad Tarbiyat, for their stay in Britain.[85] Lynch invited Taqizadeh and Mo'azed al-Saltaneh to come to the House of Commons to meet with members of the Persia Committee, where they were given assurances that neither Russia nor Britain was planning intervention in Azerbaijan. They were urged to counsel their Azerbaijani compatriots to maintain public order and thus deprive the Russians of any excuse for intervention.[86] And on October 29, 1909, both addressed the House of Commons at Lynch's invitation.[87] During a brief visit to Paris in early December 1908, Taqizadeh met with the moderate constitutionalists and was encouraged to write, with Mokhber al-Saltaneh, the political exiles' official letter of reconciliation to the shah. Addressing the monarch in respectful terms, they blamed the foreigners for "separating him" from his nation, promising that the "threat to the Crown" would dissolve with the restoration of the Constitution.[88]

Taqizadeh's radical collaborators objected to his remaining in England, however, arguing it was a waste of time and could potentially prove harmful. He was warned that "people talk[ed]" about his contacts there and was reminded of his own conviction that one rifle sent to Tabriz was worth thousands of articles published in Europe.[89] Other members of the *Sur-e Israfil* group expressed their weariness of his alleged "opportunism." Dehkhoda, however, though recognizing this particular characteristic of Taqizadeh, opted to defend him. At least, he stated, Taqizadeh is active in the right direction, and he is making the most of the strong backing Browne and others are offering him; if each of his detractors were to have one-tenth of the support he gets, all problems would be solved.[90] Dehkhoda fully appreciated the sincerity and value of Browne's devotion to their cause, despite the professor's early disagreement over the publication of Dehkhoda's fiery "Charand parand" article.

Taqizadeh's Transcaucasian/Armenian Connection

Following the meeting in Paris in December 1908, Browne and the Persia Committee sent Taqizadeh to Tabriz to organize the national reconciliation efforts and to act as the liaison between Tabriz and the political exiles in Europe. He was instructed to reach his destination via Trebizond in Anatolia. However, unbeknownst to Browne and his other British sponsors, he took another detour to visit Baku and Tiflis, where he met other radical members of the Iranian Anjoman-e Azerbaijan: Mohammad Reza Musavat, Hasan Roshdiyyeh, the Rashti brothers, and Hosain Khan Kasma'i.[91] The Hemmatists, Moslem Social-Democrats of Russian Azerbaijan, especially Nariman Narimanov and Mohammad Amin Rasulzadeh, and other liberal members of the local intelligentsia offered their help. The Transcaucasian connection acquired a vital role in the resistance movement directed from Tabriz, where members of the Iranian Social-Democratic faction had remained to undertake the armed struggle together with the two by then legendary heroes of Tabriz, Sattar Khan and Baqer Khan. As the Russian envoy to Tehran reported to St. Petersburg, "Sattar Khan's camp would have laid down arms a long time ago had our Transcaucasians not assisted them."[92]

Indeed, the Russian authorities failed to stop the flow of arms and volunteers crossing the border. Armenian, Georgian, and Russian revolutionary groups hailed the Iranian resistance leaders as the torchbearers of the oppressed nations fighting a war of liberation. Karl Kautsky, the prominent Social-Democrat theorist, had conceded that the socioeconomic conditions in Iran precluded a proletarian revolution but encouraged his Iranian contacts, mostly of Armenian background, to participate in the ongoing "bourgeois and petit-bourgeois democratic struggle," the preliminary phase of the ultimate revolution.[93] Kautsky, like other Russian socialists who watched events in the region, firmly believed that "Persia and Turkey, by struggling for their liberation, struggle for the liberation of world proletariat."[94] In fact, the coup of 1908, in which the tsarist government was directly implicated, helped the Russian revolutionaries convince their Iranian comrades that they shared a common enemy.

Since the late nineteenth century, Transcaucasian Armenian political parties formed their own militias in several towns in Iranian Azerbaijan, which they used as a "launching ground" for their military operations across the border in the eastern provinces of the Ottoman Empire, enjoying the Qajar government's tacit approval. "Persian soil became a mecca for [Armenian] revolutionaries" struggling for national liberation, writes Houri Berberian.[95] They published their own newspapers and reportedly founded a weapons factory in Tabriz in 1891. As we shall see, Armenians of different socialist parties began to give serious support to the Iranian constitutionalists in late 1908 and early 1909. Basically, a dual Marxist-nationalist and anti-Russian ideology colored their perception of the Iranian struggle. They were also initially supportive of the Young Turks' newly established government.[96]

In October 1908, a group of some thirty Social-Democrats of Tabriz voted to penetrate the "democratic revolutionary" ranks and support the armed insurrection in northern Iran. Armenians joined other Transcaucasian volunteers in the Azerbaijan and Gilan battles, inspired by the slogan "The love of freedom has no fatherland."[97] In Azerbaijan and Gilan, Yeprem Khan and Stepan Stepanian, two Armenian militants born in the Caucasus who in 1896 had fled to Tabriz to escape Russian arrest, had secretly agreed to work with radical members of the Anjoman-e Azerbaijan covertly.[98] Two separate Armenian socialist parties, the Dashnakist and the Hnchakist, established close working relations with Taqizadeh.

Resistance in Azerbaijan and Gilan

By early January 1909, Taqizadeh and fellow radicals were back in Tabriz, which royalist forces had kept under siege for months. They resumed publication of journals and pamphlets, working with the local radical *anjoman* members and the new Transcaucasian volunteers. Their rhetoric was aggressively revolutionary, inciting the populace to revolt and lend support to Sattar Khan and Baqer Khan's armed struggle. Mohammad Reza Musavat, in the first issue of his paper *Musavat* published since its closing in June 1908, picked up his polemical attack on the shah from where he had left it nine months earlier. Comparing Mohammad Ali Shah to the "pharaoh of ancient Egypt," the article warned of his imminent "crushing defeat" unless the monarch acknowledges that he owes his crown to the will of the people. "Do not torment your people, lest you destroy your own basis of support."[99] At about the same time, a pamphlet circulating in town incited revolt against the tyrannical ruler. "The people have the right to use all means to put an end to his evil rule and replace him with a worthier one."[100] A dynasty may be necessary, a monarch needed, but, the pamphlet's author insisted, he must abide by the laws of justice and equality. A nation that does not revolt and erase violence and despotism cannot ever trod the path of progress and civilization. Prior to the French Revolution, it went on, eighteenth-century philosophers had enlightened people regarding their rights, inspiring them to desire independence and liberty. And it praised the Ottoman nation, which had joined hands with the military to attain liberty, progress, and civilization. It concluded with a call to the entire nation of Iran to follow Tabriz's example and raise the standard of revolt before it is too late. Neither the Russians nor the British will intervene, it stated; they will just watch and see who triumphs.

Within a few weeks of his return to his native town, Taqizadeh renewed his contacts with Armenian leaders. According to the Azerbaijan Dashnak Central Committee documents cited by Houri Berberian, Iranian Social-Democrats and liberals led by Taqizadeh reached an agreement with the Dashnakists to form a new party modeled on the Armenian party's own.[101] While maintaining these contacts, Taqizadeh was simultaneously planning with the rival Hnchakists to found another Iranian party. Judging from Taqizadeh's private papers edited by Iraj Afshar, two personalities came to play a dominant role in the formation of a future party. Vram Pilosian and Tigran Ter Hacobian figured among a small minority of Hnchakists who defected from their party. Whereas the majority of Hnchakists decided to carry on the social-democratic agenda, Pilosian and Tigran decided to join forces with Taqizadeh and his fellow Iranian constitutionalists. In January 1909, the idea of a Democrat Party took shape, with both Tigran and Pilosian as its main ideologues and organizers. Although the party and the program, stripped of its socialist slogans, would remain secret until the summer of 1910, in fact its ideological foundation was established in Tabriz in the winter of 1909.

The social-revolutionary Dashnakists and the social-democratic Hnchakists continued to support the insurgents' battle against royalist troops, recruiting and organizing popular revolts among mostly peasants and some workers. The Hnchakists, again according to Berberian's Armenian sources, had agreed with the Tabriz–Baku Social-Democratic Party founded on the eve of the Constitutional Revolution in 1905, "pledging to uphold social-democratic principles."[102] Taqizadeh's agreement with Pilosian and Tigran did not prevent him from also working with the two Armenian parties. His correspondence of the winter and spring of 1909 amply demonstrates his involvement in promoting the armed insurrection then raging in Gilan. The insurrection was directed by the newly established Sattar Khan Committee, which was dominated by Social-Democrats and Dashnakists and included the Rashti brothers Karim Khan and Abdol Hamid Sardar Mohiy; Hosain Kasma'i, a former religious student who had exchanged his turban and long clerical garb for the Caucasian mojahedin (holy warrior) outfit; Mohsen Najmabadi, a Tehran activist and grandson of Shaikh Hadi Najmabadi, the reform-minded religious scholar of the pre-revolution period; Mehdi Nuri, the rebel son of the *mojtahed* Fazlollah Nuri; Ali Mohammad Tarbiyat, brother of Mohammad Ali Tarbiyat, who was married to Taqizadeh's sister; Haidar Khan Amu-Oghli; and Yeprem Khan.

After the royalist coup in July 1908, Haidar Khan had fled to Baku, where he contacted the Hemmat Party leaders Nariman Narimanov and Amin Rasulzadeh and raised funds to purchase weapons. He also rallied many Caucasian and Iranian fighters to the resistance cause, bringing them along to Tabriz in the winter of 1909 to join Azerbaijan's Social-Democratic group. He was especially close to the Armenian Dashnakists.[103] This group also included the Bulgarian-born Russian subject Panoff (his full name is not known)[104] and Sergey Ordzhonikidze, the Georgian Social-Democrat who participated in the bloody events of Gilan. Firebrand revolutionaries established in Tabriz a laboratory for manufacturing explosives, expertly handled by Haidar Khan, who was then known as the "bomb maker." They addressed local peasants about class struggle and their right to revolt against tyrannical landowners.[105] Sattar Khan and Baqer Khan fought the reactionary olama, expelling *mojtahed* Mirza Hasan and the *imam jom'eh* from Tabriz.

A common short-term goal, the overthrow of Mohammad Ali Shah, forged an alliance of disparate Caucasian, Armenian, and Iranian groups. Calling themselves mojahedin or *fedayan* (devotees), they were radical secular fighters with ties to Baku, Tiflis, and Tabriz who more often than not distrusted one another. Following a fierce battle on February 8, 1909, Transcaucasian volunteers and local mojahedin dressed alike in Caucasian attire and set up a truly revolutionary regime in Rasht and Anzali, Gilan's most important towns.[106] All were to play a prominent part in the battle of Qazvin and the fall of Tehran in the following spring and summer. In her detailed analysis of these fateful events, Janet Afary concludes that the "revolutionary social movement" in the North involved people who had transcended class, religious, ethnic, and gender divides, struggling in unison against despotic rulers and foreign imperialists.[107] Yet fierce rivalry between various personalities controlling the province marred their short-lived unity and rule. As we shall see, once their common objective was attained with the restoration of the Constitution and the overthrow of Mohammad Ali Shah, most would part company to support different newly empowered, rival political personalities.

Taqizadeh, the Reconciliatory "Moderator"

Taqizadeh, the "moderate" Persia Committee's man sent back to Iran to help stage a "national reconciliation," was contacted by Abdol Majid 'Ayn al-Dowleh, the royalist commander in Azerbaijan whose notorious policies had triggered the national uprising in 1905. A series of private letters between the two, dated January and February 1909,[108] reveal Taqizadeh's personal ambiguity regarding his role as mediator and 'Ayn al-Dowleh's surprisingly deferential tone. Apparently believing the young politician of humble social origin was London's special envoy for national reconciliation, the royal prince assured Taqizadeh of his friendship and cooperation in their joint effort to save the nation. "*Dowlat* [government] and *mellat* [nation] are one," he wrote, one cannot exist without the other.[109] Taqizadeh's response adopted a similar flattering tone. "I dare say that those in favor of peace with honor are no less worthy than victorious warriors the like of Alexander or Napoleon." He nonetheless firmly stated his unwillingness to carry on negotiations in the "futile" and "hypocritical" language of diplomacy and politics.[110] Taqizadeh and 'Ayn al-Dowleh first met alone in the office of the radical, antimonarchist *Musavat* paper for a preliminary discussion. Taqizadeh then tried to plan a meeting in Tabriz between 'Ayn al-Dowleh's personal emissaries, some members of the Tabriz *anjoman*, and a "neutral" foreign envoy, French or American, as an observer. He insisted that minutes be taken according to official protocol and signed by all participants.

'Ayn al-Dowleh's verbal promises of cooperation rapidly reached a stalemate, while the siege of Tabriz continued to take its heavy toll on its population. Frustrated, on February 9, 1909, Taqizadeh composed an angry letter, directing his wrath at the shah's arrogant self-view that his "imperial grandeur and honor" depended on "spilling one spoonful of my blood and that of others like me."[111] In fact, Taqizadeh had plans for an alternative course of action. The Persia Committee, realizing the shah's resistance to any concession unless forced to, approved this plan. A coordinated march into Tehran by Bakhtiyari-led troops from Isfahan in the South and mojahedin militia from Rasht in the North was deemed the most effective means to threaten the royalists in the capital.[112] Since early March 1909, Taqizadeh had begun to encourage the mojahedin in Rasht to conquer Qazvin on their way to Tehran. Mirza Ali Theqat al-Islam, the Tabriz constitutionalist *mojtahed* who had begun separate negotiations with 'Ayn al-Dowleh even before Taqizadeh's return to Tabriz, was left uninformed of the new strategy. This bruising rebuff of the venerable but vulnerable religious leader left him with a sense of betrayal that destroyed his trust in Taqizadeh and other members of the Tabriz *anjoman*. More significantly, it underscored the nationalist leaders' disunity and weakness in their attempt to prevent the colonization of their country in all but name. Committed but helpless constitutionalists of all colors, from moderate to radical, had to experience again the stark reality of their dependence on an overwhelming foreign power interfering in their behalf.

Anglo-Russian Negotiations

The departure from Tehran of Nikolai Hartwig, the Russian ambassador and mastermind of the royalist coup of 1908, and his replacement by Evgeni Sablin facilitated a mostly cordial collaboration with Sir George Barclay, the British envoy. By late December–early January 1909, the strategic necessity of an Anglo-Russian policy allowed a more flexible Russian government diplomacy in Iran. Sablin was instructed to cooperate with his British colleague to compel the shah to restore the constitutional government. The shah's hands, though, were often tied in having to contend with Hartwig's persistent reactionary influence in shaping St. Petersburg's policy, which rendered Barclay's task daunting. The shah, still confident of Russian backing, as evident in Izvolski's public speeches, resisted the demands made upon him. Moreover, the royal forces besieging Tabriz enjoyed the Russian consul general's support, demonstrating Russia's impatience and continued desire to control the situation militarily.

Barclay and Sablin prepared for the shah a joint proposal of reforms as a condition for Anglo-Russian provision of financial support and protection for him personally and for his throne. The proposal took months of intense Anglo-Russian negotiations over details and precise wording. Only toward the end of April was the final draft officially presented to the court.[113] The shah was to proclaim publicly the partial restoration of the Constitution; to promulgate as soon as possible the electoral law to be drafted by a competent committee that would include nationalist representatives; to prepare for a speedy Majles election; to dismiss from office notorious reactionary officials; and to distance himself from Fazlollah Nuri and Nuri's fellow anticonstitutionalist *mojtaheds*. In addition, a council of advisers was to be established to begin much needed administrative and financial reforms. The shah was also to decree a general amnesty for all political insurgents, though specifically excluding individuals involved in criminal acts committed under political guise. Should the shah genuinely accept this proposed program and promptly act upon it, Britain and Russia would offer a substantial sum as the advance of a loan. However, its expenditure was to be strictly supervised by a small committee composed of the Tehran directors of British and Russian banks; Joseph Bizot, the French financial adviser currently employed by the government; and representatives of the reconvened Majles. Bizot would immediately have "every facility for studying the financial" situation in the country to provide "proper security for the regular payment of the loan interest."[114]

Izvolski and Grey believed that the establishment of the National Assembly in its previous shape was not desirable. It relied too much, they argued, on revolutionary *anjomans* that were deemed incapable of governing the country. "Without in any way departing from the basic principle of nonintervention in domestic affairs," Izvolski explained, a common plan of action was necessary to help the shah and "men of merit" draft a new law establishing a "legislative body fitting historical customs of the Persian people and their religious beliefs."[115] The Russian minister in fact meant to exclude most of the liberal reforms the constitutionalists advocated. Joint diplomatic pressure compelled the shah to install a council of state composed of sixty councilors and given considerable power, but Barclay declared his skepticism regarding its possible effectiveness. The appointed councilors, he informed Grey, were "ignorant and reactionary" with the exception of a couple of them, who "regard the council as a farce."[116] The two envoys had selected Javad Khan Sa'ad al-Dowleh as their interlocutor for their program to induce the shah to restore constitutional government. Originally hailed as the much-admired "father of the constitution," Sa'ad al-Dowleh had rapidly distanced himself from the first Majles and joined the royalist ranks after the coup. Barclay described him as a man with "a record in the past . . . far from stainless" and possessing "in a degree unusual even for a Persian the faculty for intrigue." Nonetheless, the British diplomat accepted him as a "strong man" who "for the moment" endorsed the nationalists.[117]

However, the intrusive role of the British and the Russians in determining the new government's composition continually raised objections from both the royalists and the constitutionalists. The reactionary court officials objected to the selection of Sa'ad al-Dowleh as interlocutor, viewing him as a "liberal" British agent planted in their midst. Their hostile court intrigues slowed down the negotiations, boosting the shah's negative stance against the reform proposal. Barclay and Sablin persistently demanded Sa'ad al-Dowleh's appointment as prime minister and Abol Qasem Khan Naser al-Molk as financial minister. The latter, an Oxford-educated member of the aristocratic elite, was very hesitant to return to Tehran and give up the personal safety he enjoyed in Europe, where he resided at the time. Both Barclay and Sablin devoted time and energy to persuade him to assume the important cabinet post, offering him guaranteed protection if ever needed. They never relented on that particular choice, but Naser al-Molk would not return until after the overthrow of Mohammad Ali Shah and the inauguration of the second Majles. The two legations further recommended the inclusion of moderate "nationalists" to form with the shah's appointees a special committee within the council established to prepare the electoral law. Sadeq Khan Mostashar al-Dowleh, the liberal Azerbaijani deputy in the first Majles who was being held under arrest in the royal military camp, figured prominently as a British choice. Barclay arranged for his release from detention, together with that of Morteza Qoli Khan Sani' al-Dowleh, another constitutionalist deputy of the first Majles. Both statesmen would play a prominent role in the Electoral Committee and as deputies in the second Majles.

Thorny issues raised by all concerned parties delayed the restoration for several months. The reactionary elements at the shah's and the tsar's courts disagreed with British demands for the expulsion of the court official Amir Bahador and the *mojtahed* Fazlollah Nuri, the shah's most ardent supporters. And the then Persian prime minister, echoing Ayatollah Nuri, seriously challenged the religious validity of parliamentary government as "inconsistent with Mohammedan law."[118] Barclay nonetheless identified Nuri as "the most prominent reactionary mujtahid, who had been so active of late in condemning the re-establishment of the constitutional regime."[119] Russia, however, strongly advised against Nuri's banishment on the basis that it would not be "prudent."[120] Sir Arthur Nicolson, the British ambassador to St. Petersburg, agreed that Nuri was too influential in Tehran to be expelled. "It might cause turbulence," he wrote to Grey.[121] Barclay regretfully gave up the idea, judging it not worth fighting for.

Financial aid to the shah proved to be a more virulent source of Anglo-Russian disagreement. Russian officials gave priority to strengthening the central government's authority by providing its troops with regular payment and preventing a total administrative collapse due to lack of funds. Izvolski favored granting a substantial joint Anglo-Russian loan to the shah.[122] Moreover, he did not share the British decision to "wait and see . . . whatever element in the country is strongest and gains the day." He thought there was "no such single element in sight," and he never failed to express his skepticism that a constitutional government would alone restore peace and order.[123] Nicolson would invariably respond that his government was "immovable on the question of giving an advance to the shah" before the latter fulfilled the conditions attached to it.[124]

Heated discussions between the two envoys and their respective governments dragged on, allowing the royalists' time to prolong their combat in the North and to rally the anticonstitutional front in the capital. At times, some Russian officials would even threaten to revoke the Anglo-Russian Convention of 1907. British officials then agreed to offer only an advance to the loan, conditional on the shah fulfilling his promise to implement their proposed reforms in deed and not just in words. The money, Barclay proposed, would be deposited in a joint account in both diplomats' names, to be paid in installments and used to pay the soldiers' arrear salaries, while the sums allocated for the administrative reforms would be advanced only when the reconvened Majles approved the transaction. "Until the regime is working, the shah must be starved."[125] Russia reluctantly gave up the idea of a substantial loan but insisted on exercising a strict control that should look "as innocent as possible and as little official as possible."[126] That was an unrealistic wish, given the vast international network of dissidents scrutinizing all details of the negotiations available to them. The Persia Committee leaders escalated their "media war" in defense of the constitutionalists' cause, referring to the constitutionalists' legitimate demands for the restoration of the Constitution in its integrity, and against granting a loan to the shah until then.

Rumors spread rapidly in Tehran based on foreign-press reports that the British and Russian envoys intended to play a dominant role in Persian internal affairs through the appointment of foreign advisers. A "leading member of the first majles [*sic*]" informed Barclay that the new nationalist government would be interested in foreigners' advice; however, under no circumstance would they accept "the imposition of foreigners" by the two powers.[127]

On their own, however, members of the shah's entourage endeavored to raise funds elsewhere in order to circumvent Anglo-Russian financial tutelage. Some court officials contacted a German diplomat offering concessions in return for a loan, with no success. The German was mindful of the Anglo-Russian Convention, which he was unwilling to challenge.[128] In fact, the British and Russian envoys watched with apprehension the noticeably increased German commercial penetration of the country, worrying about its potential political implications. The alleged German "threat" would further complicate the intricate balance of international power they had so painstakingly achieved in the country. As we shall see, France played a significant part in fueling anti-German sentiments in Britain and Russia, anxious as it was in maintaining a viable European alliance between the two powers against its German nemesis. Its diplomat in Tehran was instructed never to deviate from this principal role of honoring the convention and sustaining Anglo-Russian close collaboration. The appointment of a French treasurer general and French financial inspectors to the Persian government notwithstanding, both British and Russian envoys insisted that "no third party," not even France, "could be admitted to deal with Persian Affairs on an equal footing with Great Britain and Russia."[129] In London, Lord Grey categorically asserted: "If there were any risk . . . of such an action leading to interference on the part of any foreign Power, Russia would have our support . . . for the prevention of any alteration in the situation that may adversely affect British or Russian interests."[130] This policy was similarly applied to any other European effort to engage in mediation between the nationalists in Tabriz and the royalists, as a newly arrived German consul reportedly attempted.[131] The two powers threatened to cut short their mediation should such a third party be involved.

Bizot's confidential report on Iran's financial state was highly pessimistic, based on his findings of a severely depleted Treasury as well as of government, court, and individuals' indebtedness to foreign banks. He urged the appointment of a European treasury general as soon as possible and the advance of substantial sums to run the country.[132] Barclay continued to express his doubts on the usefulness of such a loan but conceded to Russia's insistence on an immediate advance.[133] 'Ayn al-Dowleh, the commander of royalist forces in the North, was sent a large sum for the operation in Azerbaijan. He reportedly managed to appropriate for himself part of the sum sent.[134]

These complex, secretive Anglo-Russian negotiations that took no real Iranian interests into consideration played out as the nationalist resistance was gathering momentum in the North and while Lynch and other British individuals supportive of the constitutional cause were staging a national reconciliation.

The Insurgency

The worsening situation in the North shifted the two powers' focus of discussion from financial aid to military intervention. The bloody battles intensified in Azerbaijan and especially in Gilan with the increased participation of Transcaucasian mercenaries. Alphonse L. M. Nicolas, the French consul in Tabriz who was in daily contact with all major players, noted also the "revolutionary party's constant contact" with the Young Turks' CUP.[135] British diplomats confirmed the Young Turks' aid to the insurgents in secretly sending men and arms cross the border.[136] The siege of Tabriz, however, also further alienated a starving population from the local foreign residents. Wild rumors spreading in town raised the Europeans' concerns regarding possible attacks on their life and property, despite vigorous denials by *anjoman* leaders. Nicolas accused the Russian consulate of "manufacturing" false and "sensationalist" news and "alarming rumors."[137] Like Barclay in Tehran, he persistently debunked such disinformation, pointing at the insurgents' utmost care to avoid provoking foreign intervention. However, fear-mongering proved to be a convenient means for some Tabriz *anjoman* members as well as for the Russian government to further their respective goals. The former desired British mediation to put an end to the Russia-backed royal troops' siege of Tabriz, which they were unable to end decisively, and force the shah to comply with their demands. The latter seized the situation in Tabriz as a pretext for sending troops, arguing that its chief motive was to protect European residents. Despite Russian public denials, signs abounded of military preparation for intervention in the conflict, a move that the shah and his reactionary court believed would maintain their power. Britain's delicate position in the midst of all involved parties, guided by its own conflicting interests, kept its diplomats engaged precariously in a highly volatile situation that risked unraveling its promises to honor its separate commitments to the different groups involved in the struggle.

The constitutionalists had initially won some battles waged against royal troops in Azerbaijan as well as against the notorious tribal leader Rahim Khan and his tribal allies. It was widely believed that Rahim Khan was the royalists' mercenary who also received orders from the Russians. The nationalists' two commanders, Sattar Khan (declared the "Persian Garibaldi" by his admirers) and Baqer Khan, were the heroes of the resistance to tyranny, enjoying great popularity in Tabriz. Both were the "undeniable and absolute authority in Tabriz," wrote Nicolas, and all "patriots" wore on their chest a medallion bearing the portrait of one or the other, though he cautiously added: "This popularity will be maintained as long as they are successful."[138] The exhilarating sense of victory did not last long as looting and extortion by armed gangs further aggravated the besieged population's dire situation. Nicolas himself quickly revised his opinion of Sattar Khan and Baqer Khan. He now portrayed the latter as a "sinister brute," "unintelligent" and "savage," living off the people in a grand style; the former, though more intelligent, "had no sense of what the revolution was all about."[139]

On April 20, 1909, the constitutional forces suffered a decisive defeat in a daring assault on royal troops. Two foreign sympathizers, the British journalist Arthur Moore and the American Howard Baskerville, joined the fighters. Baskerville, a Princeton graduate and a freedom-loving and idealist teacher at the Tabriz Presbyterian mission, had recruited and trained his students to participate in the resistance. The Persia Committee had dispatched Moore as special correspondent for several liberal newspapers, including the *Manchester Guardian*, his expenses collectively paid by the committee and the press. Walter Smart, the British consul in Tabriz, though deploring Moore's "reprehensible conduct" in participating in the fight, recognized the journalist's good influence on the insurgents. "These gentlemen," he wrote, "behaved with the greatest pluck, but their men failed to support them and they reached the royalist positions with only the merest handful of followers."[140] Baskerville was killed, but Moore escaped unharmed and returned to London, where the committee dismissed him for writing highly critical reports on the Tabriz fighters for the *Manchester Guardian*. Sattar Khan and Baqer Khan, who had cowardly fled the battle, lost the glorious aura they had previously earned. Sattar Khan began to drink heavily, and Baqer Khan, living up to his reputation for opportunism, was widely believed to be ready to sell himself to the highest bidder.[141] The *anjoman* of Tabriz, until then reluctant to accept an armistice arranged by the two powers with the shah's final consent, declared a cease-fire. 'Ayn al-Dowleh gave up the struggle upon hearing the news of Russia's decision to send troops to Tabriz.

Tabriz's nationalist leaders had already lost hope for a victory on the battlefield days before the disastrous defeat, at a time when the two envoys in Tehran were pressing their respective consuls in the Azerbaijan capital to bring their mediation between royalists and constitutionalists to a rapid conclusion. The insurgents' goal to stage their return to power on their own terms had by then waned considerably. They sent cables to the shah, imploring him not to allow Tabriz to fall into the hands of a foreign power and promising to support him should he stand by them and protect the nation. The Tabriz *anjoman*, Barclay informed Grey on April 17, 1909, was now "willing to accept whatever terms the British and Russian governments might suggest to the shah, there being no hope but in intervention by the two Powers."[142] Rumor was spreading that Sattar Khan and Baqer Khan, fearing a popular uprising, might create a crisis by attacking foreign consulates. British and Russian diplomats in Tabriz took this alleged threat seriously. Barclay was ready to send an ultimatum to the shah that if he did not act immediately upon the two envoys' reform proposal, he would be held responsible for "anything that happens to the consulates" in Tabriz. By April 19, 1909, the British diplomat had also urged his Russian colleague "to cable the military authorities in Tiflis to be ready to proceed to Tabriz."[143] Nicolson and Grey went along with the decision. In fact, Russian troops had already gathered at the border. Izvolski issued the order to escort and "facilitate the entry into town of necessary provisions; protect the consulates and foreign subjects, and assist those wishing to leave town."[144]

Russian Intervention

The Russian military invasion was officially declared a humanitarian measure to lift the siege of Tabriz, protect foreign lives and property, and restore order, while denying any intention to favor either party in the struggle. London adopted the same argument. In response to Browne's vehement protest against the invasion, the Foreign Office tried reassurance: "The Russian advance into Persian territory is of a temporary nature and solely undertaken with a view to allay disturbance and prevent bloodshed."[145] Both powers, despairing of the shah's continued resistance to their demands for reforms, hoped that the crossing of Russian troops over the border would also force him to concede.[146]

In Tabriz, Sattar Khan immediately ordered a cease-fire; the *anjoman* went along, though some members remained suspicious that the Russian troops, numbering two thousand, would turn into a long-term occupation force. Taqizadeh most fiercely opposed the military intervention, literally begging the two envoys to stop the troops' advance. He urged them to exert more pressure on the shah to agree to the *anjoman*'s demands: restoration of the Constitution in its entirety, universal and complete amnesty for the insurgents, removal of all government troops, and appointment of a governor general of their choice—all terms to be guaranteed by the foreign powers.[147] Both diplomats, however, trusting neither royalists nor nationalists, were not willing to offer that guarantee or to stop the troops' arrival.[148] Barclay was convinced that Taqizadeh and some fellow *anjoman* members used the news of impending arrival of Russian troops as leverage in negotiations with the shah. On April 30, the troops approached Tabriz under the command of General Snarsky (full name not known). Thoroughly discouraged, Taqizadeh then felt "it was all over"; the country was lost.[149]

Until then, Barclay worked more harmoniously than not with his Russian colleague, whom he often praised in his dispatches to London. Meanwhile, Grey was impressed with Izvolski's "moderation, restraint, and adherence to the spirit of the Anglo Russian Convention which he has shown since the Persian coup d'etat [*sic*] of the summer, under very trying and provocative circumstances."[150] Both were naturally alarmed by the rumor that Hartwig might resume his post as envoy to Tehran, which would complicate the British effort toward national reconciliation. Overall, the military intervention raised the tension between the two governments, further delaying the restoration of the Constitution. It was then apparent that the Russian imperial government was severely divided over its foreign policy, specifically concerning Persian affairs, with the Ministry of Foreign Affairs under Izvolski pitted against hard-liners within the Ministry of Defense and the military authorities in the Caucasus. Commander Lyakhof and his fellow Russian officers commanding the Cossack Brigade, though officially no longer under Russian but Persian government authority, persisted in pursuing Russian hard-line national interests. During his thirteen-year service in Tehran, Lyakhof had succeeded in forming a strong, well-disciplined force, detaching it totally from the host country's authority and rendering it virtually a Russian brigade. He fired some Persian officers and replaced them with Russians, rewarding those Persians he kept on with promotions and good salaries but using them as spies. Major Claude Stokes, the British military attaché in Tehran, confirmed this fact and acknowledged that Cossacks were employed to "shadow British officers in this country."[151]

General Snarsky and his troops treated Tabriz as a conquered city, imposing harsh rules on its population that exceeded their initial instructions only to restore peace and order. The Russian officers also overruled or overstepped Russian diplomatic authority in Tehran. Baqer Khan and Sattar Khan sought refuge in the Ottoman consulate; many others were arrested throughout Azerbaijan, creating total disarray among the resistance ranks and causing the Tabriz *anjoman* to demand general amnesty.[152] The *mojtahed* Mirza Hasan and the *imam jom'eh* returned to Tabriz and formed the Anjoman-e Islamiyeh (Islamic Anjoman), an anticonstitutional Islamic center enjoying the Russian consul's full support. Lyakhof would send alarmist reports printed in the Russian press on alleged anarchy prevailing in the country. The viceroy in Baku would fuel hard-liners' hostility with his own alarmist news of Caucasian revolutionaries commanding events in Azerbaijan and Gilan. The Russian press, meanwhile, would publish official government denials of any interested motives concerning the Persian government. The Russian troops were in Tabriz, it claimed, to protect foreign lives and property and would remain there until order was restored.[153]

The Anglo-Russian Convention was more than ever determining the nation's fate. Most of the action was located in the northern provinces and Tehran, the declared Russian zone of influence. Hence, as the envoy of a partner in the convention, Barclay had to acquiesce more often than he wished, while deploying all the diplomatic skills he could muster to bring about what officially was termed the "national reconciliation" of all parties concerned. Until shortly before the fall of Tehran in mid-July 1909 and despite his own better judgment, he went along with Russia's determination to maintain Mohammad Ali Shah on the throne at all costs. Constitutional activists began to circulate pamphlets, expressing outrage and total disillusionment with the European powers' quiescence, if not complicity. One such text addressed directly the British and Russian envoys, "respectfully" reminding them of their pledge of noninterference in the country's internal affairs. "What is the nation to do? For sure, you are not Moslems, and do not believe in the Day of Judgment. However, you believe in order and justice, civilization and law. Why should you tolerate that our nation be subjected to such tyranny?"[154]

3

The March to Tehran

RUSSIAN INTERVENTION had not prevented the revolutionaries' advance elsewhere in the country. The movement was by then spreading rapidly in various provinces with its own local leaders, be they genuine constitutionalists or mere opportunists joining the cause for personal reasons. Isfahan had fallen under the powerful Bakhtiyari tribal khans' control, with Najaf Qoli Khan Samsam al-Saltaneh seizing the governorship despite the shah's refusal to acknowledge him as such. His brother, Ali Qoli Khan Sardar As'ad, who returned to Iran via Khuzestan, where he had forged an alliance with the local tribal leader Shaikh Khaz'al, was preparing his armed tribesmen to march to Tehran. In Rasht, Social-Democrat revolutionaries extended their rule to several parts of the province of Gilan. They seized control of the road to Tehran, setting up roadblocks and demanding from all travelers a pass issued by the "war committee." The Rasht–Tehran road was privately owned by a Russian company that had exclusive right to levy tolls. The governor was murdered in his house by a group of Georgians, Armenians, the Bulgarian Panoff, and local Gilani mojahedin. Sardar Mohiy, one of the Rashti brothers, reportedly played a crucial role in the bloody act.[1] Red flags were displayed everywhere in town, though many houses had the Russian flag flying over their roofs, signaling foreign protection. "The entire movement in Rasht was planned in the Caucasus,"[2] wrote George Percy Churchill, the secretary at the British legation in Tehran in charge of Middle Eastern and Asian affairs. His statement was not entirely accurate.

The Multifaceted Constitutionalist Leadership

Internal conflicts divided the ranks of the constitutionalist leadership in the North, diluting its revolutionary character. A new governor for Gilan was chosen from among the local elite. Mohammad Vali Khan Naser al-Saltaneh, the Sepahdar, a wealthy landowner, had fought alongside the royal troops before defecting to the constitutionalist camp in his native province. A paternal cousin of the Rashti brothers, he had convinced the local Social-Democrats of his genuine constitutionalist credentials, promising to respect and enforce their decisions. He would thus emerge as one of the prominent official figures rallying all forces and conveying an aura of legitimacy to the disparate and unruly mojahedin. Factionalism, personal rivalries, sedition, and plundering had marred the revolutionaries' accomplishments, wrote a contemporaneous source.[3] Furthermore, the Sepahdar was known as a "Russia man," who had accepted the governorship upon the Russian envoy Evgeni Sablin's advice, with Barclay's approval.[4] Both envoys still believed in the possibility of enforcing a "national reconciliation" and preventing the shah's overthrow. The Sepahdar's large estate was located in the Russian zone, so he was vulnerable to Russian threats of retaliation should he act against Russian interests. The Sepahdar was caught between the Russians' powerful grip and the no less forceful revolutionaries' control, so his conduct in subsequent events would reflect the negative effects of both pressures exerted on him.[5]

The Russian envoy Sablin instructed his consul in Rasht to urge the Sepahdar, "in the interests of a speedy reconciliation between the shah and his people, to hold the advance" along the Rasht–Tehran road.[6] On May 2, the shah had at last decreed the restoration of a "limited" constitution. But because of strong protests raised by nationalists active in Tehran and by the revolutionaries, the text of the decree was rectified to mean the restoration of the Constitution "in its integrality," without the slightest change.[7] The decree also announced the formation of a special committee to draft an electoral law and that the committee would include nationalists who had the confidence of the government and the nation. Sadeq Khan Mostashar al-Dowleh, Morteza Qoli Khan Sani' al-Dowleh, Hosain Qoli Khan Navab, and Abdol Hosain Mirza Farman-Farma, among others, figured in the list.[8] The two envoys instructed their consuls in the "various centers of revolt" to inform the "nationalists" that "it is now their duty to do everything in their power to secure a reconciliation between the Popular party and the shah."[9] The leaders decided otherwise.

On May 5, 1909, the Gilan militia, composed of a couple hundred fighters led by Yeprem Khan, the Rashti brothers, and Hosain Kasma'i, enjoying Taqizadeh's full support,[10] had conquered Qazvin with little bloodshed, and they all waited for Taqizadeh's signal for the final assault on the capital. The Bakhtiyari khans were also preparing to march to the capital. Barclay at last realized that the nationalists, as he persistently referred to the revolutionaries, were aiming at dethroning the shah; Lord Grey agreed. However, the two envoys continued to negotiate with Mohammad Ali Shah, insisting on the formation of a cabinet with candidates they deemed suitable, including Sa'ad al-Dowleh and Naser al-Molk, who still refused to return to Tehran.[11] In addition, the envoys demanded the expulsion of the "mischief-makers"; the lifting of telegraph censorship; the disarming of all groups in the capital but leaving the Cossacks solely in charge of maintaining order; and the decrease and eventual evacuation of all Russian troops from Tabriz. The demands fulfilled many but not all of the constitutionalists' own wishes: they also desired the immediate evacuation of Russian troops.

While intensive negotiation Barclay conducted between the shah and the constitutionalists was taking place in Tehran, in Najaf some olama supportive of the Constitution were adamant in their demands for the shah's absolute surrender and in their denunciation of Russian military intervention. Surrounded by young activist mollahs, who had representatives in Istanbul's Anjoman-e Sa'adat and extensive networks with revolutionaries in Iran and abroad, Mohammad Kazem Khorasani made official political pronouncements that often reflected their views. A French army officer, Capitaine Anginieur (full name not available), known in Tabriz constitutionalist circles as highly sympathetic to their cause, had traveled to Najaf and Karbala in December 1908. A delegate of the Young Turk CUP arranged an exclusive interview with Ayatollah Khorasani on December 27, 1908. In a report sent to Raymond Lecomte, the French ambassador to Tehran, Anginieur related his conversation with the cleric, who denounced the opponents of the Constitution as "infidels" and claimed to be in favor of women's education and their right not to cover their face. Unimpressed, Anginieur described him as undeserving of his reputation as a man of great intelligence. The young mollahs of Khorasani's entourage, he remarked, were "more superior [*sic*]" to him; in fact, they "led" him. He mentioned in particular Seyyed Ali Mohammad Kashani (the brother of Mo'ayyed al-Islam Kashani, the editor of *Habl al-matin*), "a remarkably intelligent and extremely liberal" man.[12] On the whole, the French officer noted the *mojtaheds*' general reluctance to interfere in politics unless absolutely necessary. Russian occupation demanded their intervention, however. Obviously guided by the activist elements of their entourage, Khorasani and Abdollah Mazandarani sent a personal letter to the French ambassador in Constantinople pleading for support against Russian "unlawful intervention." "We bring our complaints to your government," they wrote, "which had always shown itself as the protector of liberty, justice, and human rights. We plead with you to remember the suffering endured by your noble nation at the time it fought for its liberty and to help the Persian people to prevent Russian intervention."[13]

Meanwhile, Sablin and Barclay dispatched a joint message to the *mojtaheds*, appealing to their patriotism and assuring them of the shah's concessions for the restoration of constitutional governance and political reforms. Seeking their support for the reconciliation plan, the message asked them to help the shah restore order and calm in the country and to instruct the people to give up "fratricide struggle." The shah's objective, the two envoys assured the *mojtaheds*, was to establish peace and security in conformity with the advice of the "two friendly Powers." Khorasani and Mazandarani's response was respectful in tone and appreciative of Anglo-Russian help in restoring the Constitution. "It is well known to the civilized nations," they asserted, "that the defense of the independence of the motherland is one of the greatest religious obligations of Moslems. . . . We therefore appeal to the sense of justice and neighborly duties of the two governments that they will not allow the awakened feelings of the Persian nation to be trampled upon." They called for the evacuation of Russian troops, which were causing great disturbances and disorder.[14]

The French consul in Baghdad worried about a possible decree calling for holy war against Russian troops and suspected the Young Turks' influence in this direction. His British counterpart shared this worry that Najaf and Karbala would use all their influence to "make untenable" the Russian position. The French consul also described Shaikh Kazem Yazdi, the influential Karbala *mojtahed* who had persistently opposed the constitutional movement but also vehemently protested Russian occupation, as a leader capable of using his considerable clout to cause anti-Russian disturbances in the Caucasus.[15] With the rapid unfolding of events, the *mojtaheds* in Najaf and Karbala continuously informed British and French diplomats they would not help restore calm until the withdrawal of Russian troops.[16] Public demonstrations, meetings, lectures, and publication of articles encouraged the constitutionalists in their last efforts to restore their power and to resist further foreign encroachment in national affairs. Barclay, who received similar reports from the constitutionalist olama in Tehran, informed Grey, "The ulama resent what they call our present passive attitude, contrasting it with our former support of the constitutional elements."[17]

Barclay foresaw Sablin possibly jeopardizing his (Barclay's) effort to stage a reconciliation between the shah and the nationalists. In fact, Sablin did exert pressure on the Sepahdar to check the revolutionaries' advance from Qazvin, threatening him with "material and moral ruin" should he fail to "pacify" them.[18] Smart, then British consul in Tabriz, had observed that the Sepahdar was "no nationalist" and a "reluctant figure-head" who, while in Qazvin, sought the shah's pardon through the Russian legation.[19] The Sepahdar, who was heavily indebted to a Russian bank, in desperation told Smart the revolutionaries were beyond his control and that he did not wish to be assassinated. He suggested the Russian envoy should talk to them because they were Russian subjects.[20] Abdolhosain Nava'i's chronicle of the fall of Tehran confirms the Sepahdar's dilemma. "Moderate and cautious," he wrote, the Sepahdar favored a diplomatic resolution to the conflict, and he distanced himself from the "extremists," causing a long-lasting rift between himself and them.[21] Indeed, the Sepahdar had communicated to Mostashar al-Dowleh, the constitutionalist mediator in Tehran, his intention to "safeguard the rule of our crowned father," for whom his Gilani militias were ready to shed their blood.[22]

Rising Anglo-Russian Tension

Meanwhile, the occupying forces' repressive conduct in Tabriz further heightened Anglo-Russian tension. Lord Grey criticized Russian intervention against the nationalists, warning it would "eventually result in our being compelled to interfere in their favor. . . . It will become necessary for me to admit, if questioned in Parliament, that Great Britain and Russia are no longer acting in concert in Persia." He asked the Russian government to put an end to the situation.[23] In St. Petersburg, Izvolski, equally anxious to avoid any disastrous consequences that such "divergence of views" might entail, assured Nicolson that the Russian government attached great importance to Anglo-Russian good relations, and he blamed General Snarsky personally for the troops' conduct in Tabriz.[24] Barclay informed the British foreign minister "very confidentially" that Alexander Izvolski had "rebuked" Miller (full name not available), his consul general in Tabriz.[25]

Facts on the ground in Azerbaijan further aggravated the situation as Snarsky was determined to wage war against Russian volunteer revolutionaries engaged in "unlawful" activities, inciting rebellion, and publicly insulting Russian government officials and even the emperor. Many were arrested and immediately deported to the Caucasus. At that time, the Young Turks' new regime in Istanbul continued to openly support the constitutionalists. In Tehran, the Ottoman legation had offered sanctuary to constitutionalist activists.[26] In Tabriz, some small groups representing the CUP at Salonika had reportedly carried to the Tabriz *anjoman* letters of encouragement and weapons while the fight was still ongoing against royal troops.[27] Ottoman passports were offered to combatants for protection, and Ottoman flags were hoisted on roofs of private homes. The Ottoman consul general in Tabriz criticized the Russian military's treatment of the local leaders: "The dictates of a foreign official cannot be forced on men who are the leaders of a whole nation and who have shed their blood in the cause of their country's independence."[28] Turkish military incursions in Azerbaijan, ostensibly to protect its borders against Kurdish tribal raids, further complicated an already volatile situation in the province. Russia suspected the Young Turks' design to annex Azerbaijan border territories to their empire, thus infringing on Russia's own sphere of influence. That suspicion would increase as Turkish military incursions in the Russian sphere would continue unabated until the end of the second Majles and beyond.

Anglo-Russian attempts to stage a reconciliation between the shah and the nation and to force the appointment of cabinet ministers to their liking, not to mention the endless discussions over providing the struggling nation with financial help, were eventually to prove futile. Activists in Tehran distributed pamphlets throughout the city, moderate or revolutionary in tone depending on their anonymous authors' political tendency but unanimously expressing angry dissatisfaction with the royal concessions. "All this bloodshed and turmoil were not intended for a mere piece of paper and a few sentences of words devoid of meaning!"[29] Some texts reflected Social-Democratic ideology, identifying the "nation" with the "toilers," peasants, grocers, drapers, butchers, carpenter, porters, hard-working people of all trades, "who own this country." They alone have the right to vote and govern, the pamphlets argued; they alone can represent and protect the "oppressed" from the grandees' tyranny; and they must be "our kind" of people.[30] An increasing number of such popular pamphlets were circulating in mosques, the bazaar, and public places, expressing skepticism regarding the sincerity of the shah's intentions and distrusting his motives.[31] Other texts were milder, more conciliatory, guaranteeing the preservation of the monarchy should the shah honor his promises.[32] Similarly, telegrams were sent from Qazvin to the foreign legations in the capital, denying any intention to cause a bloody confrontation and expressing loyalty to the shah and concern for the security of foreign residents.[33]

Grey and Barclay began to envision the high probability that the shah would demand asylum in one of the legations. But Izvolski opposed any kind of neutrality in the conflict, declaring the march to Tehran an unjustified act of hostility. He informed his British counterpart that the Cossacks would be ordered to fight the insurgents to protect the shah, the capital, and its residents. Rumors spreading in Tehran of imminent mob attacks on Armenians and foreigners served the Russians' purpose. Sablin was by then in favor of military intervention in the capital to protect foreign lives and property and to secure the Rasht–Tehran road. Orders were given to the viceroy in Baku to have fifteen hundred troops cross the border to Anzali and from there march to Qazvin; these troops were not to proceed to Tehran, however, unless foreigners were attacked. Lord Grey expressed his apprehension of the terrible consequences of such Russian intervention to keep the shah on the throne at all costs. Whatever form the new government would take, he wrote, "it would probably prepare the way to a better state of things, without any diminution of Russian influence in Persia." Otherwise, he stated bluntly, "we shall be unable to affirm that the policy of non-intervention can be maintained, and the whole course of policy with regard to Persia will undergo a serious change."[34]

Izvolski attached great importance to the Anglo-Russian Convention of 1907. However, he cynically dismissed the national movement as nonexistent. He regarded the "real Persian people as an apathetic, ignorant herd, who ask only to be protected against excessive extortion and oppression, and so, far from being fired with any enthusiasm for constitutional ideals [they] have no clear notion of what the term means."[35] Barclay soon believed that Izvolski had fallen under the influence of hard-line Russian diplomats in St. Petersburg, especially Hartwig, and that he would use Russian troops to reestablish order by imposing measures that, although likely to bring an end to anarchy, were not consistent with the principles of nonintervention.[36] In Tehran, Sablin espoused the hard-liners' view and continued to send alarming messages concerning threats to foreigners' safety in the capital. Without consulting his British colleague, he advised Izvolski to send troops to Qazvin to "clear[] out the revolutionaries now collected" there and thus to avoid "the necessity of occupying Tehran."[37] Barclay, vigorously denying there was such a threat, reached the conclusion that Sardar As'ad and the Sepahdar were after all justified in considering the dispatch of a large force to the capital.[38]

Yet both envoys exploited the threat of Russian intervention in their last attempt at negotiating with the leaders of the militias. For several weeks in June and July 1909, they sought to prevent the constitutionalists' advance to the capital from the north and the south. They sent their respective consuls from Isfahan to Qom, where Sardar As'ad and his troops were stationed, to try to dissuade him from a "foolish" act that might, they claimed, result in another civil war. But Sardar As'ad confided to the British consul general in Isfahan, R. B. Graham, that the march could not be stopped; much money had been spent, and he could no longer expect forgiveness from the shah.[39] Barclay surmised that the tribal leader might have some "ulterior motive," and "in that case, we can do nothing more, but must let matters run their course."[40] In fact, Sardar As'ad was initially reluctant to engage in military combat against royal forces, but the Bakhtiyari leader, while in Europe, was influenced by the exiles and their British supporters. Moreover, due to a long-lasting power struggle dividing the ranks of the tribal *ilkhan*s (top tribal chieftains), which included Amir Mofakhkham, a royalist Bakhtiyari, Sardar As'ad was reluctant to engage in a tribal civil war.[41] However, his relative Amir Mofakhkham's relentless refusal to join the constitutionalist side, despite offers of a high position once the battle was won, would eventually wipe out all of Sardar As'ad's hesitation. Barclay had already given up on Sa'ad al-Dowleh, who, beleaguered by reactionaries in the cabinet and fearing the constitutionalists' hostility toward him, periodically offered his resignation from the position of prime minister. The British diplomat determined: "His Excellency is no longer useful."[42]

Taqizadeh's About-Face

Sadeq Khan Mostashar al-Dowleh, one of the prominent Tabriz deputies in the first Majles, was the most effective member of the reform council set up upon Anglo-Russian advice. A moderate by then acting as the chief royal adviser for constitutional affairs and as a liaison to the constitutionalists in the provinces and abroad, he favored staging the restoration of the Constitution without bloodshed. In 1907–8, with Taqizadeh he had led a group advocating the most secularizing legislative reforms, but without condoning the political radicals' tactics or ideology. With the Constitution restored, he contacted Taqizadeh in Tabriz directly through the government-controlled telegraph system.[43] Taqizadeh, reassured, received his initial cable with enthusiasm and gratitude. He then vested his hope in the person of Mostashar al-Dowleh, affectionately referred to as "the soul of Iran."

However, Taqizadeh's own leadership was acknowledged in the capital, and Mostashar al-Dowleh's deferential tone in his dispatches to Taqizadeh clearly reflected this new status his former Majles colleague had acquired. It was at this point that Taqizadeh's notorious about-face reportedly took place, which was inexplicable to his radical comrades, who had trusted his commanding opinion. Taking seriously the Russian threat to occupy Tehran should the "Qazvinis" (the armed militias assembled in Qazvin) invade the capital, Taqizadeh changed his instructions and exerted pressure on all to halt the march to the capital and ensure public security and safety of foreign lives and property.[44] Fear regarding the preservation of national independence once more induced moderation. Taqizadeh, even more than Dehkhoda and his circle, felt the strong impact of Anglo-Russian push-and-pull tactics.

Taqizadeh's historic attempt at restraining the revolutionary forces had a double-edged impact on his comrades and followers and was eventually to tarnish his image in contemporaneous Persian chronicles. He was fully aware of the "unhappiness" he had caused the mojahedin with his request for restraint.[45] He dispatched a lengthy cable to inform them of the painful choice confronting them: to launch a final assault or to disband and return home.[46] Admitting that the choice constituted a complex, divisive issue, he presented what he regarded as the conflicting views of the two existing parties (using the English word *party* in transliteration). One advocates a national reconciliation with the government, given the domestic and international circumstances, even though corruption still prevails and treasonous ministers collaborate with the foreign powers. Proponents of reconciliation call for unity with the government by all means, if only in appearance, convinced as they are that a real constitutional system cannot yet be founded in Iran. A perfect example of such an accommodation, he explained, is to be found in the current cooperation between the British and the Russians, who, overlooking their divergent interests, are taking into consideration the European balance of power and the commonly perceived German threat. The second group, Taqizadeh stated, regards this policy of reconciliation as a devious conspiracy against the constitutional cause, aiming at preserving the status quo, with Russian occupation in the North and prevailing domestic despotism. This group favors a definitive attack on Tehran and the total destruction of the roots of all evil, fearing neither the English nor the Russians. Taqizadeh then acknowledged that he belongs to the first group, while confessing that he might lean this way out of lack of better judgment or personal shortcoming. He assured them he did not wish to impose his decision on them, emphatically ascertaining his reluctance to assume the burden of responsibility for their decision. And he bitterly referred to the voluminous dispatches sent to him from Iran and the Caucasus, protesting his decision and claiming that he was preventing the Sepahdar's troops from liberating Tehran. There is no way, he wrote, to find out which opinion is the best, where the truth lies. But one thing is certain: "the fancy" idea of revolution, as it originated in an advanced nation such as France and accomplished in the Ottoman Empire, where Europeanized military forces already existed, cannot work in Iran. This is a nation, he asserted, where a third of the population consists of tribal, tent-dwelling marauders and savage plunderers, whose mojahedin possess attributes he would be too ashamed to mention here. And he warned: to wage war is tantamount to committing suicide. Iran has no schools to educate the nation and undertake the necessary reforms needed to confront the enemy from within and abroad. A bloody revolution can only prolong the war, and in war there is no chance to set up schools.

The politically moderate reformist Taqizadeh, the "reconciliatory" leader, had thus eclipsed the radical Taqizadeh, silencing his alternative, social-democratic voice. As we shall see, once elected to the second Majles, together with other radical deputies he would fight hard for the enactment of reform bills modernizing social and cultural institutions that he lamented were lacking to accomplish a political revolution. But in the spring of 1909, when the various armed groups were ready to march into Tehran, Taqizadeh's new instruction divided their ranks. Some accepted the idea of making a peaceful overture, responding favorably to Taqizadeh's "philosophical telegram," assuring him of their concern for national unity, and promising an orderly "liberation of the country from its enemies."[47] They would stand by, awaiting the Tabriz *anjoman*'s and Taqizadeh's commands. Others, especially the radical Transcaucasians, remained ready for armed assault.

Meanwhile, the Young Turks had reportedly sent their representative to Qazvin urging the troops to pursue the battle to its final end.[48] By late April 1909, following a short but bloody battle against Sultan Abdul Hamid's military countercoup, the Young Turks had consolidated their power in Istanbul. The new regime's victory greatly impressed and inspired many of the Iranian constitutionalist leaders in exile in Istanbul.[49] The British envoy in the Ottoman capital informed the Foreign Office about the Young Turk regime's increasing interest in developments in Iran, noticing the local

Anjoman-e Sa'adat's close contacts with the CUP. The Young Turks, he explained, think the British government is "deceived" by the Russians, whose occupation of Tabriz will be permanent "unless Turkey comes to the rescue by sending troops to places in Azerbaijan"; the Turkish troops would withdraw when the Russians do. The consul also asserted "there would seem little doubt that the Young Turks have advised the Persians to imitate their action" in deposing Mohammad Ali Shah as the Young Turks had deposed Abdul Hamid.[50]

The continued Russian military presence in Azerbaijan further exacerbated the rising tension within the activists' ranks. The appointment of a new governor proved to be another sensitive issue for all interested parties involved in the multilateral negotiations in Tehran and Tabriz. Still insisting on justifying their role as peacemakers, the Russians reportedly had assured Sa'ad al-Dowleh that they would evacuate their troops as soon as the selected official was installed in Tabriz and order was restored.[51] Tehran wished to appoint Ahmad Ala' al-Dowleh, a notoriously reactionary Qajar official whose governorship in Fars prior to the coup in 1908 included support of the anticonstitutionalist local feudal lord, which was not easily forgotten.[52] Tabriz constitutionalists were appalled; they had settled on Mehdi Qoli Khan Mokhber al-Saltaneh as the most acceptable candidate for the post. A constitutionalist governor, Taqizadeh argued, would gain popular trust, in contrast to an "ancient type," who would fail to establish public order and safety. We are willing to accept royal help, he wrote to Mostashar al-Dowleh; however, we, too, have labored hard and have risked our lives to calm down Qazvin, Rasht, and Isfahan, to halt the assault on Tehran, and to reconcile the nation with the government.[53] But Mostashar al-Dowleh's influence in the selection of new officials was too limited. In his response to Taqizadeh, he confessed: "On this issue which I shall not name," obviously referring to government appointments, "I am alone," and being alone meant having no voice in the matter. Expressing his growing pessimism and despair, he counseled Tabriz to give up Mokhber al-Saltaneh's nomination.[54] The recent death of Mostashar al-Dowleh's oldest son, who had joined the mojahedin, had added a personal dimension to his anguish.

Paranoia and impatience with the slow progress in Tehran heightened the tension among the mojahedin amassed in Qazvin and within the ranks of the Tabriz *anjoman*. Talk of conquering Tehran in three days, on the one hand, and threat of massive arrests of nationalist leaders, on the other, renewed the pressure on Taqizadeh, who began to doubt the worth of his own moderate approach. "We are running out of time," he wrote to Mostashar al-Dowleh.[55] But the latter, under comparable pressure in Tehran government circles, wondered whether, in "these dark times" and given the clashes of views and personal whims prevailing at his electoral committee level, it was useful for him and fellow constitutionalist committee members to state their opinion freely. He worried about rumors circulating in the capital about the mojahedin's imminent attack, which would play into the hands of "those who seek pretexts" to crush the whole movement. "We must be aware that a loss of national independence would be the worst problem," he wrote, once more advising Taqizadeh to soften all harsh views.[56]

But Taqizadeh was losing patience, and he threatened to withdraw from the world of politics. In a long, highly emotional response, he bluntly asked: Toward whom should he soften his stance? Would Sadeq Khan Mostashar al-Dowleh, the friend with whom he communicated so intimately, blame Azerbaijan for anything, or was the government to be blamed for the country's problems? Had the government lifted the siege earlier, the foreigners would not have intervened. The government had destroyed the Majles and left the country at the mercy of two foreign governments and an arbitrary rule. It failed to appoint Mokhber al-Saltaneh, the only man capable of forcing the ouster of the Russian troops. Now it has become obvious, Taqizadeh went on, that all national affairs are in foreign hands. The foreigners, he warned, desire to uproot the seeds of constitutionalism and liberty in Iran, substitute a pro-Russian Iranian for a Russian general, and have a despot rule over the people, tying their feet and hands. He predicted that Azerbaijan would not calm down.[57]

Taqizadeh had by then come to realize how the strong political pressure exerted on his friend had induced him to practice self-censorship. Adopting an ironic tone, he remarked that Tehran is rumored to have no liberty, *constitutionalism* being just a word devoid of meaning. "How can I understand what your real opinion is?" How can the people trust the reliability of individuals put in charge of government affairs and believe they are expressing their views freely? Here, Taqizadeh did not hesitate to boast of the vital role he had played in recent events. "Yes, I dare say that it was I who have completely calmed down Gilan and Qazvin and prevented the Qazvin mojahedin, despite all their forceful impulse, from launching a final assault on Tehran to finish the job once and for all. Otherwise, they would have defeated Tehran in barely three days. I wish you had read all my cables to Qazvin on this matter." Now, as a result, the mojahedin resent him, he observed bitterly. Yet he still felt confident that they could be totally quieted down if government officials would not impose their candidates for governorship or allow foreigners to intervene in national affairs. In conclusion, he expressed his trust in Mostashar al-Dowleh, if the latter were indeed free, advising him to resign from his post if he were not.[58]

Taqizadeh's suspicion was indeed justified. The European press was informing its public on an ongoing Anglo-Russian program that aimed at establishing the two powers' dual supervision over domestic affairs in Iran with Tehran's consent. Indeed, as already stated, the appointment of cabinet ministers was subject to the Russian and British envoys' approval; all foreign loans and commercial concessions required the two powers' permission; overall administration of the various ministries was to be entrusted to foreign experts of their choice; the shah's personal safety and property were to be guaranteed by and put under their protection. The Tabriz *anjoman* requested confirmation from Tehran as to the veracity of these reports, warning that it would never agree to such terms, which amounted to surrendering national sovereignty, and threatening a renewed armed struggle.[59] Most important, it insisted that no loans should be contracted before elections were held for a new Majles and the people's representatives were in place to consider the matter.[60]

The issue of foreign loans was a particularly delicate one because a severe shortage of ready cash deprived the constitutionalists of the necessary financial resources to carry on urgent public tasks and services in Azerbaijan and thus prolonged the Russian "guests'" stay in the province. Some members of the Tabriz *anjoman* contemplated negotiating a loan from the Russian Banque d'escomte et des prets (hereafter "Russian Bank") with the active participation of the British consul in Tabriz.[61] But the Russian Bank was dragging on the process as events were by then rapidly unfolding. The absence of both financial means and a governor of their choice fueled the constitutionalists' frustration, particularly as their interlocutor in Tehran, Mostashar al-Dowleh, was by now admitting his helplessness. His graphic description of the government scene in the capital tells it all: "The disease is so advanced, there exists no physician knowledgeable enough to find a cure, and there is even no accord among the available physicians themselves."[62] The situation worsened when the electoral law was published on June 23, 1909. A two-round election was allowed only in cities and towns, excluding rural areas, and a minimum income or literacy and property ownership were required to register to vote.[63] This electoral setup was a far cry from the universal, direct elections the constitutionalists had hoped for.

Further Russian Intervention and the French Connection

In fact, Barclay and Sablin and their respective diplomatic attachés were the only "physicians" involved in finding remedies. They would press the shah to restore the Constitution, and then they would closely watch events unfold, controlling the situation as much as possible so as not to allow the "reformist," "nationalist movement," as Barclay persistently viewed the constitutional struggle, degenerate into a revolution. Lord Grey was reconciled with the moderate constitutionalists' demands for a parliamentarian regime, even though he had no faith in the Iranians' ability to succeed. His acceptance of the overthrow of the shah came later in the summer of 1909, when the Bakhtiyari tribal forces and the mojahedin were ready to march into Tehran. The tsarist government accommodated itself to London's new policy, but it reserved for itself the right to act preemptively in defense of its interests within its own sphere of influence. Thus, while Grey was scornfully skeptical of the Iranians' competence and ability to run their own affairs, the Russians were determined to repress brutally any action perceived as a direct challenge to their imperial prerogatives. With the mojahedin advancing from Qazvin north of Tehran and the Bakhtiyari amassed in Qom to the south, the Russian embassy informed the Persian government that it was sending its troops to Qazvin to ensure the safety of foreign lives and property and the security of the Anzali–Tehran road, deemed vital for Russian trade. On July 7, 1909, eight hundred to fifteen hundred Russian soldiers (depending on the source) landed in Anzali and moved to Qazvin via Rasht, their commanders proclaiming the troops would remain in Qazvin unless troubles occurred in the capital that would necessitate their march to Tehran as well.[64]

In between British skepticism and Russian cynicism, French contempt and equal determination to promote France's national concerns from within the broader context of European balance of power further developed that country's vigorous policy of indirect intervention in Iranian affairs. With the arrival in Tehran of Raymond Lecomte, the new French ambassador, in the summer of 1908, France had begun to play an active part in local politics. Stephen Pichon, the French minister of foreign affairs, had assured his Russian counterpart that the new envoy would be as cooperative with the Russian legation as his predecessor. The French minister had indeed instructed his new ambassador to maintain on all occasions an equal balance between

Russia and England and to safeguard their agreement.[65] The French strategic policy to isolate Germany, France's nemesis, was to consolidate the Anglo-Russian Convention. Many officials in the French Ministry of Foreign Affairs shared Lecomte's great fear, verging on paranoia, of an Anglo-German rapprochement, to the detriment of Russia, Britain's traditional ally in post-Napoleon Europe. Some officials in the Quai d'Orsay, however, were less convinced of the danger of German political design in the region. Furthermore, Pichon the Freemason was not so adamantly in favor of the Russian conduct in Iran. "Whatever our friendship for Russia, it is not up to us to facilitate its acquisition of Persia, which would be a rather sad gift to offer her."[66] But Lecomte felt no sympathy for the constitutionalists, even though he had astutely evaluated the prevailing climate in the Iranian capital, as his reports show.

His earliest appraisal of the sociopolitical situation in Tehran, noting the poverty and hopelessness of the masses, had realistically concluded that the widespread misery could prove to be a strong factor in promoting a popular uprising and that the "Persian Louis XVI" would be dethroned on the day the revolution-in-the-making erupted. However, he immediately downgraded the possibility of such an event, dismissing it as a "parody of French history," and he predicted that the republic that some of the more educated Iranians dreamed of "would be nothing but anarchy."[67] His accurate analysis of the climate of fear gripping the capital helped him assess the potential to manipulate the situation. The royalists feared reformist ideas, he explained, while the reformers' physical fear of the shah's power paralyzed their resistance. He also correctly depicted both camps' unspoken desire not for foreign intervention but for "inspiration from a friendly Power" to show them the way out of their impasse.[68] However, Lecomte also defended the Russian military intervention, arguing that the mojahedin then stationed in Qazvin constituted a "revolutionary band," well trained, equipped, and organized under the leadership of the Armenian Yeprem Khan, having the destruction of Russian imperial power as their sole objective. He considered them more dangerous than the Bakhtiyari tribes, whose traditional reputation for plunder was well established among the Tehran population, he wrote, while the mojahedin's success had galvanized the revolutionaries. He also accused England, "blinded by its own constitutional liberal convictions and its distaste for Russian politics," of encouraging a "moral disorder" conducive to civil war and threatening Russian interests.[69] He strongly believed that Russian military intervention was fully justified and urged Paris to convince London of its necessity.[70] In fact, in Great Britain, despite the strong objections raised in Parliament among members of the Liberal Party and the opposition, Lord Grey opted to defend Russia's "self-protective" measures as "not an unreasonable caution." Both British and French governments assured their public that the Russian troops would not meddle with the local unrest.[71]

Up to the last days prior to the fall of Tehran, the mojahedin continued to insist on their nation's sovereign rights, reminding the people of Najaf's rulings condemning foreign occupation.[72] As Taqizadeh wrote to Mostashar al-Dowleh, the mojahedin had nothing more to fear. "He who is already wet should not fear rain."[73] Sa'ad al-Dowleh, in contrast, promised the Russian envoy a complete withdrawal of the mojahedin and Bakhtiyari troops and a cancellation of their march to Tehran if the Russians would evacuate Tabriz and other places in the country on a definite date.[74] But the intervention had already taken place, and British and Russian diplomats met with the Sepahdar and Sardar As'ad to warn them against provoking further foreign intervention.[75]

Until the fall of Tehran, the British and the Russian diplomats and their representatives were intensively engaged in negotiations with the insurgents' leaders. Barclay had come to believe that the shah's acceptance of the Anglo-Russian program had brought some détente and that the prospect of an imminent Bakhtiyari–mojahedin march on Tehran was "remote." His bewilderment with the subsequent turn of events contrary to his expectations was tangible. "The prompt and striking manner in which events have contradicted this statement affords a somewhat disheartening illustration of the difficulty of correctly gauging the situation in Persia," he wrote to Lord Grey.[76] With news of the mojahedin approaching Tehran, Graham, the British consul general in Isfahan, went to Qom to ask Sardar As'ad to give the restored Constitution a "fair chance" for the sake of peace and order; his effort was to no avail. Graham described Sardar As'ad as a man whose "intellect is clouded," for he "speaks like a person possessed with an *idée fixe* and appears incapable of admitting anyone except himself can gauge rightly the real situation in Tehran."[77] As late as July 4, the envoys once more attempted to stop the march to Tehran, sending their delegates to Karaj, where the Sepahdar militias were stationed, rejoined by Sardar As'ad and his Bakhtiyari fighters. The militia leaders responded with demands that the diplomats deemed "unreasonable": they would come armed to Tehran to negotiate the dismissal of several "traitors," including Nuri; the evacuation of all foreign troops from the country; the appointment of government ministers by the *anjomans* throughout the nation until the reopening of the Majles; the minister of war's assumption of command of all military forces; provincial authorities' nominations of their own governors; and the disarmament of royal troops.[78] This last attempt at negotiation failed. Both the Sepahdar and Sardar As'ad, however, promised to avoid unnecessary confrontation and to swiftly restore order in the capital upon their arrival.

The Fall of Tehran

Yeprem Khan and the Rashti, Azerbaijani, Armenian, and Transcaucasian militias, following a swift conquest of Karaj, subsequently suffered a disastrous defeat when the Russian-commanded Cossack Brigade disseminated their forces in successive bloody encounters. Further advance succeeded only when the Bakhtiyari troops joined their forces, with Sardar As'ad changing his tactics to enter Tehran from the south, as originally planned. They finally struck a severe blow to the royalist regiments stationed a few miles outside the capital, with some losses on both sides. They entered Tehran at dawn on July 13, 1909, encountering no resistance at the gate. Gunfire was exchanged at the royal palace, the Cossacks' headquarters, and the Majles building. A cease-fire, however, was quickly negotiated. Concerns about looting and, more important, the need to co-opt the Cossack Brigade as the basis for the future national army determined the invaders' official decision to stop the fight. In fact, as a secret source informed Barclay, the Russian and Persian officers of the Cossack Brigade had planned not to oppose the advance to the capital. The British diplomat had accurately predicted that the insurgents "might very probably win an almost bloodless victory."[79] A few weeks later the Cossacks' Russian commander, Lyakhof, left the country.

Though the insurgents entered Tehran without opposition, fierce fighting occurred in some parts of the city, with casualties numbering anywhere from sixty to seventy to thousands, depending on the source. However, the mojahedin nominal leaders honored their promise to the diplomats, for within three days of their arrival a cease-fire negotiated by Churchill, the British legation's secretary of Oriental affairs, was enforced. The shah and his entourage took refuge in the Russian legation, the Cossacks were brought under the new rulers' command, and foreign life and property were safeguarded.[80] By July 23, peace was restored in the city. The "civil war," as some Persian sources label the street fights, lasted barely three days. Either Yeprem Khan and his Armenian–Georgian troops or the Sepahdar or Sardar As'ad or the collective revolutionary forces, again depending on the source, are credited for the triumphant conquest of Tehran. Eyewitnesses and contemporaneous Persian accounts generally hail it as the people's victory over tyranny and celebrate the mojahedin leaders as national heroes restoring freedom in the country. In contrast, Lord Grey, "livid with anger," held Lynch and the Persia Committee members responsible for the constitutionalists' victory.[81] Barclay's final analysis reflected his bewilderment in his late realization of the true nature of the rapidly unfolding events that he and his Russian colleague had tried so desperately to control. It is worth quoting in full:

> It would be interesting to know something of the inner history of this movement and why it occurred just when it did. The plea that the restored constitution was a sham, whether believed or not by those who put it forward, was not true. . . . I see no reason to doubt that had the Bakhtiyari and *feda'i* [plural *fedayan*, alternative name for *mojahedin*] kept quiet the Assembly would have met in due course. Apart from the agitation against the Russian occupation, things were proceeding unusually smoothly at Tehran. . . . It was only when the revolutionaries started from Kasvin [*sic*] and the mission of our consul-generals at Kum [*sic*] was known to have failed that it was generally realized that the movement might after all be more than a mere demonstration. Its seriousness became more and more evident as time went on, and it was known that preparations were actively proceeding for sending reinforcements from Isfahan and Rasht. . . . The revolutionary leaders were receiving urgent advice from abroad. It is, indeed, abundantly clear that the revolutionaries have been in close touch with certain persons in London and Paris, and also of course with the Anjoman in Constantinople . . . urging the Bakhtiyaris to finish the business quickly for fear of the foreigners. What the business is remains to be seen.[82]

Barclay's expressed puzzlement would reoccur throughout this period, revealing his repeated incomprehension of events and the personalities involved.

Persian chronicles of the revolution view the overthrow of Mohammad Ali Shah as the final triumph of the heroic national struggle against tyranny. In contrast to the essentially bloodless events in 1905–6 that led to the promulgation of the Constitution by Mozaffar al-Din Shah, they argue, the fall of Tehran in 1909 resulted from months of civil war, demonstrating to the world that Iran indeed had accomplished a revolution according to the French meaning of the term. This time the nation "took" its freedom, having earned it in bloody battles. Some foreign observers, however, attribute the triumph of the "nationalist cause" to outside intervention and to some tribesmen who, "with the exception of their leaders, had no interest in the question of constitutional government."[83] According to this view, skeptical bordering on the cynical, the nationalists fighting in Tabriz "had only to sit behind walls and do a little shooting to maintain their position,"[84] receiving no backing from the people in town; and when they succeeded in surrounding the royal camp in Tehran, they made no attempt to capture the shah. "They had no desire to fight, but merely to force compliance with their wishes."[85] In fact, most European reports at that time depict the turning point in favor of the nationalists as occurring when the Russian government decided to cease its support for the shah and to accept the British suggestion that an overture be made to the nationalists[86] and when the Russian envoy subsequently began negotiating for the surrender of the Cossack Brigade.

The diplomats' analysis merely covered up their respective governments' intensive manipulation of the fateful events that paradoxically allowed a renewed experimentation with constitutional rule in Iran. As a new government was installed, the Oriental secretary Churchill candidly admitted: "One cannot but recognize that a constitutional regime established independently of the two Powers, and inaugurated by the dethronement of a detested and worthless sovereign, stands a very good chance from one obtained for the country by outside pressure which stopped short of demanding the thing most needed, a change of sovereign." He went so far as to express his sense of "rejoice at the failure of our program. . . . Mohammad Ali Shah is now deposed, and the field lies for a second and more promising experiment in parliamentary government."[87] In sharp contrast to this sanguine view, Izvolski was convinced that the country would descend into anarchy, "which would certainly compel Russia to intervene on a large scale."[88]

The nation's history in the early twentieth century, as elsewhere in the Middle East on the eve of World War I, is part of the global history of European imperialism. The nationalists' capture of Tehran and their return to power undoubtedly could not have happened without British and Russian belated approval, following a failed attempt at checking the revolution's development. The nationalists had very little room to maneuver in freedom, their revolutionary rhetoric masking a grim reality: they were either to perish or to survive in a highly diminished form. Thus, they took action out of lack of choice, in response to foreign pressures bearing down on them. This predicament was already apparent months before the fall of Tehran, when the major players, still in exile, planned their comeback with the helping guidance of some European advisers.

The loosely labeled "nationalists," "constitutionalists," and "reformers" combined their forces in a common effort to restore the Constitution. However, they were under no monolithic political organization. The militias consisted mostly of Armenian and Transcaucasian fighters, with some Iranian Azerbaijani and Gilani mojahedin. Their leaders' political ideologies ranged from Russian-inspired social democracy to West European–type liberal democracy and Freemasonry. Demographically, they were mostly reform-minded aristocrats, educated middle class, powerful tribal chieftains, and middle-ranking constitutionalist members of the Shi'a religious institutions, some of whom had exchanged their clerical garb for the European "coat and trousers." They were former Majles deputies or government officials, writers, journalists, preachers, publicists, and various other types of professionals. Their networks overlapped, and, ultimately, many directly or indirectly followed the instructions of their European mentors—British, French, Russian, German, as well as Young Turk—which hampered their ability to speak in one voice or to form their own autonomous plan of action acceptable to all. Nonetheless, with the exception of some opportunistic individuals, the unspoken motive of each group that willingly or expediently followed European guidance was a search for inspiration, supportive but friendly advice, not foreign intervention, as Lecomte astutely observed. Indeed, Great Power politics more than battlefield realities ultimately determined the fall of Tehran. That the European powers manipulated the constitutionalists' vulnerability to promote their own respective interests in no way detracts from the intelligentsia's genuine commitment to a surprisingly uniform nationalist political culture that they envisioned for a transformed country, a new Iran. The heterogeneous ethnic/ideological composition of the diverse leadership, despite the hurdles it created for the legislators in the second Majles, would not obstruct the enactment of far-reaching and enduring reforms.

4

Prelude to the Second Majles

IN AN INTERVIEW with the Tbilisi paper *Zakafkaz* (Transcaucasia) dated July 31, 1909, Lyakhof, the former Russian commander of the Cossack Brigade, acknowledged that the "progressives" had won a bloodless victory over the "traditionalists." But how long will it last? he asked. He predicted that only factions with financial backing and political support would ultimately triumph.[1] In interviews of him by the British press, however, Lyakhof openly stated that royalist officials in exile were plotting to destabilize the new regime, inciting sedition and creating political turmoil.[2] French diplomats in Tehran were even more skeptical in their diagnosis. In his dispatches to Paris, Lecomte did recognize the relatively orderly and self-disciplined conduct of the militias who had swiftly seized power in the capital. However, although acknowledging the existence of abundant "men of action," he noted the short supply of qualified politicians to effectively occupy important government posts. Hence, he remarked sarcastically, the paradoxical character of the revolution: both the victors and the vanquished were handsomely awarded with important positions in the new cabinet, bringing together former reactionary ministers and revolutionaries.[3] Lecomte continued to defend Russia, arguing that it had conceded much in the recent negotiations for the restoration of the constitutional regime, and he again dismissed what he called the English "blind cult of parliamentarian institutions."[4] British official opinion was, by and large, equally pessimistic. David Fraser, the *Times* correspondent in Tehran who published his account of the revolution in 1910, described the Persian environment as "inimical to the growth of individualism" and commented that the "frame of mind of the Persians and the national character do not seem to constitute a soil suitable for the development of representative institutions."[5] However, Lord Grey, though as committed as the French to the Anglo-Russian Convention and equally cynical about the constitutionalists' prospects, agreed to give the constitutionalists a try. His decision to respond positively to the forceful request made by the Persia Committee members in Parliament, led by Lynch, was more commercially oriented, driven by British business interests in the region. He supported the Lynch Brothers' lucrative construction and transportation projects in the Persian Gulf in agreement with Bakhtiyari tribal leaders, who stood to gain substantially.

Lynch, in a concerted effort with Browne, never missed an occasion to press for a debate in Parliament to review the Anglo-Russian Convention, which they perceived to be potentially disastrous for both Iranian and British interests.[6] They encouraged journalists they had befriended to publish positive articles to counter the generally negative British press reports on events in Iran, especially in the *Times*. Browne was successful with the *Morning Post*, whose editor was a fellow liberal friend.[7] The *Daily News*, the *Daily Chronicle*, and the *Manchester Guardian* also published favorable accounts of events in Iran. Browne was mostly concerned with winning British public opinion in favor of what he persistently termed the "Persian Nationalist Reform Movement." His influence upon the constitutionalist movement's leaders proved to be a determining factor in coordinating an international public-relations campaign in Tehran, Istanbul, Najaf, Paris, and London. For a while, it succeeded in bringing together some of the radicals, moderates, and members of the former regime now turned constitutionalists. The task was daunting, indeed, given the prevailing international political climate, competing European powers' intervention in Iran, and the novelty (for Iran) and difficulty of the constitutionalists' enterprise, which had to deal with diverse political groups, domestic obstacles, and royalist ambushes. Crisscrossing alliances and rivalries among the dominant players would influence the decisions surrounding the formation of successive constitutional cabinets.

Sorush

Among the numerous new Persian publications established during the struggle for the restoration of the Constitution, *Sorush* (Glad Tidings) best exemplifies the exiles' common effort to inform the public on crucial issues challenging the construction of the New Iran. Sponsored by the Anjoman-e Sa'adat in Istanbul, *Sorush* was Dehkhoda's brain child and received vital support from the newly empowered Young Turks he had met while in Paris. Upon his arrival in the Ottoman capital, he had joined the Anjoman-e Sa'adat and almost immediately began working on the new publication that was to be the *anjoman*'s official organ. By that time, the *anjoman* had toned down its radicalism, and Dehkhoda had endorsed a similar policy of moderation in support of constitutional monarchy while promoting far-reaching institutional reforms, aimed at secularization and modernization of the state. Within a few months of his collaboration with the *anjoman*, Dehkhoda rationalized his ideological shift on the basis of the harsh military facts on the ground, the Russian occupation of Azerbaijan and Qazvin. In a letter to an acquaintance in Tehran, he elaborated at great length his new stand. New tactics had to be adopted, and his earlier radicalism that insisted on a "fast speed" strategy had to be replaced with more pragmatic tactics to rally all "true patriots," regardless of their background, round the common national cause. The first two years of constitutional government, he lamented, lost the opportunity to establish the much needed institutional reforms. Now is the time to do it, he wrote; now is the time for reconciliation. Now is also the time to face reality and give up old attitudes of "victimhood" and such sentiments as heroism; in Europe, such attitudes can gain no currency. Would the tears of some patriots or the lamentation of some opportunists keep England quiet or satisfy Russia? "Material civilization" is the only means to meet the challenge of Europe's onslaught. We need reason, science, and hard work, he stated. Philosophy and theology are respectable fields of knowledge, but to govern a country today it is essential to be well informed about political and administrative matters. Even a short stay in a modern school or an imperfect knowledge of foreign languages would be better than mastery in the old disciplines. "We have no Bismarck," he stated matter-of-factly; therefore, "should we wish to dust off" some "rotten" legacies, there is no other way but to increase our knowledge of Europe. "We need to send a greater number of young people to study there" and then recruit them to fill government posts.[8]

The first issue of *Sorush* came out on July 1, 1909, with Dehkhoda named as both director of publication and editor. He held both posts until mid-October 1909, when an Ottoman official took over the direction of the publication in compliance with a new government press regulation requiring Ottoman ownership of all foreign papers.[9] Dehkhoda retained the general editorship until his return to Iran. The paper eulogized the Young Turks as pathbreakers to freedom and independence and as a source of inspiration for the Iranian exiles' own struggle. Acknowledging with gratitude their support, it borrowed their motto: "Unity, accord, progress." It explained to the reader its main editorial objectives: the dissemination of the world's new thought, its origins, its teachers, and their enlightening impact in combating ignorance and spreading freedom and rational truth. It proclaimed that despotic monarchy constituted the biggest obstacle to progress. It promised to write about major events and political movements that helped shape the modern world and to seek models to emulate from among thousands of hard-working individuals who had sacrificed their lives to attain their ultimate goals. England, France, the United States of America, Germany, Austria—all are advanced nations showing the way to those aspiring to reach their level of civilization.

Sorush contributors openly referred to the "Revolution of Iran," defining its major events and leadership as revolutionary. In an article entitled "The Nations of Asia Are Waking Up," a regular contributor, Hosain Kazemzadeh, stated that it was now Asia's turn to follow the path of progress and that the traditional concept of divine right to rule had lost its legitimacy and was to be replaced by the French revolutionary concepts of the Declaration of Human Rights. Soon after the fall of Tehran and the subsequent abdication of Mohammad Ali Shah, the paper published the picture of his son, Ahmad Mirza, bearing the title "constitutional monarch" and accompanied by a Persian poem composed for the occasion a month earlier. The "newly *selected* shah" was advised to learn important lessons from his "father's ugly deeds" and avoid his fateful "hellish suffering." Should he follow the "pure path together with us," he would attain glorious fame and receive the support of the entire nation.[10]

Turkey was recognized as the first Moslem country to have eradicated an absolute dynastic regime in the region.[11] Dehkhoda, however, felt the need to draw a distinction between the Ottoman and the Iranian revolutionary processes. Our revolution, he wrote in an editorial, differs from the Young Turks' in the sense that all classes of our nation have collectively joined in the struggle to bring about changes, whereas theirs was "restricted to the military." He was referring to the civil revolt against the Ottoman sultan, which ended in victory only when Ottoman military officers based in Salonika joined the revolt's ranks and overthrew the reigning monarch. In contrast to the Turks, Dehkhoda proclaimed proudly, our urban, rural, and tribal population, our peasants, merchants, out-of-office government officials, and writers participated in the holy war, earning their share in the victory. Thus, he remarked, Iran's Constitution is more liable to last as long as Iranians exist on earth.[12] In a lengthy article, Ahmad Beg Aqaev, the Baku-born intellectual modernist who had met with the Persian exiles in Paris before coming to Istanbul, eulogized Iran and Persian cultural contributions to human civilization. Iran has survived centuries of calamities as a result of tyranny corrupting its nature, values, and religion, he wrote. However, "the soul of Iran is still alive in the midst of ruins," its Iranian identity (*iraniyat*) intact, for, indeed, its people are the "chosen creatures of God." The dark past should remain a lesson for all involved in the construction of a better future. All roots of tyranny must be destroyed first, before Iran can enjoy the fruits of liberty, independence, and constitutionalism.[13]

Leading articles developed the themes of modern civilization, insisting on the primacy of an intellectual revolution laying the ground for a political revolution. French history and the French Revolution provided ample evidence for the authors' arguments. The French political revolution, Kazemzadeh explained, was successful because, with the philosophy of the Enlightenment, the nation had undergone an intellectual revolution beforehand. Iran must follow the same path and go through a "general intellectual revolution"; otherwise, the Constitutional Revolution will have no lasting effect.[14] Numerous columns were devoted to lengthy exposés of the history of European revolutions and constitutional governance. In one such editorial, Dehkhoda emphasized the importance of education and called for the establishment of a new ministry of science and education that would send students on government scholarships to Europe. He advocated the policy of choosing students from among the underprivileged classes and no longer from among the elite. Rich children, he argued, have had their opportunity to bring about necessary changes, and not much has come of it. Educating the poor would challenge the rich to do better. Thus, fifteen- and sixteen-year-old youths, selected from among graduates of the religious schools, would be more morally committed to serve their country, greatly appreciating the opportunities offered for good jobs on their return from abroad.[15] Moralizing, self-critical essays echoed themes that an earlier generation of Persian nationalists had innovated. Thus, Ahmad Bey Aqaev deplored Iranians' anarchist nature that "thrives on chaos." Rich or poor, members of the elite or the poorest individuals in the realm, they all have the tendency to discard the law. The rule of law, he wrote, functions in England because all, regardless of their social status, abide by it. Iranians must exert self-discipline, learn to obey the law, and help the government in enforcing it. The government must, in turn, closely connect with the nation, for both the nation and its government constitute two interdependent forces; one cannot last without the other.[16]

The issues of national sovereignty, independence, and territorial integrity filled many of *Sorush*'s pages, often becoming lead stories meant to arouse public hostility to Russian occupying troops. Yahya Dowlatabadi repeatedly stressed the slogan "Iran rightfully belongs to Iranians" alone; no individual Iranian or group of officials has the right to sell it out to the foreigners. The Anglo-Russian Convention of 1907, he argued, cannot go on pretending to safeguard Iran's sovereignty and territorial integrity; that has never been its intention. This responsibility must be assumed by the Iranians, who are now awakened to their rights with the rising consciousness of their own national identity. Their neighbors' power can no longer erase their rights.[17] In a fiery nationalist editorial, Dehkhoda proclaimed erroneously that Iran is an ethnically, religiously, and linguistically homogeneous nation, which, he added correctly, had conquered other glorious ancient civilizations and had endured Greek, Arab, and Mongol invasions without ever losing its identity. It will never give the Russians any chance to "satiate its greed"; Iran will prove to be too big a "morsel" to "swallow." Furthermore, the Russians' divisive tactics will never succeed in breaking it up. Current disputes among the various political groups, he ascertained, are not grave enough to cause serious disunity. In fact, it is Russia that needs to heed imperial breakdown, ethnic conflicts, and a humiliating military defeat by Japan, the rising power in the East. Dehkhoda further argued that Russia wished at all cost to prevent the spread of the "new European civilization" in Iran in order to enchain Iran to its own despotic rule. Yet in the past four years, he stated, brave Iranian warriors have been fighting to win back their national independence and to "create anew the history of France in the heart of Asia."[18] A long, well-informed article discussed in detail the Anglo-Russian rivalry in Iran and Afghanistan leading to the convention, displaying a high degree of political sophistication and knowledge of intricate international affairs that were missing in the press of the first Majles.[19]

Dehkhoda and fellow contributors were weary of British imperial designs, but they chose to pick on Russia as their most-favored enemy. Of the two European "neighbors" (Britain considered as such by virtue of its rule in India), they feared Russia most because of its direct military intervention, which threatened to last indefinitely. More important to an understanding of this tactical choice is the fact that imperial Russia provided the political radicals and the moderate constitutionalists alike as well as the anti-Russian subjects of the tsar in Azerbaijan and the Caucasus with a common adversary. Thus, Panoff—the Bulgarian revolutionary who had participated in some of the crucial events involving the Social-Democrats both prior to the coup of 1908 and subsequently in Gilan and Azerbaijan and who was then deported to Moscow, where he was arrested—tried to arouse his comrades' sense of international brotherhood. Echoing the standard Russian Social-Democratic Workers Party antinationalist slogans, he emotionally proclaimed there is neither Bulgarian nor Iranian in this world; they all are brothers enslaved with chains. "Without religious or national distinction, we all must shed our blood" for the common cause.[20] Panoff's transnational message, however, failed to resonate much in the paper's columns. Issues related to patriotism, national sovereignty, and distinct Persian identity continued to overshadow Russian Social-Democrats' ideological priorities. *Sorush* periodically published olama's cables calling for the evacuation of Russian troops, and Najaf kept strong networking ties with the Anjoman-e Sa'adat, insisting on national unity in combating the Russian occupation of the fatherland.[21]

British officials and individual supporters consciously cultivated a self-image as protectors of Iran's independence. They never missed the chance to remind the exiles of this imminent Russian danger, if only to prevent their "reform movement" from turning into an extremist revolution and thus offering Russians the perfect pretext for further intervention. The tactics succeeded in many quarters, including the Anjoman-e Sa'adat. Dehkhoda would repeatedly assure his readers:

> Today, in my capacity as an influential and popular writer, well informed on the state of the nation['s] sentiments, the world being my witness, I wish to deny any belligerent intention attributed to us. The sole purpose of the Iranian nation is to rejuvenate the land and serve the circle of world civilization. In the past year I have said and still say that we desire for Iran a constitutional government and no other. We totally deny any intention to change the royal dynasty or its monarch, as our enemies claim.[22]

Dehkhoda was responding to numerous rumors spreading in Europe by reactionary forces depicting the Anjoman-e Sa'adat and the constitutionalists in general as "nihilists" and "extremists." The despots are still trying to return to power, a constitutionalist wrote from Paris to Abol Hasan Mo'azed al-Saltaneh, mentioning some reactionaries who had come to France. They are, he noted, striving to create a crisis situation to keep foreign troops in the country and to ruin the reputation of the constitutionalists abroad, discrediting them to the eyes of European powers.[23]

Kazemzadeh cited international laws forbidding foreign interference in a nation's domestic affairs and deplored the European powers' violation of their lofty principles. Russia, he wrote, offers the perfect example of military might and political power so forcefully trampling these laws. He also condemned concessions granting foreign governments exterritorial rights to protect their subjects' commercial interests in the country. International trade is based on voluntary not obligatory deeds, he argued. "No government can use its subjects' commercial losses or deal breaking as a pretext for intervention."[24] In the same issue, Dehkhoda called on all Iranian patriots to boycott Russian imports. "Trade," he wrote, "is the most effective weapon for defeating the enemy, even more powerful than a mighty army." The day the Iranian nation boycotts Russian sugar, tea, oil, and textiles is the day thousands of Russian factories will stop working; millions of its workers, rendered unemployed, will then join hands with Russia's enemy. Such a chain of events leading to a government paralysis would have worse repercussions for the tsarist government than a military defeat. He then asserted that Iran's worst betrayers are the importers of Russian goods and its consumers. The time has come for the merchants to fear the nation that has now opened its eyes and found out that all its misfortunes are caused not only by the Qajar monarchs, the treacherous ministers, and the Russian government but also by those individuals who have failed to develop trade and industry in our country and worked instead with the foreigners as mere middlemen, causing the nation to sink into debt.[25]

By the end of the summer of 1909, *Sorush* felt the need to warn Tehran's victorious constitutionalists against too much complaisance. A Dehkhoda editorial acknowledged that "for the time being" Russia has suffered defeat at the hands of brave Iranian nationalists. "But how long will their defeat last, given the widespread ignorance prevailing in our midst?" The Russians are patiently waiting to see Iranian battle fatigue and complaisance undermine their newly acquired strength. Domestic conflicts and intrigues will further erode it, providing the enemy with an "excuse to remain on our soil." Independence is not part of Russian agenda for Asia, he noted. Europeans in general are busy planning their future policies a century ahead. "The life of nations, like human life, is a vast battlefield. He who has the most weapons and the most power shall win the race." He urged the new government to quickly establish order, consolidate national institutions, and enforce the Fundamental Law.[26] In a highly colorful article, Hosain Danesh, an Ottoman-employed Iranian expatriate, observed dramatically that Iran was now on a battlefield where the ideas of the "enlightened civilization" are clashing with centuries-old "traditions of superstitions," where forces of light combat forces of darkness, and where the "sane Aryan nature" fights the "frightening nonsense of alien countries." Who will rescue Iran, he asked, and help it stand on its own two feet again? Where is the gardener who will save the tree defoliated through centuries of neglect and now rotten to the core? Which model of expertise and statesmanship will the nation choose?[27]

Sorush, the Anjoman-e Sa'adat's mouthpiece, more than any other publication of that time enunciated the concrete agenda for the second Majles legislative reforms pertaining to such issues as national sovereignty; nationalism, or the novel idea of national identity superseding tribal, ethnic, or religious communalism; emulation of European education and the spread of modern sciences; and promotion of domestic trade and industry to compete with and reduce foreign imports.

The New Government in Tehran

With the fall of Tehran, the big question was, indeed, Which players and instructors should assume the responsibility to build the national institutions anew? In general, essays, pamphlets, and public speeches consistently promoted the concept of a highly centralized system of government with strong national institutions and a powerful Majles enacting modernizing reforms; a centralized command of all disparate armed militias, including the Cossack Brigade, to establish law and order and defend national borders; evacuation of Russian troops to ensure national sovereignty and independence; and financial reforms to help accomplish all these tasks. The nationalist leaders, however, lacked all the basic social tools and financial means necessary to undertake their self-imposed tasks. Moreover, cautious diplomatic tactics forced them to collaborate with the coalition of forces initially forged for the "national reconciliation" movement, and Anglo-Russian pressure was felt at all levels.

On July 15, 1909, the shah and his family moved out of the palace to seek temporary residence in the Russian embassy, thus effectively abdicating his throne. A High Council of five hundred men—which included former Majles deputies and cabinet members, merchants, tribal leaders, and members of the aristocracy turned constitutionalists—took over provisional authority to run the country. It appointed a special committee of some twenty of its own members to assume government tasks until elections were held for the second Majles. In addition to members of the olama, some merchants, and a son of a Bakhtiyari leader, the committee included constitutional old guards such as Morteza Qoli Khan Sani' al-Dowleh, Hasan Khan Vothuq al-Dowleh, Sadeq Khan Mostashar al-Dowleh, Ibrahim Khan Hakim al-Molk, Hosain Qoli Khan Navab, Abdol Hosain Vahid al-Molk Shaybani, and Nasrollah Taqavi as well as the militia leaders Yeprem Khan, Mirza Ali Mohammad Tarbiyat, Hosain Kasma'i, the two Rashti brothers Abdol Hamid Sardar Mohiy (formerly known as Mo'ez al-Soltan) and Karim Khan, and their influential cousin Sardar Mansur.[28] The committee then assigned cabinet positions to a select few: the Sepahdar (Mohammad Vali Khan Naser al-Saltaneh), minister of war; Sardar As'ad, minister of the interior, with Ahmad Khan Qavam al-Saltaneh as his deputy; Naser al-Molk (who was still in Europe), foreign minister; Hosain Mirza Farman-Farma, minister of justice; Sani' al-Dowleh, minister of education; Mirza Hasan Mostowfi al-Mamalek, minister of finance; Sardar Mansur, minister of post and telegraph; Yeprem Khan, head of the police. Mokhber al-Saltaneh was finally appointed governor of Azerbaijan as a consequence of the Tabriz *anjoman*'s and Taqizadeh's relentless request. Najaf Qoli Khan Samsam al-Saltaneh, who had seized power in Isfahan, was officially confirmed its governor. The notorious Asef al-Dowleh, formerly governor of Khorasan before acquiring that post in Fars during the turbulent months of the Lesser Despotism, was dismissed and replaced by Ala' al-Dowleh. The no less notorious 'Ayn al-Dowleh, however, enjoyed more favorable treatment. Refusing to seek asylum at the Russian embassy, he surrendered to the new authorities and was pardoned with a "gift," the governorship of Khorasan.[29] Thus, whereas the committee was composed of both the constitutionalist old guard and political newcomers, the cabinet and provincial governorships were, with a handful of exceptions, almost exclusively occupied by aristocrats and the former shah's officials.

The newly installed provisional government's first task was to officially depose Mohammad Ali Shah and "appoint" his son to accede to the throne. The Sepahdar and Sardar As'ad jointly cabled the olama in Najaf to inform them of the new development. The response was prompt: "The deposition of Mohammad Ali Mirza, due to his great betrayal of religion, government, and nation, is obligatory by *shar'* [religious] and *qanun* [constitutional] law."[30] The mojahedin and Russian embassy officials escorted the new monarch, Ahmad Shah, a fearful youth taken away from his royal parents against his will, to the palace. There the new leaders of the nation, in the presence of olama, royal members of the family, and other grandees, proclaimed him shah in accordance with clauses 36 and 37 of the Fundamental Law, which bestowed on the nation's representatives the power to enthrone the new monarch. They also appointed the eldest Qajar prince, Azod al-Molk Nayeb al-Saltaneh, regent.[31] The constitutional monarchy was restored in Iran. The government then negotiated with Mohammad Ali Mirza the terms of his exile. As a result of skillful Anglo-Russian mediation, the government was compelled to bear a heavy financial burden in exchange for the restitution of royal properties and the valuable Crown Jewels the former shah had taken with him. The imperial crown, which was pawned at a European bank, was redeemed later.[32]

Thus, the nascent government, presiding over a near bankrupt Treasury, had to assume royal debts to foreign creditors amounting to millions of tomans,[33] some at 12 percent interest. They also agreed to pay the departing shah an annual pension of one hundred thousand tomans; the agreement, bearing his signature and dated September 7, 1909, stipulated that payment would cease should he ever fail to honor his promise not to stage a comeback.[34] Members of the committee leading the negotiations, including Taqizadeh, Navab, Vothuq al-Dowleh, and Mostashar al-Dowleh, signed the protocol. Barclay believed the terms were advantageous to the shah but gave the new government a "moral" and "political" advantage.[35] However, the financial liability would prove to be a burden, and the Russian guarantee of the former shah's promise not to interfere in political affairs was too lightweight to be taken seriously, as subsequent history would amply demonstrate. ʻAyn al-Dowleh reportedly donated ten thousand tomans to help pay the first installment of the royal pension, and two wealthy Armenians loaned the rest of the sum.[36] Furthermore, Russian officials would not commence the shah's departure until the newly installed authority in Tehran guaranteed payment of his three-million-ruble debt to the Russian Bank.[37] The deposed shah finally left on September 9, 1909, accompanied by British and Russian representatives and escorted by Russian, British Indian, and Iranian troops to the port of Anzali. From there, he sailed to exile in Odessa, taking with him, among others, Amir Bahador Jang, Arshad al-Dowleh, Mojallal al-Molk, and Movaqqar al-Saltaneh, four of his most reactionary court officials. They left behind a country in dire need of order and public safety, a depleted Treasury, and a political situation threatening a general state of anarchy if not swiftly controlled.

The new government's first task concerned the fate of former court officials. Many of them acquired cabinet posts or governorships, as the list given earlier shows. A great number of them, such as Saʻad al-Dowleh and other politicians, were allowed to go abroad without any questions asked; others paid a ransom and stayed. Many more acquired a foreign legation's protection and by hoisting its flag on the roof of their houses enjoyed complete immunity from prosecution. In those days, Zargandeh, the village outside

Tehran where the Russian legation had its summer residency, was considered Russian territory. It rapidly turned into a refugee camp for the supporters of Mohammad Ali Shah and their entourages. Among them was Hajj Isma'il Maghazeh'i, one of the big merchants who had initially supported and financed the constitutional movement and who after the coup in 1908 had defected to the royalists' camp.[38] Two lower-ranking olama who had collaborated with Nuri were spared, despite their well-known involvement in the bloody assaults on the constitutionalists in 1907. In contrast, Majd al-Islam, the constitutionalist cleric who had renewed publication of *Neda-ye vatan* (Call of the Fatherland), was arrested when it was revealed he had collaborated with the "despots" following the coup. He spent a year in prison before his release and banishment to his native Kerman. In Tabriz, Mir Hashem, the lower-ranking "*clerc*" who had quickly defected to the reactionary camp as early as 1907, was also arrested.[39]

With the remarkable exception of Nuri, though, surprisingly very few were brought to trial, few enough to raise Kasravi's suspicion: "Who supported them?"[40] The issue is not adequately debated in the chronicles, nor is it fully documented. Privately, however, leading voices expressed their disenchantment, if not outrage. From Geneva, Mirza Aqa Farshi, the Tabriz deputy in the first Majles and member of Taqizadeh's circle, wrote an angry letter to Sadeq Mostashar al-Dowleh, complaining about some reactionaries' promotion in the new government. "Is 'Ayn al-Dowleh not to be sentenced to death? Did he not destroy the city of Tabriz? . . . If a person like 'Ayn al-Dowleh, who has committed all sorts of crimes, is appointed governor of Khorasan, why then don't we consider Shaikh Fazlollah Nuri guarantor of the sharia? . . . How can you find excuses that you had no other choice? If, indeed, you have acquired power, you should distinguish . . . those who served [the cause] from those who betrayed it. . . . Otherwise, we shall have no other fate than hopelessness, despair, and extinction."[41] Farshi ended his letter pointing to the Young Turk government's example in purging the state of its former officials. A few days later, an unsigned note to Mostashar al-Dowleh from the Anjoman-e Sa'adat in Istanbul lamented the fact that both Sardar As'ad and the Sepahdar were included in the cabinet and warned against potential conflicts and social turmoil.[42]

In a more optimistic letter sent a week after the fall of Tehran, the Persian ambassador in Paris, Samad Khan Momtaz al-Saltaneh informed Mostashar al-Dowleh about the Freemasons' involvement in the events of the days after the fall of Tehran. Conveying the ambassador's hearty congratulations for the "restoration of national rights" and for Mostashar al-Dowleh's vital role in the process, Momtaz al-Saltaneh mentioned the "friends" meeting regularly "at the place you know," who were full of praise for his achievements. But, he added, they all were worried about the fate of some "true friends," referring to many royalist members of the aristocracy who had joined different French lodges, and they had contacted the French minister of foreign affairs. Pichon, "who is one of our friends and is a person of great humanity," had then called the French envoy in Tehran, requesting "safety of life" for the "friends," and the envoy promptly cabled his assurances. Momtaz al-Saltaneh also mentioned that Dr. Schneider and "some other friends you do not know" share the worry over such "friends" then in need of protection despite their opposition to the constitutionalists. Some individuals must not be allowed back to Iran because they are a threat to *sécurité publique* ("public security," given in transliterated French in the text); others have committed treason from within Iran, and they must be punished. "Can you see what secrets would be unveiled in these trials?" Even if some of them are already out of reach, having taken asylum abroad or at a foreign legation, the nation can nonetheless pronounce the necessary religious decree in their absence, after having summoned them to come to court. Momtaz al-Saltaneh ended the letter urging Mostashar al-Dowleh to press for trials. "Without punishment nothing can be accomplished in the future, and justice shall not be restored." Nonetheless, he hastened to add, the result of the revolution is to be enjoyed, and instruction to support the new regime has been given to all, especially to politicians and the press in France and England. "You will see how much praise they will bestow" on the newly installed regent, Azod al-Molk. The Iranian diplomat's enthusiasm displayed a naive faith in French support, uninitiated as he was in his host's diplomatic double game. "The French government is very, very much on our side," he wrote.[43]

The cryptic text of this letter sounds puzzling, and it certainly needs decoding. Samad Khan Momtaz al-Dowleh, his brother Isma'il Momtaz al-Dowleh, and Mostashar al-Dowleh were members of several Masonic lodges. The term *friend* definitely was a substitute for the Masonic *brother.* The French foreign minister and many in his ministry at that time were Freemasons; so was Dr. Schneider. Samad Khan was thus relating the Freemasons' concerns for the safety of some of the royalists, who were also "brothers" and so possessed some of the lodges' secrets, which needed safeguarding. He was also expressing the French Masonic interest in the Constitutional Revolution following its due course and consolidating its gains.

Public trials of some of the reactionaries, unaffiliated to any Masonic lodge, would symbolize the constitutionalists' newly acquired power. Finally, in his letter the ambassador mentions only one person by name, Ibrahim Khan Hakim al-Molk, who was the number two leader of the Réveil de l'Iran lodge prior to the coup in 1908 and who was to play an equally important role in the lodge when it reopened. Hakim al-Molk would also assume chairmanship of important committees in the second Majles, such as the Education and Electoral Law Committees.

Nuri's Trial

Here one question begs to be raised: Did the French Masons encourage Nuri's trial? It is important to remember that the Réveil de l'Iran was affiliated with the Grand Orient, which, as stated earlier, was the most radically anticlerical of all Masonic organizations in France. At the turn of the century, it had engaged in a fierce battle against the Catholic clergy in France and Rome for the official separation of church and state. The law that ensued in 1905 marked the apogee of the Grand Orient's power in public affairs because it was initiated by some of the organization's most important leaders. Moreover, by the spring of 1909, months before the fall of Tehran, Paul Henri Morel, Hakim al-Molk, and Mohammad Ali Khan Zoka' al-Molk had sent a letter to the Grand Orient Supreme Council in Paris urging it to use all its influence with the French Ministry of Foreign Affairs to have the authorities select the replacement for the departing French consul to Tehran from among "those whose ideas would at least be favorable to the Constitutional Movement." A French envoy, they asserted, could "in times of crisis effectively protect the life of our threatened brothers, without causing any diplomatic complication. Other foreign legations exercise daily that right to give protection." They pleaded for a new envoy who would not be "clericalist" like his predecessors or a resolute adversary of Freemasonry.[44] In the Réveil de l'Iran file at Rue cadet, there is a note attached to that letter and addressed to the "Masonic Brother, President," conveying the "expressed wishes of our friends in Tehran to have a new envoy sympathetic to their movement."[45] The request was apparently received favorably by the French government, for the new consul was a Mason who, as an ex officio director of the Alliance française school Central Committee, closely collaborated with the Réveil de l'Iran lodge. The lodge was officially reopened in January 1910, when it received permission from the Grand Orient in Paris. However, Morel, its energetic leader, did not wait that long to resume its activities. In

December 1909, a special session was devoted to commemorate the "martyrdom" of the three constitutional members of the lodge executed in July 1908 for heretical adherence to Babism: Malek al-Motakallemin, Jamal al-Din Va'ez, and Jahangir Khan.[46]

The lodge could not have been the only element in favor of Nuri's trial. It must be remembered that since the eventful summer of 1907, Nuri had proven to be the most dangerous opponent of the Constitution; no royal court official had his immense power to damage its champions, as Barclay had repeatedly observed with consternation. However, the Grand Orient's interests were not necessarily identical to those of the Iranian "brothers," no matter how genuinely the Tehran lodge desired to support the constitutionalists. And Lecomte was adamant about safeguarding Anglo-Russian interests in the country. The Réveil de l'Iran itself included among its esteemed members many moderate constitutionalists as well as royalist turncoats. Moreover, the mojahedin, the Social-Democrats, Taqizadeh, and his fellow radicals simultaneously belonged to several ideological groups with diverse programs of action. They were united in their independent resolve to push for the marginalization of the olama in public affairs, and they had a constituency among some of the intelligentsia and low-ranking clerics, no matter how numerically insignificant they were. This anticlerical agenda would prove to be the most significant source of tension within the constitutional ranks, alienating many members.

When Mohammad Ali Shah sought refuge at the Russian embassy and numerous disgraced officials were given asylum in various embassies, Nuri refused to follow them. "My religious status does not allow me to follow such a course of action," he reportedly told his anxious entourage.[47] Warned that his life was in danger, he turned down many offers to hoist the Russian flag on his roof for protection. He dismissed with contempt the example of the *imam jom'eh* of Tehran, a son-in-law of the shah, who had joined the royal group going to the Russian legation and then to exile in Europe.[48] "Alas!" the *mojtahed* reportedly lamented, "what remains of Islam, now that the foreigners can say the olama of Islam . . . have gone to take refuge in [the abode of] heresy."[49] In a letter to the regent Azod al-Molk, he explained that he believed only in the protection of God, while hoping his trial judges would be fair.[50]

Nuri waited at home, attended by a few relatives and domestic servants. People who normally crowded his residence—his students and theological disciples, his political admirers and followers—had fled the scene. On

July 29 or 30 or 31, 1909, depending on the source, the mojahedin, led by Yeprem Khan, escorted Nuri to the improvised court. All sources confirm Nuri's calm composure, serene dignity, and moral strength while entering the building where the trial was held, surrounded by armed guards, who were duly impressed and in awe. A hastily formed tribunal had already sentenced to death two court officials, the leader of the royalist ruffians and the deputy governor of Tehran, charged with the murder of many constitutionalists. In self-defense, both claimed they were merely carrying out Nuri's instructions. Outside the court, in Tupkhaneh Square, a tangible "festive" air reigned, galvanizing an excited and excitable mob who waited to hear the verdict and were fully enjoying the "entertainment." Mohammad Mehdi Sharif-Kashani comments: "In truth, what a strange situation this is nowadays. The hand of divine power is taking revenge, and no lesson is taken" to prevent further wickedness.[51] On that day, a leaflet circulated town, informing the public that the "eyes of the Jeunes Persans [given in transliterated French in the text] are wide open, and till the end of their life [they] will strive to protect the country's independence and preserve the constitution. Long live liberty! Long live equality! Death to the despots! Long live the Jeunes Persans faction."[52]

The presiding judge was a constitutionalist middle-ranking cleric by the name of Shaikh Ibrahim Zanjani. Shaikh Ibrahim was born into a modest family in the province of Zanjan. According to his autobiography, he pursued his religious education in Najaf with respectable but by no means the most celebrated *mojtahed*s and was careful, he wrote, to avoid the worldly and corrupt elements prevalent in the holy cities. Arriving there as an idealistic young man, he had viewed the religious profession as the loftiest and most inspiring of all, looking up to its high-ranking leaders as a source of emulation. He studied hard and read voraciously all assigned works and beyond, but within a couple of years he lost all his illusions. "Seeing the prevailing conditions there and the situation of the famous olama and their students, I lost that naive belief that they, indeed all inhabitants of the holy cities, were like pure angels," disinterested in material and worldly power. The place revealed itself to be a "center of rapacious people" betraying the most fundamental principles of Islam. "Of religion, only the name had remained."[53]

Whatever his real experience in Najaf was, however well founded his perception that provoked such a moral revulsion toward the olama, Shaikh Ibrahim returned to Zanjan intellectually transformed. He eventually obtained a modest mosque, where he taught and preached, rapidly acquiring a controversial reputation for propagating novel and alien ideas. He admits in his memoirs that he began to read underground Persian social and political treatises and newspapers mostly published abroad by Iranian exiles as well as European novels recently translated. Such readings helped him discover the world at large and increased his desire to know more about European sciences; it also reinforced his conviction that political tyranny and religious corruption were the chief causes of national decline. He rose in defense of equality of all human beings, regardless of their religious, ethnic, linguistic, and class differences. He thought all should enjoy equally their human rights, freedom of thought and opinion, the universal right to education, the right to seek knowledge "all over the world, even in China" and among the unbelievers.[54] Repeating some of the contemporary Persian, Arab, and Ottoman Moslem reformers' apologist rationale, he argued that Europeans and Americans, who were then the most advanced people in the world, had merely borrowed from Islam all their principles at the time when these very basic Islamic concepts, including liberty, equality, and fraternity, were kept obscured from the Moslems by corrupt rulers and olama.[55] His religious radicalism, however, was more rooted in other dissenting religious movements. Echoing Babi doctrine, he adamantly denied the legitimacy of a "specific religious class" endowed with supreme religious or temporal authority. "Islam recognizes no ecclesiastical class," and no one or no group can intercede with God on behalf of His creatures.[56] *Taqlid* (unquestioningly following the religious instructions of a *mojtahed*) and blind worship must be abolished, he emphatically asserted, and replaced by individual reasoning: one must first understand one's creed rationally, then believe and act accordingly.[57] Furthermore, he believed all past and present Moslem governments, be it Sunni or Shi'a, have always fallen into the hands of warriors seizing power by force. The sword has always ruled over religion, he stated, dismissing the concept of monarchs ruling by divine right. Shaikh Ibrahim was emphatic in recognizing the people's right to choose and accept their ruler through their elected representatives. The ruler must be knowledgeable in both the rational and religious principles, be honest and just, and be aware of and dedicated to the common good.[58]

A few travels took Shaikh Ibrahim to Baku, where he met "interesting people" and admired modern cultural institutions and schools, and to Arabia by way of Ottoman territories, where he encountered "intelligent and broad-minded" Turkish officials. He befriended many reform-minded individuals, but he was closest to Akhund Mullah Mohammad Kazem Khorasani, the most important constitutionalist *mojtahed* in Najaf, whom he met during his student years and with whom he regularly corresponded. In his self-serving autobiography, Zanjani claims that the *mojtahed* Khorasani trusted no one else in Tehran and preferred Zanjani's account of events in the country over others'. In 1906, Shaikh Ibrahim was elected Zanjan deputy to the first Majles, joining other militant constitutionalists in Taqizadeh's radical group, and was to be reelected to the second Majles. He had also joined the Réveil de l'Iran lodge.

At the trial, Shaikh Ibrahim gave Nuri no consideration for his religious rank or social status. The jurors included Vahid al-Molk, Mirza Ali Mohammad Tarbiyat, representatives of the Sepahdar, and Sardar As'ad, among others. Shaikh Ibrahim and a member of the radical mojahedin faction, Ali Mohammad Tarbiyat, set the tone of the trial. By most if not all accounts, Nuri's fate was decided even before his arrest, and his sentence a forgone conclusion. There exist no official minutes of his interrogation, a surprising fact given the numerous newspapers that had resumed publication by then, as Ahmad Kasravi indicates.[59] Either no notes were taken during the trial, or they were subsequently destroyed. Available accounts such as Mehdi Malekzadeh's, Mohammad Torkaman's, and Mehdi Ansari's are based on verbal reports by individual eyewitnesses and thus should be read with caution. Zanjani's charges against Nuri, however, were published in leaflet form and distributed freely within days of the trial.[60] Nuri was accused of turning against the very constitution he had initially endorsed, especially clause 2, stipulating the right of a council of five *mojtahed*s to review all laws enacted. He was also charged with inciting people to assail the Majles and its deputies, wrongly declaring innocent deputies heretical Babis, causing chaos and lawlessness in the Tupkhaneh Square in the summer of 1907, and gathering a "corrupt assembly" to target the constitutionalists.[61] In addition, he was accused of taking bribes, instigating civil strife, collaborating with the despotic ruler, sabotaging the restoration of the Constitution, and, consequently, facilitating foreign invasion.

According to the eyewitnesses who provided accounts to Malekzadeh, Nuri calmly rejected some charges as fraudulent and insisted on his right and prerogatives as a *mojtahed* to pronounce judgments in conformity with the law of Islam. As to his alleged role in unleashing the reactionaries' violence against the constitutionalists, he serenely stated that the people were in no need of incitement, so powerful was their hostility. Nuri is also reported to have downplayed the substance of his quarrel with the constitutionalist olama, stressing instead the power politics that allowed the two constitutionalist *mojtaheds*, Seyyed Abdollah Behbahani and Seyyed Mohammad Tabataba'i, to "appropriate" the Constitution, denying any share in its achievement and keeping him out of the decision-making process. The trial was summarily brought to an end with Zanjani sentencing Nuri to death for "corruption on earth" and national treason. On either the same day or the following day, depending on the source, Nuri was hung in the public square. The crowd watched, some crying, some applauding. Malekzadeh refutes Browne's reported rumor that Shaikh Mehdi, Fazlollah Nuri's revolutionary son, joyfully hailed his father's death. To the contrary, Malekzadeh writes, Shaikh Mehdi went to a corner and wept.[62]

News of Nuri's execution was likened to a bombshell within Iran and abroad. It stunned and perplexed people, Sharif-Kashani writes. How could one hang a *mojtahed*?[63] Taqizadeh stated in his autobiography, "No one could have imagined that a grand *mojtahed* would be killed," adding, "but they killed him."[64] Dowlatabadi was appalled by this "senseless killing" of a high-ranking cleric whose only crime was to oppose the nationalist government. It did not bode well for the nation, he asserted apprehensively, especially since it was undertaken by Armenians and Christian Georgians.[65] Several constitutionalists shared his view, morally shocked and fearing the potentially explosive consequences of such an action. Indeed, many eyewitnesses cited by secondary sources expressed dismay at not only the death sentence but also at the fact that it was planned and executed by non-Moslems. The Sepahdar was fiercely opposed to the execution, which only increased his personal fear of the radical mojahedin. Generally described as a weak, emotional, and indecisive man, he reportedly reached for his Mauser gun upon hearing the news while in a meeting with other government leaders and pointed it at Ali Mohammad Tarbiyat, who was then standing next to him. "He kills everybody," he screamed, dashing to the exit door. As Tarbiyat tried to block him with his own Mauser, the Sepahdar fled the scene.[66] The regent Azod al-Molk, many other grandees and politicians, as well as olama were equally outraged by what they saw as an unnecessary act of violence against a religious leader.

In response to the uproar, a pamphlet justifying the sentencing was distributed all over town. "Following the execution of Shaikh Fazlollah, the destroyer of the pure sharia," it stated, "the corrupt hypocrites" have objected to the hanging, igniting sedition and disturbances, even though his deeds were no secret; the shah's and his courtiers' evil doings were based on his instructions. Therefore, the "nation's victors and the mojahedin who follow the path of Islam" called for a public execution to serve as a lesson to all.[67] Interestingly, *Ruznameh-ye Majles* (Majles Journal), the major newspaper that had resumed publication by then and would become the Moderate Party's official organ, deliberately omitted mentioning the *mojtahed*'s execution, while justifying the execution of the two court officials for "waging war against God" and "corruption on earth." General pardon is not for all, it stated; there are those who should be punished.[68] In his dispatch to London, Barclay did not mince words. On those executed, he wrote, "none call for any pity. . . . All had murders to their account. . . . This, perhaps, cannot be said of Nuri, but he has been one of the most unscrupulous enemies of the constitutional cause, and, though no proper account of his trial has appeared, he is believed to have been plotting for the restoration of Mohammad Ali." Barclay was keenly aware of potential royalist conspiracy as a "real" danger. Nuri's followers, he warned the Foreign Office, could "provoke an outrage upon foreigners in order to bring about foreign intervention" in the royalists' hope of restoring absolute monarchy. "Shaikh Fazlollah," he concluded, "was a danger to his country, and Persia is well rid of him."[69]

One question needs to be raised here: Was Nuri a *mojtahed* genuinely rising in defense of the holy law? If so, did he prove to be vulnerable to manipulation by the reactionary elements, who sought in him a lofty justification for their onslaught on the Constitution and the Majles? It would be difficult for the objective analyst to assess his historic role purely on the basis of his religious proclamations and treatises. His religious, moral, and intellectual motives were convincingly authentic. Indeed, the Constitution and some of its champions presented a great threat to Shi'a Iran's religious tradition and political culture, and the olama stood to lose many of their prerogatives and social influence. Undoubtedly, Freemasons, controversial religious ideologues, and secular Social-Democrats, all deemed heretical by religious leaders, had a share in the constitutional movement. But there exists enough historical evidence to demonstrate Nuri's deliberate choice of supporting Mohammad Ali Shah's dynastic interests to the bitter end, collaborating with his notorious officials, and accepting their financial support for the relentless campaign against their constitutionalist adversaries. The shah had certainly mobilized Nuri and other conservative olama, taking advantage of their rivalry with Behbahani and Tabataba'i for his own ends. By providing these olama with material and financial support, the shah enabled them to unleash their virulent attacks against the constitutional movement. The fact that Nuri continued to oppose the Constitution even when the shah, upon Anglo-Russian pressure, reinstated it in May 1909 in no way diminishes the grave charges of collaboration. Vanessa Martin summarizes best Nuri's position: "He acted as the ideologue of the absolutist cause," therefore "confirming the shah as one of the executive authorities of the religion."[70] Any revisionist attempt to rehabilitate his political role in Iranian history must take this fact into serious consideration.

The stand taken by Mirza Ali Theqat al-Islam, the Tabriz *mojtahed* who stood on the other end of the political spectrum in favor of the Constitution, was no less founded on Islamic principles.[71] Whereas Nuri represented mainstream Shi'a jurisprudence, Theqat al-Islam symbolized an updated Islamic tradition of dissenting thought. Through the centuries, both disciplines, often at war with each other, have enriched Islamic cultures in all their diversity. However, both *mojtahed*s became victims of their partisanship, drawn as they were to power politics, which in modern times was too complex for them to survive unscathed. Activist olama had traditionally drawn support and established their respective power base not from within religious institutions, but within the ranks of the lay ruling elite, to whom they were closely related by birth, marriage, and socioeconomic ties. Theqat al-Islam proved vulnerable to manipulation by the revolutionaries in Tabriz, having accommodated some of his socioreligious views to modernist ideas; Nuri allowed himself to be Mohammad Ali Shah's instrument, lending his religious aura to the monarch's political survival. Both Nuri and Theqat al-Islam paid a heavy price for their partisanship: Nuri executed by the radical constitutionalists in 1909 and Theqat al-Islam by the reactionary forces under Russian command two and a half years later.

The Tehran constitutionalist *mojtahed* Mohammad Tabataba'i never recovered from the coup of 1908. The "blows" he then endured at the hands of the reactionaries caused a state of "fear" and "despair" in him that, compounded by physical illness, ravaged him for the rest of his life, he wrote in his short autobiographical notes.[72] In early September 1909, upon his return to Tehran from Mashhad, where he was banished for the entire period of Lesser Despotism, he deliberately stayed away from politics. Shaikh Fazlollah Nuri and Seyyed Abdollah Behbahani, one an opponent and the other a friend of the constitutional movement, Tabataba'i wrote, "have ruined the affair," adding that the Constitution was restored and the Majles reinstated, "but not the way I wished it to be."[73] He died of a prolonged illness a decade later in his country home in Vanak, disillusioned, bitter, and utterly lonely.

His son, Mohammad Sadeq Tabataba'i, a reformist now attired in Western clothing, would become the rising star of the Moderate Party, playing a dominant political role in the period of the second Majles and subsequently.

The Mojahedin in Tehran

Within the provisional government, the news of Nuri's execution brought equal shock and fear among some of its members, further fueling the mutual distrust that prevailed. Most sources blame the mojahedin for the state of chaos then reigning in the capital. Their ranks were already severely divided before their conquest of Tehran. Ethnically diverse, ideologically disparate, inexperienced in the finer military arts, yet armed to the teeth, unruly, and highly belligerent, they spread terror in the capital. Yeprem Khan led a militia composed mostly of Christian Armenians and Georgians. The Tabrizi Ali Mohammad Tarbiyat and the Rashti brothers had their respective armed groups of Azerbaijani, Gilani, and Transcaucasian Moslems. Pamphlets circulating in the capital weeks before the militias' arrival in Tehran had tried to reassure the population regarding their trustworthiness and good behavior.

However, the mojahedin, with their distinct garb, fur hats, and weapons in hand, created a sensation. They appeared like the living symbol of "divine wrath," wrote an eyewitness, avenging the oppressed and retaliating against the oppressors but also "killing people indiscriminately" and terrorizing both innocent bystanders and members of the old regime. No one had the courage or power to protest.[74] They roamed the streets freely, bullying the populace, taking ransoms, and refusing to follow orders. According to Fereydun Adamiyat, their total number reportedly was nine hundred, of which six hundred followed Abdol Hamid Sardar Mohiy and three hundred followed Haidar Khan Amu-Oghli.[75] Their numbers greatly accrued with the so-called Saturday mojahedin, Tehran inhabitants who, wearing the same Caucasian garb, opportunistically joined the militias upon the fall of Mohammad Ali Shah. Yeprem Khan, as the appointed chief of police, tried to discipline them, but they were out of control. Within days after the departure of the shah, reportedly one thousand armed Bakhtiyari tribesmen, having their own traditionally unsavory reputation as lawless plunderers, and many more mojahedin arrived in Tehran, swelling the ranks of their respective leaders.[76] Barclay praised Yeprem Khan as a good "police chief" but deplored the prevailing chaos and lawlessness in the capital due to the Armenians' and other Caucasians' behavior. "The Persian government has to figure out how to dispose" of them, he wrote to Grey, recognizing the difficulty of removing them "at present."[77]

The new regent, Azod al-Molk Nayeb al-Saltaneh, joined hands with the two publicly acknowledged national leaders, Sardar As'ad Bakhtiyari and the Sepahdar, to urge Taqizadeh to come back to Tehran immediately and exert his control over the unruly mojahedin.[78] Taqizadeh arrived in the capital a week after Nuri's execution. In fact, he was partial to Ali Mohammad Tarbiyat, his relative. Although acknowledging the latter's ideological radicalism and personal "killing instinct," he stood by him and immediately entrusted him with the formidable task of unifying all militias under his sole command, thus antagonizing the Rashti brothers and the influential Sardar Mansur, who was close to the Sepahdar, his fellow Gilani. Ali Mohammad Tarbiyat, Taqizadeh wrote, had no social base of support, no powerful backing; he possessed only personal bravery. Furthermore, Taqizadeh insisted the Sepahdar had been selected merely to be a figurehead leader of the mojahedin and was tolerated by the militias because of his social status. In those days, Taqizadeh claimed, it was not possible to have an "individual without any social standing put in such a position."[79] The Sepahdar was merely a nominal leader, he asserted again and again.

A realignment of constitutional forces was taking place even before the reopening of the Majles, defying any ideological explanation. Moslems and Christians, Iranians and Transcaucasians had worked together to raise funds for weapons purchased and smuggled into the province from the Caucasus, receiving support from the Baku and Tiflis Social-Democrats, some of whom were affiliated with Lenin's Bolsheviks. Hosain Khan Kasma'i's correspondence with Taqizadeh at the time the latter was still in England confirms the close collaboration between the two in the clandestine armed struggle against Mohammad Ali Shah's troops in the northern provinces.[80] As already stated, Taqizadeh had adopted an alternating radical/moderate approach upon his return to Tabriz. However, once the Rashti brothers reached Tehran, they shifted their alliance, rallying round the Sepahdar, their cousin and fellow Gilani. Together with Sardar Mansur, another Gilani relative, they were responsible for convincing the Sepahdar to assume the nominal leadership of the militias' triumphantly marching to Qazvin and then to Tehran. They were now siding with the largest landowner in the province, whose "Russian sympathies" had "brought him into discredit" with Taqizadeh and his circle, as Barclay readily admitted.[81] Thus, the hostilities that were soon to erupt among some of the major players in the constitutional struggles had their roots in tangled ethnic identities and kinship ties, superseding any party loyalty or ideological affinity.

Taqizadeh's Rise to Power

Taqizadeh was initially welcomed by all factions, including the Sepahdar and Sardar As'ad, who quickly included him in the twenty-member special committee they had formed. "I became its most influential member," he boasts in his memoirs.[82] He lost no time in restructuring the committee, reducing its number to twelve, with his close collaborators well placed to form a majority, all under his control.[83] It was renamed a "directorate," often referenced so by the term *directoire* in transliterated French in the sources, alluding to Napoleon Bonaparte's seizure of power with the formation of the Directoire. Indeed, some accounts mention the allusion, but with apprehension rather than with admiration. Dowlatabadi claims that Taqizadeh had set up the Directorate with the help of his supporters and fellow radicals, people who were obedient to him, creating the dubious impression that he wished to emulate Bonaparte.[84] Many constitutionalists who remained true to their initial radicalism remembered his notorious about-face in the spring. Furthermore, the "great," "extraordinary" respect generally accorded Taqizadeh upon his arrival aroused some envy and resentment among others. Sharif-Kashani, who was close to the Sepahdar, perceived Taqizadeh as young and inexperienced in the art of statesmanship, despite his intelligence, oratorical talent, and knowledge acquired in his European exile. All these signs of respect will cause him trouble, Sharif-Kashani predicted, for it will incite him to mischief, and it will be difficult for everybody to submit to his will.[85] Indeed, all sources agree that Taqizadeh's arrival in the capital and his assumption of political authority far exceeding that of others deepened the rift that had already appeared with the appointment of the Sepahdar and Sardar As'ad to the highest government posts.

Taqizadeh's supporters, however, greatly outnumbered his detractors by the time he reached Tehran. Private letters from individuals and officials addressed to him display the reverence and self-ingratiating language of people recognizing in him the man of the time, "the sole hope for Iran and Iranians."[86] Furthermore, it was to Taqizadeh that Mas'ud Mirza Zell al-Soltan, the Qajar prince and former governor of Isfahan who had fled to Europe, turned for assistance against the Gilani mojahedin blocking his landing in Anzali. The cabinet formed before Taqizadeh's arrival increasingly lost ground as the Directorate, which Taqizadeh dominated, turned into a powerful center for decision making, even though the membership lists of both the cabinet and the Directorate overlapped. Some cabinet ministers—Sardar As'ad, the Sepahdar, and Sani' al-Dowleh—were also included in the Directorate; so was Yeprem Khan, the chief of police. But the Directorate often made decisions without even bothering to inform the Sepahdar or Sardar As'ad. The two leaders, Barclay surmised, were included in the Directorate to keep them under control, for they had often acted independently, especially the Sepahdar, who "seems to be scheming against the directoire."[87]

The militias, refusing to disarm, maintained a high profile on Tehran's streets, engaging in lawless acts, their meager pay, or rather nonpayment, increasing their notorious inclination toward extortion and plunder.[88] Taqizadeh's selection of Ali Mohammad Tarbiyat as overall commander met with stiff resistance from the Armenians and Georgians who had rallied round Yeprem Khan as their sole leader, while the Rashti and Qazvini mojahedin preferred to follow Abdol Hamid Sardar Mohiy.[89] Taqizadeh admitted that "from that day on" Sardar Mohiy and his mojahedin "became our enemies." They remained supportive of the Sepahdar, who would increasingly resent Taqizadeh's assumption of power.[90] Sardar As'ad, according to Dowlatabadi, would eventually choose an alliance with Taqizadeh out of expediency: they shared a common adversary in the person of the Sepahdar.[91] Of equal significance to understanding the deepening divide within the ranks of the mojahedin were the profound mistrust and skepticism that the Armenians, be they Dashnakists or Hnchakists, felt regarding Taqizadeh's revolutionary credentials, a sentiment that would only increase once he assumed power in the Majles, as we shall see.

Taqizadeh's immediate concern was to restore order and establish the rule of a central government to be abided by all in the capital and provinces—a daunting task, to say the least. Thus, he cabled the *anjoman* of Gilan a long message deploring the state of "anarchy" still prevailing there. Now that the "lawful revolution" has accomplished its goal, he told the *anjoman*'s leaders, it is the obligation of all to obey the new government, as the olama have ordered by proclaiming the "end of the revolution." Any challenge to this command, he warned, would be tantamount to national betrayal and opposition to religious edicts. He condemned the Qazvin mojahedin and the *anjoman* of Rasht for their responsibility in the reigning lawlessness there. The "lion and sun," he explained rather colorfully, have now replaced the "red pawns,"[92] using the Persian imperial emblem and the chess piece to underscore the radicals' irrelevance in the new political arena: the established constitutional authority has now "checkmated" the revolutionaries. Taqizadeh and his close collaborators also began to decrease their communication with the Anjoman-e Sa'adat. Its leaders in Istanbul began to resent the paucity of information they received and to worry about being sidelined. In response to the scattered news reaching them, they expressed their dissatisfaction with the committees being formed and complained that they were not given important positions in the new government and did not even figure in the list of potential candidates for the Majles, despite the significant role the *anjoman* had played in the successful restoration of the Constitution. Hosain Danesh, the Iranian expatriate, member of the Anjoman-e Sa'adat and contributing writer to *Sorush*, bitterly protested the rejection of his nomination for a seat representing Azerbaijan. The *anjoman* was rapidly losing its importance, Abol Hasan Mo'azed al-Saltaneh was told; it existed only in name.[93] *Sorush*, too, began to publish articles critical of persistent dissention in the constitutionalist ranks and of what its editors perceived as slow progress in achieving stated goals in the capital.[94]

In the capital, however, the new leaders were not idle. Popular despite his rivals' hostility, self-assured, and self-assertive, Taqizadeh did not waste time; he began working seriously on altering the country's power structure. He openly denounced the appointment of former officials to new posts, insisting on the formation of a new government composed of "Jeunes Persans." He declared the old rules guiding the selection of officials and cabinet ministers obsolete, dismissing what he contemptuously termed "leadership bones," the old notion of hereditary entitlement to high positions. He refuted with equal vehemence the prevalent belief that the new government could not succeed without the cooperation and collaboration of "experienced wise old men" representing the old system. The nation cannot reform itself, he asserted, unless new, worthy men are entrusted with the great tasks lying ahead of them.[95]

The Directorate, which Taqizadeh controlled, along with Hosain Qoli Khan Navab, Mirza Ibrahim Khan Hakim al-Molk, Mohammad Reza Musavat, and the Qajar prince Solaiman Mirza, among others, acted as a powerful committee overseeing the executive branch and laying down the legal foundation of the electoral procedure. It was also instrumental in the selection of Majles candidates, aimed at obtaining a majority for their group, and in the appointment of governors, rejecting previous British and

Russian nominees and thus angering the Russian envoy and worrying the British. Barclay observed that since Taqizadeh's return to Tehran "there was a noticeable tendency to give governorships to men who are new to provincial administration rather than to those who have had large experience of it in the past," in the hope that "the corrupt methods" of the past may be abolished.[96] However, "it would have been wiser," he commented, "in deference to the wishes of Russia, to waive any objections there may be to the employment of men of the old school." In this matter, he opined, the government is "least judicious."[97] In fact, the British diplomat had underestimated the new leaders' radical intention to completely reform the political power structure.

Financial and Political Hurdles

The Directorate instituted several subcommittees in charge of important issues that needed immediate attention. The Finance Committee, headed by Saniʿ al-Dowleh and including two European financial experts, a Frenchman and a Belgian, as well as a Zoroastrian merchant and an Armenian merchant, first tackled the budget problem. The negotiation of government loans from foreign banks encountered several obstacles, necessitating more time and political maneuvering. Russia persistently refused to advance a loan to a government it viewed as hostile in attitude. "There was nothing to show that the new regime was less witless, corrupt or worthless than the old," the Russian government complained to the British envoy to St. Petersburg.[98] Barclay perfectly understood the nationalists' prevailing anti-Russian sentiment as "natural and intelligible" but viewed it as a "foolish blunder" now, when "Russia was naturally sensitive at the change in the balance of the two Powers' [*sic*] influence."[99] Russia finally consented to offer a joint Anglo-Russian loan only if the two powers retained control of its expenditure; the Directorate refused the terms. Attempts to seek loans from foreign banks were also obstructed by some members of the cabinet.[100] The Sepahdar had reportedly "begged" the Russian envoy in Tehran "not to grant any money and prevent any advance of cash" to the new government.[101]

The dire need for ready cash was initially solved with a systematic collection of ransom from grandees and former officials, who willingly paid the asking price in return for their freedom. Barclay tacitly approved the practice as "fair game" and even complained that many who "deserve squeezing" were spared due to foreign protection.[102] Vast sums were thus raised to pay for urgent government expenses. Zell al-Soltan was denied permission to stay in the country but was allowed to go back to Europe after paying a hefty sum. Great abuse of the practice was reported, but by and large it proved to be a speedy and efficient way to raise funds. Mohammad Taqi Vakil al-Ro'aya, the Hamadan deputy in the first Majles who was to be reelected to the second, was put in charge of the ransom system. In addition to the ransoms, individuals were asked to donate as much financial assistance as they could. The olama were requested to organize meetings in their mosques for this enterprise.[103] The constitutionalist *mojtahed* Khorasani cabled from Najaf a decree calling on the nation to resume paying taxes.[104] Mokhber al-Saltaneh and governors of other provinces took over the management of confiscated royal estates and properties of grandees who had fled the country.[105]

These measures, however, were short-term stopgaps; the central Treasury remained in dire need of ready cash to fulfill its financial obligations and carry on the necessary changes the new leadership had vowed to institute. Moreover, political disunity among the new leadership's ranks further compounded the financial problems. The personal rivalry between the Sepahdar and Sardar As'ad was common knowledge in the various political circles; and it was often kindled and manipulated by their respective opponents for their own ends. Both would often find themselves in an untenable situation, and each in turn offered to resign, to no avail. Of the two, the Sepahdar was the more politically unstable. Perceived as aristocratic, arrogant, mercurial, and childish, he often missed important meetings, sulking at home and refusing to cooperate. No one paid any attention to his views, Sharif-Kashani explains.[106] Reportedly fearing for his life, he resented the appointment of Yeprem Khan as chief of police and came to trust only the Rashti brothers, Sardar Mohiy and Hosain Khan, and their relative, the wealthy and highly influential fellow Gilani Sardar Mansur.[107] The international power play was also a decidedly disruptive factor in Tehran politics of the time. If the Sepahdar was viewed as too close to the Russians, the Bakhtiyari Sardar As'ad was deemed too close to the British. Thus, the two leaders' fierce rivalry further polarized the political climate in the capital.

When the Directorate was dissolved due to incessant discord among its members, it left the cabinet even more helpless in resolving problems that needed immediate attention, so the cabinet, too, was dissolved. This first cabinet had lasted only two and a half months. However, it was replaced by a second on September 30, 1909, that was almost identical to the first. The Sepahdar was appointed prime minister, but moderate members of the cabinet urged both the Sepahdar and Sardar As'ad to work closely with

Taqizadeh and his collaborators in anticipation of the influential faction the latter would form in the new Majles.

Parti-Bazi (Party Game)

The concept of an ideologically cohesive political group with a selected leadership following a defined program of action was too novel to be understood by most people in Iran at the time. From the start, the European term *party*, nationally adopted in transliteration, acquired a pejorative sense in the popular mind in being linked to *bazi*, "game": the political party game assembled individuals sharing common self-interests and targeting rival groups.[108] In fact, the combined though disparate groups involved in the revolution were now competing for power and maneuvering to place their respective allies in sensitive government positions. The still invisible but distinct Democrat and Moderate Parties had not yet emerged publicly, but the main players on both sides were already positioning themselves, provoking mutual criticism and subjected to the wrath of concerned observers.

In Istanbul, a committee calling itself Sa'adat-e Iraniyan (Iranians' Happiness) promulgated a manifesto addressed to national leaders in Tehran, warning them that the country was in danger of imminent annihilation, unless they gave up the divisive *parti-bazi*. The Russian and the English, they were told, have now reached an accord over the division of "our sacred homeland" among themselves. Kindled by their sense of honor and their *iraniyat*, "Iranian-ness," they must form a united national front, giving up *parti-bazi*. Highly emotional in tone, at times romantically nationalist, the manifesto text carries a forceful, urgent message of impending disaster should the new government fail to establish national unity and rise in defense of the nation. "If national sovereignty is lost, in the name of which nation would the freedom seekers acquire progress and liberty?"[109] *Sorush* articles continued to call for united action, with Dehkhoda, by now distancing himself from Taqizadeh and his group, even insisting on the tribes' right of representation in the new Majles. They constitute half of the population, he wrote.[110]

The critiques had in fact started much earlier. Barely a few weeks after the fall of Tehran, pamphlets began to circulate in the capital and were posted to leading politicians, olama, and merchants. The number of pamphlets, eleven in all, and the virulence of the attack in fact underscored the importance Taqizadeh had acquired in the country. One of them, titled *Cry of the Fatherland* and addressed directly to the new ministers, rose in defense of the

Sepahdar and against Taqizadeh and members of the Directorate. It praised Sattar Khan, Baqer Khan, the Sepahdar, and Sardar As'ad for having risked their lives in resisting despotism and defending the rights of the nation, thus earning Iranians' respect. In contrast, it accused Taqizadeh and his group of *parti-bazi*, a power game forcefully imposing its policy on all others. It was this very *parti-bazi*, the pamphlet alleged, that had destroyed the first Majles and ruined the reputation of its deputies, with many shamelessly having to seek refuge in foreign embassies and foreign countries. Have they not learned the bitter lessons of such *parti-bazi*? Now, it is enabling Taqizadeh to grab power, control the Directorate, and install his relative, Mirza Ali Mohammad Tarbiyat, an "inexperienced youth," as commander of the mojahedin, "the nation's saviors."[111] Sardar As'ad is also reprimanded for *parti-bazi*, giving away positions to collaborators of despots. Noting Iran's display of collective pride and honor never witnessed before and perhaps never again, the anonymous author expressed his fear of the possible loss of the resulting good opportunity and positive conditions to achieve constitutional goals.[112] Another pamphlet explicitly defined national leaders' military and political triumphs strictly on the basis of the "nation's favorable opinion and popular acceptance," stressing the fact that the Sepahdar's "glorious deeds" would not have taken place without the support of the people of the Caucasus, Rasht, and then Tehran. Favorable public opinion played, it insisted, and still plays a role, raising Taqizadeh, a bookstore owner of modest social background, to the rank of the people's representative, helping him gain other statesmen's acceptance of the *directoire* (as given in transliterated French in the text) he had proposed. And yet, it lamented, this *directoire* is governing with absolute power, the state of the nation is daily getting worse, and corruption keeps on breeding more corruption.[113]

Taqizadeh was no less vehement in his defense of a strong political authority necessary for nation building. Now is the time to restore law and order, he asserted. Knowledgeable and trustworthy people act as a provisional government; the government's mandate is to meet the challenging tasks of checking foreign intervention and instituting domestic reforms. Mojahedin, tribesmen, religious leaders, and Cossacks, all have to obey without questioning, setting aside personal interests. Opposition is the prerogative of the would-be lawfully elected deputies and no one else, he proclaimed emphatically. It is an imperative to earn the "praise" of the "world watching us" so that "it will consider us worthy of governing our own fatherland."[114]

Taqizadeh's opponents were a politically disparate group. It included some olama, with different motives and objectives, and politicians who, regardless of their political background and social rank, adopted a religious tone in reaction to the radicals' predominantly secular rhetoric. "The sword of religion," Dowlatabadi remarks, was a useful weapon to wage war against rival factions and undermine their credibility.[115] Dowlatabadi, the former Azali-Babi converted to constitutionalism and a modernist reformer, had already while in Istanbul kept his distance from the "extremists" or "revolutionaries," as he labeled Taqizadeh's group. Upon his return to Tehran in early November, he chose to work more closely with the moderates but candidly admitted his own affinity to the radicals, who were more "genuine freedom seekers." In fact, he believed the moderates "were, willingly or unwillingly, the despots' instruments."[116] Even more surprising was Dehkhoda's defection to the moderates' camp upon his own return to Tehran at about the same time. This group, after all, was composed mainly of former officials of the deposed shah and of the *dowleh*s and *saltaneh*s that Dehkhoda had, while still in exile in Europe, refused to consider to be genuine constitutionalists. The choice made by Abol Hasan Mo'azed al-Saltaneh and Mohammad Sadeq Tabataba'i was less surprising; both became important members of the Moderate Party in the making. They were joined by Mostashar al-Dowleh, Momtaz al-Dowleh, and Nasrollah Taqavi, with whom they had collaborated while in exile in Europe, as well by lesser-ranking turncoat constitutionalists. Abdollah Behbahani, the constitutionalist *mojtahed* who played an important role in the first Majles period, would also join their ranks upon his return to Tehran.

Until the summer of 1910, all the major political actors would continue to offer to the public a semblance of unity, and, as we shall see, government officials would persistently play out the same game of musical chairs in four successive cabinets until the closing of the second Majles. Outwardly, a precarious political balance of power would be maintained in Tehran, until politics, rather than policy, significantly widened the tactical divide between the radical and moderate factions. Elected deputy to the Majles, Taqizadeh would retain his center-stage political role, using it most effectively to fight for the reforms all had initially called for. The second Majles period would eventually, by the spring of 1910, witness some of the fiercest power struggles, with Taqizadeh bearing the brunt of the social conservatives' assaults. However, it must be noted here that from the very beginning of their return to power, the constitutionalist reformers, regardless of their separate alliances, which defy definition in ideological terms, were united in their shared vision of a "new Iran," a vision that inspired the elected deputies' reform program. The conventional labels *Moderate* and *Democrat* attributed to the two parties that would emerge out of these earlier factions need closer scrutiny. One fact is indisputable: the hostility between the two factions only gradually gave way to official, organized party platforms that essentially advocated almost an identical modernist program. Divergent political views that emerged in the summer of 1910 were to some extent also about personalities and their ability to navigate competing interests, their personal beliefs, and their political ambitions as well as, no less significant, about Anglo-Russian interference in internal affairs. In the turmoil of the next few months, each individual would try to ride the tide; many would flounder, and some would perish. No revolution has ever proven to be smooth sailing; this one would be no exception.

5

The Parties

POMP AND HIGH HOPE marked the inauguration of the second Majles, on November 14, 1909, almost eighteen months after the destruction of the first Majles and the subsequent suspension of the Constitution. It was opened by the young Ahmad Shah accompanied by royal princes, high-ranking olama led by the *mojtahed*s Abdollah Behbahani and Mohammad Tabataba'i, wealthy merchants, and other members of the social elite. All the foreign embassies were also duly represented. Cabinet ministers as well as some sixty-five newly elected deputies took their assigned seats. The regent Azod al-Molk formally declared the opening of the National Consultative Assembly "in the name of God the Freedom Giver" and the Imam of the Age. In a speech written for him by Taqizadeh in collaboration with Sadeq Khan Mostashar al-Dowleh,[1] Azod al-Molk expressed his joy in witnessing such an event marking the end result of the nation's three-year-long travails and sufferings, ushering in a "new era." This second phase of the "age of renewal," he stated, will lead the nation to the path of progress. He acknowledged with gratitude the help provided by "friendly nations" and individual "good wishers," supportive European press and committees, as well as the foreign envoys in Tehran. He also specifically thanked the constitutionalist olama Behbahani and Tabataba'i, the nationalist leaders Sattar Khan and Baqer Khan, Sardar As'ad Bakhtiyari, the Sepahdar, as well as the mojahedin and the "martyrs" for their immeasurable devotion to the cause. He promised to lift the people's worries over foreign troops then occupying the country by engaging in friendly negotiations for their evacuation so that the government could begin in earnest its tasks, reforming and organizing its ministries "in accordance with the principles of advanced nations." The national objectives, he asserted, were to implement constitutional laws "in conformity with the spirit of Islam." The tone and content reflected a moderate, all-inclusive national agenda aiming at institutional reforms inspired by European models.

The regent's speech was followed by speeches by several others, who, in contrast to the prince's conciliatory terms, emphatically proclaimed the Majles the center of the nation's political power, reflecting the popular will. The Iran of today, they stated, is different from last year's Iran: today the law has supreme authority over the executive power, and military officers and grandees have come to the seat of the legislative power to pledge allegiance to the Constitution.[2] The speeches, including the regent's, called for national progress and development, expressing the leaders' readiness to steer the nation toward modernity, which was acknowledged as a European phenomenon.

The Elected Second Majles

Tehran elections for the second Majles reportedly took place in an exceptionally peaceful and safe manner, supervised by a committee that included Hakim al-Molk, Sani' al-Dowleh, Mostashar al-Dowleh, Nasrollah Taqavi, and Hosain Mo'tamed al-Molk, the brother of Abol Hasan Mo'azed al-Saltaneh. They met at Dar al-Fonun to select candidates deemed fit to represent the people, without encountering much opposition.[3] The new electoral law, promulgated on July 1, 1909, was written by a committee composed mainly of these same individuals, with the addition of Abdol Hosain Mirza Farman-Farma, Nasrollah Khan Moshir al-Dowleh, and Hosain Qoli Khan Navab and in consultation with the Anjoman-e Tabriz. A total of 120 deputies were to be elected in two rounds, eliminating class and professional categories that had formed the social base for the first Majles electorate. Voters had to be Moslem property owners, earn a minimum income, or pay minimum taxes, unless they were educated, and the minimum age was lowered from twenty-five to twenty years. To be eligible to run for election, candidates had to be Moslem, at least thirty years old but no older than seventy, literate, morally of good standing and trustworthy, with some knowledge of public affairs. Qajar princes directly related to the shah, be they brothers, uncles, or sons, were automatically eliminated from eligibility for elected office. Foreign subjects, women, apostates (Moslems who renounced their religion), individuals declared bankrupt, and indicted criminals were denied the right to vote or be elected.[4] Jewish, Zoroastrian, and Armenian communities as well as the Bakhtiyari, Qashqa'i, Torkaman, Shahsavan, and, collectively, the five smaller tribes (Khamseh) in the South were entitled to one representative each.

The Electoral Committee had decided on a two-round procedure for the general elections: each quarter in a city or town would vote for three times the number of candidates officially allotted, and those with the highest number of votes would then select the deputies from among themselves. In areas where only one person was to be elected, a single round would be practiced. Rural people would vote in the town nearest to their village. Fifteen seats were allotted for Tehran instead of the sixty in the first Majles. Azerbaijan got twenty seats instead of the previous twelve, a change that marked the ascendancy of that province as a result of its vital role in the resistance to royal despotism. More importantly, it highlighted the predominant part that Azerbaijani deputies, led by Taqizadeh, were to play in the Majles until his political demise in July 1910. Taqizadeh, however, was elected as a representative from Tehran. Furthermore, the law stipulated that a vacant seat due to death or resignation could be filled with a nonresident of the province he represented and be elected by Majles deputies. Sadeq Khan Mostashar al-Dowleh writes in his memoirs that the Electoral Committee sought "foreign experts'" advice in formulating the laws pertaining to each cabinet ministry that were to be drafted after the elections.[5]

Mansoureh Ettehadiyeh argues that the new legislature was by far more politically conservative than its predecessor, with the old elite turned constitutionalists acquiring power they did not have then. It was also less representative in its social composition.[6] Indeed, with the abolition of the class-based electorate, neither the students nor the guilds were represented collectively. Zahra Shaji'i counted twenty former deputies; some twenty-two olama; eighteen landowners, government officials, merchants; four Qajars; and a few educated journalists and physicians. Five *mojtaheds* were to be included in the list for the clerical council in charge of reviewing the laws before their enactment, in compliance with clause 2 of the Constitution.[7] The constitutionalist olama of Najaf reportedly had cabled their peers in Tehran and other religious centers in the country, urging them to nominate twenty *mojtaheds* deemed worthy and qualified, impartial and acceptable to all, and, more significantly, "cognizant of the exigencies of the time." The Majles was to select five from among them to form the clerical council.[8]

By the time the Majles was forcefully closed in December 1911, the total required 120 deputies had not yet been elected. Practically no Majles session enjoyed full attendance owing to delayed elections, some deputies' late arrival to the capital, some deputies' subsequent appointment to government posts, or some deputies' absenteeism. The council of five *mojtaheds* played no role because the selection of its members encountered serious obstacles in the Majles. The olama elected as deputies had very little influence compared to their counterparts in the first Majles. Similarly, the big merchants who had figured so prominently in the early phase of the revolution played only an indirect part through their elected proxies in the events of the second Majles period. The elections were by no means free.[9] Theqat al-Islam bitterly complained they were rigged in Azerbaijan, and, consequently, the province came to be represented by "unworthy individuals." He figured in the first- and second-round lists of successful nominees, but he chose to withdraw his candidacy. He had distanced himself from the radical local *anjoman* and Taqizadeh, whose tactics and agenda he profoundly distrusted. In a moment of bitter realization of his own predicament, he came to admit that at no time was any serious attention ever paid to the "turbaned class" (referring to clerics, who wear a turban) and that he had been "foolish" to believe it was his duty to get politically involved. The government, he wrote, attained its objectives at the expense of the "turbaned"; therefore, "it is of no use to kill oneself for them."[10] In Tehran, rumors were widely spread that secret meetings were held at Dar al-Fonun to prepare the list of candidates, who, according to some eyewitness accounts, were not all qualified, causing "irrevocable damage."[11]

The nationwide lists were not formally based on any party affiliation because the Democrat and Moderate Parties were not officially formed until after the opening of the Majles, even though the Democrat Party was in fact secretly in the making months earlier. However, as discussed in the previous chapter, the political schism had already emerged prior to the elections, dividing the ranks of the constitutional leadership. Mehdi Malekzadeh writes that the conflicts that divided the constitutionalists in the second Majles were sown in the first Majles, grew in exile during the period of the Lesser Despotism, and erupted in Tehran with the restoration of the Constitution.[12] The group that was to form the secretive Central Committee of the Democrat Party had covertly organized the preparations for the elections, selecting individual candidates to the exclusion of the Gilanis, who had played a vital role in the bloody resistance.[13] Once the Majles was inaugurated, the Central Committee maintained its secretiveness, while issuing a stern order to its followers to respect in words and deeds all religious faiths and customs of the general population. Under no circumstances, it warned, should the olama be given any pretext to raise any objection to Democrats' actions. Yet it also instructed its followers to call on "people fervently attached to the basic principles of the sharia" to give up their "superstitions" and their trust in the religious leadership and draw their attention to the "harm of its despotism." The Central Committee also proclaimed its support for the current government, offering to cooperate in its effort to consolidate the central authority for as long as necessary for the protection of the country and until "better social conditions."[14]

Throughout the period of the first Majles and until the return of the constitutionalists to power, political activists used the term *ferqeh* (faction) mainly in reference to their organizations. Subsequently, the European word *party* was translated into *hezb*, and *hezb* and *ferqeh* were used interchangeably in political circles. Originally a Qur'anic term meaning "army of God" or "companions of God," *hezb* in its modified interpretation acquired a secular, modernist significance suitable to its users' goals. The Democrats and the Moderates then dominated national politics, defining all debates and policies, even though their parties would not officially be recognized as such until 1910. For the sake of convenience, the names "Democrat" and "Moderate" are used here to identify the factions even prior to their emergence as official parties.

The Democrat Party (Hezb-e Democrat)

From the start, the Democrats acquired a numerically disproportionate power in the new Majles. They held only twenty-seven seats, with twelve from Azerbaijan,[15] two from Khorasan, and one from Kermanshah. Significantly, Isfahan and Gilan had none, despite the local presence of active party cells. Neither the Sepahdar, the Gilani landlord, nor Sardar As'ad, the Bakhtiyari tribal chieftain, would tolerate selection of "extremists" for their respective political turf. Various factors allowed the well-organized, highly motivated small group of Democrats opportunities to effectively establish an authority far exceeding the party's relative size.

The Democrat group formed a viable organization, with a competent leadership, an executive committee, and its own rules and regulations. It had a political manifesto, a program of action, and its own newspaper, *Iran-e now* (New Iran), which began publication almost three months before the opening of the Majles. Though based mainly in Tehran, Tabriz, Rasht, and Mashhad, the party tried to extend its networks throughout the provinces and cultivated ties beyond the nation's border into the Caucasus. Its membership, though Moslem in majority, included non-Moslems, in particular

Armenians and Georgians, and though its members were mostly of middle-class background, it also included some wealthy merchants and landowners as well as two Qajar princes.[16] Overall, the party's membership number remained insignificant. In January 1910, it counted a mere 390 members.[17]

The Democrat Party was formed, or rather reconstructed, from the older Social-Democratic faction by a group that included Hasan Taqizadeh, Hosain Qoli Khan Navab, Mohammad Reza Musavat, Ibrahim Khan Hakim al-Molk, Shaikh Mohammad Khiyabani, Haidar Khan Amu-Oghli, Mohammad Amin Rasulzadeh, Mohammad Ali Khan Tarbiyat, Isma'il Nobari, Shaikh Ibrahim Zanjani, Solaiman Mirza, Abdol Hosain Khan Vahid al-Molk, Mahmud Mahmud, and others. Judging from Vram Pilosian and Tigran Ter Hacobian's correspondence with Taqizadeh, these two men were the main initiators of the party and organization. As early as August 1909, Pilosian urged Taqizadeh to recruit and organize the group, establish a central committee, and push to ensure the election of its members, and he offered a list of suitable candidates.[18] Furthermore, an Armenian by the name of Joseph Basil was the original founder and financier of *Iran-e now*, until it was closed temporarily in July 1910. Rasulzadeh, the Moslem Social-Democrat from Baku, was its editor, and Tigran a regular contributor.[19] Pilosian was also the author of the Democrat group's rules and regulations.[20]

The Central Committee was established in October 1909, weeks before the inauguration of the Majles, and was composed of Taqizadeh, Vahid al-Molk, Solaiman Mirza, Musavat, Rasulzadeh, Mahmud Mahmud, Navab, and Hajji Mirza Baqer of Baku, with Hosain Parviz acting as its secretary. The list varies slightly according to the sources,[21] and there seems to be no consensus as to the identity of the Central Committee's director—Haidar Khan or Navab or Mahmud Mahmud. Haidar Khan was rapidly declared "indispensable" to the group, a "good organizer and a good propagandist," who had to remain in Tehran and whose time was not to be wasted in joining government forces fighting rebels in the North. He was reportedly instrumental in founding a local Democrat committee in Mashhad and in encouraging the local poet Mohammad Taqi Bahar Malek al-Sho'ara to establish his paper *Now bahar* (New Spring) as the party's official organ along with *Iran-e now*.[22] The Central Committee initially enforced utter secrecy over its membership and activities. Taqizadeh even asked Pilosian to send two separate letters in correspondence about party business, one addressed to the Central Committee and one to him personally.[23] All members chose Tehran as their base; all shared a common educated, middle-class background, with the exception of the Qajar prince Solaiman Mirza. Taqizadeh, Solaiman Mirza, Vahid al-Molk, and Musavat were elected Majles deputies, with Taqizadeh assuming leadership of the Majles faction until his political demise eight months later.

According to the party's program, each of five chosen individuals was to direct a ten-member cell in different parts of the capital and throughout the country, each cell linked to its regional center, which would report directly to the Central Committee. Membership of each cell was to remain unknown to other cells, and utmost secrecy was to be kept over the party's activities and views. Members had to be at least eighteen years old, honorable, incorruptible, their views thoroughly tested in three separate interviews before admission. They had to abide by the rules and regulations of the party and refrain from abusing party patronage or pursuing self-interests. They were charged with the important task of spreading the principles of democracy as instructed by their leaders and recruiting new members. Members of the ruling class were not eligible, unless exceptionally approved by the Central Committee. More important, individuals "professionally engaged in business related to religion"[24]—that is, the religious classes—were also excluded. Malekzadeh remarks that the party omitted terms such as *socialism* and *social democracy*, even though their program was based on the Social-Democrats' and was "to a certain extent, revolutionary." It enunciated two radical goals: the destruction of the feudal system and the separation of politics from religion.[25] However, it must also be noted that the program shared many if not most European liberal, secular values and policies but omitted the specific Russian Social-Democratic principles of class warfare and anticapitalism.

Ettehadiyeh surmises that the party's program, first published in 1909, was written by Amin Rasulzadeh.[26] However, as already stated, it was the Armenian Vram Pilosian who claimed authorship. The program dealt with politics, civil rights, electoral laws, justice, education, religious affairs, national defense, and basic economic principles. Though it broadly copied with some variation the Iranian Social-Democratic program of 1907, as translated by Nariman Narimanov into Persian from the original Russian,[27] it adopted a more radical policy than its predecessor on issues related to the judiciary, education, and religion. The program of 1907 had prudently omitted mentioning freedom of religion as it figured in the Russian text, only advocating freedom from forced conversion: "in accordance with the holy *shariat*, that no one should be forced to renounce his religion or adopt another."[28] Equally cautious was the call for freedom of opinion and of the press as long as they were compatible with Islamic principles. However, the text written in 1909 categorically proclaimed the total separation of political affairs from religion. Furthermore, it reiterated the clauses of the Supplement to the Fundamental Law of 1907 that granted all citizens equality before the law regardless of their ethnic or religious affiliation, freedom of speech, and freedom of the press, while erasing the constitutional restriction "in conformity with the religious law" attached to them. The Democrats pronounced education to be compulsory and free to all, again omitting the constitutional statement "unless forbidden by the holy law," and added a potentially controversial call for special attention to be given to women's education. The Supplement had conceded to the newly established High Court and to the lower courts judiciary power in matters of public affairs, leaving the olama in charge of matters pertaining to religion, thus implicitly eliminating religious jurisdiction over public affairs.[29] The Democrats' program openly declared a separation of the two and granted equal justice to all citizens on trial, regardless of their religious affiliation. Moreover, it brought all religious endowments, *owqaf*, under government jurisdiction, their funds to be spent on public education and charities.

Though by no means irreligious, the Democrats were opposed to traditional olama authority in public affairs, which they viewed as obstructing their modernizing legislative reforms. In that sense, their brand of secularism was closer to the French concept of *laicisme*, protecting individuals' civil rights in public affairs from clerical interference, than to the US secularism that, with no single officially declared state religion, sought to protect freedom of all religions.[30] Taqizadeh would later explain his views to Browne in very explicit terms. In a letter written in 1911 from Istanbul during his second exile, anxious as he was to clear his party of any charges of extremism and revolutionary intentions, he compared it to the British Liberal Party. "It would be like Conservatives in England labeling the Liberals anarchists," he wrote ironically. He expressed his due respect and gratitude to some of the olama for their "patriotic services" to national independence. "I even believe that the results of their support for Iran's freedom were by far greater than those of people like me." And he acknowledged that their honored historic role deserved a glorious space in the revolution's annals. However, he insisted, "no individual or group belonging to any profession or ethnicity can be awarded legal rights surpassing the human rights and natural law common to all subjects." He informed the English scholar that he had equally rejected the Armenians' demand for three representatives in the Majles (instead of one constitutionally granted to each minority group) as recognition of their great sacrifices in the resistance struggles.[31] He apologized for making such an "unacceptable comparison" in his attempt to clarify his view that equality must prevail. He adamantly denied special privileges, consideration, or national-political rights to the olama class in general just because of services rendered by "a handful of its patriotic members." The olama, he argued, had always wielded "sufficiently great" social influence; they could retain it.[32]

In a separate Democrat treatise that discussed the traditional power structure of the ruling elite in Iran, the olama were depicted as a privileged class on a par with landlords, big merchants, and the reigning dynasty.[33] The revolution, it stated, has destroyed this structure and brought about a class-based balance of power institutionalized and secured by the law, guaranteeing equality to all subjects. Any powerful social class, it warned, would nonetheless attempt to preserve its prerogatives at the expense of the people, whose helplessness and ignorance had been reinforced by their traditionally enforced belief in the "Shadow of God." To illustrate its argument, the essay pointed to clause 2 of the Supplement to the Fundamental Law enacted in 1907, which underscores the olama's entitlement to intervene in political affairs solely on the basis of what radical constitutionalists perceived as the olama's excessive influence in traditional society. The essay concluded with an affirmation of the people's newly acquired ability to fight for their rights and interests through active participation in an organized political party; democracy must prevail. This statement clearly emphasized the Democrats' intention to categorize the olama no longer as a privileged class possessing special religious authority, but rather in terms of their function as equal to any other worldly profession or trade. It also underscored the distinction of the state law from the sharia. The olama thus emerged in the Democrats' program as defined solely by their expertise in religious affairs, stripped of their traditional exclusive authority over the judiciary and education, and denied a special authoritative role in public affairs. The Democrats' political detractors would soon conveniently use this principle, even though it was fought in less radical language, to brand them as "extremists" and "revolutionaries," despite the fact that they all, Democrats and their detractors alike, shared in common the modernizing reform project.

The Democrats' program pursued the same concept of equality in their determination to abolish all other socioeconomic privileges the ruling elite had traditionally appropriated. It expressed an unwavering conviction that premodern allegiances (dynastic, sectarian, tribal, and ethnic) belonged to the dustbin of history. Inspired by the European conception of progress, it compared universal human progress to a river flooding its banks, wiping away "all remnants of ignorance mired on its shores."[34] As history has demonstrated to the world, the text argued, this "flood of liberty," which traces its origins to Europe at the time of the rise of capitalism, has destroyed the "dams of feudalism" with an extraordinary force. Scientific and industrial achievements have triumphed over the Dark Ages, and various peoples have united to build great nations. These nations are now striving to form united international groups, transcending religious and national differences, to continue their march toward the era of happiness, liberty, and equality. The East, it went on, which is still trapped "under the iron claws of despotism and slumber-induced feudalism," cannot escape the "contagious" effect of this march. "The twentieth century is to the East what the seventeenth century was to Western countries." Iran likewise cannot avoid inevitable changes, and Iranians in the past few years have "torn their chain of captivity" to attain their human rights. In order to reach the "caravan of progress" and join the world in its fast forward race at an equal pace, the fatherland must first be developed. Hence, the Democrat Party includes learned patriots, whose "essential existence," though numerically still insignificant, is of utmost importance for the preservation of liberty and national independence. Their mission is to establish a strong, highly centralized constitutional government, extending its executive authority through newly formed administrative institutions to the remotest corner of the country. This government represents the nation's "commoners," who constitute the majority of the population.[35]

Pursuing these lofty ideals, the first clause of the first section of the Democrats' program declared the abolition of all political privileges. It designated the Majles as the center of state power and the sole authority to legislate and rendered the cabinet of ministers, selected from among elected deputies, accountable to it alone. In its economic section, the program insisted that state laws were to be applied equally to all landowners and peasants, banning forced expulsion of peasants from their domiciles. It called for state land, *khaleseh*, to be distributed to cultivators along with the necessary farming tools through an established Agriculture Bank, and it insisted on the necessity to nationalize rivers, forests, pasture land, and mineral resources. These stated reforms, in addition to others regulating the working conditions of peasants and laborers, echoed the French Revolution's slogans as well as some European Social-Democratic labor laws. They dramatically targeted the social, economic, and political prerogatives and interests of the traditional elite classes. Here, however, it is worth noting that Morteza Qoli Khan Sani' al-Dowleh, the nonpartisan member of several cabinets and a member of the old political elite, would effectively push for the Democrats' nationalization program, as we shall see.

Ettehadiyeh observes that all the earliest parties formed in Iran in this period, including the Democrat Party, were essentially inspired by contemporary Russian socialist parties.[36] However, it is important to note here that the Democrats' program was more in tune with program of the Baku Moslem Social-Democrat Party and its Iranian counterpart than with the program of the Russian Social-Democratic Workers Party.[37] The economic section dealt more with issues related to the peasants' equal rights with landowners than with abolition of private property,[38] calling for labor laws rather than denouncing capitalism, national unity rather than class struggle, the fatherland rather than the proletariat, social justice rather than a classless society. A pamphlet dated 1912 and attributed to Taqizadeh during his exile in Istanbul,[39] reiterated all the basic principles of the Democrat Party program, insisting on equal social justice for all, peasants and landlords, grandees and commoners, with the law applied uniformly all over the country. It emphasized the need to abrogate any landlords' prerogatives deemed unlawful, such as their absolute power over the peasants living or working on their lands. In fact, despite some borrowed Marxist slogans and terminology, the entire program, as enunciated in 1909 and 1912, focused more on accomplishing a western European–inspired sociocultural and political transformation of society than a socialist economic revolution. As we shall see, the second Majles debates and its legislation confirm that observation.

Nonetheless, the Democrat Party's Central Committee followed the Russian socialist autocratic model. Indeed, its whole theoretical structure was hierarchical, dominated by a handful of individuals, who laid down the rules and regulations and made all decisions. Originally written by Pilosian in French in September 1909, the committee's program established strict rules and regulations for its members.[40] The committee would select candidates to run in the elections; the party's Majles faction would execute its ideas, which were to be discussed in special meetings of all deputies and party leaders prior to each session. The deputies would also submit to the committee a yearly report, which would be presented to all party members at the party's annual congress. Members of the party were to be loyal and devoted to the cause and were forbidden to divulge party secrets to nonmembers.[41]

In contrast to the secret Social-Democratic faction covertly active in the period of the first Majles, Democrat deputies of the second Majles took the opportunity to openly experiment with the European model of parliamentarian governance. They now had power, which they intended to exercise. In the beginning, Taqizadeh and his group enjoyed both tacit British support through Browne's connections and some, but not all, Armenian-Caucasian Social-Democrats' help. The latter group seized the moment, capitalizing on Taqizadeh's fame and popularity to try to realize the changes they and other reformists of all ideological shades had worked for since the late nineteenth century. Their daunting task was to translate novel and basically alien concepts into concrete laws, institutionalize them, give them an aura of national legitimacy, and thus ensure their swift execution. Hence, the Democrats had to navigate two currents simultaneously: that of the ideologues who wrote down the theoretical program and that of the nation builders who actually held public office. In reality, many Democrat politicians would pragmatically push their way through the ideological labyrinths of the constitutional landscape, gaining supporters and collaborators across the porous party fences. Taqizadeh would continue to be a master manipulator, making choices and shattering many of his diverse supporters' trust. Moreover, some of the radical Marxist-inspired slogans calling for the distribution of land to the peasants, who were entitled to own the soil they cultivated, were destined to remain mere abstractions. The issue of land reform would not be conclusively debated in the Majles, nor would it incite peasant revolts similar to the events in Gilan during the period of the first Majles and in the subsequent resistance struggles.[42] Nonetheless, the Democrats' detractors would find in the party's more radically activist wing a convenient justification for their relentless adversarial stand within both the Majles and the cabinet as well as in the lively press coverage.

The Social-Moderate Party (Ejtema'iyun-e E'tedaliyun)

The Moderate Party was officially formed in the summer 1910, though many of its adherents' political alignment had already taken place months earlier. Ettehadiyeh cites a source naming the new regent, Abol Qasem Naser al-Molk, who succeeded Azod al-Molk upon the latter's death that year, as the party's originator, aiming to offer a moderate alternative organization to the Democrat Party.[43] Indeed, as we shall see, the party was formally established upon Naser al-Molk's demand for the formation of a multiparty parliamentary system, and its program was then written down and promulgated upon the Democrats' demand. Though it included many members of the ancien régime—aristocrats, olama, wealthy landowners, merchants, and most ministers of the cabinet—it can by no means be identified exclusively with the former upper-class elite. The social rank of many of its members, such as Ali Akbar Dehkhoda, Sadeq Khan Mostashar al-Dowleh, Abol Hasan Mo'azed al-Saltaneh, Mohammad Sadeq Tabataba'i, Mirza Aqa Farshi, Nasrollah Taqavi, and Vakil al-Ro'aya, defied any strict class analysis. Mo'azed al-Saltaneh and Mohammad Sadeq Tabataba'i directed it and planned its program. They took over the *Ruznameh-ye Majles*, the formerly nonpartisan constitutionalist paper of the first Majles period, as its official organ. It had resumed publication on July 21, 1909, a few weeks after the fall of Tehran and a month before the publication of *Iran-e now* began. Sadeq Tabataba'i was its publisher, and Shaikh Yahya Kashani its editor.

In its first issues, the *Ruznameh-ye Majles* quite significantly adopted a general nationalist, constitutionalist tone, advocating modernizing reforms. Like the Democrats, it expressed its faith in progress and freedom. However, in contrast to the Democrats' belief in a natural social force powerfully propelling humanity forward, the Moderates' articles stressed the role of historic individuals, national heroes who either through great personal courage or brilliant intellect led their nations on that glorious path. They cited Napoleon, Bismarck, and other similar rulers in Europe, whose "names shall remain glorious in eternity." They pointed to several such "glorious names" in Iran's history from pre-Islamic times to the present: Achaemined Ardeshir of the pre-Islamic period; the Buyid sultans in medieval Baghdad; Nader Shah, the eighteenth-century monarch; and Aqa Mohammad Khan, founder of the Qajar dynasty. Lamenting the fatherland's subsequent decline, these articles proclaimed that now the "Divine Will has decreed that the nation renews itself" under the guidance of the two new heroes: the Sepahdar and Sardar As'ad.[44] The journal did not fail to praise the Najaf ayatollahs Mohammad Kazem Khorasani and Abdollah Mazandarani for their support to the cause of national rights and for the abolition of tyrannical rule. It depicted ignorance and lack of knowledge of the "new world" as well as the sale of national sources of wealth to foreign concessionaires as the major causes of corruption and military defeats. "It is now up to us to show the way to reforms, and it is up to those in charge of the government to act" accordingly.[45] It emphatically disqualified the old type of officials who, armed solely with the knowledge of Persian and Arabic literature but none of the new political and social sciences, believed they could govern the country. "The era of ignorance and the uninformed" is over, the *Ruznameh-ye Majles* stated categorically.[46]

In contrast to the Democrat Party, which had existed in different social-democratic shapes in prior times, the Moderate Party was new. The choice of the name "Ejtema'iyun-e E'tedaliyun" is both puzzling and revealing. On the one hand, the name distinguished the party members' moderation from the Democrats' radicalism; on the other hand, its basic program was no less progressive than the Democrats' in its reformist outlook. Ironically, at that time, the word *ejtema'iyun*, "socialist," which was selected as part of the party's name to highlight its concerns with social issues and which the Democrats had deliberately dropped from the name of their own party, could only denote a "socialist" context. It therefore constituted a contradiction in terms. As we shall see, the Moderate Party's opponents would not miss the chance to point to such a paradox inherent in the "incongruous" name choice.

The Moderates' program was first issued in a brief one-page form summarizing its policy point by point.[47] Progress and independence of any government, it asserted, rests on "the consolidation of the foundation of civilization," which can be achieved only through "rallying all national forces together." It insisted on "unity and accord" as an imperative to attain a common course of action and common objectives. The people of Iran, united in their common faith in Islam, were in the past unable to assemble all forces to a common cause. But now the beneficial "light of knowledge" and freedom was helping them form national unity of purpose. The program included:

1. Implementation of the principles of an evolutionary-progressive transformation of society

2. Centralization of all procedures related to national affairs

3. Due consideration to be given to the living conditions of all toilers and provision of the necessary means to improve their livelihood

4. Development of economic potentials for increased wealth

5. Compulsory school education

6. Organization of expanded military forces in accordance with modern principles

7. Maintenance of good political, economic, and commercial relations with foreign nations

In their swift response to this diminutive program, the Democrats harshly dismissed its basic assumptions. Rasulzadeh, the Baku-born editor of *Iran-e now*, most imbued with Russian social democracy, wrote a fiery rebuttal that reads like a socialist manifesto.[48] He denounced the Moderates' program as essentially part of an "intrigue" (using this term in transliterated French in the text) plotting to safeguard the interests of the traditionally privileged classes. Abandoning the caution that Democrats generally adopted in their public pronouncements, he emphatically stated: world progress cannot be stopped; its march cannot be prevented. It constitutes the strongest force capable of moving the wheel of history in a mutable order, and no other force can stand in its way without suffering defeat. Thus, the privileged classes will gradually be forced to relinquish their prerogatives, as evidenced in the history of advanced nations. Today all constitutional and republican states in Europe form one type or another of national governance that has militantly snatched power away from the claws of the privileged classes. However, these classes, facing such bloody revolutions, do not relinquish so easily their rank and status. Once despotism collapses and constitutional liberty is established, they try to halt their losses by forming political parties to keep the government in their hands and to reconsolidate their power. Thus, in France the nation is not yet totally free of its aristocracy, which has retained much of its former privileges.

The pamphlet went on to predict that "our beloved fatherland," deprived for so long of the benefits of the law of progress, will follow the same path: despotism has come to an end as a result of the bloody constitutional revolution of the past few years, and the class-based government is now changing into a national government. The "patriarchal rights" of the shahs have been transferred to the nation. The aristocrats, now realizing the full impact of these irreversible changes, are using the new political system to find means to preserve some of their feudal prerogatives. They are forming "their own conservative party to promote their tyrannical advantages hidden behind the veil of the Constitution." This is what the Moderate Party is all about, Rasulzadeh claimed. It reminded him of a similar situation in Russia, when the tsarist government deceived the reformists who were clamoring for change, telling them, "First public security, then reforms," and then going on to arrest the constitutionalists. The term *moderation*, he remarked, sounds like the Russian use of the term *security*, a deceptive cover for *reactionary*. Likewise, British officials in India support moderate parties, which they fully control, and denounce all other nationalist parties as "extremist" and "revolutionary."[49]

The critic carried further his argument in labeling as "deceivers" and "cheaters" the Iranian and Ottoman Islamic organizations that use the holy religion to conceal their worldly agenda, as he said the "moderates" are doing. Since the term *moderate* is novel in Iran, he wondered whether "an old belief and conservative purpose are hidden behind it." He denounced the Moderates' insistence on unity in one religion and its sacred purpose, which implicitly does not recognize members of religious minorities as Iranians. "The dispute between despotism and constitutionalism," he rhetorically stressed, concerns "a dispute over rights, the equal rights of all children of Iran regardless of ethnic or religious differences."[50] Political freedom, he added, necessitates a multiparty system, like the ones in England, the first free nation in the world, and France, the model for all European revolutions. Furthermore, he went on, the Moderates' slogan, "Unity and accord," cannot eliminate conflicting political and social views in a class-based society, even if spiritually imbued with a common faith. A Moslem farmer, he explained, cannot avoid economic clashes with a Moslem landowner or avoid remaining defenseless because of the lack of laws to defend his rights. He pointed at the contradiction inherent in the terms *social* and *moderation*: one is socialist, underlining the proletariat's rights; the other is bourgeois and capitalist. One combats the other, he ascertained, fighting a class struggle, leading to the inevitable triumph of the proletariat and the abolition of private property, as Karl Marx had predicted.

The pamphlet was a transparent, pure socialist manifesto, rarely expressed so directly in this period. Rasulzadeh deliberately provoked the Moderates: "Are they fighting Iran's capitalists? Do they want to hand our government over to Iran's proletariat? Are they willing to bring our women out of their black veil and allow them seats in the National Assembly? Would they accept that private lands be distributed among the cultivators and establish labor laws for the country's workers?" No, he responded, for there exists in Iran neither capitalism nor a proletariat; feudalism still prevails. "In a country like Iran, socialism is a fantasy"; by calling itself "moderate and socialist," the Moderate faction is in fact "professing a lie," creating a "new socialism" that would provoke the European socialists' derision and mockery. Socialists, in all their variations, are internationalists not nationalists. "Nation, religion, fatherland, language, all is just a means for the property owners and capitalists to attain their ends."[51]

Rasulzadeh dismissed the Moderates' program as consisting of broad, meaningless generalizations: "It is all mere words."[52] In fact, he stated, the party that bears the strange name "Social-Moderate" is established to safeguard the former elite's privileges to the detriment of the common people. Its future may lie in its transformation into a true conservative aristocratic party, but right now it is a group that cannot even be labeled conservative, for it is temporary, expediently formed by different individuals with diverse self-interests. He called on the "naive members of this faction" to get to know as soon as possible its true nature lest they end up helping the opponents of their own aspirations and interests.

At no other time did Rasulzadeh ever write such a radically provocative, unabashedly socialist treatise, not even in *Iran-e now*. However, its impact on the legislature and society in general was practically nil. It only served his political adversaries' purpose to denounce all Democrats as extremists and ultimately caused his own banishment from Iran.

The Moderates eventually produced a lengthier program,[53] giving it a broad explicitly modern European sociological/philosophical framework. Dismissing the methodology of Marx and Engels and their "unrealizable desires and impossible hopes," it acknowledged the works of Henri Bergson as its preferred source of inspiration.[54] Thus, like the Democrats, the Moderates espoused a universalized understanding of history, adopting a progressive, evolutionary narrative. This understanding detects three general phases of human development, from the earliest period of human life at its "barbarian" stage through the beginning of socialization and on to the current era of universal human "awakening" to its rights to liberty and independence, guided by an innate sense of good and bad. This natural development, the Moderates' program argued, was hampered by the prevailing selfishness and greed of some groups, who, subjugating the weaker multitude, came to form the ruling classes and to establish kingdoms and empires. Societies consisting of rulers and ruled, masters and slaves, were for centuries sustained tyrannically through such an "artificial power." Divine revelations and monotheistic prophets sent to redeem human suffering did not put an end to it because religion was co-opted to conceal unlawful rule in the guise of lawful principles. However, "natural human disposition" could not tolerate such an "artificial situation." "True powers" rose in defense of victims of tyranny and confronted "artificial powers"; at last, human societies have found the "straight path to progress and self-improvement." Because evil and selfishness periodically occurred to prevent the attainment of human liberty, political circles and reform parties were established. Despite their differences in outlook, despite their respective mistakes and errors in judgment, such parties readily acknowledge each other's rights. They have worked to lift all obstacles obstructing social progress and improve human social conditions. Since 1905, the essay continued, Iran has begun this historic march based on natural law and not on class struggle. However, "natural circumstances" have caused ideological conflicts and political opposition, dividing society into various parties and numerous factions.[55]

The Moderates insisted their party is spiritually compatible with the "sacred truth of Islam," which is based on the lofty principles of liberty, brotherhood, equality, and human cooperation. The party strives to offer the best and most complete plan for human happiness and progress, to protect its nation and religion. The text of the program generally asserted that the "social spirit" of any society finds its most perfect form in religious truths. The Moderate Party, it stated, has likewise based its program and ideas on the general character and beliefs of its people, relative to their conditions and the exigencies of their specific place and time. It promised that the party program itself would periodically undergo changes in accordance with the exigencies of time and new situations, sustaining forever the "principles of evolution and gradual renewal." And it categorically rejected any revolutionary program as "unnatural" and "destructive." New institutions must first be solidly established before condemning old ones. Again and again, the program emphasized the merits of moderation: With every action at any place, moderation is the basic condition for good health and safety, for "human truth can only be reached when divorced from extremism."[56]

Paradoxically, despite their insistence on moderation and a gradual process for change, the Moderates in effect offered a far-reaching program of social reforms no less radical in its scope than the Democrats' program. Written in response to the Democrats' demand, it displays an almost identical faith in progress as a historical process inevitable and unstoppable. The text often reads like a verbatim translation of European sources, with here and there a more specifically Islamic-Iranian variation inserted. Like the Democrats' platform, it expressed concerns with the plight of the peasants and the poor, a desire to lift their standard of living, and proposed to offer them better opportunities commensurate with their abilities and merit. It equally enforced the novel concept of supreme political authority transferred from an absolute monarchy to a "national sovereignty" centered in the Majles of elected representatives, who are empowered to legislate and appoint government ministers accountable solely to the Majles. The Democrats consistently rejected the formation of an unelected second chamber, or Senate, fearing its appointed members would perpetuate the existence of the old aristocratic elite. The Moderates, in contrast, insisted on the formation of a Senate through national elections, thus ensuring its democratic composition.[57] Their party platform recognized people's right to participate in the process through their right to vote, which it conceded unequivocally; it also denied any individual, political group, or class the right to tyrannically monopolize power. No public office is to be inherited or kept indefinitely in the hands of single individuals. Freedom of assembly, press, opinion, work, residence, and travel is guaranteed as long as it does not impair the freedom of other individuals or disturb social order. However, a "moderate" consideration reminiscent of the Supplement to the Fundamental Law of 1907 is displayed in the stipulation that all laws to be enacted have to be compatible with prevailing common mores, morality, and religion. In addition, perhaps having in mind the relatively inferior number of Democrat-occupied seats in the Majles, the Moderate program declared that the majority vote in parliamentary proceedings should be binding upon all deputies.[58] As we shall see, that was precisely the intention of the new regent, Naser al-Molk, who returned to Tehran in February 1911, at the time of heightened political crisis threatening the precarious balance of power between the Majles and the executive branch of the government.

The Moderate program, embodying the core contradiction of its party name, seemed to want to craft a modern program while defending traditional Islamic cultural norms. The party's leaders wished to protect their sociocultural and moral values, but their views were fundamentally inspired by European thought. Echoing the Democrats and the earlier generation of modernist intellectuals, the program's authors accepted the modern European conception of history as universal, encompassing all human activities that transcend cultural particularities in an inexorable evolutionary march toward progress and liberty. Despite what seemed to be warring narratives, both parties' programs were in fact complementary, and both Democrats and Moderates seemed to understand that, in the last analysis, their disputes were not so much a clash of ideologies as a clash of opposing strategies in a common pursuit. While the Democrats kept on chastising their critics for "old ideas," the Moderates condemned the Democrats for being essentially "extremist," "revolutionary," "nihilist," and "irreligious." Contrasting their moderate, gradual pace for transformative change to the Democrats' speedier one, some elements of the Moderate Party undertook an intensive slander campaign against the Democrats. The Democrats responded that they had no need to defend themselves: their program is their evidence, for it speaks for itself. Their party is a party for all the commoners, wishing to bestow upon all citizens the right to participate directly in their government through their elected representatives and through egalitarian laws that do not favor a particular class or profession: that is democracy.[59]

In a published essay responding point by point to allegations of extremism, its anonymous author denied the accusation that the Democrats were fighting to seize the privileged class's wealth for distribution among the poor and claimed they rather wished to restore the rights of the poor and lift the bondage that the powerful had imposed on them. Furthermore, he strove to demonstrate the compatibility of the Democrats' views with Islam. He claimed the Democrats are "rejuvenating Islamic principles," lost since the Umayyad dynasty (661–750) had reinstalled the old pre-Islamic despotism, and are restoring the original spirit of equality. Rising in defense of the controversial program of separation of religion and politics, the writer erroneously attempted to demonstrate the Islamic legitimacy of this radical innovation by blaming the Abbasid caliphs (750–1258) for the emergence of a distinct olama privileged class put in charge of the judiciary. Prior to their rule, he explained, all individual Moslems were under the obligation to acquire religious knowledge and had the right to teach and apply the law. With the rise of the Shi'a monarchy in sixteenth-century Iran, he went on, the olama established their institutional power separate from the sovereign's, assuming exclusive prerogatives over various functions: education, justice, social guidance, charity endowments. Thus, by force of historical circumstances, there came about a separation of power, even though not totally complete: monarchs and government officials interfered in matters pertaining to religious authority; the olama interfered in political affairs. The complete separation of the two powers, the author asserted, is necessary to delineate each power's prerogatives. However, he conceded the possibility that a *faqih*, a specialist in Islamic jurisprudence, might hold office in a political institution, provided his intervention in politics is not carried on behalf of religion, but he denied politicians the right to intervene in religious affairs. Addressing another controversial program regarding the special attention to women's education, the essay argued that mothers' prevalent ignorance constitutes the most important cause for moral corruption and national misfortune. Echoing most Moslem male feminists of the time, the anonymous writer stated: women must be educated in order for them to raise better their children.[60]

Such carefully calculated arguments from the Democrats aimed at refuting accusations of extremism would fail to convince many Moderates, who found in *Iran-e now* ample evidence for their denunciations. The paper would often publish articles calling on the Democrats to rise in defense of the exploited classes of society, distinguishing the poor from the rich, the landowner from the peasant, the tyranny of the one and the misery of the other.[61] It also wrote fiery polemics on issues of imperialism, warning the public against the machinations of both Russian and British involvement in the country, insisting on national sovereignty.[62] The two parties fought their battles rhetorically despite their fundamentally identical goals in constructing the new Iran. However, Anglo-Russian interference in internal affairs would turn their polemical disputes into a serious political crisis.

The Armenian/Caucasian Socialist Connection

The Democrat Party program and ideological framework were, indeed, the brain child of Armenian Social-Democrats, with the editor of *Iran-e now*, Mohammad Amin Rasulzadeh, the party's most outspoken publicist, and Haidar Khan Amu-Oghli its most militant revolutionary warrior, fighting with militias composed of Russian subjects from the Caucasus. Ideologically, Georgian and Armenian volunteers perceived the Iranian revolution as a necessary early stage for international socialism, though more mercenary motives undoubtedly also colored their decision to join the combat. Of greater significance was their staunch animosity to tsarist imperial rule, which they viewed as oppressive and exploitative and vowed to destroy. This animosity motivated them to carry on their struggle across the border. The Armenian press warned Iranians against Russian intentions, fueling their fear and mistrust of their northern neighbor.[63] The message conveyed was clear: Russians, Armenians, other Caucasians, and Iranians were all victims of the same tyrannical imperialist government. The identification of a common enemy, however, by no means succeeded in forging an Armenian united front. Political and personal conflicts caused the emergence of several groups that often engaged in communal strife. Theirs was a history of violence compounded by some murky relations with Russian authorities and Moslem political leaders.[64] Armenian/Moslem ethnic conflicts in Russian Azerbaijan, at times bloody, had also marred that history, threatening to spread across the border into Iranian Azerbaijan. Persian chronicles show how ethnic brushfires were skillfully put out in time, despite recurrent attempts to rekindle them. Constitutional leaders accused Caucasian refugees and Iranian agitators returning from Baku of instigating such acts of violence on behalf of tsarist officials with the intention to foment trouble among the "freedom fighters."

Armenian parties most active in Iran were basically socialist in orientation but differed in their primary goals and the approaches they took to achieve them. Hnchakist intellectuals Vram Pilosian, Tigran Ter Hacobian, and Sedrak Banvorian, who had seceded from their party to join the Russian Social-Democratic Workers Party, and Vasso Khachaturian, a Baku member of the Russian party who had come to Tabriz, helped found the Democrat Party in 1909, as others had previously done with the Tabriz Social-Democratic faction in 1905. In 1909, as in 1905, the issue of bourgeois nationalism versus international socialism troubled many Armenian ideologues. Armenian Social-Democrats of Tabriz, led by Khachaturian and acting upon the belief that Iran already had a small class of workers and artisans that could be mobilized, decided to fight to arouse "class consciousness for the socialist struggle" in Iran, while simultaneously cooperating with the bourgeois Democrats. The majority present at a meeting in October 1908 where debates on bourgeois nationalism versus international socialism took place, accepted the proposal to fight. A minority led by Pilosian and Tigran, arguing that Iran lacked the social basis for such a struggle, insisted that the minority led by Pilosian and Tigran should instead join the revolution as its "most radical elements."[65]

The Dashnakists, in contrast, though also socialist oriented, preferred to give priority to Armenian national liberation issues while still fighting despotism and imperialism. Their detractors, Hnchakists and Social-Democrats alike, accused them of using socialism as "the selected weapon to battle national oppression rather than as the inevitable stage in economic development."[66] Some Hnchakists even dismissed what they saw as the Dashnak Party's false socialist pretensions, but they themselves were subjected to attacks by more radical Social-Democrats for their inherently dualist, contradictory, nationalist agenda.[67] Mutual accusation often underscored personal animosity masked as ideological disputes, rendering the political climate even murkier and more confusing to the noninitiates. As a consequence, a climate of general mistrust would inevitably undermine their participation in the revolution alongside the constitutionalists.

Social democracy in the early twentieth century was essentially internationalist. Armenian socialist ideologues lived in minority communities in the Russian and Ottoman Empires as well as in Iran. Their struggle was by force of political circumstances a dual struggle for national emancipation/liberation and international socialism. With very few exceptions, ethnicity rather than class necessarily defined the identity of their constituency. The Dashnak Party's insistence on ethnicity was in part an assertion of self-determination, a declaration that no Armenian could be politically neutral. This ideological dichotomy created tension within the Armenian socialist ranks, fueling the competition between individual leaders. In a personal letter addressed to Taqizadeh, the Social-Democrat Tigran Ter Hacobian explicitly denounced such Armenian nationalist tendencies. "In Persia," he wrote, "we must recognize neither Armenian, nor Jew, nor Tatar, nor Persian. We must create a new nationality that will be Iranian. That it speaks different languages, worships a different God, we do not mind. For us, there must be no difference in nationality."[68] This conception of one nation with a common citizenship for all its inhabitants was not shared by the majority of the Dashnak Party, however, a fact that would further aggravate dissention within the broad-based secular-nationalist factions, especially among some Moslem constitutionalists.

For centuries in this region, a majority of Moslems and a small minority enclave of Christian subjects had formed totally distinct communities sharing very little in common. Cultural misunderstanding was bound to occur. Moreover, the ideological self-definition of the politically activist Armenians remained rather confused, judging from Houri Berberian's account based on the Dashnak archives found in Watertown, Massachusetts. Some people's identification with the Dashnaks' program, others with the Social-Democrats', and still others with Russian Social Revolutionaries' merely highlighted the essential ethnic/class dichotomy that typically characterized not only the Armenians of the region but also other minority subjects—Jews, Christian Chaldeans, and ethnically diverse Moslems—constituting what Lenin had termed "the nationality question." Much of the tension, not to mention the conflicts that would erupt between Democrats and their Armenian/Caucasian revolutionary comrades-in-arms, could be traced to this fundamental problem. And yet, despite ideological and ethnic differences, both the Dashnakist Party and the Hnchakist Party cooperated with fellow Caucasian and Iranian Social-Democrats. Among other considerations justifying the Armenian community's participation in the Iranian constitutional revolution, Berberian cites its strong objections to clauses in the Supplement to the Fundamental Law pertaining to religion and religious-minority status. Clause 1 declares Shi'a Islam as the official state religion; clause 2 forbids the enactment of any law deemed incompatible with the sharia by a council of five *mojtaheds*; clause 58 bars non-Moslems from cabinet positions. These articles, Berberian writes, "indicated the inferior position of non-Moslems in Iran."[69] For the Armenians and others, pursuing the constitutional struggle, therefore, was the logical means to attain an ultimate goal: the separation of religion from political and public affairs in general.

Taqizadeh and the Armenians

Depending on the source, the Dashnakists initiated or responded to a request for joint action with Iranian constitutionalists as early as July 1907, when a certain Mirza Hosain, "the dentist" originally from Qarehbagh, first contacted Stepan Stepanian, the Tabriz Dashnak leader.[70] The Armenians, however, were more interested in contacting Taqizadeh directly. In September 1907, Hovsep Mirzayan, acting as the official representative of the Tehran Dashnak Committee, and someone named Rostom (full name not available) from the Baku Committee met with Taqizadeh and five other Majles deputies to discuss mutual interests in a collaborative accord. The discussion of issues ranging from Ottoman military incursions on the border to socialist objectives and Iranians' concerns for a positive image of the Constitutional Revolution in Europe reportedly led to a semiofficial agreement reached in meetings held from December 30, 1907, to January 4, 1908.[71] The fact that neither group actually signed the "pact" between them, in addition to the opposition from within the Dashnak ranks to any accord, amply demonstrates the lack of trust and need for prudence that characterized the relationship between the Dashnaks and the Iranian constitutionalists from the very beginning. On the one hand, Armenians viewed Iranian fellow revolutionaries with condescension, pointing at the Iranian movement's alleged disorganization and its "fanatic" and "chauvinist" tendencies,[72] while Iranians generally felt the need to downplay, if not conceal, their alliance with non-Moslems, which might discredit their movement among the more pious members of their constituency. Two members of the Dashnak Party consistently and vigorously were involved in the discussions, Stepanian and Yeprem Khan.[73] Both were born in the Caucasus, both took part in militant excursions into Ottoman Armenian-populated territories, and both were arrested by Russian border authorities and sent to prison in Siberia, from which they escaped before coming to Tabriz in 1896. They joined the Dashnak Party, Stepanian in Tabriz and Yeprem in Rasht, where he had eventually settled.

The royalist coup of June 1908 dramatically changed the situation for all groups. Overcoming all previous objections to working with the constitutionalists, a majority of Dashnakists in Azerbaijan decided to participate overtly in the Iranians' struggle for freedom, arguing that "it would provide the Iranian–Armenians with the opportunity to ask for true equality as 'children of the same fatherland.'"[74] In August 1908, a pact was agreed upon and this time duly signed by Dashnakist leaders, including Stepanian and Sattar Khan, the Tabriz resistance warrior. As previously discussed, Yeprem Khan and his militia of Armenian and Caucasian mojahedin, also known as *fedayan* (devotees to the cause), played a historic role in the resistance in the North and in the final march into Tehran. Back in Tabriz in the winter of 1908–9, Taqizadeh requested a meeting with Rostom and members of the Dashnak Azerbaijan Central Committee to plan the formation of a party.[75] By September 1909, with the shah overthrown and sent into exile, "the situation looked promising," as Berberian remarks. Success in Iran, she writes, increased the Dashnakists' hope for improvements in the quality of Armenian cultural and economic life as well as better relations with Moslems in Iran and in the neighboring empires.[76] However, close ties with the Democrats were not officially sanctioned with a signed agreement in Tehran.

Taqizadeh had also made similar plans with the Dashnakists' rivals, the former Hnchakists Pilosian and Tigran. Judging from Pilosian and Tigran's personal correspondence,[77] there can be no doubt that the two were, indeed, the chief ideological architects of the Democrat Party program and rules. In a letter to Taqizadeh dated August 19, 1909, Pilosian wrote: "The era of political party formation in Persia has begun." He urged Taqizadeh to set up a central committee that would include educated people willing to join the action. An organized Democratic majority must be formed in the Majles, he argued, for without it peace cannot be achieved; people are tired of the revolution and general unrest. Writing about "our projects" being carried out by Tabriz "secondary groups," who were recruiting new "partisans" and fighting against "Theqat al-Islam, Jalal al-Molk and Co.," he accurately predicted that "our people" will win the Tabriz elections. The "adversaries," he commented, "are not active men" and cannot work seriously.[78] But Pilosian was unaware of or misinformed on the facts developing on the ground in Tehran. He mentioned a list of twenty-two desirable Majles candidates that included Dehkhoda and Mostashar al-Dowleh, oblivious to the fact that neither would join the Democrats, preferring the Moderate Party. Moreover, Taqizadeh, deeply involved in power politicking in the capital that concerned other players and different issues, would have no time to respond to Pilosian with an equal sense of urgency.

Though complaining of the lack of communication, Pilosian throughout the fall 1909 continued to advise Taqizadeh and warn him against dangers prevailing in the provinces and treacherous political intrigues. Domestic unrest and the presence of foreign soldiers, he wrote, threaten the integrity and independence of the country. A "handful of patriots cannot save Persia" if they are not backed by a strong and well-organized party outside the Majles. Reminding Taqizadeh of the case in Turkey, where the CUP fully supported its Parliament, he stated emphatically: "We must devote all our energy to the formation of a Democrat party."[79] When news of the official organization of the party rather belatedly reached Tabriz, Pilosian exuberantly expressed his delight. "The Democrat Party is no longer a dream," he wrote to Taqizadeh, "it really exists."[80] Worried about the party being in majority if not exclusively Azerbaijani, he suggested the inclusion of Persians to avoid a "provincial character."[81] Pilosian also looked for a Persian term to substitute for *democrat* in the party's name, which, he argued, is too foreign and too identified with "social-democrat." Similarly, Tigran insisted on promoting one national identity embracing all religious and ethnic communities: one inclusive nation for all citizens equal before the law—all Iranians.[82] Pilosian was even more adamant in his objections to the Dashnakists' attempt to join their party. He explained it would create a conflict of interest, for one cannot be a member of two organizations, hold two citizenships, or be loyal to two committees. Perhaps too anxious about rival Armenian groups' interference in the new party, Pilosian conveyed his readiness to come to Tehran with Tigran to offer their services to the party's cause. Months later, when the Democrat Party Central Committee was duly formed and functioning, Pilosian pleaded with Taqizadeh to keep all its works and decisions "entirely secret" and warned him against contacting Armenians, especially Dashnakists, without first consulting him or Tigran. "Just as we do not know the Persians well, you do not know the Armenians."[83]

Tabriz Democrats acknowledged Taqizadeh's leadership role in the party in the capital by coordinating their tasks, following instructions, and rendering their provincial branch accountable to the Central Committee. They respected and honored his expressed wishes to keep secret their correspondence with him and other members of the committee. Pilosian explicitly assured Taqizadeh that he himself read the letters and shared them with no one else, his knowledge of Persian, "the official language of our country," having sufficiently improved.[84] He would not talk about Taqizadeh or the party in the presence of persons Taqizadeh deemed "inappropriate," and he even scolded a Georgian individual, recently arrived from Tehran, for talking openly about "these matters." Pilosian, though, cultivated such "inappropriate" acquaintances "in order to have them at our disposal and ready to act, in times of need, for the good of the public and the party."[85] Basically, the Armenian–Taqizadeh connection was kept as secret as possible.

The Entanglement of Party Politics

Though persistently denounced as extremists, the Democrats in power would prove to be more pragmatic in working with constitutionalists who were not associated with the Armenian ideologues. Taqizadeh referred to Ibrahim Khan Hakim al-Molk as "the pillar of the Democratic cabinet,"[86] and he worked equally well with unaffiliated, well-born officials committed to modernizing reforms, such as Morteza Qoli Khan Sani' al-Dowleh and Hasan Khan Vothuq al-Dowleh. Despite his intense dislike of Sardar As'ad, he also cooperated with the Bakhtiyari leader, who expediently shifted his political alliance according to the exigencies of the immediate moment. In that sense, the Democrats were no different from the now Moderate Dehkhoda, who throughout the period of the first Majles had published a series of fiery articles about the plight of the urban and rural poor, proposing land reforms, but then conveniently joined the "*dowleh*s and *saltaneh*s" in the Moderate Party, those very persons he had vehemently opposed while in exile in Europe. Similarly, Taqizadeh and his parliamentary faction quickly distanced themselves from their Social-Democratic past, dropping the term *socialist* from their party's official name. They went so far as to forbid anyone to claim membership in the old Social-Democratic faction,[87] which was now declared defunct. Mansoureh Ettehadiyeh surmises that this move may have been just tactical, determined as the Democrats were working to consolidate their hold on the Majles and thus were reluctant to display any association with a revolutionary, foreign-based party. She also argues that the Democrats needed to dilute their socialist creed in order to appeal to Iran's Moslem constituency.[88] Thus, the party, she states, consisted of two wings: a constitutionalist, liberal nationalist wing and a socialist wing rising in defense of the poor and the toilers.[89]

However, one question needs to be raised here: How strong and cohesive was the interaction between the two wings? Taqizadeh and some of his close collaborators may have been ideologically ambivalent. His correspondence with the Social-Democrats in Tabriz, on the one hand, though less frequently kept once he returned to Tehran, does reveal his reluctance to break his ties with them. His correspondence with Browne, on the other hand, shows his equal wish to maintain friendly relations with the Cambridge scholar and Browne's influential British political and press contacts. It is also important to note that the majority of Democrats were liberal nationalists more in the western European parliamentarian tradition than in the Russian Social-Democratic revolutionary mold, though political inexperience and intellectual confusion often led to mistaken views and attitudes. Embedded in both the Democrat and Moderate Party programs was the radical idea that Iran should take Europe as a model for its modern nation-building reforms, though they often reverted to doublespeak to soften the idea's implication. The alternative national program the Moderates proposed was premised on the belief that only gradual evolutionary development, solidly based on national religious-cultural values, could achieve the outcomes both parties favored. Rasulzadeh's fierce critique of the Moderate program essentially constituted, as already stated, a socialist manifesto,[90] but its goals were carefully couched as an ideal far beyond the reach of Iran at that time, given the absence of all socioeconomic conditions necessary for a socialist revolution. Both parties expressed concerns about the plight of the poor, yet neither would seriously work for legislative reforms to improve that class's economic conditions. The few debates devoted to the *khaleseh* (state land) did not contemplate its distribution to the landless peasants, as we shall see. Secular liberals such as Dehkhoda and others who strongly advocated the formation of public institutions separate from olama jurisdiction had renounced revolutionary goals. However, when it came to institutionalizing and executing reforms conceived as vital to both programs, members of both parties would often interact with one another as genuine reformers, transcending any ideological barrier. It would be a mistake to highlight too strongly some of the Democrat Party's socialist-sounding rhetoric at this early stage in modern Iranian history.

If anything, uncompromising secularism and anticlericalism defined the Democrat Party leadership's so-called extremism and alienated the socially conservative religious elements. Compounded by the Democrats' relentless denunciation of Russian military occupation and political influence in domestic affairs, especially in Khorasan, Azerbaijan, and the northern provinces,[91] this "extremism" would anger many politicians who tread cautiously given the prevailing treacherous climate of international power politics. From Istanbul, some still active members of the Anjoman-e Sa'adat expressed their worries that some clauses of the Democrat Party's program were incompatible with the present situation in Iran and, if implemented, could be potentially dangerous, even if they were right. Assadollah Mamaqani, Najaf's representative in the Anjoman-e Sa'adat, also took to task the program's clause concerning landownership. Don't its authors know that right now landowners are too powerful to combat successfully? he asked Mo'azed al-Saltaneh. True, these reforms are needed, he admitted, but it is not the appropriate time to implement them.[92]

Mo'azed al-Saltaneh, the leader of the Anjoman-e Sa'adat until he returned to Tehran, would not join the Democrat Party. Sadeq Khan Mostashar al-Dowleh, one of the most important writers of the new electoral law, who had collaborated with Taqizadeh in writing the regent's speech for the inauguration of the second Majles, would part company with the Democrats in his selection of party affiliation. Though neither pro-British nor pro-Russian, he was undeniably pro-French through his affiliation with the Grand Orient. Dehkhoda, the former radical, also parted company with Taqizadeh, the man with whom he shared strong anti-Russian sentiment and many secularizing reform ideas and whom he had supported while both were in exile, despite his perception of the Tabrizi's opportunism. It is worth noting here that the former editor of *Sur-e Israfil*, the fiery poet who had devoted his pen to the revolutionary cause, would adopt a low-key political profile in the second Majles; his presence was mute, at least judging from the minutes recorded in the official record of Majles business, *Mozakerat-e Majles-e dovvom* (Parliamentary Debates of the Second Majles). In fact, he was recorded absent in most sessions, even when important bills were debated.

Personality issues and differences over strategy and over the means employed to attain common goals would thus further divide the constitutional players' ranks. Whereas the Moderates were generally inclined to avoid unduly antagonizing the Russians, the Democrats adopted a more hostile, bellicose attitude toward them that reinforced their detractors' accusation regarding their "extremism." The politics of implementing the reforms that both parties mostly agreed upon remained entangled, eventually helping some of the Democrats' domestic and foreign adversaries to covertly undermine their influence in the legislature and within the cabinet.

One must also consider the fact that the whole concept of political parties with distinct ideological differences constituting the very foundation of parliamentary governance was still alien not only to the Iranian public at large but also even to many members of the Majles. A polemical essay written in defense of representative government criticized the multiplicity of parties, condemning *parti-bazi*, which the author believed favored rampant cronyism and a patronage system that allowed distribution of public positions to acolytes.[93] *Iran-e now*, in contrast, would instruct its readers on the utmost importance of a multiparty system for a free and independent political life, rebutting those who confused it with *parti-bazi*. A political *ferqeh* does not play games, it asserted, for it is not personal; it has a specific ideology and program, and no free country can survive without it.[94]

The Smaller Parties

Several small parties emerged in this period, some in support of either the Democrats or the Moderates, with not much ideological differentiation. Thus, the Accord and Progress Party (Ettefaq va Taraqi) was formed explicitly to support the Moderates in the Majles and to help them acquire majority votes, whereas the Democrat-Socialist Party (Democrat-e 'Amiyun) rose in defense of the Democrats, refuting their detractors' accusation that they were combating Islamic principles.[95] Several other smaller parties offered a moderate program of reforms that would respect the religious values of the country while calling for no less radical transformation of the nation's political culture. The Association of Iran's Liberals (Jam'iyat-e Azadi Khahan-e Iran), for instance, had a program similar to the Moderates', respectful of Islam and its leadership but with an equally forceful national plan to secularize, modernize, and Persianize the entire country.[96]

Whatever their ideological differences, the small parties raised one general question, echoing Lenin's: "What is to be done?" Reading through their respective programs, as compiled by Mansoureh Ettehadiyeh, one cannot avoid reflecting on the remarkable similarities among them. Despite the complex and convoluted relationship that characterized the parties, a few persistent common themes transcended their mutual enmity and enabled them to work together in accomplishing the reforms they all deemed necessary. These reforms, pertaining to social, cultural, and political affairs, were radically progressive in scope, aiming at transforming what was then a traditional, multiethnic, multilingual, and mostly Moslem Shi'a society.

6

Legislative Reforms

MANY CONSTITUTIONALIST LEADERS, be they Democrats or Moderates, who had traveled to Europe, some having spent time there in exile or studying there, were acquainted with the merits of its modern culture and liberal political system as well as its imperialist faults. Seeking ways to meet the challenge and combat colonial powers' encroachment in national affairs, the constitutionalists relied on those powers' ideas, while bitterly acknowledging the difficulty of the trade-off between emulating European models and national independence. They inevitably ushered in an era of secular nationalism that was cloaked in dramatic contradictions. In this particular historic era, when the eighteenth-century philosophy of the Enlightenment and French revolutionary ideology irresistibly appealed to countries in Africa and Asia, there appeared to be no alternative for them to turn to. In his letter to Taqizadeh written months before the inauguration of the second Majles, the Persian ambassador to Paris, Samad Khan Momtaz al-Saltaneh, said it all in plain words. He strongly recommended the hiring of European advisers, for "just as we learn from the *mojtaheds* all about our religious laws, we must now turn to foreigners to learn from their expertise" on matters pertaining to government administration, commercial and civil laws, engineering and other professions. Hired experts must, he insisted, be given complete responsibility over their respective domain.[1] Architects of the new Iran believed that ideas could not endure without institutional reforms and the creation of a modern political culture, which required an overhaul of the entire educational and judiciary structures. While struggling to translate their ideas into legislative reforms and innovative policies, they had to face European powers that were adamantly resolved to unravel any national development plan that ran counter to their interests.

Under Naser al-Din Shah's reign in the 1870s and 1880s, feeble attempted reforms had resulted in the formation of a Ministry of Justice to replace an informal *divan khaneh* (government court). However, Qajar princes were appointed to top positions. Similarly, the notorious Joseph Naus, the hired Belgian official who had involuntarily triggered the constitutional revolt in 1906, was entrusted with the administration of customs services and subsequently the post office, the Treasury, and mint. His assigned task was primarily to raise ready cash for the Qajar court and payments of foreign debts. In 1906, the constitutionalists' first act was to immediately dismiss him and replace him with another Belgian, Joseph Mornard. In 1907, the French government sent Joseph Bizot to act as financial adviser, instructing him to work closely with the British and Russian envoys. Upon his arrival in Tehran in 1908, the Frenchman was reportedly appalled by the prevailing traditional modes of levying taxes, involving tribal chieftains competing with central and provincial rulers and intertribal rivals over collecting road taxes. He called for a complete restructuring of the system that would aim at the centralization of the entire country's finances under one ministry, which would have total control over tax revenues. He then requested two Europeans to be appointed as Treasury general and inspector of finance. With the restoration of the Constitution, the new government accepted his advice to independently hire special foreign advisers to modernize each ministry's system of administration.

The Majles deputies' expressed view of the "civilized nations" as a model to emulate underscored their trust in the Europeans' proven competence in the matter of governance. Until the spring and summer of 1910, when street violence and its political repercussions accentuated the Democrat/Moderate Party divide,[2] most deputies worked together in full accord to achieve legislative reforms. Judging from the second Majles minutes, the *Mozakerat-e Majles dovvom*, both factions more often than not voted in common agreement in favor of or in opposition to various bills under consideration. They aimed at modifying the political power relations by weakening the traditional dynasty/olama mutual dependence in ruling the country. As already noted in the previous chapter, the two parties' programs were almost identical in their concrete reform proposals. Although the Moderates rejected the Democrats' clause separating religion from state, the two parties' respective official stands concerning legislative changes pertaining to social functions that traditionally fell under olama jurisdiction did not significantly differ. In fact, both parties attempted to curtail institutional olama authority in public affairs, even if some felt the need to couch their views in normative religious rhetoric. In this chapter, the discussion of the reforms most intensively debated in the Majles casts light on how the deputies gave priority to achieving policy goals aimed at drastically restructuring the state apparatus, revolutionizing the judiciary and the national education and economic policies, as well as forming unified national police and military institutions.

On November 15, 1909, the second Majles held its first session. Within days, while voting in some provinces was still ongoing, all duly elected deputies pledged allegiance to the Constitution in a ceremony presided over by Ayatollah Behbahani and six other religious dignitaries. The majority voted for Hosain Mo'tamed al-Molk as Speaker and Mirza Sadeq Khan Mostashar al-Dowleh as his deputy. Four months later, the latter would assume leadership, with Seyyed Nasrollah Taqavi and Isma'il Momtaz al-Dowleh as his deputies. Like most of the representatives, all Speakers and their deputies adhered to the Moderate political faction even before it emerged as an official party, including Ali Akbar Dehkhoda, Abol Hasan Mo'azed al-Saltaneh, Assadollah Kordestani, Mohammad Sadeq Tabataba'i (the constitutionalist *mojtahed*'s son), Mirza Mohsen Khan (Behbahani's son-in-law), Mohammad Ali Khan Zoka' al-Molk, and Mirza Ali Mohammad Dowlatabadi. However, despite their inferior numbers, the Democrats rapidly formed a cohesive, self-assertive group, imposing their will through lengthy speeches and frequent interventions in the debates. Among them, Seyyed Hasan Taqizadeh, Hosain Qoli Khan Navab, Abdol Hosain Khan Vahid al-Molk, Mirza Ibrahim Khan Hakim al-Molk, Solaiman Mirza, Isma'il Nobari, Shaikh Ibrahim Zanjani, Seyyed Hosain Ardabili, and Shaikh Isma'il Hashtrudi figured prominently.

The Majles was composed of many inexperienced and politically unsophisticated members, who had to learn on the job the intricacies of parliamentary governance. There was a dire need for instruction on proper rules regulating attendance, establishing routine order, defining terminology, and following the debate and vote system. There was also the constant necessity to remind all elected representatives of the "sacred task" their electors had bestowed upon them: to safeguard national interests. From the start, Taqizadeh, the Democrat parliamentary leader, emerged as the most important deputy, with considerable clout to determine the Majles agenda. His views on parliamentary procedure were regularly solicited, and the Speaker would respectfully defer to his opinion, more often calling on him rather than on others to express it. Following Taqizadeh's months-long political activism while in exile and back in Tabriz, a renewed self-confidence had rekindled his optimism in the Iranians' ability to attain full sovereignty, self-governance without foreign interference. In the first letter he wrote to Browne after his return to Tehran, in October 1909, he stated his hope to legislate necessary reforms, if only the foreigners would cease intriguing.[3]

In fact, Taqizadeh's rising status in the Majles, perceived as based on his individual merit, had also attracted British and Russian diplomats' attention. In a lengthy report on the political climate in Tehran, French ambassador Raymond Lecomte informed Paris that the two legations "negotiated" sensitive issues with the young Azerbaijani and some of his group, often through the intermediary of government officials, "selected to save the ministers' face." Despite his cynical opinion on the revolution and its leaders, the French ambassador admitted that only Taqizadeh, "determined and audacious," popular with the public but hated by the executive government, "embodied" the idea of revolution and reforms. The young deputy, he noted, is not satisfied with the "ridiculous July victory" or the program of the "timid revolutionaries," and he loudly warns against the appointment of former corrupt royal officials to government positions. If he succeeds in establishing his "superior authority," Lecomte remarked, "we should see before long the mediocre revolution of the palace . . . melt away" as a result of profound transformation brought about by this "real democratic spirit."[4] Barclay, in contrast, initially rested his hopes not just on the Azerbaijani deputies but also on the "moderate" nationalists, "men of integrity" who, "if led properly by capable party leaders, should become a useful force for reform." By November 1909, he had already identified Mostashar al-Dowleh as a "moderate" in contrast to Taqizadeh and Navab, whom he perceived as part of the "more violent section" of the Majles that was seeking a "policy of sweeping changes."[5] He also observed favorably the "eclipse of clericalism, perhaps the most significant feature of the election."[6]

Taqizadeh and other informed deputies needed to instruct their colleagues on parliamentary protocol demanding punctuality, regular attendance, and respect for due procedure. This routine and mundane task added to their initial difficulties in properly setting up their legislative reform program. A list of all separate committees pertaining to foreign affairs, finance, justice, defense, and education had to be submitted to the Majles vote. Accumulation of committee memberships due to a shortage of representatives knowledgeable enough in constitutional concepts and practice allowed greater say to some individuals, causing resentment among others, especially when politically sensitive issues were debated secretly behind closed doors. The deputies were repeatedly told that general participation in all committees' deliberation would only delay the enactment of laws; it was a matter of speed.[7] Some also raised serious objections to the practice of secret ballots; they were told that this practice was not contrary to the Constitution because the results of the vote would subsequently be revealed to the public and thus would not remain secret.[8] Indeed, a relatively small number of deputies, affiliated with either the Democrat or the Moderate intelligentsia, rapidly acquired disproportionate clout in legislative decision making. The fact that, four months after the inauguration of the Majles, only 65 out of the required 120 deputies had actually been elected and were present in Tehran facilitated the dominant role these deputies came to play.[9] The problem lay in the complex electoral rules calling for Majles review of any elected deputy's credentials before accrediting him if his election was contested by his local *anjoman* or official authority, a frequent occurrence that left a great number of parliamentary seats unoccupied till the very end of the legislature's two-year term.

The new cabinet of ministers formed on November 30, 1909, was almost identical to the preceding one that had lasted barely two months, with the Sepahdar holding the important posts of prime minister and minister of war and Sardar As'ad the post of minister of interior; deputies continued to consider the former Russia's "client" and the latter Britain's. Both were perceived as more interested in pursuing their separate personal instead of national interests, though still enjoying a popular image as the leading champions, not to say the saviors, of the constitutional movement. Both were also known as fiercely competitive, whose rivalry was easily manipulated by their respective opponents for different purposes. Neither the intelligentsia nor the foreign diplomats held them in great esteem, a factor that would fuel the intense hostility between the Majles and the executive government and seriously hamper the execution of legislated reforms. Lecomte defined the cabinet as "heteroclite," made up of "incompetent men of yesterday and before yesterday," lacking leadership, ideas, and willpower.[10] The French ambassador had, however, failed to distinguish more competent ministers from the rest of the government. Sani' al-Dowleh, the minister of education and public works,[11] was an independent-thinking official. Though belonging to neither party, Sani' al-Dowleh was committed to reforming the nation's political and socioeconomic culture. He worked closely with the Majles's reformist leaders, who initially supported his attempts to implement his blueprint for industrial and commercial development, the Path to Salvation (Rah-e Nejat).[12]

Judging from recorded minutes of the second Majles, the deputies began their tenure in earnest, abiding by their leaders' advice to avoid past habits of "talking a lot and doing nothing."[13] A vast program (for which they often employed the transliterated French term *programme*) was conceived to formulate and enact administrative rules for all ministries, rendering all ministers accountable to the Majles. "The Majles and the ministers are like two wheels of a carriage," Taqizadeh colorfully stated, "the front wheel has to go forward for the rear wheel to advance. If the ministers do not cooperate with us, there will be no progress."[14] The deputies' first priority was to empower a highly centralized government with far-reaching national authority that would be accountable to the Majles. In fact, Taqizadeh and fellow modernizers attached great importance to the integration of all provinces into one single national entity, with Tehran serving as the political center. He never missed a chance to remind the provincial *anjomans* of their obligation to abide by the law of the country. "The *anjomans* must acknowledge the limits" of their authority, he asserted.[15] Indeed, in Tabriz the new governor, Mehdi Qoli Khan Mokhber al-Saltaneh, had by early February 1910 succeeded in reducing the once powerful local *anjoman* "to the state of insignificance."[16]

The deputies' goals were overly ambitious: they tackled major issues concerning government administration and attempted to restructure entire sociocultural and financial institutions, despite a chronically depleted Treasury and the humiliating presence of Russian troops threatening their nation's sovereignty. Many fully understood the need to approach the issues gradually, given the circumstances, by assessing what could be realistically accomplished. Abdol Rahim Talebov, one of an earlier generation of respected intellectual fathers of Iranian secular nationalism who lived in the Caucasus, expressed to Dehkhoda his skepticism that Iran, a country so poor and lacking all the necessary institutions, could progress in less than five years.[17] Similarly, a pamphlet circulating in Tehran conveyed in practical terms the general view on the matter: "Indeed, our parliament will not all at once become a European parliament; nor will Tehran become a London, Isfahan a Paris. . . . Donkeys and camels will not be instantaneously transformed into railroads or oil lamp into electrical light."[18] Nonetheless, it urged newly appointed officials and elected deputies to work together with learned people acquainted with modern systems. Renewal and change require new ideas and institutions to replace the old.

Most deputies were in full agreement that foreign experts were essential to help the ministries in implementing modernizing reforms at the national level. The ministries that were to be radically transformed included Finance, Justice, Defense (or War, as it was then called), the police portion of the

Interior, and Education and Public Works. There was general consensus on the need for a special budget to finance students to study in European universities. The Majles had no difficulty approving the cabinet's almost identical reform project submitted on November 30, 1909. Such reforms were also encouraged, if not initiated, by British individual supporters and diplomats. In his response to Taqizadeh's message in October 1909, quoted earlier, Browne reminded him of the difficult tasks ahead that needed to be undertaken before "poor Iran can breathe" again: making financial reforms, raising funds from trustworthy sources, establishing an army and restoring order among the mojahedin, and educating Iranian students in engineering to help develop the nation's mineral wealth.[19]

Public Security

The most pressing task demanding both the cabinet's and the Majles's immediate attention concerned the need to rapidly establish a semblance of law and order and to ensure public security in the capital and the provinces. Rival mojahedin militias attached to competing individual commanders continued to roam the streets of the capital; Bakhtiyari forces obeyed solely their tribal leaders, and the Cossacks upheld their independence from government authorities, following only the orders of their Russian officers. There was general consensus among officials and Majles deputies on the necessity to build modern military and police institutions. This ambitious and costly plan required bringing all militias and tribal forces firmly under central-government control. The early appointment of Yeprem Khan as head of the police was bitterly resented by the Cossacks, the Bakhtiyaris, and especially some mojahedin. As already stated, Taqizadeh and his group's selection of Mirza Ali Mohammad Tarbiyat as the chief leader of all mojahedin combined into one unified national force had antagonized Abdol Hamid Sardar Mohiy. Mirza Ali Mohammad Tarbiyat, Haidar Khan Amu-Oghli, and the Caucasian fighters were subsequently attached to the Democrats, while Sardar Mohiy and his Rashti followers remained staunch allies of their fellow Gilani, the Sepahdar.[20] The intensified rivalry increased their unruly behavior in the streets, which often turned into their battlefields. However, Democrat and Moderate leaders were united in their desire to eliminate the destructive elements among the mojahedin.

A partial solution was attained by sending many of them away to quell tribal or popular insurrections in the northern provinces. Sardar Mohiy and his brother Karim Khan quickly put an end to lawlessness then prevailing in Rasht before moving on to Ardabil. But the situation in Azerbaijan was more difficult to contain. In Tabriz, Russian troops were in control, keeping under surveillance Sattar Khan and Baqer Khan, who had sought refuge in the Ottoman consulate for a month. With the fall of Tehran, the two fighters renewed their unruly activities, causing political and diplomatic troubles for the governor, Mokhber al-Saltaneh, who had assumed his post on August 24, 1909. The Russian government had vigorously opposed Mokhber al-Saltaneh's appointment as governor, and its Tabriz consul never ceased obstructing many of his attempts to restore order. Walter Smart, who was then the British acting consul in Tabriz, advised the governor to expel Sattar Khan and Baqer Khan, who "have become a state within a state and a terror to all the merchants and moneyed classes." He also urged him to consider "the imperative necessity of his conciliating the Russians, without whose consideration his task would be exceedingly difficult."[21]

Ardabil was then controlled by the local *anjoman* dominated by Caucasian mojahedin, who allegedly followed no rules, acting as "thugs," plundering and terrifying the population. In the town's vicinities, Rahim Khan and his tribesmen, in alliance with the Shahsavans and enjoying Russian tacit support, raided villages and created havoc.[22] Partly in order to send him away from Tabriz, Mokhber al-Saltaneh dispatched Sattar Khan and his militia to restore public safety in the town. Sattar Khan reportedly tried to resist the order, to no avail.[23] However, once he reached Ardabil in mid-September, he joined forces with the local and Caucasian mojahedin, failing to keep peace for long. Tribesmen, rallying round Rahim Khan, renewed their bloody attacks. Rahim Khan was reportedly plotting to restore the deposed shah to power. Smart pronounced the situation to be "a reign of terror."[24] On their way to besieged Ardabil, Sardar Mohiy and his militia had similarly created havoc in villages and towns crossing their paths. They were recalled to Tehran. Yeprem Khan and his own Caucasian/Armenian mojahedin as well as Bakhtiyari troops led by Ja'far Qoli Khan Sardar Bahador (Sardar As'ad's son) were sent instead to defeat the insurgents. By then, the Russians, who had persistently refuted Mokhber al-Saltaneh's emphatic denunciation of their complicity with the tribesmen, pressed Rahim Khan to put an end to his raids. The constitutionalists were thus ensured a decisive though temporary victory.[25] Rahim Khan fled to the Russian frontier, where officials refused to deliver him to Azerbaijan authorities.[26] The Shahsavans negotiated their submission but were later routed by Yeprem Khan and his forces. The Majles hailed the mojahedin and Yeprem Khan's "heroic" achievement.[27]

Sattar Khan and his mojahedin, emboldened despite their initial failure in combat, returned triumphantly to Tabriz, where they promptly resumed their unruly behavior.[28] The rumor spread that they planned to attack Russian lives and property. George Shipley, the new British consul who had replaced Smart when the latter moved to Shiraz in early February 1910, qualified the rumor as "exaggerated." Nonetheless, the Russian government used it as a pretext to exert pressure on Mokhber al-Saltaneh and Tehran officials to expel both Sattar Khan and Baqer Khan from Azerbaijan, threatening to reinforce the Russian troops' presence in Tabriz.[29] From Tehran, Barclay supported the Russians' demand and officially requested the expulsion. Mokhber al-Saltaneh, wishing above all to prevent an armed conflict between the Russians and the mojahedin in Tabriz that might provoke further tsarist military intervention, arranged with Yeprem Khan's and Sardar Bahador's help an honorable and peaceful departure for the "two national heroes." Shops closed, and people accompanied them to the outskirts of the city to bid them good-bye.[30]

Constitutionalist elements in Tehran, however, were not enchanted with their arrival, fearing that their potential troublemaking would add to the existing turmoil. In fact, Mostashar al-Dowleh had earlier sent a lengthy cable to Najaf, asking the olama to invite both fighters to spend a few months in the holy city, until the Majles and government had reorganized the mojahedin militias and restored order. But Ayatollah Khorasani ordered Sattar Khan and Baqer Khan to proceed to Tehran instead. On March 19, 1910, they left Tabriz with their troops, marching south, fully armed, by way of Qazvin, where Russian troops were stationed. They arrived in Tehran on April 16, 1910, and, weapons in hands, arrogantly paraded in the streets.[31] Their visible presence further compounded the authorities' difficulties in establishing order in the capital.

The Majles had been clamoring for the subordination of all armed men to government police and military officers. Should they refuse to do so, the police must be empowered to punish them publicly, meting out equal treatment to mojahedin, Cossacks, and Bakhtiyaris. There must be no difference made between them, Taqizadeh told the minister of war, insisting on the importance of that policy issue.[32] The law passed on February 2, 1910, forbade all civilians to bear arms in towns and required official permits for out-of-town travelers and hunters.[33] Encountering the mojahedin's strong resistance, the Majles committed a substantial sum to buy out their weapons. Moreover, undesirable elements, labeled "pseudomojahedin," were to be dismissed and receive travel expenses to return to their respective regions of origin. The rest, the "true" and "worthy" ones who had served the revolutionary cause, were to be incorporated into the national army and given regular salaries.[34]

The process of disarming the mojahedin proved to be problematic as the prevailing lawlessness rendered public safety increasingly difficult to establish. It took almost three months after the passage of the new law for a special committee set up at the Ministry of War to implement it, but many mojahedin refused to leave. Indeed, the Ministry of War had difficulties enforcing the law, as Taqizadeh had predicted. In a special session devoted to the issue, the deliberation turned acrimonious: Nobari the Azerbaijan Democrat and Dehkhoda the Moderate rose in defense of the mojahedin, while, interestingly, the Democrats Taqizadeh, Mohammad Ali Tarbiyat, and Solaiman Mirza voted against integrating all of them into the new army.[35] Another Democrat, Shaikh Ibrahim Zanjani, suggested the dissolution of all mojahedin. "They fought to save the nation's honor," he stated, but now "they have to disband to preserve that very honor."[36] As a Bakhtiyari leader whose tribesmen formed one of the most powerful militia in Tehran, Sardar As'ad warned that the various armed groups could not be dismissed as long as they had not been properly and officially integrated into the new army.[37] Consensus could not be reached.

Issues concerning the military reforms, the Ministry of War's budget, the cost of purchasing weapons from Europe, and the kind of weapons needed remained unresolved. Iran, unlike its neighboring Ottoman state, had no centuries-long tradition of a highly centralized military institution serving the empire. Nor did it benefit from comparable military modernizing reforms that the Young Turks had inherited from the defeated government, providing them with institutional means to consolidate their power. The constitutionalists had to build from scratch a national army, still an alien concept in a country where disparate tribal forces obeyed only their respective leaders. And the mojahedin, still basking in the glory of their role fighting despotism, many of them protected by their various powerful chieftains, generated unabated chaos, fueling a rising political crisis that eventually and ironically would put an end to their freewheeling comportment in Tehran.

Education

Morteza Qoli Khan Sani' al-Dowleh belonged to an aristocratic family of Qajar high officials. He had been sent with his brother Mehdi Qoli Khan

Mokhber al-Saltaneh to study in Berlin under the auspices of the powerful German industrialist Siemens family. That connection would later facilitate their introduction to German bankers and industrial companies interested in investing in Iran. Both returned imbued with zealous determination to help modernize their country. They kept regular contact with the Siemens, a fact that would earn them the label "Germany's creatures." They joined the constitutional movement from the start, playing a dominant role in its various stages, whether in or out of government. They helped draft the Constitution in 1906 and its supplement in 1907. Sani' al-Dowleh was also the first Speaker of the first Majles, the founder of a private German-language school in Tehran, and the author of "Rah-e najat" (Path to Redemption), an essay on national development following the European industrial model. Both brothers worked with others in staging the national reconciliation that successfully restored the Constitution. The period of the second Majles provided them with a more auspicious time to seriously transform their ideas into concrete government programs. Mokhber al-Saltaneh was appointed governor of Azerbaijan, enjoying, for a while at least, the support of all constitutional factions in Tabriz, including Taqizadeh's. Sani' al-Dowleh took over the Ministry of Education and Public Works.

At that time, the Ministry of Education (then called Olum) incorporated the traditional olama-controlled school system (*ma'aref*) and the religious endowments (*owqaf*). It also included a newly founded portfolio labeled "public works," covering trade and industry, mine exploration, agriculture, forests, and road construction. The combined portfolios in one ministry offered the minister in charge vast responsibilities over some of the most important old and new institutions regulating the country's economic and cultural life. The Supplement to the Fundamental Law of 1907 had brought the religious schools and endowments under the direct control of the Ministry of Education. It irrevocably imposed government supervision over what used to be the olama's sole prerogative. The coup of 1908, however, froze all attempts to implement these drastic changes. The second Majles was determined to achieve the reforms, arguing that the Ministry of Education was as vital to the nation as the Ministries of the Interior and Defense. Without the Ministry of Education, a deputy remarked, "there is no country." Rejecting the previous practice of appointing just one minister in charge of the entire ministry, who "did what he wanted," the creation of a permanent administrative staff with a director general, whose tenure would outlast the minister's time limits in office, was suggested to manage its entire bureaucracy.

It was thought that such a broadened, fully staffed ministry would be more adequate for the present age of "renewal."[38] The Majles Education and Public Works Committee, chaired by Mohammad Ali Zoka' al-Molk, included some of the most activist Democrat reformers—Solaiman Mirza, Mohammad Ali Tarbiyat, and Abdol Hosain Vahid al-Molk; they all favored the European system as a model to emulate.[39]

Sani' al-Dowleh wasted no time in forming a proper administration. He was entrusted with the task of regulating the public primary-school system to be applied uniformly throughout the country. He urged the Education Committee to enact speedily the laws necessary for the ministry, though fully aware of the government budget constraints. Furthermore, some deputies realistically acknowledged that their reforms needed time for successful implementation and that they might take ten years to be seriously effective. However, neither this realization nor the financial constraints prevented the Majles from debating extensively the reform program pertaining to national education. "Among ourselves," Abdol Hosain Vahid al-Molk asserted pragmatically, "we are content to legislate such laws," even though they would be executed only gradually. Most deputies admitted openly again and again: they were enacting laws for the future.[40]

The debates focused on the need to establish a single nationwide uniform program applicable to both private and public schools, all under the ministry's administrative supervision. The ministry would have the right to inspect all schools and close down private schools that failed to conform. Zoka' al-Molk objected to the latter provision, arguing that private schools might offer a better program than the government and that there was no guarantee that the public system would be the best. The deputy minister of education rebutted, insisting that the country was not yet ready for independent private schools. A uniform government program is now most urgently needed, he stated; later, when more expertise is acquired, private programs would be allowed. Here, Taqizadeh vehemently protested the deputy minister's remark on the grounds of its incompatibility with the constitutionally guaranteed "freedom of educating and being educated." In an impassionate speech expressing his rejection of any kind of government control of knowledge disseminated in schools, he clamored indignantly: "People cannot be compelled to accept a government program, even if passed by majority vote." It would still be unlawful because it would undermine their freedom, he argued. "Freedom of learning," he went on, exists in all advanced constitutional nations; only despotic governments enforce exclusively its education program. Individuals must be free to develop their native intelligence and natural disposition to think freely. He warned the assembly: "Without the freedom to teach and learn," there can be no progress. Confronting rebuttals and abruptly conscious of the need to comply with some prevailing socioreligious normative values, he finally conceded that the private schools' program should be supervised by the government. And he even hastened to admit that the Constitution grants freedom of education on the condition it does not violate the basic principles of the holy law.

Taqizadeh won the debate, and the Majles voted to send the proposal back to the Education Committee to review its compatibility with constitutional principles.[41] However, a program that an unnamed woman proposed for girls' schools that would offer science courses such as physics, chemistry, and geology provoked the deputy minister of education's outrage. "She had no shame in writing this program," he told the Majles.[42] The issue was not deemed worthy of discussion, and no one picked it up. This brief interchange regarding adding sciences to the curriculum of women's education underscored the reluctance of even the most dedicated constitutionalist deputies to contemplate women's legitimate demands for equal education rights. But the women would not be silenced so easily, as we shall see.

A few days later the Majles resumed the discussion of a uniform education program supervised by the Ministry of Education; again no agreement was reached. Similarly, there was wide opposition to the ministry's ruling that all teachers, regardless of where they studied, had to pass an official exam prior to being hired. There was general agreement that good science textbooks were needed and that many had to be translated from foreign languages, but no consensus was reached over the obligation to teach religious texts in public schools. Some deputies favored teaching the principles of Islam; others denied non-Moslems the right to teach their own religious texts, though they could be exempt from studying Islamic books. The issue was sent back to the committee for further review.[43]

However, the urgent request to send two hundred young men on government scholarships to study in Europe met with unanimous approval. It was considered "vital" for the nation's future, no matter how costly and despite budget constraints. It was generally believed that they would return to serve their fatherland and assume important civilian and military posts. Mostashar al-Dowleh, then Majles Speaker, argued: "If, indeed, we are stepping into the world of modernity [*tajaddod*] and desiring to reform properly our institutions, it is important to follow a proper way" and send students abroad.[44] Abdol Hosain Vahid al-Molk added, "This is the best project," and Taqizadeh commented emphatically, "This is the best plan so far proposed to the Majles."[45] No one objected to its potential cost. The intelligentsia generally believed the educated aristocracy had failed to lead society onto a new path of progressive development. Now was the time, they thought, for the less affluent to be granted scholarships in exchange for government services to be rendered upon their return. In fact, Browne—Taqizadeh, Navab, and Vahid al-Molk's Cambridge mentor—had strongly advised them to select students to be sent abroad from among the middle class and not from the wealthy and grandees. They must study science and technology, avoid seeking their self-interests, and learn from the best principles and practices Europe could offer.[46]

Furthermore, the deputies most interested in reforming the education system received indirect encouragement from the Alliance française and the Réveil de l'Iran Masonic lodge. As already mentioned, Democrats and Moderates alike were members of the lodge. Zoka' al-Molk, the chairman of the Majles Education and Public Works Committee, at that time was also secretary of the lodge, which had close ties with the Alliance school. The collaboration between the two French institutes was further consolidated with the restoration of the Constitution and throughout the period of the second Majles. In January 1910, Dr. Paul Courbault took over from Morel, who was too ill to continue his functions, both the leadership of the Réveil de l'Iran as well as the teaching post at Dar al-Fonun. In agreement with the chairman of the Alliance school's Central Committee, Dr. Courbault wrote to the Grand Orient Order in Paris, requesting a new instructor for the school. He pleaded with its Supreme Council to "use all its influence" to have a "brother" appointed to the post. "The atelier and the Persian government," he informed them, "need the presence of a European Brother."[47] In April 1910, upon his resignation and before he returned to Paris, he dispatched another letter to the order, telling the Supreme Council that the Persian government would soon request from the French government his replacement for the teaching position at Dar al-Fonun. He urged them to have a Mason selected, who would also assume the lodge directorship. The lodge is "exclusively composed of government ministers, deputies, and high administrative officials," and it has a "considerable beneficiary impact on affairs of the country." Its active members, he added, needed "backing by a European enlightened brother."[48]

From Tabriz, French consul Alphonse Nicolas was similarly interested in promoting French cultural influence. He was a high administrative official in the Alliance française, which he represented in Azerbaijan, but had no known affiliation with any Masonic lodge. He focused on spreading the instruction of the French language in the existing foreign schools in the region and even in Moslem schools with financial support from the Alliance. The competition with other foreign schools was fierce, each vying to enroll Persian students. A French Catholic school recently established in Tabriz was successful in attracting Moslem students, provoking the "constant hostility" of the local American Presbyterian school officials, who viewed French institutions "with a cold and calculated hatred."[49] The American missionaries also strongly objected to Nicolas's project for a Franco-Persian school in Orumiyeh to be eventually developed into a college like Beirut's American College. The fierce American opposition did not block the Frenchman's ambitious academic mission to spread French *laic* schools that would counteract the Protestants' "spirit of inquisition" and their imposition of "narrow religious ideas" upon their Moslem students.[50] Nicolas was imbued with a spiritual zeal to "transform" the Persian nation, "lost with superstitions," genuinely impressed as he was by its students' potentials. Governor Mokhber al-Saltaneh encouraged Nicolas's efforts to spread the teaching of the French language, as did the Russian consul Miller until he began to worry about French instructors' "Russophobia."[51] Here, it is worth recalling that although the constitutional intelligentsia may have benefitted from such European support at that time, their predecessors in the mid–nineteenth century had called for a drastic revision of the education system long before any contact with individual European mentors or the establishment of any Masonic lodge, as Monica Ringer has documented.[52]

The Majles education reforms essentially aimed at creating a new class of modern educated civil servants capable of undertaking the immense task of nation-state building. Financial constraints were resolved with a compromise when the Majles voted for free schooling for all children of the poor to be subsidized by fees required from children of well-to-do families.[53] The resolution brought the entire private and public education system under the jurisdiction of the government Ministry of Education and made public elementary schooling universal and compulsory. Despite the political turmoil, the new law with far-reaching educational reform would pass by majority vote shortly before the dissolution of the second Majles, bringing to an end the olama's traditional exclusive authority over the country's education. The highly sensitive issue of the religious endowments, however, remained a hot issue on the Majles agenda when it was later raised for discussion again, as we shall see.

Public Works

Sani' al-Dowleh concentrated even more effort on the broader section of the Ministry of Education and Public Works that dealt with industry, mining, agriculture, and infrastructure construction. He also took in charge revenues from taxes levied on various commodities to finance government projects. Declaring it was time for people to start bearing their financial share of national services, he suggested beginning with a salt tax as a relatively light financial burden to be imposed on the population. Though agreeable to the novel idea, some deputies preferred to have individual provinces decide separately their taxation based on their specific economic circumstances. Local people know best their local needs, they argued, and Tehran's conditions are different from Kurdistan's or Azerbaijan's. Taqizadeh rejected this argument, though he admitted that conditions in different provinces varied. Remaining constant to his effort to build a strong centralized government, he insisted on imposing a single fiscal system throughout the nation. Local *anjomans* cannot have absolute authority in such essential political decision making, he told his peers. Sani' al-Dowleh, politically nonpartisan, agreed with Taqizadeh the Democrat. The Majles voted in great majority in favor of a national, uniform salt taxation,[54] establishing a precedent for a future taxation system.

Sani' al-Dowleh's interest in concessions, domestic or foreign, concerned his and his family's commercial and industrial enterprises linked to European, especially German, companies. He favored free trade and free capitalist markets to be institutionalized with an appropriate law, and he called for regulating mining concessions. In a special Majles session, he addressed the issue by referring to some countries, such as England, where mineral resources are privately owned. In other countries, he went on, natural resources are strictly government properties, but concessions are granted for exploration and exploitation provided they are profitable. In Iran, he stated, concessions to foreign companies must be encouraged to help the nation's development. Compensation should be given to the owner of the land or to the government in case of state ownership. Companies that had already obtained or would obtain permits for exploration, install factories, or trade in commodities would provide the necessary capital. Their imported tools and equipment should be exempt from customs duties. Furthermore, in case of privately owned land, he insisted, the government has absolutely no right to interfere in any way; the nation's economic development depends on free enterprise.[55]

The issue of granting concessions to foreign subjects tended to strike a sensitive cord among many nationalists, given the abuse of this practice by past Qajar monarchs. Taqizadeh had early on in the debates called for enacting laws to regulate all kinds of concessions, including trade in commodities and manufactured goods as well as land sales. The public, he added, should be informed about all financial transactions and leases to companies.[56] Similarly, concerned politicians and government officials were fully aware of the ongoing British oil exploration in the South but resented the secretive negotiations of the concessions granted to the foreign company. The local press and Persian publications abroad warned against drastic consequences of land sale as part of agreed oil concessions, which contravened the law of the country. Agreement to grant a lease, the press articles insisted, had to be revoked once the concession was terminated. The land and all the buildings constructed for its development would then return to the nation, their lawful owner. Some even suggested that trustworthy and competent "supervisors" be sent to secretly watch over the oil works in the South.[57] But, despite the deputies' concern, the terms of the oil concessions granted to European companies prior to the revolution remained secret; there is no mention of any serious and open debate on the subject in the official Majles minutes.

Deputies favoring concessions to foreigners carefully couched their argument, insisting that all companies must have Iranian partners.[58] Opponents vigorously objected to long-term exclusive rights entailing special benefits, which they denounced as detrimental to local industries. Supporters riposted that the country's industrial growth needed competition.[59] Ideological tensions at times, though rarely, surfaced openly in the national debates. Many deputies expressed their fear of trade and industry falling into the hands of wealthy "owners of capital," be they local subjects or foreigners, at the expense of those with less capital to invest in industrial or infrastructure projects. Monopoly was specifically resented; it was conceived as contrary to public interests and to the constitutional principle guaranteeing freedom of trade.[60] Sani' al-Dowleh agreed but argued that Iran was in dire need of technological knowledge and industrial expertise. Not everyone can start a factory. The government, he went on, must help and encourage industrial projects in order to eventually reduce the nation's needs for imported products.[61] As noted earlier, Sani' al-Dowleh and his brother Mokhber al-Saltaneh were known to have intensive contacts with German industrialists, with whom they collaborated to establish factories, especially textile, in Iran.

The debates were lengthy and at times impassioned. Bitter memory of past experiences fueled the opposition to concessions, though the prevailing national dependence on imported goods and technology was fully acknowledged. Many viewed trade and industrial monopoly with profound distaste yet recognized the necessity to exempt imported tools and machines from customs duties. They stated that the nation's plentiful mineral resources could in the future be exploited domestically for exports. Taqizadeh approved the granting of exclusive concession rights to import machines and tools for as long as the country does not manufacture them. "Our country," he explained, "is witnessing the dawn of the age of machines."[62] However, he also carefully distinguished domestic trade from foreign trade and rejected any exclusive right to be conceded to local entrepreneurs. Domestic monopoly, he explained, is detrimental to national development and may lead to corruption. In the end, the deputies voted in majority to exempt from customs duties all imported tools and machines needed for "vital national economic development."[63]

The actual terms for mineral concessions other than oil granted to private companies required longer debates. Sani' al-Dowleh relentlessly called for less-stringent conditions to facilitate foreign companies' capital investment. The terms of their contracts, he insisted, must be indefinite to allow them to recoup their expenses and draw profits; dividends due to the government should be reduced from the 10 percent it currently demanded to 5 percent. Vakil al-Tojjar, a merchant and Moderate deputy, denied the government any exclusive authority to grant concessions to foreign or domestic companies and asserted that Iranian individuals should play an equally important role in exploiting rich national resources. Their wealth would contribute as much to the country's development. Assadollah Mirza, a Qajar prince and Moderate deputy, seconded that motion. Referring explicitly to Sani' al-Dowleh's request for gold extraction, he acknowledged seeing no conflict of interest when a cabinet minister obtained such a concession, which would benefit the entire country. "He is also an individual seeking self-interest like anyone else," he said. Isma'il Nobari, a Democrat, though not opposed to concessions to private companies or individuals, insisted that only state-owned uncultivated land could be conceded to whoever wished it. The owners of private land, however, should be compensated generously. Most deputies agreed with the latter provision.[64]

The debates concerned the merits of capitalist enterprises, company versus individual, foreign versus national ownership. Sani' al-Dowleh's private interest in gaining concessions did not prevent Taqizadeh and his fellow Democrats from voting for his proposals. The realistic feasibility of such proposals and their ultimate beneficiary, the nation, were deemed the sole conditions for approval. Weeks later, Sani' al-Dowleh and Mo'in al-Tojjar were entrusted with determining the terms of concessions to be granted for all mineral exploration in the South of the country, which they were to submit for review to the relevant Majles committee before parliamentary ratification. The *Mozakerat* offers no further details on the issue. Nor does it mention the secret negotiations between Iranian individuals and foreign companies interested in obtaining other concessions; the Majles Financial Committee discussed the issues behind closed doors. Secret, unconstitutional deals took place, defying the deputies and their reform projects' concerns. Mo'in al-Tojjar's lengthy dispute over the Hormoz Island oxide concession that involved two British companies and the British government is a perfect case in point.

Controversial Foreign Concessions

Mo'in al-Tojjar had reportedly by royal decree acquired in 1896 a ten-year concession for the exploitation of the Hormoz Island red-oxide deposits. In 1904, he alleged that he had obtained a renewal of the concession in perpetuity. Vakil al-Ro'aya, who was in charge of the investigation of this concession, contested that claim, arguing that no period was fixed in the document. The issue was of importance because Mo'in al-Tojjar wished to sell the concession to an English company, which the British Foreign Office backed in order to "debar the trade from falling into German hands." But another company countered that it had obtained the rights to explore Hormoz Island on the basis of the original decree of 1896. Mo'in al-Tojjar failed to provide the committee with any valid document as evidence to his claim and consequently was denied any further concession rights on the basis of the new law. Unsavory and murky facts hidden from public debates marred the intensive negotiations between all interested parties, including the British envoy to Tehran. Sani' al-Dowleh, then minister of education and public works, played a large role in the negotiations. But Mo'in al-Tojjar relentlessly pursued his "legitimate" ownership case to the bitter end; it took more than a year of wrangling among all parties involved, until weeks before the closing of the second Majles. At stake was the effective applicability of the new laws pertaining to the granting of concessions to foreigners, which Mo'in al-Tojjar tried to circumvent.

The issue of land lease in Abadan to the British Oil Company (later called British Petroleum) proved to be far more complex to resolve. It involved a powerful industry that enjoyed the British Foreign Office's full support and the local Abadan influential tribal chieftain, Shaikh Khazal of Mohammereh, who was engaged in a fierce power struggle with other tribal leaders in the region, including Sardar As'ad and the Bakhtiyari's nemesis Isma'il Khan Sulat al-Dowleh, the Qashqa'i *ilkhan*. In late April 1910, Sardar As'ad, then minister of the interior, informed George Churchill, the British Oriental secretary, that Shaikh Khazal, in competition with the rival Bakhtiyari tribe, controlled much of the oil-rich region in the South but had no right to sell or lease land that was strictly government property. The state owned all, he asserted, and the shaikh was under investigation for any unlawful transaction he may have made. Sardar As'ad even threatened to forcibly appoint another chief in his place. Thereupon Churchill warned him that such action "might be prejudicial to the British Oil Company's interests" and even hinted that "His Majesty's Government might have some understanding with the sheikh by which he would be entitled to their support against the Persian Government."[65] The message to the Persian officials was quite clear.

Charles Marling, who was replacing Barclay on leave that summer, had also sent an even stronger message through J. R. Preece, a representative of a financial group seeking concessions in exchange for a loan to Iran. Preece had developed close ties with the Bakhtiyaris. On May 2, 1910, he met with Sardar As'ad to remind him of the concession terms that entitled the Anglo-Persian Oil Company to purchase or lease land without any government interference. Indeed, the company had recently paid the Bakhtiyaris £5,000 for the land needed to lay the pipeline. He insisted that Sardar As'ad, as a Bakhtiyari, "could not hold the opposite," adding that the British government "would not allow any interference" with Shaikh Khazal. Preece subsequently sent further warnings to Sardar As'ad about "the danger to his own position if he persisted in his unfriendly attitude to His Majesty's Government."[66] Thus sobered, Minister of Interior Sardar As'ad promised that his government would no longer pursue the matter. Marling believed that the minister had doubtless raised the issue in the first place in order to acquire a share in the compensation advanced to Shaikh Khazal as well as to cause his tribal enemy serious trouble with the government. The British diplomat had found out that the land in question belonged to the shaikh by "hereditary occupation," as was the case with the Bakhtiyaris' and other tribes' land ownership. However, the royal decree had explicitly forbidden the sale of such land. Another case in point involving Shaikh Khazal's successful defiance of Tehran authority concerned his dispute with the Ottoman government over his claim to land in Basra, then part of the Ottoman Empire. The Ottoman official in Basra turned down a British offer to mediate the Turco-Persian frontier. Thereupon, the Foreign Office, although favoring a status quo that safeguarded Ottoman state territorial claims, insisted on warning the official that the shaikh of Mohammereh was under British protection, which justified intervention by the British government.[67]

As the Shaikh Khazal episodes amply demonstrate, domestic intrigues and individual greed, compounded by foreign governments' interventions, further exacerbated the Majles's struggle to assert its authority in the remote provinces. In fact, Tehran had no say concerning some of its most valuable national resources. The Majles's well-meaning reform projects and expressed concerns to protect national interests could not disrupt the deeply entrenched corrupt Qajar system of secret dealings benefitting a few. Thus, while the deputies were still deliberating terms and conditions to be attached to concessions, reports of a shady deal involving the Ministry of Finance and an unknown company created uproar in their midst.

Domestic Companies

A group of Tehran merchants informed the Majles that a private company had secretly been granted a sixteen-year lease for state land in the capital. The constitutionality of the deal was raised, leading to a rare Majles debate concerning the plight of landless peasants and issues of land use, property rights, and privileges. The dividing line between private and public property was at that time still murky. The fight was even more alluring because well-born officials owned or wished to own exclusive development rights over state land for industrial and commercial projects. One deputy after another, most of them Democrats, vehemently denounced the concession for failing to consider its drastic consequences on the livelihood of Tehran's resident poor. It is our duty, one Democrat deputy loudly proclaimed, to protect the peasants' future, to improve their living conditions, and to enable them to buy property. The properties in question, he emphasized, cannot be entrusted to a company for sixteen years, thus condemning the peasants there to a life of misery for that length of time. Nobari, another Democrat, objected to the lease as incompatible with the Constitution. No Majles can ratify such a contract giving individuals total authority over a plot of land to manage as they please, he asserted. "How could the minister of finance allow it?"[68] Some Moderate deputies warned against revoking the contract, for it would cost the government dearly, financially and politically. It would also incite the peasants to rebel and reject the owner's authority. Taqizadeh objected to the old Qajar regime practice of leasing government income-producing properties to private individuals. The practice displayed a sign of government weakness, he said, and he insisted on the lawful procedure of Majles ratification for all such contracts. These debates, he further remarked, would not have taken place had all deputies abided by the rules regulating such transactions. He was deliberately pointing the finger at some of his colleagues for alleged violation of the law.[69] The Majles Finance Committee was ordered to investigate the contract leasing the state land in Tehran to a foreign company. The committee then decided to revoke it, advising the government to buy back the land in question and, should it decide to lawfully lease it to a company, obtain the prior Majles ratification. The Democrats and other nonaligned deputies won that battle in the Majles, but the issue of land reform was not addressed.

The Majles attached specific conditions for all concessions to be granted to domestic companies: official inspectors to be sent regularly for supervision; no foreign nationals to be allowed to share in the concession; all antiquities and precious-gem mines to remain exclusively state properties.[70] For instance, after lengthy debates in several sessions, an eighteen-year-long concession for the Mashhad–Barforush road construction in Khorasan was granted to Khodadad Parsi, an Iranian Zoroastrian merchant also known as Sasani.[71] The concession bore all the approved stringent measures.[72] Although this debate seemed to display overtones of ideological clashes, in fact it defies any attempt to frame it along those lines. All deputies were in favor of private capital investment in modernizing projects benefitting the nation.

The heated debates in the Majles on the terms of concession were limited to just a few domestic cases. All important industrial and commercial projects involving international concerns, including oil exploration and the construction of railway lines, were discussed by the special committees in closed-door sessions. The *Mozakerat* omitted all such references, leaving the majority of the deputies and the public in the dark, thus arousing their suspicion. The balance between national economic sovereignty and technological-financial dependence on foreign expertise was not addressed. The modernization process the nationalists advocated so unanimously would open even wider the gates to European economic penetration. Whether conscious of the dichotomy or not, the nationalists were confronting what would prove to be the biggest threat to the nation's independence. As we shall see, from behind the scenes European powers vigilantly kept the government in check, intriguing with some co-opted officials or politically maneuvering to set one against another and severely hampering the country's development of any major project needing foreign assistance.

The Judiciary

The state of the Ministry of Justice preoccupied most deputies, Democrats and Moderates alike. Many deputies openly expressed their opinion that the ministry should be reformed according to the model of "all civilized nations," though vaguely adding that it also had to conform with Islamic principles. They wished to reduce drastically the olama's jurisdiction in matters of public affairs and to abrogate some existing laws,[73] while Ayatollah Khorasani repeatedly cabled from Najaf, demanding the implementation of clause 2 of the Supplement to the Fundamental Law of 1907, requiring a council of five *mojtaheds* to ensure the compatibility of all laws to the sharia before their passage. The olama presented their list of twenty *mojtaheds*, from which the Majles would select five, but the deputies kept delaying their vote. Mohammad Hashem Mirza, the nonpartisan prince-deputy, objected to Khorasani's specific desire to limit the choice to "*mojtaheds* of high ranks," finding it inconsistent with the constitutional clause. He called for the elimination of such restrictive wording from the minutes.[74] Heated debates over clause 2 followed, dividing the Democrats from the religious conservatives and some Moderates, who thought the olama, not the Majles, should select the five *mojtaheds* from the proposed list. Seyyed Jalil Ardabili, the Azerbaijan Democrat, and Vakil al-Ro'aya, the Moderate, noted the unconstitutionality of the olama's interference in nonreligious matters, arguing it was the Majles's prerogative to select the five. It is incumbent upon all to obey the *mojtaheds*' rulings on religious-related matters, they admitted, but not their rulings on political affairs. Ardabili and Vakil al-Ro'aya recalled the olama's decree asking the faithful to abide by the Fundamental Law and declaring disobedience tantamount to "waging war against the Imams."[75]

Ayatollah Khorasani and some of his partisans in the Majles angrily denounced the alleged widespread defiance of religious prohibitions,[76] such as consumption of alcohol, gambling, the sale of lottery tickets, and the use of imported phonographs defusing music in the streets. Many deputies, Democrats and Moderates alike, stressed their concern with the proper adherence to the holy law, which embodied the moral values of the nation, but they insisted on the Majles's responsibility to enforce the religious prohibitions. Taqizadeh took the opportunity to claim for public officials equal right to enforce them. He accused the religious authorities of failing to accomplish properly their function during the period of despotism. Weeks later, when the Majles discussed a new legislation forbidding gambling, the aristocrat-deputy Fahim al-Saltaneh raised his objections on the grounds that gambling fell under the olama's jurisdiction; Nasrollah Mo'azed al-Saltaneh, the Moderate, rejected the argument on the grounds that the olama's prohibition had failed; therefore, a state law was needed to enforce it.[77] The anticlerical elements in the Majles were thus appropriating the right to interfere in matters of religious affairs by arguing that some olama were not fulfilling their obligations. The detractors of these elements began to spread rumors about some deputies' alleged antireligious tendencies, specifically targeting Taqizadeh, as we shall see.

The parliamentary Justice Committee, which included the secular-minded Qajar prince Assadollah Mirza and two prominent Democrats, Shaikh Ibrahim Zanjani and Solaiman Mirza, began a rigorous investigation of popular discontent. There were nationwide reports of recurring bread shortages due to hoarding and a fraudulent system of grain distribution. Government officials were accused of granting a company exclusive rights to purchase and sell wheat to bakers in return for cash remunerations. Taqizadeh blamed the Ministry of Interior directly for the corrupt practices and demanded those in charge to put an immediate end to it. Corrupt merchants had to be brought to trial and publicly punished to avert violent bread riots. The Majles, it was said, would no longer tolerate such fraud causing misery among the poor.[78] The bread shortage is right now the most important issue confronting the nation, the deputies told government officials. Some intriguers are using it as a pretext to foment political turmoil and raise a "wall between the nation and the Majles."[79]

Numerous letters poured in from the provinces, denouncing officials' cruel misconduct and abuse of power. Zoroastrians in Kerman and Yazd complained of discriminatory treatment by local officials. The Majles sternly admonished government ministers for failing to implement the Fundamental Law, by which equal rights were granted to all citizens, their life and property were safeguarded, and they were protected from arbitrary arrest unless lawfully charged with a crime by a written warrant signed by a court of justice.[80] Persistent public outcry accusing "some" deputies of working against public interests as though they were the "people's enemies" compelled the Majles to appoint a special twelve-member commission to investigate the validity of the complaints and to propose solutions.[81] Nasrollah Khan Moshir al-Dowleh, the minister of justice, promptly resigned and was replaced by Sardar Mansur, an ally of the Sepahdar, a fellow Gilani who was at that time minister of the interior. Moshir al-Dowleh then took over the Ministry of Trade.

The special commission investigated shortages of bread and various complaints of injustice committed by officials. Weeks later, armed with its conclusive findings, it recommended the establishment of several new judicial institutions.[82] Chief among them was a Court of Appeals (Tamiz) to allow the defendants a last resort for justice. The idea of this judicial institution had been created on paper at the time of the first Majles but never implemented. The deputies now recommended that the Court of Appeals should acquire also the power to oversee the judicial pronouncements of all judges. However, until the court was formally established, a committee of Majles deputies was appointed to carry out its functions. The legislative branch was thus allowed to substitute for the judiciary, at least temporarily, contravening the constitutional separation of powers. In addition, the Majles proposed a special judicial chamber to be formed to help all plaintiffs identify the source of the charges against them and understand the legal procedures undertaken. The twelve-member special commission also called for the nomination of some olama to be members of the Ministry of Justice in order to prevent any judgment that might "conflict" with the sharia. Last, it asked the religious courts to acquaint the government with all currently presiding judges.

Democrats enthusiastically endorsed all the recommendations, which they perceived as essential for reforming the entire judiciary. They would install a "healthy" and fair social environment necessary for the good functioning of the executive branch of government. The Ministry of Justice, Hashtrudi the Democrat insisted, should demand that the olama designate and appoint worthy religious judges, to whom all religious cases would be referred before sending them to the ministry for final sentencing. Hajj Aqa Ibrahim, a cleric-deputy, proposed reserving a special room in the ministry to be recognized as the religious court's official abode. It would prevent people from complaining that the ministry was interfering in matters pertaining to religious affairs. In contrast, Vakil al-Tojjar, who supported the proposed institutional innovations, called for eliminating the old regime government officials' widely abused practice of mediating on behalf of a defendant. Similarly, he insisted no minister should be allowed to take upon himself the right to charge, arrest, or judge anyone without solid evidence of wrongdoing.[83]

Tensions between the cabinet ministers and the Majles increased in the summer 1910. By that time, a serious political crisis also divided the ranks of the cabinet and escalated the hostility between some ministers and the Majles. Rumors that Najaf ayatollahs were raising questions of individual legislators' religious "blasphemy" began to spread more widely, chiefly targeting Taqizadeh. To turn off the harsh spotlight suddenly highlighting the radical legislative proposals, some deputies toned down their critical voice. They now hailed the revolutionary contributions of the olama, the Sepahdar, and Sardar As'ad and adopted a less-intransigent, more-prudent approach, thus delaying the implementation of the far-reaching judiciary reforms. The gap between ambitious aspiration to reform and the need for caution due to existing midsummer political reality kept on widening. Deputies were resigning from their posts in various committees, slowing down the work done by the Majles. The Justice Committee especially was losing many of its members, further reducing the pressure exerted on the Ministry of Justice to establish the Court of Appeals, a cornerstone of judiciary reforms. The twelve-member Majles special commission also saw changes in its composition to include more Moderates. Its chief tasks to supervise the administration of justice, to check potential noncompliance to constitutional rules, and to help redress the plight of "oppressed people" were challenged for as long as the Tamiz court was not in place.[84]

It is important to note here that the challenge to the twelve-member commission came from deputies irrespective of their party affiliation, though Democrats voiced their opposition more than the Moderates. Critics such as the Moderate Shaikh al-Ra'is accused the commission of assuming judiciary functions and hence running counter to the constitutional division of power. He found a surprising champion in the person of Solaiman Mirza, the staunch Democrat, who then forcefully reminded the commission that its task was to inspect the justice system and not to execute justice. The intention behind its formation, he proclaimed, was not to "blend legislative power with executive power. That would be an innovation totally contrary to the Fundamental Law." Judicial courts, he further asserted, can be reformed only once the Tamiz is established.[85] Assadollah Mirza, the prominent Moderate member of the commission who was emerging as a powerful voice in the Majles, vehemently rejected the rebuke. The commission, he retorted, was acting in lieu of the Tamiz, as originally planned. It was helping distressed people who had turned to the Majles to intervene on their behalf in preventing unwarranted judgments; it would not try to overturn any judgments. The minister of justice, he argued, is not the sole guilty party, for there were other individuals in the ministry equally guilty of not properly carrying out justice. Assadollah Mirza specifically resented the hostile attack on the commission, given the troubles it went through and the long hours of hard work spent for the sake of people's safety and well-being.[86] Other deputies rose in his defense, claiming the commission was in fact set up to reform the judiciary and not just to inspect it. Some expressed their puzzlement that Solaiman Mirza raised such objections to the very commission in which he had originally participated to resolve the bread crisis. Why should he now oppose the judicial task performed by its other members? the nonpartisan Qajar prince Mohammad Hashem Mirza asked.[87]

It was a pertinent question. By the summer of 1910, the political climate had definitely turned against Taqizadeh. Rumors were rapidly spreading that he was an enemy of Islam, unworthy to sit in the Majles. This state of affairs would force him to ask for a temporary three-month leave of absence, which was granted. He hoped to return once the dust had settled—an unrealistic hope, given the intensity of the political crisis, as we shall see in the next chapter. Most other Democrats, feeling the heat, similarly were compelled to cautiously tone down their political rhetoric favoring secular reforms and used the constitutional division of powers as a convenient justification for their sudden otherwise inexplicable about-face.

The fierce discussion about the Tamiz commission continued unabated in a subsequent session chaired by Assadollah Mirza in his capacity as recently elected deputy Speaker. He raised the fundamental question: Is the Tamiz commission in charge of implementing justice or only inspecting the judiciary? The Majles has to resolve the issue, he urgently told his colleagues. Solaiman Mirza expressed his right to oppose the commission's action. Prominent Democrats, including Taqizadeh, stood by him, denying legislators the authority to intervene in the judiciary. The committee, they stated, should limit its role to investigating the justice minister's and his staff's wrongdoing. Nobari, the Tabriz Democrat, qualified people's complaints as rumors not based on factual cases.[88] Seyyed Jalil Ardabili, one of the rare Democrats not reversing his view, recalled the ample evidence of judicial courts' "treachery" that proved the legitimacy of the victims' complaints. The commission members, he stated, had gone through three hundred cases, with much effort and time consumed. And now, he lamented, the Majles is attacking instead of supporting the commission members, "cooling their desire" to continue, and thus leaving their work incomplete. The commission, he emphasized, indeed stands in for the Tamiz and must be authorized to continue. Moderates, who were not targeted in the vicious rumormongering, supported him. Assadollah Mirza finally reminded the deputies that they had granted that authorization by majority vote. The debate ended inconclusively as the majority this time voted to postpone any decision until a growing government crisis was resolved.[89]

The political storm that was then gathering strength hampered the deputies' exercise of power in parliamentary governance. It also affected the curious positioning of the Democrats. The convoluted history of the second Majles's reforms is not easy to deconstruct, so entangled are its debates, with its various actors' professed political stands, genuinely assumed or simulated, often running counter to their proposed intentions. Moreover, foreign powers' constant involvement in the country's government and business affairs, mostly secret and not necessarily compatible with their respective public pronouncements, displayed international concerns that had no direct relevance to facts on the ground in Iran. The semblance of an independent, constitutional, and democratic National Assembly composed of different factions working in unison to create from scratch a modern state was in fact masking a harsher reality. Both invisible and sometimes visible strings were attached to the deputies and ministers alike, rendering the achievement of their stated enterprise much more complex.

7

European Interventionism

AS ALREADY STATED, the Anglo-Russian Convention of 1907, which divided Iran into three zones of influence, marked what seemed to be the end of almost a century of the two powers' rivalry in the region. They had acknowledged their respective interests while adopting, in theory, a policy respecting the country's independence and territorial integrity. The convention, however, did not lay the competition to rest. The historic reality proves the policy was sheer fiction deluding no one involved, not even the Iranians. In fact, neither power intended to treat the country as a sovereign nation: territorial integrity did not mean national sovereignty. Moreover, by consistently sustaining an attitude of mutual acquiescence, the two powers obstructed any Iranian attempt to assert even a semblance of national liberty in pursuing financial or government policies without the two powers' prior joint consent.

As amply evidenced in archival records, London and St. Petersburg maintained their control over Tehran's political scene. Russia had initially suggested establishing a second legislative chamber, a Senate, to counterbalance the Majles. Its members would be appointed rather than elected by popular vote. However, Lord Grey and Barclay thought such a chamber was of "doubtful utility" and believed it unwise to give the deputies the impression that the Russians and British were intriguing against them.[1] Indeed, the Majles voted against the proposal when government officials introduced it several months later. Taqizadeh was the most outspoken in rejecting the motion, which was endorsed by many notables, merchants, the Bakhtiyaris, and Ayatollah Khorasani.[2] The British and Russian envoys retained control, choreographing the game of musical chairs in forming successive cabinets and closely watched the Majles's undertakings. Despite his personal misgivings over Russian military action and his basic sympathy for the constitutional movement, Barclay supported tsarist imperial demands as legitimate in its zone of influence.

French diplomats pursued a consistent policy supportive of the two powers' agreement. Determined to reverse the outcome of the German victory over France in 1870, France had signed a defense alliance with Russia in 1894 and the Anglo-French Entente Cordial with Britain in 1903. Subsequently, the historic Triple Entente of 1907 consolidated the alliance of the three European powers, in part to counter the older Triple Alliance of Germany, Austria, and Italy of 1882. In his excellent detailed analysis of the intricate European alliances prior to 1914, Christopher Clark explains how the bipolar geostrategic system "structured the environment in which the crucial decisions were made."[3] As applied specifically to Iran, this "polarization of Europe" would inevitably have drastic if not fatal consequences for the second Majles.

The Great Game and the "German Threat"

Germany, Clark writes, was "in the position of parvenu" in the Great Game of that time. Its acquisitions of colonies were meager in comparison to those made by the mighty empires Britain, France, and Russia, which left no place at the "crowded table" in their exclusive "established club."[4] The intricate system of inter-European alliances compounded Germany's sense of isolation within the continent. When Germany established commercial ties with South African authorities, Sir Francis Bertie, then assistant undersecretary at the Foreign Office, who was notorious for his hostility to Germany, aggressively threatened war if it "lays so much as a finger" in that region. "The entire English nation would be behind it [war]," he told the German ambassador to England, "and a blockade of Hamburg and Bremen and the annihilation of German commerce on the high seas would be child's play for the English fleet."[5] But at that time Berlin's decision makers were creating their own policy of *Welt Politik*, enhancing Germany's presence in the non-European world despite its marginal colonial possessions. When they determinedly concentrated on expanding German economic interests in the Ottoman Empire, the European powers, especially Britain, were seriously alarmed. By the beginning of the twentieth century, Anglo-German tension intensified as German enterprises further developed commercial and industrial projects in the region. However, the terms of the Anglo-Russian Convention of 1907 persistently stifled Germany's expansion efforts in Persia and the Persian Gulf region.

The accession of Sir Edward Grey to the post of foreign secretary in December 1905, which he retained until December 1916, further solidified the influence of pro-Russian, anti-German elements within the Foreign Office, despite lingering deep distrust of tsarist imperialist ambitions. Widespread dissenting opinion was dismissed, and in the "official mind" of British foreign policy, Clark notes, quoting Bertie, that the Germans were "deliberately aiming at world predominance" with their rising economic power and at "push[ing] [the British] into the water and steal[ing] [their] clothes."[6] The extreme paranoiac perception of German policies predominated as Grey consolidated his influence by promoting officials who shared his views. Clark's intensive research in British archives led him to believe that the "invention" of Germany as "the key threat to Britain" was perpetuated by Sir Francis Bertie, the permanent secretary at the Foreign Office and subsequently its ambassador in Paris.[7] Both Sir Charles Harding, former envoy to Tehran, and Sir Arthur Nicolson, then envoy to St. Petersburg, shared Bertie's hawkish perception, enhancing Grey's resolute pro-Russia stand.

They were the three diplomats who shaped British policy outcomes in Iran in the historical period under consideration. Nicolson in particular consistently supported a close alliance with Russia, defending Russia's intervention in Iran against its detractors in London's decision-making centers. Indeed, though the Anglo-Russian Convention "muted the tensions" between the two countries, there were voices in the Foreign Office, in Parliament, and in the press who justifiably worried about the "policy of appeasement toward Russia" and warned of the "Russian threat to Britain's far-flung empire."[8] Grey's own Liberal Party and government in power were divided between the liberal imperialists and "radical elements." Before World War I, writes Clark, some among the cultural and political elite tended to be more pro-Germany, professing "a deep admiration of the country's cultural, economic and scientific achievements."[9] Many were highly critical of the Triple Entente and of the foreign minister's and his supporters' provocative anti-German policy, which they felt might encourage Germany to adopt a more aggressive stand. Such voices were often heard in Parliament, in the press, and in the British consulates in Tehran and Tabriz.[10] Nonetheless, Lord Grey worked closely with his Russian counterpart Alexander Izvolski, who enjoyed a great measure of independence within his own government in formulating Russian foreign policy. Izvolski, who had signed the convention in 1907, believed that the new relations would grant him the freedom to expand Russian power in the Turkish Straits and in Russia's Persian sphere of influence.

The Quai d'Orsay (Ministry of Foreign Affairs) similarly acquired autonomy from the rest of the French cabinet, secretively guarding information from other ministers. The two brothers Jules and Paul Cambon, the French ambassadors to Berlin and London, respectively, became important decision makers, often acting independently of the foreign minister. Paul Cambon, who kept his post in London from 1898 to 1914, reportedly would "not infrequently burn" instructions from Paris when he disagreed with them.[11] Similarly, judging from his dispatches from Tehran, French ambassador Lecomte's attitude toward Persian personalities was influential in shaping his ministry's policy, especially when Stephen Pichon was the foreign minister from October 1906 to March 1911. Pichon was known for his lukewarm interest in ministerial affairs and his regular absenteeism.[12]

Lecomte's ambassadorial tenure in Tehran lasted the same number of years as Pichon's term as foreign minister, with a brief interlude in Paris during the Lesser Despotism. He diligently watched over the sustainability of the bilateral Anglo-Russian agreement, rescuing it whenever traditional mutual distrust and political differences threatened its survival. French representatives in Iran were ordered to mediate between the two powers "discreetly" and "disinterestedly." In fact, France in that period attached great importance to a strong Anglo-Russian alliance, which it deemed vital for the balance of European power. When Nikolai Hartwig, the intransigent Russian ambassador, was recalled to Moscow prior to the restoration of the Constitution in Iran, Lecomte doubled his vigilance. He worried that the shah would feel "liberated from the heavy Russian tutelage" and ready to be "seduced by the Germans." That would create a "dangerous situation," he reported, because the new Russian envoy, Sablin, and his British counterpart, Barclay, were too "inexperienced."[13] The French, the "discreet missing link" in the regional politics to use Mariam Habibi's term,[14] thus came to play an essential part in the European interventionism that severely hampered the constitutionalists' struggles to safeguard national sovereignty.

When Sani' al-Dowleh, Taqizadeh, and Navab proved to be more independent-minded nationalists than Barclay had thought, he unequivocally labeled them "extremists." By loudly voicing their opposition to Russian troops' occupation and seeking financial sources other than the Anglo-Russian proposals to fund the nation's modernizing reforms, the nationalists found themselves pawns in a European geopolitical-economic exercise of power. These so-called extremists were to fatally encounter the powers' fierce adversity.

Anti-Russian Sentiment

In a meeting with Izvolski held in London shortly after the fall of Tehran in the summer of 1909, Grey called for a quick evacuation of Russian troops to put an end to the anti-Russian mood prevailing in the country as a whole. He assured his Russian colleague that Great Britain would comply with the convention and, when needed, would cooperate with the Russian government "to prevent changes in Persia which would be to the disadvantage of Russia."[15] Barclay, who that summer still believed that "the recent revolution was a rebellion against Russian influence," a sentiment he deemed "perfectly natural and intelligible," worried that the "nationalists had too high an expectation of a decrease" of this influence. He optimistically thought he had convinced them to follow his "counsels of moderation" and hoped the Majles "will prove as reasonable."[16] Indeed, Mostashar al-Dowleh had decided, in his capacity as Speaker of the Majles, not to allow "too heated" speeches about "neighboring powers" and had promised to "diligently supervise" the deputies.[17] Events in the following months would prove Barclay wrong and Mostashar al-Dowleh unable to do what he promised.

In February 1910, suspected Russian complicity in Rahim Khan's and the Shahsavan tribesmen's savage raids in the North exacerbated popular resentment of the continued military presence in Tabriz and Qazvin. In a special session, the Majles took to task the deputy minister of foreign affairs Mirza Isma'il Khan Theqat al-Molk, asking him to explain the government's failure to liberate the provinces. Whereas the Moderates adopted a cooler tone, mentioning the nation's "wounded hearts" and insisting that "friendly relations" be maintained in the discussions, the Democrats unleashed their anger at the Russians and the cabinet ministers alike. Taqizadeh then delivered one of his most fiery speeches, consolidating his national popularity and hence his political clout in the Majles. In what reads like a long passionate soliloquy, he referred to the occupation as a traumatic experience, inflicting a humiliation that Iranians felt deeply down "to their skin and bones." It has been nine months, he said, since the troops' arrival, a consequence of the previous regime's wrongdoing. The people of Tabriz had begged the shah to lift the siege, offering in exchange their readiness to submit to his rule, if only to prevent the Russian invasion—to no avail. The Russians had come on the pretext of establishing order and safety, but, in fact, they brought insecurity and chaos. They came to Qazvin ostensibly to protect foreign lives against possible assault by the Bakhtiyaris, but they also recently sent their troops to Ardabil, with no excuse this time. There is no more reason for the troops to remain on Iranian soil, he clamored forcefully, except to "prevent our government from functioning properly, to render it powerless." In conclusion, Taqizadeh reminded the government of their obligation to negotiate speedily the withdrawal of the troops, to be guaranteed by the British government, and keep the Majles informed. Evoking the power of the legislature to check the executive action, he insisted the negotiations not be kept secret, for the Ministry of Foreign Affairs is part of the government, and the government is accountable to the Majles. He accused Minister of Foreign Affairs Ala' al-Dowleh, who had failed to come in person to the Majles when summoned, of lying to the people and of keeping the Majles in the dark as to his real intentions and relationship with the Russians.[18]

In fact, Ala' al-Dowleh was the Russian choice for the post against the nationalists' wishes, and he was accused of grossly neglecting to protect national independence. "Our ministers," claimed another Democrat, "have facilitated their [the Russians'] occupation, contravening international law."[19] The deputy minister's denial of all charges and assurances of an imminent evacuation failed to convince them. In reality, shortly after Yeprem Khan and his militia defeated Rahim Khan and the Shahsavans and order was restored, more than three thousand Russian soldiers marched to Ardabil and East Azerbaijan despite Barclay's vigorous protests.[20] In contrast, Barclay's Foreign Office colleague in St. Petersburg, Sir Arthur Nicolson, had persistently justified Russian forces in Azerbaijan. "European representations about national sovereignty," Nicolson would often cynically argue, "do not in any way apply to the conditions of Asiatic life, and the nominal Persian government has no use except as a convenient address for diplomatic representations. It is not in a position to be really answerable for its acts; and whether we like or not, we must defend ourselves by such means as will guarantee the safety of Russians and other foreigners."[21] In Tehran, exasperated by the persistent critique of Russian policy, Lecomte dismissed the English "blind cult of parliamentarian institutions." Russia, he asserted, had the most to lose in remaining true to the Anglo-Russian Convention.[22]

On February 5, 1910, the Majles voted in majority to censure Ala' al-Dowleh; thereby, to Russia's annoyance, he was forced to resign. He was temporarily replaced by his deputy until several weeks later Mirza Ibrahim

Khan Mo'aven al-Dowleh was appointed to the post. Anti-Russian voices did not subside. Articles published daily denounced the occupation, and *Iran-e now* covered extensively the special Majles debate with the foreign-affairs minister, keeping the public informed. Najaf sent cables signed by the ayatollahs Khorasani and Mazandarani calling for the end of the occupation by foreign troops.[23] In his eyewitness account written later, Sharif-Kashani expresses the general dismay with the exposed politicians' corruption and betrayal: "How could our minister of foreign affairs be a Russian agent?"[24] For weeks on end, the press continually aroused nationalist sentiment. Some olama called on the bazaar's traders to forego celebrating Nowruz, the coming national holiday, to express their sorrow; this was no time to rejoice, they said. Azerbaijan deputies informed Tabriz of their intention to renounce the festivities,[25] and cables were sent to ask other provinces to follow suit.

As leader of the most vocal and most intransigent anti-Russian elements within the legislative assembly, Taqizadeh was able to reach out to a large public in the capital and provinces. His partisans in Tabriz had sent to Lord Grey an "earnest appeal to the English people" through the good offices of Shaikh Hasan Tabrizi, Browne's assistant in Cambridge. The note, dated March 7, 1910, takes to task the British government for not honoring its pledge to respect Persia's integrity and independence, as enunciated in the Anglo-Russian Convention. It accused the British of complicity in the Russian military intervention and continuing occupation on the pretext of restoring order and protecting foreign nationals, even though "neither now nor in the past, have Europeans been in any danger." It declared: "History will not forget that England has stained her honor in this matter, and has forgotten to be the champion of liberty or the defender of an oppressed people who had trusted that honor." The emotional message ended with the statement: "All we desire is Persia for the Persians."[26] Though its wording recalled Browne's views, the letter echoed the passionate sentiment expressed in the open sessions of the Majles and in articles published in the Iranian liberal press.

Russian troops in the North reportedly carried out harsh measures to impose its rule, obstructing Mokhber al-Saltaneh's effort to govern Azerbaijan and restore order and repeatedly threatening to reinforce Russia's presence in Tabriz. The French consul in Tabriz, Alphonse Nicolas, who, in contrast to his compatriot Lecomte in Tehran would not at that time condone tsarist policies, reported that the Russian consulate was an "active manufacturer of false and sensationalist news and alarming rumors."[27] Miller, the Russian consul in Tabriz, would later explain to his French counterpart: "We occupy so we can, at the slightest provocation, intervene militarily to defend our interests and punish our opponents."[28] The Russian official, Nicolas commented, is obeyed but feared, and other consuls in town can do nothing. Indeed, Russian imperialist policy repeatedly and blatantly exercised its principle of a fear-based power and reminded the local population of it. Thus, for instance, when on June 16, 1910, a Russian deserter found refuge in the *mojtahed* Theqat al-Islam's house, the Cossacks penetrated it without warrant or prior warning. The action was deemed a "sacrilege," stirring popular outrage; it also angered Nicolas. He protested officially against such interference in the internal affairs of the city, "where governing becomes impossible."[29] The French diplomat's protest was of no consequence; other foreign diplomats were equally helpless in countering Russian brutality, as he had earlier remarked. Theqat al-Islam, the constitutionalist *mojtahed*, remained a favorite target of Miller and General Snarsky, the military commander in Tabriz. Nicolas also blamed Miller and the occupying troops for the ethnic-sectarian violence occurring periodically throughout Azerbaijan, involving Ottoman Turks, Kurds, and Armenians. Russian aggressive politics, he wrote, terrorized one segment of the population, the Moslems, and "agitated a turbulent minority." He was convinced that foreign interventions were the real cause behind the Moslem–Christian troubles.[30]

Despite pressure from the Majles and the public, the Russian envoy consistently upheld his intransigent stand against any troop withdrawal "unless the Persian government changes its attitude."[31] Furthermore, Russian authorities turned down Tabriz's repeated request for the arrest of Rahim Khan or at least his removal far from the northern frontier. The Russians reportedly treated him as a "political refugee."[32] Although Grey worried that unrest in Azerbaijan might further damage Persian–Russian relations, his envoy to St. Petersburg seriously warned him against any inclination to disapprove of Russia's attitude or to side with the Persian government.[33] From Tehran, Lecomte continued to justify Russia's "moderately cautious" behavior in Tabriz and persisted in claiming that Germany was inciting radical Iranian anti-Russian activities.[34] As for Barclay, who was witnessing the political tension escalating between prominent deputies and government officials, he came to realize that his hope that "moderation" would prevail in the Majles was ill founded. By late January 1910, the execution of Movaqqar al-Saltaneh in a manner he considered barbaric left him with no more illusion about the "moderate" nationalists' ability to contain the "radicals."[35]

The Movaqqar al-Saltaneh Episode and Its International Effects

Movaqqar al-Saltaneh, a relative of the deposed shah and brother of Ala' al-Dowleh, had been a member of the Réveil de l'Iran lodge and had actively participated in the constitutional movement, though his Masonic "brothers" suspected his real motives for doing so. Following the coup in 1908, he took refuge in the Russian legation before departing for Europe, where he reportedly revealed Masonic secrets. He returned to Tehran in late January 1910, enjoying the Sepahdar's hospitality and expecting his former constitutionalist comrades would grant him amnesty. Instead, he was immediately arrested on charges of conspiracy to foment turmoil in the capital and tried in a court presided by several "radicals" on January 26, 1910. Expecting a lenient sentence, he apparently revealed more secrets, but he was tortured and then executed the next day.

Regardless of whoever made the decisive order for the execution, the French lodge or the radical wing of the Democrat Party, the event received bad press in London. It left the British public with the impression that "Iran is still the same Iran of the era of despotism; no humanism, no civilization, the same old savagery remaining," Browne wrote to Taqizadeh, urging him to impress upon Iranian officials the utmost need to exercise "moderation" and "compassion." Enemies abound, he added; they must not be given any opportunity to speak ill of Iran, as they had on the occasion of Nuri's execution.[36] Even before this recent execution, Browne had warned Taqizadeh of the British press turning generally hostile to the constitutionalists, and the Persia Committee by then was practically nonexistent. Lynch, he explained, one of the committee's most important founders, "whose ideas I could not share nor [*sic*] accept," had also kept aloof from its members, and the Persian embassy in Britain was "not free of the smell of despotism."[37] Expatriates in Europe were equally appalled by the negative publicity Movaqqar al-Saltaneh's execution had acquired abroad.[38]

Such warnings came from different directions at a time when the nationalists, facing insurmountable Anglo-Russian obstructions and widespread disrepute in international public opinion, were confronting another vexing issue concerning much needed loans.

The Loan Negotiations

Both Moderates and Democrats in the Majles maintained a united front in their search for vitally needed loans that would least damage their country's independence. As stated earlier, the government had raised funds from former officials and grandees in return for amnesty as well as from wealthy individuals imbued with patriotic zeal. However, those funds failed to meet the government's desperate financial needs. By mid-December 1909, it applied for an advance on an Anglo-Russian loan that was then under consideration. Ala' al-Dowleh, who was still the minister of foreign affairs, pleaded with Barclay to speed up the delivery of the loan with acceptable conditions; otherwise, he warned, his cabinet might fall, and anarchy would prevail. Barclay contemplated with "misgivings" an eventual resignation of both the Sepahdar and Sardar As'ad, whose "prestige" as "victorious revolutionary leaders" he believed helped sustain the cabinet's authority. He urged Lord Grey to offer an advance on the loan with more acceptable conditions as soon as possible.[39]

However, the Anglo-Russian loan proposal attached a list of the two powers' uncompromising demands, which seriously infringed on any semblance of financial independence the country might wish to protect: 7 percent interest rate for a period of ten years guaranteed by customs revenues; government budget to be approved by both embassies; most of the cash advanced to be spent to restore public safety on routes vital to European trade; rescheduled payments of principal and interest of existing loans; exclusive right to administer the post and telegraph; the hiring of foreign instructors for the Persian forces to be approved by the two embassies; seven French financial experts to be hired as advisers; oil concessions to be granted to British and Russian companies; preferential rights for the construction of railways to be given to the two powers; and no concessions to be given to other foreign firms without prior consultation with British and Russian governments. A few weeks later, a joint Anglo-Russian communiqué reiterated the conditions and demanded another concession for the navigation rights of Lake Urumiyeh to be given to the Russian company that owned the Tabriz–Rasht road.[40] Russia then added to the list its desire to have a Russian instructor, no other national, be appointed for the newly crowned young shah's education—a demand Barclay feared that the Majles would categorically reject.[41]

With the fall of Tehran, Hakim al-Molk, nominally put in charge of the royal court, had dismissed the two unpopular Russian instructors of Mohammad Ali Shah and his son. According to Taqizadeh, the Russian authorities had protested vehemently.[42] And Grey informed the Persian ambassador in London that the dismissal would cause the Persian government "embarrassing complications."[43] The Majles, however, persistently refused the Russians' demand, asserting its exclusive authority over the young shah's education until he came of age. By late February 1910, the political tension between the Majles and the cabinet escalated, fueled by increased anti-Russian sentiment and the conditions attached to the loan. Cabinet officials had negotiated its terms, deliberately leaving the Majles in the dark. However, Minister of Education and Public Works Sani' al-Dowleh and Minister of Finance Vothuq al-Dowleh, both of whom Barclay had labeled "ultra nationalists," had dissented. In a secret parliamentary Finance Committee meeting, the two had reportedly encouraged its members to reject the loan even before the conditions had been officially submitted to the Majles. But some representatives demanded open sessions for all to participate in the discussions.[44]

Some nationalists privately expressed their worries about the survival of national sovereignty given their dependence on foreign loans. We need to prove to the world, they wrote, that we are capable not only to attain our freedom but also to govern our nation. They urged their compatriots abroad and in Iran to donate funds, accept government taxes, and raise domestic loans.[45] From Istanbul, Hosain Danesh vehemently insisted that Iran must rely solely on itself, on the strength of its "Iranian-ness," and no one else. In a letter to Browne, he quoted a Persian proverb: "No one should scratch my back / except the nail of my own finger."[46] The Iranian press, especially *Iran-e now*, called for the outright rejection of the advance. Cables were sent to the Majles from all over the country, Najaf, Baku, and Istanbul. Individuals and organizations offered donations and expressed their willingness to accept any amount of taxes to help the nation manage its dire financial problems.[47] Tehran women's *anjomans* volunteered to help in raising domestic funds.[48] Such public demonstration of national unity further encouraged the resistance to Anglo-Russian loan conditions. Sani' al-Dowleh, who initially had urged the Majles Financial Committee to resist the terms of the loan, expressed his satisfaction with such a display of "noble and disinterested patriotism" in protest against "such ruinous and crippling conditions" attached to the loan.[49]

Browne also had strongly advised Taqizadeh to be extremely cautious and to avoid accepting loans from European powers, suggesting instead loans from Zoroastrians of Bombay, who were interested in helping Iran to develop. To raise the Parsis' contributions, he counseled, it would be best to "side" with Iranian Zoroastrians.[50] A religious ruling from Najaf, dated February 21, 1910, and bearing Ayatollah Khorasani's signature, was timely: the ruling proclaimed that it was incumbent upon all Moslems to protect the life and property of the Zoroastrians and all recognized religious minorities.[51]

Khorasani, the most prominent constitutionalist religious leader, had kept constant correspondence with the Cambridge professor, with whom he had cultivated a warm relationship based on mutual respect. Browne would later send Khorasani a copy of his book *The History of the Persian Revolution*, which the *mojtahed* admired, and even promised to have it translated for all Iranians to read.[52]

Browne's assistant in Cambridge, Shaikh Hasan Tabrizi, contacted Parsi business circles in Bombay as a possible alternative source for a loan. The negotiation took place through the Parsis' lawyers in London, with Browne acting as a supportive mediator. The Parsis, Shaikh Hasan wrote, were Iranians and friends of Iran. They could not be forbidden to undertake financial deals in what was officially recognized as British or Russian zone of influence. A loan of half a million pounds would be given in five installments, repayable in thirty years with a 5 percent interest rate and an initial 10 percent fee charged up front. In exchange, they wanted numerous concessions for textile factories, power plants, mining exploration and extraction, construction of warehouses in ports, and navigation rights in the Persian Gulf. One-third of the shares of the established Parsi company would be sold to Iranian subjects, and the Iranian government would be entitled to one percent of the net profit. These concessions were not to be sold to any other foreign firm.[53]

Shaikh Hasan deemed the conditions "easy." Eager as he was to circumvent the onerous Anglo-Russian loan advance, he overlooked the fact that the Parsis' terms were financially exorbitant. He insisted that the Parsis were no enemies and that their conditions would not destroy national independence. He favored Samad Khan Momtaz al-Saltaneh, the ambassador to Paris, to carry out the negotiations, instead of Momtaz al-Saltaneh's counterpart in London, whom he did not trust. But Momtaz al-Saltaneh refused to get involved, obviously realizing the potential objections from his host country.[54] Shaikh Hasan also counseled to keep the process in utter secrecy, fearing British sabotage and Russian interception of his correspondence. He claimed he was only conveying Browne's personal views and executing his instructions. "All this work," he claimed, "was done through the mediation of his Excellency Professor Browne. He was and is of the same opinion."[55] There exists no evidence in Browne's papers, however, that he knew the details of this loan proposal.

Sani' al-Dowleh and Vothuq al-Dowleh independently sought other alternative sources to raise loans, exploring possibilities with private European financial firms. A Paris-based group of bankers represented by Maurice Cohen offered to advance a substantial loan in cash to be guaranteed by customs receipts and, if needed, telegraph revenues, promising to handle all the diplomatic objections to its offer.[56] An international firm based in London, the Seligman Brothers, had cautiously sought the Foreign Office's agreement to its own loan proposal, which would not contravene the two powers' interests.[57] The British Oil Company, enjoying the Foreign Office's tacit approval, was also interested in granting a loan in exchange for the Persian government's shares in the company.[58] Sani' al-Dowleh and Vothuq al-Dowleh had contacted the International Oriental Syndicate earlier, a London-based company of British financiers. They tried to negotiate a loan, pledging the Crown Jewels, which were then estimated at 20 million francs at a minimum. In December 1909, the syndicate's representative, Joseph Wolf, had secretly arrived in Tehran. The company proposed to reorganize the government's finances, consolidate its debts, and redeem the loans advanced by the British Imperial Bank of Persia and the Russian Bank in exchange for the surplus of customs receipts and possibly future government income from the British Oil Company. The syndicate urged the British government to allow it to proceed, arguing that as an English firm it would consolidate British influence in the country at the expense of its rivals, while the Persian ministers assured Churchill, the Oriental secretary attached to the Tehran British embassy, that they trusted Britain more than they did Russia. They negotiated with Wolf, they told him, because "they were convinced that no other Power was behind him," certainly not Germany.[59]

Barclay promptly responded that the British government "cannot agree" to any advance other than the Anglo-Russian one; the Foreign Office dispatched an identical message to Wolf and the Seligman Brothers.[60] The British envoy attempted to discredit both Sani' al-Dowleh and Vothuq al-Dowleh by informing the Sepahdar about their independent secret talks with the syndicate. The Sepahdar then informed the Majles. In a closed-door meeting, Sani' al-Dowleh and Vothuq al-Dowleh justified their secret dealing by referring "to the Sepahdar's notorious Russian leanings,"[61] as Barclay had predicted. He did worry that the Majles's real decision making was done in secret committee meetings, leaving the majority of the deputies and the public uninformed on its proceedings. Indeed, there exists no account of the ministers' loan negotiation in the Majles minutes, hence the Persian government's official brisk response reflecting no dissenting voice: it assured that any arrangements made with Great Britain would be "fully respected," but the Anglo-Russian ongoing negotiation "cannot do away with the full power of the government over its uncharged sources of revenue."[62] Barclay feared the same secretive methods could be adopted with private financiers or a foreign power. "Therefore," he wrote, "we should bear in mind the ever present possibility of being confronted some day with a fait accompli."[63] The British diplomat's worry was well founded. In fact, as the governor of Azerbaijan, Mokhber al-Saltaneh, revealed months later to the French consul, Sani' al-Dowleh, Vothuq al-Dowleh, and Taqizadeh were secretly negotiating with a Frenchman who was offering a big sum disguised as a personal loan in exchange for the nomination of a couple of French inspectors of finance to Tehran.[64] However, there exists no other source corroborating this information, confirming the utmost secrecy the negotiators had kept over a project that obviously failed.

A greater source of British worries was the fact that Sani' al-Dowleh and Vothuq al-Dowleh also had simultaneously contacted German government officials, who were interested in acquiring a railway concession in exchange for a cash advance and the appointment of German financial advisers. The German Foreign Ministry had encouraged the Deutsche Bank to send its representative to Tehran to meet with the two ministers.[65] At that time, the powerful industrialist Georg von Siemens, who had hosted the brothers Sani' al-Dowleh and Mokhber al-Saltaneh during their student years in Berlin and had kept contact with them, was the director of the bank. Both Russian and British authorities were duly alarmed, as were the French. Although the two ministers continued to deny any secret negotiations, other members of the cabinet, Mo'aven al-Dowleh, Sardar As'ad, and the Sepahdar confirmed them. The latter strongly urged Barclay that "on no account should they be given a free hand."[66] Barclay agreed. He did not trust Vothuq al-Dowleh's "confidential" assurances that he would personally never allow the deal with the Germans, and he knew well enough that the Majles would be tempted to accept such an offer when "very few guarantees, if any, would be asked."[67] Sani' al-Dowleh and Vothuq al-Dowleh's desperate attempts to seek financial help that would circumvent the economically and politically onerous Anglo-Russian offer had no chance to succeed.

The "German Threat"

A mixture of trade and geopolitics lay at the heart of Anglo-Russian-French relations. Iran was central to Anglo-Russian dominance in Central Asia, which precluded the emergence of any other European power capable of challenging that status. France, Russia, and Britain were equally alarmed by Germany's rise to power in Europe in the early 1900s. The "German threat" and European international politics rather than the Great Game of Central Asian policies had motivated Britain and Russia to settle their respective interests in Iran and Afghanistan by delineating their zones of influence. The Anglo-Russian Convention was thus created by "painting the German devil on the wall."[68] Raymond Lecomte was relentlessly intriguing in Tehran against the real or imagined "German threat" to the convention. Already in the spring 1909, his official reports to Paris warned against Germany's activities in Persia, arguing that its agents were working to "ruin the good functioning" of Anglo-Russian "recognized influence" and that its envoys in Tehran sought to profit from any British or Russian "diplomatic setbacks," the "schadenfreude" so typically German, he wrote.[69] He particularly distrusted Sani' al-Dowleh, whom he consistently identified as a "German creature" or a "client of Germany." In contrast, British liberal politicians, including some diplomats in Persia at the time, were distrustful of Russia and more inclined to give Germany the benefit of doubt as to its imperial ambitions in the region. Thus, European geostrategic and economic interests on the eve of World War I would inevitably play a decisive part in the unfolding events in Iran at the time of the second Majles.

The long-serving chancellor Prince Otto von Bismarck, the architect of Germany's unified empire, was not interested in imperial expansion into what was then the vast Ottoman Empire. The "whole Orient," he is believed to have said, "should not be a concern of German foreign policy."[70] Upon Bismarck's dismissal from office in 1890, Kaiser Wilhelm II reversed this policy. Following two trips to the Ottoman Empire, the newly crowned German emperor developed a romantic fascination with the Orient, Islam, and Islamic civilization. He cultivated his image as the protector of Moslems throughout the world against Christian imperialists, portraying his European rivals as the Moslem world's enemies. His advisers were encouraged to foment the rise of a pan-Islamic movement headed by the Ottoman sultan-caliph to combat colonial rulers in North Africa and Asia. The overthrow of Sultan Abdul Hamid by the secular Young Turk revolutionaries did not put an end to Turkey's pan-Islamic appeal to the colonized Moslem world on the eve of World War I. The kaiser and his advisers' Orient policy at the turn of the century boosted German business interests in the region. By 1911, the German ambassador in Constantinople would proudly proclaim the Ottoman Empire a German "political, military and economic sphere of interest."[71]

German industrialists, banks, and construction firms acquired concessions in parts of the Ottoman Empire. In 1888, they had begun work on the Anatolian Railway, linking Constantinople with Ankara and Konya, which was completed in 1896. German multi-industrial, agricultural, and infrastructure projects in Anatolia eventually led to an ambitious scheme to construct a railway system connecting Berlin to the Persian Gulf, the so-called Baghdad Railway. The Ottoman government gave its consent. The project greatly alarmed the Triple Entente allies, however, who had their own separate railway plans and were adamant in obstructing a third party's competition. More specifically, both Britain and Russia viewed the German project as threatening their respective power in Asia and the Caucasus. They collaborated to consistently obstruct the German railway extension into Iran, where the nationalist reformers, led by Sani' al-Dowleh, were keenly interested in developing a national system independent of Anglo-Russian influence.

Germany had obtained most-favored-nation treatment from the Tehran government. German officials endeavored to pursue commercial interests in the country while avoiding any conflict with the Anglo-Russian special political status. In fact, they were anxious to maintain good relations with both Britain and Russia. As an Austrian official rather crudely remarked to the British representative in Vienna, "Germany was merely looking after her own interests," trying to "get as big a slice of the pudding as she possibly could."[72] Individual Iranian politicians welcomed German assistance. Walter Smart, Browne's former student and regular correspondent, fully understood Iranian intelligentsia's genuine interest in developing their nation's economic and industrial infrastructure as an integral part of their reform projects. He had observed German commercial activities in Azerbaijan, encouraged by Governor Mokhber al-Saltaneh, Sani' al-Dowleh's brother. The governor had confided that he was fully aware of the "folly of a pro-German policy," but he was not unduly worried that Germany constituted a threat to Anglo-Russian interests. Smart believed in the governor's sincerity and expressed an understanding of the region's need for foreign technical and commercial assistance for its enterprises. Russia, he explained, was not trusted, and Britain could not be relied on because of the Anglo-Russian Convention. "Therefore, by almost a natural process of exhaustion they turn to the Germans." The English, he further argued, can meet the German competition in the South but are restrained in Azerbaijan. As to the Russians, "they are very badly organized to meet German competition since they are not business men [*sic*]."[73]

Russia and Britain, however, concerted their efforts to keep Germany from establishing a solid political or commercial foothold in Iran. Despite German assurances to respect the convention, both remained adamantly opposed to a private foreign company acquiring the right to construct the railway system. Izvolski repeatedly communicated his concerns that the agent of the Deutsche Bank might obtain a railway concession at Tehran.[74] Furthermore, the Russian consul in Tabriz viewed with great alarm German weapons and textile factories set up in Azerbaijan, with Mokhber al-Saltaneh's encouragement. The governor and his brother Sani' al-Dowleh reportedly owned a monopoly on the cotton-thread-spinning industry in the entire country. Smart had informed London that the Germans planned to use the textile factory "as a sort of school for educating the benighted Persians in the art of modern industry. . . . They hope to create needs by their educative process and to act as purveyors to these needs. They evidently had grandiose ideas as to the scope of their undertakings." Smart did believe that Azerbaijan would eventually develop economically and that, at present, the Germans were the only Europeans seizing the opportunity, and he predicted that they would succeed. Quoting Mokhber al-Saltaneh, he surmised that the Russians could not prevent German commercial presence in the province, where a "popular hatred, deep and enduring," of the occupiers prevailed. He thought the only way to remove the German danger was "the English to step into the breach . . . and fight the Germans with their own weapons."[75]

Many British businessmen with commercial interests in Iran agreed with Smart's analysis, and some went even further by strongly condemning Grey's pro-Russian policy. In late May, Joseph Wolf, frustrated with the Foreign Office's reluctance to agree to the loan proposal by his company, the International Oriental Syndicate, had written a "private and confidential" letter to the minister, warning him against successful competition from Russia in expanding its economic "supreme position" in northern Iran and the capital. The prevailing political weakness in the country, he argued, severely hampered all its government's genuine efforts at consolidating and basing its power on a "sound financial basis." But he did not hold the Persians solely responsible for the situation. "It is partly, I may say, solely due to the British policy adopted in Persia," which allowed Russia and other competitors to "monopolize the trade and prestige in the country." He believed that all complications with Germany in the past few months could have been avoided and that the Persian government would not have considered any German proposal if British commercial development had succeeded in establishing a firm foothold in the country. "As long as the present state of affairs is maintained," he concluded prophetically, and the Persian government is "constantly harassed by representations that prevent it from devoting its time to the internal reorganization of the country, so long will British trade and prestige continue to decrease to the advantage and gain of Russia."[76] In response, Wolf only succeeded in obtaining the already cited curt Foreign Office rebuff of his loan proposal.

German officials resented their exclusion from trade and investment in Iran and dismissed the Anglo-Russian objection as uncalled for. Again and again they assured the two powers they had no political designs on the country but demanded a right equal to France's to participate in Iran's financial and economic development. British and Russian approval of Bizot's request for French financial experts to assist the Iranian government particularly provoked the Germans' ire, for with their appointment the French would be in a position to control and block German interests in the country. This would be "offensive" and unacceptable to the German government, the German ambassador to St. Petersburg explained in a memo addressed to Izvolski. It would assume that "Persia had totally lost its independence," even though both Russia and England had proclaimed its integrity and independence in their agreement. He firmly stated his country's legitimate determination to pursue actively its financial and commercial interests and "resolve issues without taking into consideration other Powers' [*sic*] interests." Nicolson interpreted the latter statement as rendering the Germans' assurance to respect the Anglo-Russian "special situation" in Persia "an almost empty phrase."[77]

Izvolski publicly denied the Germans' allegations, claiming the Persians could raise funds elsewhere but on stated Anglo-Russian conditions. Nicolson expressed more harshly his personal opinion: "Persia was up to her ears in debt to both of us, and so could scarcely be considered independent from a financial point of view."[78] Reportedly, the tsar expressed his anger at Germany without mincing his words. "It was quite inadmissible that a distant country with no political but small commercial interests, and who had necessarily stood aloof during the crisis, should now claim to be placed on an equality with England and Russia, and to enjoy an equal portion of the fruits of any benefits which might arise from a possible eventual re-establishment of order and tranquility."[79]

On April 7, 1910, the British and Russian envoys informed the Persian government that they had no objections to a loan from a third party provided it would not offer as guarantees the revenues from customs duties and other sources committed to servicing debts owed to Russian and British banks. Other nations, the British representative in Vienna stated, "must not assume that because Persia is technically independent, they were at liberty to misuse her rights of independence merely to create difficulties for the two Powers which had supreme interests in that part of the world."[80] But the German chancellor believed the British were in fact not honoring the "open-door" policy and exerted pressure on the Persian government to accept the Anglo-Russian conditions for a loan. Such demands, he noted, "practically do away with the open door and render Germany's acquired right to most-favored-nation treatment a dead letter."[81] Lord Grey felt the need to send an explicit warning through Count Paul Metternich, the Austrian chancellor: "Were the Persian Government to grant a third party a concession, which was prejudicial to our political or strategic interests, and thus confront us with a fait accompli, we should . . . safeguard our interests by whatever measures we thought necessary in Persia itself."[82] It was an ominous warning, especially to Sani' al-Dowleh, who was fighting hard to realize his pet project, the construction of a national railway system independent of Anglo-Russian control and with German financial and technological expertise.

Long and tense negotiations were exacerbated by polemical articles in the Russian and German press that inflamed public opinion in their respective countries.[83] Nonetheless, a moderate solution was reached through the diplomatic mediation of the Austrian chancellor Metternich. Germany proposed to give up "reluctantly" its claim to "most favored nation treatment" in exchange for an agreement with the two powers. It would give up the railroad project in Iran on the condition of receiving orders for 25 percent of the material for the railways to be built by Russia and Britain in their respective zones. It specifically demanded an agreement be reached before the British and Russian envoys pressed the Persian government for a reply to their loan offer. The German ambassador in St. Petersburg informed his British counterpart that although "it was far from their wishes to cause difficulties for them," Germany could if necessary inform the Persians on the limits imposed on their liberty to grant concessions.[84] He thus insinuated his willingness to support Persian resistance to the two powers' demands.

Anglo-Russian Pressure

The British and Russian legations sent strong personal warnings to Sani' al-Dowleh, "Germany's client": should he persist in seeking loans "irreconcilable" to the two powers' program, "we should demand his dismissal from office." Vothuq al-Dowleh, the "nationalist disrespectful of financial conventions bothersome for his country," as the French diplomat Lecomte put it, was given a similar but "slightly softened" message. Sardar As'ad and the Sepahdar were pleased, believing that the warnings would strengthen the Moderates in the cabinet. To the contrary, it created an uproar within the Moderates' ranks. Once more, when both ministers were labeled "extremists," they quickly denied any involvement with Germany.[85] But they succeeded in influencing the official Persian response, which categorically rejected all conditions incompatible with Persian independence, accepting only financial terms pertaining to the loan's interest, fund, and security.[86] Charles Marling, the British attaché while Barclay was on leave, and his Russian colleague in Tehran were convinced that the German envoy was in fact "secretly controlling relations of Persia to England and Russia." They severely warned the Persian government that it "cannot play off Germany against us."[87]

Some of the nationalists' greatest worries concerned the prospect of all of Persia's natural resources, especially oil, falling into foreign hands. "We are not poor," Vakil al-Ro'aya would remind his fellow deputies,[88] a realization widely shared among many in the various political circles, as was their awareness of their country's utter dependence on foreign help to explore and develop that wealth. They found themselves facing the inevitable dilemma: how to balance national independence with reliance on foreign financing and wide-ranging expertise needed for their modernizing programs. This national vulnerability was duly exploited by the two European powers as leverage in imposing the conditions for their proposed loan, exerting pressure on the government to stop delaying its official application.

The loan negotiations went on as the two powers, especially Russia, raised more demands and conditions while blocking any alternative offers.[89] The Tehran government, for its part, delayed its formal application for an advance, believing other private companies, such as the International Syndicate and the Seligman Brothers, would propose easier terms. Despite the Foreign Office's negative communication to the syndicate, foreign private financiers continued their secret efforts to reach an agreement with the Persian cabinet ministers. Seligman Brothers reportedly hired Arthur Moore to represent the company. Moore was the journalist who had initially joined the resistance in Tabriz before losing all illusions about the mojahedin's moral integrity and military competence. He was by now the *Times* correspondent in Tehran and the Seligman Brothers' spokesman. The International

Syndicate had J. R. Preece negotiating on its behalf in Tehran, also secretly. It is significant that Marling was privately in favor of allowing a "reputable" British firm, such as the Anglo-Persian Oil Company or the International Syndicate, to advance a loan if Tehran persisted in delaying its formal request to the two powers and if Russia did not object. His concern was to prevent the Persians from approaching a third power.[90]

The Battle of Wills

The Oriental secretary Churchill defined adequately the prevailing political situation in the capital that spring and early summer of 1910: the executive and legislative authorities as well as the "moderates" and "extremists" among them were engaged in a tenacious battle of wills to impose their respective views on the decision-making process.[91] Political intrigues and rumor mongering intensified the struggle to win over public opinion. Since its inauguration in November 1909, the second Majles carried a burden of expectations, challenged as it was to institute reforms that would speedily improve people's living conditions. Persistent shortages of bread, the prevailing lawlessness, and the lack of public safety generated anger that undermined the deputies' popularity in the streets of the capital. The legislators accused "some corrupt people" of using popular discontent as a pretext to stir political troubles and to erect a divisive wall between the nation and its representatives. Rumors spreading in town alleged serious conflicts among the deputies, forcing them to issue an official denial and to assure the public that complete accord reigned in the Majles and that all representatives were pursuing national interests.[92] The liberal press, however, kept revealing the stark reality belying such a declaration, further exacerbating existing tensions within the Majles.

The cabinet crisis, with its ministers bearing the brunt of Anglo-Russian threats, added to the general political instability. Sani' al-Dowleh was determined to oust the pro-Russian Sepahdar from the cabinet. Sardar As'ad, who was by then "coquetting with the Nationalists," tacitly went along with Sani' al-Dowleh's political scheme. The Russian and British envoys constantly worried that a reshuffle would result in a "ministry of extremists."[93] They urged the cabinet either to exclude the nationalists or to submit a written promise not to seek a loan or grant a concession that would "run counter" to their joint proposal.[94] Izvolski added his own threat that concessions to foreigners without prior Anglo-Russian approval would be considered "a hostile act" and "have serious consequences": a demand for immediate payment of

Persian government debts, occupation of all customs' posts, as well as Russian troops in Tehran.[95] The threats further deepened the divide between the "revolutionists" and the "moderate reformists" within the Democrat Party and not just between Democrats and Moderates.

The French ambassador, Lecomte, astutely depicted the political scene at that particular time. He distinguished the "progressive party" from the "party of the conservative revolution (not to say reactionary)." The former group included Taqizadeh, "the agitator," and Navab, both of whom he defined as the "only valuable men of the revolution" "capable of some initiative," as well as Sani' al-Dowleh, who was "dangerous and tenacious . . . though not without value." The "reactionary" party was led by the Sepahdar and included Sattar Khan, who had resurfaced as a "noisy" opponent of the Democrats.[96] Lecomte, of course, overlooked many other important actors whose views crossed the Democrat/Moderate divide. Churchill equally tended to judge the Majles's ideological composition as consisting of, on the one hand, a "noisy minority" of extremists who violently opposed the Sepahdar, the Russian "tool," and, on the other hand, a majority of moderates advocating "a patient attitude towards Russia" and supportive of the Sepahdar's and Sardar As'ad's leadership. Churchill, unlike his fellow British diplomats stationed in Iran—Walter Smart, Claude Stokes, and R. B. Graham—was by far less tolerant of the "progressives" and preferred to support the Moderate "conservatives."[97]

Yet, in fact, throughout that period Majles members of all factions often voted similarly on vital issues concerning modernizing reforms and financial issues.[98] Apart from some religious issues, the dividing line between the "progressives" and the "moderates" defined their respective tactical policy in encountering Anglo-Russian power. Though Taqizadeh and Sani' al-Dowleh were socially and ideologically apart, the former supported vigorously the latter's development projects, especially the need to seek sources of loans other than the Anglo-Russian offer. Most nationalists of various political coloring resented the Anglo-Russian powers' harsh conditions for the loan and menacing tone, which further aggravated their suspicion of the pro-Russian Sepahdar and his acolytes. The British and Russian envoys' joint list of suggested nominees for a new cabinet led to a fierce power struggle over its formation. Anxious that a secret deal might accommodate the foreign powers' demands, Isma'il Nobari, the Democrat deputy from Azerbaijan, exclaimed loudly what many thought: "The Majles is the guardian of the nation's independence and its law"; it has the legal right to be informed on the "state of the nation."[99] The Majles rejected the Anglo-Russian list of conditions.[100] And the new cabinet formed in early May 1910 retained the same ministers with only a minor change: the Sepahdar and Sardar As'ad traded their posts, the latter becoming prime minister and minister of war, and the former becoming minister of interior. Sani' al-Dowleh and Vothuq al-Dowleh kept their ministries. Britain and Russia failed to obtain their dismissal, Lecomte claimed, because of secret support from the Germans. Germany, he asserted, was strengthening Persia's willpower.[101] His Russian and British colleagues reached the same conclusion. They had favored the Sepahdar as head of the cabinet, for "he would be ready to give us the assurances we require," and his appointment "would be regarded as a defeat of German influence."[102]

On May 20, 1910, the two legations felt the need to send a follow-up to their April note concerning their loan proposal, reiterating all their demands. Both powers were also in agreement to respect France's wish to appoint seven more financial experts to join Bizot and the Belgian Joseph Mornard. The Anglo-Russian message was meant to be a "veiled threat"; in fact, a "boycott of the cabinet" had been seriously contemplated.[103] Yet again Sani' al-Dowleh and Vothuq al-Dowleh remained the sole negotiators for loans and concessions, tacitly supported by the Majles "extremists." By mid-June 1910, Marling was convinced that German backing had indeed strengthened the nationalists' determination to assert their independence from both powers.[104] The Anglo-Russian diplomatic power game aimed at shaking the ground under the "revolutionists" and "extremists" and thus bringing about a fundamental shift in the Majles balance of power—to no avail. The rivalry between Bakhtiyari and Qashqa'i tribal chiefs to a great extent accounted for this temporary failure.

Intrigues in the Provinces

Fars, the southwestern province that was an integral part of the British sphere of influence, was vital for the security of the British trade route in the region and the British Oil Company's fields. In addition to the traditional tribal Qashqa'i–Bakhtiyari conflict, fierce hostility between the Qashqa'i leader Isma'il Khan Sulat al-Dowleh and the local governor Qavam al-Molk often engendered political turmoil. Moreover, Bakhtiyari families' internal power struggle divided their ranks as the weaker branch forged an alliance with Sulat al-Dowleh, pledging mutual friendship and assistance. Sulat al-Dowleh had also formed an anti-Bakhtiyari alliance with the powerful Arab tribal chieftain Shaikh Khazal, who controlled much of the southwestern trade routes. The shaikh's hostility was also fueled by the Bakhtiyaris' competing claim to ownership of land being exploited by the Anglo-Persian Oil Company. All factions getting involved on one side or the other challenged the central government's authority. In the ongoing power struggle that essentially reflected personal ambitions and intrigues among the local ruling elite, some elements chose to seek the Sepahdar's support, whereas others turned to the Bakhtiyari leader Sardar As'ad.[105] Thus, the convoluted tribal/regional alliances in this remote region further accentuated the antagonism already existing between the pro-Russian Sepahdar and the pro-British Sardar As'ad. Taqizadeh and his fellow Democrats seized the opportunity to feed the animosity between the two and succeeded in winning Sardar As'ad over to their side, provoking Marling's anger.[106] The Foreign Office had rejected Marling's earlier proposal to threaten Sardar As'ad to publicly "forfeit friendship of His Majesty's Government" should he join the "extremists' camp." Grey did not favor "an open breach" with the Persian government.[107]

Meanwhile in Tabriz, the "extremist" and "moderate" elements of the nationally active *anjoman* were equally involved in a power struggle no less potentially destructive than the one in the capital. The Russian consul Miller and General Snarsky, the commander of the occupying troops, were determined to prevent Mokhber al-Saltaneh from governing in Azerbaijan. In February 1910, Snarsky had denounced the "germanophil" governor in the German journal *Asien*, accusing him of corruption.[108] The Russian's intention was to damage the governor's reputation in Germany, the country where he and his brother Sani' al-Dowleh had formed business ties with many of its prominent companies. Moreover, the French consul Nicolas was convinced that Miller was behind the antigovernor defamatory pamphlets allegedly published and distributed by the local *anjoman.* Though the *anjoman* had fought hard for the initial nomination of Mokhber al-Saltaneh to the post, a few remaining members of the Social-Democratic faction led by Shaikh Selim were by then actively engaged in denouncing him personally in mosques and public places. Similarly, the radical wing of the Democrat Party led by Tigran and Pilosian, though they had by then been sidelined by the party's Tehran parliamentarian leadership, were carrying an underground campaign to undermine constitutional moderates.[109] Mokhber al-Saltaneh bitterly complained that the *anjoman* and the Russians "are united against me. . . . I am alone, alone! Alone facing Russia represented by Mr. Miller."[110] Smart, the British consul in Tabriz until early February

1910, confirmed the governor's predicament in many diplomatic dispatches. He had nothing but high regard for Mokhber al-Saltaneh, praising his "frugality, his rectitude, his obvious sincerity, his jealous care of public money, his industry and lack of personal prejudices," virtues to be found in "few, if any, other Persian governor."[111] But the situation was hopeless; by the spring of 1910, Nicolas admitted that "terror reigns" in Tabriz, blaming Miller and his "*agents provocateurs*" for the "crazy rumors spreading like fire."[112] The Frenchman's prognosis was gloomy: "It seems to me that we are witnessing the agony of Persia . . . incapable of standing up by itself."[113]

Tehran's inability to establish its central authority in the provinces, the increasing hostility between the cabinet and the Majles, and discord within the cabinet, its members incapable of speaking in one voice, contributed to the gravity of the political crisis in the spring and summer of 1910. Of even greater consequence to the survival of the constitutional regime was the financial state of the country. The national debt to British and Russian banks gave an advantage to the two powers, which they ruthlessly employed to obstruct any official attempt to independently seek the much needed financial resources elsewhere. Britain and Russia vigorously stifled any project deemed disadvantageous to their own economic and geostrategic interests.

8

The Political Crisis

INCREASED TENSION between the Majles and the cabinet hampered the enactment of legislative reforms and their implementation. Character assassination and innuendoes thickened the climate of suspicion, poisoning politicians' relationships, thus affecting the goodwill of Democrats and Moderates to work together to achieve common goals, and dissension within each party further widened the divide. Many deputies accused fellow legislators, more specifically the deputy Speaker Abol Hasan Mo'azed al-Saltaneh, of conspiring with individual ministers to promote executive policies that allegedly contravened the constitution. Others accused Vakil al-Ro'aya, deputy member of the Committee of Financial Affairs in charge of collecting funds from donors, of fraudulent accounting, even embezzlement.[1] The malicious smear campaigns fueled the climate of distrust, often distracting the national representatives from properly accomplishing their tasks in a timely way. Similarly, repeated Majles requests for ministers' attendance to answer the deputies' queries, as required by law, were ignored. When the ministers attended, meetings were held behind closed doors among members of the different parliamentary committees. Such secret deliberations alienated the rest of the deputies and aroused their suspicion. Mostashar al-Dowleh, the Speaker, defended the practice on constitutional grounds, which granted his office the right to hold secret meetings when necessary, without the presence of journalists or spectators; he told his detractors their opinion "cannot change the law."[2] Taqizadeh "the extremist" supported the "moderate" Mostashar al-Dowleh's procedural justification, but that did not assuage the dissidents' resentment.[3]

All the while, anti-Russian sentiment in the Majles and the Iranian liberal press intensified, alarming British and French diplomats as well as hardening conditions for Russian troop evacuation. In private, Marling complained bitterly to Sardar As'ad of the nationalists' "suicidal agitation" against the Russians that "infected" public opinion. He particularly deplored the fact that "foreign relations was left entirely in the hands" of the Majles Committee of Foreign Affairs, in majority composed of Taqizadeh, Navab, Hakim al-Molk, and Vahid al-Molk, all "fanatical Russophobes" who, sitting behind closed doors, "worked [themselves] up into hysterics over fancied wrongs."[4] Marling exhorted Sardar As'ad to contact the Russian envoy and remedy the situation. The Bakhtiyari's subsequent conciliatory meeting with Stanislav Poklewski-Koziell only resulted in demands for more concessions: duty-free import of cars for the Russian privately run Rasht–Tehran road, an extension of a mining concession for a Russian company, and the restoration of the Cossack Brigade's independent status from Persian jurisdiction. The British diplomat, uncomprehending and underestimating the force of the nationalist fervor gripping many of the constitutionalist deputies, whether "extremists" or "moderates," could only note the "extraordinary folly of these people." Bewildered as well as exasperated, he observed: "They imagine they could struggle against a Power [*sic*] whose armed forces alone were equal to one-third of the entire population of Persia."[5]

Persistent news of Russian troops' ill treatment of local inhabitants in the Russian zone, of troubles in various parts of the country involving rival tribes competing with provincial governors in Fars, Lorestan, Kordestan, and Azerbaijan, of shortages of basic commodities, and of administrative mismanagement further eroded the cabinet's status in the public's eye. It also tarnished the reputation of the deputies. Democrats chose to blame the two chief ministers, Sardar As'ad and the Sepahdar, for the nation's loss of confidence in its elected representatives. News from abroad concerning Qajar princes' conspiracy to assault the Majles, overthrow the young Ahmad Shah, and crown Abol Fath Mirza Salar al-Dowleh instead added a sense of imminent danger to the beleaguered constitutionalists.[6] Salar al-Dowleh, the deposed shah's brother and former governor who had a formidable power base among Kurdish tribesmen, would repeatedly wage war against the constitutionalists, as we shall see.[7]

A warning letter sent in the name of the Tabriz *anjoman* to Mostashar al-Dowleh pleaded with deputies and ministers to work together in unison, set aside *parti-bazi*, and carry out the important task of nation building. Divisive, artificially created conflicts, they were told, would "ruin us all," offering the two powers the pretext to destroy national independence. All the past sacrifices of the nation should not be wasted for the sake of some personal conflicts. "We should learn our lessons from the Ottomans, who have so successfully attained their objectives through unity, overcoming even ethnic differences."[8] But the damage to the "national unity" that the *anjoman* so passionately and so urgently pleaded for had no quick remedy. Attitudes within the Majles were hardening. A battle for power broke out in the open within the Majles over issues concerning the separation of executive and legislative branches of government. Shaikh al-Ra'is the Moderate contended that the Majles had no legal right to interfere in government affairs, while Zoka' al-Molk insisted that it was part of its function to oversee the ministers' work. The regent, Azod al-Molk, dismissed any call for a new cabinet, informing the Majles that any change would have to include the two "national leaders," the Sepahdar and Sardar As'ad.[9] This statement only succeeded in heightening the Democrat-led Majles's animosity toward conservative members of the cabinet. Others persisted in blaming "untrustworthy ministers" and the secretive meetings among committee members, which left most of the deputies and the public uninformed about "real issues."[10]

It is important to note here that many of the ministers and former ministers had ties to one or the other parliamentary faction, acquiring positions and political clout with the factions' support. The Sepahdar, for instance, was close to some Moderates, but without sharing their reformist, progressive outlook, and Sardar As'ad, driven by his fierce rivalry with the Sepahdar, staged a rapprochement with the Democrats, but without sharing any of their "radical" ideas. More significantly, neither Sani' al-Dowleh nor Vothuq al-Dowleh belonged to any faction, but they were members of the Sepahdar's cabinet, while finding supporters among the Democrats in the Majles. In the spring and summer of 1910, factionalism, personal rivalry, and intrigues eroded the constitutionalist united front, leaving its various leaders mired in bitter personal recriminations. Denunciations of *parti-bazi* increased, inciting *Iran-e now* to define parties' significance as necessary components of parliamentary democracy. The Majles, it explained in several articles, has to have separate ideological parties to inform the public of their different programs before elections. Each party, it went on, represents a particular class, protecting its rights and its political, economic, and cultural objectives. There are parties of the right, representing wealthy property owners and "feudal" grandees, and there are parties of the left, safeguarding the rights of the poor, the oppressed toilers, and peasants and calling for equality. Without such parties, it ascertained, the Majles remains "weak."[11] The tone of these articles and the definition of each party, underscoring an intended socialist message, compelled the Democrats' parliamentary leadership to further distance itself from the "radical" and "revolutionary" wing of their party.

Marling's concern, however, was not some deputies' alleged radicalism as much as their so-called extreme nationalism. Thus, he deplored the "failure which has hitherto attended the experiment of self-government," blaming the "ultra-nationalists" in the Majles for the cabinet' inability to function properly. "Their professed intentions for the regeneration of Persia are excellent," he conceded, yet their "particular pernicious" action in foreign affairs and their "unreasoning hatred of Russia" are "intimidating" the ministers. Interestingly, although recognizing Taqizadeh's undeniable "sincerity of purpose," Marling thought the deputy's "utility to the cause of freedom of Persia ceased with the abdication of Mohammad Ali," and he wished Taqizadeh would now adopt an "almost passive part in public affairs."[12] Marling's comments, pronounced at the time of heightened political crisis in the capital, displayed the initial British perception of Taqizadeh as a moderate leader whose role in restoring the constitutional government had outgrown its usefulness to the Foreign Office. Together with his Russian and French colleagues, Marling contemplated a reshuffling of the Persian cabinet to weaken the influence of the "extremists."

Religious controversies added a new dimension to the political crisis. Clever manipulators exploited the situation, driving a wedge between the constitutionalists by pitting the "progressives" and "revolutionists" against the "conservatives," a division that earlier in the Majles debates was less starkly marked. Ayatollah Behbahani began orchestrating many moves that determined Taqizadeh's fate and ultimately his own.

The Religious Dimension of the Crisis

Behbahani had returned to Tehran from exile in early October 1909. Though received with pomp and honor, treated with due respect, and invited to attend the inauguration of the Majles, he failed to regain the illustrious fame his role as a constitutional leader had earned him prior to the coup in 1908. Close associates and acquaintances warned him against resuming political activity. Times have changed, he was repeatedly told, and his opponents, especially the so-called Europeanized constitutionalists, had ascended to power.[13] Even before his return to the capital, he was informed that the "exigencies" of the times had changed.[14] Ayatollah Mohammad Tabataba'i, the other Tehran religious leader of the constitutional movement, now bitter, disillusioned, and in poor health, had opted for political retirement.[15] Behbahani ignored the advice, seemingly oblivious to the new reality that Ayatollah Fazlollah Nuri's execution had so dramatically revealed. He chose to support the Sepahdar and his entourage, thus inevitably arousing the Democrats' and other reformists' suspicion. Shaikh al-Ra'is, on viewing a photograph of Behbahani with Zahir al-Dowleh, a constitutionalist Qajar prince and a mystic, composed an ironic poem reflecting the constitutionalists' general distrust of the *mojtahed*: "Undoubtedly, this is the beginning of a great end, the holy law and the mystical order associated. But, alas, the space in between for the image of Truth is empty."[16]

Democrats accused Behbahani of promoting his self-interests, obstructing the enactment of legislative reforms, and intervening in government matters that did not pertain to his religious function. They resented the pressure he exerted on some officials and the excessive authority he exercised in the judiciary.[17] He was believed to be behind individuals such as Assadollah Kordestani, a Majles deputy with a wide network of contacts within the country as well as in the holy cities and Europe, who was spreading rumors targeting some Democrats, especially Taqizadeh, for their alleged political and religious "extremism."[18] As we shall see, Kordestani was also responsible for informing Edward G. Browne about his former protégé Taqizadeh's "radicalism." Such allegations were also soon to be made by Shaikh Hasan Tabrizi, the Cambridge professor's assistant, by Hosain Danesh, the constitutionalist expatriate in Istanbul, as well as by many other activists who had until then supported Taqizadeh. The olama's hostile attitude was further inflamed as the liberal press intensified its anti-olama polemics, some bordering on what they considered to be anti-Islamic. The *Habl al-matin* episode, which had occurred at the time of the Directorate, then dominated by Taqizadeh and his group, was still fresh in their memory.

Antimonarchist and antireligious, the paper had a long history of radicalism that predated the revolution. At the time of the Lesser Despotism, its editor, Jalal al-Din Kashani Mo'ayed al-Islam, had joined the mojahedin fighters in combating the royalists in Rasht. With the fall of Tehran, he had renewed publication of the paper. Issue number 6 carried a fiery anti-Arab, anti-Islamic article that glorified pre-Islamic Persian history and culture, echoing late-nineteenth-century nationalist thought.[19] Persia's honor and independence, it claimed, was annihilated with the invasion of "savage, lizard-eating" Arab Bedouins. "For thirteen hundred years, the Iranian race has tried to shake the yoke of their nonsense [*khorafat*] off their back." It hailed the present era, which is witnessing the "champions of freedom" restoring national honor and prestige. Unfortunately, the article lamented, a "few worshippers of the ancient" imagine that, despite the people's awakening to liberty and progress, they can continue to "exploit the credulity of the faithful" for their own ends. Addressing the olama directly as the "real oppressors," it urged them to "have mercy for the wretched people." And it asked them to follow the example of the ayatollahs Khorasani and Mazandarani of Najaf, who supported the constitutionalists to the very end. Otherwise, the "turbaned" would be severely punished to prevent them from destroying the newly acquired freedom.[20] The article created a furor in olama circles, including Najaf's, and among government ministers. The paper was banned, and its editor was arrested and sentenced to three years in prison. The Directorate's officials rose in defense of Mo'ayed al-Islam's innocence, arguing that he should not be punished instead of the article's author, who had fled the country, and so the editor was released from prison within two months of his arrest.[21] But it was the Democrats' popular paper, *Iran-e now*, that would provoke most of the conservatives' ire and escalate the opposition's attacks, led by Behbahani.

With the enacting of laws going counter to long-standing Islamic institutional jurisprudence and practice, constitutionalist olama's animosity continued to simmer until it boiled over with *Iran-e now*'s published article discussing Qur'anic laws known as *qisas*,[22] which it declared incompatible with modern political and philosophical principles. The article outraged many pious readers and led Ayatollah Khorasani to dispatch from Najaf an urgent and confidential cable to Ayatollah Behbahani in Tehran: "Obedience to divine commands must be proclaimed to all Moslems of the world."[23] Behbahani, seizing the occasion to reassert his lost political clout, immediately notified the Speaker of the Majles, Mostashar al-Dowleh. Minister of Justice Sardar Mansur, the Sepahdar's ally, ordered the paper's closure. Fierce debates in open Majles sessions underscored the reformists' desperate attempts to safeguard the concept of freedom of the press, which they understood to be an essential component for a modern, free society. Referring to clause 20 of the Supplement to the Fundamental Law, which guaranteed that freedom, the Democrats Montasar al-Saltaneh and Solaiman Mirza proclaimed the decision to close the paper unconstitutional and unjust because neither an investigation nor a trial had been held prior to the sentencing. Taqizadeh called for an orderly procedure wherein the special committee in charge of government supervision would discuss and resolve the issue behind closed doors, without any public interference. He also demanded the personal appearance of the minister of justice to explain the matter to the nation's representatives. Other deputies, such as Vakil al-Ro'aya, who later on would self-proclaim nonpartisan, insisted that protection of the Constitution is even more important a civic duty than safeguarding national independence. The importance of the press lies in its function: informing, enlightening, awakening the nation; it is a vital "instrument of progress."[24] The majority of deputies, regardless of their affiliation, agreed that the paper should be allowed to resume publication.

The press was not attacked solely for its antireligious content. *Habl al-matin*, based in Calcutta and therefore falling under British colonial jurisdiction, was earlier severely reprimanded for its publication of some "inflammatory" political articles. The editor was threatened with expulsion and the closing of his paper. In an emotional, self-defensive letter addressed to the local authority, he expressed his "sincere sorrow" for the misunderstanding due to faulty translation. "I am devoted to the British government which is the champion of good government," he wrote. But he adamantly insisted on his patriotic right and obligation to work for the "regeneration of Persia" and its "welfare." He refuted the false claims that his policy was to agitate or "create bitterness of feelings." He conveyed his incomprehension that, with the "deep-rooted aversion of the British nation and British government to suppress a well-meaning journal," he should still be expelled "for advocating the cause of my country."[25] The editor was then acquitted.

Behbahani and his fellow conservative olama, enjoying the Sepahdar's blessings, would not relent in their attacks on the "irreligious" elements within the constitutional assembly. The Sepahdar would denounce the "lack of morality" of "certain individuals" and condemn the "evil effects" of journalists "whose nationality is unknown," asking whether they were "compatriots or foreigners."[26] Indeed, the original publisher of *Iran-e now*, Joseph Bazil, was an Armenian, as were Tigran and Pelosian and other Caucasian-born authors of some of the articles in it that were translated into Persian. Mohammad Amin Rasulzadeh, *Iran-e now*'s editor, was a Moslem, Baku-born Russian subject. The paper, by then the most important in Tehran with a circulation of two to three thousand copies, was suspended on July 11, 1910, but resumed publication a few months later, on October 24, 1910. The Sepahdar had also instigated his loyal mojahedin, led by Sardar Mohiy, to wage a fierce campaign against the Democrats. The Rashti brothers, Sardar Mohiy and Karim Khan, and their relative, Sardar Mansur, founded a paper, *Vaqt* (Time), in defense of the Sepahdar and openly hostile to the Democrats. By early May 1910, it had published articles denouncing the Democrats as revolutionaries aiming at destroying the country and referring to the Sepahdar as the patriotic "savior of the nation" who believed in "moderation."[27]

The conservatives received a formidable boost with their successful recruitment of Sattar Khan and Baqer Khan upon their arrival in Tehran. The two "national warriors" then worked to mobilize the public against the "irreligious," the "nihilists," and the "radicals."[28] Their common favorite target was Taqizadeh, considered the most anti-olama deputy, who, as the uncontested leader of the Majles Democrats, promoted far-reaching secularizing reforms. More important, his virulent anti-Russian rhetoric presented serious obstacles to Anglo-Russian designs in the country. Furthermore, his alliance with different ideological groups and his ties to the mojahedin faction led by his relative Ali Mohammad Tarbiyat, Haidar Khan Amu-Oghli, and their Caucasian fighters, all deemed "extremists," underlined his "radicalism." The bitter rivalry between the militias of Sardar Mohiy and the Sepahdar, on the one hand, and the militias of Tarbiyat and Haidar Khan, on the other, in addition to the intense power struggle between Behbahani and Taqizadeh further entangled the Democrats and Moderates' politics with religious polemics and issues of public safety.

Taqizadeh's Political Demise

Less visible but of equal if not more relevance was the Russian and French desire to undermine the "revolutionists'" political clout. The Russians' motive was the most obvious: to neutralize serious opponents of Russian imperialist policies. The French concerns were often murkier. Despite the part French Masons played and continued to play in support of the constitutionalists and their reforms, a role supported by a fellow Mason, the French minister of foreign affairs, French officials were divided over balancing their interest in spreading French democratic ideals with their geopolitical need to keep Anglo-Russian cooperation intact. Ultimately, it was the latter consideration that came to dominate their relationship with the constitutionalists, as we shall see in the next chapter. Lecomte, one of the most cynical critics of the constitutional movement, had from the start of the restored constitutional government identified Taqizadeh as the most "determined," "audacious," genuine revolutionary and the most competent political leader, hence the most dangerous to French interests in the country. But he had also predicted that Taqizadeh would not succeed in attaining his goals, given the existing "vacuum" of similarly qualified politicians and the prevailing corruptibility of many others. Therefore, Lecomte hastened to reassure Paris that Taqizadeh, despite his activities as a political "apostle" and despite his moral values, might fail; the "mediocre arrivistes" that fill the ranks of the government "will eliminate that threat." After all, he added, this is Persia, "where means to soften" moral virtues are abundant. His political preference leaned toward the Russophile Sepahdar and his cleric ally Ayatollah Behbahani. Overlooking the notorious reputation the latter had acquired even among foreign diplomats, he portrayed him as "the most venerated religious individual," with considerable political prestige in the nation, having remained "faithful to the Constitution."[29]

Lecomte's sentiment would not change as time went by, with Taqizadeh and his "small group of demagogic parliamentarians" ascending to power in the Majles.[30] Nicolas, the French consul in Tabriz, though more skeptical of Taqizadeh's political talents, believed he was unfairly attacked; he also held Behbahani in poor esteem. "This rapacious individual," he wrote, had an entourage worse than the former shah's.[31] The British view of Taqizadeh was more ambivalent. Barclay had reached the conclusion that he was the most important "nationalist extremist," whose relentless anti-Russian rhetoric hampered Anglo-Russian cordial cooperation in promoting the two countries' respective interests in Iran. Smart and Stokes, the British military attaché in Iran, had a more nuanced though more positive opinion of Taqizadeh. Both would later oppose the official British policy decisions concerning the constitutional government.

The campaign to destroy Taqizadeh had begun months before his fall, even before the inauguration of the second Majles. In early November 1909, an anonymous letter from Tabriz warned him about his "enemies'" busy conspiring to divide his supporters' ranks and forging fake letters as evidence that he, Navab, and Hakim al-Molk were working as British agents.[32] His meteoric rise to power in the national scene had provoked many of his rivals' resentment and dissent, be it personally or politically motivated. Undoubtedly, his acquired powerful status and strong personality undermined his relationship with fellow constitutionalists of all ideological shades. His proven leadership qualities threatened many among his collaborators as well as his opponents, domestic and foreign, including those who were initially attracted to him. Mokhber al-Saltaneh associated him with the virulent personal attacks of the radical elements within the Tabriz *anjoman.* Much earlier, the constitutionalist *mojtahed* Theqat al-Islam had come to distrust him and his group in the Tabriz *anjoman.* Reports were sent to

Najaf, complaining of Taqizadeh's "party" rising to power in Azerbaijan and undermining Theqat al-Islam's influence. "This arrogant youth is destroying Islam," Theqat al-Islam's brother wrote to the then Speaker of the Majles, Mostashar al-Dowleh. "His party's [influence] in the Majles must be diminished."[33] The Russian consul in Tabriz played his own part as well, sowing dissent within the *anjoman* to isolate the "extremists" and Taqizadeh through defamation of character.

Already in early February 1910, Pilosian had informed Taqizadeh that the Tabriz *anjoman* had begun to be infiltrated by "reactionaries," who, encountering no serious challenge, began a slander campaign to undermine the deputy's standing among the *anjoman*'s members. He also reported a recurring new phenomenon in town: "They are exciting the fanaticism of the black gangs [the mollahs] against the *fauxcols*," the young men who were wearing the *fauxcol*, a starched shirt collar then fashionable in Europe and favored by some modernist Iranians, and who were being beaten in broad daylight for this choice.[34] The traditional conservatives had coined the term *fauxcoli* as a pejorative designating the modernists by their European-style clothes. Pilosian was convinced that the slander was "invented" by the nation's enemies. The French consul in Tabriz, Nicolas, had reported similar allegations, attributing to his Russian colleague a pamphlet published by the *anjoman* that viciously attacked Taqizadeh, whom it accused of "*parti-bazi*" to consolidate his own power.[35]

The fierce power struggle among the Armenian parties in Tabriz and Tehran further polluted the murky political climate. As already discussed, both Dashnakist and Hnchakist leaders had initially attempted to influence the constitutionalists, chiefly through their favorite interlocutor, Taqizadeh, who had initially sought their support. However, several events and the Democrats' decision to distance their party from various Social-Democratic groups angered some Armenian personalities, turning them from allies or just friendly supporters to staunch opponents. Moreover, Taqizadeh's about-face in the summer of 1909, ordering the mojahedin to lay down their arms; his appointment of Ali Mohammad Tarbiyat as the sole commander of all the militias after the fall of Tehran; the defection of Hnchakist Social-Democrats, Pilosian and Tigran, from their Armenian party to help found the Democrat Party; and, last but not least, the personal animosity existing between various players, be they Armenian or Iranian, and transcending ideological or national policies cumulatively contributed to Taqizadeh's estrangement from many of his former supporters.

Of greater significance, the Majles Democrats under Taqizadeh's leadership were not aiming to attain all the goals stated in their Central Committee's program. They believed in a gradual process of implementation. An unabashed political warrior for institutional reforms, Taqizadeh sought compromise when confronted with occurrences potentially endangering national independence, a characteristic that rendered him vulnerable to the accusation of being a turncoat. It must also be pointed out here that the Iranian Democrats generally wished to downplay their political ties with non-Moslem Armenians, while Armenians grew more skeptical and distrustful of their Iranian political allies and comrades in arms.[36] All these crucial elements severely hampered the collaboration between various revolutionary factions and allowed their opponents' political manipulation to their own respective advantage. The opponents' goal to divide the constitutionalists, chief among them the Democrats, succeeded, though other factors contributed as much.

As early as January 1910, an issue with serious religious implications antagonized many constitutionalist olama and their moderate supporters. By Taqizadeh's own account, the olama's hostility to him began with the Isma'ili episode. In a village near Naishapur in Khorasan, a local cleric declared Isma'ilism, a minority sect in Shi'a Islam, heretical and incited the murder of two Isma'ili inhabitants. After an unsuccessful attempt to prevent the killing, the Mashhad British consul, Major Mark Sykes, informed his embassy in Tehran of the situation. Barclay then officially submitted a protest to Sardar As'ad, demanding a detailed account of the event and the punishment of the two lower-ranking clerics responsible for the crime. Lord Grey reportedly had instructed Barclay to inform the authorities that the British government attached great importance to their punishment. Sardar As'ad then decided to have the guilty men arrested and brought to prison in the capital, where Yeprem Khan was in charge of the police. The fact that Moslem mollahs were being held under Armenian authority spread rapidly in town, however, portending a potentially explosive situation. A meeting was held in the Sepahdar's house to resolve the problem. In his autobiography, Taqizadeh recalls his own intransigent demand for capital punishment of the guilty clerics, which Sardar As'ad approved. He thus angered the olama present at the meeting, including Ayatollah Behbahani, who emphatically reminded all of the tradition granting religious leaders immunity from execution. The government officials at the meeting decided instead to have one of the defendants banished to Najaf, the other imprisoned in Tehran. From that day on, Taqizadeh wrote, the olama's relentless animosity would eventually erode his political legitimacy on religious grounds.[37] Taqizadeh never tried to hide his ultimate goal to secularize essential national institutions, especially the judicial and the educational, which had traditionally been under the olama's control. Although most constitutionalist leaders within the Majles and the cabinet shared his effort to legislate secular reforms, regardless of their party affiliation, he was secularization's most vociferous advocate, a relentless warrior combating clerical opposition.

As the political crisis was gathering momentum, Taqizadeh and his faction supported Sani' al-Dowleh and Vothuq al-Dowleh in exerting pressure on the rest of the cabinet ministers to implement their proposed reforms. He escalated his opposition to the olama's political interventionism, especially Behbahani's, who reportedly cabled Najaf to denounce Taqizadeh as a heretic. Taqizadeh's enemies, genuine or enticed, escalated their character assassination. Najaf received numerous letters requesting the ayatollahs' speedy action in dealing with him. Feeling the political heat, Taqizadeh decided to withdraw from the Majles until, he hoped, the dust settled. On July 3, 1910, the Majles granted him three months' "sick leave." Just five days later, Khorasani and Mazandarani ordered his expulsion from both the Majles and Iran. In a cosigned letter dated July 8, 1910, addressed collectively to the regent, the olama of Tehran, the Majles, and the cabinet ministers, the two *mojtaheds* wrote what in fact read like a religious ruling. It stated that Seyyed Hasan Taqizadeh's views are incompatible with the Moslem community and its religious law. Therefore, his membership in the Majles is forbidden, and he is to be stripped of all political status and privileges in accordance with the holy law and the Constitution. It decreed the obligation of all olama, government officials, trustees of the Majles, military commanders, and all classes of the Iranian nation to prevent Taqizadeh from entering the Majles and from intervening in national affairs. His expulsion from Iran was pronounced of "immediate necessity," binding this "divine ruling" to its execution in Azerbaijan and all other provinces: all should be warned against cooperating with him.[38] However, it should be noted that this fatwa was not intended as a *takfir nameh*, a certificate pronouncing Taqizadeh heretical.

The press did not publish the letter immediately, nor was it read openly in the Majles. Rare were the deputies who demanded obliquely that "all written communiqués from Najaf" be read out loud in an open session for debate.[39] Taqizadeh was still enjoying the powerful deputies' tacit support, be they Democrats or Moderates. He continued to attend the Majles, expressing his opinion and insisting on correct parliamentary procedures. And he was elected member of the new Committee of Foreign Affairs, which included his fellow Democrats Navab and Vahid al-Molk.[40] Supporters in the capital rose in his defense. Some wrote to Najaf, vigorously refuting the ayatollahs' charges, asking them to reconsider their fatwa; Najaf refused to revoke it, however.

In a letter responding to one of Taqizadeh's sympathizers, Ayatollah Mazandarani condemned in even stronger terms the "secret *anjoman*," the Democrat Party's Central Committee, by then mostly inactive, which he accused of recruiting its members among "cursed Bahais," Armenians, and non-believing Moslems. The committee is emulating the corrupt European thought, he wrote and alleged that one such secret local *anjoman* of religious students was formed to spread the Europeans' evil ideas. Their intrigues and rumormongering, he complained, are now undermining the olama's authority. Nonetheless, Mazandarani clearly and unequivocally denied that the ruling regarding Taqizadeh was a *takfir* edict that would condemn him to capital punishment. Those who make that assertion are lying, the *mojtahed* wrote; it is a ruling concerning his personal political thought, which makes him unworthy of membership in the Majles and general participation in government affairs. Mazandarani confirmed that their decision was based not on a couple of individuals' judgment but on the judgment of people who are knowledgeable, worthy nationalists who had once believed in Taqizadeh but have now come to realize the corrupt nature of his views. Mazandarani, the constitutionalist *mojtahed*, carefully distinguished the "corrupt elements" from the "righteous" members of the Majles, who uphold "correct" constitutional concepts. He also blamed the radical mojahedin for the continuing presence of Russian troops in Iran.[41]

The political crisis had reached a boiling point. Mostashar al-Dowleh, the moderate and capable Speaker of the Majles, became the target of increasing personal assault. He resigned his post as Speaker on July 6, 1910, the first of many colleagues to fall within a couple of weeks. Zoka' al-Molk, a Democrat, was elected to replace him by majority vote, while intensified rumormongering about some "corrupt," "irreligious" deputies compelled many to assert their pious devotion to Islamic principles and to moderate their attitude toward their conservative opponents. However, when Sani' al-Dowleh and Vothuq al-Dowleh intensified their campaign in the cabinet, which finally induced the Sepahdar's and Sardar As'ad's resignations, the Majles swiftly appointed both former ministers as deputies and received them with great respect and honor. Even Solaiman Mirza, the fiery Democrat who was to replace Taqizadeh as the faction's leader, praised the Sepahdar's and Sardar As'ad's "sacrifices" to help achieve national freedom and progress. He hoped they would then support legislative reforms necessary for restructuring government institutions that would help the new cabinet ministers fulfill competently their respective tasks.[42]

The new prime minister, Mirza Hasan Mostowfi al-Mamalek, a former finance minister, belonged to neither faction but was respected by all, but a battle over the choice of new cabinet ministers took place inside and outside the Majles. Isma'il Nobari and Taqizadeh proclaimed that the formation of the new government was entirely the prime minister's prerogative.[43] Mostowfi al-Mamalek conditioned his acceptance of the post on his right to choose his ministers. The Democrats appeared about to win important cabinet posts, a fact that could have saved Taqizadeh, but the assassination of Behbahani on the night of July 16, 1910, decisively struck the fatal blow that brought about his ouster from the Majles, marking the end of the second phase of his political career.

Behbahani's Assassination

The assassin, a Caucasian who reportedly committed his act without the Democrats' knowledge, was associated with Haidar Khan Amu-Oghli, the most violent member of the mojahedin militia commanded by Mirza Ali Mohammad Tarbiyat, Taqizadeh's relative.[44] Haidar Khan went into hiding, while fingers immediately pointed at Taqizadeh, and letters were sent to the Majles demanding his expulsion. A recently established guilds' union sent a letter to the deputies, asserting that the assassination had proven the culpability of the "anarchists." "It is our religious and patriotic obligation," they wrote, "to follow Najaf's ruling," and they urged the Majles to "expel some deputies." The union threatened to take "some rightful steps" should the Majles fail to accomplish its duty.[45] The guilds' union organized massive public demonstrations calling for retribution for the ayatollah's murder. The ensuing turmoil in the capital forced Taqizadeh to quit attending the Majles. *Habl al-matin* desperately attempted to clear Taqizadeh's name, publishing an article that blamed the Russians and their secret agents for the murder. Their aim, it asserted, was to create a crisis situation in the country and to misinform the constitutional olama. Refuting any charge of heretical beliefs against Taqizadeh, the article begged the olama to investigate the matter properly, but to no avail.[46]

Upon his friends' advice, Taqizadeh escaped by night, heading toward Tabriz, where he waited for the opportunity to stage a comeback to the capital. Governor Mokhber al-Saltaneh reportedly received an order to bar his entrance to the city, which he could not execute, he told Nicolas, because Taqizadeh was not accused of any crime. The French consul in Tabriz was equally convinced that the deputy "had nothing to do" with the assassination.[47] Taqizadeh tried to lead his party in absentia, instructing Democrats to carry on the fight to achieve their program. Pilosian wrote a letter in French to Browne, pleading for his intervention with Khorasani to revoke the fatwa, with no apparent success.[48] News from Tehran was far from encouraging. Tigran Ter Hacobian, who had arrived in the capital to help the party, wrote of his despair in seeing the prevailing total disarray.[49] Shaikh Ibrahim Zanjani, the Democrat deputy, described a similar gloomy scene reigning in the Majles and cabinet, both of which had been marred by what he described as the officials' intrigues and betrayals. He warned Taqizadeh that as long as Najaf would not revoke its fatwa, his return would not be safe, for he was held responsible for all the wrongdoings and all the killings committed all over the nation.[50]

In Tabriz, too, a strange cabal of unlikely bedfellows formed in opposition to Taqizadeh, including Russians, Armenians, and some members of the *anjoman*, which increasingly rendered his stay there unsafe. That summer, the Tehran Dashnakist Central Committee had sent a memo to its Azerbaijan Central Committee, accusing Democrats of promoting only their self-interests. It subsequently denounced Taqizadeh as a "nationalist" who was "highly cunning and circumspect" and too close to Pilosian and Tigran in forming the Democrat Party, which had turned hostile to the Dashnakist Party.[51] In his report dated August 10, 1910, Nicolas confirmed the existence in Tabriz of a strong group opposed to Taqizadeh, with some *anjoman* members calling for the publication of the Najaf ayatollahs' ruling. He predicted: "Most probably, he would live an ugly moment should they lay hands on him."[52] In early December 1910, the disgraced deputy left for Istanbul, the second exile of his young political life.

Taqizadeh's Friends and Foes

The labels *radical*, *revolutionist*, and even *republican* followed Taqizadeh long after his departure, as many foes and even former collaborators cast him aside as too extremist. Assadollah Kordestani sent a long letter to Browne identifying Taqizadeh and his "clique" as terrorists who used the professor's respectable name to promote their views and achieve their goals. He attached to the letter a handwritten copy of the Democrat Central Committee program, which included clauses that did not figure in the publicly available one. Thus inserted was an article stipulating far-reaching land reforms that would nationalize all private lands, obviously implying the abolition of private property. Other radical measures similarly addressed the need to proclaim martial law and establish military tribunals to judge "reactionaries" as well as the need to eradicate foreign intervention with a reformulation of foreign policy.[53] In fact, it was not Taqizadeh who had written this copy of the program, but Tigran, who in a letter sent after Taqizadeh had already left Tehran proposed the formation of the National Salvation Committee, which would gather all existing constitutional parties and tribal representatives in a common effort to fight against reactionary elements.[54] The Central Committee's by-laws duplicated the Democrat Party's, with some clauses added, such as the establishment of a military tribunal to punish reactionaries in the capital and to bar anticonstitutionalists from government positions. These clauses also mention the "expulsion of all foreign forces by whatever means" and land reforms to redistribute ownership.[55]

Some moderate constitutionalists, such as Momtaz al-Dowleh, the deputy Speaker of the Majles, denied that Taqizadeh was a "traitor," viewing him as a politician with ideas as others had their own.[56] Others relentlessly smeared his reputation. Shaikh Hasan Tabrizi, Browne's assistant, now back in Tehran, began to spread negative rumors as soon as the fallen deputy was forced into exile. "I know that you esteem Taqizadeh and believe in him," he wrote to Browne, "but I personally think that he is responsible for all the bloodshed and turmoil prevailing in the capital." Claiming that all current political problems were the direct consequence of Taqizadeh's wrongdoings and "bad character," Shaikh Hasan falsely implied that Najaf's ruling was holding him responsible for Behbahani's assassination.[57] Two months later, upon Browne's further inquiry, the self-described moderate Shaikh Hasan accused Taqizadeh of "setting fire in the country" by advocating reforms incompatible with the nature of the "ignorant nation of Iran."[58] Iran, he asserted, is not France or England, which had benefitted from the rule of law for generations. By then forsaking the Democrats to join the Moderates, Shaikh Hasan founded a paper virulently defaming all Democrats, who held him in utter contempt. Indeed, the Democrat Abdol Hosain Vahid al-Molk, calling Shaikh Hasan "Cambridgi" in reference to his years spent in Cambridge, questioned the paper's financial source. "With whose money [is it funded]?" he asked, and he squarely identified the Moderates and the "supporters of Anglo-Russian politics" as its chief sponsors.[59] Claude Stokes, the military attaché in Tehran, also believed Shaikh Hasan "got hold of the muddy end of the stick about Persian politics."[60]

British and French envoys in Tehran had worried about the potential for Taqizadeh's political abilities to ruin their respective agendas. Lecomte, as already stated, considered him a leader of the fiercely anti-Russian "demagogic parliamentarians" and held him responsible for instigating Behbahani's assassination.[61] In a similar vein, Churchill, the British Oriental secretary, described Taqizadeh and his "noisy minority" within the Majles and the cabinet as "revolutionists," enemies of Russia and of the Sepahdar, whom he continued to praise. He wrote to Browne, "They do not seem to be able to grasp the fact that if Russia really loses patience, nothing on earth can save them." And he derided their "naive" belief that Germany would help them.[62] Rising in Taqizadeh's defense, Claude Stokes, the military attaché who kept his distance from Churchill, informed Browne that Taqizadeh had "wisely bowed before a storm which blew from Najaf[,] where the olama had fallen into the hands of the fugitive reactionaries and the Russian Consul (or the consulate agent) recently appointed there." Labeling Behbahani as the Sepahdar's man and the Sepahdar as the tool of the Russians, Stokes explained that Behbahani was warned "to stop intriguing, but disregarded it." Furthermore, Stokes believed the new cabinet, filled in majority with "nationalists," was dedicated and competent to govern. The Sepahdar, he thought, was by then totally discredited.[63]

In his correspondence with Browne, Khorasani repeatedly denounced Taqizadeh. In one particular letter marked "confidential" and sent when Taqizadeh had left the country, he denounced the Caucasian mojahedin, believing they had come to Iran ostensibly to uproot despotism but were in reality a "kind of Russian soldiers" penetrating the country to "destroy national character" from within. They worked with people holding similar corrupt views, such as the "Bahais and other enemies of religion" who had infiltrated all government institutions. He held this group, which included Taqizadeh, responsible for Ayatollah Behbahani's murder. He then justified his fatwa and affirmed his confidence in the newly appointed regent, Naser al-Molk, whose "honorable existence is a divine blessing for the Iranians." He concluded the letter expressing his hope that Browne would not pay attention to the Armenians and Caucasians and "other corrupt" elements: "We are working to destroy their activities."[64]

Browne was kept informed on the latest events by many of his Persian correspondents in Iran and abroad. Hosain Danesh was his most regular informer from Istanbul. Born in Isfahan, Danesh had been living in Istanbul for several years and held several official positions, such as chief translator for the Ottoman government. A member of the Anjoman-e Sa'adat, contributor to the paper *Sorush*, and modernist reformer, he shared views identical to Taqizadeh's yet disliked him personally. Already in December 1909, he had depicted the rising star in Persian politics as a man holding a "multitude of viewpoints" that would hamper national renovation.[65] Two years later, when Taqizadeh left Tehran for exile in Istanbul, Danesh claimed that Iranian expatriates kept their distance from the "leader of the revolutionaries." Yet Danesh admitted that he had spent much time with Taqizadeh and even regarded his fate as a bad omen. "His downfall after all such greatness and power in Iran constitutes a warning lesson . . . that one mollah's ruling could block his deeds and power."[66]

Browne sent a message to Taqizadeh through Hosain Danesh, expressing his suspicion of his protégé's "extremism." From Istanbul, Taqizadeh promptly sent a letter to his former Cambridge mentor dated March 30, 1911, the first in fifteen months, in which he apologized for his long silence. He was too busy with affairs of state, he wrote, and he had no time "to touch a pen or read a book." He passionately denied advocating any "extremist" ideas or revolutionary program, asserting their incompatibility with the present situation in Iran. He insisted that Democrats were opposed to terrorist acts. If some "traitors" to the nation wished to label the Democrat faction "revolutionary," despite its explicitly stated program and despite its denials, "that is another problem." He blamed "a few enemies" for causing some of his supporters' suspicion, even Browne's, and for bringing about his own downfall. He admitted that he might have been mistaken in his refusal to concede to the olama as a professional class any social or political status that might exceed other citizens'. This was not the time for expressing such views, he confessed, and he had never expressed them openly in the Majles. To the contrary, he stated, "I have paid them [the olama] due respect and honored them in recognition of their achievements." Finally, he desperately tried to convince Browne of the "purity of his sentiments," wishing to clear himself of all charges made against him by his enemies and hoping to retain "his beloved master's" trust. "You know and God knows that in this period of my political life, working to rescue the fatherland, I have not acted against any principles of my faith and convictions. Had I erred, it was unwittingly."

However, he added, his views "remain correct and respectable until proven wrong."[67] Browne immediately responded, assuring his faith in Taqizadeh's "good intentions" and "genuine patriotism" and expressing his regret that his former protégé had lost his position. Nevertheless, he had come to the conclusion that, indeed, Taqizadeh was "an extremist."[68]

It is significant that when several months later Browne received another letter from Shaikh Hasan denouncing the Democrats' radicalism and including Navab in the list, he rose in defense of the latter. Arguing that Shaikh Hasan had no proof of Navab's alleged radicalism, Browne sternly wrote that he would not hear any bad word against him. Navab, he asserted, was one of his oldest friends, "reasonable, courageous, reliable and trustworthy," whereas he had heard stories confirming Taqizadeh's "extremism."[69] Despite this disagreement, the Cambridge professor and Shaikh Hasan, his former protégé and assistant, would continue to correspond in the following years, keeping each other up to date on events in their respective countries.

Taqizadeh's Profile in the Second Majles

As a prominent deputy, Taqizadeh asserted his authority by displaying his familiarity with parliamentary procedure. He never ceased to remind his fellow deputies of the utmost importance to abide by the Constitution and to respect Majles rules of order, and he periodically called for that order. Socially, however, his standing reflected his modest background, which influenced his irrepressible hostility to politicians who, he claimed, considered themselves entitled to power by virtue of their privileged class status. Members of the former elite held practically all of the cabinet positions and some seats in Majles committees. Taqizadeh cooperated with individuals such as Sani' al-Dowleh and Vothuq al-Dowleh, among other reform-minded ministers and deputies, and endorsed their financial and economic projects, but he persistently opposed other representatives of what he called the "ancient" sociopolitical order. His relationship with Sardar As'ad remained ambiguous at best: he shared with him a common opponent, the Sepahdar, and used that rivalry between the two to win over the powerful Bakhtiyari's support when needed. In that sense, he was a prototype of the ambitious, intelligent, politically talented, modern middle-class politician who advocated far-reaching modernizing reforms yet who could compromise and reach agreement with some of his ideological opponents in order to achieve a goal essential to the cause he espoused. In present-day terminology, the term *pragmatic* would best describe Taqizadeh's short-lived tenure in the second Majles.

Here, Taqizadeh's association with the Social-Democrats begs the question: During his Majles tenure, how close was he to them, and how much did his policies and political action reflect their ideology? Do the available official records of his deeds and rhetoric represent the totality of his legacy for that brief period prior to his political demise and second exile abroad, when he was in a position of power to execute his cherished ideas for legislative reforms? There is no doubt that the prominent status Taqizadeh acquired and was conceded to him on the basis of merit as well as some influential patronage reined in his "radicalism." Acquired political power subjected him to constraints, enabling him to accommodate others' more moderate perspectives. He was a favorite protégé of Browne and benefitted from the supportive presence of Cambridge-educated British diplomats in Tehran, especially Walter Smart and Claude Stokes, neither of whom was "radical." Once elected to the Majles, he drastically reduced direct communication with his Cambridge mentor, whose counseling obviously mirrored many policies Taqizadeh advanced. He had no time for letter writing, as Browne fully understood: "I know quite well how busy you are with the reforms. . . . Your time belongs to Iran."[70]

There is no evidence that at that stage Taqizadeh ever espoused a socialist agenda or violent means to push for his program. His earlier secret overture to the Armenian groups amounted to a tactical alliance to defeat the royalist troops and restore the Constitution. The militias they assembled accomplished the alliance's initial mission; he subsequently curtailed his direct contact with the Armenian cofounders of the Democrat Party. His cooperation with them may not have been extinguished; it may have instead just gone underground. However, careful to avoid damaging his "nonrevolutionary" reformist political persona, he ceased to correspond regularly with the Armenian Social-Democrats with whom he had collaborated so closely from the earliest phase of the constitutional movement up to the inauguration of the second Majles. Tigran Ter Hacobian, the former Hnchakist cofounder of the Democrat Party, continued to send copies of his writings and to offer his advice, but Taqizadeh's responses were sporadic and often uninformative.[71] Becoming aware of the deputy's political troubles, Tigran wrote to him: "Why had you stopped writing to us? You could always have relied on Azerbaijan. Now it is too late. Had you kept us informed on your current struggles, we would have been of great use to you."[72]

It is important to recall here that, as discussed earlier, the Democrat Party program was neither truly revolutionary in Marxian terms nor in favor of political violence to attain its goals. Furthermore, *Iran-e now*, the party's organ, though basically social-democratic, only sporadically advocated radical socialist views. Instead, it published fiery anti-Russian and overtly secular, anti-olama articles; it also targeted those it deemed "reactionaries," mainly the Moderates and their friends in or out of power, thus eventually succeeding in crystallizing the two parties' divide. These views, which Taqizadeh consistently shared, energized the Democrats' detractors and provided his enemies with convenient "proof" of his "extremism." The battle over freedom of the press that dominated many Majles debates and *Iran-e now* editorials is a case in point.

Last but not least, Taqizadeh's opponents and ill-wishers did not distinguish between the various Armenian groups he associated with and therefore would mistakenly identify him with European socialists. Some Armenian Social-Democrats of Tabriz, who insisted on carrying on a socialist revolution, maintained contact with European fellow ideologists, as Cosroe Chaqueri's documented studies prove. In their organs, especially *Die Zeit* of Germany, the Social-Democrats informed their respective publics in Europe on the Iranian revolution. They kept "the left wing of European politics abreast of political developments and Anglo-Russian colonial rivalry in Iran."[73] In the eyes of the European officials closely watching the country's events, was Taqizadeh guilty by association? Probably! However, Taqizadeh was a politically complex man, impossible to reduce to the characterization "extremist"; he was no ideologue, but a man of action. One may detect conflicting interests in his political relationships but no contradictions in his political behavior and deeds. He was endowed with a strong personality and exceptional leadership qualities, and his political ambitions for the country transcended politics to allow him to side with nonpartisans' reform proposals that he agreed with or did not run counter to his own goals. In today's terminology, his decisions can best be defined as following the practice of realpolitik. However, the hostile reaction of the Social-Democrat ideologues, marginalized as they were in terms of number and influence, compounded his vulnerability to other detractors' attacks. Taqizadeh ended up being undermined by his association with them.

Taqizadeh's rise to power, which allowed him to dominate the second Majles during his tenure, was in fact facilitated by his British connections and support, but so was his downfall. He had become too "extremist," meaning "independent nationalist," for his sponsors' geopolitical agenda. He had earlier figured high on some British influential personalities' list of young Iranians to be groomed for potential government positions that would serve British interests, but after his rise to power they had no more use for him. In a European dominated world evolving historical events necessitated the elimination of such independent-minded personalities capable of finessing the situation to their and their national objectives' advantage. What we know of Taqizadeh's political life in the period of the restoration of the Constitution and, to a lesser extent, the second Majles may indeed leave ample room to question his entangled alliances with different ideological groups. But it is undeniable that his proven competence as a nationalist, modernist leader became a liability. Therefore, he was largely a hostage of European powers and of forces beyond the constitutional movement he tried to lead. He rose and fell with the tide of its history.

Here, the fierce rivalry between the Sepahdar and Sardar As'ad must be underlined as a major catalyst that kept kindling the political hostility between the Democrats and the Moderates throughout the period of the second Majles. The fact that both men were notoriously reputed to be the proxies of Russia and Britain, respectively, fueled their detractors' antagonism, while paradoxically adding weight to their political influence, which outlasted that of many other more competent constitutional leaders. It is worth noting that the French envoy, Lecomte, consistent in his efforts to maintain the Anglo-Russian collaboration, deplored the growing animosity between the Sepahdar and Sardar As'ad. He considered the Russophile Sepahdar as the "man of order" who "represented the policy of entente," and by July 1910 he feared that the Sepahdar's growing distance from Sardar As'ad, "the former client of England," would compromise "the beautiful result of perfect accord" reached between the two powers in the past two years.[74] Indeed, as Malekzadeh reports in his account of the revolution, it was Sardar As'ad's rapprochement to the Democrats that, though based on personal rather than constitutional motives, facilitated the fall of the Sepahdar's cabinet.[75] As already mentioned, neither the Sepahdar nor Sardar As'ad was disgraced; upon their dismissal from the cabinet, both were instantaneously honored with appointment to Majles seats.

Najaf's sweeping ruling on Taqizadeh was essentially a political act, the fruit of months of intrigues in Tehran and Azerbaijan by detractors with murky personal as well as political motives, some of whom were secretly encouraged by foreign powers. Politics overshadowed policies, undermining the balance of interests that had earlier existed between Democrats and Moderates in the Majles. It hampered the lively parliamentarian debates that often resulted in cross-party consensus to legislate reforms commonly believed vital for the construction of the new Iran. As the Majles minutes amply reveal, the votes had ranged across the political spectrum but for the most part were in favor of nationalists' demands, be they genuinely or expediently espoused. By early June–July 1910, the dividing line between the two parties became much more pronounced, however, and they emerged as two confrontational groups with clear-cut conflicting politics. Thus, the Moderates' official organ, the *Ruznameh-ye Majles*, accentuated their differences with the Democrats, labeling "some of them" "socialists, revolutionaries and anarchists." Such individuals, the paper argued, are divisive, ruining the reputation of the olama and respectable people. "We are religious believers; we cannot negate any religious principle." Distribution of land all at once among the peasants is dangerous, it warned, for one cannot so quickly change people's mind and character. Admitting that Iran had stepped onto the path of civilization (*tamaddon*), it nonetheless pointed to some problems resulting from that step that needed utmost caution in solving. Although acknowledging that "all institutions in Iran must be reformed," including the peasants' and toilers' situation, the paper counseled moderation and prudence in gradually improving popular culture before undertaking reforms. It insisted the Moderates were not against liberty and equality. In fact, they unequivocally asserted that "all Moslems are brothers" and declared that the holy law was based on liberty and equal rights for all people.[76]

Ultimately, the palpable fear caused by Behbahani's assassination, although inciting many in the Majles to tone down their secular rhetoric, did not compel all to close ranks behind the Moderates and reactionaries. Each party had its supporters outside the Majles, its journalists, and its militias, with whom they turned up the heat on the streets and created visible signs of unrest. Street violence would ensue.

9

The Aftermath of Ayatollah Behbahani's Assassination

THE PERIOD from the summer of 1910 through December 1911 marked the desperate constitutionalists' struggle to consolidate their shaky hold on power and accomplish the necessary reforms to build their nation-state anew. Several detrimental factors, both domestic and foreign, obstructed their path, rendering their task increasingly insurmountable. Behbahani's assassination genuinely shocked the public at large, and there was a nationwide call for the arrest and punishment of the guilty party. The bazaar, many guilds' partisans of the Moderates' leaders, and the olama came to believe the Democrats were irreligious and viewed their program, especially the clause calling for the separation of religion from public affairs, as incompatible with the holy law.[1] As a consequence, the atmosphere in the Majles changed significantly, and social conservatives seized the occasion to attack the "radicals" in their midst. Worth noting here is the fact that the execution of Ayatollah Nuri a few months earlier, though widely condemned, had not had such drastic political repercussions for the "extremists" and their associates in the Majles.

The Plot to Defame the Nationalists

The denunciation of "extremism" forced Democrats and Moderates alike to express publicly their commitment to Islamic principles, loudly ascertaining that the murder of Behbahani constituted "a blow to Islam and the Moslem world," while Shaikh Ibrahim Zanjani, the Democrat who had presided over Ayatollah Nuri's trial and execution, proclaimed the murder "the biggest event that threatens the nation's independence." Vakil al-Ro'aya, another hard-core reformist, rushed to assert that Islam offered the "best," "most beneficial" plan for the country's progress and admitted that the Majles had "to a certain extent" erred on that point. He described

Behbahani as "a great man," even glorifying him as "the founder of the principles of the Constitution," and deplored the "meaningless" though politically consequential evil act.[2] Lamenting the prevailing lack of unity of political purpose, he asked the assembled Majles: "What happened to this patriotic zeal. . . . We sit in silence, totally dumbfounded," not knowing or not wanting to know what must be done.[3] Despite his passionate eulogy, Vakil al-Ro'aya strongly opposed reading the Najaf ayatollahs' "text" in the Majles, as some were demanding. He argued that the council of five *mojtaheds* was not yet selected and that Behbahani, one of the twenty nominated candidates, had first to be replaced on the list. Vakil al-Ro'aya's objection was an oblique way of preventing the public reading of Khorasani and Mazandarani's decree condemning Taqizadeh. Many other deputies decried in a similar vein the public's loss of trust in the Majles as a result of the murder but refused to have the text read out loud in a general assembly.

The defamation campaign did not abate, leading some deputies to suspect that "corrupt" elements were manipulating the situation for their own destructive purposes. Indeed, Assadollah Kordestani, who emerged as the most vocal detractor of the Democrats in the Majles, persistently called for reading Najaf's ruling in an open session. He praised Sardar As'ad but accused some individual ministers and deputies, "the national traitors," of kindling dissention among all "freedom-seeking brothers" and causing "much disquietude between an ancient nation of Islam and its religious leadership." For nine months, he added, those "dishonorable" and "unscrupulous" individuals have threatened the ministers, forcing them to accept unlawful demands. Assadollah Kordestani was outspoken in his condemnation of the Democrat Party Central Committee, which he described as the "revolutionary center" that destroyed Behbahani, "a pillar of Islam."[4] As observed earlier, however, Taqizadeh and other fellow Democrats had much earlier sidelined the radical wing of their party, and in Tehran the Central Committee existed only in name, to Tigran's sorrow.

Political fear and paranoia prevailed in the capital through much of the summer of 1910. Massive popular demonstrations in the streets took place every day in protest against the "heinous deed," forcing the bazaar to keep its shops closed. The combustible nature of the rumormongering led the Majles deputies under attack to postpone debating any other issue so long as the police had not found and arrested the assassins. In a special session that was unanimously agreed upon to be exclusively devoted to the crime, its implications, and its potential repercussions, the discussion quickly degenerated into unrestrained quarrels. When Vakil al-Roʻaya requested full cooperation with the new cabinet, he encountered vociferous protests, with many arguing that elected deputies were meant to serve the country, not the ministers, and that they had the right to oppose the ministers' policies if need be. In response to Sardar Asʻad's expressed worries that the murder had "shaken the country's security," they stated their confidence that security was maintained throughout the nation.[5]

The disputes went on relentlessly, pitting the Democrats against Assadollah Kordestani, thus veering the debate to personal accusations and name-calling. Individual deputies took turns denouncing the abuse of the labels *moderate* and *revolutionary*. Who is what? one Democrat asked. Kordestani was challenged to name openly whom he alluded to when mentioning "traitors": "Not to mention the name is wrong! Mentioning the name would help in investigating whether this person is guilty or not and dealing with him accordingly." And this Democrat denied categorically the rumor that the Najaf ayatollahs' decree had charged "some representatives" with "irreligiosity." The olama, Kordestani was told, would not pronounce such a ruling without solid evidence, which did not exist. Kordestani was asked to define the label *corrupt* attached to some deputies. What does it mean? If it means refusing Russia's control, "then many of us here are corrupt." The Democrats blamed "the so-called moderates" for causing all this trouble and, together with some "reactionaries," for inciting the bazaar and guilds to persevere with their public protests.[6]

Sardar Asʻad, by then tactically supportive of the Majles's Democrats, echoed the self-defensive, virulent denunciation of rumormongering individuals such as Kordestani. He criticized the growing tendency to refer to "revolutionaries" in contrast to "moderates"; this *parti-bazi* tendency, he claimed, is "destroying us." He pleaded with all to set aside personal conflicts and raise their objections in private and in a calm, conciliatory tone. Insecurity is prevailing, he insisted, as armed groups frighten the population with violent threats and intimidation to extol money. He requested the Majles's full cooperation with the ministers in investigating the murder until the assassins were arrested and duly punished and public safety restored.[7]

The intensive anti-Democrats propaganda campaign, although met with no less intense ripostes from the Democrats, would not subside so easily. The Speaker Zoka' al-Molk dismissed any suggestion to replace Taqizadeh, who was then still officially on leave of absence in Tehran and had not resigned.[8] Solaiman Mirza, who was emerging as the new Democrat faction leader, fiercely defended the right of the "accused" to defend himself. Condemning such corrosive "suspicions" of the presumed innocent, he warned against their evil effects creating serious misunderstandings. He urged his colleagues to concentrate their efforts on liberating the country from Russian occupation instead of wasting time affixing such "labels." Now that the suffix *yun* (-ism) is added to our vocabulary, he further remarked, we must all label ourselves *esteqlaliyun* (independists) and collaborate to achieve our national goals.[9]

For days on end, the rumormongering ran wild, and the bazaar remained closed. Some mullahs preached holy war against Taqizadeh's party, heightening the already tense climate. There was reportedly a growing public perception of the murder as "tantamount to an open declaration of war against religion."[10] Tigran explicitly blamed Abol Qasem Naser al-Molk, who was still abroad, and his moderate partisans for obstructing Taqizadeh's return to his Majles seat.[11] Whereas Marling had reached the conclusion that the public demonstrations were a genuine and spontaneous expression of discontent, Lecomte surmised that these "artificial manifestations" may, indeed, have been incited by a group that would profit from the situation. He had noted a lack of willpower among officials to act decisively and arrest the assassins, known to be hired guns from Baku. The chief of police, he wrote in his letter, "does not dare take the initiative that may cost him his post with the future government." Lecomte, convinced that "this unfortunate country is destined to inaction on the part of the so-called men of action," went so far as to wish the Sepahdar would organize a coup d'état to dissolve the Majles and elect a new one that would be more "disciplined."[12] Both Russian and British governments were also encouraging some Persian officials' demands for the dissolution of the Majles and new elections. Marling and his Russian counterpart in Tehran were in fact secretly supporting the Sepahdar's return to power, convinced he could form a government capable of installing indispensable good relations with the two powers. Lord Grey, more skeptical about the Sepahdar's ability to restore order because of his reputation as "Russia's creature," favored encouraging Persian officials to arrest Behbahani's assassins and expel all foreign mojahedin.[13]

The renewed Russian threat to intervene militarily unless order was restored finally provoked the deputies to act decisively in unison. The guilds and retailers were promised that Behbahani's assassins would be arrested soon and were encouraged to reopen the bazaar. The Majles finally assigned the task to Yeprem Khan, instructing him to avoid all publicity and especially to keep the press out of it. Although the official reason behind such an order was to prevent alerting the murderers, who might then escape abroad, in fact fear of escalating violence lay behind it because the armed mojahedin still roamed the streets. Lecomte correctly pointed the finger at the Caucasian mojahedin, whom he accused of having introduced "contract assassination" to Tehran.[14]

Insecurity at all levels paralyzed the capital as the Democrats' adversaries seized the moment created by the assassination crisis to strike their blow. Their rhetoric was calculated to manipulate deep-rooted popular fear of widespread chaos and social uncertainties and to exploit the genuine worries of religious people, who were rendered vulnerable by their confused comprehension of alien political ideas. In conjuring the specter of destruction of Islam by "extremists," these adversaries were in fact playing two political games: exploiting public fears to boost their own political power and, deliberately or not, furthering the European imperialist Great Game advantage over Persian nationalist interests. Democrats, however, would not relinquish their hard-won influence as easily as the foreign diplomats predicted.

The New Cabinet's Travails

Mostowfi al-Mamalek's cabinet, presented to the Majles on July 26, 1910, included some of the most nationalist anti-Russian, radical reformist Democrats: Hosain Qoli Khan Navab, minister of foreign affairs; Ibrahim Khan Hakim al-Molk, minister of finance; as well as their nonpartisan allies Ahmad Khan Qavam al-Saltaneh (Hasan Khan Vothuq al-Dowleh's brother), minister of war, and Assadollah Mirza, minister of posts and telegraph. Though Sani' al-Dowleh and Vothuq al-Dowleh were no longer part of the cabinet, to the British, Russian, and French satisfaction, the Majles unanimously elected them deputies and, more important, appointed them members of the Committee on Foreign Affairs. Marling erroneously labeled the Democrats Navab and Hakim al-Molk as well as all Democrats as "socialists" and had no good word for any of the cabinet ministers, except Qavam al-Saltaneh. He predicted their fall soon enough for the Sepahdar to take over.[15]

On July 31, 1910, Mostowfi al-Mamalek submitted his program to the Majles. It would consist of hiring foreign experts, reforming the police to ensure public safety and restore calm throughout the nation, establishing a military force equipped with modern weapons, overhauling the education and judiciary systems, and instituting the Court of Appeals (Tamiz). The new cabinet's paramount task was to restore order, which entailed disarming the mojahedin once and for all. Until then, the Majles had been powerless to compel the government to disarm the lawless fighters; it lacked the ready cash to pay them off. Matters got worse when Sattar Khan and Baqer Khan, who had joined the pro-Sepahdar militia led by Sardar Mohiy, instigated the murder of Mirza Ali Mohammad Tarbiyat, the mojahedin chief whom Taqizadeh had appointed to oversee a unified national force. The murder occurred in broad daylight on August 2, 1910, in a teahouse on Lalehzar Avenue, one of the capital's main commercial streets. Marling was convinced that the crime was "purely political" in revenge for the murder of Behbahani. The assassins in the two cases, he remarked, "were the self-promoted champions of the rival parties," engaging in political warfare "carried on by revolvers."[16]

The ensuing street violence provided the government with a timely pretext to deal with the unruly mojahedin. The following day, upon the deputies' request, the ministers attended the Majles to address the urgent issue of national security. Assadollah Mirza, the newly appointed minister of post and telegraph, started the debate by expressing the national sorrow over the murders of both Ayatollah Behbahani, who "had served the constitutional movement so well," and Mirza Ali Mohammad Tarbiyat, which "has wounded the heart of all freedom seekers." He proclaimed emphatically: "Today, the enemy of the country is the Mauser," the weapon used in all the deadly fighting between the various groups, the "real enemy of national independence." He informed the deputies that he had ordered all individuals walking freely in the streets carrying a Mauser to be severely dealt with, regardless of their rank or social status, be they ministers or deputies. He included even those "whose portraits we used to kiss" in homage to their glorious past deeds, alluding to Sattar Khan, Baqer Khan, and other mojahedin leaders. Assadollah Mirza identified those bearing arms collectively as "the number one enemy" of the country, who had to be dealt with speedily to allow the Majles to function in peace. He therefore called on the deputies to gather the "very great power" they had used to destroy the "two great evils of despotism and reactionarism" and dispose of the individuals causing this "third evil," regardless of their "kinship to anyone of us or [of] previous connections in Rasht or Tabriz." He concluded: "The law is sacred and must be enforced," and "we must let the people understand that Iran belongs to Iranians," a veiled reference to the foreign mojahedin.[17] Both the minister of interior and the minister of war endorsed his suggestions.

On the same day, a fierce debate took place in the Majles over freedom of assembly and the press as well as over the cabinet's request for "absolute power" to resolve the political turmoil that was threatening national stability. The press was attacked for publishing "corrupt" articles that contravened the law and incited violence, leading to anarchy; public orators were condemned for their "inflammatory" speeches conducive to antigovernment protests; and organized meetings of "lawless" groups were held responsible for fanning public unrest. Some objected to granting the government unrestricted power to establish order. But, in general, Democrats and Moderates alike agreed that "extraordinary times" necessitated "extraordinary rulings." Isma'il Hashtrudi, the fiery Democrat, concluded the debate by proclaiming: "Now is the time for action"; all national powers were to be handed to the ministers to restore order. Otherwise, he asserted, the Majles cannot legislate the needed reforms, and "we would revert to tribalism," which would mean a total "lack of independence." Some took him to task for what they perceived to be his exaggeration of the situation, arguing that "Lalehzar Boulevard is not Iran," that order prevails in all other places, and that the country is safe and independent. Nonetheless, a resolution passed by a majority vote would allow the government to declare martial law for a period of three months, renewable if necessary, and grant it extensive power to enforce public order. It entailed the drastic measures of banning the carrying of fire arms by anyone except the military and police and of arresting those who resist; of forcefully preventing the publication of any article deemed "corruptible" or "troublemaking"; and of forbidding public meetings without government permission.[18] Hashtrudi pushed hardest for the resolution. The suspension of *Iran-e now*, the most radical paper in the capital, was sustained; it would not resume publication for another seven weeks.

The Battle of Atabak Park and Its Consequences

After consultation with the British and Russian envoys, who had demanded the immediate disarming of all militias, the government decisively gave the mojahedin forty-eight hours to voluntarily disarm. The chief of police, Yeprem Khan, rallied his government troops, composed of "orderly" mojahedin in addition to hundreds of Bakhtiyari fighters, to evict the rebel militias that had gathered their forces at Atabak Park (the present-day location of the Russian embassy). The Russian government and Colonel Vadbolski (full name not known), who had replaced Colonel Lyakhof as commander of the Cossack Brigade in the fall of 1909, decided not to intervene in the fighting that would inevitably arise with the eviction. A battle did indeed erupt on August 7, 1910, and lasted four to seven hours, depending on the source. It resulted in many dead and wounded but also in the disempowering of the radical Rashti and Caucasian mojahedin and their armed supporters. Sardar Mohiy sought refuge first in Zargandeh (at the time the location of the Russian legation's summer residence) and then in the Ottoman embassy. Sattar Khan was wounded and remained disabled until his death a few years later; Baqer Khan surrendered and forever relinquished all political action. Both would later be granted a government pension for life. Haidar Khan Amu-Oghli was arrested but quickly released by order of Democrat officials. He would remain an integral member of the national unified troops that would fight reactionary forces alongside Yeprem Khan, the appointed national commander of the mixed Armenian and Iranian armed groups. Yeprem Khan and Ja'far Qoli Khan Sardar Bahador, the Bakhtiyari commander, emerged as nationally acknowledged heroes. Behind the scenes, Marling surmised that Sardar As'ad was the prime mover in strengthening an "obviously weak" government and had emerged as the determining force behind subsequent developments.[19]

A few weeks later the *anjoman* of Rasht sent an unsigned cable to the Majles questioning the "legality" of the Atabak Park "war" on the militias. Democrats categorically denied the *anjoman*'s right to interfere, symbolically putting an end to the power it had acquired when the radicals had occupied the city. The Majles voted in majority against the request for an answer to their query.[20] The successful albeit bloody disarmament of the mojahedin did not help reduce the political tension that was tearing the constitutionalists' ranks apart, however. The Democrats had succeeded in enacting some laws with the supporting votes of many genuine reformists among the Moderates and nonpartisans. Behbahani's murder, however, unleashed the virulent hostility of anti-Democrats and reactionary forces from inside and outside the Majles. Democrats and their nonpartisan supporters were thus reduced to maneuvering within the tight constraints imposed by conservative political interests that were cleaving to the two European powers.

The Majles renewed its effort to appoint the council of five *mojtaheds* that, as stipulated in clause 2 of the Supplement to the Fundamental Law, would review all laws enacted before their passage. However, the discussion held the day after the Atabak Park battle was acrimonious. Contentious issues were raised, such as whether the *mojtaheds*' candidacy should be based on their being either "the most knowledgeable in the exigencies of the time" or "just knowledgeable"; whether the selection should be made by majority vote or appointed by lottery; what meaning a lottery would have; and what would happen if not all five nominated candidates received a majority vote. The debates often deteriorated into petty arguments over small details, even if irrelevant or concerning semantics. Endless, pointless discussions were devoted to the meaning of "most distinguished" and "distinguished," thus blocking and delaying the deputies' final vote. Some deputies suggested referring to Najaf for their specific understanding of the terms to be applied. Many, including Speaker Zoka' al-Molk, vehemently rejected that notion, arguing that the issue was a constitutional one concerning the Majles alone, not the olama.[21] For days, several attempts at voting failed. However, one important decision, to erase the word *supervisory* attached to the council on the grounds that it did not figure in the Supplement to the Fundamental Law and was therefore unconstitutional, gained unanimous consent.[22] After several more votes proved inconclusive, Solaiman Mirza won the deputies' acquiescence to appointing the five *mojtaheds* by lottery. A final list of five *mojtaheds* was reached.[23] Behbahani's murder seemingly succeeded in accomplishing what the first Majles and months into the second had not. However, as we shall see, the issue had still not been definitively resolved.

By the summer and autumn of 1910, even before the appointed new regent, Naser al-Molk, returned to Tehran from Europe, the Democrat and the Moderate groups had emerged as two distinct political entities. Thus, although their respective platforms may have differed in details and tactics but not in substance, politics trumped policies as the polemical disputes showed no signs of abating. The *Mozakerat* minutes for that summer of 1910 show the Majles as a hotbed of conflict fueled by polemical articles in the parties' respective papers. On the one hand, the Moderate paper *Ruznameh-ye Majles* criticized the Democrats' rejection of moderation, "the method of all rational people," accusing them of demeaning the term to render it "hateful" to public opinion. More important, it bitterly complained of the Democrats' occupying most government posts, as if they were entitled by "inheritance right" and could exclude Moderates. And it blamed "these gentlemen, inventors of revolution," and their allied parties for "all the corruption of the past year."[24] *Iran-e now*, on the other hand, once it resumed publication in late October, would regularly publish articles in the Democrats' defense, denying its leaders were ever revolutionary. In fact, as early as September 1909 the paper had condemned mojahedin militias, arguing that the country needed a modern army, and it would months later denounce political terrorism as counter effective.[25]

Dissenting Armenians

In Tabriz, the local Armenian-controlled Democratic faction secretly combated the opposition. Thanks to the faction's "ingenious tactics," Tigran informed Taqizadeh, the Democrats had a "considerable force" to stir the Majles by sending cables of protest. They referred to themselves as *mellatiyun* (nationalists) to appeal to nonparty members in order to "use them for our purpose."[26] When weeks later Tigran arrived in Tehran to help organize the Democrat Central Committee's activities, he was utterly dismayed to find the committee a "center of ineptitude and laziness," not up to the task of defending its Majles members then under attack. He expressed his outrage when realizing that the so-called Democratic government of Mostowfi al-Mamalek was not Democratic, and he described the state of the party as an affair "à *l'asiatique*," lacking in discipline and organization.[27] Facts on the ground proved his confidence and trust in his party agitators' competence and strength of will unrealistic, if not irrelevant to the complex situation in the capital. He had underestimated the powerful traditional religiopolitical forces hampering the possibility that the Democrats' radical wing could push its agenda ahead. Moreover, Tigran failed to comprehend that most of the Democratic officials, including Taqizadeh while still in power, were, above all, nationalist reformers and not radical revolutionaries in their strategy or ultimate goals and that his group had turned out to be a mere fringe, having lost out to the parliamentarian group that emerged as the party's mainstream. Tigran remained stubbornly oblivious, not to say contemptuous, of the current Democrat officials' pragmatic exercise of power, which required compromise, and in this obliviousness he displayed what was in fact his own total lack of understanding of the prevailing character of the constitutional movement and its main actors.

Furthermore, Tigran deplored the fact that Democrats had forged alliances with the Moderate and Dashnak Parties unconditionally. In April 1910, the Azerbaijan Armenian Central Committee had appointed Hovsep Mirzayan, a Dashnakist leader of the Tehran Committee, as its candidate for the Majles. Fluent in Persian, Mirzayan had supported his committee's proclaimed neutrality in the escalating conflict dividing the Democrats' and Moderates' ranks.[28] When Armenians in Isfahan and elsewhere in southern Iran refused to vote for him, issues were raised in the Majles over the legitimacy of his candidacy as the sole representative of the entire Armenian community in the country. Many deputies insisted Armenian candidates from all different regions had to be sent to Tehran for a second-round election in compliance with the electoral law.[29] The Majles debates were lengthy and divisive. Finally, with the expressed recognition of Azerbaijan as the most important center for all Armenians, the majority voted to accredit Mirzayan as the sole legitimate Armenian deputy on November 26, 1910.[30]

Despite Mirzayan's original skepticism regarding the viability of the constitutional movement and profound distrust of its Democratic leadership, his Majles record demonstrates his genuine interest in promoting the parliamentarian liberalism it espoused. In his inaugural speech, "Yusuf Yanes," as he is referred to in the *Mozakerat*, expressed views that fundamentally were no different from those of the Democratic faction. He considered the rule of the people, with power taken away from one class and given to all members of society regardless of their religious or ethnic background, as the most essential meaning of the term *constitutionalism*. "The individuals in power," he explained, must be "totally free intellectually" and consider all classes equal in their rights. Mirzayan declared that the deficient electoral laws must be changed in favor of universal suffrage. He required all deputies to be educated to assume legislative responsibility and called for judiciary reforms to allow all defendants legal services free of charge. One of the government's important tasks, he added, is to lift prevailing poverty with a better distribution of the country's wealth. In conclusion, he expressed his hope that eventually the slogan "brotherhood and equality," which currently exists only in words, will be realized in deeds and that all religious, ethnic, and tribal groups will unite under the umbrella of one common nation.[31] Solaiman Mirza, the new leader of the Democratic parliamentary faction following Taqizadeh's departure, enthusiastically endorsed Mirzayan's speech as the "first ideological declaration by an elected representative," a model for all to emulate.[32]

While still in Tabriz, Taqizadeh felt increasingly isolated and uninformed about events in the capital. No longer the prominent national leader who had not hesitated to negotiate with nonparty members, he reverted to the more radical rhetoric of his earlier career. He would send instructions to fellow Democrats, urging them to close ranks and ensure the swift execution of the party's "liberal" program. He warned them against the intrigues of their adversaries, the old-time government bureaucrats, who wished to tarnish the reputation of younger progressive officials, destroy liberalism and democracy, and preserve the old system. More significant was his renewed close contact with the Armenian-dominated Democratic faction of Tabriz. Indeed, they helped him during his short stay in his native town, and when he was compelled to leave the country altogether, they financed his travel to Istanbul.

Taqizadeh in exile chose to overlook the intense rivalry dividing Armenian factions, preferring to view them all as forming one politically united ethnic group. He called on all Iranian Democrats to take Armenians as a role model. The Dashnakists, he explained, are working together in support of Yeprem Khan; they consider his success or failure as the party's as well. He commended "all Armenians" who joined the party out of a sense of ethnic loyalty, regardless of their personal political preferences. He lauded their ability to take over schools, hospitals, and libraries and to administer them to control and educate the young generation. Those who do not share their ideas and refuse to join the Dashnakist Party, he claimed, are left unprotected and jobless, as evidenced by the sorry fate of Tigran and other Armenians who had preferred the Iranian Democrat Party.[33] Such statements betrayed Taqizadeh's Armenian fellow Democrats and contradicted his own defense of "freedom of learning" without central-government intervention, made when he was a prominent member of the Majles. It also ran counter to his strictly nonethnic, nonsectarian Iranian nationalism, according to which all citizens enjoy equal rights before the law.

Contrary to Taqizadeh's positive perception of Armenian solidarity, Armenian disputes were in fact aggravating the divide between the Democrat and Moderate Parties, and dissention increasingly tore apart the Dashnakists' ranks. On the one hand, Yeprem Khan, a Dashnakist, had earlier turned hostile to Taqizadeh and his group when the latter attempted to stop his militia from invading Tehran in the spring of 1909. Moreover, as evidenced in his letter to Haidar Khan Amu-Oghli, Yeprem Khan did not believe that the Democrat faction was a "real party."[34] On the other hand, many Dashnakists, including Mirzayan, resented Yeprem Khan's disarmament of the mojahedin with the exception of Haidar Khan's and the Bakhtiyaris' militias. Many complained of his distancing of himself from their party. Others, feeling betrayed, even questioned his loyalty to the Armenian community: "You are theirs [the Iranians], but perhaps first and foremost you are ours because we, by the history of blood, conceived and bore you, and your parents have a right to their demands. . . . You are *our* Yeprem, and we will not let you . . . be only theirs."[35] Yeprem Khan would resign from the Dashnak Party in early 1911.

In addition, as Taqizadeh had observed, Tigran and Pilosian, the original cofounders of the Democrat Party, were the target of a virulently hostile campaign launched by their Armenian rivals, the Dashnakists and the Hnchakists. Mirzayan had pushed hard for the Majles to allow Armenians to have more than one representative, a request Taqizadeh had consistently turned down, as Tigran had urged him to do. Tigran wished to prevent the possible presence of two Dashnakists in the Majles.[36] Taqizadeh was initially the central figure with whom all politically active Armenians wished to collaborate. His choice to work more closely with Tigran, Pilosian, and other Hnchakists turned Democrats had bitterly disappointed the Dashnakists. Though some of the Dashnakists did cooperate with him, most began "provocative attacks" in the summer of 1910, charging the Democrats with "unideological acts of violence" and declaring "neutrality" in the two Iranian parties' conflict. Though the dispute involved individual Dashnakists and Armenian Democrats, Taqizadeh was "their common focal point and target."[37]

A small party, Accord and Progress surfaced in 1910 in support of the Majles Moderates, further complicating party alignments. According to Berberian's Dashnakist sources, the new party was an offshoot of an earlier radical organization formed in Tabriz during the resistance struggles. Composed of Iranians and Dashnakists, it was modeled after the Young Turks' CUP. Dashnakists financed the party's newspaper and figured on its editorial board. The party addressed its entire polemics against the Democrats.[38] As Berberian notes, "The Dashnaktsutium, somewhat similar to the Hnchakian party, privately persisted in its belief that no Iranian political party or organization satisfied the Dashnaktsutium's requirement and/or perception of what constitutes a political party."[39] The Hnchakists had also distanced themselves from the Democrat Party on the grounds that it was not adhering to social democracy. Conversely, the Tabriz Armenian Social-Democrats accused the Hnchakists of nationalism, defending the Armenian people's interests in particular more than the proletariat in general.[40] Adding even more complexity to the parties' conflicts, some members of the Iranian Social-Democratic faction formed an alliance with the Hnchakists when the Democrats declared the Social-Democratic faction obsolete in early 1910.

Generally speaking, apart from the individuals who joined the Democrats, the Armenian groups within Iran were too mired in their own internal rivalries and political conflicts of interest to care much for the Iranian constitutionalists. Hence, a close analysis of the parties active in the second Majles lays bare a stark reality: there was in fact no consistently unified, ideologically radical Iranian-Armenian-Caucasian front that could in any way define Taqizadeh and the Democratic parliamentary faction. Similarly, any loyalty that could bind individual Democrats into an ideologically cohesive political group remained fluid. "Dissention," Browne accurately observed, "is, indeed, one of the greatest dangers which threaten Persia." As a consequence, he feared, the country might be "hampered and thwarted in her struggle" by Russia and Great Britain.[41]

The Cambridge professor's fear was well founded. While the parties' enmity increasingly came to overshadow their common national goals, indigenous and foreign intrigues seriously endangered the Majles's essential legislative tasks. Prime Minister Mostowfi al-Mamalek's effort to run a government that would be able to navigate the intensified party politicking, to bring Democrats and Moderates on board, and to meet the demands made by both Great Britain and Russia and their respective allies at a time when the country was going through a severe financial crisis was doomed almost from the start. Observing the political climate reigning in the capital, the French consul Nicolas would wistfully wish "Taqizadeh's banishment would be revoked and that he would then develop his program and explain his ideas."[42]

The Cabinet's Reformists

Though Prime Minister Mostowfi al-Mamalek did not belong to any faction, he was more inclined to sponsor the program for modernizing reforms and thus gained the Majles Democrats' and the exiled Taqizadeh's support. Similarly, the two new Majles deputies, the nonpartisan Sani' al-Dowleh and Vothuq al-Dowleh, chose to back Mostowfi al-Mamalek's policies. More important, Hosain Qoli Khan Navab, the appointed foreign minister, emerged as the most prominent cabinet figure determined to check Russia's interference in domestic affairs. He would soon come under increased fire for his "uncompromising" anti-Russian attitude.

Navab was born into a notable family originally from Mazandaran. In the eighteenth century, one of his ancestors was appointed by the reigning shah to accompany a royal Indian guest back to India, where he settled, acquiring wealth and the honorific title "Navab." By the time he was back in Iran, Hossain Qoli Khan was awarded the distinguishing British title "Companion of the Bath."[43] In his term as foreign minister, his cordial relationship with Barclay and Marling, although marked by a sense of self-confidence, nonetheless displayed a personal need for the foreign diplomats' recognition of his high official status.[44] Marling understated Navab's staunch nationalist character, portraying his anti-Russian sentiments as being influenced by his friends "in the heat of party warfare," thus putting him "in a difficult position." The British diplomat, however, adequately predicted the foreign minister's predicament: should he succeed in arranging the withdrawal of Russian troops, he would remain in good political standing, but should he fail, his enemies would accuse him of selling himself to Russia.[45] As we shall see, Marling's observation also understated Russia's role in orchestrating Navab's ejection from office.

Navab was much more independent minded in defending national interests than Marling thought. The foreign minister was often challenged in the Majles for failing to keep it informed on his diplomatic interaction with foreign powers, especially Russia. He tried to reassure the deputies that the negotiations for the evacuation were being undertaken in a "friendly" and "properly moderate" manner.[46] He would then insist on his constitutional prerogative as minister in charge of conducting foreign affairs to discuss relevant issues only in closed-door meetings. Assadollah Mirza, the minister of post and telegraph, supported him, arguing that the "diplomatic program" must not be openly debated.[47] Navab lectured the deputies on proper Majles procedure, which was in conformity with "all parliaments in the world"; after all, he reminded them, our rules and regulations are based on a foreign model that offers "the best system."[48] He would not always win that debate, despite the Speaker's support.

Navab's differences with Marling and Barclay over Russia's true intentions widened with the events that unfolded in the following few months. The British envoy attempted to stage Navab's rapprochement with the Russian envoy Poklewski but was not successful. Navab maintained a fierce nationalist resistance to Russian intervention in domestic affairs and to the unending Russian troop presence in Qazvin and Azerbaijan. The issue inevitably increased Great Britain's impatience and intensified Russia's hostility and France's suspicion. Lecomte had in fact predicted that the new government that included Navab, a former British protégé "now at the service of the Revolution [*sic*]," would be as anti-Russian as the previous one.[49] He could not repress his constant contemptuous dismissal of the Iranian leaders' "ambitious program that they flatter themselves they could realize for the glory of the revolution," qualifying the program as indicative of their "megalomania."[50]

The Europeans' obstructionist actions to undermine the nascent constitutional regime in its struggle to retain a semblance of national sovereignty did not end. Debts to British and Russian banks provided the foreign powers with a leverage they would not surrender. The negotiations would consume much of the government officials' and the Majles members' energy, distracting them from legislating and implementing the new reforms, their stated priority.

The Ongoing Loan Negotiations

The endless, time-consuming loan discussions at both the international and national levels went on for months, with the government ministers persistently delaying their submission of an official response to the Anglo-Russian proposed loan. The government was deprived of any sizable revenue not already pledged to servicing existing debts and lacked any administrative expertise to deal with the prevailing near bankrupt financial situation. Even though pressured to consent to unacceptable conditions attached to the loan, the ministers persevered in their search for alternatives. Competing foreign firms raised the ministers' hope for a loan large enough to pay off existing debts to the British and the Russian Banks and to carry on some of their reform projects. The two powers would then forcefully inform European financiers of Tehran's lack of credentials and viable financial resources. Marling would also warn of the Persian government's "notorious" behavior of "diverting" funds to "other purposes." He readily acknowledged the fact that the Majles was trying to "break down the old system" but saw no results except "chaos." He was highly skeptical of the country's prospects for obtaining a loan large enough to pay off all existing debts at a lower rate of interest.[51] Hence, the new cabinet would prove as vulnerable as its predecessors in its effort to raise a foreign loan independently.

Lord Grey, under pressure from British business firms, came to realize that safety of and restoration of order on the roads in the South needed urgent action, which in turn required an advance of ready cash. He suggested to his Russian counterpart that they revise the terms of their joint loan proposal by offering it without conditions and reducing the interest rate from 7 to 5 percent. The Russians categorically rejected his suggestion.[52] He then began to view favorably the Anglo-Persian Oil Company's proposal to offer a loan in exchange for the Persian government's shares of the company. The deal would have the advantage of keeping the company British and preempting any other foreign ownership. The oil company eagerly pursued the deal, having its representative in Tehran, J. R. Preece, conduct bilateral negotiations while simultaneously consulting the Foreign Office. In exchange for a loan of half a million pounds at 5½ percent interest, the company wanted all of the government's company shares, rights, and royalties; surplus of the customs revenue not already pledged to Britain and Russia; surplus of the telegraph revenues similarly not pledged; and all government mining shares, royalties, and percentage profit.[53]

As the discussions went on, Sergei Sazanov, the tsar's newly appointed acting minister of foreign affairs, declared he had no objections in principle to the Anglo-Persian Oil Company's negotiations, but he wished to delay their conclusion until the consolidation of the debts to the Russian Bank.[54] Yet, as evident in the Anglo-Russian diplomatic correspondence, the Russian government never tried to hide its reluctance to advance money to the Persians. Regardless of Russia's true geo-economic motive, this stalling tactic was meant to maintain Tehran's desperate pecuniary situation as long as possible. Recognizing the new cabinet's position of economic weakness, which underscored its political vulnerability, Sazanov preferred to wait till Tehran "pleaded" with the two powers for financial assistance.[55] When that wish failed to be realized soon enough, the two powers thought of sending an oral warning "to take the necessary steps if the Persian government does not see fit to fall in with [their] legitimate demands."[56]

Financial companies such as the Seligman Brothers firm, represented in Tehran by Arthur Moore, persisted on resisting British and Russian government objections to their offers of a loan to Iran. They intensified their competition for Iranian concessions while reassuring the two powers of their intention to seek only any "surplus" of pledged revenues as securities on the loan. But the Foreign Office would reply: "Such a surplus does not at present exist."[57] Lord Grey was particularly worried that non-British capital might be involved in these companies' offers. Seligman Brothers reassured him they alone and not the other European financial partners would negotiate with the Persian government, without any reference to other sources of capital. The loan was to be secured on the southern Iran customs revenue. But both Barclay, who had returned to Tehran in the fall, and Grey worried that this financial arrangement would "clearly afford a footing in the Gulf to other Powers."[58]

All the while, Iranian ministers, independently from Russian officials but with British tacit agreement, applied for a £100,000 cash advance on the proposed loan from the British Imperial Bank to be secured on the Crown Jewels. The Foreign Office had no objections, but Poklewski rejected the application. The Persian government continued to plead, in fact "begging" British officials to consider the requested cash advance seriously, desperate as it was to service its debts, cover its expenditures, and restore road safety in the South.[59] The advance was apparently secretly granted, judging from the Majles's interrogation of Sani‘ al-Dowleh months later, when he was accused of foregoing the Majles's ratification of the deal in compliance with the Constitution.[60]

In the meantime, British companies engaged in trade in the British zone of influence were losing patience with the Foreign Office. The *Times* published articles and a letter written by H. F. B. Lynch on the chaos and lawlessness prevailing in the British zone.[61] Lynch, one of the original founders of the Persia Committee, owned several family enterprises in the gulf region. The Manchester Chamber of Commerce blamed Grey for "acting in harmony and complete agreement" with the Russians, "discouraging and weakening the Persian government," and leaving it without the means or the power to restore order on the trade routes. It urged British officials to help put an end to the chaos prevailing in the South.[62] A month later, as safety on the trade routes continued to deteriorate, a British company urged Grey to take the necessary measures to help restore the confidence to do business in the area. Thus, British business leaders' increased pressure on the Foreign Office compelled Grey to discuss a joint Anglo-Russian threat of intervention to secure the trade routes unless the Persian government acted responsibly on its own to restore order. The British foreign minister, in agreement with Sazanov, considered sending Indian troops under British command to the gulf region. As we shall see, Barclay drafted a note to send an ultimatum to the Persian government in which he would "insist" on the organization of a force in the South, composed of some twelve hundred Indian soldiers under British officers' command to police the Bushehr–Shiraz–Isfahan road if within three months order were not restored. He would not submit the note till weeks later, however.

Escalation of Tensions

The Russian government relentlessly maintained a hostile attitude toward Mostowfi al-Mamalek's cabinet and refused to evacuate its troops from Qazvin unless Mokhber al-Saltaneh was dismissed as governor of Azerbaijan. Mostowfi al-Mamalek's announcement to the Majles that the withdrawal of the occupying forces would soon be secured "with the assistance of friendly Governments [*sic*],"[63] obviously meaning Germany and Turkey, had further incensed St. Petersburg officials. In addition to the dismissal of Mokhber al-Saltaneh from his post in Azerbaijan, they demanded that the Russian Road Company be allowed to bring motor cars onto the Rasht–Anzali–Tehran road and that complete Russian authority over the Cossack Brigade be restored. Navab, the most authoritative member of the cabinet, dismissed all demands. The Majles, he argued, would not grant concessions for more motor cars for it would give Russians complete control of the traffic on the northern roads. And he adamantly insisted on keeping the Cossack Brigade and its commander "subordinate to the orders of the Minister of War as regards the use to be made of the force."[64] He did not trust the brigade's Russian officers, considering them to be "*agents provocateurs*." His stand provoked British pessimistic assessment of any attempt to assuage Russian antagonism toward Mostowfi al-Mamalek's cabinet. In fact, St. Petersburg's hostility would only intensify in the following months. The Tehran government "now proving intractable," Sazanov urged Lord Grey to issue strong threats that would also include an increase in the number of Russian troops in the country.[65]

Tehran officials continued to resist the pressure. In early September 1910, Mostowfi al-Mamalek's cabinet sent the two embassies a response to the Anglo-Russian proposal for a joint loan made on May 7, which had laid out several demands and conditions. The ministers denied any intention to grant concessions to foreign companies and reminded the two powers of their "obligation to protect Persia's independence" and their repeated assurances of noninterference in its internal affairs. In the same vein, Navab assured Barclay personally of his government's friendly relations with Britain but also its determination to safeguard its national independence. The two envoys returned the note to the Ministry of Foreign Affairs with a warning of the dire consequences of noncompliance to their demands.[66] Iranian diplomats and journalists at home and abroad pursued a relentless public denunciation of Russian occupation. Persian diplomats in European capitals reportedly were instructed to inform the local press about the harsh behavior of troops in Tabriz and Qazvin. Similarly, *Habl al-matin*'s editor regularly condemned British support of Russia's aggressive policies. In the issue of September 12, 1910, the paper promoted the idea of forming an alliance between secret societies and Russian revolutionaries to foment troubles that would force a Russian evacuation. It also contemplated guerrilla warfare and encouraged the olama to proclaim a boycott of Russian goods until all troops evacuated.[67]

On October 2, 1910, the Russian consul general in Baghdad dispatched a letter to the *mojtahed* Khorasani, asking him to resort to his "unerring judgement" and not act on the words of some "unpatriotic" Persians proposing to wage a holy war and boycott Russian goods or on the words of "some Europeans" intriguing against Russian commercial interests. Warned of an "unavoidable defeat by the mightier Russian military" and the "severe repercussions" for Persia's own commercial interests, Khorasani was urged to consider "the disastrous results" of such actions. Khorasani's son replied on his father's behalf. Assuring the consul of Persian officials' friendly relations with Russia, he stated they were concerned only with safeguarding national independence. Denying that a religious war was being promulgated, he nevertheless warned that as long as the Russian troops remained in the country, "it is the imperative duty of every Persian, or rather every Moslem and especially all spiritual authorities of Islam . . . not to leave any stone unturned . . . for the defence of Moslems rights and Islamic dominions."[68]

British Ultimatum of October 14

In contrast to Poklewski, Barclay was friendly to the cabinet ministers who were closer to the Democrats, persevering in his assessment of their party as the only body "bearing any semblance to a party in the accepted sense." He was doubtful that a "less inconveniently nationalist" cabinet could be formed, given the "nationalist minority" controlling power in the Majles. And he confessed his pessimism regarding a possible Persian–Russian conciliation because Russia could not expect the same "subservient attitude" from the Persians displayed by the previous regime. In fact, he did not dismiss the possibility of Russia "permitting intrigues among her influential protégés," mentioning the Sepahdar in particular, to provoke an intervention.[69]

With the anti-Russian political climate giving no sign of abating, on October 14, 1910, Barclay sent the Tehran government the note he had drafted earlier, giving it three months to restore order in the South. Failure to do so, he warned, would force the British government to take the necessary steps to secure the southern roads' safety by sending Indian troops under British command. Expenses would be covered by a one percent surcharge on custom duties on all goods imported at the southern ports and from the revenues of Fars. Russia, considering such a force a legitimate counterpart to the Cossack Brigade, agreed.[70] The note provoked turmoil in Iran and among anti-imperialist elements in Europe. It was denounced as blatant evidence of an Anglo-Russian plan for a de facto partitioning of Iran. Navab angrily responded within ten days, writing down a long list that outlined the country's dire situation, including a depleted Treasury and unacceptable loan conditions damaging the nation's sovereignty, royalists' intrigues to bring back the exiled shah, and, referring to Behbahani's assassin, criminals escaping justice by pretending to be foreign subjects. He assured Barclay that British trade had no reason to complain and that, in fact, the volume of trade had increased since the restoration of the constitutional government.[71] The Lynch Brothers Company informed the Foreign Office that the trade figures had indeed increased by 30 percent over the previous year.[72]

The loan negotiations between all the parties went on, delaying a satisfactory result for any of them and further aggravating Tehran's dire financial situation. In fact, the various loan proposals were invariably economically disadvantageous to the Persians, especially with respect to the conditions attached. Moore had informed Barclay that after the Persian government paid all the outstanding debts to Russian and British creditors, not much of Seligman Brothers' loan would be left at its disposal. The director of the British Imperial Bank concurred: "By the time the Persian Government has finished with Seligman's [loan]," he wrote the Foreign Office, "they would realize what their money cost them."[73] The bank was then ready to make a counteroffer of £1.25 million pounds at 5 percent based on customs receipts at all Persian Gulf ports. By mid-October, all three major lenders competed fiercely for their respective loan proposals. The Anglo-Persian Oil company offer added two more conditions: (1) the installation of a telephone line deemed necessary for its enterprise in the South and (2) use of its own barges in navigating the Karun River. Vakil al-Ro'aya, the deputy head of the Majles Financial Committee, and all cabinet ministers except Navab reportedly accepted the oil company's loan terms. The foreign minister, however, objected to the terms on the grounds that they would violate the indisputable right of his government to construct the country's means of communication and transport. He also opposed the Imperial Bank's proposal.[74] Barclay began to reverse his view of Navab, believing he had become, since Taqizadeh's exile, "the leader of the Extremist [*sic*] section of the Nationalist Party, notorious for its anti-Russian attitude."[75] Foreign Minister Navab and his allies' resistance to the Anglo-Russian loan centered not only on its onerous terms but also on the further erosion of national sovereignty that the two powers' economic juggernaut would prove to be. Grey was adamant in his refusal to support any proposal "likely to prejudice the interests of the British Bank." As a consequence, any other loan offer was "quashed" by Russia and Britain.[76]

Moore subsequently remained in Tehran, resuming his journalistic career as correspondent for the *Times* while continuing to support Navab's search for other loan prospects. Moore intended to discredit the British Imperial Bank and to reopen negotiations with the Seligman Brothers. The Majles would later reject a last-minute condition added to the British loan, which demanded the payment in full of a £40,000 debt resulting from the cancelled lottery concession of 1889. The Democrats, led by the Speaker, categorically refused to assume the fallen regime's decades-old debt. The Russian government would not relinquish its demand for the consolidation of Persian debts to its bank before giving its consent to the British loan. Grey continued to insist "the [Imperial] Bank must be left free to make a firm offer to the Persian government."[77]

Navab's "intransigence" persisted. In a letter dated October 23, 1910, also signed by Mostowfi al-Mamalek, Qavam al-Saltaneh, and Assadollah Mirza, the foreign minister requested the opening of the Russian-owned Jolfa–Tabriz road to Persian-owned cars and demanded transit right through Russia for Persian nationals. In addition, he claimed the Persian government's right to regulate the tariff for motor-car services, and he asserted that a three-year extension of a mine concession would be effective only after Russia's withdrawal of its troops from Qazvin. Russia had to "show her goodwill by first withdrawing her troops" before his government could "show good marks of goodwill," he wrote.[78] In the meantime, on October 30, Mostowfi al-Mamalek reshuffled his cabinet. Sani' al-Dowleh was reinstated as head of the Ministry of Finance, and Navab remained in charge of the Ministry of Foreign Affairs. The appointments of two Qajar princes, 'Ayn al-Dowleh and Farman-Farma to the Ministry of Interior and the Ministry of War, respectively, would not tilt the government toward a more "moderate" political stand.

Worldwide Condemnation of the British Ultimatum of October 14

In Tehran, the local press published translated texts of foreign-press articles depicting the ultimatum as constituting a loss of Persian sovereignty and frequently calling for Germany to "take great interest in Persia."[79] On November 17, 1910, a massive protest against the British ultimatum and Russian military occupation, in defense of the Constitution and national independence, and in favor of international solidarity in combating imperialism was held at Tupkhaneh Square. Barclay reported that the "Nationalist [*sic*] elements in the majles [*sic*]" had organized it.[80] In contrast, in the European and Turkish press the Anglo-Russian note was seen in some circles as evidence of Britain and Russia's intention to occupy and partition Persia. Rome reacted in a similar way but expressed its reaction more diplomatically. The Turkish press viewed the Anglo-Russian-French Triple Entente alliance as a direct threat to its government's interests in northwestern Iran. It justified Turkish military activities there as measures taken to protect its resident nationals, compatible with British and Russian policy in their respective spheres of influence. On October 23, 1910, a conference of Moslems was organized in Istanbul, calling for Moslem and Eastern countries' alliance against European imperialism.[81] Some Young Turk officials sent cables to Najaf and Karbala, asking the Shi'a olama to rise in defense of fellow Moslems. And they decided to appeal to the German emperor, who was perceived as "the champion of the downtrodden" Moslems, to rescue Persia and Islam.[82]

On October 23, 1910, a group of protesting Persians and Turks met in Berlin to denounce British policies and to hail Germany and the emperor "as the only true friends" of Moslems. On November 1, 1910, in an article entitled "The Partition of Persia and German Trade There," the influential paper *Berliner Tageblatt* discussed extensively the potential advantages for Germany of the struggle over Persia. Citing rumors spread by Persian expatriates in Berlin about their country's potential boycott of British goods in response to the ultimatum, the article predicted Persia would turn to Germany as its favorite trade partner.[83] The German press increased its virulent anti-British articles, trying to persuade the public of the Anglo-Russian intention to partition Persia. Foreign-affairs officials in Germany, however, saw "no cause for anxiety" as long as its commercial interests were "not ignored."[84]

In a letter scolding Barclay for the threatening wording of the October ultimatum, which had led to such European and Turkish press speculation, Grey denied he had expressed a wish for a policy of "active intervention," except when necessary to protect Britain's citizens and trade.[85] By November 9, Barclay, too, came to regret his wording and apologized for having gone further "than was intended in threatening the Persian government."[86] In reality, the Foreign Office never contemplated occupation, and Grey continually instructed his diplomats to avoid any such thought. His government, he repeatedly informed his diplomats, would not assume the obligations that occupation would entail. And he pressured Russia to consent to the

British Imperial Bank loan. "Unless the Persian government is to be allowed to collapse completely," he argued, "it is essential" for Persian officials to have the necessary means to restore order in the South, "without involving a British occupation of territory."[87] In a confidential note to his envoy in St. Petersburg written on November 18, he observed that Russian troops' "indefinite stay" would be "inconsistent with the maintenance of any native government at all in Persia when combined with refusal or prevention of all financial help."[88] A day later, the Imperial Bank submitted the loan contract to the Persian government, knowing that its signing would take enough time to allow the consolidation of debts owed the Russian bank, which St. Petersburg insisted upon.[89]

The Majles, indeed, prolonged the loan debate that began on December 6. Vakil al-Ro'aya assured the Imperial Bank that his Majles committee accepted its offer. Navab and Sani' al-Dowleh fought hard to win some amendments, which the bank then conceded to: the reduction of the interest rate from 7 to 5 percent and the redeeming of the loan in five years instead of fifteen. Sani' al-Dowleh urged the Majles to vote in favor, but many deputies demanded a look at the complete, detailed government budget, as yet to be submitted. They could not, they argued, approve sight unseen a contract without knowing the budget, which should determine the amount of the requested loan. Shaikh Assadollah Kordestani, the Majles's regular agent provocateur, even went so far as to deny the need for such a loan. The Imam Jom'eh (as referred to in the *Mozakerat*), the traditionalist cleric-deputy, categorically rejected the contracting of any foreign loan. Reminding his colleagues of the disastrous consequences of the late Mozaffar al-Din Shah's loans, he predicted that a similar corruption would occur. "Anyone who agrees with contracting a [foreign] loan is sharing in the nation's blood," he warned gloomily. He concluded that as usual no one would agree with him, but "it is my duty to say this."[90] Moderates such as Mostashar al-Dowleh and Assadollah Mirza, acknowledging the need for borrowed money, required more detailed information on the loan's management and expenditure. "Borrowing without control," Assadollah Mirza asserted, "is unacceptable. And the loan proceedings cannot be left without close supervision of its proper spending."[91]

The Majles voted in favor of forming a special joint committee of Moderates and Democrats to review the bank's contract. The committee, which would include two officials from each ministry as well as a European adviser, was charged with the proper distribution of sums allocated to each ministry. It would control all expenditures and prevent corruption.[92]

Germany and the Railway Project

The construction of a national railway system was an important part of the constitutionalists' reform program, without which, they were convinced, their modernization project would be incomplete. Persian officials ideally wished to grant a railway concession to anyone they could trust, provided it was a commercial enterprise independent of the two major foreign powers, Russia and Britain. Sani' al-Dowleh favored German firms. But no such project could avoid passing through either the British or the Russian zone of influence. Anglo-Russian maneuvers to keep German enterprises from gaining a solid footing in Iran had continued unabated. Britain and Russia were determined to block Germany's projected extension of the Baghdad Railway into Iran. In Russia, a syndicate of financial firms had in the summer of 1910 proposed to connect Indian and Russian railroad systems through Iran to "effectually compete with, if not kill, the Baghdad Railway." The idea was to create an Anglo-Russian "world railway" with an "uninterrupted line" linking Asia with Europe and "ourselves to go right into Persia, and not wait passively till foreign goods . . . destroy our monopoly."[93] Paradoxically, the syndicate vigorously denied the possibility of using this "world-wide" transport system as a "weapon of local politics."[94] That statement belied the underlying motives of the entire project, as explained in the syndicate's memorandum, which specifically indicated that its objective was to compete with the German Baghdad Railway project. Economic considerations in that period were intrinsically entangled with geopolitical interests. The syndicate, fully aware of Persian officials' distrust of any British or Russian project in their country, seriously contemplated including French and Belgian participants to mask its Anglo-Russian identity.[95]

The British response to the proposal was, on the whole, quite positive. But the German and Russian emperors' projected meeting in Potsdam in early November 1910 raised serious concerns in London and Paris. The Quai d'Orsay worried Sazanov would secretly reach an agreement with German foreign-affairs officials that would irrevocably damage the Triple Entente system of alliance. The Foreign Office also suspected that the Russian foreign minister would allow a Baghdad Railway extension into Iran's so-called neutral zone. Grey instructed his envoy in St. Petersburg to insist that Sazanov first consult Britain and France before the meeting and that he remind the Germans of the Anglo-Russian "exclusive" political interests in Persia, which "have always been recognized"; Sazanov agreed.[96] However, the Russian foreign minister doubted that the two powers could prevent Germany from obtaining a railway concession in the neutral zone terminating in the gulf port of Bushehr.

The intricate and often secretive international diplomacy before the outbreak of World War I sometimes crisscrossed existing alliances. In the labyrinthine European corridors of power, governments sought their respective interests regardless of their commitments to their official allies. The Potsdam conference aimed at resolving the geostrategic issues confronting the Russian and German imperial governments, including the Baghdad Railway line to the Persian Gulf. Upon his return from the meeting, Sazanov reported to Hugh O'Beirne, the British diplomat in St. Petersburg, that Britain's demands were satisfactorily met; more specifically, the neutral zone was declared a matter that "could only be treated *a trois*."[97] In an interview by the Russian press, Sazanov went further, stating categorically that all discussions were "based on recognition of the absolute inviolability of the foundations of the existing political situation." Russia would not renounce its alliance with France or its agreement with Britain.[98] Sazanov also openly admitted to the French ambassador in St. Petersburg that the existing system of alliances and entente was an "established principle," even though Germany and Russia "might seek a settlement of their differences."[99] The Potsdam participants agreed that Germany would renounce all political advantages in Persia but would be granted commercial equality. In return, Russia would consent to the construction of the future Baghdad Railway line passing through the Russian zone to a junction in Khanekin on the Persian border with Ottoman Iraq, where it would be linked to Tehran via the future Persian railway. The Munich press hailed the Russo-German railway agreement as representing "a severe blow to British diplomacy."[100]

For Sani' al-Dowleh and his fellow reformists, however, that Russo-German agreement was not a promising sign for the Persians' own national project: their worst adversary was concocting a project with the country in which they had vested their hope for financial and technological help.

10

Battling for the Future

THE SECOND MAJLES, dubbed the "nation's holy shrine," was intended to complete the legislative reforms stipulated in the Supplement to the Fundamental Law of 1907 and to enact each ministry's rules and regulations, thus establishing a more orderly and sustainable system of governance than the preceding legislature. In attempting to accomplish their "sacred" task, the deputies had learned important lessons after the debacle of 1908: not translating lofty words written on paper into action would leave the nation as weak and vulnerable to tyranny and foreign encroachment as ever. However, inexperience, corruption, a depleted Treasury, and the novelty of alien political and cultural concepts accentuated the fragility of the new system they were building from ground zero. Arduous efforts to enforce the administrative reforms so far enacted constantly encountered numerous obstacles. The constitutional regime's ability to raise the money needed to implement them was, as already shown, severely restrained. Moreover, the attempted enforcement of its authority throughout the country met with unabated resistance in the provinces, where tribal conflicts and power struggles among the local political elite underscored the central government's weakness. The reformists in both the Majles and the government were, indeed, facing attacks from all directions while simultaneously challenging foreign powers' political and financial pressure. The insurmountable obstacles did not, however, stop them from trying to accomplish their all-important legislative tasks; in fact, the obstacles strengthened the deputies and ministers' intention to enact the necessary reforms deemed essential to the construction of the new Iran. The second Majles was battling for the future, as many deputies often reminded their colleagues.

In late July 1910, Mostowfi al-Mamalek had sent to the Majles his new cabinet's program for approval. It concerned hiring foreign experts, reforming the police and security systems to ensure peace and public safety throughout the nation, establishing military forces equipped with modern weapons, reforming the judiciary and instituting the Court of Appeals (Tamiz), and reforming the education system.[1] In open sessions, deputies deliberated the reforms pertaining to various ministries, chief among them Education, Justice, and Finance.

Ministry of Education and Public Works

The Majles had debated the need to divide the Ministry of Education and Public Works into two separate entities. Assadollah Mirza vehemently rejected the motion, asserting his conviction that both must be part of the same ministry, upon which the nation had set great hope for the country's development.[2] By December 1910, the ministry still carried the dual function, divided into several sections, including education and antiquities, religious endowments, forests and parks, mines and water, roads and transportation, among others. All sections were to follow their respective rules and regulations, although the latter were still under discussion. Some issues pertaining to education had already been heatedly debated in previous open sessions, leading to the formation of an advisory board to resolve issues arising from conflicts between religious and public schools, their respective programs, and assigned textbooks for both. Traditionally, the terms *maktab* and *madreseh* applied to religious schools. The Majles began to differentiate them, however, the former for religious schools and the latter for public schools.

The majority had voted in favor of rules that would reorganize the entire system, in effect laicizing it and bringing it under the centralized authority of the ministry. Universal primary and secondary schooling was declared free; its textbooks were to be selected by appropriate staff and were to be used uniformly nationwide. Even the *owqaf* institutions, which had for centuries remained solely under religious management, were brought under the Ministry of Education to administer their private funds and supervise their expenditures.[3] At that stage, in contrast to traditionalist lay and olama's destructive contention decades earlier, there were no serious objections to this radical departure from traditional practices, according to the *Mozakerat-e Majles dovvom*, the minutes of the parliamentary debates. It is worth mentioning here that these official minutes periodically omitted dissenting arguments, judging from many deputies' registered protests regarding this omission.[4] However, it must also be noted that in the summer and fall of 1910, Democrats led by Solaiman Mirza and other nonpartisan reformists such as Sani' al-Dowleh, at that time a Majles member, controlled the debates. They were thus able to pass many bills despite some traditionalist conservatives' objections.

However, the case of the Imam Reza religious endowment, one of the most important in the country attached to the Mashhad mosque and named after the local shrine of the eighth Shi'a Imam, engendered some heated discussions. The Ministry of Interior had sent a "modern-minded"[5] and "pious" representative to audit the endowment's books. Seyyed Hosain Ardabili, the nonpartisan deputy, deplored the delay in implementing the newly legislated reforms; the deputy minister in charge conceded that the audit had not yet started and that the endowment's affairs were run "as in old times." The new law, he explained, required the reorganization of the entire system to become a "model for the rest of the *owqaf* throughout the country." It could not be achieved in a short time, given the current shortage of experienced personnel and lack of necessary funds to pay their salaries.[6] This particular, highly sensitive religious issue was not put to rest until much later, when the Majles was struggling for its survival, as we shall see.

Similarly, the question of sending students to study abroad, though passed unanimously, was not yet resolved by January 1911 for lack of funding. Solaiman Mirza in particular passionately argued for a speedy submission of the government budget to finance the selected students' travel to Europe. Education has top priority over all other projects, he said, pronouncing it a "sacred goal" for the nation's development. And, once more, he insisted on preferably selecting poor but qualified rather than socially privileged young men. Past experience, he claimed, has shown money was wasted on the rich, who acquired the European lifestyle and manners but no professional skills or scientific knowledge. Vakil al-Tojjar, objecting to the high cost of studies abroad, argued that the money could be spent instead on schools in the country to educate hundreds of students or even to bring teachers from abroad, thus preserving Iranian youths' moral values. Solaiman Mirza angrily rebutted, pointing to the lack of qualified teachers and the students' ignorance of foreign languages, which meant they wouldn't understand their foreign instructors. Besides, he added, most academic institutions in Europe are free of charge or require minimal fees. Shaikh al-Ra'is supported the Democrat on the need to "rejuvenate the nation's spirit." He refuted some deputies' religiously based objection that sending young Moslems to study abroad is incompatible with their religious values. Acquiring knowledge of the French language, he further claimed, would help the olama when conversing with foreigners and members of the "protected religions" (as the country's Jews and Christians were referred to). Conversely, he added, the government should also send students to study religious sciences at the holy centers to help the Ministry of Justice enforce proper compliance with the holy law.[7]

Hakim al-Molk, then minister of education and public works, had requested the Majles to immediately choose Dar al-Fonun graduates to study at the university in Paris. They would return home with their degrees and work for the government.[8] Of great significance is the fact that the issues then debated chiefly concerned lack of sufficient funds and the long delay in finalizing the foreign-loan proposal rather than religious obstruction serious enough to defeat the project.

The Ministry of Education was also charged with establishing museums, public libraries, scientific and historic institutions, as well as a school of arts to help restore ancient Persian and Islamic arts.[9] Interest in archaeological excavation was rising, reflecting the nationalists' growing realization of the value of such findings. Its advocates in the Majles eloquently spoke of the newly discovered antique objects as precious parts of the ancient Persian culture that should be exhibited in museums. There were calls for sending students abroad to study archaeology and in the meantime hiring foreign archaeologists to excavate the sites, as the Greeks and Egyptians had been doing. However, the greater interest was attached to the antiquities' commercial value. Though the government was officially the custodian of all sites in the country, some deputies fiercely debated the exclusive right of the owner of the land where the site was located to dispose of all found objects in complete freedom, including selling them to dealers for export. Shaikh al-Ra'is proposed a 5 percent tax on the cash value of the antiquities. A modern educated prince-physician-deputy, Dr. Haydar Mirza, challenged the motion, accusing the "ignorant" and "greedy" property owners who, not knowing the value of their possessions, were selling out the national cultural heritage to foreigners. All archaeological sites, he proclaimed, belong to the nation and should be protected by state regulations and administered by the Ministry of Education. To those who rose in defense of private property, Behjat al-Olama, the religious conservative deputy from Arabestan who was in favor of government jurisdiction over the sites, retorted: "The law always limits freedom when needed."[10] The Moderate Shaikh al-Ra'is no less emphatically countered that freedom is restricted solely when the holy law is contravened and if a person's right is infringed upon. He reminded his fellow deputies that the counsel of five *mojtaheds* was not yet formed to resolve these critical questions, thereupon raising the continued vexing issue of the religious council.

Though twenty candidates for the council had already been chosen, the withdrawal of some from nomination delayed the entire procedure. Many new questions were raised, and endless discussions on tedious interpretations of clause 2 of the Supplement to the Fundamental Law led an exasperated deputy to express his suspicion: "There are some who want to suppress" the creation of this council, directly referring to Mohammad Hashem Mirza, the nonpartisan liberal prince-deputy.[11] In fact, many more deputies, regardless of their political affiliation, supported clause 2 in only a lukewarm way, to say the least. Two days later the Majles finally voted to replace the candidates who had withdrawn their nomination, resorting to the selection by lottery because the voting failed four times to reach a majority.

Most deputies defended all private enterprise against increasing government regulations, to Sani' al-Dowleh's dismay. The finance minister, formerly in charge of the Ministry of Education and Public Works, repeatedly objected to any suggestion of maintaining the time-honored practice of private ownership of water, forests, and roads. "It is my duty to insist," he said, "that all matters concerning water" pertain exclusively to government jurisdiction. Responding to the proposal by the deputy minister of education and public works to grant an individual investor the right to repair *qanat*s (underground water canals) and water distribution, he asserted: "It is wrong to entrust a company or an individual" with such a vital public resource. And he emphatically proclaimed all matters concerning infrastructure renovation or new construction, including dams and water distribution, must be administered by the government, which is solely responsible for all public services. His intensive centralization program would include roads, transport, and means of communication as fundamental parts.[12] He strongly believed that only the representative government should assume the authority on behalf and in the interest of the nation to deliver such public services, thus departing from long traditional practices honored until then. But Sani' al-Dowleh also considered private commercial and industrial enterprises necessary for national development. He and his family were the most prominent entrepreneurs at that time.

The Ministry of Justice

The deputies received numerous complaints of alleged injustices committed by corrupt judges or other officials and of unconstitutional arrests of individuals without warrant. They summoned the minister of justice to question decisions undertaken without prior consultation with the Majles. Hosain Dabir al-Molk, the minister, blamed the deputies for not completing the promised judicial reforms and vigorously justified his right in the meantime to dismiss some judges and replace them with knowledgeable, reform-minded individuals. Weeks later, when summoned again to answer deputies' complaints, he accused the Majles Judiciary Committee of not fulfilling its task properly and lamented both the existing shortage of knowledgeable men and financial constraints. Although rising in the minister's defense, Solaiman Mirza nonetheless blamed the ministry for not following the lawful procedure in appointing judges.[13]

Such debates highlighted the government's dire financial situation: the ministries had no budget to implement their ambitious programs or even to pay the salaries of the functionaries they currently had or to recruit new ones. Some deputies asserted that no reforms could be implemented without adequate financing, not even those pertaining to the military and security affairs, an assertion that provoked a severe reprimand from Assadollah Mirza, minister of post and telegraph. Reforms must be legislated, he retorted, regardless of the availability of funds; "money should be found," no matter how.[14] He had earlier asked candidly: Where do we get the money?[15] The requested loans were not forthcoming; the negotiations were still mired in international economic and geopolitical conflicts beyond the deputies' control. Moreover, customs duties levied in the southern and northern ports, the largest sources of revenue, were pledged to pay off the nation's current debts to foreign banks. Provincial authorities disposed of local taxes willy-nilly, skimming off most of the money taken in before sending the remainder to the central Treasury. Taxes levied in Arabestan, for instance, were distributed among the Bakhtiyaris, local notables, and various cities in the South. Not a dinar reached the government, deputies lamented in the Majles; it was all "wasted."[16]

The budget remained the cabinet's responsibility before sending it to the appropriate Majles committee for discussion behind closed doors. However, by January 1911 Minister of Justice Dabir al-Molk had resigned, and deputies continued to complain of the slow progress in implementing judicial reforms. They expressed their disenchantment with a system in a state of total disarray. They desired the speedy consolidation of centralized institutions to establish equality of all before the law throughout the country in accordance with the constitutional mandate. But they were aware that unpaid salaries only maintained officials' tradition of raising funds locally, which allowed diverse, long-standing court systems in different provinces to prevail. Local customs thus endured, bypassing the central government's authority.[17]

Tax Reforms

As stated in the previous chapter, taxes were levied on some basic commodities, including salt. By January 1911, there was general agreement in the Majles on the need to raise state revenues by levying new taxes on opium. The deputies' major concern was the widespread consumption of the narcotic, defined as a "deadly poison" that afflicted especially the poor and weak members of society, so its production had to be drastically curtailed. Taxing it would therefore benefit society and the Treasury. But deputies and government officials disagreed on all other matters concerning that issue, such as the new rules to regulate both domestic and foreign sales. Vakil al-Ro'aya, among many others regardless of their political allegiance, favored tax-free trade in opium and poppy seeds, with no government intervention, thus preserving the merchants' exclusive commercial rights. Khorasan deputy Kashef (full name not known) asserted that the opium trade in Iran "belongs to the merchants," free of government interference. A government monopoly, he went on, would not only infringe on the merchants' exclusive commercial entitlement but also cause drastic financial losses. Therefore, he said, "we must not inflict damages to their wealth."[18] Similarly, Vakil al-Ro'aya fiercely opposed a motion to grant the government the exclusive right to regulate and control the production and domestic sale of opium. Doing so would "dishonor" the government, he and others argued rather dubiously, because the ayatollahs have condemned opium as "unlawful and forbidden," like alcohol. How, therefore, could the government get involved in this trade? he asked. The minister of interior agreed, yet he believed a government monopoly would constitute the best means to prevent consumption of the "deadly poisonous" substance. Sani' al-Dowleh proposed only two options worth considering to prevent consumption: "Either taking the trade away from the people" and transferring it to a government monopoly or imposing a heavy tax to render it prohibitive. The physician-deputy Dr. Ali Khan was the sole voice favoring the total ban of opium consumption in any form. Another deputy responded cynically: neither of the suggested preventive measures will bear fruit, regardless of the common agreement between the "people of science and the people of holy law" regarding opium's deadly side effects; opium is too addictive for the problem to be solved with reforms alone.[19]

In fact, despite the publicly acknowledged religious prohibition, the opium trade was too lucrative for the legislators and the ministers to enact any rules that would "damage" its commercial value. They all agreed to subject it to taxation, but some opponents of any kind of government control requested delaying the tax's implementation. Time is needed, Kashef explained, for the people to get used to the idea and for the addicted to adjust to the new prohibiting law. Besides, he added, corrupt officials have always abused their function in collecting taxes.

Indeed, prevailing widespread corruption in levying taxes was well known; so was the fact that collectors often were met with popular protests that sometimes degenerated into bloody confrontation. Whereas some deputies favored delaying the enforcement of new tax laws, others suggested maintaining the traditional system until the new laws could be executed uniformly throughout the nation and thus allowing current local officials to continue "taking their dues" in accordance with traditional customs. The conservative cleric-deputy, the Imam Jom'eh, had at an earlier point vigorously challenged the compatibility of a highly centralized taxation system with the sharia. And now, once again aware of his lone dissenting voice in the constitutional assembly, he nonetheless proclaimed it his duty to pronounce the new laws "have no legal basis" because they contravene the Islamic law. The other deputies paid no attention to his remarks and went on arguing in favor of allowing administrative officials to bring about necessary changes in matters under their respective jurisdiction without having to wait for Majles's prior approval. There was general agreement that new institutions needed consolidation to be fully functioning; in the meantime, the ministers' hands "must not be tied."[20]

Much of the discussion reflected the constitutional aspiration for a reconstructed nation-state where the rule of law is enforced and justice prevails. References to European practices to be emulated often prompted several rebukes from those who in fact did know the true origin of their legislative reforms. Arbab Kaikhosrow, the Zoroastrian deputy, strongly advised against mentioning European models or using foreign terminology. "It would cause difficulties," he noted.[21] "I am not a fanatic," Behjat al-Olama once exclaimed, but there is no need to refer to foreign practices in order to justify our views. "We, too, are in the process of founding such a constitution. Other countries' laws are irrelevant to us."[22] However, some legislators continued to defer to European institutions as a source of inspiration, employing those institutions' terminology, despite their colleagues' distaste.

The Bureau of Accounts

There were endless discussions over the formation of Bureau of Accounts (Divan-e Mohasebat), modeled on the French *court des comptes*, to audit all government financial records, inspect all revenues and expenditures, and ensure the proper management of all ministries' budgets in the capital and the provinces. The bureau's director general was to be chosen by the Majles based on his professional merit and upon the minister of finance's recommendation. After much debating, the minister was granted the right to select all bureau officials, who had to fulfill certain basic personal requirements: Iranian citizenship, religious piety, moral integrity, loyalty to the fatherland and commitment to promoting national interests, knowledge in matters pertaining to the assumed post, and thirty years of age minimum. However, the *divan* would have total independence from the minister of finance and be accountable solely to the Majles, though it would be part of the Finance Ministry, which would pay its officials' salary. Many sessions were devoted to the bureau's structural hierarchy and functions and the rules of its officials' conduct in accomplishing their task.[23] An oversight committee to review the government budget was to be formed of twelve members from the bureau, the Majles, and the Senate. Sani' al-Dowleh, the finance minister, as well as Solaiman Mirza and Vahid al-Molk, the Democrat deputies, forcefully denied the not yet established Senate any right to intervene in budget matters. Vahid al-Molk argued that the Belgian Constitution, on which theirs was based, does not confer on the Senate any power to oversee financial affairs. The resistance to concede such a power to the Senate reflected the second Majles's deep distrust of an institution that constitutionally required half its membership to be appointed by royal decree. Such a system, it was feared, would unavoidably allow an Anglo-Russian role in the selection process, a fact all genuine nationalists abhorred. An emotional deputy, anticipating the two powers' potential interference, loudly proclaimed that the Majles's task was to establish financial reforms, a "heavy yoke on the deputies' shoulders," which bore the burden of "lifting millions of unfortunate citizens" from their abject living conditions.[24]

As was the case with the debate on the selection of students to send abroad, the deputies discussed the class composition of the *divan*'s officials. Was the son of a grocer qualified to assume such a responsible post? Was he knowledgeable enough compared to a well-born and wealthier individual whose social background supposedly better prepared him to acquire experience and knowledge in financial affairs? Was potential competence simply based on social and economic status? The "grocer's" qualifications were defended by some but not others, again depending on the deputies' political views; but the question did not absorb too much of their time or attention in one of the sessions devoted to the council. The issue was raised later with more heated arguments, revealing usually muted ideological differences. One unprecedented ruling under consideration called for the requirement that each council member, especially if a poor educated young man were put in charge of handling cash money or tangible properties, had to have an individual well-to-do guarantor who would pay back the government if the council member cheated or embezzled. The requirement was meant to prevent corruption and to ensure the good functioning of government financial affairs. Some dismissed the ruling; others defended it by referring to past and current instances of corruption, explaining that "people's ethics" have yet to be improved. Thus, Hajj Aqa Ibrahim dismissed the possibility of entrusting the country's finances to a poor man without a guarantor. How do we know he is honest? he asked. Yusef Yanes (Hovsep Mirzayan), the Armenian delegate, strongly objected to the rule. Enforcing it, he said, would be tantamount to declaring the prospective employee guilty of wrongdoing until proven innocent. It would also mean, he added, that young people who have professional merit but are poor would not be eligible for government service, which is unfair. In response to those who claimed there are wealthy individuals willing to offer guarantees for such competent but poor young men, Yanes sarcastically wondered aloud about such an optimistic view of "capitalists." Which capitalist, he asked, would pass over his children's, relatives', or acquaintances' financial entitlement to his estate and support instead a young educated man "without means" (*bi chiz*)? The lengthy animated discussion was turning into an ideologically supercharged and class-oriented dispute, unnerving many conservative and moderate deputies alike. They put an end to it, reminding the Speaker that the debate on "the rich and poor" is irrelevant to the subject of the bureau under consideration. The controversial motion was objectionable to many for different reasons, and so the Majles voted in majority against it.[25]

Military Reforms

Despite the urgent need for a standing army to ensure security and to enforce the rule of the new law, the Majles tackled military reforms much later than other issues, not until mid-February 1911, judging from the *Mozakerat* records. In sharp contrast to the country's contemporary Ottoman and Egyptian neighbors, the Persian government had no reformed military institutions and no significant numbers of new cadres of officers trained in European-style academies. In addition to the Cossack Brigade, which obeyed Russian commanders, the existing tribal forces, who paid allegiance only to their leaders, and the poorly equipped, unruly militias composed of hired mercenaries were poor substitutes for a national army with an overall central command. The idea of compulsory national conscription was first broached on February 11, 1911, in an open Majles session attended by the then minister of war. The minister proposed the idea of compulsive, universal military service as a national obligation for all young men, regardless of religious, ethnic, or linguistic differences, for a period of three years. He declared it a long overdue duty for all male citizens, a service imposed "without exceptions" in the "whole world."[26]

The minister, however, acknowledged it would take ten years to set up the system successfully, only after a national census was completed and the appropriate budget was provided. In the meantime, he informed the deputies, the government would recruit soldiers from among the tribes. Each clan of thirty families was to send one mounted fighter (*savar*), equip him with one gun, and assume the cost of his salary and his horse maintenance as well as the financial needs of his family in his absence for a three-year military service. Sardar As'ad, the Bakhtiyari khan, immediately protested. Speaking on behalf of the southern tribes, he told the minister: "You cannot keep the *savar* [away from his tribe] for three years"; that period is too long and the expenses too heavy for the families to bear. The minister could not contain his sarcasm when he retorted that surely the Bakhtiyaris have enough mounted warriors and guns to put in the service of their country and people. In general, the deputies, including the Qashqa'i representative, were in favor of the suggested centrally organized recruitment, provided all tribes were treated equally. To some warnings that the tribesmen would resist the order, the minister insisted there would be no exemptions for anyone.

Behjat al-Olama, the deputy from Arabestan, suggested that the Arab tribes should be included as well. The Armenian deputy, speaking in the name of his coreligionists, passionately insisted all citizens should fulfill their national obligation, to which Seyyed Hasan Modarres the cleric-deputy, vehemently replied: "The *dhimmi* people [adherents of officially recognized religions—Christians, Jews, and Zoroastrians] must never provide soldiers" to a Moslem army. They pay their dues, and the Moslems give them protection, he sternly added. But Yanes persisted in arguing in the name of the "political laws" of the country, not the Islamic sharia. The Constitution, he reminded Modarres, grants equality to all, including with respect to the obligation to serve the nation. "Diverse people," he stated, have fought for the nation, are equally patriotic, and are ready to join their forces with all others. They have to be accepted in an Iranian military force for the sake of the common good.[27] His message was loud and clear and highly controversial for the traditionalists: the diverse peoples of the country abiding by the rule of one nation-state and forming an armed force in defense of the common fatherland.

In sharp contrast, the Zoroastrian delegate Kaikhosrow strongly refuted his Armenian colleague's pronouncement. Though cautiously declaring that he was not speaking in the name of the Zoroastrians, he nonetheless chose to define them all as "not accustomed to war." Clause 8 of the Supplement to the Fundamental Law, he stated, grants equality before the law to the entire population, yet nowhere does it specify equality in military services. Modarres had the last word. Grandiosely self-proclaiming himself representative of all Moslems in Iran, Najaf and Karbala, Afghanistan, India, and the Caucasus, he declared that the compulsory military service should not apply to non-Moslems; exceptions would be acceptable only if they volunteer. Though recognizing the differences between religious and political laws, he categorically pronounced, "The Supplement cannot possibly be contrary to the Islamic law." Most deputies approved his speech. Yanes withdrew his objections, conceding that the motion was, after all, about recruiting mounted warriors, not foot soldiers.[28]

The subject of national conscription was closed, but the minister of war felt the need to warn that from now on everyone in Iran must understand that military service is compulsory, as in the rest of the "advanced nations," even though it would take ten years to enforce it. "We have to start with what we proposed today; this law is temporary for the next seven to eight years."[29] That proposal won the majority vote, once more reflecting the generally acknowledged understanding that the laws they were currently enacting, although difficult to implement in the present, were meant for future implementation. The limited legislated military reforms produced no immediate results, of course, because the government lacked the financial means to implement them. The government's effort to restore order in the South also bore no fruit. Isma'il Khan Sulat al-Dowleh failed to deliver on his promise to establish safety on the roads, as the British diplomats had foreseen. More important, fighters sent to combat unruly tribes and private militias were not paid their salaries and were thus reduced to plundering the caravans transporting goods that they were sent to protect. Shiraz had not received the funds sent to pay them. Walter Smart, then British consul in Shiraz, believed the recent military reforms changed the soldiers' position "very disadvantageously." "With its usual mania of putting the cart before the horse," he remarked, the Majles exchanged the old village system with one paid by a government the soldiers no longer trust.[30]

Combating Corruption and Concessions

Persistent corruption at all levels of the economy was a most vexing problem confronting the reformers. Mineral concessions granted to individuals or companies angered many deputies. The Majles again and again denied the government the right to dispose of national resources without prior Majles ratification. It set up detailed rules regulating its contracts with foreign and domestic companies, fixing the owners' annual dues payable to the government and subjecting them to the Bureau of Accounts (Divan-e Mohasebat) for inspection.[31] Dubious commercial transactions between local merchants and foreign companies that contravened newly enacted laws sparked Majles opposition.

The already mentioned notorious case of Mo'in al-Tojjar is a case in point. His dispute over his ownership right to dispose of oxide mines on Hormoz Island embroiled British government officials. The Majles denounced the controversial concession as illegal, thus provoking heated debates.[32] The disputed concession was finally settled in late December 1910. Sani' al-Dowleh informed the Majles that Mo'in al-Tojjar's concession had long expired, so he was now obligated to pay the government 75 percent of the sales profits. He told the deputies that the issue was now closed.[33] In fact, the problem had been resolved earlier, in mid-November 1910, with the Persian government signing the new contract with the winning British company and assuming responsibility for any lawful claims the losing company might have because of the older contract Mo'in al-Tojjar had signed with them. Sani' al-Dowleh conceded to the Majles the right to ratify the contract, a mere formality to ensure its quick passage.[34] The government gave Mo'in al-Tojjar a lump sum of £24,000 in compensation. The issue was not really put to rest with that, however, because the original concessionaires continued to demand their rights for months until Sani' al-Dowleh's tragic death put an end to the dispute.[35] Hormoz Island, with its wealth in mineral resources and strategic position in the Persian Gulf, had acquired a strategic-economic importance for British interests in the region.

Concessions granted even to Iranian individuals and companies provoked equally heated debates, with several representatives, mostly Democrats, adamantly opposed to acquired exclusive rights. The Rabi'zadeh Company, for instance, had requested a concession for the exclusive right to fabricate soap and leather. Proponents argued that this concession needed government support to encourage industrial development and thus reduce foreign competition. Opponents objected to the excessive advantages contractually accorded to the company in the concession: a seven-year tax exemption, free land and water, state protection that excluded other companies. All deputies in common agreement opposed the monopoly right, although the term *monopoly* was not used in the debate. The Democrats refused to grant tax exemption. Similarly, the issue of foreign capital invested in the project raised equally passionate discussions. When some deputies asserted no country can develop and progress without foreign capital, Behjat al-Olama, the Moderate cleric-representative of Arabestan, responded: "We are not forbidding foreign capital to penetrate our country. Right here, we are loudly proclaiming that we have opened the doors of Iran so that foreign nationals can bring their money and develop trade with our cooperation." But he denied them the advantages granted Iranians; foreigners, he stated, are in no need of tax exemption or other benefits. They should get "facilities" and no more. After lengthy discussion, the Majles voted in majority to grant Rabi'zadeh Company the requested tax exemption provided no foreign capital were involved.[36] Weeks later, when discussing a concession granted to Sani' al-Dowleh while he was still a deputy, the Majles passed a bill in support of the Democrats' insistence on the Majles's prior approval of foreign participation in national enterprises.[37] Upon his return to government post as financial minister, Sani' al-Dowleh relinquished the concession to avoid any conflict of interest.

From the start of the revolution, the majority in the Majles were adamant about retaining control over the decision-making policy regarding most concessions. As already noted, the constitutionalists wished to prevent the recurrence of the ancien régime's abuse of such sales to foreigners.[38]

With the fall of Mostowfi al-Mamalek's government in early February 1911, though, the rush of European companies seeking lucrative concessions in the country would seriously challenge the reformists' resolve. This debate, like most others recorded in the *Mozakerat*, displays the thoroughness of the deputies' endeavor to legislate rules and regulations for good governance and to enforce the rule of law uniformly across the country, even though the country had no financial means or human resources to implement the legislation. It demonstrates their apparent desire, when formulating the details, to preempt official incompetence and corruption. They charged the Ministry of Finance with the task of submitting to the Majles each ministry's budget, including concessions.

Yet many important issues debated either were omitted altogether in the *Mozakerat* or were simply not submitted for discussion in open meetings, despite much loud outcry against the secrecy guarded by government officials and committee leaders. Thus, oil concessions seldom figure in the recorded minutes. In one, indeed rare, instance when the subject was raised openly in the Majles, the discussion dealt with the Anglo-Persian Oil Company's noncompliance with the concession's conditions: failing to employ Iranians, preventing Iranian individuals from buying company shares, not disclosing the location of its headquarters. The minutes registered the deputies' complaints that the company had "occupied" the southern port Bushehr, built railways, and telephone wires, all without informing the government. In fact, the government had allowed such construction, but the Majles resented being kept deliberately in the dark.[39]

Public complaints constantly reached the Majles concerning widespread hoarding of grains and the resulting shortage of bread and rice, unlawful transactions in basic commodities, and middlemen's extortionate profiteering practices. Hoarding in order to create artificial shortage and thus to justify higher prices was unanimously condemned in compliance with the Islamic ban on such a practice. However, most deputies wished to protect freedom of trade in agricultural produce, defending the right of individual owners to store as much grain for as long as they wished without suffering any kind of government retribution. Rising in defense of landowners and merchants, many deputies, again regardless of their party affiliation, insisted the merchants and landowners were not to be subjected to the new antihoarding regulations; their private property should be immune from government confiscation. Only in case of real shortage, they admitted, should officials seize the grains and enforce its sale at a fixed price, but without further punishing the proprietors. It was a tricky argument that would not necessarily prevent corruption. Sani' al-Dowleh, the free-market champion, adamantly denied the Majles had the authority to debate such issues or to specify rules regulating the markets. Islamic law pertaining to hoarding is clear, he commented, sufficiently covering its punishment, which was applicable to all, with its enforcement falling under municipal jurisdiction. Some deputies refuted his argument. The Moderate deputy Kashef, for instance, declared that the long-prevailing tradition of hoarding left the poor at the mercy of landowners and merchants, who accumulated their wealth at the poor's expense. The resulting shortage, he said, is inciting popular revolts; it must be resolved once and for all with new laws. No agreement was reached; the bill was sent to the appropriate committee for further consideration.[40] The Majles kept hearing of consistent recurrences of unlawful hoarding of basic agricultural commodities and the selling of those commodities at inflated prices, allegedly with the complicity of municipal officials, including the mayor of Tehran.[41]

The most urgent cases of corruption were repeatedly brought to the Majles's immediate attention: lack of financial accountability in the provinces and the smuggling of goods in southern and northern ports to avoid paying customs duties. Summoned to respond to people's widespread petitions for help, Finance Minister Sani' al-Dowleh would not deny the complaints' veracity. Instead, he used the occasion to call for swift Majles-approved government action to send inspectors to establish order in the messy fiscal situation in the South and to install customs institutions to regulate the tariffs of traded goods crossing the nation's various borders. The finance minister did not need to remind the deputies of the impending date October 14, by which time they had to restore order in the South to avoid direct British military intervention there.

Turmoil in the Provinces

The Qashqa'i and Bakhtiyari leaders' tribal rivalry over their respective territories went on unabated and unchecked by powerless Tehran authorities. In Shiraz, the long feud pitting the Qavami family against Isma'il Khan Sulat al-Dowleh, the resident Qashqa'i tribal leader, extended to their respective local supporters and the Tehran-appointed governor. Shiraz and Isfahan thus were enmeshed in the incessant intrigues of local governors, grandees, and tribal chieftains, allowing bandits of all types to engage in relentless and bloody raids that endangered the safety of the trade routes. Government officials in the capital, especially Sardar As'ad, the Bakhtiyari ally of the Qavami family and enemy of Sulat al-Dowleh, as well as British diplomats concerned with British trade in the South were also involved in local politics. Similarly, the Shiraz *anjoman* organized anti-British and anti-Qavami public demonstrations, allegedly incited by Sulat al-Dowleh. The Qashqa'i *ilkhan* was also implicated in fomenting attacks on the Jewish quarter, according to Smart, who was compelled to intervene on behalf of the local Jews.[42] Sulat al-Dowleh even contemplated marching into Tehran to force the government to appoint him governor of Fars.[43] The Majles questioned the government on the prevailing unrest in the South, taking it to task for not sending appropriate authorities to restore order. Some directly named Sulat-al Dowleh, whose personal interests concerned neither the nation nor the Constitution, as the chief cause of the turmoil.[44]

By late October 1910, Smart reached the conclusion that time had come to "depart from our policy of neutrality in Fars politics." He believed Sulat al-Dowleh was opposed to establishing security on the southern roads because he derived considerable revenues from tolls levied on passing caravans. And Smart suspected the Qashqa'i leader of encouraging his tribesmen and local supporters to raise havoc. Though he was fully aware of the Qavamis' notorious reputation as troublemakers, he favored them and defined them as "townsmen," not "tribal chieftains," who are in favor of a strong government in Tehran, in contrast to the Qashqa'is. The decision to restore security on the southern roads with British officers from India, Smart wrote to Barclay, "must be accompanied by removing Soulat [*sic*] al-Dowleh." Suppressing Sulat al-Dowleh's power, he asserted, would "simplify" British intervention in avoiding the "gradual development of policing the roads into a general occupation."[45] Despite British official denial, Smart had understood the general implication of Barclay's October note to the Persian government as signifying interference in Persian internal affairs. Thus, deploring the help that the British had provided to Sulat al-Dowleh in the past, Smart suggested replacing him with his brother, who was related to the Bakhtiyaris by marriage.[46] But the Bakhtiyaris themselves were torn by interfamily conflicts and power struggles, and some of their leaders' alliance with Sulat al-Dowleh was deepening the rifts among them. Barclay did not give his consent to interfere in the Persian government's relations with Sulat al-Dowleh.

A few days after sending his report to Barclay, Smart was confronted with another serious riot in Shiraz, involving sectarian violence and tribal intrigues. On the morning of October 30, 1910, a mob attacked government buildings, clamoring for justice for the murder of a Moslem woman allegedly by some Jews. Then the mob attacked the Jewish quarter, killing eleven, wounding fifteen, and destroying many houses. The guards sent to quell the disturbances instead joined the plunder, and many Qashqa'i tribesmen followed suit. The local authorities, including the governor Qavam al-Molk, proved to be powerless and too frightened to put an end to the riot. It was finally suppressed in the early evening when the Cossacks intervened. "The riot," Smart reported, was started by "artificial" means. It turned out that the body was not that of a Moslem woman but of a Jewish woman dug out of the cemetery. He accused Sulat al-Dowleh of fabricating a crisis situation to frighten the populace, subdue them to his power, and thus force Tehran to accede to all his demands. This violent episode, Smart concluded, was a perfect example of the Qashqa'i tactics in the South. He called for the immediate appointment of a governor general to help local authorities.[47] He favored 'Ayn al-Dowleh, the hated former commander of the royalist forces in Azerbaijan. On November 15, 1910, pressed by British officials, a Majles special committee ordered the Ministry of War to dispatch within a week a police guard to escort the Italian general Maletta (full name not known) charged with establishing order to Shiraz and securing its trade roads in the South. He was to be followed within two weeks by two thousand troops. The ministry was also asked to send to Fars all salaries due to the troops. The Majles had rejected separate Qashqa'i and Bakhtiyari offers to send troops to establish order in the South. Hiring local armed men was deemed "unacceptable."[48]

Other tribes in other provinces also engaged in power struggles chiefly motivated by personal or regional interests, all equally challenging Tehran and its local representatives. Shaikh Khazal of Mohammereh, the powerful Arabestan chieftain who enjoyed British support, fought on several fronts: in alliance with Sulat al-Dowleh and other auxiliary southern tribes; against the local governor over disputed land ownership; against Ottoman authorities over Turco-Persian borders; against the Majles decision opposing a concession for the construction of a dam in Ahvaz with European financial support. More important, Shaikh Khazal independently negotiated the selling or leasing of his land to the Anglo-Persian Oil Company, which, with other British commercial firms working in the region, cultivated good rapport with him.[49] G. E. Wilson, the British consul based in the Persian Gulf, desired British protection for Shaikh Khazal. In a letter collectively signed by British officials stationed in the South and addressed to London, Shaikh Khazal is credited for his "wise administration" in a region where the central government's authority is "almost non-existent." Were he to be deprived of British support, the signers claimed, "various British enterprises on the Karun [River] and in the South-West would be seriously hampered."[50] The Foreign Office assured Shaikh Khazal of British protection. However, upon Grey's instruction, Barclay denied this fact when Navab inquired about such "rumors." The Persian foreign minister was told explicitly that Shaikh Khazal had "special relations" with the British government that were "contingent upon his observance of his obligation towards the Persian Government" and that only "in case of any encroachments on his rights" would he receive support. Barclay further reassured Navab that such caveats demonstrated British "consistent intention to respect the independence and integrity of Persia."[51]

Much of British capital was invested in the South, more so than in the rest of the country. British officials, therefore, considered the keeping of the local Arab tribes united under Shaikh Khazal "of supreme importance." Barclay often warned Sardar As'ad that "any disturbances of the status quo" in Shaikh Khazal's territory "would be a matter of serious concern to His Majesty's government."[52] But he also warned the Arab chieftain and his co-conspirators, Sulat al-Dowleh and smaller Arab tribes, against disruptive intrigues and mischief targeting the Bakhtiyaris and their allies.[53] Lieutenant Ranking (full name not known), the British military attaché in the gulf region, had informed Barclay that intertribal power struggles rendered the restoration of safety on the southern roads a much more complicated problem than could be solved by armed troops.[54] He was confirming Smart's opinion on the situation. However, contrary to Smart's advice, Nezam al-Saltaneh Mafi was appointed governor of Fars. By early January 1911, the Persian government, ignoring the Majles's objections, officially empowered Sulat al-Dowleh with securing the Bushehr–Shiraz road. While Barclay was highly doubtful of the Qashqa'i khan's genuine interest in accomplishing the task, the minister of the interior assured the Majles that, indeed, raids and plunder had dramatically decreased in the South.[55] The minister was, like Sulat al-Dowleh, one of Sardar As'ad's nemeses.

Elsewhere in the country, constant news of tribal unrest reached Tehran periodically. As we shall see later, the Qajar prince Abol Fath Salar al-Dowleh was busy recruiting Kurdish and other tribes on behalf of his brother, the deposed Mohammad Ali Shah. The Torkaman tribe similarly conspired to restore the former shah to his throne, organizing revolts in its region. Rahim Khan, the notorious troublemaking tribesman in the North, had returned to Azerbaijan from the Russian frontier in early December 1910. The Shahsavans fomented serious disturbances, raiding and plundering villages and defeating the Ardabil governor's troops.

Moreover, various Kurdish tribes in the Northwest engaged in fighting one another when not fighting both Ottoman and Persian troops and plundering villages, which provoked more Turkish military incursions. Russian officials, convinced the Germans were encouraging the Turkish presence, protested against it. The Young Turk official commanding the Ottoman troops active in the area defended his government's policy: "Turkey had too long neglected to assert her sovereign rights" there, he stated, expressing satisfaction that the Persian government was "fortunately not in a position to do more than protest."[56]

Continued Resistance to Russian Demands

Russia's military occupation in Qazvin and Azerbaijan continued to cause anger among Persian politicians and the press. Banished from Tehran, Taqizadeh resumed his earlier radical rhetoric, keeping contact with fellow Democrats in Tehran. He encouraged them to uphold their party's program, but there is no evidence that he incited them to wage open warfare in deeds and not just words. In his correspondence with Taqizadeh, Shaikh Mohammad Khiyabani, an Azerbaijani deputy, specifically acknowledged the new rules of the game. Now that we have laid down arms, he wrote, we have begun our opposition with words, following the "rules of logic and knowledgeable philosophers." And he cited Taqizadeh's own dictum: "Each time has its own conditions and its appropriate pace [of action]."[57] Taqizadeh's contacts in Tehran, cautious and fearful of being labeled "extremists," followed dutifully his request to tear up his letters once they read them. Yet caution was not unanimously adopted, not even by Taqizadeh himself, who reverted to his tactical alliances with groups advocating divergent political programs. Thus, there were reports of his secret negotiations with CUP members in Salonica for a Turco-Persian alliance,[58] despite the Turkish military incursion in the northwestern part of the country. Simultaneously, he supported a pan-Islamic movement originating in Istanbul that called for a joint Sunni–Shi'a struggle against Anglo-Russian imperialism. Indeed, as already noted, such Ottoman political propaganda, directly encouraged by the German kaiser and his close advisers, was spreading in the Moslem world. Poklewski confirmed that rumor.[59] Barclay, however, remained highly skeptical of the success of such a movement in Persia; history would prove him right. Nonetheless, more concrete reports provide evidence of such efforts to mobilize the faithful to combat Russian occupation.[60]

By all accounts, the internal political situation in Tehran was increasingly precarious. It even worried French officials to the point of exasperation with what their Tehran envoy described as Anglo-Russian ineffective diplomacy. Lecomte's reports persistently displayed his utter contempt for Persian officials, whom he deemed conspiratorial and untrustworthy, especially Navab the "fanatic "Russophobe," nationally considered "the light of the cabinet, the hope of the Persian revolution." Dismissing the government's genuine fear of the former shah's possible return, Lecomte only saw intrigues, "the old Persian weapon," to corrupt, discredit, and defame. Angry and scornful of his British and Russian colleagues' diplomacy, he believed they were wasting time and energy quarrelling with the Persians over the distribution of posts to foreigners, demeaning themselves with this "wretched kingdom," and sending threats that the Persian government "receives ironically." Lecomte believed the Persian government was "convinced of the powerlessness of these two giants, tied to one another to the point of not daring to make any move, and both paralyzed by their fear of Germany."[61] This caustic French analysis covered up the intricate reality of the international game being played out in the country, in which France was no less a determining factor.

It was Navab, the foreign minister, and his close allies in the Majles who desperately resisted Russia's objectionable demands, no matter the consequences. A minor diplomatic incident in Kashan blatantly demonstrated the futility of his combative effort to counter a no less stubborn Russian determination to crush him. On November 14, 1910, the residence of the local Russian consul, a Persian national, was raided by the local police chief looking for an "offender," who was not found. The whole house, including the women's quarters, was searched. Sazanov seized on the occasion to bring about Navab's downfall. He instructed his envoy in Tehran to demand reparation and the dismissal of the police chief "for this insult to the Russian flag" as well an apology from Navab in person at the Russian embassy, wearing his official government minister attire. He also requested Barclay to suspend any interaction with the Persian minister, a request the British diplomat dismissed. With Navab in office, so hostile to Russia, "the situation was worse than ever," O'Beirne informed Grey. Two days later Navab apologized in a written response, but no more, arguing that his government did not recognize the Persian subject as acting consul for Russia because he had "no proper consular status."[62] The response did not satisfy Poklewski. On December 1, with Barclay exerting pressure on him to accede to all Russian demands, Navab finally complied and made a personal appearance in official uniform at the Russian embassy.

Navab knew the price he had to pay for his forced acquiescence to Russian intransigence: the loss of credibility among fellow Democrats and others in the Majles, where he was repeatedly summoned to account for the continuing presence of Russian troops. And he, the Democrat reputed for his so-called anti-Russian extremism, would have to respond in vague terms, assuring them the troop withdrawal would be undertaken in a friendly and "properly moderate" manner. "It is our duty," he would say, "especially mine," to achieve it speedily.[63] Tension between deputies, especially those excluded from committees' deliberations, and some cabinet members would intensify toward the end of the year. The fact that the Kashan Russian consul was an Iranian national holding a dual Russian citizenship further aggravated the case. Both Navab and Majles deputies had been condemning the practice of holding a second passport, refusing to accept its legitimacy. Vakil al-Tojjar would go so far as to pronounce it "dishonorable," tantamount to selling out one's religion and nationhood.[64]

Deeply humiliated by the experience, Navab also came to realize the power dynamics defining his relationship with Barclay, proving his belief in the diplomat's friendly support unfounded and rather naive. On December 24, 1910, Barclay sent him a letter to remind him of the October deadline to restore order in the South. Despairing of safeguarding national independence, Navab resigned his post a day later. Barclay regretted losing a minister he deemed reliable enough to administer effectively the loan to enforce security of the southern roads. Furthermore, he was skeptical that any change in the government would improve relations with Russia.

However, the demise of Navab, Sazanov's bête noire, helped improve the Persians' negotiations with Russia to the latter's satisfaction. Mirza Mehdi Mohtashem al-Saltaneh, appointed to the vacated ministry, quickly concluded the consolidation of debts owed the Russian Bank. Within a couple of weeks after Navab's departure, the consolidated Russian loan contract was signed, to be redeemed in fifteen years at a 7 percent interest rate and secured by northern customs revenues. The charges included the exiled shah's pension and the maintenance expenses of the Cossack Brigade.[65] The Russian demand for concessions in the North was also granted. The British Imperial Bank was thus expecting Russia's green light to grant the Persian government an advance of £100,000 on the proposed Anglo-Russian loan, but the money would not be available till later in the spring of 1911. Russia would later express its willingness to negotiate an Anglo-Russian combined loan for the construction of a Trans-Persian railway line starting in the North, explicitly stating that the question of the loan was "intimately connected" with that of the railway construction. Both issues were to be "treated simultaneously."[66]

Sazanov, "anxious to give Persia a proof of the disinterestedness of the Russian government," was then ready to withdraw Russia's troops from Qazvin.[67] However, the public announcement of the evacuation was delayed upon Naser al-Molk's request. The new regent had reportedly "begged" Poklewski to wait until his return to Tehran and the formation of a new government "likely to reciprocate this friendly step." Naser al-Molk was determined, upon his arrival in the capital, "to utilize the evacuation to attain his goal: a new cabinet under the Sepahdar."[68] The Democrats and fellow nationalists' influence would wane further upon Naser al-Molk's return to the country. His proxies and allies would conspire to foment the erosion of their power in government and the Majles.

Political Dissent

When Regent Azod al-Molk died on September 22, 1910, the Foreign Office initially favored Sardar As'ad to replace him. However, fearing possible disturbances among rival tribes, especially the Qashqa'i, it chose Abol Qasem Khan Naser al-Molk, despite his reputation as a "weak" man who fled Tehran and sought refuge in Europe whenever the political climate turned too unstable. Naser al-Molk had left the country at the time of Behbahani's assassination and would not come back until February 1911. The Democrats fiercely opposed his candidacy, distrusting him as an Oxford-educated aristocrat with dubious constitutional credentials, who, they alleged, was mostly responsible for Najaf's fatwa condemning Taqizadeh.[69] Barclay's hope rested primarily on Naser al-Molk because he believed the latter would adopt a "saner policy" toward Russia and influence even the "extremists."[70]

Naser al-Molk delayed his return until early February 1911. However, while still abroad, he had stated that certain conditions needed to be met before his arrival, thus displaying his desire to assume greater authority than his predecessor. He discreetly directed his commands at undermining the "extremists'" influence. His constituency was composed chiefly of the old Qajar ruling establishment turned constitutionalist, the Sepahdar and his supporters, influential conservative olama, some Moderate deputies, and Sardar As'ad, who by then was scheming to bring about Mostowfi al-Mamalek's downfall.[71] More significant was the fact that Naser al-Molk enjoyed both Britain's and Russia's full backing.

In a secret meeting with a Majles committee, the Bakhtiyari leader Sardar As'ad had threatened to withdraw all his troops securing the capital and send them back to their territories unless a new government more friendly to the two powers was formed.[72] Once more reversing his political alliance, he had then distanced himself from the Democrats. His objective was to install a pro-Russian government in compliance with British demand, his economic interests in the oil-rich southwestern region outweighing his animosity toward the Gilani politician, the Sepahdar. He had supporters in the Majles among deputies highly critical of the Democrat members of the cabinet. The Moderate Abol Hasan Mo'azed al-Saltaneh, who had played an important role forging the alliance of exiled constitutionalists in combating Mohammad Ali Shah, sounded the alarm. In a highly emotional speech on January 5, 1911, he related his encounter with some ministers, whom he had warned against the "malevolent group" busy conspiring to bring the "reactionaries" back to power. He had told the ministers that the "reactionaries'" proxies, in conjunction with foreign sponsors, including Russia, were organizing chaos throughout the nation, a catastrophic replay of the coup in 1908 that would end with the destruction of the country's very foundation.[73] A heated debate on the state of the nation consumed the various deputies that day. Some echoed Mo'azed al-Saltaneh in blaming Mostowfi al-Mamalek's cabinet for the general unpopularity of the government and called for its dismissal. Others deplored the fact that the Majles had wasted its hard work enacting laws that were proving to be fruitless because not executed.

However, the nationalist reformer Sani' al-Dowleh, then finance minister, urgently asked for Majles support of the government, which, he asserted, the cabinet needed in order to accomplish its tasks. The legislative and executive powers must work together to protect the nation, he told them; the Majles must stop obstructing the government's work. Legally, he argued, the prime minister must resign when the regent assumes his post, and only then can the latter authorize the formation of a new cabinet. The current ministers, he added, are unable to make any progress due to the dire financial situation: "It is not their fault."[74] Mohammad Hashem Mirza similarly defended the cabinet and condemned deputies whose hostile views reflected some mud-raking press articles. No newspaper should have such power to cause the demise of an entire cabinet. "I consider any such attempt by individuals . . . poisonous."[75] The minister of post and telegraph reminded the deputies that they had entrusted Mostowfi al-Mamalek with their unanimous support in selecting his ministers. Progressive change, he stated, needs not just time but also financial resources.

Dissent within the government and the Majles intensified. The press and some deputies, especially the relentless intriguer Assadollah Kordestani, fueled the divisive contentions, whether out of legitimate dissatisfaction with the slow progress in the implementation of reforms or in the attempt to fulfill a secret political agenda. By the end of January 1911, in anticipation of the regent's imminent return, dissension within the Majles heightened. Zoka' al-Molk, the Democrat Speaker of the Majles, was now the main target. Assadollah Kordestani held him responsible for arbitrarily selecting some issues for debate and neglecting others. More explicitly, he accused him of partiality to "one faction" in particular, thus failing to observe strict neutrality as constitutionally required. Zoka' al-Molk angrily refuted the accusation, arguing that his critics' conception of neutrality was purely subjective and based on their own political motives. He offered to resign, but the Democrats and many of the Moderates, with the exception of "ten to fifteen" deputies, tried to stop him from acting on such a precipitous decision. Hashtrudi, another Democrat, went so far as to threaten that all Azerbaijani delegates would return to their province unless Zoka' al-Molk's good reputation were restored in the Majles. The majority of the deputies voted to acknowledge the Speaker's neutrality in carrying out his duty; "three to four" voted negatively, according to the *Mozakerat*. And Mohammad Hashem Mirza, enjoying most deputies' support, rose to condemn Assadollah Kordestani's "repulsive" opinion.[76]

Two days later, when Kordestani in self-defense referred to his constitutional right to express freely his opinion and demanded evidence of his critics' rebuttal of his view of Zoka' al-Molk's lack of neutrality, Mo'ez al-Molk told him he could not use "parliamentary freedom as a sword" to promote his personal agenda.[77] Nonetheless, Zoka' al-Molk ended up submitting his resignation in writing. Solaiman Mirza seized the occasion to defend the existence of ideological differences between parties as essential to "national progress." All participants in government affairs and the Majles, he stated, have the right to adhere to a political party with an ideology of their choice and to proclaim it publicly. However, he went on, both the regent and the

Speaker of the Majles are under the obligation to maintain strict political neutrality and non-partisanship. He declared himself ready, as a member of the Democrat Party, to accept any self-proclaimed nonpartisan candidate for the Speaker's post. The majority voted for two nonaligned deputies: Momtaz al-Dowleh for the vacant post of Speaker and Matin al-Saltaneh.[78]

The Assassination of Sani' al-Dowleh

On February 4, 1911, Russian officials' other bête noire, Sani' al-Dowleh, dubbed "Germany's creature," was assassinated. Though he was by no means an "extremist," his personal integrity and nationalist political independence had aroused French and Russian animosity. Both had perceived him as a competent Persian reformer, energetically combating corruption, qualities that in their perspective were liabilities. His reform projects, they suspected, ran counter to their geopolitical and economic interests in the country. Barclay, although recognizing Sani' al-Dowleh's prominent role in the constitutional movement since its early stages, acknowledged his "decidedly German leanings" and identified him as a "staunch supporter of Persian independence," determined to free the country from Anglo-Russian "oppressive attentions." He considered Sani' al-Dowleh's goals—the construction of a railway system connecting the Persian Gulf to Tehran and the Caspian Sea, to be financed independently from European governments, and the repayment of all Persian debts to Russian and British banks—"eminently unpractical" and unlikely to be successful.[79]

Sani' al-Dowleh was above all a nationalist, believing in the possibilities of thoroughly restructuring the country's socioeconomic and political institutions to meet the advanced European standard of modern nation-states. He had even urged the Majles to adopt the solar instead of the "Arab" lunar calendar, arguing it helped in better keeping track of financial bookkeeping; and he suggested choosing Nowruz, the ancient Persian festive day marking the solar equinox, as the first day of the New Year.[80] This centuries-old feast that had survived the advent of Islam was yearly celebrated throughout the country. Like most of his projected reforms, the calendar reform was not undertaken nationwide until two decades later. The assassin eliminated the most competent Persian nationalist reformer, whose program threatened the Great Game players' vital interests in the country.

The assassin and his accomplice, an Armenian and a Georgian, respectively, but both Russian subjects native of the Caucasus, were arrested.

Officials from the Persian Ministry of Foreign Affairs and the Russian embassy attended their interrogation. Persian officials, observing the prisoners' fear, were skeptical of their explanation of the alleged nonpayment of a debt the victim owed one of them and immediately suspected a political motive. There were calls for rigorous investigation, particularly from Azerbaijan, where the victim's brother, Mokhber al-Saltaneh, was the governor. In the Majles, the Democrat Montasar al-Saltaneh, referring to Sani' al-Dowleh as "the martyr for the sake of liberty," dramatically claimed the bullet that killed him had in fact also hit every Iranian, the whole nation![81] The assassin was found with cash in his pocket; questions were raised. Who paid him, who instigated the murder, who provided the gun? Some pointed the finger at Russia, which had requested the extradition of the assassin and his accomplice. Once more the issue of dual nationality, real or fake, gave rise to virulent protests in the Majles. Criminals pretending to be Russians are sent back to Russia and thus escape punishment, Solaiman Mirza noted angrily.[82]

The timing of the murder, corresponding with the imminent change of government and the pro-Russian Sepahdar's return to power, was seen as more than sheer coincidence. Months later, when the assassins were extradited to Russia, to the national representatives' outrage, the regent and the pro-Russian foreign minister, Mohtashem al-Saltaneh, personally assured them of the Russian government's "trustworthy" promise to stage a swift trial and punishment. Skepticism prevailed, especially because one of the two prisoners was reported to have committed suicide while crossing the Caspian Sea.[83] Inquiries were periodically made regarding the trial supposedly being held in Russia; each time, reassurances were given that the investigation was being diligently pursued. Finally, in April 1911 the foreign minister announced in the Majles that the trial was completed and the assassin was to be punished publicly. However, he added, the politically sensitive investigation of who instigated the murder of the "political martyr" could not be successfully undertaken. Follow-up questions regarding the assassin's punishment received a similarly vague response, and the minister of foreign affairs finally went so far as to admit that "nothing is known" about the instigator.[84] No further discussion of that issue is recorded in the *Mozakerat*.

By the time Naser al-Molk reached Tehran on February 8, 1911, the political stage was set to further erode the so-called extremist nationalists' influence in government.

11

The Summer of Discontent

A CAUTIOUS, Oxford-educated aristocrat and a close friend of both Lord Grey and Lord George Curzon (one of the architects of the Anglo-Russian Convention), Abol Qasem Naser al-Molk was imbued with the spirit of the British system of constitutional monarchy he ideally wished to transplant to his country. He had occupied the post of finance minister during Mirza Ali Khan Amin al-Dowleh's short-lived cabinet (1897–98), when he hired the Belgian Joseph Naus to direct the customs services, the bête noire of the constitutional movement. Grey favored Naser al-Molk's appointment as the new regent; so did Grey's Russian colleague, Izvolski. The French ambassador, Lecomte, however, depicted him as an "opportunist" seeking his self-interest. Other eyewitness accounts viewed him as a pro-British politician, weak in character and lacking sufficient constitutional credentials.[1]

Moderate by temperament and political disposition, Naser al-Molk did not adhere to Taqizadeh's or Navab's firebrand of nationalism, nor was he inclined to promote an uncompromising, anti-Russian policy. His greatest problem, as attested by most foreign diplomats in Tehran, was his obsessive fear of the Democrats allegedly threatening his life, an obsession bordering on paranoia. In his account of the successive constitutional governments, Abdolhosain Nava'i holds him chiefly responsible for Najaf's ruling against Taqizadeh and the defamation of the Democrats. Mostashar al-Dowleh, by no means an extremist, characterizes him as the chief and most disruptive intriguer, plotting to undermine national sovereignty and conspiring against the Majles.[2] In fact, the regent's political preference was to work with the two powers, believing cooperation with them would ensure stability in Persia.[3] He therefore persistently endeavored to stifle virulent opposition to Russian intervention of any kind.

The Two-Party Parliamentary System

Naser al-Molk arrived in Tehran on February 8, 1911, raising Russia's hope that the nationalist Persians would adopt a more conciliatory attitude.

Within a few days of his return, he had explicitly promised Barclay he would "work in the closest touch with His Majesty's Legation as he had always done."[4] And he promptly informed the Majles of his determined wish to have it comply with the conditions for his assumption of the regency that he enunciated while still in Europe. The unexpected resignation of Prime Minister Mostowfi al-Mamalek the day after Naser al-Molk's arrival in Tehran had angered the latter. He urged the ministers to continue running the government until a new one was formed, and he purposively delayed his first visit to the Majles, sending a letter instead, in which he restated his conditions. In a meeting held in the royal palace on February 12, he urged the deputies to form regular parties with definite programs instead of wasting their time in "unprofitable" discussions of "international *haute politique*" (in transliterated French in the text). Privately he told Barclay, who had attended the meeting, that the lack of a "stable majority" in the Majles was "paralyzing" the government. And he dismissed the "visionary" program of the Democrats, whom he labeled "the noisy minority," democratic only in name, their party being a "puppet" of self-serving persons, carrying disruptive goals with the help of hired Caucasian revolutionaries.[5] Furthermore, the regent resented the Majles's self-proclaimed right to "dictate" the composition of the cabinet and wished for a "solid group" governing "unhampered" by legislators' interference in administrative affairs.[6]

After a lengthy discussion in an open session, the deputies responded to the regent's letter, expressing their willingness to support the government in combating terrorism and hoping he would appoint a prime minister who would inspire confidence.[7] Two days later the foreign minister appeared in person, informing them that the cabinet was now reduced to four ministers; all others had resigned. The regent, he explained, was waiting for the Majles to identify two distinct parties, representing the majority and minority members, and to provide complete lists of their adherents and their respective detailed programs. Only then, the minister told them, would the regent appoint a new prime minister, as stipulated in all constitutional laws of the "advanced nations." The sooner the better, he added, for the cabinet, currently reduced to four ministers, could not function properly.[8] With the increased pressure exerted on them and following tense recriminations between some deputies and individual ministers, the Majles officially presented two lists of membership, consisting of twenty Democrats and forty-eight Moderates. The Moderates explicitly pronounced their party a composite of several small ones, which included Accord and Progress, the radical Armenian-dominated socialist party turned anti-Democrats.[9] A majority coalition was thus conveniently formed for the expedient need to comply with the regent's demand.

Indeed, the Moderates' coalition list gathered together deputies who did not necessarily share a similar ideological background. Ali Akbar Dehkhoda, Mohammad Sadeq Tabataba'i, Sadeq Khan Mostashar al-Dowleh, Mirza Assadollah Kordestani, Ali Qoli Sardar As'ad, the Sepahdar, and others formed a heteroclite group, to say the least. Their program was then hastily drafted, pressed as they were to deliver it "the sooner the better" and avoid the regent's possible retribution. Eftekhar al-Va'ezin, whose name appears in neither list, explained that the small parties have realized that the "country would not advance" without such a majority coalition of deputies supporting a common program of action. Kashef, whose name is also absent from both lists, though he presented himself as a Moderate, further underscored the fact that the coalition's program did not represent any party's ideology; it represented the collective program of diverse groups united in one common objective: the urgently needed appointment of a prime minister.[10]

The coalition's modernizing reform program, however, was almost entirely identical to the Democrats', as already stated.[11] It also bears noting that the Sepahdar was chosen to be the new prime minister, with Anglo-Russian full support, long before the regent's return, whose tactics in delaying the official appointment was to exert pressure on the Democrats and further diminish their power as a "minority" party in the Majles. It was Naser al-Molk who months before his arrival in Tehran insisted on the formation of an official two-party system with distinct programs. He requested the Majles deputies to identify their party affiliation, arguing that a parliamentary government had to follow strict rules, regulations, and procedures in conformity with governance in the "civilized" world. Compliance with this order was easy, writes Malekzadeh, for it was just a matter of a seating arrangement for the deputies to be identifiable by their party membership.[12] In conformity with the French National Assembly, the Democrats sat left of the chamber's aisle, and the others on the right. Indeed, Democrats' identity was already distinct from the Moderates well before Naser al Molk's official proclamation. The proclamation merely formalized what already existed, highlighting the deputies' political affiliation. But it succeeded in entrenching the constitutionalists' political divide, despite the fact that their respective proposals for reforms, except on issues related directly or indirectly to religion, remained almost identical.

On February 18, 1911, the factional divisions in the Majles exploded in full force, displaying the ideological battles that had until then been fought anonymously, if not altogether suppressed. It is therefore worth quoting at great length the debates that took place in long open sessions, lasting several consecutive days. All of the deputies did agree with and supported the regent's insistence on applying correct Majles procedure. Deputies figuring in either list as well as the nonaffiliated deputies took turns to speak up, praising or denouncing one another, assessing their respective accomplishments or failures. Both Montasar al-Saltaneh and Solaiman Mirza, who had officially emerged as the parliamentary leader of the Democratic Party, supported the regent's constitutional demand for a multiparty Parliament. The regent only wishes to abide by the constitutional rules and proceed accordingly, they stated, and that meant the rule of the "confirmed majority" in the Majles replacing the old system of royal tyrannical rule. They called for strict party discipline to be followed by all party adherents. Deputies have to proclaim their party membership; each party is to occupy one section of the chamber, to the left or the right, and appoint its official spokesman; no single deputy can express personal ideas different from his party's. Thus, ironically, the Democrats seized on the demands made by the regent, whose constitutional credentials were seriously questioned by most players in this historic event and whose illiberal agenda belied his publicly uttered faith in parliamentary governance.

A proper, consolidated two-party system was installed. However, the Democrats called on the diverse parties hiding within the coalition to identify themselves and their respective programs. Solaiman Mirza challenged Eftekhar al-Va'ezin for asserting the existence of a majority claiming power. What has prevailed since the beginning of the second Majles, the Democrat argued, is an "incomplete" and "shaky" majority. All votes taken so far have not been based on a majority- or minority-party views but rather have represented sometimes the ideology of the left, other times the ideology of the right. And, he implied, government decisions so far, including Mostowfi al-Mamalek's, have followed individual deputies' personal views. He declared it was time for those who remain "behind curtains" to identify themselves. Today, he proclaimed defiantly, is day one of the constitutional era. The self-appointed majority of forty-eight coalition deputies must now reveal themselves as thirty members of the Social-Moderate Party, six members of the Progress Party (Taraqi), and four members of the Accord and Progress Party. He called on all members of the three separate parties forming the coalition to identify themselves and produce their own respective programs. Then Solaiman Mirza, the staunch Democrat, praised Naser al-Molk as the "most knowledgeable," "best-informed" man in the country who has prescribed the best "cure for the national ills" and whose wishes the Majles must grant. A multiparty Majles, he stated, is the only democratic system allowing the minority in opposition to challenge policies or political actions deemed unlawful.[13]

Morteza Qoli Khan Matin al-Saltaneh, the new deputy Speaker and a member of the coalition list, approved Solaiman Mirza's basic criticism that the political opinion of the majority had had no impact on the country's actions so far undertaken by the government—for obvious reasons, he said. The minority party had a program based on a definite ideology. As a consequence, the minority's ideas "willingly or unwillingly" influenced the government, and their party ruled. Currently, he remarked, no single party constitutes an absolute majority, not even the Moderates. And so, he confidently added, factions sharing similar views have coalesced to form the majority, promoting a common program of action and working with the regent to establish a properly functioning cabinet of ministers. He categorically rejected Solaiman Mirza's demand that the coalition's diverse ideological composition be publicized, adding that there exists no precedence and no law in the entire world that would justify doing so. He also claimed that preparation of a written program takes time and so should be left for the future. Right now reforms are urgently needed, hence the effort to bring together deputies, regardless of their party affiliation, to accomplish that task.

Interestingly, Matin al-Saltaneh delivered, for the first time since the inauguration of the second Majles, a solid argument in favor of a Senate. The Senate is an important institution to oversee the Majles, he observed. The Majles is accountable to the nation, yes, but how? he asked. Only through a second chamber, he ascertained.[14] The issue of the Senate was politically sensitive; its institutional function and prerogatives as stipulated in the Constitution were rarely brought up because of the Democrats' strong resistance to its formation. They feared its potential overpowering authority, with 50 percent of its members selected by the regent and subjected to Anglo-Russian prior approval.

Mohammad Hashem Mirza, the Qajar prince deputy who had so far supported legislations sponsored by the Democrats and other secular nationalists, strongly denied that the Moderate faction had until then exceeded the Democrats in number. Proclaiming his nonpartisanship, he explained that he adheres to no party to the left or to the right because he cannot support either program in its entirety. Nor does he belong to the coalition, whose program he has not even seen. Yet, he admitted, he stands "to the left," and so he seconded Solaiman Mirza's call on the deputies to identify their party affiliation. In the next elections, he insisted, people have to vote for a deputy representing a party and its program. Voting for an individual would be tantamount to several individual deputies voting for despotic rule: one hundred twenty tyrants replacing one tyrant.

At this point, the tone of the debate turned highly contentious, exposing ideological differences that were so far repressed. Hajj Aqa Ibrahim, a conservative cleric member of the coalition list, unleashed his anger at the Democrats. Asserting that all deputies have read the various programs, including the Moderates', and therefore know what "each one is all about," he highlighted the religious-secular party divide. If one person insists on keeping the judiciary under the olama's jurisdiction or demands that the cabinet include olama, that person cannot be a Democrat, he stated; conversely, if one person calls for the separation of religion from politics, he is a Democrat. In response, the Democrat Shaikh Reza, another cleric, violently protested: "This is not so! This is a calumny!" But Hajj Aqa went on unperturbed, further pointing to the Democrats' ideological program, which, he alleged, grants peasants the right to dispose of land independently from the landowners and asserts the peasants' "superior opinion" over the aristocrats'.[15] Needless to say, no such ideas explicitly figured in the official Democrat program.[16]

"We are divided ideologically," Hajj Aqa stated, "so let us proclaim our opposition to the Democrats"; nothing should remain "veiled" anymore.[17] Echoing Solaiman Mirza, but from a different perspective, he acknowledged the fact that the Constitution had not been implemented, that previous governments had ruled without representing the majority, and that during Mostowfi al-Mamalek's tenure the nation had reached a state of anarchy, with murders committed in broad daylight. His ministers, he went on, were chosen to please some individuals or groups and not on the basis of any party allegiance. It is time to implement the Constitution properly, he concluded and recognize the separation of powers. The executive branch governs;

the legislative branch is composed of an opposition party and a supportive party. The deputies do not need to identify their party membership; their vote would sufficiently indicate it. The conservative cleric's speech, echoing the newly installed anti-Democrat regent, succeeded in formalizing the ideological divide, cementing the two main parties' oppositional stand. Their cooperation in enacting reformist laws endured the fierce power struggle inside and outside the Majles, but the religious controversy and the politics it engendered deepened the schism.

The lengthy and raucous session was finally brought to an end inconclusively; the simmering tensions did not subside. Four days later in another stormy "special" session, Najaf Qoli Khan Samsam al-Saltaneh, the selected leader of the majority, presented its deputies' membership list and a short note enunciating the "common program of action." The list is incomplete, he warned the assembly, and the diverse parties included in the coalition have not yet prepared their respective programs for publication. Shaikh Isma'il Hashtrudi, the Azerbaijan deputy who had so far voted with the Democrats but now declared himself belonging to neither group, accepted the short program; Solaiman Mirza objected. A membership list does not constitute a party, nor would a program based on reform projects that all agree on anyway replace a party ideology. The majority is simply a parliamentary bloc, he argued, so they need to know its various components' political stand. Here, Shaikh Reza, the fiery Democrat, rose in defense of the Democrats and of Solaiman Mirza in particular, insisting that Islam calls for the elimination of all privileges. The Democrats, he added, attest to the Oneness of God and protect the rights of all irrespective of their social status, a shah or a beggar. He declared openly: "We are the supporters of the lower [classes]" and would no longer permit the aristocrats to oppress them. Then he defiantly mentioned the clause of the Democrat's program that, he alleged, allows land to be taken from its owner and given to the peasants that toil on it. Shaikh Reza's radical, lengthy statement provoked the Speaker's rebuke and, more important, fellow Democrats' rebuttal. The clause in question was read out loud, stipulating the establishment of an agricultural bank that would finance the peasants' purchase of state land (*khaleseh*) and provide them with the necessary means and tools to cultivate it. Nowhere is there a mention of the peasants' use of force, it was pointed out, and in case of buying private land the landowner's consent is in fact required.[18]

The following day, in another special session a letter from the regent was read out loud, expressing his satisfaction with the official formation of a majority party that would determine the selection of the prime minister. Affirming the constitutional monarch's responsibility to ensure a harmonious relationship between the legislative and executive branches of government, he warned against conflicting interpretations of the Constitution, including perception of the regent's political status. He demanded a distinct program for each party that would shun all personal interests and thus avoid a system reminiscent of the "gangs in older days." Yet he insisted on underlining the commonly accepted path leading to national progress, minimizing ideological differences. In Islam, he wrote, there exists diverse branches with minor differences; the fundamental principles remain identical. He wished the same for the parties, deliberately downplaying the fundamental differences between religious dogma and political ideology.[19]

Many deputies, including the Armenian deputy Yusef Yanes (Hovsep Mirzayan), welcomed the regent's message. The majority was officially acknowledged as a coalition of Moderates and smaller groups (*hay'at-e mottahedeh*) and not a single party, confirming Solaiman Mirza's and his fellow Democrats' initial observation. The coalition then presented the list of its deputies' membership, which they declared incomplete because the coalition remained open to other smaller parties that shared its views. Solaiman Mirza, offered a general program of action with which, he believed, all agreed regardless of ideological differences. The program listed various bills already debated in the Majles, many of them successfully enacted as legislated reforms: reforming the judiciary and the military; enforcing public safety; combatting corruption; providing universal, compulsory elementary school education; sending students abroad; setting up a council of accounts. The program also ordered all parties that were part of a coalition to present their respective ideological program and identify their members. Each party had to have a representative leader, even when abiding by the overall coalition leadership. The Democrat Party leader declared the majority coalition in power and the minority in opposition assuming full legal right to challenge any failed policy or action. He emphatically declared his party's adherence to the Islamic principles of freedom of life and property, "inasmuch as each principle grants it," and landowners' right to freely dispose of their land. Solaiman Mirza's pronouncement categorically distanced the party from the radical Shaikh Reza, who had in the beginning of the session dismissed Solaiman Mirza's leadership as not representing the Democrats.[20]

Sadr al-Olama, a cleric who wished to explain his inclusion in the Democrat list, described himself as a humble man with a modest and even frugal standard of living. He supported the Constitution and a centralized government unifying all tribal and sectarian communities, and guaranteeing freedom and equality to all before the law. "We all are brothers in our fatherland," he told his colleagues. He grew up in a rural area where he witnessed the harsh treatment the peasants endured at the hands of their landlords, working hard for a miserable subsistence livelihood, "cruelly robbed" of the fruits of their labor. He vowed to work "to the last drop of my blood" to eliminate such widespread misery—a vow, he added, that determined his choice to "sit on the left side" of the aisle.[21] Sadr al-Olama's unadorned eloquence and genuine appeal to lift the abject economic conditions of the peasantry could not fail to attract the general assembly's sympathy; the praise for his speech was unanimous.[22] It must be remembered here that both the Democrats' and the Moderates' programs had included a clause to ameliorate the landless peasants' livelihood, even though that issue was rarely mentioned in the parliamentary debates and no legislative reform had so far been enacted. More important is the fact that the political terms *left* and *right* had gained currency in the parliamentary discourse as never before. Ideological diversity had thus acquired respectability, at least in principle. It justified Solaiman Mirza's repeated complaint that the Moderates' extended program, which had just been published, was too general, lacking specifics and uncontroversial because all parties in the Majles agreed with it anyway (see chapter 5). It is the ideological specifics, he insisted, that differentiate one party from the other. But Najaf Qoli Khan Samsam al-Saltaneh, the majority leader, defended its general character as "essential" to attracting the membership of different people and groups sharing common views.[23]

Interestingly, many deputies continued to resist joining any party. The Zoroastrian representative Kaikhosrow, for instance, proclaimed his independence, voting to his liking on bills and not on a party basis; so did Dr. Ali Khan and Vakil al-Ro'aya, despite their mostly liberal-democratic voting pattern. Shaikh Mohammad Khiyabani, the Tabriz representative, claimed he had initially joined the Social-Democratic faction for its freedom-fighting cause but had come to reject its socialist ideology. He declared his nonpartisanship, even though he admitted attending the Democrats' meetings, despite his ambivalence toward some of that party's views. "I still do not understand the meaning of 'Democrat,'" he told the deputies; he would condemn it if it means "republican." Furthermore, he disagreed with the conception of the law as changeable, a mostly translated version of the Europeans law. Our law, he said, must be immutable and compatible with our sharia.

He would adhere only to the party that enacts laws based on it.[24] Judging from the recorded minutes, however, Khiyabani did not always adhere to this publicly declared principle; in fact, more often than not he voted alongside the Democrats and their allies. Similarly, as already stated, Mohammad Hashem Mirza, who regularly voted to the "left" of the ideological spectrum, resisted joining the Democrat Party, and the same goes for Hashtrudi, the Azerbaijan deputy. The Armenian deputy Yanes, a Dashnakist, had his own program, which he did not present to the Majles. Of equal significance is the ideological conversion of the Tabriz *anjoman*. Initially one of the most radical groups active in the revolution and the period of Lesser Despotism, it adopted a moderate political voice by the time Naser al-Molk assumed the regency. In a cable sent to the Majles on the very day the new prime minister attended it to present his cabinet's new program, the *anjoman* referred to the regent respectfully, praising his religious disposition and his knowledge in diagnosing the nation's ills. It expressed its full confidence in his ability to lead the combat against terrorism, to safeguard national independence, and to enforce the principles of the holy law.[25]

A close analysis of some deputies' refusal to identify their party affiliation reveals a fear of being implicated in "extremist ideology" or perhaps just a reluctance to commit to a party that, at this early formative stage of multiparty experimentation, was still personally dominated by an individual or a small group. The presence of religious "traditionalists" and clause 2 of the Supplement to the Fundamental Law further discouraged many of them to transgress acceptable religious norms. The regent's requirements, enjoying tacit Anglo-Russian agreement and backed by a majority of his supporters in the Majles, politically sharpened the rivalry between parties and intimidated many deputies who voted mostly with the Democrats. Efforts to sideline identifiable Democrats and non-Democrats deemed "extremists" or "radical nationalists" persisted, despite the Democrats' and Moderates' shared program.

The new configuration of forces in the Majles drastically reduced the predominant influence the Democrats had enjoyed until then. And the radical wing remained a fringe of the Democrat Party, having lost out to the parliamentary mainstream group; it played no vital role in shaping the legislative reforms. In this process, Solaiman Mirza had become aware of the complex and sometimes insidious interplay of politics, policy, and power. He would tone down his social-democratic rhetoric and refrain from venting his radical ideas in the debates unless absolutely necessary. Adjusting to the novel role of leader of the minority party in opposition to the government in power, he saw his status constitutionally legitimized, giving him the right to express his objections to policies without suffering undue consequences, even with the Sepahdar and Naser al-Molk holding the executive reins. A particularly confrontational encounter with Assadollah Kordestani clearly demonstrates Solaiman Mirza's confidence in his new status as the leader of a legitimate parliamentary minority faction.

In an early spring session, Solaiman Mirza questioned the fairness of a previously passed law that had imposed a sales tax on salt. It has turned out to be a burden for the poor, he explained, and has led to an increase in duty-free imported salt, to the detriment of the locally produced salt. His Democrat parliamentary faction proposed the elimination of the sales tax and its replacement by a property tax that would not affect the poor. Assadollah Kordestani vehemently dissented. Accusing the minority with failure to consult the majority prior to the assembly meeting, he charged them with contravening the proper Majles procedure and potentially causing party conflicts with the government. He also recalled the dominant role the Democrats played in passing that salt tax. Solaiman Mirza rebuked him, pointing to the minority's responsibility to challenge the majority's decisions when necessary; he was not inciting any conflict. Should the minority remain mute to avoid being accused of sedition? he asked. "If that is so, then the majority . . . should vote that the minority is to keep silent" and that the majority should be allowed to "do whatever it wants."[26] The proper procedure for any bill to pass, he reminded his critic, is for it to be signed by a number of deputies before it is sent to the appropriate committee and then debated in an open session. It passes if it wins a majority vote.

Solaiman Mirza once more seized the occasion to confront the forged coalition, questioning its composition. The majority party is not a single party, he asserted; it is a bloc made out of small factions and individuals with diverse views. How many are Social-Moderates or Social-Democrats or Accord and Progress members? he wondered aloud. And he denied that the Democrat Party had ever formed a majority in the Majles; the salt tax was enacted following a majority vote that passed in accordance with the "nation's desire" to pay a tax rather than take foreign loans with onerous consequences to national independence. He ended: the Democrats are not to be blamed. The majority is now in power; they, not the minority, are accountable to the nation.[27] Matin al-Saltaneh, member of the majority, fully endorsed the Democrat leader's suggestions. The salt tax was eventually enforced but at a lower rate to help alleviate the burden on the poor.[28]

Judging from his private talk with Barclay, the regent intensified his expression of utter contempt for the Democrats. He labeled them all "terrorists" responsible for recent murders by assassins imported from the Caucasus and acting as their proxy to kill their designated targets. He believed Ayatollah Behbahani's murder and the violence that had recently rocked the capital were commandeered by Taqizadeh, spreading a "reign of terror." He implicated Navab and Hakim al-Molk, arguing that, although not directly responsible, they nevertheless attended secret meetings where discussions of assassination were taking place; and he deplored Momtaz al-Dowleh's and Mostashar al-Dowleh's "exceedingly liberal" views. The term *terrorism* thus attached to *extreme nationalism* and *liberal* was added to the regent's and his supporters' vocabulary in justification of their anti-Democrat attacks. Naser al-Molk's excessive paranoia led him to the firm conviction that all Democrats and their allies were his enemies and that the political situation was already "exceedingly hopeless."[29]

Barclay worried the regent might soon resign. Yet the British envoy was observing the rapid weakening position of the "ultra-nationalists," who were "handicapped" by the loss of their prominent members, Taqizadeh, Sani' al-Dowleh, Navab, and Assadollah Mirza. Though he described the majority coalition as consisting of small groups formed around individuals such as the Sepahdar, Sardar As'ad, 'Ayn al-Dowleh, and Farman-Farma, all with doubtful constitutional credibility, he believed "it may last longer than its somewhat artificial origin might lead one to expect."[30] Within several weeks, the regent and the Sepahdar dismissed Democrats or anyone allegedly associated with them from government positions, and through their proxies in the Majles they relentlessly tried to undermine self-proclaimed Democrats. Militias affiliated with the Democrats were punished and deported, whereas those attached to the Moderates were "left unharmed."[31]

This overt discrimination would backfire later in the summer. Morgan Shuster, the American financial adviser eventually appointed as the Persian government's treasurer general (introduced in this chapter and discussed more fully in chapter 12), would then blame the regent for the "strife and bitterness of party rivalry [that] had not entered into their [the deputies'] proceedings" prior to the regent's return. Shuster unequivocally asserted as a "historical fact" that Naser al-Molk was "the father of factional hatred in the Persian Parliament."[32] Indeed, although ideological differences preexisted the official emergence of parties, the regent's political meddling fueled the deputies' mutual distrust, despite their common agreement in legislating needed reforms. Politics increasingly overshadowed policy; tactics eclipsed the national strategy to attain shared goals. And the entire procedure of nation-state building would bear the brunt of its architects' conflicts.

The New Sepahdar Cabinet

On March 4, 1911, Naser al-Molk came to the Majles to be sworn in as regent in the presence of high-ranking olama, the Speaker, and all deputies. His speech conventionally adhered to the concepts of constitutional monarchy and parliamentary governance, seemingly flowery rhetoric more than expressed conviction. He declared his political neutrality and his nonadherence to any party. He briefly reviewed the status and authority of the Majles to enact laws to be signed by the monarch, who, he assured his audience, possesses neither power to revoke them nor any other claim to authority in political affairs. The ministers, he went on, are accountable to the Majles, which has the right to dissolve the cabinet in case of loss of confidence. He expressed his hope that the legislative and the executive branches would work harmoniously, setting aside personal conflicts that had previously marred their respective work and establish law and order peacefully. He asked all citizens to respect the rule of law, proclaiming: "Today, the power of the government rests on the power of the entire nation," which cannot be opposed. He ended his speech on a somber note, threatening to resign should the deputies fail to fulfill their obligation in improving the situation in the country. He then announced the appointment of the Sepahdar, Mohammad Vali Khan Naser al-Saltaneh, as the new prime minister.[33]

In reviewing that speech, Barclay observed that the regent "showed a misapprehension of his position,"[34] which was strictly honorific in that the Constitution bestowed upon the Majles the power to approve the appointment of the prime minister and his cabinet ministers. One can add here that Naser al-Molk was actually rejecting personal responsibility for any potential political failure in ensuring stability and security in the country, while at the same time fomenting dissension among the nation's representatives, whose authority he had sworn to respect.

Seven days later the Sepahdar attended the Majles and delivered a speech blaming the Majles for having taken power unconstitutionally, leaving the government utterly unable to function properly, with dire consequences for the nation's security and stability. He presented the new cabinet: Ahmad Ala' al-Dowleh, minister of education and public works; Sadeq Khan Mostashar al-Dowleh, minister of the interior; Isma'il Khan Momtaz al-Dowleh, minister of finance; Mirza Ibrahim Khan Mo'aven al-Dowleh, minister of trade, post, and telegraph; Nasrollah Khan Moshir al-Dowleh, minister of justice; and Mirza Mehdi Mohtashem al-Saltaneh, minister of foreign affairs. The prime minister retained the Ministry of War temporarily.[35] Reportedly, Sardar As'ad had played an important role in forming the cabinet, with the full approval of the regent, who favored the selection of the Sepahdar to lead it precisely because of the Sepahdar's well-known close ties to Russian interests. Barclay, though sharing many deputies' distrust of the Sepahdar, believed the closeness was natural, given his debt to the Russian Bank and the location of his estates in the Russian zone.[36] Contrary to the regent's denigrating comments, however, Barclay praised Momtaz al-Dowleh, Mostashar al-Dowleh, and Moshir al-Dowleh, describing them as European-educated "representatives of the Young Persian School" and not part of Navab's group of "extreme nationalists known locally as the Democratic Party."[37] The British diplomat's ambivalence regarding Russia's entitlements and all the main Persian players in the political drama unfolding under his eyes would remain constant to the very end.

In his speech to the Majles, the prime minister declared his top priorities to be combatting sedition and "terrorism" (using that transliterated French term), which he identified with "elements opposed to the Constitution," and restoring peace and security. In view of this "extraordinary responsibility," he demanded "full powers" for his cabinet to accomplish its task, which included punishing indicted criminals and organizing well-disciplined government institutions, especially the military. In addition, he wanted to implement temporary emergency press laws to eliminate various newspapers' excessive abuse of their "ill-conceived freedom," which had endangered the nation's security. The Sepahdar also presented his cabinet's general program neatly itemized in sections: establishing national security; sending armed forces where needed in the provinces; proposing a new budget; establishing good relations with "friendly nations"; pursuing the previous cabinet's loan negotiations; initiating financial reforms with hired foreign help; setting up a special committee to consider temporary laws pertaining to municipal issues not yet legislated; making judicial, educational, and commercial reforms. He threatened to resign should the Majles fail to ratify his program. Mostashar al-Dowleh, the new minister of the interior, pleaded for complete cooperation between the Majles and the ministers, foregoing past practice of secretive policy making that, he believed, had had such disastrous consequences.[38] In fact, most of the new cabinet's program was practically identical to the previous cabinet's. The deputies had no hesitation in approving it, but the prime minister's demand for full power raised fierce objections a few days later.

On March 15, the prime minister and members of his cabinet returned to the Majles, bringing their program for approval and repeating the threat to resign should it be rejected. Vahid al-Molk and Solaiman Mirza, the two most outspoken Democrat champions of the Constitution, pronounced it unacceptable. Nowhere in the Constitution, Vahid al-Molk asserted, is there a mention of "full powers" to be assumed by any of the three separate branches of government; in fact, "the Fundamental Law has eradicated" these terms from its lexicon. This government, he reminded the cabinet officials, is a government for the people, whose rights are clearly defined. No one can be arrested and condemned without due legal process; "in no way could we even touch any clause of our Constitution." Moreover, he argued, this martial law would revoke the people's newly acquired freedom guaranteed by its elected representatives. It would reverse the slow process of their fully comprehending and adjusting to the novel, revolutionary concepts it entails. Vahid al-Molk and his fellow reformers were, indeed, conscious of the fact that parliamentary governance was held together by the strength of their ideas; suspending liberties now would threaten its precarious sustainability. He rebutted the prime minister's contention that the prevailing state of chaos and anarchy was a consequence of the legislature's failure to enact appropriate laws; he blamed instead the executive branch's incompetence. And he passionately defended freedom of the press, "the most basic right that helps a country attain a high degree of civilization."[39]

The Sepahdar denied that his cabinet aimed at seizing power "by the sword" and reiterated his threat to resign. Interior Minister Mostashar al-Dowleh, whose constitutional credentials were uncontested, pleaded for the Majles's trust. The government, he said, needs the deputies' consent to assume such authority. Only when thus empowered could the ministers combat the lawlessness and sedition prevailing in the provinces and succeed in restoring order and implementing the new laws. He ended with a solemn promise that the cabinet would not abuse the authority granted; it would use that authority judiciously. Although expressing his particular trust in Mostashar al-Dowleh, Solaiman Mirza nonetheless vigorously opposed granting full powers to the cabinet, recalling past experience of such abuse. Arresting and punishing criminals and terrorists, he said, are a normal part of the government's function, with no need of full power to be exercised. Voting in favor of full powers would be tantamount to revoking the Constitution and all the rights it bestows on the people; it would lead inevitably to the Majles's closure. He asked the ministers to submit a detailed definition and explanation of the requested powers: What for, for how long, against whom? In addition, he conditioned his acceptance of the part in the program related to "friendly relations with foreign nations" on those nations' reciprocal respect for Iran's independence.[40] At the end of that long session, despite the passionate objections raised by the two Democratic deputies, the cabinet's program passed by an absolute majority vote: forty-seven for, seventeen against, and nine abstentions.

Although the Democrat Party leadership was defeated in this instance, the majority vote confirmed that the Majles had made solid gains in its experimentation with the novel parliamentary governance, albeit perhaps only in appearance. The executive had requested the legislature's assent to acquire full, extraordinary governing power, which was granted by majority vote after lengthy debate. Predictably, the majority was created in compliance with the regent's request to fulfill its obligation to support government policies. Nonetheless, for the mostly inexperienced deputies in attendance, beneath the trappings of parliamentary democracy lay important learned lessons on its proper functioning.

Earlier, on February 25, Foreign Minister Mohtashem al-Saltaneh had informed the Majles on the excellent relations existing between Iran and concerned foreign nations since the regent's return. Russia, he told them, having established a "most friendly and close" relationship with the new government, had announced the recall of its troops in Qazvin. It had also, the minister reported, expressed its willingness to cooperate with Persian officials to ensure security and order in the country and promised to extradite the insurgents and criminals who had fled to its territories. He counseled the national representatives to appreciate these friendly relations.[41] Many deputies had welcomed the minister's message, unaware of the fact that Russia's decision to withdraw its troops from Qazvin was decided before the regent's return to Tehran and, upon his request, simply postponed until the Sepahdar's cabinet was installed.

Contentious Religious Discussions

Within a month of Naser al-Molk's return, fierce opposition to some reforms pertaining mainly to education and the judiciary erupted in the Majles. The regent's quick reversal to a traditional rhetoric encouraged social conservative elements to voice their objections to certain reforms. A man reputed for his admiration of British parliamentary governance, which was often reflected in his public speeches and letters to the Majles, and desiring a governmental structure modeled on the European system, Naser al-Molk paradoxically began to object to proposed reforms that he now deemed incompatible with Iran's social and moral norms. In a new letter to the Majles, he went so far as to criticize the translation of European constitutional texts. Laws, he wrote, are always pertinent to a country's social, political, and cultural background; he urged the deputies to abide by the Islamic law when legislating reforms.[42] In that same session, a letter from Najaf signed by the constitutional *mojtahed* Abdollah Mazandarani in support of the regent's view and condemning reforms emulating foreign laws that were incompatible with the holy law was read out loud. Mazandarani specifically complained that the deputies had not yet revised article 27 of the Supplement to the Fundamental Law of 1907, which separated judicial courts pertaining to public affairs from the religious courts and thus effectively secularized laws related to the nation's public life.[43] Days later the regent sent another letter blaming the parties for the government's shortcomings in establishing and consolidating political institutions. These parties, he claimed, are essentially good subjects for political and philosophical textbooks, expressing "hopeful," wishful thinking, but not relevant for urgently needed action. All parties, he commanded, must give up their conflicting views and concentrate on formulating administrative reforms. Here again he stressed the imperative to respect the country's moral values and customs.[44] Barely a few days passed after the regent sent this letter when the *mojtaheds* Khorasani and Mazandarani dispatched a joint cable praising the regent and expressing their satisfaction that the previous era of "personality cult," personal conflicts, and "self-interested theatrics" had come to an end. They hoped that under his guidance the "true patriots," the olama, princes, and aristocrats would eliminate "class hatred" and defuse tensions prevailing in the country.[45] Thus enjoying the backing of high-ranking political and religious conservative authorities, some fractious conservative lawmakers felt secure in raising contentious religious issues.

One of the first of such serious issues recorded in the *Mozakerat* concerned the personal qualifications of hired employees for the Registrar Bureau, located in the Ministry of Justice and functioning as the depository of official census and all personal and commercial documents. Citizenship, Moslem religion and knowledge of Islamic jurisprudence, literacy in the

Persian language, and a minimum age of twenty-five were required qualifications for all bureau employees. Hajj Ibrahim Aqa, the religious traditionalist member of the majority, had inserted the additional religious requirement to the bill while the bill was debated. Yanes strongly objected to the exclusion of non-Moslems. He was offended by that exclusion, he told his colleagues, because the bureau jobs do not require knowledge of religious law. The Constitution, the Armenian deputy stated, grants equality to all citizens without mentioning Moslem identity; to be Iranian is sufficient. The Constitution grants all Iranians equality as citizens as well as equality under the law; otherwise, he warned, non-Moslems would be considered unequal to Moslems, tantamount to being "in captivity." Kaikhosrow, the Zoroastrian deputy, adopting a milder tone, accepted the need for Islamic law experts, but he contemplated the possibility of a non-Moslem acquiring that knowledge, which would then qualify that person for a position in the bureau. Shaikh Ibrahim Zanjani, the Democrat, totally denied the need for religious qualification; Eftekhar al-Va'ezin, the unaffiliated representative, declared it "superfluous"; Vakil al-Tojjar, the Moderate, deemed it necessary only when and if the olama's signature was required. Kashef, a member of the coalition, and Mohammad Hashem Mirza, the nonpartisan who voted mostly with the Democrats, supported the requirements. Finally, Imam Jom'eh, addressing Yanes and Kaikhosrow as "our two brothers," assured them that, indeed, they are equal citizens, but in matters concerning Islamic law non-Moslems are "naturally" not qualified.[46] The bill with its added religious requirement passed by majority vote without any reference to article 27 of the Supplement, which unequivocally separates laws pertaining to public and government affairs from the sharia.

The educational reforms provoked a livelier debate as the promoters crisscrossed ideological or party lines, rallying the support of most if not all deputies favoring sociocultural changes. Several sessions in March and April were devoted to formulating the rules regulating the newly reformed Ministry of Education, which also included the religious endowments. The ministry was declared the sole institution responsible for the national school system—its programs, standards, textbooks, and teachers' qualifications. Shaikh Assadollah Kordestani, the member of the coalition reputed for his periodic provocative opposition to the Democrats' policy proposals, ignited the controversy this time. He vigorously objected to the subjection of religious schools, financed by the religious foundations, to the ministry's supervision. Reminding his colleagues of their debates concerning the exemption of private schools from government control, he defined the independently financed *maktab* (religious school) as private. Therefore, they do not fall under the ministry's jurisdiction, and the *maktab*'s "special requirements" must be implemented by the trustees of the endowments. Hajj Ibrahim Aqa, the cleric-deputy and member of the coalition, further argued that each religious school is subject to specific conditions raised by the endowment that finances it. It has to be exempt from government supervision in order to avoid contravening the donors' wishes. Seyyed Hasan Modarres, the nonpartisan cleric-deputy, amplified these two deputies' argument, but Dr. Ali Khan, also a nonpartisan, refuted it. There exist no possible conflicts, he told them; the *maktab* is kept under the *waqf*'s (religious endowment's) jurisdiction, but the ministry must ensure compliance to its rules concerning, for instance, exams and proper student behavior. Mohammad Ali Zoka' al-Molk, the Democrat, defended the ministry's right to supervise all kinds of schools, including the private ones, to enforce the execution of the system of national education. "The ministry, after all, is the Ministry of Education and Religious Endowment," he told them.[47] The bill was sent back to the appropriate committee for further review. Weeks later Imam Jom'eh demanded the regent's seal of approval for the new rules regulating the ministry to ensure its accordance with the holy law. The Constitution, he stated, requires all laws enacted to be reviewed by the religious council before their passage.[48] But the education bill had already passed; Hosain Mo'tamed al-Molk (brother of Abol Hasan Mo'azed al-Saltaneh), the newly elected Speaker,[49] had "saved" it, according to the British report.[50] Solaiman Mirza in particular had praised the Speaker's impartiality and leadership in speeding the enactment of needed laws in an orderly fashion.[51]

The judiciary reforms similarly raised the objections of the religious traditionalists and their political allies. Their concern here was to sharply distinguish religious laws pertaining to personal and moral affairs falling under the olama's jurisdiction from laws pertaining to public and political issues. At stake was the fundamental issue of who had juridical authority, the olama or state officials, to police moral crimes. The two most outspoken cleric-deputies, Imam Jom'eh and Hajj Ibrahim Aqa, opposed government imposition of price control as a preventive measure combating hoarding. Hajj Aqa insisted the hoarding issue falls under religious jurisdiction, though the provincial *anjoman* is consulted on pricing matters to ensure no abuse is committed.[52] Both deputies wished to create a new public-defendant position to be charged with the implementation of religious laws, including the antihoarding laws that were then intensively debated. Modarres fully endorsed their proposal, insisting on a religious rule holding the public defendant solely responsible for "people's affairs." A religious judge, he ascertained, and no one else should appoint the public defendant. Neither the *anjoman* nor the *parlement* (as given in transliterated French in the text), he said, can interfere, not even the municipality; it is not part of their function.[53]

That was the first time the Majles openly and publicly voiced an official determination to sharply delineate the religious realm, *shar'i*, from the public-political realm, *orf*. Both religious law and laws based on local customs traditionally coexisted, and their respective exercise of judicial power underscored their complementary status. Here, however, the term *orf* emerged as broadly defining state laws. In fact, Modarres felt the need to stress the distinction between the two realms. In comparison to the "specific details" of this religious position, he said, the concerns of the *anjomans* and the *parlement* are "wider" in scope. His effort to clarify his statement is important to note here because it signaled the growing acceptance of the new conception of a man-made law, *qanun*, separate from the sharia, even though the concept was articulated in a confused and even ambiguous speech.

Indeed, the central issue debated then was the government decision to control prices of basic agricultural commodities to prevent hoarding. The opponents of that regulation were not only the religious traditionalists but also reformists who championed landowners and merchants' right to dispose of their produce freely, without any government intervention. Government price fixing is contrary to the sharia, they proclaimed in unison.[54] Ibrahim Zanjani, the Democrat, angrily rebutted their statement and denounced the proposed position of a public defendant as unprecedented in Iran. Nasrollah Khan Moshir al-Dowleh, the reform-minded, Moderate minister of justice who was then in attendance, intervened to explain that the punishment for an unlawful commercial transaction falls under government jurisdiction; it is a separate case from an immoral deed considered not permissible in religious law. Although people know their religious values and principles, he explained, not all are well acquainted with government laws; this requires all functionaries to be knowledgeable in *orf* laws.[55] The minister of justice employed a similar argument when confronted with the traditionalists' insistence on basing all commercial laws and rules regulating currency transactions on the sharia. When dealing with international trade and money transfer, he informed them, the "science of law," "not our religious jurisprudence," is applicable. Admitting that "our merchants" are exposed to inevitable conflicts between the two, he nonetheless recognized the necessity to reconcile them.[56] In an earlier session, Solaiman Mirza had in fact mentioned that the parliamentary Judiciary Committee, to which he belonged, regularly consulted the olama when reviewing judicial laws to be enacted.[57] The subject was put to rest inconclusively.

Legislative Reforms: A Process in Progress

By and large, the religious traditionalists and other deputies not necessarily associated with them tried to obstruct any legislation that attempted to impose restrictions on trade and private property. They defended the rights of landowners and merchants as well as of many wealthy olama who owned large estates and invested in commercial enterprises against government interference. Behjat al-Olama and fellow cleric-deputies, for instance, objected to the government granting the British Imperial Bank of Persia the monopoly right to mint silver coins, viewing it as detrimental to the merchants' interests. The government had signed a contract with the bank, while assuming all the expenses and paying the bank a commission.[58] Conversely, most deputies favored a strong central government uniformly applying legislated reforms that would ultimately change the nation's political culture. The Arabestan (present-day Khuzistan) representative Kashef, for instance, insisted on centralizing all state institutions and equally implementing the laws governing them, be it in Tehran or Arabestan.[59] And there was no recorded objection to the employment of a modern permanent cadre of civil servants in the various ministries in the capital and the provinces, with equal benefits such as salaries, pensions, and annual vacations. Efforts to establish government institutions, well regulated, well managed, and staffed with experienced, incorruptible employees, met with no opposition.

And there were serious discussions to improve international means of communication to facilitate international trade, with no recorded dissension.[60] Similarly, a law passed requiring all physicians practicing in the country to have their medical diplomas certified by the Ministry of Education, an unprecedented regulation. It was to be applied first in Tehran and eventually throughout the country when qualified government officials were sent to different provinces, as was generally the case when enforcing all legislated reforms.[61] Significantly, given the multiethnic and multilingual demographic composition of the country, the imposition of Persian as the sole official language for all registered documents and translated texts, including those requiring the olama's signatures, passed with no problems.[62] Kaikhosrow, the Zoroastrian deputy, turned out to be the most eloquent champion of the national language, even deploring any borrowing of European terminology by his fellow deputies. Nor were there serious disputes over sending thirty students to Europe. And it was agreed that graduates of the French schools (the Catholic St. Louis and French Alliance schools) as well as of the German School and Dar al-Fonun were the most qualified students to study abroad. Some deputies, including Modarres, expressed some concerns over the potential influence of immoral values on the students living in foreign environments, causing them to lose their Islamic moral compass. That issue was resolved with the appointment of a "guardian" to watch over their behavior while abroad.[63]

Despite the increasingly politically motivated acrimonious accusations and counteraccusations in the Majles, reading the *Mozakerat* reveals the vigorous legislative power exercised in accordance with the novel multiparty parliamentary system. Moreover, many laws passed or failed to pass following votes that more often than not transcended the parties' ideological differences, demonstrating the deputies' general support for the innovative reform program they shared in common. Thus, the great majority finally voted to provide necessary funds to send thirty students and their supervisor to Europe, despite the government's dire financial situation. Half of them were to enroll in education institutes, a quarter in military academies, and the rest to study agriculture and chemistry. The majority also voted for the establishment of a school of fine arts, despite some deputies protesting its "irrelevance" to the country's current needs. Reforms finally passed to bring the entire school system, including the schools attached to the *owqaf*, under the Ministry of Education's control, with strict rules affecting financing, textbooks, and programs. In effect, a modernized administration was to take control of the entire national education system. The government would also establish schools for non-Moslem subjects to be educated according to their respective religions, and if attending regular public schools, they would be exempt from taking Islamic courses, as discussed in the concluding chapter.

Similarly, a majority passed a bill regulating the opium sales tax and banning the consumption of opium within seven years, thus allowing the addicted time for detoxing. But a general ban on the cultivation of opium was never considered. The majority voted for the government's right to collect all opiate derivatives in exchange for minimal payment to the producers, marking the defeat of the opponents of government interference in domestic trade. But the wholesale, tax-free international trade in opium was left in the merchants' hands; the majority agreed that this trade constituted a lucrative business, especially with its exports to India and China.[64]

The reform related to publicly owned land (*khaleseh*) was a more sensitive issue, though not unduly divisive. As already explained, both parties had endorsed a similar project to improve the poor peasants' living conditions. The subject was not raised again until April 1911, when Shaikh Gholam Hosain, a Democrat, pleaded on behalf of peasants for a speedy government resolution. The government reportedly had months earlier signed a contract granting a fifty-year lease to a private domestic company to develop a plot of land located outside Tehran. "These unfortunate peasants," the shaikh asked, "are they deprived of their Iranian and human rights?"[65] The issue was not discussed further until nine days later. During a highly combative session, the nonaligned Eftekhar al-Va'ezin denounced the contract. He expressed his worries that it would leave the peasants cultivating the land at the mercy of the private company and lead to hoarding and to a price increase for all the land's produce. He favored keeping the land under government administration, even though in principle he was not opposed to leasing the land to a private company or individual. He only questioned the moral and ethical qualifications of some members of the contracted company, which included 'Ayn al-Saltaneh, a notorious absentee landlord on whose land the peasants were particularly oppressed. Mohammad Hashem Mirza, the pro-Democrat, basically shared the same view, adding that the government had signed the contract unconstitutionally, without first consulting the Majles. Kashef, a member of the majority, argued that a contract bearing a government signature must be honored.[66]

Opposition to the contract was general, led by Democrats. Whereas Shaikh Gholam Hosain repeated his earlier opposition on the grounds that the contract would increase peasants' oppression, Solaiman Mirza eloquently defended a new concept of land "small ownership" (*khordeh malek*). The land is most profitable, he stated, only when a "small owner" cultivates it, reaping the fruit of his own labor. This is what the Majles is all about, he reminded his colleagues, to work to improve the living conditions of the "weak" by "lifting the heavy yoke of oppression" traditionally maintained by the "influential" members of society. The Majles should implement the basic constitutional principle of justice for all by instituting an innovative system of leasing public land to the peasants, first in the vicinities of Tehran and gradually reaching out to the rest of the country. This is the best means, he assured his fellow deputies, to combat hoarding and artificial price increase.[67] That issue, often debated in many sessions in response to frequent bread riots occurring in the capital and provincial towns, was not resolved. Any kind of land reform was left unaddressed, despite the two parties' expressed advocacy of it.

Other issues raised in the Majles, specifically those regarding its procedure, left the Democrats at a disadvantage strictly on the basis of their smaller number. Article 7 of the Fundamental Law of 1906, written at a time when not all of the 120 twenty deputies were as yet accredited, let alone elected, stipulated that 61 deputies were needed in attendance to inaugurate the first Majles. It also stipulated that two-thirds, or 80 deputies, had to be present to start a debate, and three-quarters, or 90, were necessary for a quorum to vote. Ambiguities were noted, leading to contentious interpretations. As Zoka' al-Molk accurately observed, the required total number of 120 representatives was never achieved then, nor has it been presently. He suggested dismissing all requisite numbers until the new electoral law currently being written down was completed. The deputies finally decided that only the ballots of those present in the Majles would be considered admissible.[68]

Solaiman Mirza wished to change the electoral rule concerning the replacement of a deceased or resigned deputy, who, according to the existing rule, was to be elected by the Majles. With the official establishment of parliamentary factions forming a majority/minority divide, he explained, this rule cannot be applied anymore. It is contrary to the Constitution and would give the majority excessive influence in the selection of new deputies. Therefore, he announced, Democrats will not vote for a deputy chosen by the majority, which would increase the latter's number. The "majority always rules," no matter how important or minor is the issue, he lamented.[69] And it did when the proposed British Imperial Bank loan, an issue of greater political significance with more vital repercussions for the fate of the second Majles, was ratified.

Foreign Advisers

Both the legislative and executive branches of the Persian government acknowledged their need for foreign expertise to help implement administrative reforms. Britain and Russia shared this concern, but the problematic issue of the advisers' country of origin delayed their hiring. Highly intricate negotiations between the two powers over which nation would provide experts to advise which ministry were undertaken without consulting Persian officials. Both worried that other countries, especially Germany, would be incited to claim equal rights to send their experts. The possibility of German advisers also alarmed France, who then would soften its demands for equal rights to advise the Persian government.[70] Britain and Russia's relentless objection to the appointment of any German national was also extended to the Italians, whom they viewed as Germany's allies. However, judging from the archival documents, close cooperation prevailed between the major European powers in accommodating French interests and excluding Germany's. Thus, Rome, when Tehran contacted it, deferred to London and St. Petersburg's opinion despite its close relationship with Berlin, seriously taking into account Anglo-Russian geopolitical prerogatives in the region. Grey and Izvolski insisted on the employment of subjects of "smaller" European powers, such as Denmark or Holland, "in order to avoid international jealousies and competition."[71] Of great concern to the Anglo-Russian joint interests was the possibility of German officers employed in the Persian gendarmerie, which would, it was claimed, create "troubles of all kinds for the two Powers."[72] In fact, Russia considered the country's military reorganization to be exclusively the task of Russian officers. Similarly, London preferred to keep the Frenchman Joseph Bizot in charge of finances, with an additional number of Belgian experts to assist him, if France saw no inconvenience in that. But Bizot was not interested in resuming his Tehran post, as we shall see.

The Majles, however, was determined to search independently for prospective candidates, devoting several sessions to the issue. Some deputies raised questions over the suitability of the experts' national background to the Iranian socio-cultural environment; most dismissed the relevance of this concern, emphasizing the importance of the experts' qualifications and working conditions.[73] The majority voted to hire military advisers from Italy or France.[74] There were disagreements over the choice of advisers for the Ministry of Justice. In response to those who selected Egypt, a Moslem country well versed in Islamic jurisprudence, Vahid al-Molk contended that the objective is to seek administrative and not legislative expertise. "We do not need anyone to enact our laws. . . . We need an administrator of justice," he said, opting for French advisers as the most suitable for the conditions in Iran.[75] The minister of justice agreed with him but proposed hiring from Egypt an additional Moslem expert, well acquainted with the French judicial system, and the majority voted in favor of his proposal. Some deputies expressed their misgivings about potential consequences of hiring experts from different countries, who would advocate the adoption of diverse systems that may or may not fit the nation's conditions, leading to the "internationalization of

Iran." Assadollah Mirza, the minister of post and telegraph, dismissed the idea of hiring all experts from one "great, neutral" power instead. "No such thing is possible," he told the deputies.[76]

Of particular importance was the hiring of a financial adviser. Many deputies favored a neutral country that championed no European power currently involved in Iran. They favored the United States as best fulfilling their requirements; some disagreed. Assadollah Mirza preferred hiring Frenchmen, who were better acquainted with Iran's situation, having served for many years in the country and having started drafting reform programs based on the French model. Americans, he argued, may be a good choice, but they will need time, at least a year, to acquire enough knowledge of their new surroundings. Furthermore, the French centralized system suited Iran better than the American federalism, which granted the states autonomy for local affairs. Besides, he added, there was the problem of language. Many Iranians have learned French, not English. Despite these arguments, the majority voted in favor of soliciting the United States for a financial adviser.[77]

Navab, while still minister of foreign affairs and enjoying strong support from the Majles Foreign Affairs Committee, had undertaken secret discussions with Washington. The US government was officially informed of the request for a financial adviser on September 22, 1910. Its ambassador in Tehran, Charles W. Russell, had convinced his Persian interlocutors that only the Americans are honestly distanced from international intrigues. Both Russia and Britain had initially given their consent to the hiring of an American financial adviser. American officials reportedly had assured the two powers that if hired they would not object to Anglo-Russian involvement in protecting Anglo-Russian interests; it was a cordial agreement. The Persian chargé d'affaires in Washington, DC, recommended W. Morgan Shuster, a lawyer with experience in fiscal reforms who had previously advised Cuba and the Philippines. Until his resignation in late December 1910, Navab would personally conduct most of the Persian–American negotiations.

The government concluded the negotiations weeks after Navab resigned. Ironically, given the subsequent British opposition to the American adviser, Barclay believed the United States had no political interests in the country. Sazanov, however, was not as agreeable to the choice, suspecting the Germans were behind the Persians' attitude and the stiffening of their resistance to the two powers. Informed that the Majles Foreign Affairs Committee had in mind Swiss financial experts in case of the American's rejection of the request, British and Russian envoys found the contingency plan undesirable, especially if the experts were German Swiss. They warned the Persian government that they would seriously object to the "engagement of others less welcome to us than Americans and Frenchmen"; should their advice be dismissed, they would demand the hiring of their own nationals.[78] Sazanov was then reconciled with an American candidate, though he continued to have serious misgivings. Viewing the United States as a "Big Power," even though not European, he still worried about a potential German demand for equal opportunity to send experts. "The result would be that an international administration would be established in Persia," he told the British ambassador in St. Petersburg, "a complication" he wished to avoid.[79]

But it was too late. Shuster had contacted President William Taft to seek his approval, and the Persian attaché sent an official note to the State Department requesting Shuster's formal hiring in the service of the Persian government as treasurer general. By January 29, 1911, the terms of the contract, for a minimum period of three years and a maximum of five, were finalized, and the names of the Americans to assist Shuster were promulgated: Charles I. McCaskey as inspector of the provincial revenues and Bruce G. Dickey as inspector of taxation. They were the first Americans to be hired as official advisers to the Tehran government. According to Robert McDaniel, "The Persian government had pulled off quite a coup in carrying out the negotiations in the United States."[80] Russell, the American ambassador, was actively but secretly involved in promoting the choice of his country. It occurred at a time when Washington was emerging from the periphery of world politics centered in Europe and becoming a global power. Barclay expected that Russell would "assume great importance" when the American advisers arrive in Tehran, realizing "all his [own] tact will be needed to reconcile their activities with the interests" of Britain and Russia.[81]

The British envoy to Washington, James Bryce, warned Lord Grey of potential conflicts the American advisers would engender in Tehran. In a confidential report describing Shuster's personality, he remarked: "It indicates the kind of difficulties which may await him if he should unfortunately attempt to play a part in Persian politics." This is a "man of considerable force and unquestioned integrity," he added, but "with rigid methods," and therefore it will be necessary "to guide any laudable wish he may evince to protect the interests of the native Persians into channels consistent with the desire of His Majesty's government to attain the same object by well-chosen methods suitable to Oriental conditions."[82] The report did not elucidate such methods, leaving unsaid what was "suitable to Oriental conditions" according to the Europeans' perception.

The Loan Agreement

Following five combative debates in the Majles held in late April and early May 1911, the Imperial Bank loan contract was finally signed. It should be pointed out that the contract, prepared and modified by Sani' al-Dowleh, had gained majority support, but upon Naser al-Molk's request its signing was postponed until the Sepahdar's cabinet was formed (see chapter 10). The late financial minister had carefully drawn up a list of expenditures and set up a system of control for the proper management of the money.[83] The loan of £1.25 million at a 5 percent interest rate was to be converted into Persian bonds, redeemable as of 1916 and to be paid back over a period not exceeding fifty years. It was to be serviced by all net customs receipts at "all parts or places" in the Persian Gulf. Should the amount of receipts prove short to cover the loan payments, other sources of Persian revenue, including the telegraph, would be assigned. The bonds would be exempt from taxation, and the bank "would not undertake any pecuniary liability" toward the bondholders, but it would receive British government "diplomatic support" in implementing the contract. The loan would settle debt due to the British bank, service the new debt, purchase weapons, pay arrear salaries to soldiers and to diplomats serving abroad, and improve security in the South. After outstanding debts and charges were paid off, a balance of only £418,000 would be available to the government.[84]

Solaiman Mirza seriously objected to the loan terms. The loan proceeds, he insisted, should be spent on future development projects and not on past debts, and he requested an itemized list of those debts. Montasar al-Saltaneh and Vahid al-Molk supported their fellow Democrat. Similarly, Mohammad Hashem Mirza also requested an itemized list for review. The minister of foreign affairs attended the following meeting to inform the deputies that a ship carrying British troops had anchored at a Persian Gulf port, insinuating it was ready to intervene in the South should the situation there worsen; the loan contract therefore needed immediate approval. The Democrats and their allies were not duly intimidated. Solaiman Mirza rose to proclaim an official declaration on behalf of the Democrat parliamentary faction: It is not opposed to any "commercial" loan that is free of political conditions; in fact, it is in favor of foreign capital invested in the country to help in its economic development. Nor is it, in principle, opposed to the current loan under discussion. However, he remarked, all the nation's financial issues are subject to Majles supervision in compliance with the Constitution. The present loan, though numerically insignificant, is of "historic importance." His faction, he went on, insists that the loan's proceeds be spent on essential national institutional reforms and therefore is firmly opposed to paying off salaries in arrears or to doing anything with the loan that has not been submitted beforehand to the Majles for review. Then he added that all future expenditures must first be approved by the Majles, and all decisions as to where and how to spend the proceeds must be delayed until the arrival of the European and American financial and security advisers. The minister of foreign affairs responded that, given the urgent need for ready cash, the foreign advisers currently employed are quite capable of inspecting and controlling the expenditure.[85] The issue was not put at rest, as discussions occupied several more sessions.

The Democrats were repeatedly reminded that they had ratified the contract when Sani' al-Dowleh had submitted it, and they knew the country had no choice but to borrow. Mohammad Hashem Mirza repeated the Democrats' viewpoint that priority should be given to the future, not to the past, to finance infrastructure projects ensuring national development, such as railways and roads. At this point, the Speaker read out loud an anonymous cable from Azerbaijan, demanding that the deputies reject the "deplorable" and "unconstitutional" loan proposal. Mo'tamed al-Molk, the respected Moderate Speaker of the Majles, attributed the message to the Tabriz *anjoman*, addressing its Azerbaijani representatives; he called on Solaiman Mirza to dismiss the advice. The cable was obviously sent by the Democrat Party's small radical wing headed by Tigran, who had earlier informed Taqizadeh of its secretive antigovernment incitement. Solaiman Mirza, however, responded that his faction would not walk out if it could reach a compromise with the coalition. The Speaker proposed to deposit the loan proceeds in the bank and "not touch it" until the Majles reviewed the itemized list of expenditure and given its approval; the Democrats turned down the proposal. Exasperated, the Speaker admonished the Democrats, telling them they were representing the province of Azerbaijan and not its *anjoman*, and he threatened to resign should they follow the cable's advice. Hashtrudi immediately retorted that he considered himself a national deputy and not merely a deputy of Azerbaijan, adding, "I will sit in the Majles, I will not leave, but I shall abstain from voting." Another Democrat deputy of

Azerbaijan, Aqa Mirza Ahmad, vehemently protested against the Speaker's threat, accusing him of condemning Azerbaijani Democrats before proving them guilty. He voted according to his own judgment, he said, and abstention does not contravene Majles rules. The Imam Jom'eh suggested they wait until the foreign advisers' arrival. In the meantime, he counseled that a cash advance on the loan be requested to cover payment of the most urgent bills.[86]

The discussions could not but reveal the country's stark reality: its utter dependence on foreign money and foreign financial expertise. Fahim al-Molk, a member of the coalition, voiced the assembled representatives' predicament in just a few words: in this domain, he admitted, "we are students, not teachers." However, he noted that the Americans cannot accomplish miracles, nor should one expect it from them. They do not know Iran as the Europeans do; moreover, their system is so different from Iran's that it will take them a long time to get acquainted with the general situation here, especially in the provinces. "We do not have to wait for the Americans. . . . The Europeans could go on doing the job," he concluded.[87] In the following session, Fahim al-Molk went so far as to defend the loan, qualifying the conditioned terms as "not political" and "not to the government's disadvantage"; to the contrary, he asserted, it is to the government's advantage. Vahid al-Molk refuted all of Fahim al-Molk's statements.[88]

As the tension escalated between the deputies arguing for or against the loan's provisions, more objections were raised over other details: the exorbitant up-front fees and charges, the high interest rate, the lengthy five-year time needed before they could begin to redeem the debt. When the finance minister again reminded them of the late Sani' al-Dowleh's hard-won improvements to the initial loan proposal, Solaiman Mirza impatiently remarked that this was no valid reason why the present government could not further negotiate for better terms. A more important reason lay behind the Democrats stonewalling: they trusted Sani' al-Dowleh's personal integrity but not the Sepahdar's. More important was the Democrats' resentment of the financial compensations going to the Imperial Bank, a 12½ percent commission up front for issuing 12,500 bonds, each to be sold for £100, without assuming any future potential liability. And even though the bonds, which would not bear the bank's name but that of the Iranian government, would then be sold at higher prices, the government would not receive any part of the profit. The Democrats believed the government should hire the bank only to issue the bonds and pay it a commission plus expenses, and then Iran would sell the bonds in the international market, thus retaining all the proceeds; all transactions ought to be under the supervision of a government representative. Fahim al-Molk reminded them that only two banks, the British and the Russian, could determine the rate of exchange; therefore, there can be no competition from a third bank to lower the costs of borrowing money. All suggested changes to the contract failed to pass, but the Democrats, led by Vahid al-Molk and Solaiman Mirza, continued relentlessly to challenge the government. They passionately opposed giving away all of the revenues of the Persian Gulf ports and the telegraph receipts as securities for the loan. Solaiman Mirza desperately pleaded that the Majles wait until the Americans reviewed the financial situation before disposing of the proceeds. In response, he was told once more that the Americans would need time to get acquainted with the situation before offering sound advice, and the emergency expenditures in need of cash could not wait. Vahid al-Molk, in a moment of despair, wondered, Why then bother to hire foreign experts? What a waste of money, he exclaimed.[89]

In the end, on that same day, May 2, 1911, the Majles voted to ratify the loan; out of sixty-eight deputies present, thirty-eight voted for, nineteen against, and eleven abstained. The government signed the contract on May 6, 1911. It bore no changes desired by the Democrats. The endless discussion was, indeed, a show of force, a point–counterpoint debate in which the minority dissenting voice was stifled by the majority's stern retorts: our credit worthiness in the international financial market is very low; we lack the necessary expertise; the dire shortage of cash is paralyzing the government's effort to establish public safety and order, especially in the South, where the British had threatened to intervene with troops. Hence, the Democrats, whose reform projects enjoyed the endorsement of most members of their rival party, found themselves numerically isolated when they criticized the loan terms. The majority coalition and the cabinet who defied the Democrats' objections failed the litmus test of their proclaimed support for the reforms. England and Russia's powerful influence behind the scenes loomed large within the walls of the National Assembly. The majority's response to the Democrats' challenges often echoed the two foreign powers' insistence on full payment of debts in arrears and on giving top priority to funding the military and security forces in the South. Furthermore, the debate in the Majles regarding American versus European financial expertise and their respective suitability to the country's situation specifically reflected the misgivings of the Russian government concerning a third power's intervention in its exclusive sphere of influence and what that intervention might mean for Russia's interests.[90] The politics surrounding the loan controversy and its outcome did not augur well for the battles that would emerge soon after the American advisers reached Tehran a few days after the signing of the contract.

The Democrats continued to clamor against the government's secretive financial decisions. The Fundamental Law specifically stipulated that the Majles would hold the purse strings and dictate how the ministries were funded, thus rendering the government accountable for its expenditures. The Democrats' parliamentary leadership was seriously apprehensive about the ministers' disposing of the loan proceeds without prior consultation with the nation's representatives. Sani' al-Dowleh had drawn up a list of expenditures and had set up a system of control for the proper management of the money in order to preempt corrupt handling of it, but Solaiman Mirza complained that the budget and its expenditure were kept secret. He also reiterated his opposition to paying back the soldiers' and diplomats' salaries in arrears, arguing those salaries should be paid from the national revenues. He related his recent encounter with the British Imperial Bank, which refused to comply with his request to see the balance sheet of the loan proceeds deposited there. In a remarkable confrontation with the minister of finance, he dramatically cried out: "I protest [using this transliterated French term] in the name of the nation's suffering people," who would in the future bear the brunt of that debt and have to work hard to pay it back.[91] The finance minister responded that as a mere individual deputy, Solaiman Mirza cannot have access to the bank's file; only the Majles Financial Committee—a committee headed by a coalition member—has that right. Solaiman Mirza, thus provoked, denounced the rule of the majority, which sidelined the minority, leaving it constantly uninformed about the state of the country's financial affairs.

In the same session, Solaiman Mirza again unleashed his anger when the formation of a special committee for financial control and inspection of the loan proceeds was discussed. The Committee of Financial Inspection would be composed of a "mixed" group of foreign experts and government officials, including the current director of customs, Joseph Mornard, a Belgian national, and would be headed by the minister of finance and his deputy. Mornard was known as an official who worked too closely with the British and Russian legations, enjoying their tacit agreement and support in controlling the customs revenues. Morgan Shuster, Solaiman Mirza reminded all in attendance, has arrived in town. He was hired to take over the supervision of all financial affairs, including the customs; he is the treasurer general and should be the undisputed director of the committee. Here, too, the minister of finance rebuked the Democrat. The Americans, he said, have to be well informed about the situation in the country, and that takes time. They will have to seek advice from the existing European advisers who have worked here for many years, sit in the committee meetings, and gather as much knowledge as possible; until then, the Belgian will remain director of customs and head of the Committee of Financial Inspection.[92]

In a long speech, Hajj Ibrahim Aqa, the cleric-deputy, sternly corrected Solaiman Mirza: the majority is representing the nation and acts in its name, "voting for its interests and well-being." But Solaiman Mirza vehemently denied he was invalidating the majority vote—quite the contrary. He insisted on the minority's responsibility to air its objections when necessary while debating parliamentary bills, whether such objections were successful or not in winning votes. The Democrat's critique was predicated on his conviction that it was the minority's constitutional right as a legitimate opposition party to reach across the partisan divide and present the public with an alternative viewpoint. His counterargument was rejected, and the minister's proposal to establish the Committee of Financial Inspection passed with majority vote.[93]

Interestingly, as late as February 15, when Shuster's contract was already approved, St. Petersburg informed Paris about Naser al-Molk's preference that Joseph Bizot return to Tehran and resume his position as financial adviser. The French were reportedly agreeable, but Bizot was not.[94] Barclay was doubtful the Persian government would go along "unless pressure is exerted upon them to do so from outside." Grey then informed the French he had no objection to Bizot's return, provided the Persians requested it, which they did not.[95] Naser al-Molk's and the Russians' covert attempt to sabotage Shuster's hiring did not bear fruit, even though some coalition deputies defended the continued employment of only European financial experts. By proclaiming Shuster the sole authorized controller of the country's finances, the Democrats had succeeded in creating a polarized climate that was not promising for the American about to assume his post; political jockeying was casting a dark cloud over the mission he was hired to accomplish.

12

Political Intrigues and Royal Conspiracy

BY THE TIME the American financial adviser reached Tehran, other newly hired foreign experts were already in place. The Swedes took charge of instituting a gendarmerie, and the Italian general Maletta had arrived in Shiraz to organize the police force in Fars Province that would restore calm and order as well as secure the southern trade routes. However, both security tasks proved daunting.

Political Turmoil in the Provinces

In the South, the fierce power struggle opposing the Qavami family and Sardar As'ad Bakhtiyari to Isma'il Khan Sulat al-Dowleh Qashqa'i and his new ally, the governor of Fars, Nezam al-Saltaneh, in addition to other recurring tribal conflicts, showed no sign of abating. Insecurity along the trade routes increased. The government had entrusted Sulat al-Dowleh and his armed tribesmen with the security of Shiraz–Bushehr road and the Bakhtiyaris with the safety of the Ahvaz–Isfahan route. Barclay temporarily went along with this arrangement until a gendarmerie would be ready to take over the entire security system in the South. The central government had already sent soldiers for that purpose. However, there were reports of robbery and plunder by the soldiers charged to restore order.[1] General Maletta, arriving in Shiraz in mid-April, was duly pessimistic of any possibility of restoring order.[2]

The new Fars governor's first move was to arrest the two Qavami brothers, Naser al-Dowleh and Qavam al-Molk, thus fueling the Bakhtiyari/Qashqa'i enmity. Sardar As'ad, furious, intervened with the government to have them released, threatening to join the Democratic faction in the Majles and cause the fall of the Sepahdar's cabinet.[3] The government ordered the governor to release the Qavami brothers and allow them to leave Fars, an order

Governor Nezam al-Saltaneh chose to ignore. That deliberate refusal underscored yet again Tehran officials' powerlessness in the remote provinces, where local political players preserved their autonomy, even when nominally abiding by the Constitution. Fearing Bakhtiyari reprisals that would precipitate the prime minister's resignation, Barclay sent a message to the Fars governor, expressing the "hope he will see his way to obey" Tehran's instructions.[4] The governor agreed to allow the brothers to leave town. However, on their way out of Shiraz, Naser al-Dowleh was murdered, reportedly by Sulat al-Dowleh's order. His brother, Qavam al-Molk, escaped and sought asylum in the British consulate. He was to remain there until October 1911.

The bloody incident only complicated British policy in support of Nezam al-Saltaneh, who, with Maletta's agreement, wished to postpone the formation of the gendarmerie. In fact, the allotted money, some 80,000 tomans, was diverted, and little reached the soldiers, who were eventually disbanded. General Maletta's compliance with the governor's disposal of the sum raised "the suspicion that he shared in the planned diversion of funds."[5] Sardar As'ad renewed his effort to oust Sulat al-Dowleh and Nezam al-Saltaneh from their positions and refused to take any more responsibility for the safety of the Ahvaz–Isfahan road. Peace in the South was not restored, adding to the British merchants' discontent. Nonetheless, the Foreign Office refused to send British Indian troops, as the merchants' requested, arguing that the local authorities needed time and that the British "scheme" would be premature.[6] Though convinced of Nezam al-Saltaneh's complicity in Naser al-Dowleh's murder, Barclay believed that as long as Nezam al-Saltaneh was governor and Sulat al-Dowleh in charge of security in Shiraz, the city would remain calm. He feared their dismissal would lead to a state of anarchy and "unpleasant eventualities," so he used his influence with the cabinet ministers and the regent to retain Nezam al-Saltaneh in his position, and he warned Sardar As'ad of "Qashqa'i jealousy" that would be "dangerously aroused."[7] Within barely a week, his prognosis regarding the maintenance of calm if the governor and Sulat al-Dowleh remained in place proved to be totally wrong.

Reports of agitation in Shiraz pointed to Nezam al-Saltaneh and Sulat al-Dowleh as allegedly inciting the local *anjoman* and Qashqa'i agents to provoke unrest. Street demonstrations took place, demanding Qavam al-Dowleh's surrender and protesting against Tehran's instructions. The British consul, Walter Smart, was also exposed to verbal abuse. Lord Grey immediately ordered Barclay to warn the Persian government and Nezam al-Saltaneh that any violence against the consulate would have "serious consequences" and that Qavam al-Dowleh would surrender only on condition of his getting a fair trial or sent out of the country; until then, he would be protected.[8] Barclay threatened the governor that he would "reconsider" his support for him in Tehran.[9] But unrest prevailed, and Manchester firms continued to complain. The political climate worsened when in early June hundreds of fully armed soldiers entered the British consulate, ostensibly seeking asylum in protest against nonpayment of their salaries. In the melee, shots were exchanged with the consular guards, three men were killed, and two wounded. The break-in was apparently instigated by an anti-Qavami faction led by the Shiraz chief of police in a deliberate attempt to seize Qavam al-Dowleh.[10]

Internal Bakhtiyari rivalry further complicated the endless Bakhtiyari/Qashqa'i feud involving their respective supporters in the capital. There were other fights among smaller tribes and local factions competing for the right to control territories in the South. Power and the lucrative lease of land to foreign entrepreneurs seeking to explore the region's mineral wealth were strong motivations to perpetuate tribal wars. The region's preeminent shaikh, Khazal of Mohammereh, who enjoyed British protection, relentlessly fought to extend his influence in vast areas in Arabestan and contiguous provinces. Renewed disturbances thus repeatedly threatened British trade routes.

Elsewhere in the country, political tumult generated by tribal insurrections and local grandees' intrigues likewise prevailed. In the northern Russian zone, there were reports of Shahsavan tribal fighters advancing to Ardabil and defeating the local forces, leading the British consul Shipley to remark: "I am not alone in deeming it fortunate that the Russian troops are still here."[11] And in Gilan, people protested against the governor's "unjust rule," sending desperate cables to the Majles.[12] Unrest in Isfahan was also believed to be instigated by reactionaries and some local olama. The central government's authority was simply disregarded in the various provinces, and the enforcement of constitutional authority was seemingly limited to the capital, despite its partisans' effort to constrain the existing centuries-long traditional power structure.

Tumult in the Capital

In Tehran, political intrigues to destabilize the Sepahdar's government intensified, despite the full power it had acquired and the systematic elimination of most Democrats and their sympathizers from within its ranks. Moreover, many ministers felt seriously hampered in executing the policy program they had submitted to the Majles. Sadeq Khan Mostashar al-Dowleh, the appointed minister of the interior and initial author of the program, would soon realize that the enormous obstacles he encountered were far more complex than ideological opposition or even party politics. He officially was a member of the Moderate Party and virulently opposed to "extremist troublemakers" associated with the radical wing of the Democrat Party, such as *Iran-e now* editor Mohammad Amin Rasulzadeh and the militia fighter Haidar Amu-Oghli. But he was not hostile to the Democrats, judging from his own published account. A nationalist and genuine constitutionalist reformer, he was in fact ideologically closer to the Majles Democrats than to most members of his own party. Thus, he seriously mistrusted many members of his cabinet, including the Sepahdar and Vothuq al-Dowleh. He characterized the former as "Russia's man" and the latter as "Britain's man." He also thoroughly despised Yeprem Khan, who was retained as chief of police and whom he accused of double-crossing the government. He felt a closer political affinity with Minister of Post and Telegraph Momtaz al-Dowleh, Minister of Foreign Affairs Mohtashem al-Saltaneh, and Minister of Justice Moshir al-Dowleh. But he was even more distrustful of the regent, Naser al-Molk, whom he depicted as the chief and most disruptive intriguer, plotting against the Majles and the nation's sovereignty.[13]

Mostashar al-Dowleh's memoirs describe in detail the Sepahdar's cabinet torn from within, its functioning marred by intrigues, while out of office politicians indulged in the "national hobby" of criticizing those in power. The ministers' meetings, he explained, were always attended by staff members and servants, who spied for their respective masters; nothing remained secret. Yeprem Khan reportedly would periodically alert Mostashar al-Dowleh to false rumors of impending antigovernment activities, submitting a long list of conspirators to be arrested. Included in the list were powerful "pro-British" political personalities such as Ahmad Khan Qavam al-Saltaneh, Hasan Khan Vothuq al-Dowleh, Abdol Hosain Mirza Farman-Farma, and Abdol Majid 'Ayn al-Dowleh. But Mostashar al-Dowleh dismissed the allegations, sensing a trap set to blame him for the political demise of prominent, "protected" grandees. When the prime minister and the regent counseled him to treat the chief of police "gently," given the government's need of his services in fighting tribal insurrections, Mostashar al-Dowleh defiantly retorted, "As the minister of the interior, I cannot agree with the wishes of an Armenian anarchist, whose secret motives and mission" are to foment troubles in Tehran and, he surmised, to execute Dashnakist goals.[14] He even offered to resign rather than follow their advice.

Several incidents prevented him from doing so; chief among them was the Sepahdar's sudden departure from the capital in early May 1911. The prime minister had acquired the habit of retreating to his vast estates in Qazvin and Gilan whenever he was displeased, Mostashar al-Dowleh notes sarcastically in his memoirs. Many, if not most observers similarly depicted politicians' sudden decision to "go to Europe" when exposed to dissidents' attacks, leaving the political scene—either as a threat or as a face-saving action—until the dust settled. Mostashar al-Dowleh believed the regent was complicit in the Sepahdar's staged "comedy" in which a government crisis was created and his triumphant return orchestrated. He recounted how two unnamed Moderate Party leaders were held captive in a meeting with Naser al-Molk, like "flies caught in a cobweb," unable to find their way out of the regent's verbal "legalese labyrinth." Mostashar al-Dowleh was convinced the incident was a plot targeting the Democrats.[15]

A more dangerous political threat was also taking place as rumors spread widely of the deposed shah's active intention to regain his crown. Fear of an imminent anticonstitutional coup was palpable in the capital and some major cities. It was learned that in October 1910 the former shah had traveled to Europe, where he had met with Persian exiles to discuss plans for his return to power and that in early June 1911 he had again left Odessa for Baden, near Vienna. At the same time, Abol Fath Mirza Salar al-Dowleh crossed the frontier and was stirring up the Kurds to fight on behalf of his brother, the deposed shah, to regain his throne.[16] Moreover, reactionaries in the capital, both lay and clerical, had formed the well-organized Sacred Islamic Society (Anjoman-e Moqaddas-e Islami), openly recruiting members to engage in sedition. Denounced in the Majles as a "disreputable" organization bearing a "respectable name" to recruit "disreputable" members, it caused serious alarm among Majles deputies and some cabinet officials.[17] Accused of aiming at restoring despotism, many in the society were arrested, but its founders were soon released. The deputy minister of the interior assured the Majles that Iran was now a free constitutional country. The government arrested all reactionaries regardless of their social status, he stated, except those with no prior criminal record or in ill health, who were released but kept under police surveillance. The minister's chief concern then was to prevent a hostile anti-olama debate provoked by the Islamic organization. Thus, he tried to convince the deputies that the reactionaries had falsely identified themselves to "fool the people." Solaiman Mirza challenged him, remarking bitterly that those kept in prison were poor students of humble birth with no powerful patrons, whereas the "*dowleh*s" and the "*saltaneh*s" were promptly freed. The Democrat leader was not allowed to question the minister further when the Speaker Hosain Moʻtamed al-Molk rebuked his "discourtesy" and his "lack of trust" in the government, and many deputies joined the Speaker in voicing the same concern. Solaiman Mirza retorted ironically: "Obviously, the majority's responsibility is to preserve its own cabinet."[18]

By that time, June 1911, however, the Sepahdar had stopped attending important Majles sessions, including this one. The infighting in the Majles further exacerbated the growing loss of confidence in his cabinet and created an inauspicious environment that would fatally entangle Morgan Shuster's assigned task with Tehran's divisive politics. To quote Firuz Kazemzadeh, the American, "energetic, idealistic, and honest to a fault, swept into the summer heat of Tehran like a thunderstorm" and found himself "in a head-on collision with all the vested interests" that had profited from the corruption of the old administration.[19]

Shuster and the Politics of Distrust

On May 12, 1911, Morgan Shuster arrived in Tehran with his family and two assistants, Charles I. McCaskey, to serve as inspector of provincial revenues, and Bruce G. Dickey, to be inspector of taxation. On his way, he stopped in Istanbul, where he met with Taqizadeh and other Democrats in exile, who briefed him extensively on the situation in the country, warning him of foreign interference in domestic affairs and the foreign proxies' anticonstitutional machinations. Taqizadeh advised him to work closely with Hosain Qoli Khan Navab, the former minister of foreign affairs. Impressed, Shuster reached the conclusion that the Majles was the most important political institution in the country. By all accounts, including his own memoirs, Shuster was naturally and ideologically disposed to side with the liberal nationalists, espousing their struggle to defend, against all odds, their freedom and national sovereignty. His short tenure in Tehran was thus characterized by a staunch determination to deal with the Democrats and their sympathizers within and outside the Majles and to resist European, especially Anglo-Russian, diplomatic pressure to conform to their policy demands.

By temperament and professional ethics, Morgan Shuster had no patience for the diplomatic corps and their intricate social maneuvering to draw him to their tea parties and bridge circles, an impatience that would hamper his efforts to accomplish the task he was hired to do. He scorned what he called their diplomatic balance of the world, criticizing their diplomatic language and social interaction. He was determined to avoid the mistakes of his French predecessor, Joseph Bizot, who, he believed, was too close to the British and Russian envoys, thus allowing the financial situation to go from bad to worse. The Frenchman, he wrote, was "too entranced . . . by the numerous social festivities . . . that he completely forgot the trifling fact that he had gone to Persia to reform the finances of that country, and not merely to drink tea, play bridge and ride out for his health."[20] To his dismay, he observed that the Tehran diplomats, whom he described as gentlemen with pleasant and polished manners, professionally carried out distasteful duties.[21] His private correspondence with Barclay, the British envoy, displays their mutual respect and personal friendliness despite their ultimate disagreement over their respective policies.[22] His disillusion was to be even more bitter when he eventually lost Barclay's tacit support for his reform projects.

Shuster was equally dismissive of the corrupt financial officials, the *mostowfis*, and of most cabinet ministers. They were, he wrote, "not suited by character and disposition, to undertake the thankless task of stamping out corruption and venality which marked the administration of Persian finances."[23] But he lavishly praised his trusted supporters, who helped him to navigate the treacherous waters of local politics and to sustain his persistent resistance to playing the game by Anglo-Russian and their Persian proxies' rules. He mentioned Navab, the "high-minded gentleman and a patriot of unfailing devotion to the interests of his country"; lauded Kaikhosrow, the Zoroastrian Majles deputy, for his "inflexible integrity," calling him the "best and truest friend" he had in the country; named Momtaz al-Dowleh as another trusted supporter who resigned his position in the cabinet rather than collaborate with the Sepahdar; and expressed his gratitude to the "undivided support" of the local press, especially *Iran-e now*.[24] As we shall see, of equal significance is his portrayal of the Persian women, many of whom offered him great help against his opponents, warning him about potential threats and playing a vital role in defense of the Constitution and liberty.[25]

Regardless of its strategic merit and moral validity, the decision not to play the political game set Shuster at the center of domestic and international conflicts that predated his arrival. His mission, his personality, and his choice of nationalist, mostly Democratic allies thus conveniently rendered him a target for domestic and international intrigues. As he noted, quoting a fellow American's remarks following his dismissal, his mission was "doomed at its inception, seeing that a prosperous Persia would have brought about a weakened Russian control."[26] From the start, his opponents resorted to a smear campaign in their efforts to undermine him and his efforts to achieve professional task. For instance, a rumor was spread alleging that the American advisers adhered to the Bahai faith and that their intention was to proselytize; it took a while before that rumor subsided. During his short eight-month tenure as treasurer general, Shuster encountered "countless intrigues and chicaneries . . . employed to distort the truth, to falsify the record, and to discredit publicly a few men who refused to become the mere tools of alien political interests."[27] The unfailing support given to him by the Democrats and nationalist reformers would sustain his resolution to the very end.

Rampant Intrigues

As already stated, barely a few days after Shuster's arrival, the Majles voted for the formation of the Committee of Financial Inspection to oversee government expenditures. Because it was headed by the minister of finance as chairman and Joseph Mornard as his deputy, Shuster's allies surmised it was meant to undercut the newly arrived adviser's influence in financial affairs.[28] Fully warned of its potential threat to his authority, the American sent a memo to the Majles within less than a month of assuming his post, requesting what amounted to full powers over all financial decision making, which would allow him to overrule the committee. On June 11, 1911, a memorandum written by his staunch supporter, Minister of Finance Momtaz al-Dowleh, prior to his resignation, was read in an open Majles session. Noting the "regretful" state of the nation's finances due to incompetence, lack of knowledge, and lack of qualified personnel, he urged the deputies to grant Shuster "full powers" to accomplish his task. Shuster was, after all, the appointed "custodian of the national Treasury." The memo then presented twelve demands deemed necessary to thoroughly reform the financial system. It amounted to granting the treasurer general absolute authority in inspecting, reviewing, and deciding all financial matters, including the auditing of all transactions, commercial concessions, taxes, banks, and loans. No government expenditure could occur without his personal signature. His program was to be executed without delay, and all ministries' officials and staff were to provide him with any information he requested. Furthermore, he was to have the authority to select his staff members. More important, the legislature was forewarned of an impending drastic cut in the government budget. Shuster was to submit to the government a quarterly financial report and present to the Majles a proposed list of planned reforms.[29]

In closed-door sessions lasting three days and attended by the finance and justice ministers as well as by Shuster on the third day, the Committee of Financial Inspection reviewed the memo. Then, in a general session dated June 13, 1911, it was debated in detail, item by item. There were heated arguments over the immense request for unlimited power, many wondering whether it would in fact revoke the functions of the newly established Bureau of Accounts (Divan-e Mohasebat) and overrule the cabinet's authority and implicitly the Majles's as well. Some expressed their worries over the resulting loss of national sovereignty in financial affairs. Nonetheless, most significantly, an absolute majority of the deputies, regardless of their party affiliation, voted for Shuster's list of demands in its entirety.[30] The Majles thus showed its complete trust in the American adviser, granting him the nation's seal of approval for financial reforms he had not yet enunciated. That trust underscored the deputies' common desperate need for reforms deemed essential for the construction of the "new Iran." As a consequence of this vote, Shuster's full authority to manage the country's finances to the detriment of both the local grandees and foreign interests would ignite fierce battles in the Persian corridor of power in the summer and winter of 1911. The minority party came to play a vastly enhanced role in the country's financial and political affairs. Its political clout within the Majles, temporarily eclipsed when the coalition majority was formed upon Naser al-Molk's assumption of the regency, was fully restored.

Shuster retained Navab as his special adviser, who counseled him to recruit mostly Democrats for his Treasury department. He would also hire Major Claude Stokes, the British military attaché in Tehran who was on loan from the British Indian army. An overt defender of the constitutional cause, closely associated with the Democrats, and known for his anti-Russian stand, Stokes was to command a newly created Treasury gendarmerie. Furthermore, Shuster's first significant act was to set constraints on cabinet officials' disposal of state revenues as well as their access to the cash deposit in the British Imperial Bank. He used his legitimately acquired power of the purse to reject or cut the ministers' respective budget requests and resisted any demand that he considered financially unsound. Furthermore, Shuster, exposed from the start to foreign geopolitical thinking, would vigorously dismiss it as contrary to Persian national interest.

One of his first crucial changes was to bring the entire loan deposited in the Imperial Bank under his exclusive control. Barely a couple of weeks after the Majles vote empowering Shuster with such great authority, Mornard, the Belgian director of customs and deputy chief of the recently established committee in charge of supervising government expenditures, challenged his orders. He instructed all post offices to send their revenues not to the central Treasury, by now under Shuster's jurisdiction, but directly to the central post office, which he controlled; he would then deposit it in the bank. But the Belgian's referral for a withdrawal from the bank was rejected, further aggravating his hostility toward the American newcomer in Persian financial affairs. At that early stage, whereas Barclay favored Shuster's financial reform endeavors, Poklewski sided with Mornard, accusing Shuster of "seeking popularity with the nationalists." The Russian envoy would not miss a chance to verbally intimidate the American adviser in "most bellicose and unmeasured terms."[31] Reportedly at that time, Lord Grey, unwilling to support the Russian position on the matter, instructed Barclay to give Shuster tacit support.[32]

Shuster did not trust Mornard, who was cooperating openly with the Russians. His chief concern in centralizing all the financial operations in the country was to control the customs revenues, until then administered by Mornard. Moreover, in practice the minister of finance was given no role in the American adviser's program.[33] Mornard continued to resist Shuster's new rules, arguing that as director of customs he headed an independent bureau, accountable solely to the minister of finance. Mornard's position was guaranteed by Britain and Russia because customs revenues were used to pay back the loans Persia had taken out to their respective banks. But Shuster, regarding Persia as a sovereign nation, refused to consider the two powers' vested interests. And he insisted that all government employees, including Mornard, had to abide by the law the Majles had recently passed, allowing him effectively to be the sole authority in the nation's financial affairs. Without consulting the British or Russian envoy, he instructed the British Imperial Bank that no government expenditure could be approved without his signature, and he demanded that all customs receipts be deposited to his credit as treasurer general in both the British and Russian banks. That demand was interpreted in Tehran as a direct rejection of the two interested powers' financial prerogatives.

The power struggle between Mornard and Shuster was finally resolved diplomatically when the cabinet ordered Mornard to abide by the

Majles-enacted law, and, for his part, Shuster assured the two powers he would not "mingle" the customs revenues with the government funds until all debts and charges to foreign creditors had been fully paid back. Mornard was reminded of the "grossly irregular" procedures found in his accounts, thus hinting at potential corruption charges.[34] Shuster's victory, though, was not without a high price; he would eventually pay dearly. Many *mostowfi*s in charge of collecting taxes in the provinces, he noted in his memoirs, organized an anti-American movement, and employees of various ministries were encouraged to strike against his authoritarian management.[35]

Toward the end of May, Shuster had obtained from the Imperial Bank a cash advance to meet urgent domestic expenditure and prevent a bread riot then threatening the capital. The Sepahdar immediately presented him in person with an enormous bill to cover military expenses. The treasurer general at first refused to pay, suspecting possible embezzlement, and then compromised by offering one-third of the requested sum.[36] His refusal to comply with subsequent requests effectively resulted in undermining the prime minister's standing in the Majles. Conversely, Shuster's perceived integrity and resistance to some officials' corrupting influence succeeded in consolidating the Majles deputies' consensual support for his reform projects, severely weakening the coalition majority that had until then supported the prime minister. The latter once more left town, feeling "his task had become impossible" with "intrigues and disunion" within his cabinet and even among his allies in the Majles. His departure "dissolved the majority," which was already split as a result of some cabinet ministers' disagreement with the Sepahdar's policies.[37]

Barclay, however, believed the prime minister's real reason for leaving Tehran this time was his reluctance to accept Morgan Shuster's "vigorous financial control."[38] The regent, too, fearful of the new political climate that favored the Democrats, warned Barclay of his imminent departure for Europe, which the diplomat understood to imply an intention not to return and prompted Barclay's alarmed message to Lord Grey: Naser al-Molk's resignation would be "little short of a calamity for Persia."[39] With the Russian envoy, he persuaded the regent not to leave the country. Lord Grey also wrote Naser al-Molk a friendly letter urging him to remain in Tehran. Equally apprehensive of the possible destabilizing effects of the regent's resignation, Shuster was also in favor of his presence in the capital.

As unrest persisted throughout the country, political intrigues deepened the prevailing general state of mutual distrust. The Sepahdar's script and that of other conservative bureaucrats closely followed Russia's agenda. In his memoirs, Mostashar al-Dowleh fully blames the Sepahdar for instigating riots in Qazvin, which resulted in widespread lawlessness and endangered the all-important Tehran–Qazvin–Tabriz–Rasht trade route. That tactic would encourage Russia to send more troops, ostensibly to restore order in its zone of influence. Mostashar al-Dowleh suspected the regent had conspired with the prime minister in staging the latter's temporary departure to manufacture a political crisis and thus to allow him to reshuffle his cabinet.[40] The regent in turn put the blame squarely on the interior minister's shoulders for failing to secure the roads and ensure public safety. Angry and helpless, Mostashar al-Dowleh resigned; Moshir al-Dowleh and Momtaz al-Dowleh would also resign. All three were the most genuine Moderate constitutionalist members of the cabinet, supportive of Shuster and severe critics of the Sepahdar.

In Rasht, the Sepahdar's home base where he had a loyal constituency, the local *anjoman* allegedly prevented him from traveling to Europe and requested the regent to summon him back to Tehran.[41] The Sepahdar returned on July 9, after almost a month-long absence that had left the government without its prime minister. By that time, several armed groups loyal to the former shah were preparing to battle to regain the peacock throne. This imminent threat galvanized the Majles's effort to stage a united front with the cabinet ministers and confront the reactionaries' attempt to restore the old regime of absolute monarchy. In an open assembly session, Solaiman Mirza proclaimed the deputies' bipartisan support for all cabinet decisions pertaining to security, military defense, national borders, and purchase of weapons. He called for the formation of a bipartisan parliamentary delegation to visit the regent and demand the selection of a new cabinet. His proposal received unanimous agreement.[42] Yet three days later the prime minister appeared in person in an open session, assuring the deputies there was never nor will there ever be any shortcoming on his part in fulfilling his national duties. His absence was due to physical indisposition, he claimed. The Speaker in turn assured the prime minister of all the deputies' cooperation, regardless of their party affiliation, with his cabinet in matters concerning security and public safety. All rumors to the contrary must be denied, he added. In the same session, the Majles agreed to cable Sardar As'ad, who had left for Europe a few weeks earlier, to request his speedy return. "All the deputies will be happy to see you back," they wrote to him.[43] The former shah's imminent threat to the constitutional regime galvanized all to close ranks, regardless of personal or ideological differences.

It took the Sepahdar another three days to personally present his new cabinet to the Majles. He retained the post of prime minister but appointed Najaf Qoli Khan Samsam al-Saltaneh as minister of war, Hasan Khan Vothuq al-Dowleh as minister of the interior, Ibrahim Khan Hakim al-Molk as minister of education and public works, Ahmad Khan Qavam al-Saltaneh as minister of justice, Nasrollah Khan Moshir al-Dowleh as minister of post and telegraph as well as commerce, Mirza Ibrahim Khan Mo'aven al-Dowleh as minister of finance, and Mirza Mehdi Mohtashem al-Saltaneh as continuing minister of foreign affairs. No protests were raised against any appointment. Once again, the Speaker offered on behalf of the entire Majles the deputies' full cooperation on issues of "essential reforms" and national security.[44] The threat of a counterrevolutionary attack fortified the Majles–government reconciliation, subduing the parties' divisiveness. Existential issues pertaining to the protection of the Constitution and the defense of national independence overcame political conflicts.

Royal Conspiracy and Its Consequences

In early July 1911, Nikolai Hartwig, the former Russian envoy to Tehran in 1906–9 who had engineered the coup against the first Majles in 1908, met with the deposed monarch in Vienna. He informed him of the Russian government's tacit but indirect support for his plan to retake his throne. However, it would deny any involvement in case of failure.[45] In an interesting passage in his memoirs, Shuster recounts his conversation with the Russian envoy in Tehran, in which the latter asked him bluntly "whether I would not be willing to remain under Muhammad Ali, when he was restored to power, and be Treasurer-General with full powers such as I then possessed. . . . It was plainly proposed that I should cease to aid or to advise the existing Persian Government, allowing it to hurry into bankruptcy and ruin, and take service under a cruel and vicious monster who would be the cringing slave of [the] St. Petersburg cabinet." Shuster, shocked by the proposition, rejected it, telling the Russian envoy: "I had agreed to serve the Persian Government to the best of my ability, and whatever the outcome might be, I would not think of remaining under Muhammad Ali."[46]

News of the counterrevolutionary plot reached Tehran, despite Russian denials and Lord Grey's dismissal of the rumors that the deposed shah was distributing large sums of cash to the Shahsavan and Torkaman tribal chieftains. From Europe, Sardar As'ad sent urgent messages to warn Samsam al-Saltaneh and the Majles of the deposed shah's conspiracy. From the provinces in the Northwest, news rapidly spread of the former shah's brother Salar al-Dowleh reaching Hamadan, where he assembled multitribal armed forces. He had established an alliance with a Kurdish leader who controlled a vast territory around Kermanshah, and his agents had recruited the Shahsavan and other Torkaman tribes. Thus, the conspirators reportedly expanded their combined powerful presence in the North and Northwest of the country, where tribal elements routinely resisted central-government authority and local grandees still favored the pre-revolution traditional power structure granting them autonomy in local political and financial affairs. Meanwhile, Sardar Arshad al-Dowleh, a former military commander in the previous regime, arrived in Baku, where the former shah joined him. Together they crossed the Caspian Sea on July 17 or 18, depending on the source, and reached Astarabad three days later, accompanied by the former shah's brother Malek Mansur Mirza Sho'a' al-Saltaneh and two of his former officials, Amir Bahador Jang and Sa'd al-Dowleh.[47] By July 22, all the local notables had joined Mohammad Ali's allies, and the Russian consul, while maintaining the official fictitious non-interference policy, gave him full support.

The tangible threat was alarming enough to enable the new cabinet's drastic security measures to pass unanimously on July 18. The measures were in fact proclaiming martial law throughout the country: the establishment of military courts, presided over by military officers; the arrest of all anticonstitutional activists and trial in martial courts; the raiding and searching of the homes of individuals suspected of antigovernment conspiracy; the forceful closing of any newspaper guilty of publishing antigovernment articles if it did not heed a first warning and the sentencing of its editor in martial court; the order for all *anjomans* and political organizations, without exception, to stop their activities; the prohibition of all public assembly; and the banning of all firearms, except those carried by security officials.[48] Three days later the Majles voted for the formation of a group composed of nine deputies to act as a liaison with the government.

Thus armed with extraordinary power, Samsam al-Saltaneh emerged as the de facto military governor of Tehran. He wasted no time in preparing a list of known or suspected conspirators, charging Yeprem Khan with their arrest. Shuster, noticing the Sepahdar's "lukewarm support for the national resistance," blamed him for the chief of police's delay in carrying out his order.[49] And some cabinet ministers and Majles deputies similarly suspected the Sepahdar and Minister of Foreign Affairs Mohtashem al-Saltaneh of complicity with the conspirators.[50] Their suspicion was later proven right, as we shall see. Mostashar al-Dowleh, in contrast, accused Yeprem Khan of devious motives and brutal means in arresting some of the suspects. However, many of these suspects took refuge in the British or Russian legation, and following a ten-day negotiation with Russian diplomats, the government issued a letter guaranteeing immunity to all. All the while, the prime minister in fact remained politically inactive, choosing to stay in his house located in Zargandeh, near the Russian legation's summer residence. The Majles deposed him and Mohtashem al-Saltaneh by unanimous vote on July 24; the Sepahdar finally resigned the following day.[51]

On July 25, 1911, the cabinet was reshuffled. Samsam al-Saltaneh was now prime minister and minister of war, Vothuq al-Dowleh minister of foreign affairs, his brother Qavam al-Saltaneh minister of the interior, Hakim al-Molk minister of finance, Dabir al-Molk minister of post and telegraph, and Ala' al-Saltaneh minister of education and public works.[52] In an emotional speech denouncing the conspirators for their "treasonous" activities, the Democrat Solaiman Mirza then welcomed the new prime minister with effusive praise of his family, reminding all of the illustrious role the family had played in the restoration of the constitutional government, shedding blood for the cause of freedom. "Is there any corner in the country," he asked, "where Bakhtiyari blood was not shed?" Somewhat bombastically, he promised the sun would again rise to brighten the world and the country; the treasonous individuals would meet their death, as in the days of Louis XVI, and then "we will shout: long live the Constitution." The entire assembly overwhelmingly hailed his speech. Mo'azez al-Molk, a coalition deputy, took his turn to proclaim eloquently: "I come here to say out loud to the nation of Iran: wake up. . . . Iran's representatives are united and in accord, standing up as one individual to protect" the country with "its last drop of blood." The entire world is watching us, he went on, to see whether Iran is worthy of a constitutional government, whether it has acquired such a government "rightfully" or "accidently." People are wrong to believe the Iranian people "will fall asleep again," he concluded.[53] The Majles publicly offered a substantial cash award to whoever arrested or executed the deposed shah and his two allied royal princes on charges of "corruption on earth."[54] On July 31, the British and Russian envoys acknowledged that the former shah had landed in Persia, thus forfeiting his right to a pension, but cautiously stated that their governments "will in no way interfere" in the domestic conflict. Upon Navab's advice, Shuster suspended payment of the royal pension.[55]

A "national army" was levied with combined mojahedin militias and Bakhtiyari tribesmen, commanded by Yeprem Khan and Ja'far Qoli Khan Sardar Bahador, respectively. The government attempted to recall the previously expelled mojahedin, including Abdol Hamid Sardar Mohiy. However, as Malekzadeh remarks, "They were not the same mojahedin"; only the five hundred mojahedin under Yeprem's leadership, who had remained together since the purge in August 1910, were able warriors.[56] Sardar Mohiy reportedly demanded a large lump sum in advance, most of it likely to be pocketed as his salary. So did the Bakhtiyari khans who had begun to arrive in the capital.[57] Despite his anger with the cabinet's constant demand for substantial amounts of cash, supposedly for military expenses but remaining unaccounted for, Shuster worked to help in fighting the counterrevolutionaries' forces. Upon his instructions, necessary funds were provided for the enlistment, equipment, and training of five hundred Treasury gendarmes in preparation for the battle against the former shah's forces. He also intervened to keep at the militias' disposal two German machine guns, operated by Max Haas, a German artillery instructor who had been employed by the government for several years and whose contract, initially rejected by majority vote in the Majles, was renewed upon Shuster's insistence.[58] Students of both Dar al-Fonun and religious schools as well as young members of the bazaar were recruited and given military training.

Some 3,200 men ages sixteen and older were enlisted.[59] But not all actually turned up to fight, nor did the anticipated number of northern tribesmen who had pledged to join the counterrevolutionary forces. Moreover, both sides had their fighters engaged in different battlefields at different times and led by different commanders and initially encountered difficulties in disciplining and coordinating the action of their disparate armed groups. All sources confirm Yeprem Khan's superior abilities in leading a more cohesive "national army," with its nucleus militia composed of Armenian and Georgian battle-hardened men. His forces were matched by the numerically superior, equally experienced Bakhtiyari armed tribesmen. Despite early military setbacks, these forces gradually but decisively defeated the former shah's troops. A former governor of Ardabil, Rashid al-Molk, who had joined the Shahsavan tribesmen in support of the deposed shah, was defeated and brought to Tabriz for trial. However, the Russian consul, Miller, demanded his immediate release and sent Russian armed troops to liberate him. Rashid al-Molk then joined Samad Khan Shoja' al-Dowleh in waging war against constitutional authorities.

By then, according to Russian archival sources, Vothuq al-Dowleh sought a diplomatic compromise to gain Russia's "benevolent attitude" toward the Persian government if it conformed to all the terms of the Anglo-Russian Convention. On July 27, he asked Poklewski: Would the Russian government instruct all its agents in Persia to cease their support for the former shah? A few days later, on August 4, Prime Minister Samsam al-Saltaneh offered a more radical compromise. He privately informed Poklewski that he and his brother Sardar As'ad wished to reach an "understanding." Dissatisfied with the Majles, they would increase the power of the executive, and should the Majles resist, they would resign, allowing the restoration of the deposed shah.[60] But Lord Grey was categorically opposed to Mohammad Ali's return to power, as we shall see.

All the while, the national combined forces carried on their bloody battles in defense of the constitutional government. Ershad al-Dowleh's soldiers suffered a serious defeat at the hands of Yeprem Khan and the Bakhtiyari forces, armed with Haas's modern weapon. Ershad al-Dowleh was captured and, after a brief trial attended by *Times* and Reuters correspondents as well as by Shuster's representative, was executed on September 6, 1911.[61] The night before his death, he reportedly had confirmed Russia's role in backing the former shah's attempted effort to reclaim his throne.[62] Three weeks later, the same Armenian-Bakhtiyari forces dealt a severe blow to Salar al-Dowleh's advance to Bagh-e Shah, a mere eighty miles southwest of Tehran. By September 8, 1911, the deposed shah retreated to a small village on the Caspian Sea coast. However, he did not give up hope to ascend the throne again, nor did Russia give up its secret support of his ambitious plan.

Renewed Crisis

Russian officials' hostility to the constitutional regime intensified with Shuster's expanding influence in domestic affairs. The American's persistent disregard of their opinion on his reform projects alarmed even Sir George Barclay, who initially had supported his efforts. The "Stokes affair," thus labeled in the British press, fueled the Russians' anger. As already stated, the American had proposed to create a Treasury gendarmerie, which had received unanimous approval in the Majles, and he promptly nominated Major Claude Stokes, the military attaché at the British legation in Tehran, to command it.

At that time, Stokes had occupied the post for four years. Fluent in Persian and close to E. G. Browne, he remained a strong and forceful supporter of the liberal constitutionalists, especially the Democrats. He was also reputed to be a Russophobe and a serious opponent of Russian interventionist policies, in contrast to his conservative colleague George Churchill, the Foreign Office Oriental secretary, and to his fellow liberal diplomat Walter Smart, who was by then disillusioned with the constitutional movement and its leadership. Stokes offered to resign his British military commission to accept the new position.

The appointment received an ambivalent Anglo-Russian response. On the one hand, the Foreign Office acquiesced if Stokes suppressed his anti-Russian sentiment and treated both nations with impartiality. On the other hand, Anatol Neratov, the acting Russian foreign minister while Sazanov was on sick leave until December 1911, was more skeptical. He worried about the appointment's potential policy implications unfavorable to Russian interests. Nonetheless, Samsam al-Saltaneh's new cabinet signed the contract, and the Majles agreed on Stokes's salary and pension.[63] But soon thereafter the cabinet ministers began to increase their serious objections to Shuster's demands, which they deemed excessive interference in ministerial budgets. And Stokes was still awaiting permission from his superiors in India before officially accepting Shuster's offer.

As part of Shuster's effort to stimulate economic development and "rejuvenate" the country, his reforms consisted of a thorough reorganization of the country's finances. Stokes's chief task was to collect overdue taxes from all subjects living in the capital and in the provinces, including the powerful grandees who owned large estates. The Treasury gendarmerie was created for this specific purpose. Thus, as chief tax collector and Stokes's boss and as the controller of all sources of revenue throughout the country, Shuster centralized the entire financial system. He kept a firm grip on government expenditure, waging a forceful battle against the blatant corruption he detected at all levels of the administration.[64] That grip provoked loud outcries of protest as powerful landowners and bureaucrats alike resisted his order to pay their taxes, especially if their properties were located in the Russian zone. Moreover, many of them, including constitutionalists labeled "realists," tended to work with British and Russian envoys in recognizing the terms of the agreement of 1907. Thus, they began to directly or indirectly obstruct Shuster's endeavors.

Shuster also demanded from each minister an official estimate of his required budget. Most of the ministers, who had voted for modernizing reforms but were not yet accustomed to the exigencies of a highly centralized system, balked if his demand affected their personal interests. When a minister refused to submit his individual budget, Shuster cut or reduced the anticipated request, beginning with the prime minister's. Samsam al-Saltaneh was also in charge of the Ministry of War portfolio, which took up a large portion of the government revenue. Shuster, angry with what he termed "wholesale attempts at looting the Treasury,"[65] took over the responsibility of paying the troops and thus preventing any embezzlement. Samsam al-Saltaneh's initial friendly attitude turned hostile; the Bakhtiyari political and military leaders' opposition then escalated significantly. They stopped cooperating and even began sabotaging Shuster's orders.

Henry Seligman, director of the New York branch of Seligman Brothers Company, had contacted Shuster as soon as the American adviser's appointment was made public and informed him of the firm's interests in investing in Persia. Once in Tehran, Shuster applied for a £4 million sterling loan to finance his reforms and restructure the newly consolidated Russian debt. The negotiations were lengthy because the firm needed Anglo-Russian prior consent in conformity with the company's preceding practice to assure the two powers of its intention to respect all the convention terms. Therefore, the firm's new agent in Tehran, Colonel H. R. Beddoes, deemed it necessary to forge a more amicable relationship between the American adviser and the British and Russian envoys. On the eve of August 12, 1911, he arranged for all three to meet at a private dinner to discuss the loan, though they mostly argued about Stokes's appointment. Shuster assured his interlocutors of his good intentions and subsequently established regular friendlier contacts with the rest of the diplomatic corps.[66] Unconvinced by this change and more than ever hostile to the liberal constitutionalists, the French envoy, Raymond Lecomte, sent a negative report to Paris. He conveyed his skepticism regarding the recent thaw in the tension then existing between the foreign legations and Shuster, "this obstinate man, so imbued with his own infallibility" and badly counseled by "perfidious" individuals.[67] Yet at the same time, in stark contrast to Lecomte, the French envoy to Washington wrote about Shuster's good press in the United States, viewing him as the "only man who could, through his energy, intelligence, and tenacity, have saved Persia threatened by Russia's intervention."[68] Reportedly, the US government had officially adopted a neutral stand in the Persian crisis to avoid upsetting the two European powers.

Shuster was not willing to compromise his principles as demanded, nor was he keen on losing the ample support of the Democrats and of the Majles they once more controlled. Both Shuster's and Stokes's well-known reputation as closely identified with the "most extreme nationalists" reinforced Russia's hostile attitude toward them. By the late summer of 1911, Russia's virulent attacks on Shuster escalated and focused on sabotaging Stokes's appointment, which had become a convenient political tool to undercut the American's influence.

Shuster's Travails

Lord Grey had repeatedly instructed his envoy in Tehran to avoid any divergence of views with his Russian colleague, concerned as he was in maintaining harmonious relations between the two legations. The Foreign Office had welcomed the American adviser's reforms deemed essential to stabilize the country. However, Russian opposition and Shuster's intention to expand Stokes's activities into the Russian zone led to a British reversal in its attitude. On July 22, 1911, when Barclay had informed Shuster that Stokes had first to resign his post with the Indian army, Shuster naturally assumed that meant British acquiescence to the appointment. However, on August 8 Grey warned the Persian government against Stokes's employment in the North, threatening to take strong measures to secure Russian interests in its zone. And on August 19, the Russian government addressed similar objections in a memorandum to the Persian government. The tsar repeatedly rejected any of Poklewski's attempted compromise with the stern instruction: "no yielding." He reportedly claimed: "We are the masters in the north of Persia,"[69] a statement Grey was inclined to agree with.

Grey's foreign policy, according to most sources, to a large extent reflected his fear of German power rising on continental Europe, challenging Britain overseas with its naval ambitious plan, and competing with the colonial powers in expanding its trade and industries at their respective imperial doorsteps. Furthermore, German economic power generated the British commercial and industrial entrepreneurs' anxieties. This worry, combined with the perceived imperative to appease Russia, motivated Grey to safeguard the Anglo-Russian Convention at all cost. His anti-German sentiment was shared by many in his ministry, including Sir Francis Bertie, who was then British ambassador in Paris, working with French politicians equally hostile to Germany. Grey had succeeded in bringing in allied diplomats to the Foreign Office to counterattack the opposition to his Persia policy.

Shuster, stunned by what he perceived as the British complete about-face regarding Stokes, protested to Barclay. The two powers' attitude, he argued, was obstructing his "task of bringing order out of chaos" in the country's finances and "amounts to a virtual veto of my efforts and nullification of my chance of success."[70] He questioned these interests that, he stated, were not part of the Anglo-Russian Convention and that the Persians were not informed about, and he recalled the agreement's statement about respecting the country's national sovereignty to conduct its internal affairs. Echoing Lord Grey, who merely repeated the Russian expression regarding the "spirit" of the convention, Barclay's self-defensive response pointed to the violation of that "spirit." Shuster interpreted this argument to be a pretext for the change in attitude.[71] He clearly understood the implicit political character of Iran's partition into two spheres—hence his denunciation, at first in private then in public, as we shall see. Neither his moral nor his political principles would permit him to be complicit in such a violation of a country's sovereignty. He was accused of not being a "team player" in not abiding by Anglo-Russian Great Game rules. In fact, he chose to be a player on the Democrats and nationalist constitutionalists' team and to play by their rules, refusing to compromise the sovereignty of the country that employed him. He was hired by the Majles, to which he was solely accountable; the Majles alone could fire him. Insisting on his choice of Stokes as the best man to organize the gendarmerie, Shuster was willing to reduce the major's initial appointment to six months, during which he would be stationed in Tehran. But he left open the renewal of the contract and the possibility of spreading the gendarmerie authority elsewhere in the country, more specifically in the North.[72]

Stokes had applied to the British military authorities in India for approval of his resignation in July, but the authorities kept delaying their response while they waited for instruction from the Foreign Office. Grey believed the military officer could have been a great help in restoring order in the South, but, wishing to placate Neratov, he decided to block the appointment.[73] He instructed the India Office to reject Stokes's resignation. While the Anglo-Russian deliberation was taking place, the delayed response to Stokes's request exasperated Shuster. In a letter to Barclay dated October 5, 1911, he openly expressed his frustration: "It is [*sic*] not about time, dear Sir George, that two big Governments [*sic*] stop playing at this matter, and state plainly whether they intend to continue to oppose the employment of Stokes along the lines I have mentioned, or not?" His choice, he emphatically added, was based purely on the major's qualifications and nothing else, "no *arriere pensee*, no military expeditions, no intrigues."[74]

The India Office finally rejected Stokes's resignation on the grounds that it would not allow him to "accept service under a foreign power in circumstances which make his action detrimental to British interests."[75] It granted him instead a twelve-month leave of absence. But Stokes continued to reside in Shuster's house, advising him, while a multilateral war of attrition was taking place in the Sho'a' al-Saltaneh controversy, engaging Russia, the Democrats, the Moderates, the nationalists, and the partisans of the old regime.

The Sho'a' al-Saltaneh Controversy

On October 4, 1911, following the defeat of the former shah's forces, the cabinet ordered Shuster to seize the properties of Qajar princes who had participated in the failed coup. He then duly informed the Russian and British legations of his impending action, receiving no objections. On October 9, his gendarmes went to confiscate "peacefully" the estate of the former shah's brother Malek Mansur Mirza Sho'a' al-Saltaneh and found the Cossacks guarding it. The gendarmes evicted them, but more Cossack troops commanded by Russians were swiftly dispatched to guard the property. Shuster's personal protest at the Russian legation was unsuccessful; he was told the property was leased to a Russian subject. He then ordered a reinforced gendarmerie troop to seize the property by force, instructing the Persian gendarmes who expelled the Cossacks to "stand on the rights of Persia."[76] The evicted Russian officer complained that the gendarmes had pointed their rifles at him and had insulted officials of the Russian consulate. This episode, it turns out, also involved an internal Russian diplomatic power struggle that would have repercussions for St. Petersburg's decision concerning Shuster.

In December 1910, Ivan Fedorvich Pokhitonov was appointed to the post of consul general in Tehran. He had served for many years in northern Iran and was known as a monarchist, imperialist, and supporter of the deposed shah. As soon as he assumed his new post in the capital, he organized a separate autonomous enclave in the legation, with his own staff and a Cossack escort kept under his sole authority. Though subordinate to Poklewski in diplomatic rank, Pokhitonov ordered a group of Cossacks commanded by Russian officers, without consulting Poklewski, to expel the Treasury gendarmes from Sho'a' al-Saltaneh's property under the pretext that the prince was enjoying Russian protection. Poklewski reprimanded him in private, while informing Shuster that by confiscating the property, the Persian government had to assume the prince's debts owed to a Russian bank. Shuster's investigation and, more important, financial documents pertaining to Sho'a' al-Saltaneh's estate, obtained from one of the latter's wives, revealed that the Russians' assertions were fraudulent. The prince was a Turkish subject and not under Russian protection; his properties were not mortgaged to a Russian bank. Shuster informed Poklewski of his findings, who then restrained Pokhitonov and ordered the commander of the Cossack Brigade to refuse Pokhitonov's orders. The Persian government asked Poklewski to have Pokhitonov recalled to St. Petersburg.[77]

The Sho'a' al-Saltaneh incident further provoked Russian hostility. Two different narratives of the incident reached St. Petersburg: Poklewski's, which basically followed Shuster's account closely, and Pokhitonov's. Neratov opted to put the blame on the Persians and declared their "insolent demand" to have Pokhitonov recalled "unexampled." On October 15, Poklewski announced to Shuster that his government was definitely opposed to Stokes's presence in Tehran. But Stokes remained defiant, dismissing Barclay's advice to go to London while on leave.[78] And Shuster reacted immediately. In an interview with *Times* and Reuters correspondents in Tehran on October 17, he complained of Anglo-Russian obstructions to his reform projects. Two days later the *Times* reported his accusations, which the editor declared "unfounded."[79] Vexed, Shuster wrote a long and detailed statement denouncing in great detail British and Russian encroachment on Persia's independence and national sovereignty, which he sent as a letter to the editor. The *Times* published it a few weeks later.[80] His action to appeal directly to the European public eroded what was left of British official goodwill toward him.

On October 22, Neratov instructed Poklewski to have the gendarmes dislodged from the prince's estates and replaced with the Cossacks. And he demanded an official apology from the Persian government to the Russian consulate for the "insults inflicted on its officials."[81] If Persia refused to comply with these demands, he warned, Russia would take the necessary measures to protect its interests. Poklewski tried to convince Neratov of Shuster's correct version of the episode and urged him not to push the issue further, but to no avail. Similar counsels from Hugh O'Beirne, the British ambassador to Russia, and Count Alexander von Benckendorff, the Russian ambassador to London, were equally dismissed; the tsar supported Neratov. Pokhitonov's star ascended in St. Petersburg's political circles; his version of the Sho'a' al-Saltaneh's episode was adopted officially and passed around government circles, the imperial court, and the press. The nationalist Russian press echoed his hard-line tone. With Poklewski discredited in St. Petersburg, Pokhitonov was allowed to develop Russian policy in Persia, thus undermining the Anglo-Russian Convention and risking Grey's anger.[82]

Shuster's Clout in the Majles

In Tehran, Shuster's activities created another government crisis unrelated to the prince's estate confiscation. In early October, he appointed George New, a former British employee of the Indo-European telegraph system to reorganize the Ministry of Posts and Telegraph. New had worked for the ministry and was expecting the renewal of his contract, which the Majles had initially rejected, to the great satisfaction of the Russian envoy because New had by that time endorsed Shuster's drastic reform program. Minister of Post and Telegraph Abol Hasan Mo'azed al-Saltaneh, a Moderate, and Minister of Finance Hakim al-Molk, a Democrat, although both well-known constitutional reformists, did not favor the prospect of a Shuster associate in charge of the post and telegraph revenues. Nonetheless, upon Shuster's and the Majles Democrats' insistence, New's appointment was once more debated in the Majles in early October, this time receiving a majority vote in favor.[83] The ministers' intrigues to prevent it were to no avail. The small Democrat parliamentary group that was then enjoying high popularity among the capital's public increased its close collaboration with Shuster, while the ministers escalated their opposition to his staying in power.

On October 21, 1911, a heated Majles debate over the ongoing controversial Hormoz concession to Mo'in al-Tojjar demonstrated the strengthening clout of Shuster's Majles allies. The minister of finance had presented a new resolution to resolve the long-lasting dispute among the government, Mo'in al-Tojjar, and the two concerned British companies. Asked whether Shuster was consulted, the minister responded that the treasurer general had deferred to the Majles's decision whereby members of the coalition party insisted the issue was of no concern to the American, and both the minister of finance and the minister of foreign affairs agreed. Shuster had no right to intervene in national political affairs, they asserted vehemently; neither concessions nor related revenues fell under his jurisdiction. At that point, nonaffiliated members joined the Democrats in vigorously defending Shuster's legitimate right to review all matters pertaining to the country's finances, including concessions. Therefore, they insisted that Shuster had first to review the terms of Mo'in al-Tojjar's concession before it could be authorized. Mohammad Hashem Mirza offered a compromise solution: allow Shuster to review all financial decisions, which would then be submitted to the Majles to approve or reject if deemed "mistaken" or detrimental to national interests. The motion passed unanimously; it marked a victory for the Democrats.[84]

On October 23, Hakim al-Molk resigned his post as minister of finance in protest to Shuster's controlling influence. The prime minister sought to replace him with someone who would stand up to the treasurer general, which, given the latter's popularity, was difficult to find. "Even the Moderates would not dare provoke Shuster's resignation," Barclay wrote in his report in November 1911.[85] In a meeting at the Majles, the cabinet talked of curtailing his power, but the entire bloc of Democrats walked out without voting, depriving the Majles of the necessary quorum. The cabinet gave up the idea. The British envoy, Barclay, came to realize fully that the Majles was the "only check on unrestrained autocracy" and that a strong cabinet was an "impossibility unless it has the backing of Shuster." He believed that a cabinet working closely with the American adviser would have to include "extremists," which would drive the regent to resign and "provoke Russia beyond endurance," a scenario Barclay contemplated with dismay. However, he had to admit honestly that though he viewed the possibility of a cabinet of "ultra-nationalists" as "unpleasant and dangerous," he believed they were the "only section of public men in Persia imbued with any real spirit of reform."[86] The nationalist liberal intelligentsia were proving to be an inconvenience to Anglo-Russian interests as defined in the convention of 1907.

Barclay liked Shuster personally and had initially viewed his reforms as needed and beneficial for British interests. He maintained this basically positive attitude until the unsettling political controversies compelled him to reverse it. The other foreign legations, ignored if not snubbed by the American treasurer general, encouraged Russia's hostile stand. The French ambassador was from the beginning politically disposed to distrust the adviser, who worked so closely with the Democrats and other "extreme nationalists." Yet the escalated opposition increased Shuster's and, from behind the scenes, Stokes's determination to serve Persian interests and disregard the Russians' objections.

Shuster's actions further provoked government hostility. When he sent his gendarmes to collect arrear taxes from Ahmad Ala' al-Dowleh, the latter immediately complained to the prime minister. Samsam al-Saltaneh ordered Shuster to withdraw his gendarmes; upon the inevitable negative response, he promptly had his Bakhtiyari guards chase away the gendarmes. Shuster then asked for an official order signed by all cabinet ministers revoking their initial instruction to seize the properties. Unable to contravene the authority of the National Assembly, Samsam al-Saltaneh felt obliged to apologize, and Ala' al-Dowleh paid his taxes in full; so did other grandees. The power of the Democrats and hence of the Majles they controlled was consolidated. The treasurer general's political credentials remained intact as he would subsequently obtain majority vote in favor of his proposal to hire ten more American advisers.[87] Nonetheless, the prime minister and members of his cabinet continued to begrudge Shuster's financial management as well as his close cooperation with the "extremists." Prime Minister Samsam al-Saltaneh reportedly would have the "prominent extremists" arrested were it not for Barclay's opposition.[88]

Shuster persisted in choosing his other assistants from among British citizens, without consulting the Russians. In late October, when the British and Russian governments were seriously beginning to discuss their common objections to the American's actions, he hired two more Englishmen, one to serve in Shiraz, close to but unofficially part of the British zone, and the other in Isfahan, located close to the Russian zone borderline. Both had served in the country for several years, a desirable qualification for Shuster, who was desperate to find officials experienced in local affairs. The Russian consul in Isfahan expressed his "indignation" to a local British agent.[89] Recurring government officials' intrigues against Shuster escalated further when he appointed the British national M. Lecoffre (full name not known) to the post of financial inspector at Tabriz. Fluent in the Persian language and well acquainted with the financial system, Lecoffre had worked at the Ministry of Finance for two years. His qualifications suited Shuster's plan to combat rampant corruption in Azerbaijan, where he especially needed to have Lecoffre investigate the "misappropriation" of one million tomans of taxes due to the central Treasury in the past two years.[90] Mirza Ibrahim Khan Mo'tamed al-Saltaneh, a prominent member of the old ruling elite and father of two cabinet ministers, the brothers Vothuq al-Dowleh and Qavam al-Saltaneh, was in charge of collecting Azerbaijan taxes. He was unwilling to execute the treasurer general's instructions, but the investigation eventually led to his dismissal. Mostowfi al-Mamalek, the former prime minister, had advised Shuster against the dismissal of such a prominent official, to which Shuster reportedly retorted: that was just one more reason for the dismissal.[91] The action earned him irrevocable hostility from the brothers; they were important political players, whether in or out of office.

Shuster's letter to the *Times* editor, translated into Persian and widely circulating in the streets of Tehran in the form of a pamphlet, precipitated the beginning of his downfall. He proclaimed that he had nothing to do with that provocative circulation, to no avail. Lord Grey regarded it as a casus belli, fully justifying a drastic response by Russia. Russia increased its military presence in the North, and by the end of October Indian mounted troops were sent to Shiraz ostensibly as consular guards. Against his own better judgment, on November 2 (or November 3, depending on the source), Poklewski delivered orally an ultimatum to Vothuq al-Dowleh. The foreign minister pleaded for a delay in any action, arguing that such pressure would only increase Shuster's popularity "among unbalanced politicians."[92] But Poklewski could not acquiesce.

It must be noted here that Poklewski's objection was entirely based on the timing rather than the substance of the ultimatum. He had advised St. Petersburg to wait for another pretext other than Shuster to pursue Russian objectives. More significant, he strongly resented Pokhitonov's meddling intrigues that bypassed his authority as the chief of the Russian legation. Moreover, he did not agree with Pokhitonov's harsh method of action. However, regardless of the nuanced differences in the diplomats' personality, the episode laid bare the reality that Russia's imperialist policy in Iran was hiding behind its opposition to Shuster. It highlighted the underlying threat of Neratov's strategy to seize on whatever pretext was available to attack the constitutional regime, no matter how high the risk of wrecking the convention and jeopardizing Lord Grey's wish to defend it when confronted with opponents in the British Parliament and the press.

13

The End Stages of the Second Majles

Continued Financial Obstructions

Neratov was "anxious" that Shuster was potentially taking "total control of Persian affairs" because the American was aiming at merging the national gendarmerie being trained by hired Swedish officers with his Treasury gendarmerie. The project was approved by the Majles, but it alarmed the Russians, the Swedes, and the French alike. The European powers were no less alarmed with his attempt to obtain from the Majles full powers to negotiate loans and railway concessions.[1] The highly sensitive geopolitical question of railroad construction that was included in Shuster's reform program for Persian economic development further exacerbated the Russians' discontent.

The various attempted inter-European negotiations for the construction of railway systems had stalemated or remained inconclusive. Any project to be financed independently by international companies was considered a direct threat to Anglo-Russian interests. Thus, London refused to approve the request of a private company, the Persian Railway Syndicate, for an option to construct a line linking the Persian Gulf to Shiraz. However, when Barclay at the same time applied for a concession to construct a line in the South, the then Persian minister of foreign affairs, Mohtashem al-Saltaneh, warned him that in order to "safeguard" the nation's political and economic interests, "permission will never be granted to anyone to construct any other than a purely commercial railway in Persia." By "commercial," he meant private as opposed to government. Yet the regent had in fact counseled Barclay to propose an Anglo-Russian syndicate to apply for the concession, giving it the "more acceptable appearance of [an] international line." London would then insist that any such "commercial" enterprise in its zone of influence would have to submit to British control and employ British managers and engineers; Russia would do the same in its zone.[2] Various

British companies vying for the contract to build the system, including the Lynch Brothers, were ready to comply. Similar restrictive conditions were applied when the Persian government proposed to erect a telegraph line in the North; it had to agree not to compete with "international traffic" and would do nothing that "is not in accordance with the wishes of the Imperial Russian government, under whose benevolent protection" the line would remain upon completion.[3]

When the Seligman Brothers proposed to finance a trans-Persian railway line, that loan, too, was stalemated. The terms of the loan proposal were even more disturbing for the Russian government than Shuster's vastly ambitious infrastructure plans. Part of its proceeds would have redeemed the floating debt to the Russian Bank, which was consolidated in January 1911, and reduced the interest rate of the larger debt owed from 7 to 5 percent. That change would save the Persian government a considerable amount in interest payments, and if it were to default on the Seligman loan, that would give the British firm more encroaching influence in the Russian zone. Whereas Foreign Affairs Minister Vothuq al-Dowleh kept his distance from the negotiations, despite Shuster's request for support of his application, Grey initially favored the loan. However, the Russian government made it conditional on the British Imperial and Russian Banks' participation, a condition to which Grey conceded. Barclay also agreed with Poklewski's suggestion to insert into the contract a clause curtailing Shuster's authority. The American adviser would not be allowed to intervene in matters affecting foreign relations without the Persian government's prior consent. The director of Seligman Brothers agreed with all conditions. The Russian Bank then made compliance with all these demands, including control over the spending of the proceeds, before considering granting its agreement to the loan. Its ultimatum was, Shuster wrote, "tantamount to telling Russia to conduct the Persian Government."[4] The negotiations were halted as the political crisis intensified.

The loan project, in addition to his controversial appointments, further complicated Shuster's relationship with the two powers, marring his well-intentioned but highly ambitious reform projects. His diplomatic maneuvering to win over the foreign community led nowhere. His conflict with the two powers escalated at a time when the cabinet was determined to improve its relations with Russia and avoid military intervention. The regent's hostility toward Shuster increased as the Democrat-led Majles's close collaboration with him remained unassailable. Naser al-Molk had months earlier complained to London that Shuster "completely failed to appreciate that Persia is a country protected by Russia and Britain and it is clear that the only way to preserve the [Triple] Entente . . . is to get rid of Shuster."[5] The regent perfectly understood that the treasurer general was combating precisely this so-called protection.

British Opposition to Grey's Policy

Lord Grey began to seriously consider Shuster's dismissal, but he was apprehensive that the bipartisan parliamentary Persia Committee would then raise the Persian question and attack his policy. Composed of a group of members of the Liberal and Tory Parties, the committee echoed Shuster's accusations expressed in his now "notorious" letter to the *Times*. It was chaired by Henry F. B. Lynch of the Lynch Brothers, which had extensive commercial assets in southwestern Iran. Lynch admitted openly that he had been closely connected with the "circumstances" of Shuster's appointment, and he corresponded intensively with him regarding railway construction in Persia.[6] The committee steadfastly backed the American adviser, supporting his reform efforts even in difficult times when he was attacked from different political directions. It is also worth noting that Lynch, member of the Liberal Party and self-styled "liberal imperialist," had played a pivotal role in influencing Lord Grey's initial policy in support of the constitutional movement. And he had criticized the Anglo-Russian Convention from the very beginning, contending that England "got the worst of the bargain."[7]

On November 2, the House of Commons asked Grey to explain his support for Russian resistance to Stokes's appointment. The Persia Committee demanded to see all the relevant correspondence between the two governments and the Persian officials. On November 7, 1911, in a fully attended meeting in the House, Lynch denounced Grey's policy and succeeded in passing a majority-backed resolution asking the government to support Shuster. Grey responded: "Had I supported him, I should have been supporting him in the appointment of British officials in the Russian sphere of influence . . . breaking the spirit of the Anglo-Russian Agreement." Lynch vigorously debunked this argument.[8] Such critiques by influential members of Parliament and the liberal press rendered Lord Grey's Iran policy precarious, especially in light of the fact that the Russian government was re-enforcing its military presence in northern Iran. Grey began to warn St. Petersburg of the drastic consequences a military occupation of Persian territories might entail—namely, the collapse of the convention.

Domestic Unrest

Turmoil in the South and British measures to counter it further compounded the American's problems in accomplishing his task. Unrest escalated dramatically in various provinces, underscoring Tehran's increasing powerlessness in the remote provinces. With an allied Bakhtiyari-led government, the Qavamis acquired more power over their rivals, the Qashqa'is and the Qashqa'is' supporters, as well as over the governor of Fars Province, Nezam al-Saltaneh. Intrigues had broken down the negotiations between the two influential tribes and their respective proxies, putting an end to the relative stability achieved through a modus vivendi that Barclay had forged between the two camps. Sulat al-Dowleh relinquished his responsibility to secure the southern roads, and Nezam al-Saltaneh resigned his post. Their departure from Shiraz on October 5, 1911, heightened the danger of a deteriorating situation that the British diplomat had tried to prevent. Sulat al-Dowleh and the Qashqa'i tribesmen under his control raided British caravans passing on the Bushehr road and all around Shiraz. The newly appointed Fars governor, Ahmad Ala' al-Dowleh, put off assuming his post until Shuster gave him the cash necessary to pay the soldiers in Shiraz. Shuster, worrying about possible embezzlement, refused. He hired a British official borrowed from the Imperial Bank to act as his representative in Shiraz and to supervise all expenditures of any money he would eventually send.[9]

With the situation in Shiraz rapidly deteriorating, Grey feared the outbreak of civil war. He finally decided to implement the drastic "scheme" to send an Indian regiment commanded by British officers to protect the trade routes. On September 25, he informed the Russian government of his intention to bring more "consular guards," a euphemistic term for military reinforcement, to the southern zone. Ten days later the Russians replied that they had no objections and that they might follow suit in the North. In early October, Barclay requested the Foreign Office to dispatch three hundred armed cavalry men from the Indian army "without delay." The India Office approved the request and the following day sent five hundred instead of the three hundred originally requested. Although cautiously denying it was an "occupation force," a perception Britain wished to avoid, the official in charge stated that "it might become one in certain circumstances."[10]

The news of the imminent arrival of Indian troops in the South greatly alarmed Tehran officials, who took turns pleading with both Barclay and Grey to abandon their intention to send their soldiers, promising to hasten the departure of the new governor Ala' al-Dowleh to Shiraz and to speed the dispatch of the Persian Cossacks to restore order; their plea was dismissed. The Persian ambassador to London assured the Foreign Office that the life of European subjects was not endangered and that Sulat al-Dowleh and the Qavamis had reconciled. He pleaded with the Foreign Office that instead of sending soldiers, it should give "moral support" to the Persian government against the incessant Russian interference, which "encourage[s] malefactors and lower[s] the prestige of the government."[11] It was at this conjecture that Shuster, eager to solve the problem, offered to have Stokes accompany the new governor to Shiraz, where the British military officer would stay as long as necessary to organize an efficient gendarmerie and establish public safety. That offer was, of course, subject to the Indian army's acceptance of Stokes's resignation, which it denied.

By late October, Grey informed Vothuq al-Dowleh, who had again written a desperate letter begging him not to send troops to Shiraz, that it was too late to countermand the order. It was justified, he said, due to the "powerlessness of the central government" and the state of "practical anarchy" in the South that threatened British life and property. The nomination of a new governor and the reconciliation of Sulat al-Dowleh and the Qavamis, he added, "scarcely seem likely to have the pacifying effect anticipated."[12] At the same time, Barclay assured Vothuq al-Dowleh that if the government restored order and security on the trade routes, the soldiers would only guard the consulate and protect British lives and property.[13] Implicit in this last sentence was a warning of military intervention should the roads remain unsafe. Regardless of the British attempted justification, public protest against what was perceived as military intervention was aroused in the South. Barclay asked Tehran to instruct the local authorities to prevent any attack against the troops, even though he was aware that "public sentiment and agitation cannot be repressed by any government."[14]

Increased Russian Pressure

In the Russian capital, the British ambassador told the foreign minister he should understand that in cases when Britain could not agree with Russia's wishes, "this was not at all from any want of good will" but because of "really serious difficulties from the point of view of British interests." Neratov than assured O'Beirne of his policy objectives: territorial integrity of Persia, maintenance of the spheres of influence, and prevention of German intrusion into the country. However, when the British ambassador retorted that the statement regarding integrity was too "platonic," he was asked bluntly: "Why do you not occupy the country? I suppose it is out of regard for that phantom, the constitutional regime?" O'Beirne candidly replied: it would be difficult to withdraw troops later. The Russian agreed; he, too, was "averse to military occupation."[15] But the mood in St. Petersburg's political circles and the official press belied Neratov's statement.[16] Pokhitonov, whose ulterior motives regarding the Anglo-Russian Convention worried London, was then fully in charge of Russia's Iran policy. The number of Russian soldiers present in the country had reached almost four thousand, of which three thousand were in Ardabil and Tabriz. More had landed in Anzali to increase the number of consular guards in Rasht and Isfahan.[17] Less than a week after the conversation just quoted took place, Neratov informed O'Beirne, "The outlook in Persia is exceedingly dark," with disorder prevailing everywhere; if the "extremists" come to control power in Tehran, "there would be no authority left" to deal with. The following morning the British ambassador, seriously alarmed, sent a message "begging" Neratov to give an "earliest possible notice" if and when he reached the definite decision to take military action.[18] But the decision in fact had already been made and was just awaiting execution. The plan targeted Shuster, who relentlessly pursued his work, paying no heed to the European powers' objections.

Poklewski's verbal protest in early November demanding the withdrawal of the Persian gendarmes from Sho'a' al-Saltaneh's estate in addition to an official apology to the consulate for the alleged insult to the Russian officer had remained ineffective. Vothuq al-Dowleh turned down Barclay's advice to comply and rejected the humiliating demands. Meanwhile, Shuster had allowed the Russophobe Lecoffre to depart for Tabriz and had sent a circular letter to all Russian subjects holding a land lease in the North to report to his office. Neratov decided to act. On November 11, 1911, a first Russian written ultimatum was delivered to the Persian government. It added to the previous demands the recall of Lecoffre and threatened serious retaliation for noncompliance within forty-eight hours. Moreover, without waiting for the reply, Russian troops were instructed to be ready to march to Qazvin.

Prime Minister Samsam al-Saltaneh, yielding to Russia's demands, asked Shuster to remove his gendarmes from Sho'a' al-Saltaneh's property and said they would be replaced by the Persian Cossacks, who were nominally under the cabinet jurisdiction. Shuster refused, convinced that the prime minister, "this simple-minded old chieftain," was giving in to strong Russian pressure.[19] Shuster also refused Barclay's request to dismiss Lecoffre. He continued to enjoy Majles backing at the time when the deputies were anxious to complete their legislative reform before the end of their term on November 14, 1911. There was a palpable sense of urgency as the clock was ticking.

The Extension of the Majles Term

The approaching end of the second Majles's two-year term further complicated the political crisis in Tehran. The cabinet ministers had resigned, leaving Prime Minister Samsam al-Saltaneh and Foreign Affairs Minister Vothuq al-Dowleh alone to run the government. And the regent persistently labeled the Democrats a "revolutionary" group and not a party, declaring all nationalists to be "extremists," whether affiliated with the Democrat Party or not. Ironically, his avowed hostility only succeeded in giving the party an aura of political prominence exceeding its numerical importance. Once more threatening to depart to Europe, he submitted to Barclay his conditions for staying: changes urgently needed to be made before the end of the Majles's term; the cabinet vacant posts needed to be filled as soon as possible; and the cabinet granted accrued executive power to carry on a new program of action. Once more, Barclay and Poklewski went to the royal palace to dissuade the regent from departing.[20]

Meanwhile, the deputies spent the last two days before the legislature's official expiration date debating the expedient justification for an extension.[21] Given the fact that the electoral law was not yet completed and no election date was proclaimed, the country, many argued, could not remain without the active presence of its representatives. Both Democrats and Moderates insisted that the political crisis had created unusual circumstances justifying the contravention of the Fundamental Law, which limited each Majles term to two years. Samsam al-Saltaneh informed them he would accept an extended Majles until a new cabinet was formed, without committing himself to any further decision on the matter. Conservative members of the coalition objected to an extension on constitutional grounds: it is not up to the legislative branch but to the executive branch to rule for an extension or dissolution. Thus, Hajj Aqa the cleric insisted that any new law enacted in that prolonged period would be unconstitutional; he declared that in those circumstances he would definitely stop attending the Majles. The Imam Jom'eh agreed with his fellow cleric but offered a compromise that would allow the deputies to hold occasional sessions but without legislating. Morteza Qoli Khan Matin al-Saltaneh, the Moderate who often sided with the Democrat faction, favored dissolving the Majles but also promised to attend it if the majority voted for the extension. Another Moderate, Mirza Fazlollah Lava' al-Molk, was undecided.

The most impassioned speeches, however, were given by the Democrats, who declared their intention to sit tight until "half plus one" of the newly elected representatives arrived in the capital. "Half plus one" had rapidly emerged as the nationalists' repeated slogan, echoed in the cables sent from various provinces strongly urging the second Majles to prolong its mandate. These cables, many asserted, reflected the nation's sovereign will, to be executed by its elected representatives and not by cabinet ministers. When some deputies remarked that these cables did not represent the entire nation because they were sent mostly from Azerbaijan and other such "radical" regions, others reminded them of the importance of these regions, as amply demonstrated in the bloody fights to restore the Constitution. In rather graphic language, Shaikh Isma'il Hashtrudi, the Azerbaijan deputy, noted: "Azerbaijanis are not in love with my beard; they are in love with the Majles . . . in the principle of justice." Some Moderates went along, depicting the current cabinet as incapable of ensuring the country's national security and public safety. Only the Majles is the lawful source of national authority, the nonpartisan Shaikh al-Ra'is proudly proclaimed. Modarres, a nonpartisan Azerbaijani, pronounced the country in such serious danger that dissolving the Majles would only, "God forbid," worsen the situation. The Democrat Shaikh Reza, as always blunt in his statements, depicted the crisis as a deadly power struggle between two forces, the constitutionalists and the reactionaries. As the tone of the debate turned acrimonious, the Speaker often felt the need to call for order, asking the deputies to refrain from uttering "uncivil" words.[22]

In the middle of the debate, the regent sent a message to the Majles ordering the deputies to cooperate "totally" with the prime minister to establish peace and order in the country. It is "their obligation," he insisted, to collaborate with the ministers' executive tasks. Once more he threatened to resign should the Majles fail to set aside parties' conflicts. The Speaker, Mo'tamed al-Molk, urged them to send a small committee to work with Samsam al-Saltaneh in appointing a new cabinet while the Majles was still in session. Should the Majles be dissolved, he said, "we would at least have a proper cabinet."[23] The deputies voted in majority against his proposal, demonstrating a shared distrust of both the prime minister and the regent. The harsh political reality on the ground highlighted their grim perception: what the regent was requesting amounted to sweeping powers for the Bakhtiyari-led cabinet over a subdued Majles that would have to comply with all measures ostensibly taken for the sake of national security. Suspicion that Bakhtiyari leaders were plotting to seize government power was by then rife. While still in Paris, Sardar As'ad had even thought it necessary to deny such rumors.[24]

The debate over the Majles extension remained inconclusive; the bill was sent for further review to a committee, headed by Mohammad Ali Zoka' al-Molk. The following day, on November 12, he reported his committee's decision in favor of an extension until "half plus one" of the next elected representatives arrive in Tehran and inaugurate the third Majles. "The nation cannot remain without a Majles," he told the assembly; all government institutions must be informed of that decision, and the ministers were asked to speed the preparation for the new elections.[25] Deliberations resumed, as heated as before, each deputy restating his earlier argument. Their fierce discussions begged the question of what an extension would mean to the fate of their constitutional governance and to the survival of their national sovereignty. Each deputy sounded the alarm of a pending national catastrophe, whether defined as the end of the rule of constitutional law or the loss of political independence. In both cases, the Fundamental Law served as the ultimate reference to justify opposite views. Whereas the Moderates within the coalition favored an extension, the coalition's conservative wing continued to challenge its legality. When the Imam Jom'eh proposed that they "consult" the whole country before voting and thus abide by the law, the radical Democrat Shaikh Reza angrily asked: What would happen if Astarabad, Kermanshah, and Kordestan, three regions where the former shah's armed forces had staunch supporters, were to cable their rejection of the Constitution? "Should we close the Majles?" He emphatically reminded the assembly that the time when the population believed the shah was the "Shadow of God on Earth" was past. "We have eradicated this concept from people's mind, be they educated or ignorant, and replaced it with that of constitutional monarchy." And he stressed the fact that the Majles had become the sole legitimate authority in the country. "To safeguard the entire Constitution, it is worth contravening one law," he concluded his emotional speech.[26]

Many Moderates echoed his argument when weighing the extension's benefits against its illegality. The Speaker added his voice in refuting the dissenters' constitutional objections, pointing to the blatant fact that in both the first and the second Majles only a maximum of 80 deputies had been duly elected instead of the required 120, yet no one had ever raised that issue.[27] He finally decided to put an end to the exhausting and exhaustive deliberation. On that day, November 12, 1911, the Majles passed the bill prolonging its term until "half plus one" of the newly elected members of the next Majles arrived in Tehran. Whatever the intricacies underlying the opposition, out of 69 deputies present, 46 voted for the extension, 6 voted against it, and 17 abstained.[28] Many deputies were absent, having opted or were co-opted by the executives in power to avoid attending this important decision-making session.

The regent and his supporters lost this battle. A few days later Prime Minister Samsam al-Saltaneh resigned, and Regent Naser al-Molk again announced his intention to travel to Europe because of ill health. Forty-eight hours had expired, and no response had been given to the Russians' ultimatum.

Anglo-Russian Diplomatic Maneuvering

Stokes was still residing in Shuster's house, resisting British orders. His renewed request for a leave of absence was denied once more, but he chose to stay until practically the very end of the Majles resistance to another ultimatum. Lecoffre's departure for Tabriz had similarly dismayed the Foreign Office. Grey instructed Barclay to explain the issue to Shuster: "His Majesty's government are [*sic*] pledged to avoid any displacement of Russian influence by the British in the north, and the Russians are gaining the impression that under the cover of Shuster's administration this is being done." Grey then warned the American: the Russian government has in its power "means which would seriously impede the discharge of his duties, and which would be impossible for him to withstand."[29] Grey, while asking the Russian minister to allow more time for the Persians, had Barclay send another warning to Shuster. The Russians, the American was told, would protect their interests "if administrative posts" in their own zones are filled by British nationals, and "His Majesty's government cannot deprecate such measures, as it would be contrary to the spirit of the convention of 1907."[30] Shuster's response to the message was true to his character. He assured the British government of his readiness to consider the "legitimate interests" of Russia and other European powers, but he could not "recognize the existence in Persia of foreign 'spheres of influence' which the Persian Government had officially refused to do." Barclay took his message "like a man taking medicine."[31]

The Majles's approval for the appointment of ten more American assistants to be posted in the Ministry of Finance had reinforced Shuster's resolution to consistently disregard British warnings. He found it hard to navigate the rough international waves engulfing the country, let alone to understand the diplomatic nuances driving the decisions being made. He was neither a diplomat nor a politician. Though he was willing to conciliate the Russians, he would not allow all progress in Persian reforms to be erased. Lecoffre, he thought, was an expert in Azerbaijan finances, which was in a "deplorable condition." As tension mounted further, he was wary of the unavoidable Russian retribution as well as of its drastic and even fatal repercussions for the nationalist movement. In fact, he gloomily predicted that should the Russian threat persist, the Persians would "wait like a condemned man until he was hanged by someone stronger than him."[32]

On November 14, St. Petersburg ordered the dispatch of several thousand troops to northern Persia, and on November 19 it broke diplomatic relations with Tehran. Neratov had interpreted the ministers' resignation as a rejection of the ultimatum. In vain, Lord Grey attempted to convince the Russian government to forego its military threats to take over northern Persia, warning it of dire consequences. Grey reportedly "understood Neratov's position," but he was worried of its effect on British public opinion as well as on the fate of the convention, especially as news spread widely that the deposed shah's supporters had renewed fighting in the North and Northeast, with Russian military support. He had warned his Russian counterpart against any attempt to restore Mohammad Ali Mirza to his throne or to establish a protectorate with Russian soldiers occupying Qazvin or Tehran for any length of time. Poklewski denied the rumors, and Neratov promised he would not send the troops if the Persian government complied with his demands.[33] However, the British ambassador to St. Petersburg reported that Russian troops were ordered on November 17, 1911, to move immediately to Qazvin.[34]

Samsam al-Saltaneh, who continued to function behind the scenes despite his official resignation, desperately tried to prevent military occupation of the North. He dismissed the gendarmes at Malek Mansur Sho'a' al-Saltaneh's estates, replacing them with the Cossacks, and he assumed administrative responsibility over the property, overruling Shuster. On November 21, although abstaining from attending the assembly in person, he presented an incomplete provisional cabinet to the Majles: Vothuq al-Dowleh retained his post in Foreign Affairs, as did Abol Hasan Mo'azed al-Saltaneh in Post and Telegraph, while Moshir al-Dowleh was nominated for the Ministry of Education and Public Works. Of the three ministers, only the latter two attended the assembly. The prime minister also announced he would apologize to the Russian government for the gendarmes' action on Sho'a' al-Saltaneh's property. And, further complying with Neratov's demands, he declared his intention to strengthen the cabinet's executive power, restrict the Majles's function to its purely legislative role, and form the Senate, as stipulated in the Constitution. And yet Neratov reneged on his promise to withdraw the troops once he obtained satisfaction from the Persian government.[35]

Anglo-Russian Unfulfilled Promises

In London, Grey once again defended Russia's action, declaring the military move a "purely provisional measure."[36] In private, however, the foreign minister expressed his anger with Neratov's refusal to honor his promise. The Russian minister had explained to the British ambassador that withdrawal of the troops would leave the Russian government "powerless," and he defiantly stated his readiness to occupy Tehran to force Shuster's dismissal. George Buchanan, the British ambassador to St. Petersburg, concluded that the Russian government would "now use the troops presence on Persian territory as leverage for further demands."[37] Barclay informed Grey that, indeed, Poklewski was advising Neratov to "utilize" the presence of Russian troops to "force the Persian government to recognize the Anglo-Russian Convention in a formula agreed upon by Britain and Russia."[38] And the Russian nationalist press hailed the military presence in Persia, calling for the country's partition into Russian North and British South.[39]

On the international front, Neratov's apprehension of any negative American reaction to Shuster's forceful dismissal was put to rest. The US government, rather than rising in defense of one of its citizen officially hired to advise the Persian government, in effect gave its green light to his dismissal. The American ambassador in St. Petersburg informed the Russian foreign minister that his government was "not at all interested in the fate of Shuster."[40] Vothuq al-Dowleh, who had sought the US State Department's advice, had similarly obtained unequivocal assurance of the US government's abstention from any involvement in the matter. And the Majles's appeal to the House of Representatives, a "sister democracy," for help, received no response.[41] Grey tried a more nuanced diplomacy in convincing the American officials that Shuster was not being "unfairly treated." He described him as "evidently an able man" who "went to such an extreme of political innocence that he disregarded the peculiar situation in Persia. . . . He had become like a bull in a china shop."[42]

Neratov's decision not to recall his troops left Grey in an embarrassing diplomatic situation. The Persian ambassador in London again pleaded with him to stop Russian military intervention: "The hope of the Persian government and the entire nation rests on the ancient and traditional friendship of Great Britain, to whom they appeal to prevent the violation of the integrity of their government without the least justification."[43] Grey assured him the troops would be withdrawn once the Persian government complied with all the demands. And in Tehran, Barclay convinced the government to yield to the Russian conditions by similarly telling them the troops would then be recalled.[44] The Persian ambassador to London had encountered a similar deceptive response when he urged Grey to refrain from sending Indian troops in the South; it was not meant to be a military intervention, he was told. The troops had landed in Bushehr on October 27, 1911, where they were confronted with angry street demonstrations.

Persian officials experienced a sense of utter helplessness while still believing in the English sense of fair play. As Shuster sadly but astutely observed later, "The Persians had far too much confidence in the sacredness of treaty stipulations and the solemnly pledged words of great Christian nations of the world to imagine that their whole national existence and liberties could thus be menaced overnight, on a pretext so shallow and farcical."[45] Their disillusion came too late, he noted. The Persians' naïveté may have indeed reflected their inexperience in modern statecraft, typical of new players in the intriguing international power game. They pleaded out of desperation, hoping against hope to avoid their doom. Persian nationalists, irrespective of their political affiliation, were literally trapped in the labyrinthine politics of the great powers. They were left with two bad options: surrender to the ultimatum or lose their sovereignty.

Painfully aware of their dilemma, Solaiman Mirza often felt compelled to praise the Bakhtiyari leaders for their valuable contribution to the constitutional cause and their ongoing battles against the former shah's forces. They demonstrated their devotion to "liberty and nothing but liberty" and to safeguarding national independence, he stated.[46] The deputies had unanimously and consistently acknowledged the all-important part the Bakhtiyaris played in repulsing the former shah's military onslaught. But when the government complied with the humiliating Russian demands in order to prevent a military occupation, and that compliance brought no end to Russian troop advance, the betrayal stung. Many cabinet ministers and deputies succumbed to Anglo-Russian pressure. A relatively small group, mostly

Democrats and their nationalist allies, attempted to resist the pressure to the very end, though, and rallied round Shuster. They vested in him their last hope to rescue their country's independence.

Shuster, the Majles, and Activist Women

The treasurer general's biggest "crime" was refusing to abide by the rules of the Anglo-Russian Great Game as it was played out in its dying years.[47] He would not cooperate with the Persian government officials, mostly members of the old Qajar elite who, on their own or under British pressure, believed that the Anglo-Russian Convention of 1907 preserved their country's independence and feared the inevitable consequences of its contravention. Shuster instead relied heavily on the Democrats' alliance, convinced they were the most honest and genuine nationalist collaborators, with a better-organized, politically reliable party network of supporters. His personal account of his short stay in Tehran offers a vivid description of the prevailing political environment. It is also the only contemporaneous narrative that, unlike most other eyewitnesses' isolated references here and there, relates the extensive role that women played in the fateful fight against his opponents.[48] He portrays their courageous determination to defy the Russian ultimatum and fight for national independence, in contrast to the weakening will of some other political players.

Prior to the constitutional movement, women's activism was strictly in support of male-dominated and led public protests, such as bread riots or political cabals targeting one or another government official or policy. They had not formed a serious political movement of revolt against their social and cultural status. A rare exception is to be found in the mid-nineteenth-century Babi movement, as incarnated in the highly interesting woman known as Qorat al-'Ayn.[49] But that was primarily a religious reformist movement. Thus, there was neither a historical precedent nor a social tradition for the constitutionalist women's novel politicized action. During the period of the first Majles, their public participation was seemingly supported by the olama and lay male leaders alike in calling for a constitution and parliamentary governance. Alongside the men's *anjomans* and encouraged by their model, the female constitutionalists formed their own societies to mobilize other women. The Committee of Persian Women (Anjoman-e Zanan-e Irani) had even cabled Lord Grey asking for support against Russian intervention in their country's domestic policies, which the *Times* published.[50] At the time of the second Majles, however, more of such exclusively female societies were established, acquiring a semi-independent new direction. They founded a weekly paper in 1910, *Danesh* (Knowledge), written exclusively for women on topics of special interest to them.[51] Although still supportive of revolutionary men's cause, they also demanded the right to vote that the Constitution of 1906 denied them. These women included royal princesses, upper- and middle-class Democrat sympathizers, and relatives of other constitutional leaders; most of them were Moslem, but a few were Armenian and Azali Babi.[52]

Yet they did not necessarily receive the blessing of most of the revolution's male leadership, certainly not publicly. In fact, when the Majles was debating the new electoral law, the right to vote was denied women, despite their vocal demands. In a heated debate, Vakil al-Ro'aya raised the "daring" question: "On what logical basis" do we deprive women, "God's creatures," from the right to vote? Zoka' al-Molk qualified the issue as too controversial to be discussed in Parliament; he merely stated he was in favor of improving women's conditions in the country, even granting them the right to vote. In the midst of mounting anger caused by such "bold statements," Assadollah Kordestani shouted to end the debate, while the cleric Modarres remarked angrily, "My body is shaken [on hearing these words]." Women, he asserted, are "feeble creatures" without the ability to reason, and God has not endowed them with the necessary qualifications to vote. "Our official religion is Islam"; therefore, "they will never have the right to vote. . . . Others [men] must protect women's right as God ordains in the Qur'an." The majority voted against Vakil al-Ro'aya's "audacious" suggestion, and women, alongside minors, foreigners, apostates, financially bankrupt individuals, criminals, and the military, were declared to have "absolutely no right" to vote.[53]

Shuster's example further galvanized some women's political zeal. His book mentions the great risks they took to provide him with necessary and sometimes vital documents that helped substantiate his argument in opposition to his adversaries' (for instance, the financial documents pertaining to Sho'a' al-Saltaneh's estate that he obtained from one of the latter's wives). Some visited him secretly to warn him against unknown enemies and possible plots to cause his political demise. In their desperation, some even recurred to more drastic measures in defense of national rights. When rumors spread that the Majles was about to give in to Russian demands, Shuster wrote, the women rushed to the Majles with concealed weapons under their veils and demanded to be admitted. "These cloistered Persian mothers, wives and daughters," he observed, "exhibited threateningly their revolvers, tore aside their veils," and declared their intention to kill the deputies, "their own husbands and sons," if they "wavered in their duties to uphold the liberty and dignity of the Persian people and nation."[54] The *Mozakerat* does not record this incident. But the American enthusiastically declared that Persian women "since 1907, had become almost at a bound the most progressive, not to say radical, in the world." And he added emphatically: "That this statement upsets the ideas of centuries makes no difference. It is the fact."[55]

Whereas Shuster scornfully dismissed the cabinet ministers as invariably selected from the "very degenerate aristocracy," seeking their own self-interests and that of their friends, he lavishly praised the deputies as a "different type of men." He knew many if not most of them personally. And he considered the Majles to be "the only permanent check in the governmental fabric on reactionary tendencies of numbers of the grandees and cabinet officials, as well as on corruption among many Persian officials of all ranks."[56] However, given his intransigent temperament, he failed to forge a long-lasting cooperation with the Moderate constitutionalists, many of whom had supported his program and were in fact as inclined as he was to associate with the Democrats when legislating reforms. As studied in previous chapters, evidence of the deputies' willingness to cross party lines in enacting modernizing laws abounds. And many of the cabinet ministers had joined the Majles in granting Shuster full powers to undertake his tasks. Nonetheless, in the course of his work, his unbending use of the authority he had acquired generated hostility toward him personally even among dedicated reformers. He found his worse adversaries among the old aristocratic elite turned constitutionalists, whom he contemptuously dismissed as corrupt, self-serving officials. As already stated, by late October he had sent the disciplined and organized gendarme force to collect taxes from influential dignitaries residing in Tehran and its vicinities. He succeeded in standing firm in compelling the likes of Abdol Hosain Mirza Farman-Farma and Ahmad Ala' al-Dowleh to pay their long-overdue taxes, despite their complaints to the prime minister. Until the Russians issued their first ultimatum, the near collapse of Samsam al-Saltaneh's cabinet severely weakened its power to undercut Shuster's authority.

Working in solidarity with the Democrats, Shuster used the power bestowed upon him to chart an independent financial policy and to liberate the country from Anglo-Russian imperial tutelage. As a consequence, he continuously fanned Russian resentment while stoking Grey's fears of a possible collapse of the convention, to which the Majles had never officially given its consent. Shuster's task was daunting, as were his opponents' obstructions, but he was not one to be daunted. He was infused with a moral rectitude and a belief in the righteousness of his mission that for a long while sustained an unbreakable optimism that he and his supporters would prevail. His unabashed defiance of Russian intransigence and British compliance increased his popularity in Tehran, especially within the Majles, most notably when the Persian translation of his letter to the *Times* widely circulated in the capital. The deputies' nationalist fervor received a moral boost, and, again cutting across party affiliations, many closed ranks, allowing the Democrats and many Moderates to take control of parliamentary debates. Similarly, his political influence succeeded in consolidating the nationalists' clout in the Majles. And they, in turn, endorsed his decisions, giving him all the official support he needed. At the dangerous time of their struggle to defend their liberty and safeguard the Constitution, they turned to him, seeking his advice and leadership. He became their mentor, their source of inspiration, and a trustworthy leader in their hopeless aspirations not only to reform the country's finances but also, more crucially by now, to preserve their national independence.

Political Tumult

Shuster's pressure on the old bureaucratic elite and Qajar aristocracy only succeeded in forging their alliance with the Bakhtiyari leaders. When about to return to Tehran, Sardar As'ad, the powerful *ilkhan* constitutional member of the Majles, communicated to the British ambassador to France his intention to restore order. He now realized, he told the ambassador, it is better to "lean on Russia and England" and follow a policy accordingly, even though he opposed Russian influence in his country.[57] On November 23, 1911, the German envoy to Tehran observed: "At the bottom of their hearts the great landowners of the country, the clergy, the wealthy businessmen, are all sick and tired of the ruling parliamentary demagogy, primarily because this now begins to question even their traditional prerogatives and their most sacred possession: their freedom to steal and their freedom from taxes."[58]

In fact, as Sardar As'ad's latest state of mind demonstrates, the configuration of political forces was volatile, changing rapidly in short periods of time, reflecting the lack of cohesion and coherence in the constitutional leadership when confronting powers beyond their control. The Democrats increasingly voiced their differences with the more cautious Moderate coalition regarding

Russian intervention. Public demonstrations took place daily throughout the months of November and December. Severe bread shortages in the capital exacerbated the anger of both the poor residents rioting in the streets and the deputies, who accused government officials of incompetence in combating hoarding and of failure to enforce the recently enacted law forbidding it. The Democrat Montasar al-Saltaneh vehemently defended the treasurer general, Shuster, in charge of provisioning the capital with wheat and other grains, arguing that Shuster had efficiently reorganized the distribution of grain to all bakeries to eliminate corruption. But, he added, corruption prevailed, prices escalated, and wheat was mixed with chaff; "everything is in it but the pure wheat Shuster had provided," he lamented. He blamed corrupt elements in the government, who traded in grains for their personal benefits, and accused them of preventing any attempt to reform the distribution system. Eftekhar al-Va'ezin confirmed the suspicion of sabotage, which he believed was aimed at inciting public revolt.[59] According to his memoirs, Shuster shared that suspicion, pointing the finger at the "reactionary grandees for the two-fold purpose of enriching themselves and embarrassing the Constitutional Government [*sic*]."[60]

Rumors of a pending coup intensified the tension in Tehran's streets. The police found a petition signed by, among many others, Ahmad Ala' al-Dowleh, who in 1905 had triggered the revolution with the public bastinado of merchants, and Mohammad Taqi Bonakdar, the merchant who had acquired solid constitutional credentials at its outbreak. Addressed to the Russian government, the petition requested the restoration of the exiled shah. More reports were reaching the capital of his activities in Astarabad, supported by the local Russian consulate and encouraging Torkaman tribesmen to join the fight against government forces. Barclay also reported that a Russian gunboat had landed near Astarabad to assist the tribesmen. And Salar al-Dowleh, the former shah's brother, once more launched an attack in Lorestan, where he again suffered defeat, forcing him to retreat.[61]

Fear of a Russian conspiracy to destroy the constitutional regime spread rapidly, fueling street unrest.[62] The rumors were well founded. On November 20, Samsam al-Saltaneh visited both the British and the Russian Legations, seeking advice about staging a possible coup d'état by Bakhtiyari forces stationed in the capital, installing a Bakhtiyari government, and, if need be, restoring the deposed shah. Neratov was totally in favor of the coup d'état, but not Grey. However, on November 27, Barclay and Poklewski sent a joint memo to the Bakhtiyari *ilkhan*s, informing them of the British and Russian intension not to intervene in domestic affairs as long as the *ilkhans* respected Anglo-Russian interests.[63] The following day, Samsam al-Saltaneh, who had resigned as prime minister for the second time within a month, presented in person a new cabinet to the Majles. He retained his post as prime minister, added the Interior Ministry to his portfolio, and nominated Gholam Hosain Sardar Mohtashem, a Bakhtiyari *ilkhan*, for Ministry of War; Hasan Khan Vothuq al-Dowleh for Foreign Affairs; Mohammad Ali Khan Zoka' al-Molk for Finance; Mirza Mehdi Mohtashem al-Saltaneh for Justice; Nasrollah Khan Moshir al-Dowleh for Education and Public Works; and Abol Hasan Mo'azed al-Saltaneh for Post and Telegraph. He warned the deputies that a new cabinet alone could not restore peace and stability in the country unless it obtained their total cooperation. The Democrats and their allies, facing an imminent Russian military advance to the capital, were indeed ready to reach agreement with the prime minister. Solaiman Mirza welcomed Samsam al-Saltaneh back to his post, carefully repeating his trust in him and eulogizing the Bakhtiyari tribesmen's vital role in defeating the former shah's forces. But he would not have the Majles assume responsibility for the legislative/executive discord. As he explained, "unknown people" and their "hidden hands" had created a crisis for "unknown reason." He expressed his trust in most of the cabinet nominees except Mohtashem al-Saltaneh, declaring that the Democrat faction and its allies would not accept his candidacy.[64]

The Democrats were highly suspicious of the nominated minister of justice, who was well known for his close Russian connections. Solaiman Mirza called for a vote on each individual nominee on the basis of the nominee's trustworthiness. Eftekhar al-Va'ezin recalled the Moderate faction's decision a week earlier to support only a cabinet composed of a coalition of parties, working together responsibly. At this point, the prime minister lost his temper and denounced the Democrats as the sole instigators of the political crisis "from the beginning to the end." The Speaker intervened to stop him, desperately trying to restore order. When the Imam Jom'eh came to the prime minister's defense, the Speaker promptly asked him to step down from the tribune and go back to his seat, faulting the deputy-cleric's "emotional" outburst for stirring trouble. He then instructed the deputies to vote on the cabinet as a whole in accordance with the law and not on individual nominees. Some Moderates and nonpartisans praised the prime minister. Lava' al-Molk called on his assembled colleagues to "safeguard our *iraniyat* and *islamiyat* [Iranian-ness and Islamic identity] regardless of this one nominee," meaning Mohtashem al-Saltaneh.[65]

Barclay described the situation as "confused to a last degree," with the coalition majority rendered powerless in a Majles that was totally controlled by the Democrats and their allied deputies.[66] And yet as the Speaker stated in the midst of the shouting matches, the prime minister was prior to the meeting assured of a majority vote in favor of his cabinet. More significantly, forty-nine deputies voted for Samsam al-Saltaneh's reconstituted cabinet, eighteen voted against it, and one abstained. The remaining had not attended the assembly that day. Events were moving rapidly, with the Majles itself largely sidelined, its constitutional power drastically eroded.

The Second Russian Ultimatum

On November 29, 1911, a day after Samsam al-Saltaneh obtained the Majles majority vote for his new cabinet, a second Russian ultimatum was handed to Minister of Foreign Affairs Vothuq al-Dowleh, giving the Persian government forty-eight hours to comply. It demanded the dismissal of Shuster and Lecoffre; a pledge not to hire foreign advisers without the British and Russian envoys' prior consent; and compensation for all the costs incurred by Russia's recent military move to protect its citizens and properties. Vothuq al-Dowleh vehemently protested to Poklewski that enough time had not been given to his government to comply with thc first ultimatum and that the new demands were "clearly contrary to the independence of the State." The Russian responded in a confidential note that another ultimatum was being prepared in case of noncompliance. Additional demands entailed the forced resignation of the entire cabinet, dissolution of the Majles, new elections, establishment of a Senate, and, in case of another rejection, compulsory acceptance by military force.[67] In Tehran and London, Persian officials eagerly sought British advice but received little support; to the contrary, they were counseled to give in to all the demands, even though both Grey and Barclay viewed the demands as ill advised and unjustified. In St. Petersburg, Russian nationalists, enjoying the tsar's support, remained intransigent in their political hard-line stand, stifling the more moderate elements in foreign policy. British ambassador Buchanan reported that all the important newspapers in the capital, with the exception of one, entirely endorsed their government's action.[68]

On November 30, the cabinet convened a "special" Majles session to discuss the second ultimatum. Vothuq al-Dowleh read out loud the list of Russian demands. Failure to comply, he told the deputies, would result in Russian forces moving southward from Rasht, where they were currently stationed.

Vothuq al-Dowleh then informed the deputies that Russia considered Shuster to be the chief cause of the conflict between the two countries and added that dismissal of the American would greatly facilitate the negotiation for better terms. Last, he conveyed Barclay's strong advice to accept all conditions immediately. A boisterous debate ensued. The Tabriz deputy Mohammad Khiyabani clamored his opposition and emotionally called on all to rise in defense of the nation's sovereignty and territorial integrity. The time for colonial behavior is past, he emphatically declared; international-relations laws and the principles of human rights are universally accepted, protecting all nations' independence. Matin al-Saltaneh recognized their country's dilemma; accepting or rejecting the proposed conditions equally threatened its future. He considered the second demand, prior Anglo-Russian consent when hiring foreign advisers, by far more damaging to national sovereignty. He counseled rejecting it while acquiescing to the firing of Shuster, whether he was rightly or wrongly responsible for the conflicts. Shaikh al-Ra'is urged the cabinet to renegotiate all the demands.[69]

Solaiman Mirza once more dominated the debate from the tribune with a long and eloquent speech in passionate defense of the nation's liberty and independence. He denounced all the demands as violating the present and future rights of the entire nation. The country's progress, he argued, needs the building of institutions, including financial ones, and that necessarily calls for hiring advisers from abroad without seeking foreign powers' approval. "We are independent" in conducting our foreign and domestic affairs, he proclaimed emphatically; "we are free" to determine what constitutes our needs and interests and to decide accordingly. He then praised Shuster and his assistants for their valuable work organizing and reforming the nation's dire financial affairs, with honesty and integrity, raising hope for a better future. "Therefore, how can we accept having to fire them?" He also rejected the second demand, pronouncing it categorically unacceptable and "demeaning to our national sovereignty." He urged the foreign minister to negotiate new terms. Yanes, the Armenian delegate, who totally agreed with Solaiman Mirza, summed up the impassioned discussion: "Today is a great historic day for Iran." Whatever they decided then would affect the present and future of its population; they must not and would not act "irresponsibly." The majority of deputies present voted to reject the ultimatum but allowed the government to renegotiate better terms. It is worth noting here that twenty-five deputies were absent on that fateful day.[70]

Shuster became deeply enmeshed in the internal struggle of the nationalists, be they Democrats or Moderates, in resisting Russian demands. On November 30, Navab and Yeprem Khan came to his house, seeking advice, which he refused to give. Throughout that day and evening, many deputies visited him, and he told them all he did not want to influence them one way or another. He explained his predicament as a hired employee of the government, pointing out that whatever action the government and Majles took "would so vitally affect my own reputation and future." Yet he promised them that he and his American assistants "would abide loyally by the decision" of the Majles, "whatever that decision may be."[71] Barclay, however, reported rumors of meetings held at Shuster's house, discussing resistance to the Russian troops, and of Stokes's participation.[72] Stokes denied the allegation, but the British envoy was determined to force him out of the country and even to charge him with desertion unless he left Tehran within one week. Buchanan had reported to the Foreign Office Neratov's conviction that Stokes was the real cause of the crisis and that he had influenced Shuster's policy and was his "evil angel."[73] Left with no choice, Stokes informed Shuster he could not after all accept his job offer as his deputy. He departed a week or two later, depending on the source.

The Majles considered various options to retain Shuster and convince him to assume a public leadership role. Moshir al-Dowleh, the cabinet minister who had kept his distance from Samsam al-Saltaneh, told the American that the Speaker of the Majles, Hosain Mo'tamed al-Molk, as well as the majority of the deputies were ready to "grant him full powers" to carry on negotiations with the British and Russian envoys on their behalf. Shuster reminded the minister that he, Shuster, was one of the targets of the ultimatum and therefore in no position to do what the minister asked. Several deputies then suggested the government would dismiss him in compliance with the Russian demand, but the Majles would then appoint him as its "general adviser." Again, he turned down the offer. Subsequently, a joint committee made up of Democrats, Moderates, and Armenian Dashnakists requested his advice on how best to fight Russian forces. Recalling the "unreality" of the situation, Shuster sadly reflects in his memoirs: "A dozen men, of different walks in life . . . consulting one whom they considered an 'infidel' as to whether they should take a step obviously heroic and dramatic, yet which spell[ed] danger and death for thousands of their people and incredible physical disaster in the end." Following a three-hour conference, he felt "compelled to express the reluctant opinion" that their plan would end in catastrophic consequences for their country and people. They finally left his premises, realizing that passive resistance to Russian demands constituted their best option. And yet gunshots were regularly heard in Tehran. "A Mauser serenade occurred nearly every day," Shuster noted.[74]

Public indignation with the ultimatum escalated into violent demonstrations. On December 1, 1911, Ala' al-Dowleh, the conspirator, was assassinated, allegedly by order of Yeprem Khan,[75] the chief of police, who once more had survived several cabinet reshuffles. On December 3, the written rejection of the ultimatum was officially delivered to the Russian legation. Foreign Affairs Minister Vothuq al-Dowleh resigned, only to resume his post two days later. He carried on secret talks with Russian officials through Barclay's intermediary. He modified the formulation of the second demand, the pledge not to hire foreign advisers without Anglo-Russian prior consent. The new wording stated that the Persian government "will try to avoid any difficulties which might injure the interests of the Powers," a meaningless semantic distinction. The third demand (compensation for all the costs incurred by Russia's recent military move) was left for future calculation of the indemnity owed the Russians commensurate with the government's ability to pay.[76] Barclay believed Vothuq al-Dowleh could then win the Majles confidence to invest the cabinet with full power to negotiate with Russia. The foreign minister, however, failed in this proposed linguistic way out. In a secret Majles meeting attended by many of the ministers on December 11, the deputies declared no confidence in the cabinet and thus barring its officials from negotiating with Russia.[77] The Majles held no open session for another thirteen days.

While London attempted to gain more time to help the cabinet reconsider its decision, Russian troops were advancing southward. Neratov was in fact determined to implement his preferred option, to allow the Bakhtiyari leaders to stage the coup d'état. Sardar As'ad, who had arrived in Baku, was given free passage to cross the frontier. Grey, persuaded by his envoy in Russia that a coup was a "better option" than Russian occupation, went along with it on the conditions that Tehran was not to be occupied "except in the last resort" and that Russia make no more demands. Should they decide on more demands, he added, Britain should first be consulted. And he persisted in his strong opposition to the restoration of the former shah. Grey worried about the "Persian question" consistently raised in Parliament and about a Russian policy that "would make it impossible for the British to cooperate" in Persia. He also insisted on full protection to be granted to the regent, "whose attitude towards both England and Russia has been friendly throughout."[78] Moreover, a list of persons to be given sanctuary by the two legations was to be prepared.

While the two powers were plotting the coup, nationalist fervor reached its height as the Democrat Party organized public assemblies, where fiery speeches were given, inciting people to demonstrate against the Russians and to march in the streets carrying banners saying, "Independence or death," "Liberty or death," and "Death to the traitors." Cables were sent to European parliaments asking for support in the Persians' fight against Russian imperialist designs, and women sent telegrams to the Women's Suffragist Committee in London to enlist its members' sympathies. More important, the olama in Najaf issued religious decrees against the ultimatum, proclaiming a national boycott of both British and Russian goods. Telegraph lines were cut off, and telegraph posts were burned down, affecting banking transactions.[79] Ayatollah Khorasani, the constitutionalist *mojtahed*, left the holy city to come to Tehran to declare holy war, but he died on the way, on December 13, 1911. On that day, the Majles held an open session for the first time in thirteen days to announce the death of the "country's mightiest pillar," whose loss constituted a "tragic event for the constitutional movement." The session ended shortly afterward, with the declaration of an official period of national mourning. Rumors spread rapidly that the ayatollah was poisoned.[80] No evidence was ever provided.

In an effort to reduce the potential danger of such virulent public opposition, on December 12 the prime minister dismissed Mohtashem al-Saltaneh from his post, adding Ahmad Khan Qavam al-Saltaneh and Ibrahim Khan Hakim al-Molk to the cabinet. Though both were nominally acceptable to the Democrats, in fact they developed strong animus toward Shuster and fell in line with the rest of the cabinet. The battle between the legislative and the executive branches of power proved to be the most important constitutional confrontation in the short history of the revolution. Clashes between the two went on unabated, the Majles persisting in its refusal to grant the government the necessary authority to negotiate the ultimatum. The Russian military threat was looming large in the near horizon. Some four thousands soldiers were amassed in Qazvin, and several thousand more troops had reached Rasht in the North. There were widespread reports that the former shah's agents were recruiting fighters for high pay and that his fully armed troops were engaged in battles against government forces and benefitted from covert Russian complicity. Salar al-Dowleh, despite his earlier defeats, pursued his fight in Hamadan, the base of his loyal followers.

On December 17, accompanied by Minister of Interior Qavam al-Saltaneh and Minister of Post and Telegraph Mo'azed al-Saltaneh, Minister of Foreign Affairs Vothuq al-Dowleh, who had emerged as the chief government negotiator wrestling with Russian officials over the ultimatum demands, sounded the alarm. Russian troops are marching southward toward the capital, he told the deputies, and the situation in the North is even worse. Samad Khan Shoja' al-Dowleh, one of the fiercest and most brutal of the former shah's partisans, had brought Astarabad under his control and was currently leading a relentless battle against the constitutionalists in Tabriz. Other reactionary militias, he added, were fighting in Ardabil, Rasht, and Kermanshah, including hired Torkaman tribesmen. The foreign minister was, indeed, describing the real state of the nation. He pointed a finger at the Democrats and their allies: "We have no government" because of the domestic turmoil created by "certain groups and individuals," who are "playing with the very foundation of the country's existence." Good relations with foreign powers are essential for sustaining peace, he went on. Taking at face value Russian promises, he assured the deputies: the troops shall be recalled the moment the ultimatum is accepted, and no more demands will be imposed on the government. Conversely, should all conditions be rejected again, the cabinet would no longer assume any responsibility for the dire consequences. He ended his speech by insisting that his cabinet be granted full power to manage the political crisis effectively.[81] The deputies' reaction was once more raucous and inflammatory.

Khiyabani vehemently blamed the government instead for all the calamities the nation was enduring. As far as the ultimatum is concerned, he said, "national independence is not something we would give away voluntarily." In defense of Shuster, he asserted that opposition to the treasurer general was not about him personally but about his reforms; Russia understood quite well that financial reforms would mean national progress. And he insisted that foreign policy must be decided in consultation with the Majles, as the Constitution stipulates. Shaikh Reza the Democrat echoed Khiyabani: "The Majles's voice is the nation's voice."[82]

Mo'azed al-Saltaneh, one of the earliest constitutional leaders and now cabinet minister, justified his recent decision to block the flow of telegrams backing the nationalists. Censoring these cables, he explained, was necessary, given the Russian military threat. "I will never accept that foreign forces come to the capital;" it would be like a "bullet" shot directly into "my heart." Solaiman Mirza tried to lift the dispute to a loftier debate over separation of state powers. Reminding the legislators and ministers of the initial majority vote rejecting the ultimatum, he insisted on the Majles's constitutional right to debate foreign-policy resolutions. Vothuq al-Dowleh strongly protested that the cabinet was under no obligation to abide by the Majles's opinion, and he deplored the fact that only a handful of deputies were expressing their views. "All the others said nothing, neither accepting nor rejecting the ultimatum." He endorsed the proposal for a select committee. "My ruling would be the same as the committee's. . . . We have to resolve this issue quickly" before the situation becomes "really dangerous for us all."[83]

Most deputies present that day were, indeed, subdued, fully conscious that their vote would decide the country's fate. Almost all agreed: "Tonight is a historic night."[84] They voted against giving the cabinet full authority to negotiate on the nation's behalf. The vote for a motion to select a committee to work with the cabinet failed to reach a majority; many abstained, and many others were absent. A few days later some deputies changed their mind, opting to select a bipartisan committee to confer with the cabinet. Solaiman Mirza, Khiyabani, and Vahid al-Molk, among others, were reportedly delegated to convince the ministers to attend another session. The Majles then held a meeting in the foreign minister's presence, who then conceded that the selected deputies would be granted full power to reach a decision after conferring with the ministers. "Time is precious," he told the deputies assembled that day; it cannot be wasted with more back-and-forth consultation.[85] This time around, the dissenters, led by Hashtrudi and Khiyabani, were even smaller in number. Out of sixty present that day, thirty-nine voted for forming a committee, nineteen against it, and two abstained. The rest of the nation's elected representatives were absent. The Democrats and their allies joined the committee, intending to play along as a last chance to prevent national catastrophe.

That was to be the last session of the second Majles; the die was in fact cast. Days earlier the cabinet had devised a way to solve its problem by instigating the resignation of twenty deputies, thus weakening the Majles's resolve and facilitating its acceptance of the Russian ultimatum. Barclay was informed that twenty deputies' resignation was, indeed, assured.[86] It is important to underline the fact that many of the deputies who attended the assembly regularly had relied on the constitutional principle of checks and balances to compel the executive branch of government to seek Majles authorization to negotiate with a foreign power. The Democrats and their allies did not relinquish that legal right, so the cabinet, constitutionally powerless, yielded to Anglo-Russian pressure to stage the coup.

"The Nut between the Nutcrackers"

The British consul R. B. Graham's metaphor "the nut between the nutcrackers" graphically described the Persian nation's predicament in the early twentieth century.[87] Ultimately, all nationalists, be they "extremists," liberals, or conservatives, had no chance to escape the insurmountable pressure exerted by the two powers to crush the nationalists' second attempted experiment with parliamentary governance. The second Majles was a casualty of the Anglo-Russian Convention of 1907. The convention's terms had dictated Britain's policy, which, in the final analysis, acquiesced to tsarist Russia's rejection of a constitutional regime installed too close to its border. The efforts made by both Grey and Barclay, two self-defined "liberal imperialists," to protest Russian intransigence, albeit privately and essentially motivated by concerns for their colonial interests, bore no fruit. Barclay intensified his negotiations with Poklewski to give the Persians more time to reconsider their official rejection of the ultimatum. Sazanov, who resumed his post as foreign minister upon his return from his months-long sick leave, agreed to allow them more time for reconsideration in order to accommodate his British counterpart. Grey was increasingly confronting vociferous opposition in Parliament to his Persia policy. Denouncing it as subservient to the Russians, many members of Parliament were in fact interested in revoking the convention and establishing closer relationship with Germany.

As some official reported, "The Persian problem had become a Russian problem."[88] St. Petersburg felt the urgent need to repeatedly assure the Foreign Office that Russia had no intention to occupy Persia, categorically denying that Russian military action was aimed at restoring the former shah to the throne. Yet it cleverly added a caveat: should he take advantage of the present crisis, Russia would not recognize him as the monarch of the country "without prior agreement with the British government."[89] Sazanov was also willing to change the formulation of the second demand in the Russian's ultimatum to "the choice [of foreign advisers] shall not be such as to injure the legitimate interests of the two Powers [*sic*] in Persia."[90] And he extended the ultimatum deadline by another six days, up to December 21. Failure to comply, Tehran was warned, would result in the Russian occupation of the capital. Once again, British officials promised Persian officials that Russian troops would not advance from Qazvin to Tehran if the demands were satisfactorily fulfilled by the new deadline. This was the exact promise Vothuq al-Dowleh had delivered to the Majles, but the deputies no longer believed it.

Interestingly, though, the various international interlocutors involved were busy envisaging scenarios different from what they stated publicly or privately to one another. Soon after Tehran's official rejection of the Russians' demands, London and St. Petersburg exchanged their respective ideas about the future prospects of the Persian state once the inevitable dissolution of the Majles was accomplished. The Russian authorities did not mince their words in their confidential correspondence with their British counterparts. A Russian official stated that the "best solution" for the Persian problem was to divide the country between England and Russia: the former to annex the South, including Baluchistan, the latter the North, "without a neutral zone in between the two territories."[91] As already stated, Neratov had already expressed such a wish for direct colonization by the two powers, which Grey adamantly opposed. The Foreign Office repeatedly warned St. Petersburg of the drastic consequences of permanent occupation. Sazanov then reiterated what had become his routine pronouncement: "Oriental peoples were not persuaded by any argument but force."[92]

Judging from the Anglo-Russian correspondence, both Grey and Sazanov agreed on basic conditions for the future Persian government: Russian military occupation in the North would be provisional until order was restored; the power of the new Majles would be severely curtailed; a Senate composed of appointed rather than elected members would be established; the British and Russian envoys would consult one another in proposing a list of candidates for the prime ministry. Moreover, Russia urged Britain to give, "under all circumstances, our most energetic support for the formation and maintenance of a cabinet" and, if need be, selection of a regent "well-disposed toward Russia." Shuster was to be replaced by a foreign adviser who would be acceptable to both powers and who would have considerably less authority than the American had. Joseph Mornard, who had kept close contact with the Russian legation, emerged as the favored replacement.[93]

Practically all of these changes conformed to Russia's desire. Barclay expressed his skepticism that they could be realized without the presence of Russian troops in Tehran. These changes, he believed, could not prove successful, given the strong current of modern nationalism engulfing a "certain number of the population."[94] He was similarly doubtful that a financial adviser lacking Majles support and relying "exclusively on the moral backing of the two powers" would be effective in undertaking reforms. "It would be no more than a mockery," he wrote to Grey, in comparison to Shuster, who had succeeded in his endeavors precisely because of the expansive powers the Majles and cabinet had granted him.[95] In an earlier candid report, the British envoy predicted Shuster's dismissal would lead to even worse chaos than existed before his "able hand" took over the task of financial reforms. His remaining in Tehran, Barclay insisted, "is of such immense importance if Persia is ever to emerge regenerate as an independent country." And he believed that with Poklewski the British could have reached a "modus vivendi" with the American, making it "worth his while" to "com[e] to terms" with the demands. But St. Petersburg did not give Poklewski that opportunity, he lamented.[96] Barclay repeatedly blamed the "agent provocateur" Pokhitonov, the Russian nationalist opposed to the convention, for creating the incident at Sho'a' al-Saltaneh's property to precipitate Shuster's political demise.[97] A month after writing this sad epitaph, Barclay turned out to be an instrument in Stokes's and subsequently Shuster's dismissal.

Vothuq al-Dowleh, whose communication with Poklewski was monitored by the British envoy, suspected that an Anglo-Russian secret agreement was taking place. He told Barclay the Persian government should participate in the "conversation" regarding relations between the two powers and Persia. The ministers, he explained, should not be confronted with some agreement that they would find "impossible to accept."[98] He wanted to be part of the planning for the future government and offered the cabinet's own plan to stage the closing of the Majles. Sardar As'ad similarly expressed his hope to have the Majles "dissolve itself," leaving the cabinet with full powers to achieve a settlement with Russia.[99] But both asked for a promise that the Russian troops would not advance beyond Qazvin if the demands were complied with and that they would eventually evacuate from Persia altogether. Sazanov refused to give any reassurance beyond the troops' recall to Rasht, but not from Persia. "They [the Persians] do not deserve it," he argued, and he asked Barclay to do the same.[100]

Persistent reports of Torkaman armed tribesmen marching southward to Tehran, creating chaos on their way, of Salar al-Dowleh's renewed fighting, and of unrest in Tabriz and Rasht added weight to the perception of a national crisis out of control.[101] Similarly, Knox (full name not known), the acting British consul in Shiraz, described the local state of "misery, lawlessness and discontent" reigning in the South.[102] Feeling helpless in their effort to safeguard their country's independence, some nationalists once more sought foreign help. They wrote a letter to the Ottoman government, pleading for its intervention to prevent the partition of their country. To their chagrin, the Turkish foreign minister publicly stated his confidence in Russia's assurance that it had no intention to occupy their country. Both Ottoman and Russian governments, he claimed, were interested in respecting the "territorial integrity and political independence" of Persia.[103] Yet all the while Ottoman forces were consolidating their own military occupation of parts of northwestern Persia, proclaiming them Turkish territory, and refusing passage to some two thousand Russian soldiers already in Khoy.[104] It was, indeed, hopeless for the nationalists to stand up to all of these foreign powers.

Sardar As'ad, who had returned from Europe in early December, was included in the Majles bipartisan committee charged to work with the cabinet. He became de facto the most decisive Persian interlocutor empowered to negotiate with the British and Russian envoys. He had reportedly earlier assured Poklewski of "his friendly sentiments for Russia."[105] He was determined to crush the Democrats and their nationalist allies' opposition; once more, the pendulum swung back in favor of the Moderate/conservative coalition: many ministers and deputies were persuaded through intrigues, intimidation, or bribery to endorse the cabinet's position.[106] On December 21, the government officially accepted the second ultimatum's demands on the conditions that the troops would be recalled and no more demands be made. In reality, the Persian government, complying with British advice, totally capitulated to Russian demands. Russia had no intention to fulfill any condition that did not give it a free hand to "restore order."[107]

On December 24, 1911, the Majles was officially dissolved by a regent ordinance in agreement with Sardar As'ad and executed by the Bakhtiyari-led government. Yeprem Khan, the constant chief of police, had convinced the few deputies who had refused to evacuate the building that "public interests demand the Majles sacrifice."[108] He sent his troops to clear the building, expelling all and locking the gates. Gendarmes surrounded the Democrat Party's headquarters, where large crowds had gathered to organize public protests. All shops and offices were ordered to close, and a curfew was strictly enforced. Some deputies were arrested, others left town or went into hiding. A new Majles was not to be reconstituted until December 1914.

The Aftermath of the Coup

On December 25, 1911, Shuster received a letter from the Persian government informing him of his dismissal. Following an indignant though unsuccessful protest regarding the legality of this summary breach of his contract, he left Tehran on January 11, 1912,and headed to Europe. With Shuster's departure, the fifteen American advisers who had worked closely under his supervision refused to remain behind; they, too, left the country, to the Russians' greatest satisfaction. Joseph Mornard, the despised Belgian official notoriously close to Russia, was appointed in Shuster's place as treasurer general, despite protests made by local British financial officials, including those of the Imperial Bank of Persia and the chairman of the Anglo-Persian Oil Company. They all considered the Belgian to be incompetent and corrupt. Barclay, unwilling to push for another candidate, argued against his own better judgment that there was no proof of Mornard's corruption. Barclay had reached the realistic conclusion that another "strong nominee" with "strong character" would encounter the same difficulties Shuster had.[109]

Barclay thus ended up reversing his earlier conviction that the country needed a self-assertive personality to accomplish the necessary reforms for its rejuvenation. The dismissal of Shuster, he wrote Grey, means the "failure of this really hopeful experiment at comprehensive reforms."[110] And in a more intimate, reflective moment, he confided to a British colleague: "It is enough to make the angels weep to see Shuster's machinery fall into incapable hands. . . . I *really* liked that man."[111] Anglo-Russian interests had overcome Barclay's sound, more liberal judgment that had initially led him to appreciate the legitimacy of competent Persian nationalists' goals and their empowering support for the American. Lord Grey himself admitted in his memoirs that Shuster "attempted what was good, but what could only be done by force; and there was no force available for the purpose."[112] Neither the British foreign minister nor his envoy in Tehran was willing to provide Shuster with that "force," which would have enabled him to accomplish successfully the reforms they supposedly desired. Both preferred to give top priority to preserving the Anglo-Russian Convention and thus gave in to Russian demands that they judged to be excessive. Shuster understood quite well the power dynamics that defined that relationship, which he judged detrimental to British interests in the region.

In the North, Russia brutally consolidated its military occupation, turning Rasht into a military base until the end of World War I. Barclay reported "indiscriminate" killing in Tabriz, Rasht, and Anzali, but the local British consul in Tabriz vigorously denied that such "alleged indiscriminate slaughter" was taking place.[113] Russian archives, however, cited in Firuz Kazemzadeh's book, amply document the prevailing reign of terror. Sazanov reportedly ordered massive arrests of all "revolutionaries and nationalists" and harsh retributions to be "carried out with all necessary severity and speed . . . including monetary exactions from the population which supports actions hostile to us." The severe punishment was to serve as a warning to others.[114]

In Tabriz, the homes of militia fighters were raided, and many fighters were arrested or forced into exile; ruthless measures were taken against any kind of resistance. Russian forces bombarded the citadel, where many fighters had taken refuge, following a shooting incident provoked by the Russians or the Persians, depending on the source.[115] Rumors were spreading that Theqat al-Islam, the constitutional *mojtahed*, had called on the residents to rise in defense of their city against their enemies. The fierce street fights resulted in many lost lives on both sides and ended with Russian soldiers in complete control after having eliminated the local *anjoman*. Russian flags were hoisted over the citadel and all government buildings. Theqat al-Islam then advised the survivors to flee town, but he decided to remain in his house. He was arrested and charged with supporting radical revolutionaries and inciting them to revolt against government authority and to wage war against Russian troops. Following a hastily arranged trial, he was sentenced to death and hanged on December 31, 1911, with eight others, including the Social-Democrats Shaikh Selim, Ali Davaforush, and two sons of Ali Monsieur. Many others were summarily court-martialed and then hanged. Brutal crimes against the population were also committed by fighters loyal to the former shah, reportedly exceeding the Russians' violent acts.

Anticonstitutional olama returned to power, including the *mojtahed* Mirza Hasan. And the Tabriz *imam jom'eh* declared proudly: "We do not want a constitution, we want religion."[116] Samad Khan Shoja' al-Dowleh, the reactionary tribal leader of some of the fiercest fighters used to restore the former shah to power with Russian complicity, expected Azerbaijan's governorship as his due compensation. His candidacy was supported by all Russian officials in the northern zone, but the coveted post was given instead to the Sepahdar, Poklewski's preferred candidate. When Samad Khan stubbornly insisted on his claim, Poklewski, irritated, cabled Sazanov that both contenders failed to realize that "they serve not only the Persians but the Imperial [Russian] government as well."[117] In the end, the Sepahdar was selected as a figurehead governor, with Samad Khan his deputy. In fact, both were Russian proxies as Iran lost its sovereignty in the North. The governors of Azerbaijan, Rasht, and Qazvin were also Russian proxies, acting independently of Tehran. Russians were buying land in their zone, which was expanded to include the so-called neutral zone.[118] Many Persians were declared Russian subjects, especially the grandees in the North. The central government was left helpless to maintain its authority throughout the country and highly indebted to foreign banks.

In the South, tribal attacks on Indian cavalrymen commanded by British officers sent to Shiraz and Isfahan seriously alarmed British officials. The situation was seen as a threat to the life and property of their compatriots, especially when the consul Walter Smart was caught in one of the attacks on his way to Shiraz. For a few days or so, there was no news of his whereabouts or whether he was dead or alive, until finally he was reported to have reached Kazerun safely but slightly wounded in the thigh. In fact, Bakhtiyari tribesmen had rescued him, bringing him to the *ilkhan*'s tent, where he was nursed. Outraged, the viceroy of India cabled London, asking what punitive action was to be taken against the attacking tribes: Monetary compensation or punishment? Both Knox, the acting consul in Shiraz, and Smart favored severe punishment. Barclay, however, wanted to rely on the Qashqa'i and Qavami leadership to stabilize the situation and protect British interests in the region. Like Russian rule in the North, British rule in the South was consolidated through the empire's proxies, the shaikh of Mohammereh, the Bakhtiyaris, the Qashqa'is, and other lesser tribes. Iran had de facto lost its national sovereignty in most if not all of the country.

European Compliance to the Anglo-Russian Convention

In his account of the revolution, Malekzadeh opines that many of the cabinet ministers confused Iran's best interests with England's, naively believing the latter was opposed to Russian colonial expansion, and so, based on British advice, they readily took the Russians' warning at face value: complying with the demands would prevent a worse alternative.[119] Shuster, in contrast, believed that "fear and cupidity . . . undoubtedly played a part" in the tragedy that befell the country and its people. But he also did not hesitate to accuse Samsam al-Saltaneh and his minister of war, Sardar Mohtashem, as well as the rest of the cabinet of selling out their country to the Russians. He described Naser al-Molk as "more concerned with his own welfare and peace of mind than with the success of the difficult and complicated task which he had undertaken."[120] However, one must note here that without the imminent threat of occupation, neither the cabinet nor the Majles would have submitted to Russia's will. Moreover, Russia's unflinching resolve to destroy the Majles, by force if need be, met with no strong British objections. To quote Shuster again: "Persia was the helpless victim of the wretched game of cards," which the European powers, "with the skill of centuries of practice," played to "forfeit . . . the small nation's lives, honor and progress."[121]

Other European nations in general demonstrated their respective willingness not to jeopardize the convention. Austria, Italy, Sweden, Denmark, and even Turkey toward the end refrained from any action that would transgress its terms.[122] The Young Turk government, once consolidated, was more interested in expanding its borders within Iran than in helping its fellow revolutionaries. France, working mostly from behind the scenes to help preserve the agreement, needed Anglo-Russian approval to send advisers to Tehran. Hence, when it decided in the summer of 1911 to send two political advisers to the Persian government, it provided them with an official cover as professors to teach at the Institute of Political Science in Tehran. It could then avoid angering Britain and Russia, who seriously objected to French political interference of any kind in what they considered their exclusive domain.[123] Germany alone persistently defied the two powers in claiming the right for its commercial enterprises to work in Persia; it nonetheless cautiously vouched to respect their Anglo-Russian political and territorial interests as defined in the agreement.

St. Petersburg continued to fuel Mohammad Ali Mirza's hope to occupy the throne again, while keeping Poklewski in the dark. Rumors that the former shah was distributing large sums in cash to Torkaman tribesmen persisted. Not only Shoja' al-Dowleh but also the Sepahdar and other partisans of the ancien régime throughout the Russian zone sustained the former shah's desire. Neratov later admitted that the Sepahdar, far from being a revolutionary or a constitutionalist, was in fact "one of the secret partisans of the former shah."[124] So was Salar al-Dowleh, the undaunted reactionary Qajar prince who not so secretly strove several times to march into Tehran. But the evolving international situation and Grey's formidable opponents in Parliament and the press induced Sazanov to shift his strategy. A coalition of the Conservative, Liberal, and Labour Parties, appalled by Russia's activities in northern Persia, pushed for a rapprochement with Germany. Sazanov, though, was convinced Grey's policies were "dominated by fear and hatred of Germany, and would do nothing to alienate Russia."[125] Russia, however, needed assurance of British backing in case of war against Germany. During an official visit to London in January 1912, Sazanov obtained satisfaction. Hence, the Russian minister felt confident he could make further demands and obtain additional concessions from the Persians. He began by asking for a consolidation of the convention terms, enforcing Anglo-Russian authority in the country and limiting the size of Persian forces. Grey went along on the condition that the former shah would return to exile; Russia agreed to cease backing his ambition. So Shuster's demise and the Democrats' fall from power occurred, and the Anglo-Russian Convention of 1907 was fully enforced.

On February 9, 1912, Mohammad Ali Mirza renounced all his activities in the country. A few days later he bitterly admitted to the Russian consul in Astarabad that his intention was to grant "his acceptance for Persia of a Russian protectorate in any form." The consul, who had until then consistently supported him, admitted the former shah's restoration was "impossible" given the "circumstances."[126] On March 10, 1912, the disgraced former shah left the country for good, having obtained a large sum to pay off his followers and the restoration of his pension.[127] In Mashhad, some of his partisans stiffly resisted surrender, having taken refuge in the holy shrine. On March 24, 1912, Russian troops bombarded the shrine, killing many and forcing the rest to flee. Such a profane act stunned the country, arousing vehement protests from constitutionalists and reactionaries alike. One of the most famous Persian poets of the time, Malek al-Sho'ara Bahar, a Democrat ardent defender of the Constitution, composed a poem entitled "Tup-e Rus" (The Russian Cannon), condemning "the fire of the cannon of profanation [that] hit not the dome but the heart of Ali and the Prophet."[128] On May 29, 1912, Salar al-Dowleh's last offensive on the capital was still-born with his irrevocable defeat by Yeprem Khan and his forces. The Armenian fighter, who had played such an important part in the constitutional revolution, then lost his life on that battlefield. That summer, the regent traveled to Europe with no intention to return.

Conclusion

The Legacy of Modern Iran's Architects

IRAN'S FIRST SERIOUS EXPERIMENT with parliamentary governance was put to an end. The Anglo-Russian Convention of 1907 was undoubtedly the most important factor in precipitating the demise of the second Majles. However, independently of foreign intervention, the Persian architects of the nascent, modern nation-state also faced strong internal obstacles that impeded the implementation of their reforms. The reforms were based on foreign-inspired concepts, institutions, and laws, alien and alienating to the majority of a population still deeply entrenched in centuries-long traditional identities and way of life. One has to consider both external and internal factors determining the fateful events marking the years from 1909 to 1911.

External Factors

Christopher Clark debunks the theory that the Anglo-Russian Convention was a response to British fear of or hostility to Germany or both. "It was the other way around," he writes, "since Russia posed the greater threat to Britain across a greater range of vulnerable points; it was Russia that must be appeased and Germany that must be opposed." And he quotes then permanent secretary at the Foreign Office, Sir Charles Harding, as evidence: "We have no pending questions with Germany except of naval construction," Harding remarked to a colleague, "while our whole future in Asia is bound up with maintaining the best and most friendly relations with Russia. We cannot afford to sacrifice in any way our entente with Russia."[1] Clark asserts the same argument also applies to Russia; the convention was not directed against Germany. Only France, he adds, developed a policy aiming at checking German expansionist ambitions.

Indeed, as demonstrated in the preceding chapters, French officials strove to maintain and reinforce the existing Anglo-Russian Convention to prevent any potential Anglo-German or Russo-German alliance. They considered Germany their most threatening adversary, who had to be contained by maintaining the existing system of alliances. Russia, for its part, used the convention to internationally legitimize and consolidate its power in its Persian zone of influence and barely concealed its intentions that exceeded, even contravened, the convention's terms. And it was ready to breach the convention when circumstances enabled it to attain its ultimate goal: actually ruling over its zone and appropriating all rights to exploit its oil and other minerals, to construct roads and railways, and further expand its export market. Britain remained Russia's most formidable rival in the region, despite the convention agreements. It is worth noting here that the convention was signed just a couple of years after Russia's humiliating defeat in the war with Japan in 1905. A Russian senator confided to a British diplomat that his country had lost the "prestige" on which its international position depended. As a consequence of this loss, he stated, it would not allow this to happen in Persia, the principle outlet for its trade.[2]

Up to the fall of 1912, regardless of its official rhetorical statements, the Russian Foreign Ministry certainly did not hesitate to seek a trade agreement with Germany when such an agreement suited its purpose, as when the kaiser and the tsar in a grandiose ceremony in Potsdam promoted a signed agreement in the fall of 1910. Economic and commercial expansion had paramount importance in Russian foreign policy; it necessitated political power to impose Russia's will on the central government in Tehran. Moreover, tsarist Russia would not tolerate a strong, financially independent, territorially sovereign, constitutional Iran actively building a modern nation-state. Shuster, the primary driver of Persian financial policy, fought to replace corrupt local officials and corruptible foreign advisers easily rendered subservient to European dictates. He became the torchbearer of Persian aspirations, enjoying immense popularity among nationalists, be they moderates or "extremists." So he in turn rapidly emerged as Russia's number one enemy who had to be eliminated at all costs. In September 1910, even before the Shuster-related crisis, a member of the British Foreign Office had accurately observed: "It looks as though Mr. Poklewski and his government did not really wish to see Persia orderly and prosperous but wanted her to remain weak and disturbed so that she may be more completely dominated by Russia. This is a reversion to the attitude to which it was hoped that the Anglo-Russian Agreement had put an end, and is entirely opposed to the letter and the spirit of that instrument."[3]

Britain was equally interested in acquiring concessions, a large export market, and power to shape the composition of a friendly Persian government. In contrast to tsarist Russia, however, it could tolerate a modernized, constitutional state and initially favored Shuster's reform endeavors, but not at the cost of breaching the convention. Hence, to appease Russia Grey had to sacrifice the American adviser, acquiesce to harsh measures in closing the Majles, and allow a virtual "reign of terror" in Tabriz, despite the loud outcry of his British detractors. Shuster understood quite well Grey's political rationale. Although he did not explicitly agree with some British politicians' preference for an Anglo-German alliance, he deplored Grey's fear of Germany. "Germany has been Sir Edward Grey's *bête noire*," he lamented. As far as Russia was concerned, he remarked, the Anglo-Russian Convention was already "morally scrapped."[4]

London's power politics, which to a large extent influenced Grey's decisions, had certainly marked his unflinching stand toward Persia. His group succeeded in tightening their "grip on British policy," as Clark shows convincingly, thus provoking their detractors' hostile attacks from within the cabinet and Parliament. The detractors doubted Grey's appeasement of Russia, convinced as they were that his unnecessary provocation of Germany could "outweigh the potential benefits of friendship with the German Empire."[5] In fact, the Conservative Lord George Curzon, one of the powerful architects of the Anglo-Russian Convention, delivered the most critical speech the Foreign Ministry encountered. Grey, who considered himself a "liberal imperialist," saw his Persia policy fiercely denounced by fellow "liberal imperialists" such as Lynch and other members of the Persia Committee. His own and his group's political survival depended on the survival of the convention. For that very reason, to ward off his detractors' accusation of siding with Persian reactionaries, Grey virulently rejected Russia's attempt to bring back to power the deposed Mohammad Ali Shah. That was the only concession he belatedly succeeded in extracting from St. Petersburg. Thus, ironically, Grey's political in-fighting saved the Persian Constitution from destruction, at least on paper, de jure though not de facto. The old regime of absolute monarchy was not restored, but a Qajar shah was retained as Iran's constitutional monarch.

The Legacy of the Second Majles

When in an atmosphere of heightened pressure and threat the deputies were compelled to evacuate the Majles premises, they left behind their unfinished mission to reform the country's political and cultural institutions. With the historic fact that two successive coups forcefully interrupted their executive implementation in mind, a sober analysis of the legislated reforms is needed to fully assess the radical reforms' impact on Persian society. In the shifting sands of constitutional politics, the Majles had enacted a legal basis for the construction of a modern nation-state. Despite the frequently divisive debates among deputies, whose confrontational posturing delayed the passage of many bills, the overall picture reveals a shared vision of the "new Iran." Undoubtedly, the Majles was not truly representative. Of the 120 deputies allowed by constitutional mandate, only 80 deputies were elected by a small proportion of the population. Yet, to quote Shuster again, the Majles "was as representative as it could be under the difficult circumstances which surrounded the institution."[6] In his capacity as an official member of the government, endowed with full powers to reform the financial system, the American adviser had ample opportunities to witness the constitutionalists' accomplishments. He highly praised the educated Persian men and women he encountered, their eagerness to modernize, their writers' denunciation of tyranny, their success in establishing modern schools and a free press—all despite their opponents' hostility and the traditionalists' resistance to innovation.

The second Majles legislation regulating the function of each ministry laid the foundation of new modern institutions, which to a great extent actually redefined the country's identity, breaking many social traditions and installing a new political culture. Persian was adopted as the official national language, the sole language of instruction in schools and mandatory for all government employees. The solar calendar replaced the lunar calendar for all official government work, and the mandated tenure of the Majles was changed to two solar instead of lunar years. Laws restricting the sale of ancient artifacts found on privately owned land and proclaiming them state property, though as yet inconclusively, revealed a new national awareness and appreciation of the pre-Islamic historic legacy. Thus, the Majles tentatively redefined the official national cultural identity by juxtaposing the country's ancient heritage to its Shi'a Islamic one. The deputies overwhelmingly voted for government funding of a museum to display the glory of ancient Persian civilization. Of even greater importance is the discussion of the laws granting equality to all Iranians sharing one country with defined borders, regardless of their sectarian or ethnic background. These rights were already enshrined in the Supplement to the Fundamental Law of 1907, but their details were vigorously debated in the second Majles, highlighting their conceptually innovative significance.

The new electoral law was far from the universal suffrage Barclay understood it to be.[7] Yet it changed the system from an indirect two-round election to a direct one-round election, increasing the number of deputies from 120 to 136. It allowed Armenians to have two representatives instead of one and the rest of the religious minorities—Christian Chaldeans, Jews, and Zoroastrians—one each. In addition, each major tribe—Bakhtiyari, Qashqa'i, Shahsavan, Torkaman, and Khamseh—was given one seat. Here, Vakil al-Ro'aya used the occasion to raise a rarely discussed issue concerning Iran's centuries-long dual character, nomadic tribal and sedentary, which ran counter to the novel concept of modern nationhood. Referring to tribesmen in general as "the policemen of the nation," he explicitly expressed his hope they would soon settle down and lead a sedentary life. Seyyed Ibrahim (elsewhere referred to as "Hajj Aqa Ibrahim"), a fellow Moderate, shared this desire to see the tribesmen "ushered into civilization," leading Mo'azed al-Molk, another member of the coalition, to protest vehemently: they are part of civilization, in no need of others' help, and free to choose their representatives.[8] This politically sensitive issue abruptly ended when some allies of the Bakhtiyaris debated their right to have two seats instead of one, given their important role in fighting the former shah's forces. Mohammad Ali Khan Zoka' al-Molk, the chair of the committee in charge of drafting the electoral law, adamantly refused, claiming the allocation of seats was not based on services rendered to the country but on population.[9] His statement reflected an electoral ideal rather than the practical law the deputies enacted then. The tribal/settled dichotomy was not resolved, especially when the Bakhtiyari *ilkhans* acquired political control of the postcoup cabinet with Anglo-Russian support. The constitutional principles based on the conception of individualized citizenship replacing communal identity remained mere abstractions to be realized decades later.

The controversial decision to allocate the provinces a number of parliamentary seats on the basis of their relative historic role in the constitutional movement, the relatively lesser or greater concentration of knowledgeable and politically well-informed individuals in them, or their location in the British and Russian zones rather than on the size of their populations gave rise to highly contentious debates. An accurate evaluation of each region's inhabitants, it was generally agreed, was difficult to attain due to the lack of a national census. Thus, Azerbaijan was allotted nineteen seats, Tehran fifteen, Khorasan fifteen, Fars thirteen, Kerman and Baluchistan seven, Gilan six, Mazandaran five, Arabestan (Khuzestan) four, Kermanshah four, Yezd four. There were angry protests and challenges from representatives of provinces that were allotted less seats than others.[10] The representation of tribal and religious minorities was fiercely contested as depriving their members of their right to vote directly: "Collective representation is contrary to progress," many argued. Zoka' al-Molk, the chairman of the Majles Electoral Law Committee, admitted that universal suffrage was certainly a "[more] correct system" than one based on class, guild, or tribe, but he insisted that given the current circumstances "its time had not arrived."[11] Most deputies participating in the debate shared his opinion.

A much more heated debate over the electoral law took place a few days later, when Yusef Yanes (Hovsep Mirzayan), the Armenian deputy, refuted coalition traditionalist Seyyed Ibrahim's suggestion to allot one identical representative to the Armenians and Chaldeans because they all are Christians. The Armenian deputy Yanes protested, pointing out their ethnic and linguistic differences as well as their different culture and lifestyle. More importantly, he denounced communal representation as contravening the constitutional right of all to vote individually as Iranians, regardless of their sectarian, tribal, or ethnic origins. Armenians, he said, share the same responsibilities and rights as Iranians; they vote as individuals, whether for an Armenian or a Moslem. "We all are members of one fatherland," and unity strengthens the people in combating their enemies. Zoka' al-Molk again agreed in principle though not in practice, pointing to the country's present political and social reality.[12] This is the "beginning of constitutional governance," Dr. Sa'id al-Otaba responded, and individuals prefer to elect a representative from among themselves, someone acquainted with their traditional customs and mores. Should the minorities participate as individuals in the general elections, he added, naturally Moslems will acquire the majority of votes, leaving the minorities without any deputy to defend their communities' special interests.

Interestingly, the cleric-deputy Modarres chose to define the term *mellat* inclusively as "nation" in the modern European sense, embracing all different religions. The term was traditionally applied to a religious community enjoying autonomy in conducting its communal affairs under the protection of the Moslem state. He declared: "We, members of the olama, do not form a separate *mellat*; we all belong to one nation," which includes Christians. None of us, he further explained, wishes to be "cut off" from the rest by virtue of our religious differences; similarly, diverse ethnicity does not constitute national difference. Here, then, Modarres's modern definition of the conventional term traditionally used in many Moslem countries in premodern times reflected the intelligentsia's own modern conception. And he went further by assuring all present in the assembly that neither ethnicity nor religion was considered a factor in preparing the electoral law.[13] That was, in fact, a disingenuous denial: regional, tribal, and religious identities determined the distribution of seats, their locations, and the locations of the election poll centers.

The establishment of modern social institutions proved to be the Majles's greatest accomplishment. Elementary education was rapidly declared universal, compulsory for boys and girls and free (for the poor), in schools adopting a modern curriculum taught by modern educated teachers. The entire system was centralized and brought under the Ministry of Education. Funding was provided by the government, though rich students paid fees, and local landowners in the rural areas assumed basic costs. The government also subsidized Dar al-Fonun as well as foreign schools in Tehran: the French Catholic St. Louis and the Alliance française schools, the German and the American Protestant schools. But it was still short of the immense budget needed to implement the new rules throughout the nation. The *waqf* schools were financed by their donors, respecting their personal wishes, but were part of the Ministry of Education and had to adopt government-printed textbooks and follow the centralized national standard of teaching and examination. Five new schools in Tehran were to serve as the model for all other schools to be founded in the rest of the country. Secondary education was to follow.[14] Most of the deputies consistently favored teaching European languages, sending students to European universities, and hiring European instructors and administrative advisers.

Dar al-Fonun, the institute of higher education founded in the mid–nineteenth century, continued to employ foreign instructors with the Majles's full consent. Some deputies lamented the fact that even after fifty years Dar al-Fonun had failed to produce competent and knowledgeable Iranians to replace foreigners. Some suggested hiring others who might be "more suitable" to the country's conditions, such as Iranian graduates of European schools now residing in Istanbul or Zoroastrians from India.[15] But many of their colleagues, irrespective of their party allegiance, underlined the country's continued dependence on European experts: "It will take another ten years until we no longer need foreign employees," Vakil al-Ro'aya asserted.[16]

Zoka' al-Molk, the chair of the Education Committee, went further in stressing the importance of French, English, and German as the "scientific languages," stating matter-of-factly, "Nowadays, fortunately or unfortunately, they are more advanced than Persian." It would remain so, he predicted, until knowledge has sufficiently progressed in Iran and Iranian scientists have advanced into the "scientific circles," which recognize no national borders. A traditionalist member of the coalition, the cleric-deputy Aqa Mirza Ibrahim,[17] denounced the Dar al-Fonun as a "militant center" more involved in politics than in studying, proclaiming it was time to teach in Persian and dispense with the foreigners. Zoka' al-Molk countered: "We have to wait until groups of students sent abroad to pursue their higher education return to teach in Persian and translate European textbooks, not before."[18] The long-term need for foreign expertise, administrative as well as scientific, was almost unanimously considered vital for national progress. The process of modernization emulating the European model had reached a point of no return.

The list of individuals banned from voting similarly raised strong objections among many deputies, mostly Democrats and their allies. Included in the list were immediate members of the royal family, women, minors, foreign nationals, apostates and those "known for their corrupt ideas," criminals, those earning less than a minimum income, those who do not pay taxes or do not possess property or have acquired revenues "dishonorably," bankrupts, beggars, the military except honorary officers, and employees of security forces. An almost identical list banned individuals from running for a Majles seat. The inclusion of three categories of people forbidden to vote or be elected—apostates, criminals, and the poor—was vigorously disputed. Recalling cases of false accusations of heresy maliciously spread to smear the reputation of particular individuals or groups without any evidence, some deputies insisted the law had to explicitly define what constitutes apostasy and verify the charges with concrete evidence. *Takfir*, denouncing someone as heretic or as known to hold "corrupt thought," they stated, has been abused for personal or political ends, often landing the unfortunate with a severe sentence. The Democrats' ally Mohammad Hashem Mirza asserted: "We have seen with our own eyes" how "righteous individuals" were wrongly defamed as antireligious. Zoka' al-Molk agreed, but Modarres severely rebuked Mohammad Hashem Mirza: "The Majles is sacred," and its members must uphold "sacred morals." He emphatically proclaimed a deputy "known as corrupt in his thought" would do no good for his country.[19]

Solaiman Mirza seized the opportunity to address the general issue of the tangled interplay of religious sin (*gonah*) and crime (*janayat*), blurring the lines between criminal law and religious sins. The Democrat leader wished to disentangle them and introduce the innovative legal conception of social justice distinct from the sacred law. He pleaded for concrete criteria to adequately distinguish minor offenses from serious crimes. One may commit a minor religious offense and be punished, but does that mean one is thereafter deprived of all civic and political rights? he asked.[20] Solaiman Mirza could not challenge too overtly the established religious legal norms, by far more complex for the legislators to debate accurately, without sound knowledge of Islamic jurisprudence and court procedure. His long tirade elicited Modarres's stern reminder: God allows repentance and forgives. Others picked up the Democrat's argument, asking whether adultery was worse than murder or theft, usury a greater sin than murder or theft. "The *hodud* laws are clear," they were told.[21]

The important attempt to distinguish criminal law from religious sins failed, so confused and confusing was the deputies' juridical argument. The debate on the subject went on for days with no attempt made to openly discuss the radical idea of separating religious law from *qanun*, civil law pertaining to worldly, public affairs. The stakes were high because the political fight intensified the religious traditionalists' resistance to the advance of the reformists' agenda, which the traditionalists perceived as potentially harmful. The cleric-deputy Seyyed Ibrahim (Hajj Aqa Ibrahim) mentioned the possibility of separating the sins or crimes covered by the *hodud* law from other crimes; the clause concerning who was forbidden to vote and run for office was sent back to the Electoral Law Committee for review.

In the midst of this week-long fiery debate, Ayatollah Mohammad Kazem Khorasani sent an urgent letter to the regent and the Majles. He severely reprimanded the "foolish individuals" who have given the Constitution a "bad reputation" by abusing the system for their evil ends. And he lamented that nothing was being done to condemn their misdeeds. Though the letter did not identify either these individuals or their misdeeds, the Speaker's response was clear. He reminded the deputies that the foundation of the Majles was the holy law, and the Majles had no other objective than to spread those holy principles.[22] It was another disingenuous attempt to revert to traditional normative rhetoric, belying the factual evidence on the legislature's ground. The *Mozakerat* did not record any discussion of the letter, if one ever took place. However, Khorasani's warning affected the tone of subsequent debates, inflaming the religious rhetorical controversy and the traditionalists' assault on "foolish individuals."

The committee in charge of the electoral law suggested redefining apostates to "those contravening *hodud* laws," who would lose forever their civil rights, but Zoka' al-Molk categorically refused to have them forever denied their civil rights even after rehabilitation.[23] When Hajj Aqa Ibrahim reiterated his wish to retain the wording "known for their corrupt thought" or "known as irreligious," Shaikh Reza, the fiery Democrat, took his turn to challenge the whole notion of "corrupt thought." Referring to the Shi'a imams declared heretical by their Sunni opponents and to the constitutionalist olama in Tabriz and Najaf criticized by reactionary olama, he angrily dismissed any arbitrary definition of "correct" that pronounces all dissenting views as "corrupt." The traditionalist cleric-deputy Imam Jom'eh, interpreting Shaikh Reza's pronouncement as tantamount to a belief in the moral equivalence of all "thoughts," rebuked him. The cleric asserted there can be no "correct thought" other than Islam. Mo'azez al-Molk, a Moderate member of the coalition, retorted: a false accusation can rapidly lead to someone being "known as irreligious." Toward the end of the session, Shaikh Reza, put on the defensive, felt the need to rectify Imam Jom'eh's understanding of his statement. He was not expressing his belief in the equivalence of every thought, he told him; he was instead drawing attention to the existing religious "differences" in the country: Sufis, Twelver Shi'as, Shaikhis, all mutually exclusive, each accusing the other of "corruption." Seeking a valid compromise to reconcile both points of view, Hajj Aqa Ibrahim attempted to define the whole issue as pertaining solely to *orfi* matters, thereby putting it squarely in the realm of politics rather than of religious jurisprudence. Mohammad Hashem Mirza dismissed the suggestion. Once more the clause was sent back to the committee for further review.[24] Two days later the revised version presented a slightly changed wording: it banned from voting and office those individuals adhering to "corrupt religious beliefs" as well as those committing apostasy if attested to by religious judges on the basis of solid evidence. The clause finally passed by majority vote.[25] The rewording did not alter the clause's substance as much as the modernist reformers wished. Admittedly, they did not even try to speak up overtly for the drastic judiciary reforms they covertly desired. The prevailing political and religious climate on the eve of the second coup against the Majles rendered speaking freely much too dangerous for their personal survival.

The modernists were more successful in bringing about potentially less-inflammatory changes in another category of individuals banned from voting. Solaiman Mirza and allies vigorously objected to excluding from the list those who earn only a minimum wage, own no property, or pay no taxes. Iran's new "national government" cannot deprive the poor of their right to vote, the leader of the Democrat faction clamored loud and clear. They have played an integral part in fighting for the Constitution and are equally entitled to participate in the political life of the country. Referring to the Prophet's companions, who were among the poorest of his followers, he asserted: poverty does not prevent the exercise of a constitutional right. Zoka' al-Molk denied that was his intention and expressed his willingness to eradicate that condition. The clause listing those not allowed to vote was sent back to the committee, where this category was eliminated.[26]

Individuals accused of anticonstitutional deeds or plotting against national independence were equally barred from voting. The debates concerning the drafting of a list naming specific officials and government employees accused of counterrevolutionary action brought about a surprising reversal of roles among constitutional champions. It is notable that the deputies who most objected to that ban intended to protect royal conspirators from public exposure by invoking constitutional principles. Thus, the Qajar prince Mohammad Hashem Mirza, one of the most outspoken defenders of constitutional governance and a nonpartisan, though a consistent ally of the Democrats, insisted on publicizing an extensive list identifying all. In contrast, conservative members of the coalition, Hajj Aqa Ibrahim and Shaikh Assadollah Kordestani, contested the ruling, arguing that partisanship can play a role in arbitrarily disqualifying advocates of different political ideas. Espousing different political views, they stated, does not constitute a crime; moreover, anybody, even deputies, can be falsely accused of "reactionary" deeds without any evidence. Moderates such as Eftekhar al-Va'ezin and Arbab Kaikhosrow opposed the ban as adamantly. The Zoroastrian representative feared some officials' possible use of the list for revengeful retributions targeting personal adversaries. Other moderates from within both parties, including Zoka' al-Molk, indirectly supported their contention, insisting that "reactionaries" also have the right to vote, and some even asked to delete the word *reactionary* from the political vocabulary.

This issue, less religiously controversial and more politically sensitive, reflected the politics of the moment, as the Democrats and their nationalist allies, all championing Morgan Shuster, were engulfed in the hostile environment of a fierce battle relentlessly waged by the cabinet and its foreign supporters against them. Implicit in the long and at times feverish deliberations was the broader question of ideological diversity inserted into both the conservatives' and the Moderates' defense of suspected "reactionaries" in the name of parliamentary democracy. Shaikh al-Ra'is argued in defense of law-abiding officials legitimately opposed to constitutional governance, mentioning how the monarchists in the French Republic were allowed political participation. Nonetheless, significant as the discussion was, the democratic principle entailing ideological diversity did not go far enough in the debate as recorded in the *Mozakerat*. There was consensus that the Majles's task was to judge the crime itself but leave it up to the government to investigate and charge accordingly the individuals suspected of anticonstitutional deeds or plotting against national independence. The chairman of the Electoral Law Committee, Zoka' al-Molk, dissented. A suggestion to form a parliamentary committee to lead the investigation failed to gain sufficient support. So did the motion to change the clause whereby suspects would be charged only on the basis of strong, valid evidence. The clause was sent back to the committee for revision, but no conclusion on this particular issue was reached.[27] European-style ideologically diverse, liberal democracy predictably failed to attract enough genuine partisans to support its implantation.

The question of dual nationality or foreign protection gave rise to another heated debate, especially with the respect to the Anglo-Russian role in protecting their Iranian proxies. Assadollah Kordestani proposed a motion to withdraw the right to vote from Iranians officially under foreign protection. Mohammad Hashem Mirza vehemently opposed that proposal. They all are Iranian citizens, he said, though he was willing to deny the right to vote to those who acquired a second nationality.[28] That particular issue directly concerned members of the political and economic elite. Many connected with Russia or living in the Russian zone were indeed granted Russian protection, if not nationality—the Sepahdar being one of the better known among this group. In the southern zone, Shaikh Khazal, sometimes deferentially called "Sir Khazal Khan" in some British diplomatic correspondence, was granted protection and immense power in his region, provided he promoted and protected British interests. Neither European power could efficiently control the country and protect its own economic interests without the close collaboration of local allies. Those allies were well remunerated in cash, property, and commercial and customs tariff privileges, in addition to being given political protection. Because the Constitution severely restricted government concessions to foreigners, many local allies cooperated with European companies after obtaining government concessions for various industrial or trade projects, which facilitated their foreign partners' legal expansion of commercial enterprises.

The second Majles devoted numerous sessions to individual concessions granted to Iranian subjects and the prohibition of direct foreign ownership. Yet practically no deputy objected to the principle of an economic "open policy" that admittedly required foreign capital and expertise. European-style, capitalist shareholding companies began to emerge, often adopting the term *kompani* in French transliteration. The whole endeavor was conceived as part of national development, a modernizing process that necessitated "opening wide the doors to world trade." The chairman of the Trade and Economic Development Committee, Vakil al-Ro'aya, confirmed this fact when he reviewed a Nobel Company request to construct an oil pipeline in the North and denied that it constituted a monopoly type of concession. He preferred to call it a "permission" to prevent the project's detractors from associating it with the "bad experiences of previous regimes." Matin al-Saltaneh and Modarres agreed. But the Democrat Montasar al-Saltaneh strongly opposed it precisely on that ground: it is a concession, he retorted, because the conditions attached to it preclude Iranian competition. "I oppose this permission, this monopoly that would result in the pauperization of Gilan's merchants," he emphatically stated. Solaiman Mirza equally denounced the proposal as a concession to be granted to a foreign company, putting Iranian merchants at a disadvantage. If all national sources of wealth are given away piece by piece, he argued, nothing will be left for Iranians. Others countered that concessions would encourage and promote national enterprises and benefit the government. Vakil al-Ro'aya pleaded with all deputies: "We must be far-sighted." The Majles voted in majority to grant the concession to the Nobel Company. The Democrats' demand for more time for deliberations went unheeded.[29]

Many Iranian merchants or would-be entrepreneurs, including some members of the Majles, such as Kaikhosrow, requested similar concessions for privately owned companies to manufacture leather goods, to construct short railroad lines to transport agricultural produce, or to extract gold, coal, and other minerals. Domestic companies were encouraged as a means to reduce foreign imports and promote national industries. However, the local companies' demand for duty-free import of needed machinery and chemicals and their monopoly-like long-term contracts, no less steep than the foreign concessions', were equally challenged. Yusef Yanes, the Armenian deputy, objected to concessions in general if they included exclusive rights over the exploitation of natural resources or undercut domestic competition. He called for comparable restrictions. Thus, he condemned Mo'in al-Tojjar's disputed Hormoz Island red oxide concession, regarding which the deputies finally reached a solution acceptable to all parties involved. Most Democrats and their allies similarly objected to the conditions attached to the controversial concession; nonetheless, it passed by majority vote.[30] There were serious, though again inconclusive, proposals to renounce the granting of concessions and to allow only short-term, strictly regulated licenses. Licenses would not be exclusive monopolies, the proposal's proponents thought, and would forbid the owners to sell shares to foreigners unless approved by the government and the Majles. Mirza Fazlollah Lava' al-Molk insisted that domestic companies must be entirely in the hands of Iranians and no other nationals: "[A domestic company's] Iranian identity must be proven beyond any shade of doubt." His motion was defeated when the chairman of the committee, Vakil al-Ro'aya, defended foreign capital as beneficial to national development: "One must not fear foreign companies."[31]

The Majles's intention was ideally to regulate the economy and prevent government or individual corruption. However, rampant corruption prevailed, especially as the central government lost control of remote provinces, where powerful regional leaders drew benefits from foreign patronage. Worth mentioning here is the case of Shaikh Khazal of Mohammereh. "Sir Khazal Khan" was reportedly "not enthusiastic" about a government project to construct a railway system in his realm in southwestern Iran. It would "not benefit him "because it would "open up his country" and make it accessible to the central government. "They could easily send a couple of regiments down on the pretext to curb" his power, he lamented, expressing his preference that a British company rather than the Persian government be in charge of the railway system.[32] He never missed a chance to ask the British for more "protection allowance," complaining that his compensation in cash was not enough for keeping order. In the North, Russia was in complete control of its zone, with naturalized or protected Persian local merchants and notables acting as its proxies. The coup against the second Majles doubled the pressure exerted on the weakened government, compelling it to give away all the concessions that Russia had requested earlier but had been denied by the Majles nationalists, irrespective of their party affiliation.

The Majles formulated in national rather than communal terms the emerging identity of all individuals, living in one country and abiding by a constitution that grants them all equality before the law, albeit in theory and not yet in practice. Throughout the debates of the second Majles, the deputies referred to the "national identity" that was gaining currency in the country, propelled as it was also by the press and the parties. Through the enactment of laws regulating each cabinet ministry, the deputies were building what they saw as a bright future. They were transplanting foreign laws and systems that needed time to find solid roots in their traditional society. They knew it would take a long time for their reforms to bear fruit. It would take time, Dr. Sa'id al-Otaba remarked; people are not yet "connected" to one another and do not comprehend the meaning of such a novel relationship that supersedes the centuries-old traditional communities. Indeed, the legislators repeatedly referred to their fellow countrymen's unfamiliarity with democratic culture and justified their reforms as the only means to safeguard their nation's independence and ensure a better future for their descendants.

The intelligentsia aimed at fulfilling what they saw as a fundamental human aspiration: to live in freedom, peace, and security. In practice, they were emulating European concepts of the Enlightenment: equality of all citizens; separation of church and state; freedom of opinion, the pen, and religion. These values were difficult to import, necessitating a slow process beginning with education, economic development, and the creation of a new political culture. Constitutionalists of all shades were fully aware that to succeed they initially needed an expertise that could come only from Europe. All, without exception, agreed to hire European advisers to help them achieve this grand, ambitious national project. But the selection of the advisers became an object of dispute between the various powers involved.

From the start, therefore, the fate of the constitutional movement became entwined with the survival of the existing European international system of alliances, more specifically the Anglo-Russian Convention of 1907. It was this system, fiercely defended by the two powers, that Morgan Shuster, the American financial adviser, refused to honor, encouraged as he was by the nationalists. Fatally, the second Majles ended as a casualty of the convention. Britain, the liberal democratic constitutional monarchy that had initially supported many Persian reformers, must bear the brunt of the blame for the tragic interruption of Iran's authentic and in many ways positive experiment in parliamentary governance. The construction of the "new Iran" was halted, its sovereignty violated, by the complicity of some European liberal elements that had initially provided the Persian "architects" with a model they admired and aspired to emulate. French and British mentors of the constitutionalist leaders, including the Freemasons, ultimately failed to support the Persians' attempt to realize some of the universal values these mentors had encouraged them to espouse. With just a handful of exceptions, the "liberal imperialists" proved to be first and foremost "imperialists."

Alphonse Nicolas, the French consul who advised and supported the Tabriz *anjoman* from the beginning of the revolution, was one of the first to turn his back on the entire movement. He became disillusioned with its leadership, and his original enthusiasm converted rapidly into cynicism. Nothing has been accomplished, he wrote as early as October 1910. He described "the spirit of the lie, intrigue, deviousness, and cunning" as innate in all Persians, who are "good for nothing" and whose "personal interests come before the country's general interests." "It will always be so in Persia," he added.[33] He characterized a Persian pamphlet circulating in Tabriz in protest against a British threat to send troops to the South as "childish, ignorant, and stupid."[34] As troubles increased, constantly threatening the demise of the constitutional government, the consul dismissed the revolution as a "sinister farce" resulting from the "stupidity" of previous Qajar successive governments.[35] He portrayed Hasan Taqizadeh as an "excellent young man who imagined he had penetrated all secrets of civilization and politics because he had spent six months in England, where he had provided Mr. Browne the somewhat fanciful elements for a book on the Persian Revolution."[36] He scornfully rejected the validity of the Cambridge scholar's analysis, deciding it was based on nothing but bazaar rumors and gossip as well as tales told by "an individual [Taqizadeh] who is just a common and naive man whom the English have elevated too highly." He branded Browne as "essentially a superficial man" not measuring up to "our own great Orientalists," and he complained of the influence Browne had on English official policy concerning Persia. He even shared with the Russian consul a strong wish for Browne's expulsion from Cambridge University. In fact, the French consul praised his Russian counterpart, with whom he had established friendly relations, and often defended his policy in Tabriz, which Browne relentlessly condemned in the British press.[37] Nicolas was also friendly with Mokhber al-Saltaneh, the embattled governor of Azerbaijan. He often praised the governor's integrity, yet he considered him too weak and indecisive an official to run the province competently.

In sharp contrast to the French consul, Major Claude Stokes, the military attaché at the British legation, sustained his faith in the revolutionary movement till the end. He was a liberal anti-imperialist who "deplored the fact that money has to be spent on armies and navies instead of social reform." And he denounced the Anglo-Russian Convention, openly criticizing Sir Edward Grey's policy of accommodating Russia at all costs. He was angry with the foreign minister and his "falsehoods," seeing "no distinction between the methods of the Foreign Office and [the methods of] the Russian foreign ministry; both suppress the truth."[38] Like some other officials in the Foreign Office and members of Parliament, he favored an Anglo-German alliance against Russia in the grand scheme that would ultimately lead to war, which he predicted. Practically until the closing of the second Majles, he worked tirelessly with nationalists and Shuster to safeguard the Persians' constitutional rights and national sovereignty against all their adversaries from within and abroad. His association with Shuster tainted his reputation in Tehran's diplomatic circles and, more importantly, in the Foreign Office, where he provoked the ire of Grey and his group. His extensive correspondence with his former professor Browne, which he wished to keep secret, provided the latter with relevant information to denounce publicly Anglo-Russian policies and enlist the support of Lord Curzon. Curzon's anti-Grey speech in Parliament, hailed by other parties in opposition, alarmed Foreign Minister Grey while raising Shuster's hope. It is a "splendid speech," Shuster wrote to Browne, possibly leading to an "amelioration of the treatment now being accorded by Russia and England to this helpless nation."[39]

That was not to be. Stokes and the three British diplomats stationed in Iran at the time, Smart, Shipley, and Graham, saw their hope for a rejuvenated Persia crushed in late December 1911. Graham had months earlier graphically compared the part the Persians' played in the Great Game as that of a "nut between nutcrackers."[40] Smart had developed a strong attachment and even appreciation for the Persians and Persian culture while living in their midst during his diplomatic tour in their country. While still in Shiraz, Smart recounted to Browne his brief experience living with the Bakhtiyaris. When he was wounded in the battle near Kazerun, Bakhtiyari tribesmen had rescued him and took him to their *ilkhan*'s tent. The narrative of his three-day stay there, nursed and nourished by his hosts, smoking opium and drinking a local alcoholic beverage, talking late into the small hours of the morning, is almost lyrical. "We would listen to sonorous recitations from the

Shahnameh [the national epic of Iran by Ferdowsi], at times to the plaintive melody of the Persian pipe. It was a strange romantic scene." Contrasting the open-air, free horseback rides up the mountains to the squalid industrial urban life lived by the British, the English diplomat turned romantic. "And the civilized West wishes to change all this. . . . Instead of the black goat's hair tent, pitched in the boundless freedom of the desert, we would substitute the cramped, ill-ventilated hovels of our city slums."[41] Years later, writing to Browne from Tangiers during World War I, Smart mourned the tragic fate that had befallen "our second fatherland," wondering how the war had affected it. He concluded the letter with a devastating epigraph to the cause they both had helped develop, a righteous cause they saw "cynically trampled underfoot to suit the convenience of those for the moment in predominance. . . . Poor Persia! She does not stand to gain much by our quarrels."[42]

The "enlightened" Persian leaders, the *rowshanfekran*, woke up to realize they were nothing but pawns in the European Great Game. Sadeq Khan Mostashar al-Dowleh, one of the architects of the restoration of the Constitution, an important deputy of the second Majles, and a member of successive cabinets, reached the conclusion that Tehran's domestic politics of the time could be understood only within the broader context of the Anglo-Russian Convention and the European balance of power on the eve of World War I. Lord Grey, he asserted, was anxious to accommodate Russian policy in Iran, yet he also wanted to make sure that pro-British ministers would be included in the cabinet. Hence, Mostashar al-Dowleh lamented these "ironies," "paradoxes," and "comedies" that characterized the political game of revolving chairs in the formation of successive cabinets.[43] The betrayals stung them all.

Already in the summer of 1911, months before the coup, Abdol Hosain Khan Vahid al-Molk had expressed his bitterness to Browne in a letter written in Persian and marked confidential. Responding to the professor's constant call for "moderation," he angrily asked: "If it were not for those extremists, revolutionaries, ultra-nationalists, extra-nationalists [epithets then used at the Russian embassy and by moderate constitutionalists], where would Iran's independence now be? . . . If those very extremists had not raised obstacles to the loans, had they not fought in the Majles, . . . had they not obstructed the corrupt, treacherous deeds of the 'sellers of the fatherland' [*vatanforush*] abroad[,] . . . had they allowed Iran to sign and seal with their own hands its own enslavement, then even the friends of Iran abroad" would have realized the game was over, and Iran would have become a protectorate of the two powers. Vahid al-Molk then questioned Brown directly: "Have you ever asked yourself what is the meaning of moderation . . . what is the meaning of extremists in a country like Iran where the people are poor, ignorant, oppressed, and where it is not possible for them to attain their rights even in years and years to come?. . . . What is the meaning of extremist, revolutionary?" Communicating his fear that "something was cooking," he told his former mentor: "You and others abroad are not aware of what is happening here." He recalled the mysterious circumstances of the assassination of Sani' al-Dowleh, "one of the best Iranian nationalist freedom lovers," wondering about the true motive of his murder. "We are not terrorists," he categorically stated.[44] Months after the coup of 1911, Vahid al-Molk sent Browne a gloomy letter, displaying his sense of helplessness over the present "dark days" and his bitterness regarding Russia's "extraordinary hostility" toward Iran's constitutional governance and England's hypocrisy toward Asian countries, especially Iran. It was obvious from the beginning, he wrote, that Shuster had become the main problem. Praising the American's book on his experiences in Iran, *The Strangling of Persia*, which had just been published, he graphically expressed his satisfaction: "He has peeled away the English and Russian's skin," unmasking the infamy of their politics in Iran.[45]

With the forceful closing of the second Majles, the deputies' assumed task to enact social reforms and build new modern institutions remained unfinished, but their quest for change remained alive. Their basic ideas and the institutional edifice that helped shape the identity of the "new Iran" survived on the intellectual outlook of a new generation of educated citizens, albeit small but growing. Their successors had to chart their own course in the shadow of the post–World War I international power structure that favored the rise of a modernizing new dynasty implementing reforms but discarding the democratic principles the *rowshanfekran* had struggled against all odds to implement. The rest is history, as the saying goes.

Glossary of Persian Words

Notes

Bibliography

Index

Glossary of Persian Words

anjoman. Political association

Anjoman-e Islamiyeh. Islamic *anjoman* established by clerical and lay anticonstitutionalists in major cities

Anjoman-e Ma'aref. Private educational and library association, owned and managed by reform-minded intelligentsia

Anjoman-e Sa'adat. Council of Happiness; constitutional *anjoman* established in Istanbul to fight for the restoration of the Constitution in 1908

Azali. A follower of Mirza Yahya Sobh-e Azal (1831–1912), a successor of the Bab

Babi. A follower of Mirza Ali Mohammad, the Bab (1819–50), founder of a religion declared heretical by Muslim religious leaders

Dar al-Fonun. Educational institution founded in Iran in 1851, teaching a modern curriculum and European languages

Dashnak. Short for "Dashnaktsutiun," the Armenian political party

dhimmis. Officially recognized religions, non-Muslim subjects of an Islamic state—that is, Christians, Jews, and Zoroastrians

Divan-e Mohasebat. Bureau of Accounts, based on the French Cour des comptes. A judicial court overseeing the nation's financial affairs

dowlat. Executive branch of government, the cabinet

esteqlaliyun. Independists

faqih. Religious scholar of *feqh*

Faramushkhaneh. House of Oblivion, a pseudo-Masonic lodge created by Mirza Malkom Khan (d. 1908)

fatwa. Religious decree issued by a *mojtahed*

feda'i, pl. ***fedayan***. Devotee of a cause

feqh. Islamic jurisprudence

ferqeh. Political faction

gonah. Sin

Hnchak. Armenian political party

hodud. Qur'anic law punishing apostasy, murder, theft, adultery, usury

hoquq. Plural of *haq*, legal, political rights; also meaning "laws"
ilkhan. Tribal chieftain at the top of the hierarchy
imam. Shi'a legitimate successor by hereditary right to the Prophet Mohammad
imam jom'eh. Title of the high-ranking Friday prayer leader; used as a name, "Imam Jom'eh," in Majles minutes
Imam of the Age. Twelver Shi'i's Twelfth Imam expected to return some day and restore righteous Islamic rule
Iran-e now **(New Iran).** Title of the liberal constitutional paper; also the name of the future "new Iran" reformers envisioned to construct: modern, democratic, secular
iraniyat. Iranian-ness; Iranian identity
janayat. Crime
khaleseh. Public land
khan. Title of a tribal chieftain and grandee
madreseh. Traditionally Islamic institution of higher learning, before educational reforms, when it also referred to public schools under state jurisdiction
Majles. Iranian Parliament
maktab. Elementary school traditionally administered by the olama
mardom. People
mashrutiyat. Constitutionalism
mellat. Nation
mellatiyun. Nationalists
mojahedin, sing. **mojahed.** Fighters for the constitutional cause
mojtahed. High-ranking cleric, specialist in Shi'a Islamic jurisprudence
mollah. Low-ranking cleric
monavvar al-fekr. Arabic for "enlightened thinker"
Mozakerat-e Majles Dovvom. Official recorded minutes of the second Majles debates
olama, sing. **'alem.** Religious leaders
oqala. Arabic for "rational thinkers"; in the constitutional period, referring to lay intellectuals
orf. Customary law, traditionally under state court jurisdiction
parti-bazi. Political party game, originally a pejorative term denouncing parties by the constitutionalists' detractors; nowadays referring to a powerful connection
qanat. Centuries-old traditional system of underground water canals for irrigation
qanun. Man-made law, distinct from religious law
rowshanfekr, pl. ***rowshanfekran.*** Enlightened thinker, intellectual
saltanat. Monarchy
savar. Mounted warriors
Shaikhism. An eighteenth-century Twelver Shi'a semimystical school of thought that recognizes a living religiospiritual, supreme leader for each age, condemned by mainstream Twelver Shi'a olama

sharia (*shari'*, *shari'at*). Islamic holy law based on *feqh*

Sorush **(Glad Tidings).** Constitutional newspaper published in Istanbul in 1909

Sunni. Muslim adhering to a majority sect that considers succession to the Prophet is by appointment and not a hereditary right

Sur-e Israfil **(Trumpet of Israfil).** Constitutional newspaper published in Tehran during the first Majles period, then in exile in Europe during the period of the Lesser Despotism

takfir. Charging with heresy

Tanzimat. Nineteenth-century Ottoman reform project

vatan. Fatherland

vatanforush. Traitor to the fatherland

waqf, pl. *owqaf.* Religious endowment

Notes

Abbreviations

Browne Papers	Edward Granville Browne Papers, Pembroke College, Cambridge
Constantinople/Tauris	Correspondences diplomatiques, Nantes, France; Files Constantinople/889 and Tauris/7, 8, 9, 10, Archives Nationales
FO	Foreign Office Papers, Correspondence Respecting the Affairs of Persia, FO 416/40–51, 881/9535, 9540, Public Records Office, London
Grand Orient de France	Archives du Grand Orient de France, correspondence: Orient de Constantinople, FM2 865, Bibliothèque Nationale, Paris
Mozakerat	*Mozakerat-e Majles dovvom* (Parliamentary Debates),vol. 2, 1909–11
Perse	Correspondances politiques et commerciales, Nouvelle Série: Perse, vols. 3–7, Archives du Ministère des Affaires Étrangères, Courneuve, France
Réveil de l'Iran	File 1871, Tehran: Le Réveil de l'Iran, 1907–11, Bibliothèque du Grand Orient de France, Paris

Names of Months in Islamic Lunar Calendar

Moharram	Jamadi I	Ramazan
Safar	Jamadi II	Shawwal
Rabi' I	Rajab	Zu'l Qa'edeh
Rabi' II	Sha'ban	Zu'l Hejjah

Introduction

1. Le Goff, *Les intellectuels au Moyen Âge.*

2. In order to be consistent with the transliteration system I use in the text and to be phonetically more compatible with the Persian pronunciation, I have opted to use the spelling "Moslem" instead of the conventional "Muslim."

3. Rahman, *Islam*, 78.

4. Quoted in Garthwaite, *The Persians*, 121.

5. Garthwaite, *The Persians*, 156.

6. See Bayat, *Mysticism and Dissent.*

7. Quoted in English translation in Keddie, *Islamic Response to Imperialism*, 107.

8. Sharif-Kashani, *Vaqe'at-e ettefaqiyeh dar ruzegar*, 1:48–49, 63–64; all translations are mine unless otherwise noted.

9. Quoted in Mohit-Mafi, *Moqaddamat*, 113.

10. Pamphlet included in Sharif-Kashani, *Vaqe'at-e ettefaqiyeh dar ruzegar*, 1:82, 93–95.

11. Sharif-Kashani, *Vaqe'at-e ettefaqiyeh dar ruzegar*, 1:119–20, 55–58.

12. Sharif-Kashani, *Vaqe'at-e ettefaqiyeh dar ruzegar*, 121–22.

13. Quoted in Mohit-Mafi, *Moqaddamat-e mashrutiyat*, 361.

14. Mohit-Mafi, *Moqaddamat-e mashrutiyat*, 401.

15. Quoted in Mostashar al-Dowleh, *Khaterat va asnad*, 1:45.

16. Quoted in Mostashar al-Dowleh, *Khaterat va asnad*, 1:45.

17. Rahimi, *Qanun-e asasi*, 83.

18. Cited in Mohit-Mafi, *Moqaddamat-e mashrutiyat*, 273.

19. Mostashar al-Dowleh, *Khaterat va Asnad*, 2:235–39; Kermani, *Tarikh-e bidari-ye iraniyan*, 2:331.

20. Sharif-Kashani, *Vaqe'at-e ettefaqiyeh dar ruzegar*, 1:221–22, 2:238–39.

21. Quoted in Sharif-Kashani, *Vaqe'at-e ettefaqiyeh dar ruzegar*, 1:204–5.

22. Mohammad Hosain Na'ini, *Tanbih al-omma wa tanzih al-mella*, cited in Bayat, *Iran's First Revolution*, 256–57.

23. Quoted in Sharif-Kashani, *Vaqe'at-e ettefaqiyeh dar ruzegar*, 1:246–51. This essay borrows its argument from an essay written in 1906 by the constitutional reformist Nasrollah Taqavi-Akhavi and included in Mohit-Mafi, *Moqaddamat-e mashrutiyat*, 150–60.

24. Sharif Kashani, *Vaqe'at-e ettefaqiyeh dar ruzegar*, 1:209–10.

1. Freemasonry and the Constitutional Revolution

1. Bayat, *Mysticism and Dissent*, chap. 5.

2. Chevallier, *Histoire de la Franc-maçonnerie française*, 2:149.

3. Chevallier, *Histoire de la Franc-maçonnerie française*, 2:299.

4. Chevallier, *Histoire de la Franc-maçonnerie française*, 2:10.

5. Chevallier, *Histoire de la Franc-maçonnerie française*, 2:26.

6. Chevallier, *Histoire de la Franc-maçonnerie française*, 2:325.

7. Chevallier, *Histoire de la Franc-maçonnerie française*, 2:43.

8. Chevallier, *Histoire de la Franc-maçonnerie française*, 2:18.

9. Chevallier, *Histoire de la Franc-maçonnerie française*, 2:65.

10. Chevallier, *Histoire de la Franc-maçonnerie française*, 2:329.

11. Dumont, "La Turquie dans les Archives du Grand Orient de France."

12. Hanioğlu, *The Young Turks in Opposition*, 33–34.

13. Dumont, "La Turquie dans les Archives du Grand Orient," 180.

14. Louis Amiable, the venerable of the lodge, to the Supreme Council, Oct. 23, 1872, in Dumont, "La Turquie dans les Archives du Grand Orient," 180.

15. Dumont, "La Turquie dans les Archives du Grand Orient," 190–91. See also Hanioğlu, *Young Turks in Opposition*, 34 n.5; Algar, *Mirza Malkum Khan*.

16. "Tehran: Le Réveil de l'Iran," 1907–10, 1911–19, file 1871, Grand Orient de France.

17. The most comprehensive study to date of Freemasonry in Iran is Ismail Ra'in's *Faramushkhaneh va Framasonri dar Iran*. The book, though highly informative, must be read with caution, however. It is recklessly filled with factual errors, chronological confusion, and the tendency to view all Masons, with very few exceptions, as agents of European imperialism who plotted the Constitutional Revolution to subjugate Iran to the Europeans' power through Iranian Masons turned traitors to their fatherland. See also Katira'i, *Framasonri dar Iran*. Both are cited in Algar, "An Introduction to the History of Freemasonry in Iran."

18. Ra'in, *Faramushkhaneh va Framasonri dar Iran*, 1:306–12.

19. Shirazi, *Majmueh-ye Safarnameh-ye Mirza Saleh Shirazi*.

20. *Bulletin du Grand Orient de France*, 15:396–97.

21. Malekzadeh, *Tarikh-e enqelab-e mashrutiyat-e Iran*, 1:119; Ra'in, *Faramushkhaneh va Framasonri dar Iran*, 1:119–21 and sources cited there.

22. Browne, *The Press and Poetry of Modern Persia*, 18.

23. See list in Ra'in, *Faramushkhaneh va Framasonri dar Iran*, l:513–14; see also Algar, *Mirza Malkum Khan*, 49–50.

24. Algar, *Mirza Malkum Khan*, 38.

25. Ra'in, *Faramushkhaneh va Framasonri dar Iran*, 1:508 and sources cited there.

26. Royal prince to Malkom Khan requesting him to write on the prince's behalf to lodges in Paris and Berlin, in Ra'in, *Faramushkhaneh va Framasonri dar Iran*, 1:519–21.

27. Ra'in, *Faramushkhaneh va Framasonri dar Iran*, 1:560.

28. Mirza Malkom Khan, "Ketabcheh-ye faramushkhaneh," included in Ra'in, *Faramushkhaneh va Framasonri dar Iran*, 1:546. See also Bayat, *Mysticism and Dissent*, 150–52, and Algar, *Mirza Malkum Khan*, 39–40.

29. Algar, *Mirza Malkum Khan*, 71.

30. Ra'in, *Faramushkhaneh va Framasonri dar Iran*, 1:479.

31. See account of the honors bestowed on Mozaffar al-Din Shah in Hardinge, *A Diplomatist in the East*, 288–89.

32. Quoted in Algar, "An Introduction to the History of Freemasonry in Iran," 287.

33. Quoted in Algar, *Mirza Malkom Khan*, 143.

34. Quoted in Bayat, *Mysticism and Dissent*, 152.

35. *Qanun*, nos. 6, 17, 25.

36. *Qanun*, nos. 9, 15, 29.

37. Mirza Fathali Akhundov, "Alefba-ye jadid va maktubat," in *Mirza Fathali Akhundov*, ed. Mohammadzadeh, 292.

38. *Qanun*, no. 8.

39. Quoted in Algar, *Mirza Malkum Khan*, 240.

40. Quoted in Algar, *Mirza Malkum Khan*, 252.

41. Algar, *Mirza Malkum Khan*, 253.

42. See Bayat, *Iran's First Revolution*, 194–95.

43. See the list of the Political Science Faculty's administrators and instructors in Ra'in, *Faramushkhaneh va Framasonri dar Iran*, 1:452–53.

44. Nateq, *Karnameh-ye farhangi va farangi dar Iran*, 83–114. Nateq does not connect the Alliance with the Freemasons.

45. See list in Nateq, *Karnameh-ye farhangi va farangi dar Iran*, 86–87.

46. Nateq, *Karnameh-ye farhangi va farangi dar Iran*, 88–89. See also the secret report written for Amin al-Soltan about the Alliance activities in Ra'in, *Faramushkhaneh va Framasonri dar Iran*, 2:33–36.

47. Nateq, *Karnameh-ye farhangi va farangi dar Iran*, 90.

48. Ra'in, *Faramushkhaneh va Framasonri dar Iran*, 1:255.

49. Nateq, *Karnameh-ye farhangi va farangi dar Iran*, 95–96.

50. Nateq, *Karnameh-ye farhangi va farangi dar Iran*, 94.

51. Nateq, *Karnameh-ye farhangi va farangi dar Iran*, 63–80.

52. Nateq, *Karnameh-ye farhangi va farangi dar Iran*, 106–7.

53. Nateq, *Karnameh-ye farhangi va farangi dar Iran*, 94; *Bulletin de l'Alliance française* 22 (Oct. 15, 1905): 286 (quotation).

54. Dowlatabadi, *Hayat-e Yahya*, 1:304.

55. The *Bulletin du Grand Orient* for the year 1889–1990 mentions a lodge in Iran; in the order's archives, Julien Bottin is listed as having been, together with Entezam al-Saltaneh, a member of the Orient de Tehran since 1898, a lodge of the Spanish rite. However, in a letter responding to Ismail Ra'in's query, the Grand Orient categorically denies a lodge was ever founded in Tehran in the nineteenth century (Ra'in, *Faramushkhaneh va Framasonri dar Iran*, 2:16).

56. Archival materials for the Réveil de l'Iran lodge are scarce. At the Grand Orient de France library on Rue Cadet in Paris, there exists a rather thin file of correspondence, "Tehran: Le Réveil de l'Iran," file 1871. The information gathered from these exchanges between the Supreme Council and the Tehran lodge members do not reveal much about the lodge's activities or even its agenda. However, the list of its membership and the requests made by individual "venerables" and secretaries are quite illuminating. As other researchers on Freemasonry in the Middle East have noted, the archives keep their secrets. But one can nonetheless read between the lines to gather a more or less clear idea of some of the Réveil de l'Iran's activities. Ra'in offers more detailed information gathered from private interviews with Iranian Masons and articles written by other Masons in Persian journals. Again, his analysis must be read with caution, so sweeping are his generalizations. Mahmud Katira'i's book *Framasonri dar Iran* is less informative on the lodge. Paul Sabatiennes's essay "Pour une histoire de la premiere loge Maçonnique en Iran" is based on the Grand Orient's archives; however, Sabatiennes omits all the information available in the correspondence regarding the lodge's direct activities in the politics of the time.

57. Paul Henri Morel to the Supreme Council, Mar. 1907, "Réveil de l'Iran" file.

58. Charles Lattes to the Supreme Council, Oct. 19, 1910, "Réveil de l'Iran" file.

59. The lists of the Grand Orient Archives mention a total of 168 members in the Réveil de l'Iran's sixteen years of existence. Ra'in lists 120 members (*Faramushkhaneh va Framasonri dar Iran*, 2:446–53).

60. Mohammad Sadeq admitted in an interview with Ra'in that both he and his father were members of the Bidari Lodge (*Faramushkhaneh va Framasonri dar Iran*, 2:251).

61. Grand master of the Clemente amitie to Adib al-Mamalek (in French), Mar. 24, 1908, in Ra'in, *Faramushkhaneh va Framasonri dar Iran*, 2:61–63.

62. Morel to Supreme Council general secretary, Nov. 22, 1907, "Le Réveil de l'Iran" file.

63. Ra'in states that the French texts were translated into Persian three times, two in a summary form in 1908 and the third in 1912 in full (*Faramushkhaneh va Framasonri dar Iran*, 2:120–21).

64. Ra'in, *Faramushkhaneh va Framasonri dar Iran*, 2:123–38, 294–99, 628–35.

65. Kermani, *Tarikh-e bidari-ye Iraniyan*, 2:46–48.

66. Kermani, *Tarikh-e bidari-ye Iraniyan*, 2:33.

67. Kermani, *Tarikh-e bidari-ye Iraniyan*, 2:43.

68. Hakim al-Molk, "Dar Sahneh-ye enqelab-e mashrutiyyat-e Iran," *Ettele'at-e Mahyaneh* (1327/1948), cited in Ra'in, *Faramushkhaneh va Framasonri dar Iran*, 2:181–82.

69. Morel to the Supreme Council general secretary, June 11, 1908, "Le Réveil de l'Iran" file.

70. Morel to the Supreme Council general secretary, July 17, 1908, "Le Réveil de l'Iran" file.

71. Bayat, *Iran's First Revolution*, 74–75 and sources cited there.

72. Bayat, *Iran's First Revolution*, 192–95.

2. The Politics of the Restoration of the Constitution

1. Bonakdarian, *Britain and the Iranian Constitutional Revolution.*

2. Sir Arthur Nicolson to Sir Edward Grey, Dec. 22, 1908, FO 881/9535.

3. Nicolson to Grey, Jan. 4, 1909, FO 881/9535.

4. George Barclay to Grey, Jan. 8, 1909, FO 881/9535.

5. List of exiles, in *Mobarezeh ba Mohammad Ali Shah*, ed. Afshar, 17–19.

6. Ali Akbar Dehkhoda to Abol Hasan Mo'azed al-Saltaneh, Nov. 15, 1908, in *Namehha-ye siyasi-ye Dehkhoda*, ed. Afshar, 21–26; see also Dehkhoda to Mo'azed al-Saltaneh, n.d., in *Mobarezeh ba Mohammad Ali Shah*, ed. Afshar, 30. Islamic dates are not provided in citations if they are not given in the documents cited.

7. Dehkhoda, in *Mobarezeh ba Mohammad Ali Shah*, ed. Afshar, 29.

8. Hanioğlu, *The Young Turks in Opposition*, 18, 20, 21.

9. Berkes, *The Development of Secularism in Turkey*, 305–7.

10. Quoted in Berkes, *The Development of Secularism in Turkey*, 308 n. 20.

11. Hanioğlu, *The Young Turks in Opposition*, 4.

12. Hanioğlu, *The Young Turks in Opposition*, 202.

13. *Journal officiel*, Dec. 18, 1907, cited in Dumont, "Une délégation Jeune-Turque," 316; Dehkhoda to Mo'azed al-Saltaneh, Nov. 15, 1908, in *Namehha-ye siyasi-ye Dehkhoda*, ed. Afshar, 21–26; see also the group photograph of La Fraternite Musulmane members wearing European-type clothes in *Mobarezeh ba Mohammad Ali Shah*, ed. Afshar, 24.

14. Cited in Dumont, "Une délégation Jeune-Turque," 317.

15. Quoted in Dumont, "Une délégation Jeune-Turque," 322.

16. Dumont, "Une délégation Jeune-Turque," 321–24.

17. Dehkhoda to Mo'azed al-Saltaneh, Jan. 7, 1909, in *Mobarezeh ba Mohammad Ali Shah*, ed. Afshar, 74–75; Dehkhoda to Mo'azed al-Saltaneh, n.d., in *Mobarezeh ba Mohammad Ali Shah*, ed. Afshar, 113; see also Dehkhoda to Mo'azed al-Saltaneh, in *Namehha-ye siyasi-ye Dehkhoda*, ed. Afshar, 32–35.

18. "*Les États Unis de Perse*," *Revue du monde Musulman* 8 (1909): 292–94.

19. Mo'azed al-Saltaneh to brother (no name given), Dec. 19, 1908, in *Mobarezeh ba Mohammad Ali Shah*, ed. Afshar, 48–49.

20. Dehkhoda to Mo'azed al-Saltaneh, n.d., in *Mobarezeh ba Mohammad Ali Shah*, ed. Afshar, 25–28.

21. Mo'azed al-Saltaneh to Anjoman-e Sa'adat, n.d., in *Mobarezeh ba Mohammad Ali Shah*, ed. Afshar, 20.

22. Dehkhoda to Mo'azed al-Saltaneh, Jan. 20, 1909, in *Mobarezeh ba Mohammad Ali Shah*, ed. Afshar, 57–58, document 26.

23. For a comprehensive analysis of Browne's role in the revolution, see Bonakdarian, *Britain and the Iranian Constitutional Revolution* and sources cited there. See also Gurney, "E. G. Browne and the Iranian Community in Istanbul."

24. Bayat, *Iran's First Revolution*, 244 and sources cited there.

25. See Mojtahed Mohammad Kazem Khorasani to the Persia Committee, Rabi' II 3, 1327/Apr. 24, 1909, in Sharif-Kashani, *Vaqe'at-e ettefaqiyeh dar ruzegar*, 1:264–65; Khorasani to Edward Granville Browne, Apr. 26, 1909, expressing his gratitude, box 9, Browne Papers (all letters to Browne from Iranians were written in Persian); and Browne, *The Persian Revolution*, 423–24.

26. William Barber to Browne, Feb. 26, 1909, box 9, Browne Papers.

27. Barber to Browne, Mar. 11, 1909, box 9, Browne Papers.

28. Barber to Browne, Feb. 24, 1909, box 9, Browne Papers.

29. Khorasani quoted in Mostashar al-Dowleh, *Khaterat va asnad*, 2:237–38.

30. Combes, *Histoire de la Franc-maçonnerie*, 2:331.

31. Henry F. B. Lynch, memorandum, Feb. 9, 1909, enclosure, FO 881/9535.

32. Bonakdarian, *Britain and the Iranian Constitutional Revolution*, 176.

33. Report, July 6, 1909, Perse, 6:26–27.

34. Lynch, memorandum, Feb. 9, 1909, FO 881/9535.

35. Lynch to Browne, July 16, 1909, box 9, Browne Papers.

36. Lynch to Browne, Dec. 4, 1908, box 9, Browne Papers.

37. See letter by Hosain Danesh, a moderate constitutionalist working in Istanbul, dated 1909 (month and day not available), box 1, Browne Papers.

38. Lynch, memorandum, Feb. 9, 1909, enclosure, FO 881/9535.

39. Browne to Mo'azed al-Saltaneh, Dec. 30, 1908, in *Mobarezeh ba Mohammad Ali Shah*, ed. Afshar, 196, document 97.

40. Mo'azed al-Saltaneh to Mohammad Ali Shah, cable from Paris, Dec. 22, 1908, in *Owraq*, ed. Afshar, 430–31.

41. Dehkhoda to Mo'azed al-Saltaneh, Jan. 7, 1909, in *Namehha-ye siyasi-ye Dehkhoda*, ed. Afshar, 32–35.

42. Documents 28 and 31 in *Mobarezeh ba Mohammad Ali Shah*, ed. Afshar, 69–72, 74–75.

43. Dehkhoda to Mo'azed al-Saltaneh, Dec. 30, 1908, in *Mobarezeh ba Mohammad Ali Shah*, ed. Afshar, 18–20, 23–24.

44. Dehkhoda to Mo'azed al-Saltaneh, Jan. 9, 1910, in *Namehha-ye siyasi-ye Dehkhoda*, ed. Afshar, 32–35.

45. Mirza Aqa Farshi to Dehkhoda, Dec. 17, 1908, in *Mobarezeh ba Mohammad Ali Shah*, ed. Afshar, 208–9, document 104.

46. See, for instance, Momtaz al-Dowleh to Mohammad Ali Shah from Paris, Dec. 22, 1908, in *Mobarezeh ba Mohammad Ali Shah*, ed. Afshar, 187, document 88.

47. Mo'ayyed al-Islam Kashani to Mo'azed al-Saltaneh, Jan. 27, 1909, in *Mobarezeh ba Mohammad Ali Shah*, ed. Afshar, 281, document 146.

48. "Tabi'at-e saltanat chist?" *Sur-e Israfil* 2, no. 1 (1909).

49. Mokhber al-Saltaneh to Mo'azed al-Saltaneh, Feb. 3, 1909, in *Mobarezeh ba Mohammad Ali Shah*, ed. Afshar, 186, document 87.

50. Browne to Mo'azed al-Saltaneh, Feb. 10, 1909, in *Mobarezeh ba Mohammad Ali Shah*, ed. Afshar, 201–3, document 100.

51. Dehkhoda to Mo'azed al-Saltaneh, n.d., in *Mobarezeh ba Mohammad Ali Shah*, ed. Afshar, 69–70, document 28. See also Dehkhoda to Mo'azed al-Saltaneh, Jan. 3 or 4, 1909, where he threatens to give up writing should this article not be published, in *Namehha-ye siyasi-ye Dehkhoda*, ed. Afshar, 25–28.

52. Document 47, n.d., in *Mobarezeh ba Mohammad Ali Shah*, ed. Afshar, 114–16.

53. Mir Javad (Taqizadeh's brother in Istanbul) to Cambridge, Shawwal 22, 1326/Nov. 17, 1908, in *Owraq*, ed. Afshar, 402–10. See also Bayat, *Iran's First Revolution*, 254–55 and sources cited there.

54. Bahar, *Tarikh-e mokhtasari*, introduction.

55. Reports dated June 16, July 17 and 30, 1908, as well as July 20, Aug. 1 and 5, 1909, Constantinople/889, Constantinople/Tauris. Khorasani's spontaneous enthusiasm had led him to initially write a letter to Sultan Abdol Hamid praising him for restoring the Ottoman Constitution, hailing him as the "Caliph of Islam," the "benefactor of all Moslems," who has proven that "Islam triumphs" with the destruction of despotism, but the sultan was soon deposed by the Young Turks. See translation of the letter in G. Rouet, report, Aug. 6, 1908, Constantinople/889, Constantinople/Tauris.

56. Anjoman-e Okhuvat-e Iraniyan branch in Baghdad to the Anjoman-e Sa'adat, Jamadi I 7, 1327/May 27, 1909, in *Mobarezeh ba Mohammad Ali Shah*, ed. Afshar, 374–75, document 207.

57. Unsigned letter bearing the heading of the Iranian consulate in Istanbul to Mo'azed al-Saltaneh, Ramazan 4, 1327/Sept. 19, 1909, in *Mobarezeh ba Mohammad Ali Shah*, ed. Afshar, 392–95, document 217. See also Shaikh Assadollah Mamaqani to Mo'azed al-Saltaneh, Ramazan 2, 1327/Sept. 17, 1909, in *Mobarezeh ba Mohammad Ali Shah*, ed. Afshar, 396–97, document 218.

58. Bahram from Baku to the Anjoman-e Sa'adat, Jamadi II 6, 1327/June 25, 1909, in *Mobarezeh ba Mohammad Ali Shah*, ed. Afshar, 384, document 212.

59. Dowlatabadi, *Hayat-e Yahya* 3:35–37, 68.

60. Dowlatabadi, *Hayat-e Yahya* 3:74, 99.

61. Bahram from Baku to Anjoman-e Sa'adat, Jamadi II 6, 1327/June 25, 1909, in *Mobarezeh ba Mohammad Ali Shah*, ed. Afshar, 385, document 212.

62. Taqizadeh, *Zendegani-ye tufani*, 124; see also Kasravi, *Tarikh-e hijdah saleh-ye Azerbaijan*, 24.

63. Taqizadeh, *Zendegani-ye tufani*, 107; Bonakdarian, *Britain and the Iranian Constitutional Revolution*, 125.

64. French consul's report from Constantinople, July 20, 1909, Constantinople/889, Constantinople/Tauris.

65. The name "Jeunes Persans" also appears in political pamphlets published in the Caucasus and spread in Tabriz in the period of the first Majles. See Adamiyat, *Fekr-e demokrasi-ye ejtemai*, 25, citing a British report from Tabriz dated July 14, 1906.

66. The article is reprinted in Mostashar al-Dowleh, *Khaterat va asnad*, 2:132–35. See also Malekzadeh, *Tarikh-e enqelab-e mashrutiyat-e Iran*, 3:1277.

67. Dowlatabadi, *Hayat-e Yahya*, 3:38–42.

68. Dehkhoda to Anjoman-e Sa'adat, Safar 25, 1327/Mar. 18, 1909, in *Namehha-ye siyasi-ye Dehkhoda*, ed. Afshar, 43–54.

69. "Politics" is given in transliteration in the text.

70. Dehkhoda to Anjoman-e Sa'adat, Safar 25, 1327/Mar. 18, 1909, in *Namehha-ye siyasi-ye Dehkhoda*, ed. Afshar, 43–54.

71. Mirza Qasem Tabrizi to Mo'azed al-Saltaneh, Mar. 15, 1909, in *Mobarezeh ba Mohammad Ali Shah*, ed. Afshar, 139, document 61.

72. Mo'azed al-Saltaneh to Dehkhoda, Mar. 28, 1909, in *Mobarezeh ba Mohammad Ali Shah*, ed. Afshar, 46–49, document 24.

73. Dehkhoda to Mo'azed al-Saltaneh, Apr. 1909, in *Nameha-siyasi-ye Dehkhoda*, ed. Afshar, 58–62.

74. Hasan Taqizadeh to Browne, Oct. 19, 1908, box 1, Browne Papers.

75. See Smart's letters to Browne in Bayat, *Iran's First Revolution*, 243–44 and sources cited there.

76. Taqizadeh to British officials (in Persian), n.d., in *Owraq*, ed. Afshar, 102–9.

77. Taqizadeh to Sattar Khan, Rajab 22, 1326/Aug. 20, 1908, in *Owraq*, ed. Afshar, 132–36.

78. Taqizadeh to Sattar Khan, Rajab 22, 1326/Aug. 20, 1908, in *Owraq*, ed. Afshar, 132–36.

79. Browne to Taqizadeh, Dec. 2, 1908, in *Namehha-ye Edvard Browne*, ed. Zaryab and Afshar, 19.

80. Taqizadeh to Browne, Nov. 30, 1908, box 1, Browne Papers.

81. First draft of "*Times* Manifesto," in *Owraq*, ed. Afshar, 77–82.

82. Second draft of the "*Times* Manifesto," in *Owraq*, ed. Afshar, 117–18.

83. English translation of final draft of "Persian Nationalists: Manifesto from Refugees," in *Owraq*, ed. Afshar, 609–14.

84. Cited in Bayat, *Iran's First Revolution*, 246.

85. Bonakdarian, *Britain and the Constitutional Revolution*, 164.

86. Lynch to Taqizadeh, Oct. 18 and 26, 1908, in *Owraq*, ed. Afshar, 519–21.

87. The text of the speech that Taqizadeh and Mo'azed al-Saltaneh gave to the House of Commons is included in Bonakdarian, *Britain and the Iranian Constitutional Revolution*, 133.

88. Exiles' letter of reconciliation to the shah, Dec. 1908, in *Owraq*, ed. Afshar, 124–28.

89. Saheb Nasq (in Paris) to Taqizadeh, Oct. 1908, in *Owraq*, ed. Afshar, 421–28.

90. Dehkhoda to Mo'azed al-Saltaneh, Jan. 29, 1909, in *Mobarezeh ba Mohammad Ali Shah*, ed. Afshar, 79–80, document 35.

91. Taqizadeh, *Zendegani-ye tufani*, 107–16.

92. Quoted in Bayat, *Iran's First Revolution*, 241.

93. Bayat, *Iran's First Revolution*, 242 and sources cited there; correspondence of Armenian Social-Democrats with Karl Kautski and Georgi Plekhanov, reprinted in *The Armenians of Iran*, ed. Chaqueri, 313–47.

94. Quoted in Berberian, *The Love of Freedom Has No Fatherland*, 89.

95. Berberian, *The Love of Freedom Has No Fatherland*, 48.

96. A French diplomat confirmed this rapprochement in a letter dispatched on November 18, 1908 (Constantinople/889, Constantinople/Tauris). He also noted that Azerbaijan militants sought Young Turks soldiers' and Caucasian volunteers' active participation in the struggles in Tabriz. Şükrü Hanioğlu denies the Dashnak Party's claim that the congress of Ottoman opposition parties in 1907 and the resulting alliance between the Young Turks and Dashnakists played a significant role in the revolution of 1908. "For practical purposes," he writes, "it [the alliance] was worthless" (*Young Turks in Opposition*, 209).

97. Berberian, *The Love of Freedom Has No Fatherland*, 89.

98. Berberian, *The Love of Freedom Has No Fatherland*, 126, 130–34.

99. *Musavat*, Moharram 1, 1327/Jan. 23, 1909.

100. French translation in *Revue du monde Musulman* 7 (Mar. 1909): 287–94.

101. Berberian, *The Love of Freedom Has No Fatherland*, 134–35.

102. Berberian, *The Love of Freedom Has No Fatherland*, 143.

103. On the origins of the Iranian and Transcaucasian connection, see Bayat, *Iran's First Revolution*, chap. 4 and sources cited there.

104. Berberian, *The Love of Freedom Has No Fatherland*, 132–34; Kasravi, *Tarikh-e hijdah saleh-ye Azerbaijan*, 7–21. On Panoff, described by some as an "adventurist" who started as a Russian spy, and his controversial role in Gilan, see Bayat, *Iran's First Revolution*, 243, 252, and sources cited there. See also Harold Williams (*Morning Post* correspondent in St. Petersburg) to Browne, Feb. 16, 17 and May 6, 1909, box 9, Browne Papers.

105. Vijuyeh, *Tarikh-e enqelab-e Azerbaijan*, 164–68.

106. For a detailed analysis of the civil war in the North, see Afary, *The Iranian Constitutional Revolution*, chap. 5.

107. Afary, *The Iranian Constitutional Revolution*, 227.

108. Abdol Majid 'Ayn al-Dowleh to Taqizadeh and Taqizadeh to 'Ayn al-Dowleh, Jan. and Feb. 1909, in *Owraq*, ed. Afshar, 151–57.

109. 'Ayn al-Dowleh to Taqizadeh, n.d., in *Owraq*, ed. Afshar, 151–52, 154.

110. Taqizadeh to 'Ayn al-Dowleh, n.d., in *Owraq*, ed. Afshar, 55.

111. Taqizadeh to 'Ayn al-Dowleh's representative Hosain Qoli Khan, Moharam 18, 1327/Feb. 9, 1909, in *Owraq*, ed. Afshar, 150.

112. Farshi to Mo'azed al-Saltaneh, Mar. 6, 1909, in *Mobarezeh ba Mohammad Ali Shah*, ed. Afshar, 211–12.

113. Text of the final draft of the two envoys' proposal in Nicolson to Grey, Apr. 16, 1909, FO 881/9540.

114. Barclay to Grey, Dec. 29, 1908, FO 881/9535.

115. Alexander Izvolski, memorandum, Jan. 3, 1909, FO 881/9535.

116. Barclay to Grey, Jan. 18, 1909, FO 881/9535.

117. Barclay to Grey, Jan. 18, 1909, FO 881/9535.

118. Barclay to Grey, Feb. 21, 1909, FO 881/9535.

119. Barclay to Grey, Jan. 25, 1909, FO 416/43.

120. Barclay to Grey, Feb. 21, 1909, FO 416/43; Nicolson to Grey, Mar. 8, 1909, FO 416/43.

121. Nicolson to Grey, Mar. 18, 1909, enclosure, FO 416/43.

122. Izvolski, memorandum submitted to Nicolson, Jan. 17, 1909, FO 416/43.

123. As reported in Nicolson to Grey, Feb. 10, 1909, FO 416/43.

124. Nicolson to Grey, Feb. 22, 1909, FO 416/43.

125. Barclay to Grey, Feb. 21, 25, 1909, FO 416/43; Grey to Nicolson, Feb. 25, 1909, FO 416/43.

126. Nicolson to Grey, Jan. 17, 1909, FO 416/43.

127. Barclay to Grey, Jan. 19, 1909, FO 416/43.

128. Barclay to Grey, Dec. 31, 1908, FO 416/43.

129. Nicolson to Grey, Jan. 26, 1909, FO 881/9535.

130. Grey to Nicolson, Feb. 17, 1909, FO 881/9535.

131. Nicolson to Grey, Apr. 16, 1909, FO 881/9540.

132. Bizot's report is included in Barclay to Grey, Mar. 22, 1909, FO 416/43.

133. Barclay to Grey, Mar. 22, 1909, FO 416/43.

134. Barclay to Grey, Mar. 28, 1909, FO 416/43.

135. Alphonse L. M. Nicolas, report, Dec. 29, 1908, Tauris/7, Constantinople/Tauris.

136. Nicolson to Grey, Mar. 20, 1909, FO 881/9535.

137. Nicolas, reports, Jan. 4, Feb. 15, 1909, Tauris/7, Constantinople/Tauris.

138. Nicolas, report, Dec. 29, 1908, Tauris/7, Constantinople/Tauris.

139. Nicolas, report, Dec. 30, 1908, Tauris/7, Constantinople/Tauris.

140. Vratislav (full name not known) to Barclay, May 2, 1909, enclosure 1, FO 881/9540; on Moore's daily contacts with the Tabriz *anjoman*, see also Taqizadeh, *Zendegani-ye tufani*, 118–19.

141. Nava'i, *Fath-e Tehran*, 178. Despite his eulogy for Sattar Khan and Baqer Khan as legendary heroes and selfless leaders, Abdolhosain Nava'i admits success affected their behavior, changing their personalities for the worse.

142. Barclay to Grey, Apr. 17, 1909, FO 416/44. See the texts of the Tabriz *anjoman*'s cables reflecting a sense of total despair, anger, and frustration with the constitutionalists' negotiations in the capital, which did not represent Tabriz's priorities but instead accepted terms of reconciliation identical to the two envoys', in Mostashar al Dowleh, *Khaterat va asnad*, 4:92–97, 99–101.

143. Barclay to Grey, Apr. 19, 1909, FO 881/9540.

144. As reported in Barclay to Grey, Apr. 20, 1909, FO 881/9540.

145. FO document, Apr. 26, 1909, box 9, Browne Papers.

146. Barclay to Grey, Apr. 20, 1909, FO 881/9540.

147. Taqizadeh, *Zendegani-ye tufani*, 126–28.

148. Barclay to Grey, Apr. 16 and 26, 1909, FO 881/9540.

149. Taqizadeh, *Zendegani-ye tufani*, 129.

150. Grey to Nicolson, Jan. 20, 1909, FO 881/9535.

151. As reported in Barclay to Grey, Aug. 13, 1909, enclosure marked "secret," FO 416/41.

152. See Tabriz *anjoman* cables of Jamadi I 10, 11, 1327/May 20, 21, 1909, in Mostashar al-Dowleh, *Khaterat va asnad* 4:122–24.

153. Nicolson to Grey, May 7, 1909, FO 881/9540.

154. Quoted in Sharif-Kashani, *Vaqe'at-e ettefaqiyeh dar ruzegar*, 1:321–22.

3. The March to Tehran

1. Sharif-Kashani, *Vaqe'at-e ettefaqiyeh dar ruzegar*, 2:388–90.

2. George Percy Churchill, memorandum, enclosure in Barclay to Grey, Mar. 23, 1909, FO 881/9535.

3. Sharif-Kashani, *Vaqe'at-e ettefaqiyeh dar ruzegar*, 2:390. Sharif-Kashani claims Yeprem Khan and the Armenian militia he headed were not involved in the lawless acts and blames Panoff and other unruly Caucasians (1:345–47). See also Bayat, *Iran's First Revolution*, 252 and sources cited there.

4. Bayat, *Iran's First Revolution*, 260.

5. Sharif-Kashani's account of the Sepahdar's role in these early events, based on the latter's personal notes, attributes to him a greater, more independent action than do other sources (*Vaqe'at-e ettefaqiyeh dar ruzegar*, 2:384–410).

6. As reported in Barclay to Grey, May 6, 1909, FO 881/9540.

7. The text of the decree is printed in Mostashar al-Dowleh, *Khaterat va asnad*, 1:290.

8. Barclay to Grey, May 5, 10, 1909, FO 881/9540; Barclay to Grey, June 17, 1909, FO 416/41; text of the notes related to the draft of the electoral law in Mostashar al-Dowleh, *Khaterat va asnad*, 1:152–54.

9. Barclay to Grey, May 10, 1909, FO 881/9540.

10. *Nessim-e shomal*, Safar 17, 1327/Mar. 10, 1909, in *Owraq*, ed. Afshar, 29.

11. Dowlatabadi, *Hayat-e Yahya*, 3:96.

12. Capitaine Anginieur, report, n.d., Constantinople/889, Constantinople/Tauris; see also Bayat, *Iran's First Revolution*, 253–58 and sources cited there.

13. French translation of Persian text of letter dated Rabi' II 9, 1327/Apr. 30, 1909, enclosed in French consul in Baghdad to ambassador in Constantinople, May 6, 1909, Constantinople/889, Constantinople/Tauris.

14. Barclay to Grey, June 11, 1909, enclosures 2 and 3, FO 416/41; Nicolson to Grey, May 23, 1909, enclosure, FO 881/9540; and G. Lowther to Grey, July 26, 1909, enclosures 1 and 2, FO 416/41.

15. Lowther to Grey, Aug. 4, 1909, enclosure, FO 416/41.

16. Lowther to Grey, July 2 and 6, 1909, enclosure 2, FO 416/41.

17. Barclay to Grey, July 14, 1909, FO 416/41.

18. As reported in Lowther to Grey, May 12 and 15, 1909, FO 416/41.

19. As reported in Lowther to Grey, Sept. 9, 1909, enclosure, FO 416/41.

20. Lowther to Grey, May 17, 1909, FO 881/9540; Ettehadiyeh, *Peydayesh*, 184.

21. Nava'i, *Fath-e Tehran*, 10.

22. Naser al-Saltaneh Sepahdar to Mostashar al-Dowleh, Rabi' II 20, 1328/June 11, 1909, in Mostashar al-Dowleh, *Khaterat va asnad*, 4:90–92; see also unidentified document in *Owraq*, ed. Afshar, 33–36.

23. Grey to Nicolson, cable, June 3, 1909, FO 416/41; see also Grey to Nicolson, June 7, 1909, FO 416/41.

24. Nicolson to Grey, June 5, 1909, FO 416/41.

25. Barclay to Grey, June 4, 1909, FO 416/41.

26. Detailed account in Sharif-Kashani, *Vaqe'at-e ettefaqiyeh dar ruzegar*, 1:316–20.

27. Barclay to Grey, Apr. 19, 1909, FO 881/9540.

28. As reported in Barclay to Grey, June 3, 1909, FO 881/9540.

29. Quoted in Sharif-Kashani, *Vaqe'at-e ettefaqiyeh dar ruzegar*, 1:311–14.

30. Quoted in Sharif-Kashani, *Vaqe'at-e ettefaqiyeh dar ruzegar*, 1:314–16.

31. Sharif-Kashani, *Vaqe'at-e ettefaqiyeh dar ruzegar*, 1:323–24.

32. Document 25, in *Mobarezeh ba Mohammad Ali Shah*, ed. Afshar, 125–285. See also relevant discussion in chapter 2.

33. English translation of the text in Barclay to Grey, July 25, 1909, FO 416/41.

34. Grey to Hugh O'Beirne, July 1, 1909, FO 416/41.

35. As reported in O'Beirne to Grey, July 8, 1909, FO 416/41.

36. As reported in O'Beirne to Grey, June 30, 1909, FO 416/41.

37. As reported in O'Beirne to Grey, June 30, 1909, FO 416/41.

38. Barclay to Grey, July 2, 1909, FO 416/41.

39. As reported in Barclay to Grey, July 5 and 6, 1909, FO 416/41.

40. As reported in Barclay to Grey, June 29, 1909, FO 881/9540.

41. Nava'i, *Fath-e Tehran*, 68; Churchill's memorandum enclosed in Barclay to Grey, Aug. 31, 1909, FO 416/41.

42. Barclay to Grey, June 25, 1909, FO 881/9540.

43. Mostashar al-Dowleh, *Khaterat va asnad*, 1:88. See series of cables between Taqizadeh and Mostashar al-Dowleh dated Rabi' II 13, 1327/May 4, 1909, to Rajab 11, 1327/July 29, 1909, in Mostashar al-Dowleh, *Khaterat va asnad*, 2:161–95.

44. For details of Taqizadeh's decision and the resulting controversy, see *Owraq*, ed. Afshar, 25–43.

45. Mostashar al-Dowleh, *Khaterat va asnad*, 2:162.

46. Taqizadeh's cable is included in Mostashar al-Dowleh, *Khaterat va asnad*, 2:36–40.

47. Mostashar al-Dowleh, *Khaterat va asnad*, 2:41–43.

48. Amirkhizi, *Qiyam-e Azerbaijan va Sattar Khan*, 201. In his negative account of Taqizadeh's role in that episode, Ahmad Kasravi claims that British and Russian diplomats had communicated their opposition to the march and that Taqizadeh then tried to dissuade the mojahedin from proceeding to Tehran. He also believes that Taqizadeh did not want the Rashtis to acquire all the credit for the victory (*Tarikh-e hijdah saleh-ye Azerbaijan*, 28–35). Iraj Afshar, in contrast, argues that Taqizadeh and his group within the Anjoman-e Tabriz, having witnessed directly the occupation of their province, had to moderate their stance (editor's comment in *Owraq*, ed. Afshar, 26–27).

49. See detailed account in Dowlatabadi, *Hayat-e Yahya*, 3:chaps. 9, 10.

50. Lowther to Grey, July 7, 1909, FO 416/41.

51. Mostashar al-Dowleh, *Khaterat va asnad*, 2:244–45.

52. Mostashar al-Dowleh, *Khaterat va asnad*, 2:212–15, 4:189–94.

53. Taqizadeh to Mostashar al-Dowleh, Rabi‘ II 23, 1327/May 14, 1909, in Mostashar al-Dowleh, *Khaterat va asnad*, 2:167–69; see also other constitutionalists' cables sent from Tabriz to Tehran requesting the appointment of Mokhber al-Saltaneh in Mostashar al-Dowleh, *Khaterat va asnad*, 4:89–90, 98–99, 105–6, 151.

54. Mostashar al-Dowleh to Taqizadeh, Rabi‘ II 24, 1327/May 15, 1909, in Mostashar al-Dowleh, *Khaterat va asnad*, 2:170–72.

55. Taqizadeh to Mostashar al-Dowleh, Rabi‘ II 26, 1327/May 17, 1909, in Mostashar al-Dowleh, *Khaterat va asnad*, 2:173–74.

56. Mostashar al-Dowleh to Taqizadeh, Jamadi I 11, 1327/May 31, 1909, in Mostashar al-Dowleh, *Khaterat va asnad*, 2:181–82.

57. Taqizadeh to Mostashar al-Dowleh, n.d., in Mostashar al-Dowleh, *Khaterat va asnad*, 2:181–82.

58. Taqizadeh to Mostashar al-Dowleh, Jamadi I 12, 1327/June 1, 1909, in Mostashar al-Dowleh, *Khaterat va asnad*, 2:183–88.

59. Tabriz *anjoman* to Tehran, Jamadi I 15, 1327/June 4, 1909, in Mostashar al-Dowleh, *Khaterat va asnad*, 4:131–32, 2:188–89; see also Raymond Lecomte to Stephen Pichon, July 7, 8, 1909, Perse, 6:69–72.

60. Tabriz *anjoman* to Mostashar al-Dowleh, Jamadi I 24, 1327/June 13, 1909, in Mostashar al-Dowleh, *Khaterat va asnad*, 4:134–35.

61. See series of cables from Sadeq Tabataba'i to Mostashar al-Dowleh dated Rabi‘ II and Jamadi I 1327/late April–May 1909, in Mostashar al-Dowleh, *Khaterat va asnad*, 4:97–125.

62. Mostashar al-Dowleh to unknown recipient, n.d., in Mostashar al-Dowleh, *Khaterat va asnad*, 4:128.

63. Rahimi, *Qanun-e asasi-ye Iran*, 108. English translation of the complete text in Barclay to Grey, Aug. 16, 1909, enclosure, FO 416/41.

64. Mostashar al-Dowleh, *Khaterat va asnad*, 4:247.

65. Pichon to Lecomte, July 10, 1908, Perse, 3:207.

66. Pichon's handwritten note on the margin of Lecomte's report, July 2, 1909, Perse, 6:7–11. See also Pichon's response of July 6: "France must maintain its equal distance between Russia and Britain" (Perse 6:23–24).

67. Lecomte to Pichon, June 17, 1908, Perse 3:115–21.

68. Lecomte to Pichon, June 17, 1908, Perse 3:115–21.

69. Lecomte, report, July 2, 1909, Perse 6:7–11.

70. Lecomte, report, July 6, 1z909, Perse 6:22.

71. As noted in Lecomte, report, July 6, 1909, Perse 6:75–79; see also article in the *Times* (London), July 7, 1909.

72. Cable to Mostashar al-Dowleh, Jamadi II 20, 1327/July 12, 1909, in Mostashar al-Dowleh, *Khaterat va asnad*, 4:159.

73. Taqizadeh to Mostashar al-Dowleh, n.d., in *Owraq*, ed. Afshar, 161–62.

74. Mostashar al-Dowleh, *Khaterat va asnad*, 2:246.

75. See the account of these meetings in Nava'i, *Fath-e Tehran*, chap. 1.

76. Barclay to Grey, July 12, 1909, FO 416/41.

77. Barclay to Grey, July 12, 1909, enclosure 1, FO 416/41, italics in original.

78. Barclay to Grey, July 12, 1909, enclosure 3, FO 416/41.

79. Barclay to Grey, July 1, 1909, FO 416/41.

80. Nava'i, *Fath-e Tehran*, 79–86, 178–93; Malekzadeh, *Tarikh-e enqelab-e mashrutiyat-e Iran*, 3:1174–230; Sharif-Kashani, *Vaqe'at-e ettefaqiyeh dar ruzegar*, 2:389–408; Berberian, *The Love of Freedom Has No Fatherland*, 143.

81. As reported in Lynch to Browne, July 16, 1909, box 9, Browne Papers.

82. Barclay to Grey, July 12, enclosure 3, FO 416/41.

83. Fraser, *Persia and Turkey in Revolt*, 142.

84. Fraser, *Persia and Turkey in Revolt*, 128.

85. Fraser, *Persia and Turkey in Revolt*, 128.

86. Fraser, *Persia and Turkey in Revolt*, 130.

87. Churchill, memorandum, July 16, 1909, enclosure 1, FO 416/41.

88. As reported in O'Beirne to Grey, July 8, 1909, FO 416/41.

4. Prelude to the Second Majles

1. Vladimir Lyakhof, interview, *Zakafkaz*, July 31, 1909, reprinted in *Sorush*, no. 7 (Sept. 2, 1909).

2. Mostashar al-Dowleh, *Khaterat va asnad*, 2:98–99.

3. Lecomte to Paris, cable, July 13, 1909, Perse 6:98.

4. Lecomte to Paris, cable, July 13, 1909, Perse 6:98.

5. Fraser, *Persia and Turkey in Revolt*, 179. See Taqizadeh's rebuttal of Fraser's articles in *Zendegani-ye tufani*, 103–4.

6. Lynch to Browne, July 16, 1909, box 9, Browne Papers. See also the reports by Samad Khan Momtaz al-Saltaneh, the Persian ambassador to Paris, to Mostashar al-Dowleh, in Mostashar al-Dowleh, *Khaterat va asnad*, 2:94, 111–12, 120–22.

7. Mostashar al-Dowleh, *Khaterat va asnad*, 2:107–11.

8. Dehkhoda (Istanbul) to unnamed statesman (Tehran), n.d., in *Namehha-ye siyasi-ye Dehkhoda*, ed. Afshar, 65–74.

9. *Sorush*, no. 10 (Oct. 103, 1909).

10. *Sorush*, no. 4 (July 21, 1909), emphasis added.

11. *Sorush*, no. 6 (Oct. 19, 1909).

12. *Sorush*, no. 5 (July 28, 1909).

13. *Sorush*, no. 6 (Aug. 19, 1909).

14. *Sorush*, no. 11 (Oct. 20, 1909).

15. *Sorush*, no. 10 (Oct. 13, 1909).

16. *Sorush*, no. 10 (Oct. 13, 1909).

17. *Sorush*, no. 2 (July 7, 1909).

18. *Sorush*, no. 2 (July 7, 1909).

19. *Sorush*, no. 2 (July 7, 1909), no. 3 (July 14, 1909), no. 4 (July 24, 1909).

20. Panoff's letter printed in *Sorush*, no. 3 (July 14, 1909).

21. Barclay, in fact, depicted Najaf and Karbala as "the source for the widespread anti-Russian incitement," with some *mojtaheds* even threatening to come personally to Tehran to "preach holy war" (Barclay to Grey, Aug. 10, 1909, FO 416/41). A week later a British officer named Ramsey met with Khorasani's son and Behbahani's son-in-law, who complained of the presence of Russian troops and the British "passive attitude" (Ramsey [full name not known], memorandum, in G. Lowther to Grey, Aug. 17, 1909, enclosure 2, FO 416/41).

22. *Sorush*, no. 2 (July 7, 1909).

23. Report signed by Mohammad Reza to the Anjoman-e Sa'adat, Oct. 10, 1909, in *Mobarezeh ba Mohammad Ali Shah*, ed. Afshar, 401–2.

24. *Sorush*, no. 4 (July 21, 1909).

25. *Sorush*, no. 4 (July 21, 1909). Some preachers in Tabriz reportedly called for such a boycott of Russian trade, "but the agitation has subsided, entirely unsuccessful," Barclay wrote to Grey (July 20, 1909, FO 416/41).

26. *Sorush*, no. 7 (Sept. 2, 1909); no. 14 (Nov. 22, 1909).

27. *Sorush*, no. 3 (July 14, 1909). Here "alien countries" meant Arabs and Islam, a sentiment already found in late-nineteenth-century nationalist Persian literature. See Bayat, *Mysticism and Dissent*, chap. 5.

28. For a complete list of the committee membership, see Malekzadeh, *Tarikh-e enqelab-e mashrutiyat-e Iran*, 3:1237.

29. Malekzadeh, *Tarikh-e enqelab-e mashrutiyat-e Iran*, 3:1247, 1250–51; Kasravi, *Tarikh-e hijdah saleh-ye Azerbaijan*, 61–62.

30. Malekzadeh, *Tarikh-e enqelab-e mashrutiyat-e Iran*, 3:1252; Sharif-Kashani, *Vaqe'at-e ettefaqiyeh dar ruzegar*, 2:378.

31. Sharif-Kashani, *Vaqe'at-e ettefaqiyeh dar ruzegar*, 2:374; Nava'i, *Dowlatha-ye Iran*, 92.

32. G. Newell, confidential memo, July 21, 1909, FO 416/41.

33. The estimated exchange rate at the time was one toman to one US dollar.

34. Mostashar al-Dowleh, *Khaterat va asnad*, 1:294–98; Barclay to Grey, Sept. 9, 1909, enclosure 1, FO 416/41.

35. Barclay to Grey, Aug. 12, 1909, FO 416/41.

36. Mostashar al-Dowleh, *Khaterat va asnad*, 1:163.

37. O'Beirne to Grey, Aug. 13, 1909, FO 416/41.

38. Sharif-Kashani, *Vaqe'at-e ettefaqiyeh dar ruzegar*, 2:479.

39. Malekzadeh, *Tarikh-e enqelab-e mashrutiyat-e Iran*, 3:1278–79; Kasravi, *Tarikh-e hijdah saleh-ye Azerbaijan*, 68.

40. Kasravi, *Tarikh-e hijdah saleh-ye Azerbaijan*, 74. But Kasravi does not provide any answer to his query.

41. Mirza Aqa Farshi to Mostashar al-Dowleh, Rajab 7, 1327/July 25, 1909, in Mostashar al-Dowleh, *Khaterat va asnad*, 2:253–56.

42. Anjoman-e Sa'adat to Mostashar al-Dowleh, Rajab 16, 1327/Aug. 3, 1909, in Mostashar al-Dowleh, *Khaterat va asnad*, 2:256–57.

43. Samad Khan Momtaz al-Saltaneh to Mostashar al-Dowleh, Rajab 2, 1327/July 20, 1909, in Mostashar al-Dowleh, *Khaterat va asnad*, 2:250–52. The Persian ambassador had

months earlier written a letter to Taqizadeh, then still in London, assuring him of the active support of the French government and Freemasons for the restoration of the Constitution (Momtaz al-Dowleh to Taqizadeh, Nov. 25, 1908, in *Owraq*, ed. Afshar, 530–31).

44. Morel, Hakim al-Molk, and Zoka' al-Molk to Grand Orient Supreme Council, Apr. 16, 1909, Réveil de l'Iran file.

45. Unsigned letter, May 24, 1909, Réveil de l'Iran file.

46. Unsigned letter, May 24, 1909, Réveil de l'Iran file. Malekzadeh also briefly mentions such a memorial ceremony held in Tehran to honor the three "martyrs" (*Tarikh-e enqelab-e mashrutiyat-e Iran*, 3:1244).

47. Quoted in Malekzadeh, *Tarikh-e enqelab-e mashrutiyat-e Iran*, 3:1259.

48. For detailed eyewitness accounts of Nuri's last days, see Ansari, *Shaikh Fazlollah Nuri*, chaps. 7 and 8, and Torkaman, *Shaikh Shahid Fazlollah Nuri*, 1:17–20, 2:285–312.

49. Quoted in Ansari, *Shaikh Fazlollah Nuri*, 233.

50. This letter is cited in Martin, *Islam and Modernism*, 188.

51. Sharif-Kashani, *Vaqe'at-e ettefaqiyeh dar ruzegar*, 2:377.

52. Quoted in Sharif-Kashani, *Vaqe'at-e ettefaqiyeh dar ruzegar*, 2:377–78, where "Jeunes Persans" is given in transliterated French.

53. Shaikh Ibrahim Zanjani, *Khaterat-e Shaikh Ibrahim Zanjani*, 51.

54. Zanjani, *Khaterat-e Shaikh Ibrahim Zanjani*, 83–84.

55. Zanjani, *Khaterat-e Shaikh Ibrahim Zanjani*, 85, 88–89.

56. Zanjani, *Khaterat-e Shaikh Ibrahim Zanjani*, 29–30, 53.

57. Zanjani, *Khaterat-e Shaikh Ibrahim Zanjani*, 29.

58. Zanjani, *Khaterat-e Shaikh Ibrahim Zanjani*, 32–50.

59. Kasravi, *Tarikh-e hijdah saleh-ye Azerbaijan*, 67.

60. The leaflet is reprinted in Malekzadeh, *Tarikh-e enqelab-e mashrutiyat-e Iran*, 3:1261–68; for a slight variation of the leaflet's text, see also Ansari, *Shaikh Fazlollah Nuri*, 240–47.

61. For details of these events, see Bayat, *Iran's First Revolution*, chap. 9.

62. Malekzadeh, *Tarikh-e enqelab-e mashrutiyat-e Iran*, 3:1271–72; Torkaman, *Shaikh Shahid Fazlollah Nuri*, 2:300.

63. Sharif-Kashani, *Vaqe'at-e ettefaqiyeh dar ruzegar*, 2:378.

64. Taqizadeh, *Zendegani-ye tufani*, 138, 139.

65. Dowlatabadi, *Hayat-e Yahya* 3:111.

66. Taqizadeh, *Zendegani-ye tufani*, 138.

67. Quoted in Sharif-Kashani, *Vaqe'at-e ettefaqiyeh dar ruzegar*, 2:411.

68. *Ruznameh-ye Majles*, Rajab 14, 1327/Aug. 1, 1909.

69. Barclay to Grey, Aug. 10, 1909, FO 416/41.

70. Martin, *Islam and Modernism*, 193–94.

71. See Bayat, *Iran's First Revolution*, 148–49, 172–78.

72. Tabataba'i, *Yaddashtha-ye Seyyed Mohammad Tabataba'i*, 86.

73. Tabataba'i, *Yaddashtha-ye Seyyed Mohammad Tabataba'i*, 68.

74. Sharif-Kashani, *Vaqe'at-e ettefaqiyeh dar ruzegar*, 2:371. However, no available source mentions any significant number of people killed in the capital.

75. Adamiyat, *Fekr-e demokrasi-ejtema'i*, 144.

76. Malekzadeh, *Tarikh-e enqelab-e mashrutiyat-e Iran*, 3:1281–82; Taqizadeh, *Zendegani-ye tufani*, 135; Kasravi, *Tarikh-e hijdah saleh-ye Azerbaijan*, 73; Dowlatabadi, *Hayat-e Yahya*, 3:124; Sharif-Kashani, *Vaqe'at-e ettefaqiyeh dar ruzegar*, 2:375.

77. Barclay to Grey, Aug. 7, 1909, FO 416/41.

78. Taqizadeh, *Zendegani-ye tufani*, 121.

79. Taqizadeh, *Zendegani-ye tufani*, 136. Kasravi shares this view of the Rashti mojahedin, Yeprem Khan, and the Tarbiyat brothers as the most important leaders of the march to Tehran from the north (*Tarikh-e hijdah saleh-ye Azerbaijan*, 26–27). Armenian sources also emphasize the role played by Iranian-born and Caucasian Armenians as well as Georgians in the march (see, e.g., Berberian, *The Love of Freedom Has No Fatherland*, 133).

80. Editor's description in *Owraq*, ed. Afshar, 6–25, and sources cited there.

81. Barclay to Grey, Sept. 4, 1909, FO 416/41.

82. Taqizadeh, *Zendegani-ye tufani*, 150.

83. See list of members with slight variations in Sharif-Kashani, *Vaqe'at-e ettefaqiyeh dar ruzegar*, 2:421; Malekzadeh, *Tarikh-e enqelab-e mashrutiyat-e Iran*, 3:1256; and Mostashar al-Dowleh, *Khaterat va asnad*, 1:157.

84. Dowlatabadi, *Hayat-e Yahya*, 3:120.

85. Sharif-Kashani, *Vaqe'at-e ettefaqiyeh dar ruzegar*, 2:384.

86. Letters to Taqizadeh in *Owraq*, ed. Afshar, 523–24 (quotation), 162–63, 164, 542–44, 555–58, 573–79. See also Mirza Aqa Isfahani to Browne, Sept. 7, 1908, box 2, Browne Papers.

87. Barclay to Grey, Sept. 9, 1909, FO 416/41.

88. Malekzadeh, *Tarikh-e enqelab-e mashrutiyat-e Iran*, 3:1281–82.

89. Sharif-Kashani, *Vaqe'at-e ettefaqiyeh dar ruzegar*, 2:421–22; Dowlatabadi concurs (*Hayat-e Yahya*, 3:120).

90. Taqizadeh, *Zendegani-ye tufani*, 151.

91. Dowlatabadi, *Hayat-e Yahya*, 3:126.

92. Taqizadeh to the Gilan *anjoman*, n.d., in *Owraq*, ed. Afshar, 175–80.

93. Mirza Musa Tupchi to Mo'azed al-Saltaneh, Oct. 7, 1909, in *Mobarezeh ba Mohammad Ali Shah*, ed. Afshar, 141; Assadollah Mamaqani to Mo'azed al-Saltaneh, Oct. 9, 1909, in *Mobarezeh ba Mohammad Ali Shah*, ed. Afshar, 398–400; Hosain Danesh, letter to the editor, *Sorush*, no. 7 (Sept. 2, 1909).

94. A. A., no title, *Sorush*, no. 14 (Nov. 22, 1909); Shaikh Hasan Tabrizi, letter to the editor, *Sorush*, no. 7 (Sept. 2, 1909).

95. Malekzadeh, *Tarikh-e enqelab-e mashrutiyat-e Iran*, 3:1274–75.

96. Barclay to Grey, Aug. 12, 1909, FO 416/41.

97. Barclay to Grey, Aug. 10, 1909, FO 416/41.

98. As reported in O'Beirne to Grey, Sept. 6, 1909, FO 416/41.

99. Barclay to Grey, Sept. 13, 23, 1909, FO 416/41.

100. Barclay to Grey, Sept. 13, 23, 1909, FO 416/41.

101. As reported in Barclay to Grey, Sept. 9, 1909, FO 416/41.

102. Barclay to Grey, Aug. 10, 1909, FO 416/41.

103. Malekzadeh, *Tarikh-e enqelab-e mashrutiyat-e Iran*, 3:1288; Taqizadeh, *Zendegani-ye tufani*, 135; documents 9 to 13 in *Owraq*, ed. Afshar, 300–304; Mostashar al-Dowleh, *Khaterat va asnad*, 1:157, 159, 161, 183, and the appendix.

104. Sharif-Kashani, *Vaqe'at-e ettefaqiyeh dar ruzegar*, 2:430.

105. Mostashar al-Dowleh, *Khaterat va asnad*, 1:167.

106. Sharif-Kashani, *Vaqe'at-e ettefaqiyeh dar ruzegar*, 2:409.

107. Sharif-Kashani, *Vaqe'at-e ettefaqiyeh dar ruzegar*, 2:123.

108. The term *parti-bazi* survives to the present time in its pejorative but generally nonpolitical meaning: having "the right connections" to attain personal benefits.

109. *Bayan-nameh*, n.d., reprinted in *Mobarezeh ba Mohammad Ali Shah*, ed. Afshar, 435–46.

110. Dehkhoda (Istanbul) to unnamed statesman, n.d., in *Namehha-ye siyasi-ye Dehkhoda*, ed. Afshar, 65–74.

111. This pamphlet is reprinted in Sharif-Kashani, *Vaqe'at-e ettefaqiyeh dar ruzegar*, 2:484–86. It is worth noting that Sharif-Kashani was personally close to the Sepahdar.

112. Pamphlet reprinted in Sharif-Kashani, *Vaqe'at-e ettefaqiyeh dar ruzegar*, 2:486–88.

113. Pamphlet reprinted in Sharif-Kashani, *Vaqe'at-e ettefaqiyeh dar ruzegar*, 2:489–91.

114. Taqizadeh to the Gilan *anjoman*, n.d. in *Owraq*, ed. Afshar, 175–80.

115. Dowlatabadi, *Hayat-e Yahya*, 3:129.

116. Dowlatabadi, *Hayat-e Yahya*, 3:121.

5. The Parties

1. Several drafts of the speech are printed in Mostashar al-Dowleh, *Khaterat va asnad*, 1:185–87, 1:313–14, 2:82. The drafts are almost identical, with minimal differences. Kasravi claims that some of the speeches delivered that day mentioned Browne and Lynch by name (*Tarikh-e hijdah saleh-ye Azerbaijan*, 78–79). In *The Persian Revolution*, Browne presents a slight variation of the text in English translation as a speech given by the Sepahdar (336–38).

2. Speech by an unidentified person, text in Mostashar al-Dowleh, *Khaterat va asnad*, 2:85–87.

3. Malekzadeh, *Tarikh-e enqelab-e mashrutiyat-e Iran*, 3:1287. Sharif-Kashani, *Vaqe'at-e ettefaqiyeh dar ruzegar*, 2:425.

4. *Ruznameh-ye Majles*, Rajab 1327/July 27, 1909.

5. Mostashar al-Dowleh, *Khaterat va asnad*, 1:176. See text of the electoral law in *Ruznameh-ye Majles*, Rajab 9, 1327/July 27, 1909; see also Ettehadiyeh, *Peydayesh*, 189–91. For English texts, see Browne, *The Persian Revolution*, 385–400, and Barclay to Grey, Aug. 16, 1909, enclosure, FO 416/41.

6. Ettehadiyeh, *Peydayesh*, 189.

7. Shaji'i, *Namayandegan-e Majles*, 185.

8. Sharif-Kashani, *Vaqe'at-e ettefaqiyeh dar ruzegar*, 2:445.

9. Fathi, *Zendeginameh-ye shahid Theqat al-Islam*, 499.

10. Mirza Ali Theqat al-Islam to Mostashar al-Dowleh, July 26, 1909, and Sept. 1910, in *Nameh-ha-ye Tabriz az Theqat al-Islam*, ed. Afshar, 359–61, 371–72.

11. Sharif-Kashani, *Vaqe'at-e ettefaqiyeh dar ruzegar*, 2:376, 425; Mostashar al-Dowleh, *Khaterat va asnad*, 1:71–72.

12. Malekzadeh, *Tarikh-e enqelab-e mashrutiyat-e Iran*, 3:1322–23; see also Rezazadeh Malek, *Haidar Khan Amu Oghli*, 176.

13. See the Democrat Party's documents in *Owraq*, ed. Afshar, 348–65, 366, appendixes 1–26).

14. Appendix 10 in *Owraq*, ed. Afshar, 366.

15. Ettehadiyeh, *Peydayesh*, 190; Malekzadeh counted only twenty Democrat deputies (*Tarikh-e-enqelab-e mashrutiyat-e Iran*, 3:1329).

16. Ettehadiyeh, *Peydayesh*, 191.

17. Ettehadiyeh, *Peydayesh*, 199.

18. Vram Pilosian to Taqizadeh, Aug. 19, 1909, and Sept. 19, 1909, in *Owraq*, ed. Afshar, 243–46. Pilosian wrote all of his letters in French.

19. Unidentified document, in *Owraq*, ed. Afshar, 328–29; Ettehadiyeh, *Peydayesh*, 204. In an article dated February 28, 1910, the *Times* reached the conclusion that Armenians and Russians controlled *Iran-e now*, prompting Browne to rebut this conclusion (Browne, *The Persian Revolution*, 443).

20. And not Tigran, as Afshar surmised. See editor's note in *Armenians of Iran*, ed. Chaqueri, 115 n. 79.

21. Adamiyat, *Fekr-e azadi*, 334; Adamiyat, *Fekr-e demokrasi-ye ejtemai*, 95, 136; Bahar, *Tarikh-e mokhtasari*, 1:10; Malekzadeh, *Tarikh-e enqelab-e mashrutiyat-e Iran*, 3:1327.

22. Bahar, *Tarikh-e mokhtasari*, 2; Rezazadeh Malek, *Haidar Khan Amu Oghli*, 180.

23. Pilosian to Taqizadeh, Jan. 26, 1910, in *Owraq*, ed. Afshar, 247–50.

24. Ettehadiyeh, introduction to *Maramnameh*, ed. Ettehadiyeh, 12.

25. Malekzadeh, *Tarikh-e enqelab-e mashrutiyat-e Iran*, 3:1328.

26. Ettehadiyeh, introduction to *Maramnameh*, ed. Ettehadiyeh, 3–8.

27. See Bayat, *Iran's First Revolution*, 102–4 and sources cited there.

28. Quoted in Bayat, *Iran's First Revolution*, 104.

29. For a discussion of the Supplement to the Fundamental Law of 1907, see Rahimi, *Qanun-e asasi-ye Iran*.

30. Nonetheless, disputes arising over the exact role of religion in public affairs in the United States have never totally abated from the early days of its founding to the present. Many recent studies, including Susan Jacoby's book *Freethinkers: A History of American Secularism* and Forrest Church's work *So Help Me God: The Founding Fathers and the First Great Battle over Church and State*, attest to the recurring tension between the religious and secular tendencies in American society. Interestingly, many of the issues periodically debated in the United States were also addressed in Iranian intellectual and political circles at the turn of the twentieth century.

31. Armenians would, indeed, relentlessly campaign throughout 1909 and part of 1910 for their right to have two representatives in the Majles. See Berberian, *The Love of Freedom Has No Fatherland*, 140.

32. Taqizadeh to Browne, Mar. 30, 1911, box 1, Browne Papers.

33. Appendixes 1–3, in *Owraq*, ed. Afshar, 366.

34. The Democrats' program summarized and quoted in the editor's introduction to *Maramnameh*, ed. Ettehadiyeh, 3.

35. The Democrats' program summarized and quoted in the editor's introduction to *Maramnameh*, ed. Ettehadiyeh, 4.

36. Editor's introduction to *Maramnameh*, ed. Ettehadiyeh, 3.

37. See a similar discussion in Bayat, *Iran's First Revolution*, chap. 4.

38. Malkom Khan, the reformist intellectual, had much earlier suggested that *khaleseh*, state land, be given to peasants through a "national bank of agriculture," as Adamiyat states in *Ide'oloji*, 273, and in *Fekr-e demokrasi-ye ejtemai*, 49–50. Malkom Khan was no socialist of any description.

39. *Motahhed al-ma'al*, in *Owraq*, ed. Afshar, 353–59.

40. See two handwritten copies of the Democrat Party Central Committee's program, one in French and the other in Persian, appendixes 11–23 and 1–10, respectively, in *Owraq*, ed. Afshar, 366.

41. Summarized in editor's introduction to *Maramnameh*, ed. Ettehadiyeh, 11–19.

42. In his multivolume analysis of social democracy in the Constitutional Revolution, Adamiyat focuses on land reforms and equal distribution of wealth—in other words, on socioeconomic issues—to measure each party's and its members' progressiveness. Thus, he reaches the correct conclusion that the "radicals" failed to accomplish any serious land reform; they expressed compassion for the peasants' miserable conditions, reformed the peasants' taxation system, and banned extortion by landlords, but they did not push hard on the peasants' right to own land in the legislative debates (*Fekr-e demokrasi-ye ejtemai*, 65–66, 82–83). However, Adamiyat overlooks other equally important criteria for social change; he almost deliberately omits any discussion of the Democrats' struggle in legislating secularizing reforms, which constituted their most important contributions, as formulated in their party manifesto and program, and which eventually contributed to Taqizadeh's demise.

43. Ettehadiyeh, *Peydayesh*, 226; see also Bahar, *Tarikh-e mokhtasari ahzab*, 8.

44. *Ruznameh-ye Majles*, Rajab 3, 1327/July 21, 1909.

45. *Ruznameh-ye Majles*, Rajab 7, 1327/July 25, 1909.

46. *Ruznameh-ye Majles*, Rajab 7, 1327/July 25, 1909.

47. The text of this early statement of the Moderate Party's program is given in *Maramnameh*, ed. Ettehadiyeh, 89.

48. For the full text of the Democrats' response to the Moderates' program, see Mohammad Amin Rasulzadeh, "Tanqid-e ferqeh-ye e'tedaliyun ya ejtema'iyun- e e'tedaliyun," in *Maramnameh*, ed. Ettehadiyeh, 61–86.

49. Rasulzadeh, "Tanqid-e ferqeh," in *Maramnameh*, ed. Ettehadiyeh, 65, 67.

50. Rasulzadeh, "Tanqid-e ferqeh," in *Maramnameh*, ed. Ettehadiyeh, 68, 77.

51. Rasulzadeh, "Tanqid-e ferqeh," in *Maramnameh*, ed. Ettehadiyeh, 74, 72.

52. Rasulzadeh, "Tanqid-e ferqeh," in *Maramnameh*, ed. Ettehadiyeh, 80.

53. The text of the Moderate Party's lengthier program is given in *Maramnameh*, ed. Ettehadiyeh, 93–120.

54. Moderate Party program, in *Maramnameh*, ed. Ettehadiyeh, 96.

55. Moderate Party program, in *Maramnameh*, ed. Ettehadiyeh, 95.

56. Moderate Party program, in *Maramnameh*, ed. Ettehadiyeh, 96, 115, 102, 100, 117, 118.

57. Moderate Party program, in *Maramnameh*, ed. Ettehadiyeh, 119.

58. Moderate Party program, in *Maramnameh*, ed. Ettehadiyeh, 101.

59. Rasulzadeh, "Tanqid-e ferqeh," in *Maramnameh*, ed. Ettehadiyeh, 81.

60. "Usul-e demokrasi: Sharh-e maramnameh-ye democrat-'amiyun," in *Maramnameh*, ed. Ettehadiyeh, 33–57. Ettehadiyeh dates the essay to 1326/1908; however, it must have been written later because it refers to the Democrat and Moderate Parties' programs.

61. See, for instance, *Iran-e now*'s articles on Sha'ban 14, 1327/Aug. 31, 1909; Sha'ban 19, 1327/Sept. 15, 1909; Shawal 6, 1327/Oct. 31, 1909; Shawal 29, 1327/Nov. 13, 1909; Shawal 30, 1327/Nov. 14, 1909; and Zu'l Hejjah 22, 1327/Jan. 4, 1910.

62. *Iran-e now*, Sha'ban 2, 1327/Aug. 19, 1909, and Zu'l Qa'edeh 1, 1327/Nov. 15, 1909.

63. Berberian, *The Love of Freedom Has No Fatherland*, 75.

64. See description and analysis of these relations in Berberian, *The Love of Freedom Has No Fatherland*, chap. 3.

65. Berberian, *The Love of Freedom Has No Fatherland*, 88; text of the Protocol of the Social-Democrat Conference of October 1908, cited in *The Armenians of Iran*, ed. Chaqueri, 331–34; Afary, *The Iranian Constitutional Revolution*, 242–47.

66. Berberian, *The Love of Freedom Has No Fatherland*, 90–91.

67. Berberian, *The Love of Freedom Has No Fatherland*, 144.

68. Tigran Ter Hacobian to Taqizadeh, Jan. 21, 1910, in *Owraq*, ed. Afshar, 297, 304.

69. Berberian, *The Love of Freedom Has No Fatherland*, 98.

70. Berberian, *The Love of Freedom Has No Fatherland*, 118–21.

71. For a detailed account of these talks, see Berberian, *The Love of Freedom Has No Fatherland*, 122–25.

72. See, for instance, the sources cited in Berberian, *The Love of Freedom Has No Fatherland*, 126.

73. Yeprem Khan was highly skeptical before agreeing to Dashnak participation (see sources cited in Berberian, *The Love of Freedom Has No Fatherland*, 126–27).

74. Berberian, *The Love of Freedom Has No Fatherland*, 128.

75. Berberian cites a letter dated January 11, 1909, sent by the Azerbaijan Committee informing the Western Bureau that Taqizadeh had initiated the invitation (*The Love of Freedom Has No Fatherland*, 135).

76. Berberian, *The Love of Freedom Has No Fatherland*, 128.

77. See, for instance, the correspondence by Pilosian and Tigran in *Owraq*, ed. Afshar, 238–322.

78. Pilosian to Taqizadeh, Aug. 19, 1909, in *Owraq*, ed. Afshar, 238–42.

79. Pilosian to Taqizadeh, Sept. 19, 1909, in *Owraq*, ed. Afshar, 243–46.

80. Pilosian to Taqizadeh, Jan. 26, 1910, in *Owraq*, ed. Afshar, 247–50.

81. Pilosian to Taqizadeh, Feb. 3, 1910, in *Owraq*, ed. Afshar, 251–62.

82. Tigran to Taqizadeh, Jan. 21, 1910, in *Owraq*, ed. Afshar, 303–4.

83. Pilosian to Taqizadeh, Jan. 26, 1910, in *Owraq*, ed. Afshar, 240, and Feb. 3, 1910, 251–62.

84. Pilosian to Taqizadeh, Jan. 26, and Feb. 3, 1910, in *Owraq*, ed. Afshar, 240, 254–55.

85. Pilosian to Taqizadeh, Feb. 3, 1910, in *Owraq*, ed. Afshar, 251–52.

86. Taqizadeh to unknown recipient, n.d., in *Owraq*, ed. Afshar, 220.

87. Ettehadiyeh, *Peydayesh*, 200.

88. Ettehadiyeh, *Peydayesh*, 200, 240 n. 6.

89. Ettehadiyeh, *Peydayesh*, 200.

90. Adamiyat declares Rasulzadeh's pamphlet to be the "first published essay in Persian on record" to discuss social democracy extensively (*Ide'oloji*, 285). However, Nariman Narimanov's Persian translation of the Moslem Social-Democratic Workers Party program had been printed years earlier in the period of the first Majles.

91. Bahar, *Tarikh-e mokhtasari*, 2.

92. Assadollah Mamaqani to Mo'azed al-Saltaneh, Oct. 9, 1909, in *Mobarezeh ba Mohammad Ali Shah*, ed. Afshar, 398–400; see also Mahmud Tahbaz to Mo'azed al-Saltaneh, Sept. 1, 1909, in *Mobarezeh ba Mohammad Ali Shah*, ed. Afshar, 390.

93. "Maramnameh-ye ferqeh-ye taraqi va tamaddon tam ya kheyal-e kham baraye farib-e 'a'am," in *Maramnameh*, ed. Ettehadiyyeh, 123–30.

94. *Iran-e now*, Zu'l Qa'edeh 14, 1327/Nov. 27, 1909.

95. Editor's introduction to and texts of the parties' programs in *Maramnameh*, ed. Ettehadiyeh, 33–57, 139.

96. Association of Iran's Liberals party program, in *Maramnameh*, ed. Ettehadiyeh, 147–53.

6. Legislative Reforms

1. Momtaz al-Saltaneh to Taqizadeh, Ramazan 4, 1327/Sept. 5, 19, 1909, in *Owraq*, ed. Afshar, 573–79.

2. As already stated, the Moderate program was formulated in the summer of 1910. For the sake of convenience, I generally refer to the factions as the Democrat Party and the Moderate Party, as they came to be referred to in most chronicles.

3. Taqizadeh to Browne, Oct. 11, 1909, box 1, Browne Papers.

4. Lecomte, report on Taqizadeh, Aug. 13, 1909, Perse, 6:210–14.

5. Barclay to Grey, Nov. 21, 1909, FO 881/9633.

6. Barclay to Grey, Nov. 4, 1909, FO 881/9633.

7. *Mozakerat*, Moharram 29, 1328/Feb. 10, 1910.

8. *Mozakerat*, Rabi' I 1, 1328/Mar. 13, 1910.

9. *Mozakerat*, Rabi' I 8, 1328/Mar. 20, 1910.

10. Lecomte, report on Taqizadeh, Aug. 13, 1909, Perse, 6:210.

11. In Persian, *ma'ref va fava'ed-e 'ameh*, education and public works.

12. Malekzadeh, *Tarikh-e enqelab-e mashrutiyat-e Iran*, 3:1364. I have not seen a copy of Sani' al-Dowleh's treatise.

13. *Mozakerat*, Zu'l Qa'edeh 23, 1327/Dec. 6, 1909.

14. *Mozakerat*, Rabi' I 15, 1328/Apr. 27, 1910.

15. *Mozakerat*, Moharram 20, 1328/Feb. 10, 1910.

16. Barclay to Grey, Feb. 19, 1910, FO 416/43.

17. Quoted in Aryanpur, *Az Saba ta Nima*, 1:289–90.

18. Included in Sharif-Kashani, *Vaqe'at-e ettefaqiyeh dar ruzegar*, 2:463–64.

19. Browne to Taqizadeh, Oct. 16, 1909, in *Nameh-ha-ye Edvard Browne*, ed. Zaryab and Afshar, 22–25; see also Churchill's monthly summary ending Dec. 1909, enclosure, FO 881/9633.

20. Dowlatabadi, *Hayat-e Yahya*, 3:133.

21. As reported in Barclay to Grey, Sept. 9, 1909, FO 416/41.

22. Barclay to Grey, Aug. 10, 1909, FO 416/41. For more on the relations between Rahim Khan and the Russians, see Nicolson's dispatches from Moscow, Nov. 11, 12, 1909, FO 881/9633. See also the letter of a local official to Mostashar al-Dowleh, Sha'ban 9, 1327/Aug. 26, 1909, in *Owraq*, ed. Afshar, 561–66.

23. Barclay to Grey, Sept. 12, 1909, FO 416/41.

24. As reported in Barclay to Grey, Oct. 23, 1909, FO 416/42.

25. Barclay to Grey, Oct. 23, 1909, FO 416/42. See also the statement of the Russian minister of foreign affairs to the British envoy in St. Petersburg, expressing his doubt that Yeprem Khan really defeated Rahim Khan, which had enhanced the Persian government's prestige (Jan. 6, 1910, FO 416/43), and Smart's report, enclosed in Barclay to Grey, Jan. 27, 1910, 416/43.

26. Barclay to Grey, Feb. 5, 7, 1910, 416/43.

27. Dowlatabadi, *Hayat-e Yahya*, 1:124–25; Sharif-Kashani, *Vaqe'at-e ettefaqiyeh dar ruzegar*, 2:474; *Mozakerat*, Moharram 24, 1328/Feb. 5, 1910; Mostashar al-Dowleh, *Khaterat va asnad*, 2:278–80. These accounts, as usual, offer some variations reflecting the authors' personal biases. Furthermore, their chronologies slightly vary. Generally speaking, eyewitness accounts of the revolution fail to date various events accurately, rendering difficult the historian's task to corroborate them.

28. Kasravi, *Tarikh-e hijdah saleh-ye Azerbaijan*, 85–93; Malekzadeh, *Tarikh-e enqelab-e mashrutiyat-e Iran*, 3:1302–9.

29. British envoy to St. Petersburg to Grey, Mar. 11, 1910, FO 416/43; Barclay to Grey, Mar. 12, 1910, FO 416/43.

30. Malekzadeh, *Tarikh-e enqelab-e mashrutiyat-e Iran*, 3:1315–16.

31. Mostashar al-Dowleh, *Khaterat va asnad*, 1:188–89, 2:303; Nava'i, *Fath-e Tehran*, 188–89; Amirkhizi, *Qiyam-e Azerbaijan va Sattar Khan*, 461–80.

32. *Mozakerat*, Moharram 6, 13, 1328/Jan. 18, 25, 1910.

33. *Mozakerat*, Rabi' I 21, 1328/Feb. 2, 1910.

34. *Mozakerat*, Safar 22, 1328/Mar. 5, 1910.

35. *Mozakerat*, Jamadi II 13, 1328/June 22, 1910.

36. *Mozakerat*, Jamadi II 13, 1328/June 22, 1910.

37. *Mozakerat*, Jamadi II 13, 1328/June 22, 1910.

38. *Mozakerat*, Rabi' I 21, 1328/Apr. 2, 1910.

39. *Mozakerat*, Rabi' I 21, 1328/Apr. 2, 1910.

40. *Mozakerat*, Rabi' II 10, 1328/Apr. 22, 1910.

41. *Mozakerat*, Rabi' II 10, 1328/Apr. 22, 1910. For a detailed account of existing schools at that time, see Ringer, *Education, Religion, and the Discourse of Cultural Reform in Qajar Iran* and sources cited there.

42. *Mozakerat*, Rabi' II 10, 1328/Apr. 22, 1910.

43. *Mozakerat*, Rabi' II 15, 21, 1328/Apr. 27, May 3, 1910.

44. *Mozakerat*, Rabi' II 8, 1328/Apr. 20, 1910.

45. *Mozakerat*, Rabi' II 10, 1328/Apr. 22, 1910.

46. Browne to Taqizadeh, Oct. 16, 1909, in *Nameh-ha-ye Edvard Browne*, ed. Zaryab and Afshar, 22–25.

47. Paul Courbault to the Supreme Council, Feb. 1910, Le Réveil de l'Iran file.

48. Courbault to the Supreme Council, Apr. 1910, Le Réveil de l'Iran file.

49. Nicolas, report to the Quai d'Orsey, Mar. 4, 1910, Tauris/8, Constantinople/Tauris.

50. Nicolas, reports, Sept. 26, Nov. 5, 1910; Feb. 15, 25, 1911; Jan. 14, 1912, Tauris/8, Constantinople/Tauris.

51. Nicolas, report, Mar. 20, 1912, code 10, Tauris/8, Constantinople/Tauris.

52. Ringer, *Education, Religion, and the Discourse of Cultural Reform in Qajar Iran.*

53. *Mozakerat*, Rabi' II 22, 1328/May 4, 1910; Shaji'i, *Namayandegan-e Majles*, 140.

54. *Mozakerat*, Safar 15, 18, 1328/Feb. 26, Mar. 1, 1910.

55. *Mozakerat*, Safar 20, 1328/Mar. 3, 1910.

56. *Mozakerat*, Safar 4, 1328/Feb. 15, 1910.

57. Unknown sender to Mostashar al-Dowleh, Dec. 1909, in Mostashar al-Dowleh, *Khaterat va asnad*, 2:276–77.

58. *Mozakerat*, Rabi' I 18, 1328/Mar. 30, 1910.

59. *Mozakerat*, Rabi' II 29, 1328/May 11,1910.

60. *Mozakerat*, Jamadi I 2, 1328/May 12, 1910.

61. *Mozakerat*, Jamadi I, 7, 1328/May 17, 1910.

62. *Mozakerat*, Jamadi I, 7, 1328/May 17, 1910.

63. *Mozakerat*, Jamadi I 16, 1328/May 26, 1910.

64. *Mozakerat*, Jamadi I 25, 1328/June 4, 1910.

65. As reported in Charles Marling to Grey, May 14, 1910, FO 416/44.

66. As reported in Marling to Grey, May 14, 1910, FO 416/44.

67. Consul Crow to acting *vali* of Bussorah, May 27, 1910, FO 416/44. See also Foreign Office to Lieutenant-Colonel Cox, June 27, 1910, FO 416/44.

68. *Mozakerat*, Jamadi II 10, 1328/June 19, 1910.

69. *Mozakerat*, Jamadi II 10, 1328/June 19, 1910.

70. *Mozakerat*, Jamadi II 20, 1328/June 29, 1910.

71. In the minutes of an earlier session, Khodadad Parsi is referred to as "Shahriyar Farsi Sasani" (*Mozakerat*, Rabi' I, 21, 1328/Mar. 31, 1910).

72. *Mozakerat*, Jamadi II 22, 1328/July 1, 1910.

73. *Mozakerat*, Zu'l Qa'edeh 23, 1327/Dec. 5, 1909.

74. *Mozakerat*, Zu'l Hejjah 11, 1327/Dec. 24, 1909.

75. *Mozakerat*, Zu'l Hejjah 9, 1327/Dec. 22, 1909.

76. *Mozakerat*, Moharram 3, 1328/Jan. 15, 1910.

77. *Mozakerat*, Safar 1, 1328/Feb. 12, 1910.

78. *Mozakerat*, Safar 15, 1328/Feb. 26, 1910; *Mozakerat*, Rabi' I 26, 1328/Apr. 7, 1910.

79. *Mozakerat*, Jamadi I 4, 1328/May 14, 1910.

80. *Mozakerat*, Rabi' I 28, 1328/Apr. 9, 1910.

81. *Mozakerat*, Jamadi I 7, 1328/17 May 17, 1910.
82. *Mozakerat*, Jamadi II 20, 22, 1328/June 29, July 1, 1910.
83. *Mozakerat*, Jamadi II 20, 22, 1328/June 29, July 1, 1910.
84. *Mozakerat*, Jamadi II 29, 1328/July 8, 1910.
85. *Mozakerat*, Jamadi II 29, 1328/July 8, 1910.
86. *Mozakerat*, Jamadi II 29, 1328/July 8, 1910.
87. *Mozakerat*, Jamadi II 29, 1328/July 8, 1910.
88. *Mozakerat*, Rajab 5, 1328/July 13, 1910.
89. See the entire debate of that session in *Mozakerat*, Rajab 5, 1328/July 13, 1910.

7. European Interventionism

1. Grey to Barclay, Oct. 20, 21, 1909, and Barclay to Grey, Oct. 25, 1909, FO 416/42.
2. *Mozakerat*, Safar 1, 1328/Feb. 12, 1910.
3. Clark, *Sleepwalkers*, 123.
4. Quoted in Clark, *Sleepwalkers*, 142.
5. Quoted in Clark, *Sleepwalkers*, 149.
6. Clark, *Sleepwalkers*, 161.
7. Clark, *Sleepwalkers*, 166.
8. Clark, *Sleepwalkers*, 167.
9. Clark, *Sleepwalkers*, 203.
10. For a detailed analysis of Grey's policy "dissenters," see Bonakdarian, *Britain and the Iranian Constitutional Revolution*.
11. Clark, *Sleepwalkers*, 192.
12. Clark, *Sleepwalkers*, 194.
13. Lecomte, reports, Nov. 18, and Dec. 4, 1908, Perse, 4:81–85, 4:95–99.
14. Habibi, "France and the Anglo-Russian Accords," quotation from the article's subtitle.
15. Grey to O'Beirne, Aug. 6, 1909, FO 416/41.
16. Barclay to Grey, Aug. 10, 1909, FO 416/41; Barclay to Grey, Sept. 9, 1909, FO 416/41.
17. Mostashar al-Dowleh, *Khaterat va asnad*, 1:178.
18. *Mozakerat*, Moharram 24, 1328/Feb. 5, 1910.
19. *Mozakerat*, Moharram 24, 1328/Feb. 5, 1910.
20. Barclay to Grey, Jan. 28, 1910, FO 416/43.
21. Nicolson to Grey, Nov. 3, 1909, FO 881/9633.
22. Lecomte to Paris, cable, July 13, 1909, Perse, 6:98.
23. Texts in Perse, 6:152–54.
24. Sharif-Kashani, *Vaqe'at-e ettefaqiyeh dar ruzegar*, 2:473.
25. Sharif-Kashani, *Vaqe'at-e ettefaqiyeh dar ruzegar*, 2:476–78.
26. Hasan Tabrizi to Grey, Mar. 7, 1910, English translated text in FO 416/43.
27. Nicolas, report, Feb. 15, 1910, Tauris/7, Constantinople/Tauris.
28. Russian consul Miller to French consul in Tabriz, May 18, June 2, 1910, Tauris/8, Constantinople/Tauris.

29. Nicolas, report, June 17, 19, 1910, Tauris/7, Constantinople/Tauris. Marling's account of the incident differs: he reported a Russian version that denied that the Cossacks had unlawfully entered the *mojtahed*'s house. They had waited in the courtyard for the Russian consul general to discuss the matter with him, he wrote (Marling to Grey, June 20, 1910, FO 416/44).

30. Nicolas, report, June 3, 1910, Tauris/8, Constantinople/Tauris.

31. As reported in Barclay to Grey, Feb. 6, 7, 1910, FO 416/43.

32. Harold Williams (*Morning Post* correspondent in St. Petersburg) to Browne, Feb. 24, 1910, box 9, Browne Papers.

33. Nicolson to Grey, Feb. 13, 1910, FO 416/43.

34. Lecomte, report, July 23, 1909, Perse, 6:159–67.

35. Barclay to Grey, Jan. 30, 1910, FO 416/43.

36. Browne to Taqizadeh, n.d., in *Namehha-ye Edvard Browne*, ed. Zaryab and Afshar, 26–31.

37. Browne to Taqizadeh, n.d., in *Namehha-ye Edvard Browne*, ed. Zaryab and Afshar, 22–25.

38. Mirza Musa Khan to Taqizadeh, Rabi' I 8, 1328/Apr. 19, 1910, in *Owraq*, ed. Afshar, 412–19.

39. Barclay to Grey, Jan. 24, 1910, FO 416/43.

40. Nava'i, *Dowlatha-ye Iran*, 148–51; Barclay to Grey, Jan. 18, 1910, Feb. 16, 1910, FO 416/43.

41. Barclay to Grey, Jan. 18, Feb. 16, 1910, FO 416/43.

42. Taqizadeh, *Zendegani-ye tufani*, 140–41.

43. Grey to Barclay, Sept. 1, 1909, FO 416/41.

44. *Mozakerat*, Zu'l Qa'edeh 23, 1327/Dec. 6, 1909; Safar 13, 1328/Feb. 24, 1910; Rabi' I 3, 1328/Mar. 15, 1910.

45. Anonymous cable from Tehran to Tabriz, Safar 22, 1328/Mar. 5, 1910, in *Owraq*, ed. Afshar, 398–401. Afshar mistakenly dates the cable Safar 1329/Feb. 1911; I have amended the citation to include the correct date.

46. Hosain Danesh to Browne, Mar. 12, 1910, box 1, Browne Papers.

47. Various cables, in *Owraq*, ed. Afshar, 129; see also unnamed party in Baku to Mostashar al-Dowleh, Rabi' I 15, 1328/Mar. 27, 1910, in Mostashar al-Dowleh, *Khaterat va asnad*, 2:285–86.

48. *Mozakerat*, Rabi' I 21, 1328/Apr. 2, 1910.

49. As reported in Barclay to Grey, Mar. 11, 1910, FO 416/44.

50. See various Parsis' letters to Browne, Mar. 1910, and Momtaz al-Dowleh to Browne, Mar. 8, 1910, box 2, Browne Papers.

51. Copy of the religious ruling in box 9, Browne Papers. Mateo Farzaneh confirms Khorasani's defense of Iranian Zoroastrians in *The Iranian Constitutional Revolution and the Clerical Leadership of Khurasani*, 127 and sources cited there.

52. Khorasani to Browne, Rabi' I 26, 1329/Mar. 27, 1911, box 9, Browne Papers.

53. Shaikh Hasan to Mostashar al-Dowleh, Rabi' I 4, 1328/Mar. 16, 1910, in Mostashar al-Dowleh, *Khaterat va asnad*, 2:291–94.

54. See Momtaz al-Saltaneh's reports in *Owraq*, ed. Afshar, 580–82. Momtaz al-Saltaneh favored raising funds domestically, even suggesting a national lottery to be managed by Iranian individuals or, if need be, by a French group with experience in the matter.

55. Shaikh Hasan to Mostashar al-Dowleh, Rabi' I 8, 1328/Mar. 20, 1910, in Mostashar al-Dowleh, *Khaterat va asnad*, 2:294–97.

56. Marling to Grey, May 2, 1910, enclosures 1, 2, 3, FO 416/44.

57. Grey to Marling, May 13, 1910, FO 416/44.

58. Grey to Marling, May 12, 1910, FO 416/44; Foreign Office to C. W. Wallace, May 23, 1910, FO 416/44.

59. Barclay to Grey, Mar. 15, 1910, enclosure, FO 416/44. See also a later report in Grey to Marling, May 17, 1910, FO 416/44.

60. Marling to Grey, May 31, 1910, FO 416/44.

61. As reported in Barclay to Grey, Mar. 24, 1910, enclosures 1, 2, FO 416/43.

62. As reported in Barclay to Grey, Mar. 24, 1910, enclosures 1, 2, FO 416/43.

63. Barclay to Grey, Mar. 24, 1910, enclosures 1, 2, FO 416/43.

64. Nicolas, report, Sept. 18, 1910, Tauris/8, Constantinople/Tauris.

65. McDaniel, *Shuster Mission*, 108.

66. As reported in Barclay to Grey, Apr. 8, 1910, enclosure: Churchill's memorandum, FO 416/44.

67. Nicolson to Grey, Mar. 13, 1910, FO 416/43; Barclay to Grey, Mar. 15, 17, 1910, FO 416/43.

68. Gwynn, *The Letters and Friendships of Sir Spring-Rice*, 2:101–2. See also Churchill, *The Anglo-Russian Convention of 1907*.

69. Lecomte to Pichon, Apr. 20, 1909, Constantinople/889, Constantinople/Tauris.

70. Quoted in McMeekin, *The Berlin–Baghdad Express*, 8.

71. Quoted in Clark, *Sleepwalkers*, 335.

72. As reported in Sir F. Cartwright to Grey, May 14, 1910, FO 416/44.

73. Walter Smart, report, Oct. 3, 1909, enclosure, FO 881/9633.

74. Nicolson to Grey, Mar. 14 and 29, 1910, FO 416/43.

75. Enclosure in Barclay to Grey, Feb. 16, 1910, FO 416/43.

76. Joseph Wolf to Grey, May 25, 1910, enclosure 1, FO 416/44.

77. Enclosure 2 in Nicolson to Grey, Mar. 21, 1910, FO 416/43; Nicolson to Grey, Mar. 16, 1910, FO 416/43. See also Grey to Nicolson, Mar. 16, 1910, FO 416/43; Grey to Barclay, Mar. 17, 1910, FO 416/43; Grey to Count Alexander Benckendorff, Mar. 18, 1910, FO 416/43.

78. Izvolski's denial reported in Grey to Sir Edward Goschen, the German ambassador in London, Mar. 22, 1910, FO 416/43, and Nicolson to Grey, Mar. 27, 1910, FO 416/43.

79. As reported in Nicolson to Grey, Apr. 15, 1910, FO 416/44.

80. Cartwright to Grey, May 14, 1910, FO 416/44.

81. Report of Goschen's interview with the German chancellor, May 12, 1910, FO 416/44.

82. Grey to Nicolson, May 17, 1910, FO 416/44.

83. See confidential report to Grey from his Berlin envoy, May 20, 1910, FO 416/44.

84. As reported in Nicolson to Grey, May 10, 1910, FO 416/44, and Grey to Goschen, May 31, 1910, FO 416/44.

85. As reported in Barclay to Grey, Apr. 9, 1910, FO 416/44.

86. As reported in Barclay to Grey, Apr. 10, 1910, FO 416/44.

87. Marling to Grey, June 6, 1910, FO 416/44.

88. Vakil al-Ro'aya to Mostashar al-Dowleh, Safar 29, 1328/Mar. 12, 1910, in Mostashar al-Dowleh, *Khaterat va asnad*, 2:283–84.

89. The Russian government began to worry about the viability of the Persian financial guarantees to pay off the loan because the customs revenue might be insufficient to cover the debt's principal and interest (Marling to Grey, June 20, 1910, FO 416/44).

90. Grey to Marling, June 23, 1910, FO 416/44; Grey to O'Beirne, June 23, 1910, FO 416/44.

91. Marling to Grey, Apr. 21, 1910, enclosure: Churchill's monthly summary of events, FO 416/44.

92. *Mozakerat*, Jamadi I 4 and 7, 1328/May 14 and 17, 1910.

93. Marling to Grey, June 17, 1910, FO 416/44.

94. Barclay to Grey, Apr. 17, 1910, FO 416/44.

95. Izvolski to Benckendorff, Apr. 19 and 25, 1910, FO 416/44.

96. Lecomte to Pichon, June 17, 1910, Constantinople/889, Constantinople/Tauris.

97. Marling to Grey, Apr. 21, 1910, enclosure: Churchill's monthly summary of events, FO 416/44.

98. See, for instance, Majles debates on financial issues in *Mozakerat*, Rabi' II 21, 1328/May 3, 1910.

99. *Mozakerat*, Rabi' I 15, 1328/Apr. 27, 1910.

100. Nava'i, *Dowlatha-ye Iran*, 148–51.

101. Lecomte to Pichon, May 6, 1910, Constantinople/889, Constantinople/Tauris.

102. Marling to Grey, Apr. 29, 1910, FO 416/44.

103. Nicolson to Grey, May 3, 1910, FO 416/44; Marling to Grey, May 9, 1910, FO 416/44.

104. Marling to Grey, June 17, 1910, FO 416/44.

105. Malekzadeh, *Tarikh-e enqelab-e mashrutiyat-e Iran*, 3:1284; Smart, report to Marling, May 6, 1910, enclosure, FO 416/44; Marling to Grey, June 17, 1910, FO 416/44; Barclay to Grey, Sept. 25, 1910, FO 416/44; Shuster, *Strangling of Persia*, 97–102 and sources cited there.

106. Marling to Grey, June 17, 1910, FO 416/44.

107. Marling to Grey, Apr. 30, 1910, FO 416/44; Grey to Marling, May 2, 1910, FO 416/44.

108. Nicolas, report, Feb. 26, 1910, Tauris/8, Constantinople/Tauris.

109. See Tigran and Pilosian's letters to Taqizadeh, in *Owraq*, ed. Afshar, 238–75.

110. As reported in Nicolas, report, June 21, 1910, Tauris/8, Constantinople/Tauris; see also O'Beirne to Grey, June 30, 1910, FO 416/44.

111. Smart, enclosure in Barclay to Grey, Feb. 19, 1910, FO 416/43.

112. Nicolas, report, June 17, 1910, Tauris/8, Constantinople/Tauris.

113. Nicolas, report, Mar. 9, 1910, Tauris/8, Constantinople/Tauris.

8. The Political Crisis

1. *Mozakerat*, Jamadi I 25 and Jamadi II 24, 1328/June 4 and July 3, 1910. List of donors and their contributions as well as the expenditure in Marling to Grey, July 8, 1910, enclosure 1, FO 416/45.

2. *Mozakerat*, Jamadi I 28, 1328/June 7, 1910.

3. *Mozakerat*, Jamadi I 25, 1328/June 4, 1910.

4. Marling to Grey, July 4, 1910, FO 416/45.

5. Marling to Grey, July 4, 1910, FO 416/45.

6. Mostashar al-Dowleh, *Khaterat va asnad*, 2:301–3.

7. For an interesting study of the rebel prince, see Floor, *Salar al-Dowleh*.

8. Tabriz *anjoman* to Mostashar al-Dowleh, Jamadi I 28, 1328/June 7, 1910, in Mostashar al-Dowleh, *Khaterat va asnad*, 303–5.

9. Unidentified document, Jamadi I 28, 1328/June 7, 1910, in Mostashar al-Dowleh, *Khaterat va asnad*, 303–5.

10. *Mozakerat*, Jamadi II 29, 1328/July 8, 1910.

11. *Iran-e now*, Rabi' I 5, 1328/Mar. 17, 1910; Rabi' II 23, 1328/May 5, 1910; Rabi' II 29, 1328/May 11, 1910; Jamadi I 8, 1328/May 18, 1910.

12. Marling to Grey, July 2, 12, 15, 1910, FO 416/45.

13. Sharif-Kashani, *Vaqe'at-e ettefaqiyeh dar ruzegar*, 2:418; Dowlatabadi, *Hayat-e Yahya*, 2:127.

14. Dowlatabadi, *Hayat-e Yahya*, 2:129.

15. Ayatollah Mohammad Tabataba'i's son, Mohammad Sadeq Tabataba'i, a leading member of the Moderate Party in the Majles, requested a paid leave of absence to take care of his sick father, which was granted (*Mozakerat*, Jamadi I 28, 1328/June 7, 1910).

16. Quoted in Sharif-Kashani, *Vaqe'at-e ettefaqiyeh dar ruzegar*, 2:435. Reference is here made to the bloody conflicts between the jurists and the mystics that marred the history of Iran in the eighteenth and nineteenth centuries. Shaikh al-Ra'is was a mystic but was also suspected of Babism, the nineteenth-century "heretical" movement. Many mystics had originally joined the constitutional movement. See Bayat, *Mysticism and Dissent* and sources cited there.

17. Malekzadeh, *Tarikh-e enqelab-e mashrutiyyat-e Iran*, 3:1334–35.

18. Danesh to Browne, Feb. 1911, box 1, Browne Papers.

19. See Bayat, *Mysticism and Dissent*, chap. 5.

20. Quoted in Malekzadeh, *Tarikh-e enqelab-e mashrutiyat-e Iran*, 3:1289–92, and Kasravi, *Tarikh-e hijdah saleh-ye Azerbaijan*, 69.

21. In his self-serving account of the episode, Malekzadeh claims he was instrumental in obtaining the editor's release by intervening with Behbahani on his behalf (*Tarikh-e enqelab-e mashrutiyat-e Iran*, 3:1293).

22. *Iran-e now*, Jamadi I 8, 1328/May 18, 1910. *Qisas* are Qur'anic laws that specify the irrevocable punishment of certain crimes, such as theft, adultery, usury, murder, and apostasy.

23. Mostashar al-Dowleh, *Khaterat va asnad*, 2:306–7.

24. *Mozakerat*, Jamadi I 16, 1328/May 26, 1910.

25. Seyyed Jalaluddin al-Hussaini (Mo'ayed al-Islam) to Government of Bengal, June 29, 1910, enclosure 2, FO 416/45.

26. *Mozakerat*, Rajab 4, 1328/July 12, 1910.

27. *Vaqt*, n.d., in Ettehadiyeh, *Peydayesh*, 227–29, 245 n. 72.

28. Malekzadeh, *Tarikh-e enqelab-e mashrutiyat-e Iran*, 3:1327.

29. Lecomte, report, Aug. 13, 1909, Perse, 6:210–14.

30. Lecomte, report, July 22, 1910, Constantinople/889, Constantinople/Tauris.

31. As reported in Lecomte to Pichon, Aug. 13, 1910, Constantinople/889, Constantinople/Tauris.

32. Anonymous to Taqizadeh, Shawal 19, 1327/Nov. 3, 1909, in *Owraq*, ed. Afshar, 583–84.

33. Mahmud ibn Musa to Mostashar al-Dowleh, Rabi' I 7, 1328/Mar. 19, 1910, in Mostashar al-Dowleh, *Khaterat va asnad*, 2:297–99.

34. Pilosian to Taqizadeh, Feb. 3, 1910, in *Owraq*, ed. Afshar, 251–62.

35. Nicolas, report, June 7, 1910, Tauris/8, Constantinople/Tauris. See also a Lazariste priest's report, June 4, 1910, Tauris/8, Constantinople/Tauris.

36. For a detailed analysis of the relationship of the Armenian and Iranian parties based on Armenian sources, see Berberian, *The Love of Freedom Has No Fatherland*, especially chapters 3 and 4.

37. Taqizadeh, *Zendegani-ye tufani*, 152–56. See also Nava'i, *Dowlatha-ye Iran*, 160–62, and editor's summary in *Owraq*, ed. Afshar, 230–31, which is essentially based on Taqizadeh's account, though mistakenly dates the episode much later, July 1910. Kasravi mentions the episode in just one sentence (*Tarikh-e hijdah saleh-ye Azerbaijan*, 127).

38. The text of this letter is given in *Owraq*, ed. Afshar, 207–8.

39. *Mozakerat*, Rajab 5, 1328/July 13, 1910.

40. *Mozakerat*, Rajab 5, 1328/July 13, 1910,and Rajab 7, 1328/July 15, 1910.

41. Ayatollah Abdollah Mazandarani to Mohammad Ali Badamchi, n.d., in *Owraq*, ed. Afshar, 208–12. The petition addressed to Mazandarani by an Azerbaijani constitutionalist, Mohammad Ali Badamchi, on behalf of Taqizadeh was written a day after the ayatollahs' ruling but published months later in *Habl al-matin*, Ramazan 28, 1328/Oct. 3, 1910. See also Ayatollah Khorasani's confidential letter to Browne, Moharram 5, 1329/Jan. 6, 1911, box 9, Browne Papers, expressing the same arguments against Taqizadeh and the "extremists."

42. *Mozakerat*, Rajab 4, 1328/July 12, 1910.

43. *Mozakerat*, Rajab 7, 1328/July 15, 1910.

44. Nava'i, *Dowlatha-ye Iran*, 162, 169; Malekzadeh, *Tarikh-e enqelab-e mashrutiyat-e Iran*, 3:1336; Sharif-Kashani, *Vaqe'at-e ettefaqiyeh dar ruzegar*, 3:869–70.

45. Ettehadiyeh-ye Asnaf to Mostashar al-Dowleh, n.d., in Mostashar al-Dowleh, *Khaterat va asnad*, 2:311–12.

46. *Habl al-matin*, Ramazan 28, 1328/Oct. 3, 1910, printed in *Owraq*, ed. Afshar, 212–16.

47. Nicolas to Pichon, Aug. 13, 1910, Constantinople/889, Constantinople/Tauris.

48. Pilosian to Browne, Sept. 29, 1910, box 9, Browne Papers.

49. Tigran to Taqizadeh, Nov. 1, 1910, in *Owraq*, ed. Afshar, 311–20.

50. Shaikh Ibrahim Zanjani to Taqizadeh, Shawal 18, 1328/Oct. 23, 1910, in *Owraq*, ed. Afshar, 336–45. See also Shaikh Mohammad Khiyabani's letter to Taqizadeh giving the same advice, Shawal 25, 1328/Oct. 30, 1910, in *Owraq*, ed. Afshar, 347–48.

51. As reported in Pilosian to Taqizadeh, Oct. 9, 1911, in *Owraq*, ed. Afshar, 283, 290–91. Berberian surmises that the Dashnakists felt threatened by social-democratic elements in the Democrat Party and by Rasulzadeh, *Iran-e now*'s editor (*The Love of Freedom Has No Fatherland*, 135–36).

52. Nicolas, report, Aug. 10, 1910, Tauris/8, Constantinople/Tauris.

53. Assadollah Kordestani to Browne, Jan. 8, 1911, box 2, Browne Papers.

54. Tigran to Taqizadeh, Nov. 1, 1910, in *Owraq*, ed. Afshar, 320. However, Mostashar al-Dowleh writes in his memoirs that in a meeting with Isma'il Khan Momtaz al-Dowleh and Sardar As'ad held at his home on November 4, 1910, they swore to promote national interests and the principles of the Constitution, to strengthen national independence, to befriend friends, and to combat adversaries—all in unison for the common goals (*Khaterat va asnad*, 1:319). Neither he nor Tigran mentions one another's projects, supposedly planned at the same time and for basically an identical goal.

55. Berberian, *The Love of Freedom Has No Fatherland*, 138–39.

56. Momtaz al-Dowleh to Browne, Apr. 30, 1911, box 2, Browne Papers.

57. Shaikh Hasan Tabrizi to Browne, Nov. 30, 1910, box 1, Browne Papers.

58. Tabrizi to Browne, Jan. 10, 1911, box 1, Browne Papers.

59. Vahid al-Molk to Browne, May 3, 1911, box 2, Brown Papers.

60. Major Claude Stokes to Browne, Oct. 14, 1910, box 10, Browne Papers.

61. Lecomte to Pichon, July 22, 1910, Constantinople/889, Constantinople/Tauris.

62. Churchill to Browne, July 15, 1910, "Letters from Persia, 1910–1911," ADD 7604, Browne Papers.

63. Stokes to Browne, Aug. 31, 1910, "Letters from Persia, 1910–1911," ADD 7604, Browne Papers.

64. Khorasani to Browne, Jan. 6, 1911, "confidential," box 9, Browne Papers.

65. Danesh to Browne, received on Dec. 11, 1909, box 1, Browne Papers.

66. Danesh to Browne, Feb. 1911, box 1, Browne Papers.

67. Taqizadeh to Browne, Mar. 30, 1911, box 1, Browne Papers.

68. Browne to Taqizadeh, Apr. 5, 1911, in *Namehha-ye Edvard Browne*, ed. Zaryab and Afshar, 180–82.

69. Browne to Shaikh Hasan, Feb. 15, 1911, in *Namehha-ye Edvard Browne*, ed. Zaryab and Afshar, 172–75.

70. Browne to Taqizadeh, Oct. 16, 1909, in *Namehha-ye Edvard Browne*, ed. Zaryab and Afshar, 22.

71. See, for example, Tigran to Taqizadeh, May 23, 25, 1910, in *Owraq*, ed. Afshar, 305–6, 307–10.

72. Tigran to Taqizadeh, n.d., in *Owraq*, ed. Afshar, 267–75. The date cannot be verified; Afshar, the editor of *Owraq*, mistakenly gives it as Rabi' II 28, 1328/May 9, 1910, but that puts the letter before the religious ruling against Taqizadeh and his departure from the Majles—that is, before his "current struggles."

73. Editor's comment in *Armenians of Iran*, ed. Chaqueri, 86; the English text of one such article is given in *Armenians of Iran*, ed. Chaqueri, 193–236.

74. Lecomte to Pichon, July 8, 1910, Constantinople/889, Constantinople/Tauris.

75. Malekzadeh, *Tarikh-e enqelab-e mashrutiyat-e Iran*, 3:1331.

76. *Ruznameh-ye Majles*, Zu'l Qa'edeh 3, 1328/Nov. 9, 1910; Zu'l Hejjah 1, 1328/Dec. 6, 1910; Rajab 22, 1329/July 18, 1911.

9. The Aftermath of Ayatollah Behbahani's Assassination

1. Malekzadeh, *Tarikh-e enqelab-e mashrutiyat-e Iran*, 3:1332.

2. *Mozakerat*, Rajab 12, 1328/July 20, 1910.

3. *Mozakerat*, Rajab 12, 1328/July 20, 1910.

4. *Mozakerat*, Rajab 16, 1328/July 24, 1910.

5. *Mozakerat*, Rajab 16, 1328/July 24, 1910.

6. *Mozakerat*, Rajab 16, 1328/July 24, 1910.

7. *Mozakerat*, Rajab 16, 1328/July 24, 1910.

8. *Mozakerat*, Rajab 21, 1328/July 29, 1910.

9. *Mozakerat*, Rajab 19, 1328/July 27, 1910.

10. Marling to Grey, July 29, 1910, FO 416/45.

11. Pilosian to Taqizadeh, Oct. 9, 1910, in *Owraq*, ed. Afshar, 276–91. Afshar mistakenly dates the letter 1911. Nava'i also blamed Naser al-Molk for alarming the olama in Najaf and for their decree against Taqizadeh (*Dowlatha-ye Iran*, 173).

12. Nicolson to Grey, July 20, 1910, FO 416/45; Marling to Grey, July 22, 1910, FO 416/45; Grey to Marling, July 23, 1910, FO 416/45; Grey to Benckendorff, July 28, 1910, FO 416/45; Lecomte to Pichon, July 22, 1910, Constantinople/889, Constantinople/Tauris.

13. Grey to Marling, July 29, 1910, FO 416/45.

14. Lecomte to Pichon, July 22, 1910, Constantinople/889, Constantinople/Tauris.

15. Marling to Grey, July 29, 1910, FO 416/45.

16. Marling to Grey, Aug. 11, 1910, FO 416/45.

17. *Mozakerat*, Rajab 26, 1328/Aug. 3, 1910.

18. *Mozakerat*, Rajab 26, 1328/Aug. 3, 1910.

19. Marling to Grey, Aug. 11, 1910, FO 416/45; Malekzadeh, *Tarikh-e enqelab-e mashrutiyat-e Iran*, 3:1344–54; Nava'i, *Dowlatha-ye Iran*, 169–70.

20. *Mozakerat*, Sha'ban 24 and 26, 1328/Aug. 30 and Sept. 1, 1910.

21. *Mozakerat*, Rajab 30, 1328/Aug. 8, 1910.

22. *Mozakerat*, Sha'ban 7, 1328/Aug. 13, 1910.

23. *Mozakerat*, Sha'ban 7, 1328/Aug. 13, 1910. A discrepancy in the *Mozakerat* records can be noted here. On this date, it writes, the council of five *mojtaheds* was appointed. But later, as we shall see, the issue concerning the delay in forming the council was raised again and again. See chapter 10.

24. *Ruznameh-ye Majles*, Shawal 23, 1328/Oct. 28, 1910.

25. *Iran-e now* articles summarized in Afary, *The Iranian Constitutional Revolution*, 293–97.

26. Pilosian to Taqizadeh, May 9, 1910, in *Owraq*, ed. Afshar, 267–75.

27. Pilosian to Taqizadeh, Oct. 9 and Nov. 1, 1910, in *Owraq*, ed. Afshar, 276–91, 311–20. Pilosian sometimes signed his letters as "Dehati" or "Bahr."

28. Berberian, *The Love of Freedom Has No Fatherland*, 135–37.

29. Shortly before the forced closure of the Majles, the new electoral law would finally concede two seats for the Armenians. See the conclusion.

30. *Mozakerat*, Zu'l Qa'edeh 12, 14, 23, 1328/Nov. 15, 17, 26, 1910; Berberian, *The Love of Freedom Has No Fatherland*, 139–40. Mirzayan is mentioned as Yusef Yanes in the *Mozakerat*.

31. *Mozakerat*, Zu'l Qa'edeh 28, 1328/Dec.1, 1910.

32. *Mozakerat*, Zu'l Qa'edeh 30, 1328/Dec. 3, 1910.

33. Taqizadeh to unnamed official, Ramazan 28, 1328/Oct. 3, 1910, in *Owraq*, ed. Afshar, 218–25. The editor states that the letter was not mailed, but it is nevertheless significant because it reveals Taqizadeh's new rhetoric.

34. Cited in Berberian, *The Love of Freedom Has No Fatherland*, 137.

35. A Dashnakist leader to Yeprem Khan, July 26, 1911, quoted in Berberian, *The Love of Freedom Has No Fatherland*, 153, emphasis in original.

36. Tigran to Taqizadeh, Jan. 21, 1910, in *Owraq*, ed. Afshar, 297–304.

37. Berberian, *The Love of Freedom Has No Fatherland*, 135–37, 139.

38. Berberian, *The Love of Freedom Has No Fatherland*, 162 n. 80. Berberian states that the Dashnakists left the Democrat Party when it cooperated with the Moderates. See also Ettehadiyeh, *Peydayesh*, 235, 237.

39. Berberian, *The Love of Freedom Has No Fatherland*, 142.

40. Berberian, *The Love of Freedom Has No Fatherland*, 144.

41. Browne, *The Persian Revolution*, 339.

42. Nicolas to Pichon, Aug. 13, 1910, Constantinople/889, Constantinople/Tauris.

43. Nava'i, *Dowlatha-ye Iran*, 167–68.

44. Marling to Grey, confidential, Aug. 7, 1910, FO 416/45. Marling was replacing Barclay as the British envoy, who was on summer leave and returned to Tehran in the fall.

45. Marling to Grey, Aug. 11, 1910, FO 416/45.

46. *Mozakerat*, Sha'ban 12, 1328/Aug. 18, 1910.

47. *Mozakerat*, Sha'ban 17, 1328/Aug. 23, 1910.

48. *Mozakerat*, Sha'ban 24, 1328/Aug. 30, 1910.

49. Lecomte to Pichon, July 22, 1910, Constantinople/889, Constantinople/Tauris.

50. Lecomte to Pichon, July 16, 1910, Constantinople/889, Constantinople/Tauris.

51. Marling to Grey, July 12, 1910, marked "very confidential," FO 416/45.

52. O'Beirne to Grey, July 11, 1910, enclosure, FO 416/45; Nicolson to Grey, July 31, 1910, enclosure, FO 416/45.

53. C. W. Wallace to Foreign Office, July 27, 1910, FO 416/45; Wallace to J. R. Preece, Aug. 16, 1910, enclosure, FO 416/45.

54. As reported in O'Beirne to Grey, Aug. 16, 1910, FO 416/45; O'Beirne to Grey, Aug. 21, 1910, enclosure 2, FO 416/45.

55. As reported in Nicolson to Grey, Aug. 7, 1910, enclosure, FO 416/45.

56. Grey to Barclay, Aug. 22, 1910, FO 416/45.

57. See, for instance, Wallace to Foreign Office, July 27, 1910, FO 416/45, and Foreign Office to Wallace, Aug. 3, 1910, FO 416/45.

58. Barclay to Grey, Sept. 15, 1910, FO 416/45; Seligman Brothers to Foreign Office, FO 416/45; Grey to Barclay, FO 416/45; Barclay to Grey, Sept. 16, 1910, FO 416/45.

59. Grey to O'Beirne, Sept. 16, 1910, FO 416/45; Barclay to Grey, Sept. 19, 1910, FO 416/45; Barclay to Grey, Sept. 21, 1910, FO 416/45; and papers communicated to the Foreign Office, Sept. 14–16, 1910, FO 416/45.

60. *Mozakerat*, Zu'l Hejjah 12, 1328/Dec. 15, 1910.

61. *Times* (London), May 17, 28, 29, 1910.

62. Letter signed by twenty British bankers, merchants, and manufacturers to the Manchester Chamber of Commerce, forwarded to Grey, July 28, 1910, enclosure, FO 416/45.

63. As reported in Nicolson to Grey, Aug. 3, 1910, FO 416/45.

64. As reported in Marling to Grey, Aug. 4, 1910, FO 416/45.

65. O'Beirne to Grey, Sept. 2, 1910, FO 416/45; O'Beirne to Grey, Sept. 14, 1910, FO 416/45.

66. Barclay to Grey, Sept. 3, 1910, FO 416/45; Barclay to Grey, Sept. 5, enclosure 1, FO 416/45. Barclay was often annoyed with Navab's efforts to "put a wedge" between him and his Russian colleague, "acting as if he had British sympathy and support," an impression the British envoy would dispel in his conversations with Poklewski (Barclay to Grey, Nov. 3, 1910, FO 416/46).

67. *Habl al-matin*, Sept. 12, 1910.

68. All in Marling to Grey, report, Dec. 6, 1910, enclosures 2 and 3, FO 416/46.

69. Barclay to Grey, Oct. 6, 1910, FO 416/46.

70. Copy of the note in Barclay to Grey, Oct. 14, 1910, enclosure, FO 416/46; Grey to O'Beirne, Oct. 19, 1910, FO 416/46.

71. Barclay to Grey, Oct. 29, 1910, enclosure, FO 416/46; Barclay to Grey, Nov. 18, 1910, enclosure, FO 416/46.

72. Lynch Brothers to Foreign Office, Nov. 17, 1910, FO 416/46. However, customs receipts covering ten months up to January 21, 1911, showed a decline in southern trade.

73. Sir T. Jackson to Mr. Mallet, Oct. 19, 1910, FO 416/46; Barclay to Grey, Oct. 13, 1910, FO 416/46; see also series of letters to the Foreign Office from the prospective lenders, the Seligman Brothers, the Anglo-Persian Oil Company, and the Imperial Bank of Persia, all dated Oct. 22, 1910, FO 416/46.

74. Anglo-Persian Oil Company to Foreign Office, Oct. 18, 1910, FO 416/46; Barclay to Grey, Oct. 17, FO 416/46. On the oil company's attempt to have the telephone line installed, see its correspondence with the Foreign Office, Oct. 7, 1910, FO 416/46.

75. Barclay to Grey, Nov. 3, 1910, FO 416/46.

76. Hakim al-Molk to Seligman Brothers, Oct. 10, 1910, FO 416/46; Barclay to Grey, Oct. 25, 27, 1910, FO 416/46; Seligman Brothers to Foreign Office, Oct. 25, 1910, FO 416/46; Grey to Barclay, Oct. 26, 1910, FO 416/46; details of the Imperial Bank loan contract, dated Oct. 24, 1910, in FO 416/46; T. Jackson to the Foreign Office, Nov. 3, 1910, FO 416/46.

77. Grey to O'Beirne, Nov. 4, 1910, FO 416/46.

78. A copy of the letter is included as an enclosure in Barclay to Grey, Nov. 2, 1910, FO 416/46.

79. Barclay to Grey, Nov. 20, 1910, FO 416/46.

80. Barclay to Grey, Nov. 20, 1910, FO 416/46; *Iran-e now*, Nov. 19, 1910.

81. *Iran-e now*, Nov. 14, 15, 16, 1910.

82. As reported in Goschen to Grey, Nov. 3, 1910, FO 416/46.

83. As reported in Goschen to Grey, Nov. 3, 1910, FO 416/46.

84. As reported in Goschen to Grey, Oct. 20, 1910, FO 416/46; Budapest consul general to Grey, Oct. 21, 1910, FO 416/46; Sir Rennell Rodd to Grey, Oct. 21, 1910, FO 416/46; Lowther to Grey, Oct. 24, 1910, FO 416/46; Lowther to Grey, Oct. 26, 1910, FO 416/46.

85. Grey to Barclay, Nov. 7, 1910, FO 416/46.

86. Barclay to Grey, Nov. 9, 1910, FO 416/46.

87. Grey to the Russian chargé d'affaires in London, Nov. 5, 1910, FO 416/46.

88. Grey to O'Beirne, Nov. 18, 1910, FO 416/46.

89. Text of the loan contract in Grey to O'Beirne, Nov. 18, 1910, enclosure, FO 416/46.

90. *Mozakerat*, Zu'l Hejjah 3, 1328/Dec. 6, 1910.

91. *Mozakerat*, Zu'l Hejjah 3, 1328/Dec. 6, 1910.

92. Barclay to Grey, Dec. 27, 1910, FO 416/46; text of the Majles instructions to the committee in Barclay to Grey, Jan. 23, 1911, enclosure, FO 416/47.

93. Nicolson to Grey, July 26, 1910, FO 416/45.

94. Russian consortium on the question of the Persian Railway, Aug. 9, 1910, FO 416/45.

95. Russian consortium on the question of the Persian Railway, Aug. 9, 1910, FO 416/45.

96. O'Beirne to Grey, Oct. 30, 1910, FO 416/46.

97. O'Beirne to Grey, Nov. 9, 1910, FO 416/46.

98. O'Beirne to Grey, Nov. 9, 1910, FO 416/46.

99. Bertie to Grey, Nov. 23, 1910, FO 416/46.

100. As reported in Goschen to Grey, Dec. 2, 1910, FO 416/46.

10. Battling for the Future

1. *Mozakerat*, Rajab 23, 1328/July 31, 1910.

2. *Mozakerat*, Sha'ban 10, 1328/Aug. 16, 1910.

3. *Mozakerat*, Sha'ban 28, 1328/Sept. 4, 1910.

4. See, for instance, *Mozakerat*, Sha'ban 24, 1328/Aug. 30, 1910.

5. The term *tajaddodkhah*, literally meaning "advocate of renewal," referred to modernists.

6. *Mozakerat*, Ramazan 12, 1328/Sept. 17, 1910.

7. *Mozakerat*, Moharram 19, 1329/Jan. 21, 1911.

8. *Mozakerat*, Moharram 5, 17, 19, 1329/Jan. 7, 19, 21, 1911.

9. *Mozakerat*, Rajab 23, 1328/July 31, 1910; Sha'ban 12, 1328/Aug. 18, 1910.

10. *Mozakerat*, Moharram 24, 1329/Jan. 26, 1911.

11. *Mozakerat*, Moharram 22, 1329/Jan. 24,1911.

12. *Mozakerat*, Moharram 17, 1329/Jan. 19, 1911.

13. *Mozakerat*, Sha'ban 14, 1328/Aug. 20, 1910; see also *Mozakerat*, Ramazan 3, 1328/Sept. 9, 1910.

14. *Mozakerat*, Ramazan 3, 1328/Sept. 9, 1910.

15. *Mozakerat*, Sha'ban 17, 1328/Aug. 23, 1910.

16. *Mozakerat*, Sha'ban 24, 1328/Aug. 30, 1910.
17. *Mozakerat*, Moharram 22, 1329/Jan. 24, 1911.
18. *Mozakerat*, Moharram 19, 1329/Jan. 21, 1911.
19. *Mozakerat*, Moharram 19, 1329/Jan. 21, 1911.
20. *Mozakerat*, Zu'l Qa'edeh 9, 1328/Nov. 12, 1910.
21. *Mozakerat*, Zu'l Qa'edeh 9, 1328/Nov. 12, 1910.
22. *Mozakerat*, Zu'l Qa'edeh 16, 1328/Nov. 19, 1910.
23. *Mozakerat*, Zu'l Qa'edeh 26, 28, 30, 1328/Nov. 29, Dec. 3, 5 1910; *Mozakerat*, Zu'l Hejjah 12, 17, 19, 21, 24, 1328/Dec. 15, 20, 22, 24, 27, 1910.
24. *Mozakerat*, Zu'l Qa'edeh 19, 1328/Nov. 22, 1910.
25. *Mozakerat*, Zu'l Hejjah 19, 21, 1328/Dec. 22, 24, 1910.
26. *Mozakerat*, Safar 11, 1329/Feb. 11, 1911.
27. *Mozakerat*, Safar 14, 1329/Feb. 14, 1911.
28. *Mozakerat*, Safar 14, 1329/Feb. 14, 1911.
29. *Mozakerat*, Safar 14, 1329/Feb. 14, 1911.
30. Smart, report, Jan. 27, 1911, enclosure 1, FO 416/47; Smart to Barclay, Feb. 3, 1911, enclosures 1, 2, FO 416/47; Barclay to Grey, Feb. 22 and Mar. 9, 22, 24, 1911, FO 416/47.
31. *Mozakerat*, Zu'l Hejjah 21, 24, 1328/Dec. 24, 27, 1910, and Moharram 17, 1329/Jan. 18, 1911.
32. *Mozakerat*, Sha'ban 10, 12, 1328/Aug. 16, 18, 1910; Marling to Grey, Aug. 7, 1910, FO/ 416/45.
33. *Mozakerat*, Zu'l Hejjah 19, 1328/Dec. 22, 1910.
34. *Mozakerat*, Moharram 15, 1329/Jan. 16, 1911; Barclay to Grey, Jan. 23, 1911, FO 416/47. For more on this dispute, see chapter 9.
35. Ellinger (full name not known) to Foreign Office, Mar. 31, 1911, FO 416/47; Strick Company to Foreign Office, Apr. 12, 1911, enclosures, FO 416/48.
36. *Mozakerat*, Zu'l Qa'edeh 14, 1328/Nov. 17, 1910.
37. *Mozakerat*, Zu'l Hejjah 3, 1328/Dec. 6, 1910.
38. See chapter 6.
39. *Mozakerat*, Zu'l Hejjah 28, 1328/Dec. 31, 1910.
40. *Mozakerat*, Zu'l Hejjah 14, 1328/Dec. 17, 1910.
41. *Mozakerat*, Moharram 19, 1329/Jan. 20, 1911.
42. Nava'i, *Dowlatha-ye Iran*, 178–79, 208–12.
43. As reported in Barclay to Grey, Aug. 31, 1910, FO 416/45.
44. *Mozakerat*, Ramazan 13, 1328/Sept. 18, 1910.
45. Smart to Barclay, Oct. 25, 1910, enclosure, FO 416/46.
46. Smart to Barclay, Oct. 25, 1910, enclosure, FO 416/46.
47. Enclosure in Barclay to Grey, Dec. 6, 1910, FO 416/46.
48. *Mozakerat*, Zu'l Qa'edeh 12, 1328/Nov. 15, 1910.
49. The oil company that had purchased the concession of 1901 from d'Arcy, its original owner, had the rights to explore, extract, and export oil in Bakhtiyari and Shaikh Khazal territories. The Bakhtiyaris had demanded and obtained extra cash payments; the shaikh then followed suit. The company agreed on the condition the government would refund the sum

by reducing the number of its shares in the profit. See the company's report to London, Dec. 5, 1910, FO 416/46; Barclay to Grey, Dec. 18, 1910, enclosures 1–9, FO 416/46; Grey to Barclay, Dec. 19, 1910, FO 416/46.

50. G. E. Wilson to Marling, June 6, 1910, FO 416/44; Percy Cox to Grey, Aug. 7, 1910, FO 416/44; Mallet to Baron Gericke, Aug. 18, 1910, FO 416/45; Barclay to Grey, Sept. 8, 1910, FO 416/45; Barclay to Grey, Sept. 9, 1910, FO 416/45.

51. Grey to Barclay, Dec. 9, 17, 1910, FO 416/46; Foreign Office to India Office, Dec. 9, 1910, FO 416/46.

52. Barclay to Grey, Dec. 15, 1910, FO 416/46.

53. Details in Barclay to Grey, Dec. 15, 1910, enclosures, FO 416/46.

54. Ranking to Barclay, Oct. 28, 1910, FO 416/46.

55. *Mozakerat*, Moharram 1, 1329/Jan. 3, 1911.

56. As reported in Marling to Grey, Nov. 29, 1910, FO 416/46.

57. Shaikh Mohammad Khiyabani to Taqizadeh, Shawal 21, 1328/Oct. 26, 1910, in *Owraq*, ed. Afshar, 346–47.

58. Marling to Grey, Jan. 6, 1911, FO 416/47.

59. Barclay to Grey, Feb. 22, 1911, FO 416/47.

60. See Nicolas's French translation of the Najaf ayatollahs' fatwas calling for the unity of Turks and Persians as well as of all Moslems in defense of Islam against its enemies (Nicolas, report to Quai d'Orsay, Feb. 19, 1911, Taurus/9, Constantinople/Tauris).

61. Lecomte to Pichon, Oct. 1, 1910, Constantinople/889, Constantinople/Tauris.

62. O'Beirne to Grey, Nov. 20, 1910, FO 416/46.

63. *Mozakerat*, Rajab 23, 1328/July 31, 1910, and Sha'ban 12, 1328/Aug. 18, 1910.

64. *Mozakerat*, Zu'l Hejjah 14, 1328/Dec. 17, 1910.

65. Barclay to Grey, Jan. 20, 23, 1911, FO 416/47.

66. George Buchanan to Grey, Mar. 7, 1911, FO 416/47.

67. Buchanan to Grey, Jan. 30, 1911, FO 416/47.

68. Barclay to Grey, Feb. 12, 1911, FO 416/47.

69. Barclay to Grey, Aug. 12, 1910, FO 416/45. Poklewski to Benckendorff, cable, Aug. 15, 1910, FO 416/45; O'Beirne to Grey, Aug. 17, 1910, FO 416/45; Nava'i, *Dowlatha-ye Iran*, 173–74.

70. Barclay to Grey, Sept. 26, 1910, FO 416/45; Barclay to Grey, Oct. 11, 1910, FO 416/46.

71. Naser al-Molk later revealed to Barclay that the Bakhtiyari khan had sent him a message before his arrival in Tehran, urging him to stage a coup d'état (as reported in Barclay to Grey, Feb. 22, 1911, FO 416/47).

72. Barclay to Grey, Dec. 30, 1910, FO 416/46.

73. *Mozakerat*, Moharram 3, 1329/Jan. 5, 1911.

74. *Mozakerat*, Moharram 3, 1329/Jan. 5, 1911.

75. *Mozakerat*, Moharram 3, 1329/Jan. 5, 1911.

76. *Mozakerat*, Moharram 24, 1329/Jan. 25, 1911.

77. *Mozakerat*, Moharram 26, 1329/Jan. 27, 1911.

78. *Mozakerat*, Moharram 29, 1329/Jan. 30, 1911.

79. Barclay to Grey, Feb. 9, 1911, FO 416/47.

80. *Mozakerat*, Ramazan 13, 1328/Sept. 18, 1910.

81. *Mozakerat*, Safar 9, 1329/Feb. 9, 1911.

82. *Mozakerat*, Safar 14, 1329/Feb. 14, 1911.

83. Barclay to Grey, Feb. 20, 1911, FO 416/47; Barclay to Grey, May 10, 1911, FO 416/48.

84. *Mozakerat*, Jamadi I 10, 1329/May 9, 1911.

11. The Summer of Discontent

1. Nava'i, *Dowlatha-ye Iran*, 173–74; Mostashar al-Dowleh, *Khaterat va asnad*, 1:74; Lecomte to Pichon, Oct. 1, 1910, Constantinople/889, Constantinople/Tauris.

2. Nava'i, *Dowlatha-ye Iran*, 173–74; Mostashar al-Dowleh, *Khaterat va asnad*, 1:74.

3. Grey, *Twenty-Five Years*, 160–62.

4. As reported in Barclay to Grey, Feb. 12, 1911, FO 416/47.

5. As reported in Barclay to Grey, Feb. 22, 1911, FO 416/47.

6. Enclosure in Barclay to Grey, Mar. 6, 1911, FO 416/47.

7. *Mozakerat*, Safar 16, 1329/Feb. 16,1911.

8. *Mozakerat*, Safar 18, 1329/Feb. 18, 1911.

9. *Mozakerat*, Safar 22, 23, 1329/Feb. 22, 23, 1911. The party lists, however, are incomplete. At times in the course of a debate, a deputy not in either party would declare himself as belonging to one or the other. See also chapter 5. Taqizadeh presents a more complete list of the Democrats (*Maqalat-e Taqizadeh*, 5:51–68) that does not totally correspond to the one given in the *Mozakerat.*

10. *Mozakerat*, Safar 18, 1329/Feb. 18, 1911.

11. See my analysis in chapter 5.

12. Malekzadeh, *Tarikh-e enqelab-e mashrutiyat-e Iran*, 3:1358–60, 1366; Mostashar al-Dowleh, *Khaterat va asnad*, 1143–48; *Siècle*, Mar. 14, 1911.

13. *Mozakerat*, Safar 18, 1329/Feb. 18, 1911.

14. *Mozakerat*, Safar 18, 1329/Feb. 18, 1911.

15. *Mozakerat*, Safar 18, 1329/Feb. 18, 1911.

16. A month later *Iran-e now* printed a Democrat program offering reforms for a "new socialist order in the distant future," with a parliamentary democracy in power, favoring the economic development of the working class and peasants (in *Owraq*, ed. Afshar, 352). See Afary's analysis in *The Iranian Constitutional Revolution*, 269–71. Afary states that the program was never carried out.

17. *Mozakerat,* Safar 18, 1329/Feb. 18, 1911.

18. *Mozakerat*, Safar 22, 1329/Feb. 22, 1911. Shaikh Reza's bombastic radicalism, evident here and detected in most Majles debates, was in sharp contrast to other Democrats' usual cautious pronouncements.

19. *Mozakerat*, Safar 23, 1329/Feb. 23, 1911.

20. *Mozakerat*, Safar 23, 1329/Feb. 23, 1911.

21. *Mozakerat*, Safar 23, 1329/Feb. 23, 1911.

22. *Mozakerat*, Safar 23, 1329/Feb. 23, 1911.

23. *Mozakerat*, Safar 25, 1329/Feb. 25, 1911.
24. *Mozakerat*, Safar 23, 1329/Feb. 23, 1911.
25. *Mozakerat*, Rabi' I 14, 1329/Mar. 16, 1911.
26. *Mozakerat*, Rabi' I 5, 1329/Mar. 7, 1911.
27. *Mozakerat*, Rabi' I 5, 1329/Mar. 7, 1911.
28. *Mozakerat*, Rabi' II 11, 12, 1329/Apr. 11, 12, 1911, and Jamadi I 12, 1329/May 9, 1911.
29. Barclay to Grey, Mar. 6, 1911, FO 416/47.
30. Barclay to Grey, Mar. 22, 1911, FO 416/47.
31. Barclay to Grey, Apr. 16, 1911, FO 416/48.
32. Shuster, *The Strangling of Persia*, 236.
33. *Mozakerat*, Rabi' I 2, 1329/Mar. 4, 1911; English text of the speech in Barclay to Grey, Mar. 7, 1911, enclosure, FO 416/47.
34. Barclay to Grey, Mar. 5, 1911, FO 416/47.
35. *Mozakerat*, Rabi' I 9, 1329/Mar. 11, 1911.
36. Barclay to Grey, Mar. 21, 1911, FO 416/47.
37. Barclay to Grey, Mar. 21, 1911, FO 416/47.
38. *Mozakerat*, Rabi' I 9, 1329/Mar. 11, 1911.
39. *Mozakerat*, Rabi' I 14, 1329/Mar. 15, 1911.
40. *Mozakerat*, Rabi' I 14, 1329/Mar. 15, 1911. See also the summary of the discussion in Barclay to Grey, Mar. 20, 1911, FO 416/47.
41. *Mozakerat*, Safar 25, 1329/Feb. 25, 1911.
42. *Mozakerat*, Rabi' I 19, 1329/Mar. 20, 1911.
43. *Mozakerat*, Rabi' I 19, 1329/Mar. 20, 1911.
44. *Mozakerat*, Rabi' I 26, 1329/Mar. 27, 1911.
45. *Mozakerat*, Rabi' II 1, 1329/Apr. 1, 1911.
46. *Mozakerat*, Safar 30, 1329/Feb. 18, 1911.
47. *Mozakerat*, Rabi' I 28, 1329/Mar. 29, 1911.
48. *Mozakerat*, Rabi' II 20, 1329/Apr. 20, 1911.
49. Momtaz al-Dowleh had resigned from the post when he was appointed minister of finance in the Sepahdar's cabinet. Matin al-Saltaneh remained the deputy speaker.
50. Barclay to Grey, Apr. 19, 1911, enclosure, FO 416/48.
51. *Mozakerat*, Rabi' II 4, 1329/Apr. 4, 1911.
52. *Mozakerat*, Rabi' II 6, 1329/Apr. 6, 1911.
53. *Mozakerat*, Rabi' II 8, 1329/Apr. 8, 1911.
54. *Mozakerat*, Rabi' II 6, 1329/Apr. 6, 1911.
55. *Mozakerat*, Rabi' II 8, 1329/Apr. 8,1911.
56. *Mozakerat*, Rabi' II 18, 1329/Apr. 18, 1911.
57. *Mozakerat*, Safar 4, 1329/Feb. 4, 1911.
58. Barclay to Grey, Apr. 8, 1911, enclosure, text of the contract, FO 416/48.
59. *Mozakerat*, Rabi' II 13, 1329/Apr. 13, 1911.
60. *Mozakerat*, Jamadi I 12, 1329/May 11, 1911.
61. *Mozakerat*, Jamadi I 10, 1329/May 9, 1911.

62. *Mozakerat*, Rabi' II 15, 1329/Apr. 15, 1911.

63. *Mozakerat*, Safar 26, 1329/Feb. 26, 1911, and Rabi' I 12, 1329/Mar. 13, 1911.

64. *Mozakerat*, Rabi' I 9, 12, 28, 1329/ Mar. 10, 13, 29, 1911, and Rabi' II 22, 1329/ Apr. 22, 1911.

65. *Mozakerat*, Rabi' II 11, 1329/Apr. 11, 1911.

66. *Mozakerat*, Rabi' II 20, 1329/Apr. 20, 1911.

67. *Mozakerat*, Rabi' II 20, 1329/Apr. 20, 1911.

68. *Mozakerat*, Jamadi I 7, 1329/May 6, 1911, and Rabi' II 6, 1329/Apr. 6, 1911.

69. *Mozakerat*, Jamadi I 3, 1329/May 2, 1911.

70. Grey to Buchanan, Jan. 16, 1911, FO 416/47; Grey to Bertie, Jan. 18, 1911, FO 416/47; Grey to Goschen, Jan. 18, 1911, FO 416/47.

71. O'Beirne to Grey, Aug. 15, 1910, FO 416/45; Grey to O'Beirne, Aug. 18, 1910, FO 416/47; Marling to Grey, Aug. 17, 1910, FO 416/47; Grey to Benckendorff, Aug. 18, 1910, FO 416/47; Izvolski to Benckendorff, Aug. 19, 1910, FO 416/47; Grey to Daeschner (full name not known), Aug. 23, 1910, FO 416/47.

72. O'Beirne to Grey, Aug. 20, 1910, FO 416/47.

73. *Mozakerat*, Ramazan 1, 1328/Sept. 7, 1910.

74. *Mozakerat*, Ramazan 5, 1328/Sept. 10, 1910.

75. *Mozakerat*, Ramazan 5, 1328/Sept. 10, 1910.

76. *Mozakerat*, Ramazan 1, 1328/Sept. 6, 1910.

77. *Mozakerat*, Ramazan 1, 1328/Sept. 6, 1910.

78. Grey to Buchanan, Jan. 16, 1911, FO 416/47; Grey to Goschen, Jan. 18, 1911, FO 416/47; Grey to Bertie, Jan. 18, 1911, FO 416/47.

79. Buchanan to Grey, Feb. 1, 1911, FO 416/47.

80. McDaniel, *The Shuster Mission*, 115.

81. Barclay to Grey, Apr. 8, 1911, enclosure, FO 416/48.

82. James Bryce to Grey, Feb. 28, 1911, FO 416/47.

83. Barclay to Grey, May 16, 1911, enclosure 3, FO 416/48; *Mozakerat*, Rabi' II 22, 1329/Apr. 22, 1911.

84. Text of the signed contract in Imperial Bank to Foreign Office, June 1, 1911, FO 416/48, and Foreign Office to Imperial Bank, June 3, 1911, FO 416/48.

85. *Mozakerat*, Rabi' II 25, 1329/Apr. 25, 1911.

86. *Mozakerat*, Rabi' II 25, 1329/Apr. 25, 1911.

87. *Mozakerat*, Rabi' II 25, 1329/Apr. 25, 1911.

88. *Mozakerat*, Rabi' II 27, 1329/Apr. 27, 1911.

89. *Mozakerat*, Jamadi I 3, 1329/May 2, 1911.

90. On March 15, 1911, *Iran-e now* published all the correspondence between the British, Russian, and Persian governments regarding the loan. *Iran-e now* had obtained it from *Habl al-matin*, the liberal paper of Calcutta, whose editor had sources inside the Tehran government.

91. *Mozakerat*, Jamadi I 17, 1329/May 16, 1911.

92. *Mozakerat*, Jamadi I 17, 1329/May 16, 1911.

93. *Mozakerat*, Jamadi I 17, 1329/May 16, 1911.

94. As reported in Daeschner to Foreign Office, Mar. 23, 1911, FO 416/47.

95. Grey to Barclay, Mar. 30, 1911, FO 416/47; Barclay to Grey, Mar. 31, 1910, FO 416/47; Grey to Paul Cambon, Apr. 4, 1911, FO 416/48.

12. Political Intrigues and Royal Conspiracy

1. Barclay to Grey, Mar. 23, 1911, FO 416/47.

2. Barclay to Grey, Apr. 14, 1911, FO 416/48.

3. Barclay to Grey, Apr. 17, 1911, FO 416/48.

4. Barclay to Grey, May 5, 1911, FO 416/48.

5. McDaniel, *The Shuster Mission*, 121 n. 9 and sources cited there.

6. Foreign Office to Messrs. Ziegler & Co., Apr. 19, 1911, FO 416/48.

7. Barclay to Grey, May 10, 16, 1911, FO 416/48.

8. Grey to Barclay, May 10, 1911, FO 416/48.

9. Barclay to Grey, May 17, 1911, FO 416/48.

10. Barclay to Grey, June 10, 12, 21, 1911, FO 416/48.

11. As reported in Barclay to Grey, June 5, 1911, FO 416/48.

12. Barclay to Grey, May 18, 1911, FO 416/48; *Mozakerat*, Jamadi I 28, 1329/May 27, 1911.

13. Mostashar al-Dowleh, *Khaterat va asnad*, 1:74–83.

14. Mostashar al-Dowleh, *Khaterat va asnad*, 1:77, 79.

15. Mostashar al-Dowleh, *Khaterat va asnad*, 1:88.

16. For the royalist activities at that time, see Nava'i, *Dowlatha-ye Iran*, 214–16, and a more recent study by Willem Floor, *Salar al-Dowleh: A Delusional Prince and Wannabe Shah*.

17. *Mozakerat*, Jamadi II 12, 1329/June 10, 1911; see also a confidential letter dated Rabi' II 25, 1329/Apr. 7, 1911, addressed to Interior Minister Mostashar al-Dowleh and reporting on the formation of several pro- and anticonstitutional *anjomans* and religious organizations that were competing for political influence in Kashan (in Mostashar al-Dowleh, *Khaterat va asnad*, 2:334–35).

18. *Mozakerat*, Jamadi II 15, 1329/June 13, 1911.

19. Kazemzadeh, *Russia and Britain in Persia*, 584.

20. Shuster, *Strangling of Persia*, l, 28.

21. Shuster, *Strangling of Persia*, 30. In *The Shuster Mission*, McDaniel's analysis of Shuster's mission, echoing accounts by European diplomats in Tehran at that time, is highly critical of Shuster's undiplomatic tactics, which, he claims throughout his book, unnecessarily attracted the Europeans' hostility.

22. Shuster, *Strangling of Persia*, appendix D, 372–88.

23. Shuster, *Strangling of Persia*, 49.

24. Shuster, *Strangling of Persia*, 97, 16, 19–20.

25. Shuster, *Strangling of Persia*, 191.

26. Shuster, *Strangling of Persia*, 405.

27. Shuster, *Strangling of Persia*, 31.

28. Shuster, *Strangling of Persia*, 23–24.

29. *Mozakerat*, Jamadi II 10, 1329/June 8, 1911.

30. *Mozakerat*, Jamadi II 15, 1329/June 13, 1911.

31. Kazemzadeh, *Russia and Britain in Persia*, 584–85 and sources cited there.

32. Barclay to Grey, July 5, 1911, FO 371; Grey to Buchanan, July 6, 1911, FO 371.

33. Mostowfi, *Sharh-e zendegi-ye*, 2:344.

34. Shuster, *Strangling of Persia*, 46–47, 55, 67–68.

35. Shuster, *Strangling of Persia*, 66.

36. Shuster, *Strangling of Persia*, 56–61; see also Malekzadeh, *Tarikh-e enqelab-e mashrutiyat-e Iran*, 3:1375.

37. As reported in Barclay to Grey, June 17, 20, 1911, FO 416/48.

38. Barclay to Grey, June 17, 1911, FO 416/48.

39. Barclay to Grey, June 9, 1911, FO 416/48.

40. Mostashar al-Dowleh, *Khaterat va asnad*, 1:96.

41. Barclay to Grey, June 20, 1911, FO 416/48.

42. *Mozakerat*, Rajab 16, 1329/July 12, 1911.

43. *Mozakerat*, Rajab 19, 1329/July 15, 1911.

44. *Mozakerat*, Rajab 22, 1329/July 18, 1911.

45. McDaniel, *The Shuster Mission*, 135 and sources cited there. W. A. Moore, the *Times* correspondent in Tehran, published an account confirming Hartwig's conversation with the former shah. Shuster, further commenting on Russia's complicity, which was widely known in Russian government circles, cites Poklewski's announcement to his guest at a dinner ten days before the former shah landed in Iran that "the Persian constitutional government would cease to exist" within a few weeks (*Strangling of Persia*, 107–8).

46. Shuster, *Strangling of Persia*, 118.

47. Mostowfi, *Sharh-e zendegi-ye*, 2:353; Malekzadeh, *Tarikh-e enqelab-e mashrutiyat-e Iran*, 3:1379–86; Nava'i, *Dowlatha-ye Iran*, 214–16.

48. *Mozakerat*, Rajab 22, 1329/July 18, 1911.

49. Shuster, *Strangling of Persia*, 83, 97.

50. Nava'i, *Dowlatha-ye Iran*, 217–18; Malekzadeh, *Tarikh-e enqelab-e mashrutiyat-e Iran*, 3:1378–79, but Malekzadeh denies the Sepahdar was an accomplice.

51. Mostashar al-Dowleh, *Khaterat va asnad*, 1:94–96. This account, like most other eyewitness accounts, confuses the sequence of events or simply omits their significant dates. McDaniel has also commented on this confusion in *The Shuster Mission* (142 n. 12), though his sources also offer some slightly different dates from those given in the *Mozakerat*. I have used the latter whenever possible as the most accurate.

52. *Mozakerat*, Rajab 29, 1329/July 25, 1911.

53. *Mozakerat*, Rajab 29, 1329/July 25, 1911.

54. *Mozakerat*, Sha'ban 3, 1329/July 28, 1911; Nava'i, *Dowlatha-ye Iran*, 230. Shuster states that the idea of a cash award was his initial suggestion to the regent (*Strangling of Persia*, 89).

55. Shuster, *Strangling of Persia*, 110.

56. Malekzadeh, *Tarikh-e enqelab-e mashrutiyat-e Iran*, 3:1494; Nava'i, *Dowlatha-ye Iran*, 218–20.

57. Shuster, *Strangling of Persia*, 90–91, 114–15.

58. Shuster, *Strangling of Persia*, 94.

59. Malekzadeh, *Tarikh-e enqelab-e mashrutiyat-e Iran*, 3:1403–7.

60. Kazemzadeh, *Russia and Britain in Persia*, 610–11.

61. Shuster, *Strangling of Persia*, 127–30; Nava'i, *Dowlatha-ye Iran*, 241–43.

62. Moore, *Orient Express*, 33–34; Kazemzadeh, *Russia and Britain in Persia*, 600 and sources cited there.

63. *Mozakerat*, Rajab 9, Sha'ban 3, 1329/July 5, 28, 1911; Shuster, *Strangling of Persia*, 371–77.

64. For instance, Shuster revealed in a cabinet meeting the acting minister of war's embezzlement of sums destined to pay soldiers' salaries in arrears (Shuster, *Strangling of Persia*, 62–66).

65. Shuster, *Strangling of Persia*, 115.

66. McDaniel, *The Shuster Mission*, 149–50 and sources cited there.

67. Lecomte to Mr. de Selves, Aug. 25, 1911, Constantinople/889, Constantinople/Tauris.

68. Mr. Lefevre Pontalis to Mr. de Selves, Aug. 25, 1911, Constantinople/889, Constantinople/Tauris.

69. Quoted in Kazemzadeh, *Russia and Britain in Persia*, 591, 613.

70. Shuster, *Strangling of Persia*, 75–76.

71. Shuster, *Strangling of Persia*, 76–83.

72. Barclay to Grey, Oct. 1, 1911, FO 416/50.

73. Grey to O'Beirne, Oct. 12, 1911, FO 416/50.

74. Shuster, *Strangling of Persia*, 383; Barclay to Grey, Oct. 27, 1911, enclosure, FO 416/50, italics in the original.

75. Grey to Barclay, Oct. 9, 1911, FO 416/50; Foreign Office to India Office, Oct. 11, 1911, FO 416/50; O'Beirne to Grey, Oct. 10, FO 416/50; India Office to Foreign Office, Oct. 14, 1911, FO 416/50.

76. Shuster, *Strangling of Persia*, 158. Judging from the *Mozakerat* records dated Shawal 15, 1329/Oct. 9, 1911, the incident was not discussed in the Majles's open session. The records briefly note the interior minister's response to a deputy's question in which he dismissed the story of the incident as just "rumors," with no official confirmation of its occurrence.

77. Kazemzadeh, *Britain and Russia in Persia*, 615–19; Shuster, *Strangling of Persia*, 136–51; Barclay to Grey, Oct. 27, Nov. 2, 1911, FO 416/50; Malekzadeh, *Tarikh-e enqelab-e mashrutiyat-e Iran*, 3:1445–49.

78. Barclay to Grey, Oct. 19, 1911, FO 416/50.

79. *Times* (London), Oct. 19, 1911.

80. *Times* (London), Nov. 10, 11, 1911; Shuster, *Strangling of Persia*, 153–54, 358–71.

81. Kazemzadeh, *Russia and Britain in Persia*, 620.

82. Kazemzadeh, *Russia and Britain in Persia*, 625.

83. Barclay to Grey, Oct. 20, 1911, FO 416/50.

84. *Mozakerat*, Shawwal 27, 1329/Oct. 21, 1911 (the session was mistakenly dated Shawwal 25, so the correct date is given here).

85. Barclay to Grey, Nov. 1, 1911, FO 416/50.

86. Barclay to Grey, Nov. 1, 1911, FO 416/50.

87. *Mozakerat*, Zu'l Qa'edeh 19, 1329/Nov. 10, 1911.

88. Barclay to Grey, Oct. 22, 1911, FO 416/50.

89. Barclay to Grey, Oct. 28, 1911, FO 416/50.

90. Shuster, *Strangling of Persia*, 160.

91. Nava'i, *Dowlatha-ye Iran*, 269–70.

92. Kazemzadeh, *Russia and Britain in Persia*, 622.

13. The End Stages of the Second Majles

1. O'Beirne to Grey, Oct. 19, 1911, FO 416/50; Grey to O'Beirne, Oct. 23, 1911, FO 416/50.

2. Barclay to Grey, May 18, 1911, enclosure, FO 416/48; Greenway to Foreign Office, June 15, 1911, FO 416/48; Barclay to Grey, Apr. 18, 1911, FO 416/48. Grey, obviously following the regent's advice, had instructed Barclay to assure the Persian government that a private company would be in charge of the negotiations and that the British government "will stand aside entirely" (Grey to Barclay, May 4, 1911, FO 416/48).

3. O'Beirne to Grey, June 11, 1911, enclosures 3 and 4, FO 416/48.

4. Shuster, *Strangling of Persia*, 316; Barclay to Grey, Oct. 4, 25, 26, and Nov. 6, 7, 1911, FO 416/50; O'Beirne to Grey, Oct. 23, 1911, FO 416/50.

5. Quoted in McDaniel, *The Shuster Mission*, 178.

6. Shuster, *Strangling of Persia*, 403.

7. Bayat, *Iran's First Revolution*, 244 and sources cited there. In *Britain and the Iranian Constitutional Revolution*, Bonakdarian provides an extensive analysis of the "dissenters" to Grey's Iran policy.

8. Shuster, *Strangling of Persia*, 401.

9. Barclay to Grey, Nov. 2, 1911, enclosure: "Summary of Events in Persia for the Month of October," FO 416/50.

10. Barclay to Grey, Oct. 3, 1911, FO 416/50; India Office to Foreign Office, Oct. 9, 1911, FO 416/50.

11. Persian ambassador to Foreign Office, Oct. 13, 1911, FO 416/50; Barclay to Grey, Oct. 8, FO 416/50; Grey to Barclay, Oct. 9, FO 416/50; and Sir Cecil Spring-Rice to Grey, Oct. 6, FO 416/50.

12. Grey to Persian ambassador, Oct. 25, 1911, FO 416/50.

13. Barclay to Grey, Nov. 3, 1911, FO 416/50.

14. Barclay to Grey, Nov. 3, 1911, enclosures 3 and 5, FO 416/50.

15. As reported in O'Beirne to Grey, Oct. 14, 1911, FO 416/50.

16. English translation of article in *Novoe vremiya* dated November 10, 1911, in O'Beirne to Grey, Nov. 10, 1911, FO 416/50.

17. Barclay to Grey, Oct. 30, 31, 1911, FO 416/50.

18. O'Beirne to Grey, Oct. 19, 20, 1911, enclosures, FO 416/50.

19. Shuster, *Strangling of Persia*, 162.

20. Barclay to Grey, Nov. 8, 9, 1911, FO 416/50.

21. *Mozakerat*, Zu'l Qa'edeh 20, 21, 1329/Nov. 11, 12, 1911.

22. *Mozakerat*, Zu'l Qa'edeh 20, 1329/Nov. 11, 1911.

23. *Mozakerat*, Zu'l Qa'edeh 20, 1329/Nov. 11, 1911.

24. Sardar As'ad, letter dated November 7, 1911, read in the Majles weeks later, *Mozakerat*, Zu'l Qa'edeh 30, 1329/Nov. 21, 1911.

25. *Mozakerat*, Zu'l Qa'edeh 21, 1329/Nov. 12, 1911.

26. *Mozakerat*, Zu'l Qa'edeh 21, 1329/Nov. 12, 1911.

27. *Mozakerat*, Zu'l Qa'edeh 21, 1329/Nov. 12, 1911.

28. Barclay dated the vote on November 13, 1911; I use the more accurate *Mozakerat* date.

29. Grey to Barclay, Nov. 6, 1911, FO 416/50.

30. Quoted in Shuster, *Strangling of Persia*, 179.

31. Shuster, *Strangling of Persia*, 160–61; Barclay to Grey, Nov. 8, 1911, FO 416/50.

32. Shuster, *Strangling of Persia*, 180.

33. Buchanan to Grey, Nov. 15, 1911, FO 416/50.

34. Buchanan to Grey, Nov. 18, 1911, FO 416/50.

35. Buchanan to Grey, Nov. 22, 1911, FO 416/50; *Mozakerat*, Zu'l Qa'edeh 30, 1329/Nov. 21, 1911. Samsam al-Saltaneh's announcement of his intention to comply with the Russians' demands is not included in the *Mozakerat*, but in Buchanan's report.

36. Buchanan to Grey, Nov. 26, 1911, FO 416/50.

37. Buchanan to Grey, Nov. 26, 1911, FO 416/50.

38. Barclay to Grey, Nov. 24, 1911, FO 416/50.

39. English translation of a *Rossiya* article in Buchanan to Grey, Nov. 20, 1911, FO 416/50.

40. Quoted in Kazemzadeh, *Russia and Britain in Persia*, 629; see also Grey to Buchanan, Nov. 21, 1911, FO 416/50.

41. Yeselson, *United States–Persian Diplomatic Relations*, 119. Kazemzadeh, *Russia and Britain in Persia*, 634.

42. Grey to Bryce, Nov. 23, 1911, FO 416/50.

43. Persian ambassador to Grey, Nov. 19, 1911, FO 416/50.

44. Barclay to Grey, Nov. 24, 1911, FO 416/50.

45. Shuster, *Strangling of Persia*, 178.

46. *Mozakerat*, Zu'l Qa'edeh 30, 1329/Nov. 21, 1911; see also Solaiman Mirza's praise of the Bakhtiyaris for their military victories (*Mozakerat*, Ramazan 12, 1329/Sept. 6, 1911).

47. That is essentially the thesis McDaniel develops repeatedly throughout his book, *The Shuster Mission*.

48. See Bayat [Bayat-Philipp], "Women and Revolution in Iran" and sources cited there. Subsequent studies on the subject of women's movements in Iran include Afary, *The Iranian Constitutional Revolution*; Bamdad, *Zan-e irani az enqelab-e mashrutiyat ta enqelab-e sefid*; Sanasarian, *The Women's Rights Movement in Iran*. See also the sources cited in these works.

49. Bayat, *Mysticism and Dissent*, 110–15; Milani, *Words and Veils*, chap. 4.

50. *Times* (London), Sept. 15, 1908.

51. Browne, *Press and Poetry*, 85.

52. For a list of these women's names, see Bayat [Bayat-Philipp], "Women and Revolution"; Afary, *The Iranian Constitutional Revolution*, 186.

53. *Mozakerat*, Sha'ban 8, 1328/Aug. 5, 1911. The *Times* published a somewhat inaccurate article covering this debate in its issue on August 22, 1911. A corrected version appeared on August 28, 1911, though wrongly attributing Modarres's words to Assadollah Kordestani.

54. Shuster, *Strangling of Persia*, 198.

55. Shuster, *Strangling of Persia*, 191.

56. Shuster, *Strangling of Persia*, 241–42.

57. As reported in Bertie to Grey, Nov. 19, 1911, FO 416/50.

58. Quoted in McDaniel, *Shuster Mission*, 190.

59. *Mozakerat*, Zu'l Hejjah 3, 6, 1329/Nov. 24, 27, 1911.

60. Shuster, *Strangling of Persia*, 171.

61. Barclay to Grey, Nov. 2, 5, 16, 19, 22, 1911, FO 416/50.

62. Nava'i, *Dowlatha-ye Iran*, 282.

63. Kazemzadeh, *Russia and Britain in Persia*, 639; Barclay to Grey, Nov. 21, 1911, FO 416/50; Buchanan to Grey, Nov. 23, 1911, FO 416/50; Grey to Buchanan, Nov. 23, 1911, FO 416/50; Benckendorff to Foreign Office, Nov. 28, 1911, FO 416/50.

64. *Mozakerat*, Zu'l Hejjah 7, 1329/Nov. 28, 1911.

65. *Mozakerat*, Zu'l Hejjah 7, 1329/Nov. 28, 1911.

66. Barclay to Grey, Nov. 28, 1911, FO 416/50.

67. Barclay to Grey, Dec. 1, 1911, FO 416/50; Kazemzadeh, *Russia and Britain in Persia*, 632; Shuster, *Strangling of Persia*, 166–67. For descriptions of a detailed discussion between Neratov and Buchanan of the ultimatum in St. Petersburg, see Buchanan to Grey, Nov. 29, 1911, FO 416/50, and Barclay to Grey, Dec. 3, 1911, enclosure 1, FO 416/50.

68. Buchanan to Grey, Dec. 4, 1911, FO 416/50.

69. *Mozakerat*, Zu'l Hejjah 9, 1329/Nov. 30, 1911.

70. *Mozakerat*, Zu'l Hejjah 9, 1329/Nov. 30, 1911.

71. Shuster, *Strangling of Persia*, 176.

72. Barclay to Grey, Dec. 1, 1911, FO 416/50.

73. Buchanan to Grey, Dec. 9, 1911, FO 416/50; Barclay to Grey, Dec. 4, 5, 1911, FO 416/50.

74. Shuster, *Strangling of Persia*, 189, 190–91, 187.

75. Nava'i, *Dowlatha-ye Iran*, 282. Malekzadeh denies Yeprem Khan's role in the assassination, pointing the finger instead at members of the Democrat Party (*Tarikh-e enqelab-e mashrutiyat-e Iran*, 3:1464).

76. Barclay to Grey, Dec. 11, 1911, FO 416/50; Kazemzadeh, *Russia and Britain in Persia*, 643.

77. Barclay to Grey, Dec. 12, 1911, FO 416/50.

78. Buchanan to Grey, Dec. 1, 1911, FO 416/50; Grey to Buchanan, Dec. 2, 1911, FO 416/50.

79. Barclay to Grey, Dec. 14, 15, 17, 1911, FO 416/50; Imperial Bank of Persia to Foreign Office, Dec. 16, 1911, FO 416/50.

80. *Mozakerat*, Zu'l Hejjah 22, 1329/Dec. 13, 1911; Nava'i, *Dowlatha-ye Iran*, 285; Malekzadeh, *Tarikh-e enqelab-e mashrutiyat-e Iran*, 3:1466–70.

81. *Mozakerat*, Zu'l Hejjah 26, 1329/Dec. 17, 1911.

82. *Mozakerat,* Zu'l Hejjah 26, 1329/Dec. 17, 1911.

83. *Mozakerat,* Zu'l Hejjah 26, 1329/Dec. 17, 1911.

84. *Mozakerat,* Zu'l Hejjah 26, 1329/Dec. 17, 1911.

85. *Mozakerat,* Zu'l Hejjah 29, 1329/Dec. 20, 1911.

86. Barclay to Grey, Dec. 14, 1911, FO 416/50.

87. Graham to Browne, Jan. 22, 1911, box 9, Browne Papers.

88. McDaniel, *Shuster Mission,* 195.

89. Buchanan to Grey, Dec. 13, 1911, FO 416/50.

90. Buchanan to Grey, Dec. 18, 19, 1911, FO 416/50.

91. Conversation related by Sir A. Johnstone to Grey, Dec. 9, 1911, FO 416/50.

92. As reported in Bertie to Grey, Dec. 8, 1911, FO 416/50.

93. Barclay to Grey, Dec. 15, 1911, FO 416/50.

94. Barclay to Grey, Dec. 12, 1911, FO 416/50.

95. Barclay to Grey, Dec. 13, 1911, FO 416/50.

96. Barclay to Grey, Dec. 3, 1911, FO 416/50.

97. Barclay to Grey, Nov. 28, 1911, FO 416/50; see also Barclay to Grey, Nov. 12, 1911, FO 416/50.

98. As reported in Barclay to Grey, Dec. 2, 1911, FO 416/50.

99. As reported in Barclay to Grey, Dec. 8, 1911, FO 416/50.

100. As reported in Barclay to Grey, Dec. 14, 1911, FO 416/50.

101. Malekzadeh, *Tarikh-e enqelab-e mashrutiyat-e Iran,* 3:1470–73; Floor, *Salar al-Dowleh,* 23–69.

102. As reported in Barclay to Grey, Dec. 11, 1911, FO 416/50.

103. Statement published in *Jeune Turc,* Dec. 17, 1911; English translation of the text in Lowther (full name not known) to Grey, Dec. 17, 1911, FO 416/50.

104. As reported in Lowther to Grey, Dec. 18, 20, 1911, FO 416/50.

105. Buchanan to Grey, Dec. 10, 1911, FO 416/50.

106. Malekzadeh, *Tarikh-e enqelab-e mashrutiyat-e Iran,* 3:1473. Shuster reported that money and food were distributed among the poor people, who were told that the prevailing shortage of bread was due to the Majles's hostility to Russia (*Strangling of Persia,* 206).

107. As reported in Buchanan to Grey, Dec. 30, 1911, FO 416/50.

108. Malekzadeh, *Tarikh-e enqelab-e mashrutiyat-e Iran,* 3:1474–75; Nava'i, *Dowlatha-ye Iran,* 286.

109. Barclay to Grey, Dec. 29, 30, 1911, FO 416/50.

110. Barclay to Grey, Nov. 28, 1911, FO 416/50.

111. Quoted in Nicolson, *Portrait of a Diplomatist,* 259, emphasis in original.

112. Grey, *Twenty-Five Years,* 169.

113. Barclay to Grey, Dec. 26, 29, 1911, FO 416/50.

114. Kazemzadeh, *Russia and Britain in Persia,* 647. See also Buchanan to Grey, Dec. 30, 1911, FO 416/50.

115. Barclay to Grey, Dec. 22, 23, 1911, FO 416/50; Kazemzadeh, *Russia and Britain in Persia,* 648–51.

116. Malekzadeh, *Tarikh-e enqelab-e mashrutiyat-e Iran,* 3:1484–97, 1530–39; Nava'i, *Dowlatha-ye Iran,* 293–94; Kasravi, *Tarikh-e hijdah saleh-ye Azerbaijan,* 280, 283, 328.

117. Cited in Kazemzadeh, *Russia and Britain in Persia*, 654.

118. Kazemzadeh, *Russia and Britain in Persia*, 675–76.

119. Malekzadeh, *Tarikh-e enqelab-e mashrutiyat-e Iran*, 3:1473.

120. Shuster, *Strangling of Persia*, 199, 200, 239.

121. Shuster, *Strangling of Persia*, 204.

122. In deference to Russia's opposition, the Swedish government rejected the Persian request for an additional twenty military officers to organize a national army (Spring-Rice to Grey, Feb. 27, 1911, FO 416/47; Spring-Rice to Grey, Oct. 17, 22, and Nov. 22, 1911, FO 416/50; Barclay to Grey, Oct. 4, Nov. 11, and Dec. 16, 1911, FO 416/50). The Foreign Office turned down a Danish geographic group's request to send scholars on an archaeological project in the Persian Gulf area (Sir C. Greene to Grey, Nov. 15, 1911, FO 416/50).

123. Lecomte, report to Paris, Aug. 9, 1911, Constantinople/889, Constantinople/Tauris; Barclay to Grey, Oct. 27, 1911, FO 416/50; Grey to O'Beirne, Oct. 27, 1911, FO 416/50.

124. Cable, Aug. 20, 1912, cited in Kazemzadeh, *Russia and Britain in Persia*, 655.

125. Kazemzadeh, *Russia and Britain in Persia*, 655.

126. Kazemzadeh, *Russia and Britain in Persia*, 661.

127. Nava'i, *Dowlatha-ye Iran*, 249–50.

128. Quoted in Kazemzadeh, *Russia and Britain in Persia*, 667.

Conclusion

1. Clark, *Sleepwalkers*, 158.

2. Sir A. Johnston to Grey, n.d., FO 416/50.

3. Quoted in Kazemzadeh, *Russia and Britain in Persia*, 575.

4. Shuster, *Strangling of Persia*, 263.

5. Clark, *Sleepwalkers*, 166, 203.

6. Shuster, *Strangling of Persia*, 242.

7. Barclay to Grey, Nov. 22, 1911, FO 416/50.

8. *Mozakerat*, Shawwal 13, 1329/Oct. 7, 1911.

9. *Mozakerat*, Shawwal 23, 1329/Oct. 17, 1911.

10. *Mozakerat*, Sha'ban 20, 22, 24, 1329/Aug. 15, 17, 19, 1911.

11. *Mozakerat*, Sha'ban 10, 1329/Aug. 5, 1911, and Shawal 18, 1329/Oct. 12, 1911.

12. *Mozakerat*, Shawwal 23, 1329/Oct. 17, 1911.

13. *Mozakerat*, Ramazan 2, 1329/Aug. 27, 1911.

14. *Mozakerat*, Ramazan 14, 1329/Sept. 8, 1911, and Zu'l Qa'edeh 8, 10, 1329/Nov. 1, 3, 1911.

15. *Mozakerat*, Ramazan 26, 1329/Sept. 20, 1911.

16. *Mozakerat*, Shawwal 9, 1329/Oct. 3, 1911.

17. Elsewhere referred to as Seyyed Shaikh Ibrahim.

18. *Mozakerat*, Sha'ban 29, 1329/Aug. 24, 1911.

19. *Mozakerat*, Shawwal 11, 1329/Oct. 5, 1911.

20. *Mozakerat*, Shawwal 9, 1329/Oct. 3, 1911.

21. *Mozakerat*, Shawwal 9, 1329/Oct. 3, 1911. *Hodud* refers to a set of laws in the Qur'an that assign specific punishments for five specific crimes or sins: apostasy, murder,

adultery, theft, and usury. The faithful believe the Qur'an to be the eternal word of God revealed to the Prophet Mohammad to instruct humanity. Its *hodud* rulings are considered immutable and thus to be strictly followed.

22. *Mozakerat*, Shawwal 21, 1329/Oct. 15, 1911.
23. *Mozakerat*, Shawwal 25, 1329/Oct. 19, 1911.
24. *Mozakerat*, Shawwal 25, 1329/Oct. 19, 1911.
25. *Mozakerat*, Shawwal 27 (mistakenly dated Shawwal 25), 1329/Oct. 21, 1911.
26. *Mozakerat*, Shawwal 9, 1329/Oct. 3, 1911.
27. *Mozakerat*, Shawwal 25, 28 and Zu'l Qa'edeh 5, 1329/Oct. 19, 22, 29, 1911.
28. *Mozakerat*, Shawwal 9, 1329/Oct. 3, 1911.
29. *Mozakerat*, Ramazan 11, 23, 26, 1329/Sept. 11, 17, 20, 1911.
30. *Mozakerat*, Zu'l Qa'edeh 1, 5, 10, 1329/Oct. 25, 29, Nov. 3, 1911. For details on the Mo'in concession, see chapters 6 and 12.
31. *Mozakerat*, Zu'l Qa'edeh 5, 1329/Oct. 29, 1911.
32. India Office to the Foreign Office, June 28, 1911, enclosure 3, FO 416/49.
33. Nicolas to Quai d'Orsay, Oct. 16, 1910, Tauris/8, Constantinople/Tauris.
34. Nicolas to Quai d'Orsay, Dec. 10, 1910, Tauris/8, Constantinople/Tauris.
35. Nicolas to Quai d'Orsay, Jan. 30, 1911, Tauris/9, Constantinople/Tauris.
36. Nicolas to Quai d'Orsay, Aug. 10, 1910, Tauris/8, Constantinople/Tauris.
37. Nicolas to Quai d'Orsay, Feb. 9, 1911, Tauris/9, Constantinople/Tauris.
38. Stokes to Browne, Dec. 6, 1910, box 9, Browne Papers.
39. Shuster to Browne, Dec. 6, 1911, box 9, Browne Papers.
40. Graham to Browne, Jan. 22, 1911, box 9, Browne Papers.
41. Smart to Browne, May 1, 1912, box 1, Browne Papers.
42. Smart to Browne, Jan. 5, 1915, box 1, Browne Papers.
43. Mostashar al-Dowleh, *Khaterat va asnad*, 1:94.
44. Vahid al-Molk to Browne, June 1911, box 1, Browne Papers.
45. Vahid al-Molk to Browne, Mar. 6 and Aug. 22, 1912, box 1, Browne Papers.

Bibliography

Archival Sources

Archives du Ministère des affaires étrangères, Courneuve, France. Correspondances politiques et commerciales. Nouvelle Série: Perse, vols. 3–7.

Archives Nationales. Correspondences diplomatiques, Nantes, France. Files Constantinople/889 and Tauris/7, 8, 9, 10.

Bibliothèque du Grand Orient de France, Paris. File 1871, "Tehran: Le Réveil de l'Iran, 1907–1911."

Bibliothèque Nationale, Paris. Archives du Grand Orient de France, correspondence: Orient de Constantinople, FM2 865.

Browne, Edward Granville, Correspondence. Cambridge Univ. Library.

Browne, Edward Granville, Papers. Pembroke College, Cambridge Univ.

Mozakerat-e Majles-e dovvom (Parliamentary Debates of the Second Majles). Vol. 2. Tehran: Government of Iran Publication, 1909–11.

Public Records Office, London. Foreign Office Papers. Correspondence Respecting the Affairs of Persia. FO 371; 416/40–51; 881/9535, 9540, 9633.

Periodicals

Balkan Studies
Bulletin de l'Alliance française
Comparative Studies in Society and History
Comparative Studies of South Asia, Africa, and the Middle East
Bulletin du Grand Orient de France
Encyclopedia Iranica
Habl al-matin
Iran: Journal of the British Institute of Persian Studies
Iran-e now
Iranian Studies
Middle Eastern Studies
Musavat
Neda-ye vatan
Qanun
Rahnamah-ye Ketab
Revue du monde Musulman
Revue de l'Université de Bruxelles
Ruznameh-ye Majles
Siècle
Sorush
Sur-e Israfil
Times (London)
Vaqt
Yaghma

Published Primary and Secondary Sources

Abrahamian, Ervand. *Iran between Two Revolutions*. Princeton, NJ: Princeton Univ. Press, 1982.

Adamiyat, Fereydun. *Fekr-e azadi va moqaddameh-ye nehzat-e mashrutiyat*. Tehran: Amir Kabir, 1961.

———. *Fekr-e demokrasi-ye ejtemai dar nehzat-e mashrutiyat-e Iran*. Tehran: Payam, 1975.

———. *Ide'oloji-ye nehzat-e mashrutiyat-e Iran*. Tehran: Payam, 1976.

Afary, Janet. *The Iranian Constitutional Revolution, 1906–1911: Grassroots Democracy, Social Democracy, and the Origins of Feminism*. New York: Columbia Univ. Press, 1996.

Afshar, Iraj, ed. *Mobarezeh ba Mohammad Ali Shah: Asnadi az fa'aliyatha-ye azadikhahan-e Iran dar orupa va Istanbul*. Tehran: Tuss, 1981.

———, ed. *Namehha-ye siyasi-ye Dehkhoda*. Tehran: Bahman, 1979.

———, ed. *Nameh-ha-ye Tabriz az Theqat al-Islam beh Mostashar al-Dowleh*. Tehran: Farzan, 1999.

———, ed. *Owraq-e tazehyab-e mashrutiyat va naqsh-e Taqizadeh*. Tehran: Javidan, 1980.

Akhundov, Fathali. *Alefba-ye jadid va maktubat*. Edited by H. Mohammadzadeh. Baku, Azerbaijan: Talebov (Talebzadeh), 1963.

Algar, Hamid. "An Introduction to the History of Freemasonry in Iran." *Middle Eastern Studies* 6, no. 3 (Oct. 1970): 276–98.

———. *Mirza Malkum Khan: A Study in the History of Iranian Modernism*. Berkeley: Univ. of California Press, 1973.

Amirkhizi, Ismail. *Qiyam-e Azerbaijan va Sattar Khan*. Tehran: Tehran Press, 1960.

Ansari, Mehdi. *Shaikh Fazlollah Nuri va mashrutiyt*. Tehran: Amir Kabir, 1990.

Aryanpur, Yahya. *Az Saba ta Nima*. Tehran: Jibi, 1972.

Bahar, Mohammad Taqi Malek al-Sho'ara. *Tarikh-e mokhtasari Ahzab-e siyasi-ye Iran*. 2nd ed. Tehran: Jibi, 1978.

Bamdad, Badr al-Moluk. *Zanan-irani az enqelab-e mashrutiyat ta enqelab-e sefid*. Tehran: Ibn Sina, 1968.

Bayat, Mangol. *Iran's First Revolution: Shi'ism and the Constitutional Revolution of 1905–1909*. New York: Oxford Univ. Press, 1991.

———. *Mysticism and Dissent: Socioreligious Thought in Qajar Iran*. Syracuse, NY: Syracuse Univ. Press, 1982.

——— [Bayat-Philipp, Mangol]. "Women and Revolution in Iran, 1905–1911." In *Women in the Muslim World*, edited by Nikki R. Keddie and Lois Beck, 295–308. Cambridge, MA: Harvard Univ. Press, 1978.

Beck, Lois. *The Qashqa'i of Iran.* New Haven, CN: Yale Univ. Press, 1986.

Berberian, Houri. *The Love of Freedom Has No Fatherland: Armenians and the Iranian Constitutional Revolution of 1905–1911.* Boulder, CO: Westview Press, 2001.

Berkes, Niyazi. *The Development of Secularism in Turkey.* Montreal: McGill Univ. Press, 1964.

Bonakdarian, Mansour. *Britain and the Iranian Constitutional Revolution of 1906–1911: Foreign Policy, Imperialism, and Dissent.* Syracuse, NY: Syracuse Univ. Press, 2010.

———. "British Suffragists and Iranian Women, 1906–1911." In *Women's Suffrage in the British Empire: Citizenship, Nation, and Race,* edited by Ian Christopher Fletcher, Laura E. Nym Mayhall, and Philippa Levine, 157–74. New York: Routledge, 2000.

———. "The Persia Committee and the Constitutional Revolution in Iran." *British Journal of Middle Eastern Studies* 18, no. 2 (1991): 186–207.

———. "A World Born through the Chamber of a Revolver: Revolutionary Violence, Culture, and Modernity in Iran, 1905–1911." *Comparative Studies of South Asia, Africa, and the Middle East* 25, no. 2 (2005): 318–40.

Boroujerdi, Mehrzad. *Iranian Intellectuals and the West: The Tormented Triumph of Nativism.* Syracuse, NY: Syracuse Univ. Press, 1996.

Browne, Edward Granville. *A Brief Narrative of Recent Events in Persia.* London: Luzac, 1909.

———. *The Persian Revolution of 1905–1909.* 1910. New edition with an introduction by Abbas Amanat and supplementary documents by Mansour Bonakdarian. Washington, DC: Mage, 1995.

———. *The Press and Poetry of Modern Persia.* Cambridge: Cambridge Univ. Press, 1914.

———. *The Reign of Terror at Tabriz: England's Responsibility.* London: Taylor, Garnett, Evans, 1912.

Chaqueri, Cosroe, ed. *The Armenians of Iran: The Paradoxical Role of a Minority in a Dominant Culture: Articles and Documents.* Cambridge, MA: Harvard Univ. Press, 1998.

———. *Origins of Social Democracy in Iran.* Seattle: Univ. of Washington Press, 2001.

Chelkowski, Peter. "Edward G. Browne's Turkish Connection." *Bulletin of the School of Oriental and African Studies* 49, no. 1 (1986): 25–34.

Chevallier, Pierre. *Histoire de la Franc-maçonnerie française.* 3 vols. Paris: Fayard, 1974.

Church, Forrester. *So Help Me God: The Founding Fathers and the First Great Battle over Church and State.* Orlando, FL: Harcourt, 2007.

Churchill, Rogers P. *The Anglo-Russian Convention of 1907*. Cedar Rapids, IO: Torch Press, 1939.

Clark, Christopher. *The Sleepwalkers: How Europe Went to War in 1914*. London: Allen Lane, 2012.

Combes, Andre. *Histoire de la Franc-ma*çonnerie au XIX *siècle*. 2 vols. Monaco: Rocher, 1999.

Dowlatabadi, Yahya. *Hayat-e Yahya*. 4 vols. Tehran: Attar, 1983.

Dumont, Paul. "Une délégation Jeune-Turque à Paris." *Balkan Studies* 28, no. 2 (1987): 321–24.

———. "La Turquie dans les Archives du Grand Orient de France: Les loges maconniques d'obédience française à Istanbul du milieu du 19iemme siècle a la veille de la premiere guerre mondiale." *Colloques Internationaux du CNRS* 601 (1983): 171–202.

Ettehadiyeh (Nezam Mafi), Mansoureh. "The Council for the Investigation of Grievances: A Case Study of Nineteenth Century Iranian Social History." *Iranian Studies* 22, no. 1 (1989): 51–61.

———. "The Khaleseh of Veramin." *International Journal of Middle East Studies* 25, no. 1 (1993): 5–15.

———. *Majles va entekhabat az mashruteh ta payan-e qajariyeh*. Tehran: Nashr-e Tarikh-e Iran, 1995.

———. *Majmu'eh-ye motun va asnad-e tarikhi*. Tehran: Nashr-e Tarikh-e Iran, 1982.

———, ed. *Maramnameh-ha va nezamnameh-ha-ye ahzab-e siyasi-ye Iran*. Tehran: Nashr-e Tarikh-e Iran, 1982.

———. *Peydayesh va tahavvol-e ahzab-e siyasi-ye mashrutiyat*. Tehran: Gostareh, 1982.

Fakhra'i, Ibrahim. *Gilan dar jonbesh-e mashrutiyat*. Tehran: Jibi, 1974.

Farzaneh, Mateo. *The Iranian Constitutional Revolution and the Clerical Leadership of Khurasani*. Syracuse, NY: Syracuse Univ. Press, 2015.

Fathi, Nosratollah, ed. *Majmu'e-ye athar-e qalami-ye Theqat al-Islam shahid-e Tabriz*. Tehran: Anjoman-e Athar-e Melli, 1976.

———. *Zendeginameh-ye shahid Theqat al-Islam*. Tehran: Amir Kabir, 1974.

Ferrier, R. W. *The History of the British Petroleum Company: The Developing Years, 1901–32*. Cambridge: Cambridge Univ. Press, 1982.

Floor, Willem. *Salar al-Dowleh: A Delusional Prince and Wannabe Shah*. Washington, DC: Mage, 2018.

Foran, John. "The Concept of Dependent Development as a Key to the Political Economy of Qajar Iran (1800–1925)." *Iranian Studies* 22, nos. 2–3 (1989): 5–56.

Fraser, David. *Persia and Turkey in Revolt*. Edinburgh: Blackwood, 1910.

Furughi, Mohammad Ali. *Khaterat*. Tehran: Sokhan, 2017.

Garthwaite, Gene R. *Khans and Shahs: A Documentary Analysis of the Bakhtiyari in Iran.* Cambridge: Cambridge Univ. Press, 1983.

———. *The Persians.* Oxford: Blackwell, 2008.

Gharavi Nuri, Ali. *Hezb-e Democrat-e Iran dar dowreh-ye dovvom-e Majles-e showra-ye melli.* Tehran: Ferdowsi, 1973.

Gheissari, Ali. *Iranian Intellectuals in the Twentieth Century.* Austin: Univ. of Texas Press, 1998.

Gooch, George, and Harold Temperley, eds. *British Documents on the Origins of the War, 1889–1914: The Anglo-Russian Rapprochement, 1903–1907.* Vol. 4. London: His Majesty's Stationary Office, 1929.

Grey, Edward. *Twenty-Five Years, 1892–1916.* London: Hodder and Stoughton, 1925.

Gurney, John. "E. G. Browne and the Iranian Community in Istanbul." In *Les Iraniens d'Istanbul,* edited by Thierry Zarcone and Fariba Zarinbaf-Shahr, 149–75. Istanbul: Institut français de recherche en Iran, 1994.

Gurney, John, and Negin Nabavi. "Dar al-Fonun." *Encyclopedia Iranica* 6 (n.d.): 662–69.

Gwynn, Stephen, ed. *The Letters and Friendships of Sir Spring-Rice: A Record.* 2 vols. Boston: Houghton Mifflin, 1929.

Habibi, Mariam. "France and the Anglo-Russian Accords: The Discreet Missing Link." *Iran* 41 (2003): 291–307.

Hanioğlu, M. Şükrü. *The Young Turks in Opposition.* New York: Oxford Univ. Press, 2001.

Hardinge, Sir Arthur. *A Diplomatist in the East.* London: J. Cape, 1928.

Hinsley, Francis H., ed. *British Foreign Policy under Sir Edward Grey.* Cambridge: Cambridge Univ. Press, 1977.

Jacoby, Susan. *Freethinkers: A History of American Secularism.* New York: Metropolitan, 2004.

Kasravi, Ahmad. *Tarikh-e hijdah saleh-ye Azerbaijan.* Tehran: Amir Kabir, 1976.

———. *Tarikh-e mashruteh -ye Iran.* Tehran: Amir Kabir, 1984.

Katira'i, Mahmud. *Framasonri dar Iran.* Tehran: n.p., 1968.

Kazemzadeh, Firuz. *Russia and Britain in Persia, 1864–1914: A Study in Imperialism.* New Haven, CN: Yale Univ. Press, 1968.

Keddie, Nikki R. *An Islamic Response to Imperialism: Political and Religious Writings of Sayyid Jamalad-Din "al-Afghani."* New ed. Berkeley: Univ. of California Press, 1983.

———. *Sayyid Jamal ad-Din "al-Afghani": A Political Biography.* Berkeley: Univ. of California Press, 1972.

Kermani, Nazem al-Islam. *Tarikh-e bidari-ye iraniyan.* 3 vols. Tehran: Bonyad-e Farhang-e Iran, 1983.

Khazeni, Arash. "The Bakhtiyari Tribes in the Iranian Constitutional Revolution." *Comparative Studies of South Asia, Africa, and the Middle East* 25, no. 2 (2005): 379–98.

Le Goff, Jacques. *Les intellectuels au Moyen Âge*. Paris: Seuil, 1985.

Malekzadeh, Mehdi. *Tarikh-e enqelab-e mashrutiyat-e Iran.* 7 vols. 4th ed. Tehran: Sokrat, 1949.

Martin, Vanessa. *Islam and Modernism: The Iranian Revolution of 1906*. Syracuse, NY: Syracuse Univ. Press, 1989.

McDaniel, Robert A. *The Shuster Mission and the Persian Constitutional Revolution*. Minneapolis, MN: Bibliothec Islamica, 1974.

McMeekin, Sean. *The Berlin–Baghdad Express: The Ottoman Empire and Germany's Bid for World Power.* Cambridge, MA: Harvard Univ. Press, 2010.

Menashri, David. *Education and the Making of Modern Iran.* Ithaca, NY: Cornell Univ. Press, 1992.

Milani, Farzaneh. *Words and Veils: The Emerging Voices of Iranian Women Writers*. Syracuse, NY: Syracuse Univ. Press, 1992.

Mirza'i, Gholam Reza. *Bakhtiyariha va Qajariyeh.* Isfahan, Iran: Il Publications, 1994.

Modarres, Ali. *Vijehnameh-ye shahid Modarres.* Tehran: Mo'aseseh-ye Pajuheshi va Motale'at-e Farhangi, 1995.

Mohammadzadeh, H., ed. *Mirza Fathali Akhundov (Akhundzadeh).* Baku, Azerbaijan: Alefba-ye Jadid, 1963.

Mohit-Mafi, Hashem. *Moqaddamat-e mashrutiyat.* Tehran: Ferdowsi, 1984.

Mokhber al-Saltaneh, Mehdi Qoli Khan. *Khaterat va khatarat.* 3 vols. Tehran: Amir Kabir, 1950.

Moore, Arthur. *The Orient Express*. London: Constable, 1914.

Mostashar al-Dowleh, Sadeq Khan. *Khaterat va asnad.* 4 vols. Tehran: Ferdowsi, 1982.

Mostowfi, Abdollah. *Sharh-e zendegi-ye man ya tarikh-e ejtema'i va edari-ye Qajariyeh.* 3 vols. Tehran: Amir Kabir, 1982.

Murray, Gilbert. *The Foreign Policy of Sir Edward Grey 1906–1915*. Oxford: Clarendon Press, 1915.

Nahid, Abdolhosain. *Zanan-e Iran dar jonbesh-e mashruteh.* Tehran: n.p., 1981.

Na'ini, Mohammad Hosain. *Tanbih al-omma wa tanzih al-mella*. Tehran: n.p., 1955.

Nateq, Homa. *Karnameh-ye farhangi va farangi dar Iran.* Paris: Khavaran, 1996.

———. "Negahi beh barkhi neveshteha va mobarezat-e zanan dar dowran-e mashrutiyat." *Ketab-e jom'eh* 30 (1979): 45–54.

Nava'i, Abdolhosain. *Dowlatha-ye Iran: Az aghaz-e mashrutiyat ta ultimatum.* Tehran: Babek, 1976.

———. *Fath-e Tehran*. Tehran: Babek, 1977.

Nicolson, Arthur. *Portrait of a Diplomatist: Being the Life of Sir Arthur Nicolson*. Boston: Houghton Mifflin, 1930.

Oberling, Pierre. "The Role of Religious Minorities in the Persian Revolution, 1906–1912." *Journal of Asian History* 12 (1978): 1–29.

Paidar, Parvin. *Women and Political Participation in Twentieth-Century Iran*. Cambridge: Cambridge Univ. Press, 1995.

Persia Committee. *The Persian Crisis of 1912*. London: Persia Committee, 1912.

Rahimi, Mostafa. *Qanun-e asasi-ye Iran va osul-e demokrasi*. Tehran: Sepehr, 1978.

Rahman, Fazlollah. *Islam*. New York: Holt, Rinehart and Winston, 1966.

Ra'in, Ismail. *Faramushkhaneh va Framasonri dar Iran*. 2 vols. Tehran: Amir Kabir, 1976.

Rezazadeh Malek, Rahim. *Haidar Khan Amu Oghli*. Tehran: Donya, 1973.

Rezvani, Homa, ed. *Lava'yeh-ye Aqa Shaikh Fazlollah Nuri*. Tehran: Nashr-e Tarikh-e Iran, 1983.

Rezvani, Mohammad Ismail. "Bist-o-do resaleh –ye tabliqati az dowreh-ye mashrutiyat." *Rahnamah-ye Ketab* 12, nos. 7–8 (1969): 371–77.

Ringer, Monica. *Education, Religion, and the Discourse of Cultural Reform in Qajar Iran*. Costa Mesa, CA: Mazda, 2001.

Rowshan, Mohammad. *Mashruteh-ye gilan az yaddatha-ye Rabino*. Rasht, Iran: Ta'ati, 1973.

Sabatiennes, Paul. "Pour une histoire de la premiere loge Maçonnique Iran." *Revue de l'Université de Bruxelles* 1977:415–42.

Sadr-Hashami, Mohammad. *Tarikh-e jarayed va majallat-e Iran*. 4 vols. Isfahan, Iran: Kamal, 1985.

Safa'i, Ibrahim. *Rahbaran-e mashruteh*. 2 vols. Tehran: Javidan, 1984.

Sanasarian, Eliz. *The Women's Rights Movement in Iran: Mutiny, Appeasement, and Repression from 1900 to Khomeini*. New York: Praeger, 1982.

Shaji'i, Zahra. *Namayandegan-e Majles-e showra-ye melli dar bist va yek dowreh-ye qanungozari*. Tehran: Mo'asseseh-ye Motale'at va Tahqiqat-e Ejtema'i, 1965.

Sharif-Kashani, Mohammad Mehdi. *Vaqe'at-e ettefaqiyeh dar ruzegar*. 4 vols. Edited by M. Ettehadiyeh and S. Sa'dunian. Tehran: Nashr-e Tarikh-e Iran, 1984.

Shirazi, Mirza Saleh. *Majmueh-ye Safarnameh-ye Mirza Saleh Shirazi*. Tehran: Nashr-e Tarikh-e Iran, 1985.

Shuster, William Morgan. *The Strangling of Persia: A Personal Narrative*. 2nd printing. New York: Century, 1920.

Tabataba'i, Mohammad. *Yaddashtha-ye Seyyed Mohammad Tabataba'i dar enqelab-e mashrutiyat-Iran*. Tehran: Abi, 2005.

Taj al-Saltaneh. *Crowning Anguish: Memoirs of a Persian Princess from the Harem to Modernity.* Edited by Abbas Amanat. Washington, DC: Mage, 1993.

Taqizadeh, Hasan. *Maqalat-e Taqizadeh.* 4 vols. Edited by I. Afshar. Tehran: Shokufan, 1970–74.

———. *Zendegani-ye tufani.* Tehran: Elmi, 1989.

Tavakoli-Targhi, Mohammad. "Refashioning Iran: Language and Culture during the Constitutional Revolution." *Iranian Studies* 23, nos. 1–4 (1990): 77–101.

Torkaman, Mohammad. *Shaikh Shahid Fazlollah Nuri.* 2 vols. Tehran: Khadamat-e Farhangi, 1983.

Vahdat, Farzin. *God and Juggernaut: Iran's Intellectual Encounter with Modernity.* Syracuse, NY: Syracuse Univ. Press, 2002.

Vijuyeh, Mohammad Baqer. *Tarikh-e enqelab-e Azerbaijan va balva-ye Tabriz.* Tehran: Simorgh, 1976.

Wright, Denis. *The Persians amongst the English: Episodes in Anglo-Persian History.* London: I. B. Tauris, 1985.

Yaghma'i, Eqbal. "Talebov" (Talebzadeh). *Yaghma* 4 (1951): 214–21.

Yeselson, Abraham. *United States–Persian Diplomatic Relations, 1883–1921.* New Brunswick, NJ: Rutgers Univ. Press, 1956.

Zanjani, Shaikh Ibrahim. *Khaterat-e Shaikh Ibrahim Zanjani: Sargozasht-e zendegani-ye man.* Edited by Gh. Mirza Saleh. Tehran: Kavir, 2000.

Zarcone, Thierry, and Fariba Zarinbaf-Shahr, eds. *Les Iraniens d'Istanbul.* Tehran: Institut de recherches en Iran, 1994.

Zargarinejad, Gholam Hosain, ed. *Rasa'el-e mashrutiyat.* Tehran: Kavir, 1995.

Zaryab, Abbas, and Iraj Afshar, eds. *Namehha-ye Edvard Browne beh Seyyed Hasan Taqizadeh.* Tehran: Khvarazmi, 1972.

Zinoviev, Ivan A. *Enqelab-e mashrutiyat-e Iran: Nazarat-e yek diplomat-e rus.* Translated by Abol Qasem E'tesami. Tehran: Eqbal, 1983.

Index

Mangol Bayat is an independent scholar of modern Iran. She received a BA in English literature from the American University in Cairo, BA Honors in history from the School of African and Asian Studies, University of London, and a PhD in history from the University of California at Los Angeles. She has taught at the University of Shiraz, Iran; Harvard University; MIT; University of Iowa at Iowa City; and the University of Bonn, Germany. She was awarded a fellowship at the Princeton Institute for Advanced Studies and another at the Wilson Center for International Scholars in Washington, DC. A two-year International Research & Exchanges Board grant helped her devote time to study Russian intensively. She has participated in numerous international conferences in the United States, Europe, the Middle East, and Baku, Azerbaijan. She is the author of *Mysticism and Dissent* (Syracuse University Press, 1982) and *Iran's First Revolution: Shi'ism and the Constitutional Revolution, 1905–1909* (1991). She has also published numerous articles in different scholarly journals and has contributed chapters to various books of collected essays.